Murder at
Morija

Reconsiderations in Southern African History
Richard Elphick and Jeffrey Butler, Editors

MURDER AT MORIJA

Faith, Mystery, and Tragedy on an African Mission

Tim Couzens

University of Virginia Press
Charlottesville and London

University of Virginia Press
Originally published in 2003 by Random House (Pty) Ltd., Johannesburg, South Africa
© 2003 by Tim Couzens
All rights reserved
Printed in the United States of America on acid-free paper

First University of Virginia Press edition published 2005
ISBN 0-8139-2529-0

1 3 5 7 9 8 6 4 2

Library of Congress Cataloging-in-Publication Data

Couzens, Tim.
 Murder at Morija : faith, mystery, and tragedy on an African mission / Tim Couzens.
  p. cm. — (Reconsiderations in southern African history)
 Originally published: Johannesburg : Random House, 2003.
 Includes bibliographical references and index.
 ISBN 0-8139-2529-0 (pbk : alk. paper)
  1. Jacottet, Édouard, 1858–1920. 2. Missionaries—Lesotho—Biography. 3. Missionaries—Switzer-
land—Biography. 4. Murder—Lesotho—Morija. 5. Société des missions évangéliques de Paris—
History. I. Title. II. Series.
 BV3625.B5J33 2005
 266'.0234406885—dc22

2005014985

for

Edmund

Raymond   Kate   Jack

Hal

(Daniel)

Io lascio qualque cosa di caro nel mondo

Byron

Aeschylus (525–456 BC). The Father of Greek tragic drama. The titles of seventy-two of his plays are known, but only seven are now extant. The Oresteian Trilogy – *Agamemnon*, *The Libation Bearers* and *The Eumenides* – deals with murder and revenge in the royal family of Argos. According to comic legend, Aeschylus died when an eagle dropped a tortoise shell on his bald head, mistaking it for a stone.

—∽—

The truth is, we die through our ancestors; we are murdered by our ancestors. Their dead hands stretch forth from the tomb and drag us down to their mouldering bones. We in our turn are now at this moment preparing death for our unborn posterity.

Richard Jefferies, *The Story of My Heart*

Contents

Dramatis Personae

House of Jacottet
Henri-Pierre Jacottet, father of Édouard
Louise-Isabelle Jacottet (née Favarger), mother of Édouard
Édouard
Henri — sons of Henri-Pierre and Louise-Isabelle
Gustave, a doctor
Isabelle
Hélène — daughters of Henri-Pierre and Louise-Isabelle
Cecile-Louise
Louise Jacottet (née Barrelet), wife of Édouard
Henri
Gustave — sons of Édouard and Louise
Claude
Marcelle
Rose-Germaine — daughters of Édouard and Louise
Madeleine
Marguerite
Eugène Hoffet, husband of Isabelle, Édouard's sister

House of Moshoeshoe
Peete, grandfather of Moshoeshoe
Mokhachane, father of Moshoeshoe
Moshoeshoe, founder of the Basotho nation
Letsie the First
Molapo — sons of Moshoeshoe
Masupha
Lerotholi, son of Letsie the First
Letsie the Second — sons of Lerotholi
Griffith

British Administration in Basutoland
Edward Garraway, Resident Commissioner
Charles Griffith, Governor's agent 1871–81
Marshal Clarke
Godfrey Lagden — Garraway's predecessors as Resident
Herbert Sloley
Robert Coryndon
F.L. Foord, Assistant Commissioner to Garraway
D. St Pierre Bunbury, Sub-Inspector in the Basutoland Mounted Police

Missionaries
First generation
Thomas Arbousset
Katherine Arbousset, wife of Thomas
Eugène Casalis
Sarah Casalis, wife of Eugène

Constant Gosselin
Samuel Rolland

Second generation
Adolphe Mabille
Adèle Mabille, wife of Adolphe
Théophile Jousse
Frédéric Ellenberger
Paul Germond
Louis Duvoisin

Third and fourth generations
Hermann Dieterlen
François Coillard
Eugène Casalis, doctor, son of Eugène and Sarah Casalis
Ernest Mabille ⎤
⎥—— sons of Adolphe and Adèle
Louis Mabille ⎦
Henry Dyke, principal of the Normal School
Henri Bertschy
Alfred Casalis, son of Eugène and Sophie Casalis
Caroline Casalis, wife of Alfred
Sam Duby
Eva Duby, wife of Sam
Gynette ⎤
⎥—— children of Sam and Eva
Georges ⎦
Charles Christeller
Paul Ramseyer
Théo Duby, brother of Sam
Margot Duby, wife of Théo

Basotho Ministers
First intake
Job Moteane
Carlisle Motebang
John Mohapeloa

Second intake
Everitt Segoete
Bethuel Sekokotoana
Edward Motsamai
Nicolas Mpiti
Fineas Matlanyane

Third intake
Joel Mohapeloa

Doctors at Morija
Georges Hertig
Felix Augsburger

Maps and House Plan

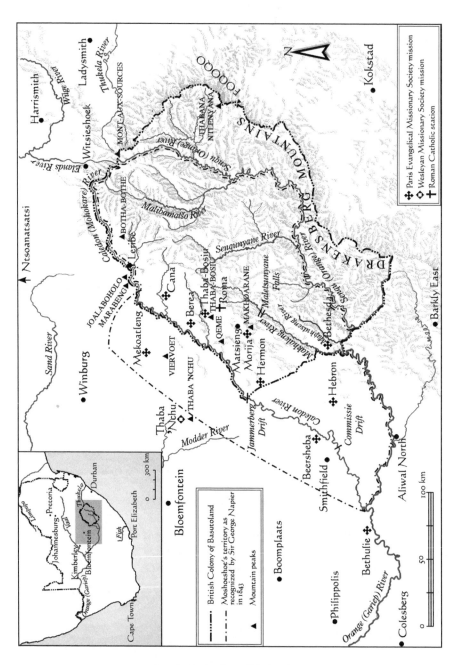

Lesotho in the time of Moshoeshoe

Legend:
- ✠ Paris Evangelical Missionary Society mission
- ◇ Wesleyan Missionary Society mission
- ✝ Roman Catholic station

Map labels:
Harrismith, Ladysmith, Thukela River, Wilge River, Elands River, Witsieshoek, MONT-AUX-SOURCES, THABANA NTLENYANA, DRAKENSBERG MOUNTAINS, Kokstad, Ntsoanatsatsi, Sand River, Caledon (Mokhotlong) River, BOTHA-BOTHE, Leribe, Malibamatso River, Senqu (Orange) River, Senqunyane River, Maletsunyane Falls, Barkly East, Cana, Berea, Thaba-Bosiu, THABA-BOSIU, Roma, MAKHOARANE, JOALABOHOLO, MARABENG, Mekoatleng, QEME, Matsieng, Morija, Hermon, Bethesda, Winburg, VIERVOET, THABA NCHU, Thaba 'Nchu, Modder River, Caledon River, Hebron, Commissie Drift, Tammerberg Drift, Beersheba, Smithfield, Aliwal North, Bloemfontein, Boomplaats, Be. Bethulie, Philippolis, Orange (Gariep) River, Colesberg

Inset map: Pretoria, Johannesburg, Kimberley, Bloemfontein, Durban, Port Elizabeth, Cape Town, Vaal, Orange (Gariep) River, Thukela, Limpopo

Inset legend:
- ····· British Colony of Basutoland
- ─·─ Moshoeshoe's territory as recognized by Sir George Napier in 1843
- ▲ Mountain peaks

Scale: 0 — 300 km; 0 — 50 — 100 km

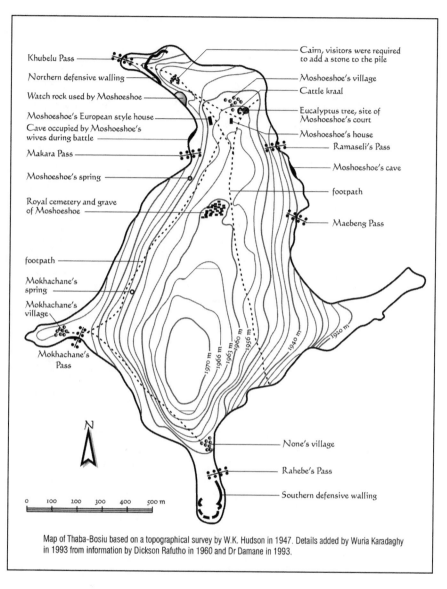

Khubelu Pass

Northern defensive walling

Watch rock used by Moshoeshoe

Moshoeshoe's European style house

Cave occupied by Moshoeshoe's
wives during battle

Makara Pass

Moshoeshoe's spring

Royal cemetery and grave
of Moshoeshoe

footpath

Mokhachane's
spring

Mokhachane's
village

Mokhachane's
Pass

Cairn, visitors were required
to add a stone to the pile

Moshoeshoe's village

Cattle kraal

Eucalyptus tree, site of
Moshoeshoe's court

Moshoeshoe's house

Ramaseli's Pass

Moshoeshoe's cave

footpath

Maebeng Pass

None's village

Rahebe's Pass

Southern defensive walling

N

0   100   200   300   400   500 m

1970 m 1966 m 1963 m 1960 m 1956 m 1946 m 1920 m

Map of Thaba-Bosiu based on a topographical survey by W.K. Hudson in 1947. Details added by Wuria Karadaghy
in 1993 from information by Dickson Rafutho in 1960 and Dr Damane in 1993.

Thaba-Bosiu

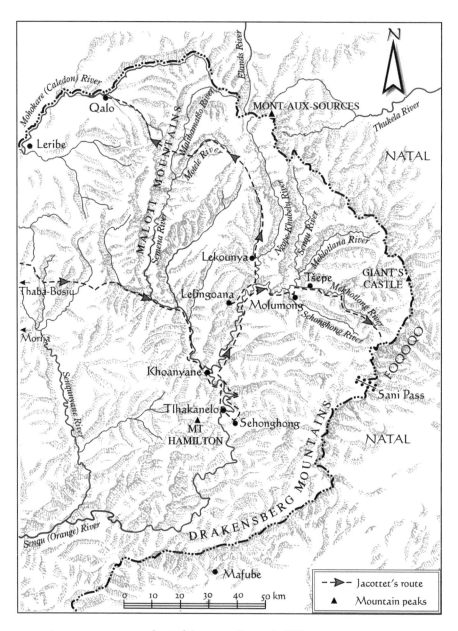

Jacottet's journey to Foqoqo in 1893

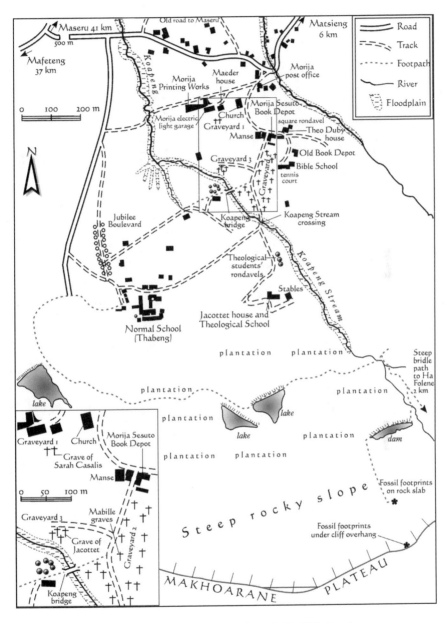

Morija (based on an original map drawn by David Ambrose)

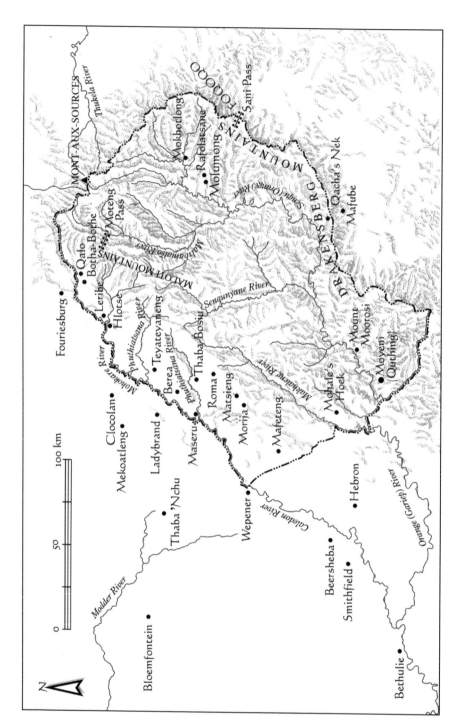

Places of importance 1830–1920

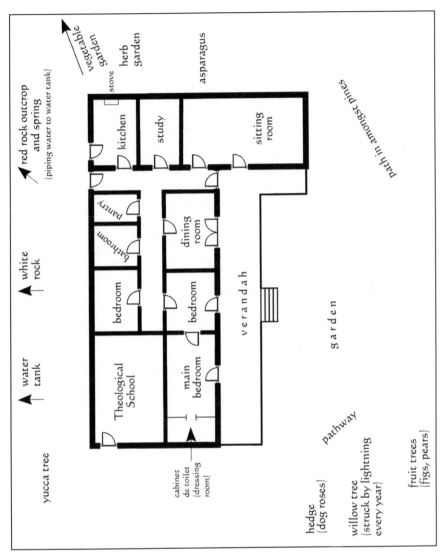

Impressionistic plan of the Jacottet house based on photographs and the memories of Dorothy Hall and Hélène Nixon

Note on Usage and Pronunciation

An inhabitant of Lesotho (pronounced *Lesutu*) is a 'Mosotho' (pronounced *Mosutu*), and inhabitants collectively are called 'Basotho' (pronounced *Basutu*). The language of the country is 'Sesotho' (pronounced *Sesutu*).

The 'oa' in words like 'Bakoena' and 'Batlokoa' is pronounced *wa* (in South Africa, they are spelled 'Bakwena' and 'Batlokwa').

The country is usually called 'Basutoland' when the colonial period is being referred to, and usually 'Lesotho' for other times. Similarly, the title 'Paramount Chief' is used for the colonial period and 'King' for the pre-colonial period.

Many of the people who appear in the book were baptized by the Paris Evangelical Missionary Society and given French names. Sometimes these were also Anglicized or Sotho-ized, so that the name of a single person might be spelled in three different ways.

Similarly, the names of places ('Lesotho', 'Basutoland', 'Thaba-Bosiu') elicited a wide, often wild variety of spellings ('Lessouto', 'Basuto Land', 'Thaba Bosigo'). The name of King Moshoeshoe (pronounced *Moshweshwe*) was often written as 'Moshesh'.

For the sake of clarity and ease of reading, some standardization has been introduced, but absolute consistency is not possible and variants have been used where they seemed appropriate.

Part One

THE FLESH

———⌾———

> And what a father –
> A priest at sacrifice, he showered you
> with honours.
>
> Aeschylus, *The Libation Bearers*

CHAPTER ONE

THE PLACE OF SACRIFICE

Lieutenant Colonel Edward Garraway, Resident Commissioner of Basutoland, kept a regular diary. On Thursday 23 December 1920, he noted that he had had to give up typing that morning, on account of his eyes; so instead he bottled some of his 'John Jameson' – he was an Irishman. That day, and the preceding days, had been hot, but he was looking forward to leaving Maseru, the capital of Basutoland, and crossing the Caledon river into South Africa next morning to meet a friend arriving at Marseilles siding.

His reverie was interrupted when one of his aides came in to tell him that Rev. Monsieur Édouard Jacottet of the Paris Evangelical Missionary Society had died at Morija the previous night. Jacottet was the Director of the Theological School at the mission. Although Jacottet had irritated him somewhat the last time they met, Garraway was saddened by the news. Jacottet was a proud and knowledgeable man, and his death would be a huge loss to the mission. Garraway arranged for a telegram to be sent to the High Commissioner in Cape Town informing him of the event. That afternoon there was a very heavy thunderstorm and quite the best rain of the season settled the dust in Maseru. Hopefully, it meant the drought was broken at last.

Later, Garraway walked down to Douglas How's and warned the policeman that he would have to come out with him to Morija the following day. Garraway realized he would have to send an African subordinate across the border to meet the train in his place. That outing would have been a pleasure: Jacottet's funeral was a matter of duty.

—◦○◦—

As it happened, Garraway was late for the funeral. He and How got off at 9.30 for the hour-long journey, but they were delayed by a puncture on the road. After passing the World, the Flesh and the Devil, three dumpy hills on the outskirts of Maseru (the last the largest), and crossing the Phuthiatsana river, they also took the trouble to pick up an old African painfully making his way to Morija and the funeral. It was a fine morning as they drove south along the main road, one of those Lesotho mornings when the air is clear as crystal, sharp to the touch. All over the fields flitted the little grasshoppers known as the litsitoe. To the west spread the plains of the Orange Free State, dotted with great rocky hills and plateaux; to the east, parallel to them, stretched the unbroken chain of the first range of the Maloti mountains, vertebral, like the spine of a somnolent prehistoric monster. Garraway noticed with sadness the dongas that spread across the countryside like the maze he had once visited at Hampton Court.

As they approached Makhoarane, beneath which the mission sheltered, the mountain began to impose its massive presence on them. To the right, a few kilometres away, they could just glimpse the Anglican mission at Masite. Soon the details of Morija mission came into focus. Most prominent was the old redbrick church completed in 1857, with its simple, elegant spire, added in 1905. Passing between the church and the post office, and glancing at the Book Depot, the Printing Works and the Bible School all to the left, they approached the churchyard, where the funeral had already begun and the coffin was being lowered into the grave. Amongst the large crowd, Garraway saw many people he knew, black and white. In the centre stood Jacottet's three daughters, caryatids in black, with the weight of Makhoarane on their shoulders.

Marcelle. Madeleine. Marguerite.

—◦◦—

The service had begun a few hundred metres up the hill at the Jacottet house, which was the highest on the hillside. The news of the missionary's death had spread the previous morning like summer lightning, leaving the church, the community, the nation struck dumb with the enormity of the misfortune, unable to comprehend why God had made His mission more difficult. To whom could they turn for support and advice, now that Jacottet was gone?

Next to the house, prayers had been said by Rev. Bethuel Sekokotoana, a former student of Jacottet's. The simple appeal of Sekokotoana began the ritual of renewal, remembrance and forgetting. Jesus, momentarily forgotten, he reminded them, was their King, the one who saves. Rev. Jacottet, oh, if we could just find the truth and receive salvation!

The coffin had then been taken down to the graveyard where most of the mourners waited, silently. Rev. John Mohapeloa read a few words from the Bible, and the people sang hymns of grief. Jacottet's open grave lay next to his late wife's sealed one.

—◦◦—

Just as the community was stricken, so were Jacottet's colleagues. They rode in from other stations: Victor Ellenberger from Leribe, Georges Dieterlen from Berea, Louis Germond from Thabana-Morena, and Paul Colin from Thaba-

Bosiu. From Morija there were Charles Christeller, Samuel Duby and his brother Théophile, as well as Jacques Zurcher, the printer. Henri Bertschy, who had arrived in Basutoland in 1885, less than a year after Jacottet, began as master of ceremonies. 'The end of a man's life on earth,' he said, 'is when his remains are entrusted to his grave.' He then invited the Resident Commissioner to begin the speeches.

Garraway, in his imposing voice, recalled his three-year friendship with Jacottet, in which time he had come to trust the missionary's advice: 'He knew the Basotho people. You, the Basotho nation, have been fortunate indeed to have him because he loved you dearly. He worked unselfishly to bring you education. During his life he lived for you and it can be said that he died for you as well.'

He also read a telegram he had received from the High Commissioner, Prince Arthur of Connaught: 'The nation has lost a true and trustworthy friend and the government has lost an assistant and loyal adviser. Kindly send my condolences and sincerest sympathy to his children and fellow missionaries.'

As their distinct shadows arched away from the east, one of the three sisters looked towards the mountain, up to the small stream flowing strongly because of the recent rain, up past their house surrounded by young pines to the spring that fed it water, and past the cairn of travellers' stones, up higher to the cave. Basking in the sun, the rocks, ancient, stoic, enigmatic, guarded their secrets. Halfway up, on a huge rock, were the dinosaur prints, 'Nonyana ea Makhoarane', the Giant Bird of Morija mountain. Amongst all those creatures of the past that had come this way, why had this one left its mark? Was it running, flying, mating, hunting, when it alighted on the rock? Why did this print survive to be discovered and rediscovered by the children on picnics?

The daughter of Jacottet brooded. Mourning became her. Blue-eyed and solemn, she contemplated the journey between cave and grave.

Amongst the shadows were also shades.

Absent friends and relatives. The three telamones, Henri, Gustave and Claude, the sons of Jacottet, a world away.

Louise. Rose-Germaine. The dead.

Also absent was the Basotho king, Griffith Lerotholi. But then he was a Catholic, and there had been some tension … and a secret, whispered when not even a fieldmouse could hear.

Perhaps there was a more innocent reason. Two of his chiefs were present. Chiefs Leloko Lerotholi and Lerotholi Mojela, the former speaking with solemn dignity: 'Servants of God of the French Church, sons of Moshoeshoe and the nation, His Highness the King has sent me to bid farewell to this minister of Moshoeshoe. He says that even if Jacottet is dead, his work will always be remembered.'

The chief's words echoed in the great amphitheatre.

—◦⊙◦—

Canon Spencer Weigall, who had been friends with Jacottet for twenty-seven years, had come from nearby Masite. Sorrow kept his speech brief. He emphasized his friend's work on the Basutoland Board of Education, and the great loss his death would mean to intellectuals and writers. 'Even if we had differences,' he said, 'my friendship with Jacottet was very close.'

It was fitting, too, that Rev. W.A. Norton, Professor of Bantu Philology at the University of Cape Town and a former missionary himself, happened to be visiting. In his speech, Garraway had drawn attention to the fact that Jacottet had recently turned down the offer of a chair in African languages at the University of the Witwatersrand in Johannesburg, because he could not bear to leave his beloved Basotho. Norton was therefore the right person to acknowledge the support Jacottet had offered the Free State missionary centres and the valuable assistance of an academic and scholarly nature he had given to local institutions, and also to laud 'his fame throughout the world as a comparative philologist and threnographist, whose help several universities sought'.

Norton's own threnody listed some of Jacottet's written achievements: his numerous articles for the mission newspaper, *Leselinyana la Lesotho*, his Sesotho grammar and his monographs, as well as his work as Sesotho examiner for schools and universities in Basutoland and South Africa.

—◦⊙◦—

After the things of the intellect came the things of the heart. As Director of the Theological School of the mission, Jacottet had taught all the early Basotho ministers – Job Moteane, Carlisle Motebang, John Mohapeloa, Everitt Segoete, Nicolas Mpiti, Joel Mohapeloa, and a score of others. Edward Motsamai stepped forward in loco discipulorum, the one for the many.

'I am standing here,' he said, 'to speak on behalf of the students of Rev. Jacottet. I just don't know what to say, nor do I know what to leave out. We learned a lot from Rev. Jacottet, both when we were still at the School, and after we became ministers. If you want to know what Rev. Jacottet was really like, you can learn it simply enough from the Basotho ministers he has taught.

A teacher is recognized in his students. We thank God for him. We learned from him not only about God and the ministry, but also a lot about his own soul and feelings. He loved us and we always went to him for advice.'

Motsamai added that he always remembered Jacottet's words to them on their last day at the School. Having taught them all about the Kingdom of God and shown them the trials that Christ went through, Jacottet presented them with a choice. 'You have now heard all about the Church of God and the way it lived and the way it was made,' he told them. 'So go and give it life if you can or kill it if you want to.'

After offering the condolences of the Church of Basutoland to Jacottet's daughters and placing them, with love, in the hands of God, Motsamai addressed his last words directly to the gathering: 'You ministers and people, your right hand has been cut off. But be comforted, and know that from today this church, with the help of God, is now in *your* hands.'

—◦◦—

There were two more speakers. Rev. Colin grieved on behalf of the congregation at Thaba-Bosiu, which Jacottet had served for over twenty years, and on behalf of the Swiss town of Neuchâtel, of which both he and Jacottet were native sons. M. Bertschy concluded by saying that he had known Jacottet for thirty-eight years, since they had been together at school (by which he meant the Theological Faculty in Neuchâtel). He quoted Psalm 43 – 'Why art thou cast down, O my soul?' – and exhorted the crowd to believe in the things that Jacottet had taught. Above all, he cajoled them to repent: 'If all of your chiefs and all of you could but repent! A person's salvation is repentance, therefore a people's salvation is repentance. There is no people that can do without the word of God.'

The service was at an end and the people turned away from the graveside with pain in their hearts. All is well, said one voice, we must thank God for those who remain on this earth.

—◦◦—

Garraway left behind a community in shock, edging towards panic. He had been moved by the simple burial, but he had no wish to linger at Morija and so he turned down invitations to luncheon. He was quiet on the way home. It was, after all, Christmas Eve, and next day there would be a new celebration of an old birth.

CHAPTER TWO

THE SOUP

On Wednesday 22 December, at midday, M. Jacottet sat down to table in his own house with five other people: his daughter, Madeleine; M. and Mme Paillard from the Swiss Mission in Mozambique, who were staying with him; and Mr Frederick Reid, a school inspector, with his son Harold, who had been detained at Morija by a big storm that had broken towards the end of the morning. M. Jacottet was, as usual on such occasions, very cheerful and in high spirits.

Soup was served, and no one noticed that it had any peculiar taste. M. Jacottet even took a second helping. This unlucky soup was no sooner swallowed than the six people who took it fell suddenly ill. Three of them, including M. Jacottet, left the table and rushed out of the house, racked by extremely violent vomiting. The two other guests, who bravely tried to stay at the table, were eventually forced from it by the same terrible discomfort. The six people had been poisoned!

Fortunately, Madeleine Jacottet, who had eaten very little of the soup, was well enough to send two messengers, one to Dr Felix Augsburger, the other to the Book Depot down the hill. The sick, who were found scattered helplessly here and there in the garden, were taken back to the house and each was laid out on a bed. Everything their condition demanded was done right away, and the treatment was continued throughout the afternoon. Dr Augsburger did his utmost, going from one room to the next to see all his patients. Sometimes one, sometimes another, gave cause for serious concern; pulses became irregular, hearts slowed. Terrible hours never to be forgotten!

By seven or seven thirty in the evening, five of the victims could be considered almost out of danger; but the sixth, Jacottet himself, who had often worried the doctor during the afternoon, was stricken. About this time he lost consciousness, in spite of injections given by the doctor to revive him. He then slept peacefully, seemingly without suffering, until three o'clock in the morning. His eldest daughter, Dr Augsburger and I were at his bedside when he surrendered his last sigh. M. Jacottet was dead!

These were the exact words (in translation) of a colleague of Jacottet, Sam Duby, in a letter he wrote to Dr Jean Bianquis at mission headquarters in Paris on the 27th. Duby was the Director of the Bible School at Morija and also ran the Book Depot, where Jacottet's eldest daughter Marcelle was his assistant. Alfred Casalis, Vice-President of the Missionary Conference and now Acting President since Jacottet's death, was on sick leave in Johannesburg, and so it was natural for Duby to report to Paris. On the morning of the 23rd, within a few hours of his colleague's death, Duby had sent a cable to Dr Bianquis at the headquarters of the Paris Evangelical Missionary Society at 102, Boulevard Arago, in the 14th Arrondissement. For some reason, Duby's cable suggested to Bianquis that Jacottet had died of a heart attack.

This is curious, as Duby was present at the death and knew that several people had been violently ill. Garraway certainly came away from the funeral the following day believing that there had been ptomaine poisoning. Perhaps Duby was reporting what Dr Augsburger had told him was the *final cause* of death; perhaps, too, he did not want to spread alarm before there was definite confirmation of exactly what had happened.

The news of the death came just in time to be mentioned in the pending issue of the journal published by the PEMS. The *Journal des Missions Évangéliques* stated that Jacottet was too important a person for a hasty obituary, and promised that suitable valedictions would appear in the following issue. For now, it could only record its profound sorrow.

Sorrow turned into bewilderment in the next issue. A number of eulogies of Jacottet did appear, but the *Journal* had to contradict the heart attack version and replace it with an admission that he had died of poisoning. Intriguingly, the new account went one step further than mere food poisoning, but, in doing so, asserted that the death was accidental. 'All thoughts of criminal malice must, it seems, be dismissed,' said the *Journal*. 'It was only a matter of the foolishness and disastrous negligence of a native servant.'

But readers of the *Journal* must have been puzzled and intrigued.

As he wrote the letter to Paris, Duby was physically and psychologically shattered. The circumstances in which the death had taken place were impressed upon his mind. He described parts of the funeral and deeply mourned the passing of his colleague, who had been in the middle of correcting the Sesotho examination papers for the University of South Africa and had also been preparing a truly scientific Sesotho grammar, as complete as possible. 'The name of Jacottet,' Duby concluded, 'like those of Arbousset, Casalis and Mabille, will always remain linked to the Mission of Lesotho.'

Duby also wrote that the five other victims were back on their feet, though it was a miracle they had survived. But the mission was in disarray. Jacottet had been in Basutoland since 1884 and was the senior and most authoritative figure of the mission. He had been President of the Missionary Conference for the year, and Alfred Casalis, the Vice-President, was away in Johannesburg. At this stage nobody knew the exact nature of the poisoning, although samples of the ingredients had been sent for analysis.

Duby complained that he had had sleepless nights since the disaster and found himself unable to concentrate on his various duties. He seemed genuinely mystified by the event: 'What happened at this fatal meal? What was this poison whose action was so quick and violent, and placed the lives of five people in serious danger and killed the sixth? How did it come to be in the soup when the native servant had tasted it without harm? This servant claims, in fact, that she drank in the kitchen some of the soup that was left over in the tureen after the accident.'

These were good questions, but whether by chance, ignorance or design there were a number of omissions and silences in Duby's account. To be fair, he might not have known the whole story. Either way, he could probably have written a book about it.

By the time the next issue of the *Journal* appeared, bewilderment had turned to consternation. Bianquis had been informed that his friend Jacottet's death was neither a heart attack, nor food poisoning, nor accidental poisoning. It was murder.

CHAPTER THREE

SUSPICION

Summoned by Madeleine Jacottet at two o'clock on the day of the disaster, Dr Augsburger arrived soon after. He noted the terrible state all the party were in. Then he set about his task of trying to save them, as his vocation dictated.

——◦◦——

Felix François Auguste Augsburger was something of a controversial character. He was about forty at the time, from a poor family, since his teacher father had died when he was only three. He studied Latin and Greek at the University of Neuchâtel, then medicine and surgery under the famous surgeon Roux at Lausanne. He also gained some knowledge of dentistry and ophthalmology.

Sent by the Swiss Mission to Lourenço Marques (he worked at Rikatla, Manjazaza and Chikhoumbane), he did not want to go home after five years, so he was lent to the PEMS at Morija, where he also stayed for some five years.

His son found him to be a hard, proud, somewhat haughty man, but just and straightforward. There was a touch of bitterness in his make-up: he could not believe in a God of love, he said, because he had seen too much suffering. He read the Bible in Latin and Greek, and spoke Portuguese, French, German and English, as well as two African languages. Once, when his son fell on some corrugated iron and cut his hand badly, Augsburger closed the wound so well that the boy kept the use of his fingers.

To this day, however, Rev. Paul Ellenberger remembers screaming in pain when his tonsils were removed, with Augsburger slapping him and shouting, 'Stop it! Stop it!' The likelihood of this was confirmed by the doctor's son, who said that, when his teeth were being done, his father had a way of calming him by slapping him! Yet Augsburger did not flinch when he operated on his own son for appendicitis. And seventy years afterwards, Joel Mohapeloa remembered how Augsburger examined his eyes by candlelight and gave him his first specs.

More damning was Alfred Casalis in his diary. In November 1920, Casalis was suffering from lumbago, pains in the kidneys, and heart strain. The regular doctor, Georges Hertig, whose reputation was as whimsical as Augsburger's, was on a month's leave in order to 'chasser le gros gibier' – hunting big game was his passion – so Augsburger was called in for an 'auscultation'. Mrs Caroline

Casalis had asked the doctor not to tell her husband anything definite if he discovered any serious condition, for fear of upsetting him. So, after poking around the offending organs, Augsburger delivered his verdict to her alone. What torture she endured when she heard this eccentric, this 'hurluberlu', declare that, in addition to her husband's known complaints, his right kidney was dangerously inflamed, he had a tumour of a pernicious kind, his heart was very sick, and he had general anaemia. Augsburger's opinion was that Casalis should return to Europe immediately.

Since Casalis had just come from there, he dismissed this abracadabran diagnosis with a disbelieving laugh and drove himself off to Maseru to consult Doctors Long and Dyke. They declared that his right kidney needed some care, with a binding, and that rest would cure everything else. Within a few days, Casalis felt much better, but it is not surprising that over Christmas he went to Johannesburg on leave, perhaps to consult specialists. Hence his absence at the time of the Jacottet crisis.

When he arrived at the house, Augsburger went first to Jacottet's room. There he found Samuel Duby in attendance, and Jacottet conscious but in obvious distress. Madeleine tried to assist him with her father, but was too sick herself to do much. Injections of camphorated oil eased the plight of Mr Reid and his young son, as well as one or two others of the party. But a similar injection had no effect on Jacottet, who had partaken so freely of the soup.

At five o'clock, with all the others out of danger, the doctor administered another injection of camphorated oil to Jacottet. The missionary then said something so startling that it must have given the doctor much pause for thought and confirmed his prevailing suspicions. Soon afterwards, the stricken man lapsed into unconsciousness and the doctor retired for an hour, leaving Marcelle alone at her father's bedside, with instructions that she was not to leave him.

Jacottet did not regain consciousness. At 3.10 the following morning, Marcelle, Duby and Augsburger heard his death sigh.

Whatever his reputation as a diagnostician, Augsburger suspected poison almost immediately. It is possible that he caught a whiff of garlic as he bent down to hear his patient's last remark. And he was of the opinion that the poison had been administered deliberately. He had three suspects or groups of suspects. His first suspect was the King of Lesotho!

The morning that followed Jacottet's death was one of fevered rumour and equally feverish activity. Dr Hamilton William Dyke, Medical Officer at

Maseru, arrived to do the post-mortem. He was accompanied by Sub-Inspector D. St Pierre Bunbury of the Basutoland Mounted Police. On arrival at the Jacottet house, Dyke met all three Jacottet daughters and Rev. Duby. He informed the eldest daughter, Marcelle, of the official purpose of the visit, and she replied, 'Certainly, we want to know what has poisoned our father.'

Dyke performed the post-mortem in the presence of Bunbury, Augsburger and a Dr Brebnor. In his initial inspection, he found no external marks of violence on the body. He then extracted a quantity of the stomach contents, and sent one and a half ounces to the government analyst in Bloemfontein.

After the post-mortem, Inspector Bunbury went into the kitchen and made enquiries of the cook, whose name was Jerita. She would not or could not give any information as to how 'the accident' had happened, except that it was after eating the soup that everybody had taken ill.

When asked what the soup was made of, Jerita pointed to an open packet of Quaker Oats, an open bottle of Lemco (a beef extract produced by Oxo), a tin containing salt, and some remains of cooked beans. Bunbury took samples of each and sealed them.

He then went and searched the pantry. This was separate from the kitchen and rather awkwardly placed – he had to go through the kitchen door, turn right and take a few steps along the main passage, before turning into the dark room with its shelves and cupboards fronted with wire mesh, designed to let in air and light and keep out flies. On the same shelves where the soup ingredients were kept, he found some open packets of Cooper's sheep dip.

Before he left the house, Dr Dyke asked Marcelle and Sam Duby whether there was any chance of poison having been left lying about which might have got into the soup or other food. They said no, but Marcelle added that there *had* been arsenic in the house which her father had used as 'a medicine for horses', but some weeks previous to his death it had been removed. Bunbury seems to have asked Marcelle the same question, to which she replied similarly: there had been poison in the house 'for the purpose of poisoning flies', but her father had told her about a month before to remove it 'as it was dangerous to have in the house'.

After questioning some of those who had been sick, Bunbury decided to let the matter rest until the analyst's report was received.

Dr Augsburger was not so quiescent, however. His analytic, if capricious, mind sought an answer not only to the cause of death, but to how and why it might have happened, and even who was behind it.

At ten o'clock that morning, he went to look for Sam Duby. 'I wish to have a confidential chat with you,' he said. He outlined his various suspicions. He said he knew that Jacottet, as 'the head of the mission in Basutoland', had had great difficulty with the Paramount Chief and also with the Roman Catholics over a land and school dispute. Could this poisoning therefore have taken place at the instigation of the Paramount Chief? To which Duby replied, 'Yes, it is quite possible.'

Augsburger outlined another supposition. As there had been trouble at the mission's Printing Works, which had led to a strike early in 1920, might the poisoning not have been delayed revenge on the part of the strikers? The question was probably rhetorical, because Duby was non-committal.

Augsburger also asked Duby, 'Do you know of a son, Claude?' to which Duby replied, 'Yes, I know him and all the circumstances.'

Augsburger then told Duby that he had seen Madeleine the previous night in hysterics, and gave his opinion that there must be something quite abnormal in the family. He went even further. For his part, he was persuaded that the poisoning had been done by a family member.

Duby's perturbation was palpable. He asked Augsburger never to speak about this to anyone in Morija. The doctor promised that the story would be buried with him, unless his silence interfered with the course of justice.

This was an odd reaction on Augsburger's part and a strange promise. Perhaps it was a humane decision to guard a family's privacy or an attempt to protect the mission. Perhaps he was told a darker secret, or suspected one.

Clearly, however, he had nagging doubts, and he soon overrode his pledge. Jacottet's brother, Gustave, was a medical doctor at Matatiele in East Griqualand. When exactly he arrived in Morija is not certain – he had probably been telegraphed when Jacottet became ill or on the morning after his death.

Matatiele, which had once been three days' ride on horseback over the mountains, was now more easily accessible by road, although still a long journey. There is no evidence that Gustave Jacottet was at the funeral, but he may have come soon afterwards.

On his arrival, he had a long conversation with Augsburger. The latter told him of his unease. Dr Jacottet then went to have a conversation with Sam Duby, appearing, as he left for this meeting, to be in a very depressed mood. But when he returned from seeing Duby, he seemed to Augsburger to be very much more cheerful, and remarked, 'I have slept,' which presumably meant he was happy with what Duby had told him.

But all this hugger-mugger pointed to a hidden undercurrent and dark suspicions. When Alfred Casalis returned to Morija to take up the acting presidency of the Conference, he found the whole mission in a state of turmoil and consternation.

CHAPTER FOUR

SHOCK

C hristmas had passed uneventfully. Perhaps Garraway overindulged, because three days later, 'full of pain', he got Dr Dyke to 'vet' him. After New Year, the pain transferred itself to his motor car – something wrong with its wheels – so he had to put it 'in the hands of the garage people', the Maseru Garage and Motor Works, which was the sole agent for Ford cars in Maseru and the only garage in the capital.

He does not seem to have been ruffled by the news, if indeed he even registered it, that Inspector Bunbury had received the report of the forensic analyst in Bloemfontein on 7 January. He was more concerned with some unnamed malaise in the colonial service, and on 13 January, in a tête-à-tête with a Mr MacGregor (probably J.C. MacGregor, son-in-law of the PEMS missionary D.F. Ellenberger), from whom he got 'a lot of useful advice', they agreed that 'the majority of the members of this service have gone temporarily mad' and 'cannot see beyond their noses'. This prejudice must have been confirmed a few days later when, at a dinner party given by Garraway and his wife Winifred (whom he affectionately called Win), Mrs Ashton – angry at him for having passed over her husband Hugh in the recent police promotions – was 'horribly rude' to him, and practically called him a liar at the dinner table. Garraway found it most awkward and had the greatest difficulty in keeping his temper, hoping all the while that the other guests could not hear everything she said. 'The poor woman,' he concluded, 'is really not quite sane, I'm afraid.'

He had been hoping to spend the day after his dinner party duck-shooting at Teyateyaneng, but was too busy and had to content himself, two days after, with leaving the office early to go fishing.

A small time bomb was ticking, however. It was ticking in the brain of Jacottet's brother.

The forensic medical report that was handed to Bunbury on 7 January held no real surprises, but it did confirm a grim reality. There was no doubt that the soup had contained poison, and the poison was arsenic.

—⌒◡—

Five days later, on the 12th, Bunbury, a man of tact and 'perfect discretion' in the eyes of Alfred Casalis, returned to Morija, again to question Rev. Duby. He asked Duby where Marcelle and Marguerite had been on 22 December, and was informed that both had been at work in the Book Depot as usual that morning. When the storm gathered, he persuaded them to stay to lunch. Marcelle went to tell her father she was not coming home to eat, but Duby assured Bunbury that Marguerite had remained with him the whole time.

Finally, on 24 January, the police took action. Following a not unfamiliar pattern in South African society, suspicion fell first on the domestic servant. The cook Jerita had, after all, made the soup. She even claimed to have eaten the leftovers, which were sent out of the dining room, consisting of about two tablespoonfuls.

Jerita was arrested.

—◦◦◦—

Dr Jacottet may have 'slept' after his conversation with Sam Duby, but his slumbers were agitated by nightmares. He had been given some information so disturbing that he felt he had to act on it. He therefore called on Bunbury in Maseru and told him that he had some 'startling news', but that he must see his lawyer first before he could speak. Consequently, on 29 January, Dr Jacottet sent Bunbury a wire from Mafeteng, and may also have made a statement.

—◦◦◦—

That previous week had been a busy and slightly distressing one for Lt Col. Garraway. During the course of it, he had had to try four policemen for giving a man a beating, from the effects of which the sorry man had died. Garraway was fairly lenient: he sentenced three of the policemen to two years in prison and dismissed the fourth from the force.

The whole of the following day he had spent in court trying another culpable homicide case. The accused was a 'native doctor' who swore that one of his female patients had been killed by a 'tokoloshe or dwarf' and not by the medicine he had given her. Garraway feared that most of the court believed him. As the 'doctor' had not intended to kill his patient (which of us do? thought Garraway wryly), he also let him off lightly with a couple of years.

As Mrs Ashton wrote to Garraway on Saturday apologizing for her rudeness at the dinner (to which the Resident Commissioner replied at once with, 'Please forget it all'), the week ended on a higher note, all very civilized, and he looked forward to Monday with a small degree of optimism.

But his run of ill luck continued and brought a doubly bitter fruit. As he was shaving on Monday morning, his servant Ephraim came to him with the news that his thoroughbred mare, Speedy Bird, had fallen into a donga and broken her leg.

Then, in the midst of a heavy thunderstorm that matched Garraway's inner bleakness, Bunbury came to see him with a request for a search warrant and a warrant of arrest.

'I have a most delicate and unpleasant task at present in connection with the death of the late Rev. Jacottet,' Garraway mused sadly to himself that night. 'Two of his own daughters and one of the other missionaries are suspected of poisoning Jacottet and I have to order their arrest.'

Garraway spent the next morning, the first day of February, in his office, milling and mulling. At noon, he and Assistant Commissioner F. L. Foord drove out to Morija, grateful that he had taken his Ford, since the main road was 'execrable' after heavy rain. They were there most of the afternoon, the situation demanding patience and delicacy.

Garraway and Foord went to see Alfred Casalis, the 'superintendent' of the PEMS (actually Casalis was now Acting President of the Missionary Conference) to warn him of the action they were about to take. It was an awful shock and Garraway felt sorry for him, but Casalis was gracious nonetheless and thanked the government official for the consideration he was giving the case. Casalis, it was clear, had had no suspicion whatsoever as to what might have been going on.

Next day, Wednesday, Garraway sent Bunbury, another police officer, Sub-Inspector E. Strong, and a white woman wardress to Morija to execute the warrant. Their authority permitted them to search the Jacottet house as well as the residence and office of Rev. Duby. Garraway regarded it as a distinctly unpleasant job and did not envy them the task. When they got to the mission, they found that Rev. and Mrs Duby, with their ten-year-old son Georges, had gone on a picnic with the eldest and youngest of the Jacottet daughters, and their absence made the initial search much easier. The arrival of the police caused quite a stir amongst the Basotho community at Morija. The old people did not want the youngsters near, but little Bethuel Sekhesa was close to his mother Hermania (who worked for the Duby family) when she was asked where the Dubys had gone, and he saw with wide eyes a policeman stationed at the gate and another at the Jacottet house.

In the Jacottet house, Bunbury found nothing of importance except a letter dated 19 February 1919, relating to an affair of the heart and signed by one R. Wasse or Wyss. In Duby's desk in the Book Depot, he discovered a bottle labelled 'arsenic'.

On their return from the picnic, Marcelle and Marguerite Jacottet were arrested for the murder of their father. Sam Duby was also arrested for the murder of his colleague.

—⟋⟍—

The three prisoners were brought to Maseru towards evening and taken to the jail, where they were placed in the custody of Mr J.G. Green.

Meanwhile, at five o'clock, after the stress of a big day at the office, Garraway, as wise as Solomon in the ways of judgement, managed to get away and umpire three chukkas of polo.

CHAPTER FIVE

THE HEARING

On Thursday 3 February 1921, there was a hum of excitement all over the Territory at the news of the arrest of Duby and the Jacottet sisters. This was cause for concern to the Resident Commissioner, who felt the furore would grow worse before it subsided. He was no doubt anxious that judicial proceedings be conducted as speedily as possible to damp down the rumour and speculation that spawned in the late summer heat.

Accordingly, the three arrestees were formally examined the following day in the court of the Assistant Commissioner on the charge of murder. Dramatically, at the examination, Sam Duby indicated that he wanted to make a statement, but the presiding magistrate, Mr F. L. Foord, who was also the Assistant Commissioner, reminded him that it was not advisable to do so at that stage. Duby fell silent.

The accused were remanded for trial until the following week in order for them to obtain legal assistance. They were returned to Maseru jail facing the most serious of all charges.

There were no lawyers in Maseru at the time, and most legal business was done through law firms in Bloemfontein. The solicitor engaged by the accused was, according to the *Star's* report of the proceedings, a Mr Watkins. This is certainly an error on the part of the newspaper. There was neither an advocate nor an attorney of that name in the Orange Free State at the time, and there is no doubt that the solicitor referred to was W.D.E. Watkeys of the firm McIntyre and Watkeys, who had their offices at 65 Maitland Street, the main street of the judicial capital of South Africa. Watkeys was almost certainly the lawyer Dr Jacottet had consulted in Bloemfontein (taking Madeleine with him to tell her story) before informing Bunbury of the surprise facts that precipitated the arrest and trial. Now he came to represent his new clients.

Rev. Alfred Casalis went to see Duby in detention, having written to the Resident Commissioner asking for permission to do so. He had lunch with Garraway on the day before the hearing. Garraway felt sorry for him: 'These poor mission people are in a very sad state owing to this horrible case of poor Jacottet's death by poisoning.'

—◦◦—

Although initially scheduled to start on 9 February, the case appears to have begun on Thursday the 10th. In fact, it was not a full trial but a 'preliminary' or 'preparatory' examination. The significance of this will become clear in due course. The case was to be heard before Mr Foord. Witnesses were to appear, though the three accused were not required to give evidence at this stage.

The 'sensational charge' that they had read about in their local newspaper, the *Friend* of Bloemfontein, heated by the bushfire of word-of-mouth gossip, brought most of the white population to the little courthouse in Maseru. There was, of course, a journalist from the *Friend*, and the Johannesburg *Star* had a 'special representative' there too. Equally intrigued were the Basotho.

Still pacing his fields seventy-three years afterwards, at the age of 101, Meshack Kotele could remember the day well. He was a product of the PEMS and was living in Maseru at the time. He recalled that some form of announcement had come from the government to the effect that one of the 'outstanding' missionaries was involved in something serious and that all Basotho were invited to attend the case. He distinctly remembered Dr Jacottet attending, as well as Charles Christeller, the missionary in charge of Morija parish. He also noticed Nehemiah Mapetla, one of the chiefs at Masianokeng.

The crowd stirred with excitement when the prisoners arrived in a motor car, accompanied by a warder. Once the accused had taken their seats in the courthouse, the *Star* reporter had time to study them.

Samuel Duby, whose gaze remained fixed in a single direction through most of the proceedings, wore a grey lounge suit with a 'trilby collar', and a black tie. Of medium height and with an aquiline nose and fair complexion, he appeared to the observer to be a man rather advanced in years, as suggested by his grey hair and 'somewhat attenuated countenance'.

Marguerite, the youngest sister, was in deep mourning. She was petite, pretty, though with dark rings under her eyes from crying. She presented a rather innocent, girlish appearance, and at the same time looked older than she was, not yet having attained her majority.

Lastly, the senior Jacottet girl, Marcelle, 'obviously approaching 40', tall, with curly blonde hair, her deportment stiff and defiant, was clad in a greenish khaki costume, with a white composition straw hat, a linen collar and black tie, and a plain black blouse.

The spectators crammed themselves into the small, hot room. Eventually, this barnyard of the inquisitive ceased or muted its craning and gawking, scratching and squawking, the court settled, and the examination began. Mr Foord presided.

—◦◦◦—

Whoever organized the order of proceedings did a good job of it. The first two witnesses, Bunbury and Dyke, low-key and dispassionate, represented authority and science. Bunbury testified to the sequence of events leading up to the arrest of the three now before the court. He also submitted the analyst's report, which stated that the food contents of Jacottet's stomach contained one fifth of a grain of arsenic, probably administered as arsenate of soda. Dr Dyke added that the phial (meaning the bottle taken from Duby's desk) contained pure white arsenic. These two were followed by two of the victims, F.M. Reid and Frank Paillard.

Frederick Murray Reid had come to Basutoland because of his health. He had consumption – or at least that was suspected when he first coughed blood into his handkerchief. At the time, this was regarded as an almost inevitably fatal 'condition', and more often than not kept a secret, something almost shameful. The long-term prospect was horrifying – an agonizing end in a soulless institution. The air of the colonies was believed to be beneficial. Born in Bridport in Dorsetshire in 1875, Reid was in his early twenties when he arrived in South Africa.

He had trained as a teacher at Borough Road College in Isleworth, and could teach Advanced Agriculture, Geology and Physiography, in addition to the normal curricular subjects. And he had four years' teaching experience in elementary and secondary schools in England. Consequently, the PEMS had no hesitation in taking him on at the Normal School at Morija. There he taught for fifteen years.

In 1914, a crisis hit the school, however, when the headmastership fell vacant. Reid was considered for the post, but the missionaries were reluctant to appoint someone from outside the mission who had little Sesotho and less French.

So in March 1914, at the age of thirty-eight, Reid applied to F.H. Dutton, the Director of Education, for the post of Assistant Inspector in the Education Department, was accepted, and hence entered government service.

He had married Emily Payne, daughter of a well-known trader, S.H. Payne, in Wepener just across the border. Until his move to government service, they had lived at Morija (where two sons, Harold and Fred Jnr, were born) in a small but comfortable house. The garden was large, with a mealie field at the bottom.

When Reid became an education inspector he was stationed at Mafeteng, to the south. The new house was bigger, with a rambling garden that was almost a miniature farm, a hen run, an orchard, a rondavel for visitors, and a thatched pantry. It also had a row of pine trees from which hung a cooler for meat, known as a 'safe'. This home-made device had double-sided panels of wire netting holding clinkers, on to which water dripped with lazy regularity. Cooled by the wind and shaded by the trees, meat would keep in the safe for a couple of days, but a very keen sense of smell was required for the family to avoid food poisoning.

Although the Reid boys did a bit of experimental smoking, their sense of smell could be relied upon. Not so their father's. He smoked a fanatical pipe and his verdict on the meat was invariably way off the mark. F.M. Reid was therefore not regarded as a reliable detector of poisoned food!

Reid, a dignified figure with a comfortable moustache, entered the witness box. On the morning of the fatal lunch, he said, he had first gone to the Book Depot, then on to the house of Mr Jacottet. He got there about 10.30 and saw the missionary in his study, where they chatted for a while over tea. Reid had with him his twelve-year-old son, Harold. After tea Reid intended leaving for Mafeteng, and he was on the point of saying goodbye when they noticed the storm coming. Jacottet persuaded him to wait a while, which he did. Although the storm lasted only three quarters of an hour it was very heavy, and, since the roads had been rendered impassable, Jacottet suggested he and his son stay for lunch, which was taken about one o'clock.

Frank and Marie Paillard were on holiday from Mozambique, where they were missionaries under the auspices of the Swiss Mission. Life was harder in the Portuguese Territory, the climate much less hospitable than Lesotho. Their eldest son had already been left in a vegetative state by cerebral malaria. So Morija was something of a temperate heaven, hot but far less humid, healthy.

Frank Paillard had taken the opportunity to visit several acquaintances. Jacottet, in particular, was an old friend, and had visited the Paillards in Delagoa Bay. The Paillards' toddler, Jacqueline, was not very well that morning, so she did not sit down to lunch with the party but was in the house at the time.

Immediately after eating the soup (their noses detecting nothing suspicious), Reid and his son became violently ill. So, too, did the Paillards. The women of the party, it seems, did not suffer so acutely – perhaps because their helpings were smaller – and were not in so much danger. When Dr Augsburger arrived, he was immediately steered towards Rev. Jacottet, who was found lying prostrate in the garden.

The vomiting of the missionary was so severe that no stomach pump could be used. Later on, this was also the case with Reid.

Augsburger injected Fred and Harold Reid and one or two of the others with camphorated oil, which eased their condition. When he gave evidence, Augsburger said that all of the party were ill, particularly Jacottet, and, since he suspected the poison had been administered deliberately, he had contacted the authorities on the morning of Jacottet's death. He also recounted to the court the conversation he had had with Duby the same morning and how he subsequently communicated his suspicions to Jacottet's brother.

Up to this point there had been plenty for the courtroom to chew on. Small morsels of sensation had been fed at regular intervals. With the arrival next of the grey-haired woman in the witness box, the rich main course was about to be served.

CHAPTER SIX

SCHOOL FOR SCANDAL

The headmistress of Eunice High School in Bloemfontein, Edith Louisa Mary King, was a tall, middle-aged woman, strict, according to pupils who remembered her over seventy years afterwards, but charming. Born in Pietermaritzburg in 1870, she had a degree in modern languages from Oxford. For three years from 1905, she had taught Art at Eunice before joining her sister, Bertha Everard, the painter, in the Transvaal. She had returned to the school in 1913 as Principal.

For fear of the reputation of her school, her evidence at the Jacottet hearing was given with palpable reluctance. By the time she had finished, the courtroom was abuzz with scandal.

Marguerite Jacottet was certainly at Eunice in 1918, and probably much earlier. It is likely that she was not schooled in France, like her siblings, because of the War.

In 1877, although he found Bloemfontein not 'particularly beautiful', as it could boast no rapid river or picturesque hill, Anthony Trollope described the town as 'a pretty, quiet, smiling village with willow trees all through it, lying in the plains, with distinct boundaries most pleasing to the eye'. In 1897, James Bryce, a prominent Liberal member of the House of Commons, thought it might be 'the most idyllic community in Africa'. The most common adjective travellers used of it was 'neat', and neat it still was in 1920. A town of 36 000 inhabitants, of whom half were white, it was the market centre of a thriving agricultural community, with an atmosphere and light that sparkled and a climate dry and invigorating. The town proclaimed itself one of the healthiest places in the Union, with an annual 'fly campaign' and a scheme for settling soldiers gassed in the First World War. It was the seat of the Appellate Division, the highest court in the land, which set the tone for a strict morality. It was also an important educational centre.

Eunice High School was founded as Oranje Vrij Staat Dames School by the Dutch Reformed Church in 1875, a year after the opposition Anglicans had started St Michael's School, and the Catholics Greenhill Convent. Its purpose was to provide education particularly for girls of the Protestant persuasion. A 'pure Protestantism' was to be purveyed, so that the daughters of the church members would not be corrupted by rival teachings. Curiously, the school, mainly because of the origins of many of its teachers and the British rule in the Orange River Sovereignty, eventually took on an English flavour to such an extent that it provoked the ire of General Hertzog (Attorney-General and Minister of Education of South Africa at the time), who instigated something of a witch-hunt against the headmistress and staff in 1909. By the time Miss King took over in 1913, the school was what she herself described as 'very mixed' – a mélange of classes, races, languages and religions, English, Dutch, French, German, Anglican, Dutch Reformed, Presbyterian, Wesleyan and Jewish (only blacks were excluded) – though its general tenor remained Protestant, if of the Anglican variety.

For most of its history, Eunice, as it had come to be called familiarly, was cramped for space in its premises on President Brand Street. This was aggravated on 28 January 1914 when an electrical fault in the Upper House caused it to catch fire. By morning the blackened ruins lay smoking in the unblinking sunlight. The Provincial Administration immediately placed the neighbouring Residency (now called the Presidency) at the disposal of the school. This elegant building had been used as the official residence of the last three presidents of the Orange Free State and then of the Lieutenant Governor of the Orange River Colony until 1910, and many of the boarders, perhaps including Marguerite, who was probably a student at the time, were moved into the upstairs rooms. Downstairs, the drawing room became the Art Room, the dining room the Kindergarten.

Every morning at eight, in the years that followed, Marguerite and the rest of the school came to the ballroom for assembly. Miss King, plain and ladylike, said the prayers (she would already have been to church at 6.30). Then Marguerite and the others would go off to classes, where Miss Storey instilled in them a love of poetry, Miss Baxter, a big, charming South African, taught them Mathematics, Miss Holden and Miss Sandall, from overseas, Latin, and Miss Earl, Chemistry (very weakly).

Miss King taught only occasionally. But sometimes she would bring into class a whole lot of twigs, and announcing, 'I am going to teach you rhythm and rhyme today,' would get the girls to beat time with the twigs. At other times she was known to troop her whole class outside, where the painter in her would point out to them particularly dramatic cumulus clouds laced with pink or red. Three of her pupils remember her to this day as strict but fair, sort of ruling everything, looked up to, even loved.

After classes ended at 1.30 or thereabouts, the boarders went off for lunch, rest and homework, followed, after four o'clock, by sport. Marguerite played cricket for her house (they lost the final in 1920!), and tennis for the first team.

For several years, the ruins of the Upper House were an unsightly reminder of the terrible fire of 1914. But on 5 June 1918, the anniversary of the founding of the school, the celebration of which the girls always complained about since it was close to midwinter, the foundation stone of a new building was laid in the ashes and Eirene House began to rise on the old foundations.

At the ceremony, Miss King paid tribute to the founders of the school. 'It has always been a source of thankfulness to me,' she said, 'that our school has the beautiful name of "Eunice", the mother of St Timothy, type of saintly motherhood, that ours was originally a religious foundation, in the sense that all its founders desired not merely secular education, but education based upon Christianity, that they realized that man cannot live by bread alone, either physical or mental, but that he must be nurtured on the word of God, the Divine wisdom, if he is to be truly human, and Eunice still strives towards that end; she still believes that her daughters should be as the polished corners of the Temple; she still believes, and her belief is borne out by history, ancient and modern alike, that what we believe does matter, that unless we believe rightly we shall infallibly believe wrongly.' The name of the school was pronounced as in Greek, with three syllables, and meant 'happy victory', which seemed appropriate at the moment when the Allies were on the threshold of winning the Great War in Europe.

———✧———

As one of the Temple's 'polished corners', Marguerite moved into the top floor of Eunice House with a few others at the end of 1919, and the building began to fill up with boarders the following year.

When, in 1996, at the age of ninety-two, she was shown a picture of the 1920 Sixth Form, Dorothy Johnston, who was just a year or two behind the class, did not recognize anyone. But when the name Marguerite was mentioned, she immediately said, 'Jacottet!', because she had thought Marguerite was such a pretty name and the memories suddenly came flooding back. She remembered seeing Marguerite at morning prayers in the Residency ballroom, looked down upon by Bertha Everard's paintings, one of which showed a blue stream flowing through a desert: 'She was a tall, big girl, Marguerite, about five feet six inches tall. If I remember, she wore rather old-fashioned clothes, long sleeves, long skirts. She wore a long pinaforish-looking thing, frilly. I thought of them as overseas garments. She was heavily built and wasn't wonderful-looking, wasn't beautiful. She never looked sexy.'

Marguerite was not one of the seven prefects of that year, but, along with others of the Senior Sixth Form, was made a sub-prefect. In the early part of 1920, she watched the pantomime, *Babes in the Wood*, in the Residency, and spent many hours in the library sewing and pasting books ravaged by careless hands. At the first meeting of the debating society, the proposal that 'the woman who lives at home is happier than the woman who works' was defeated by a large majority.

That year, the school magazine published an essay of hers, written in Dutch and entitled, 'On a Basotho Mission Station'. She wrote that families on most of the stations were the only Europeans for many miles around. She concentrated on the life of the missionary's wife, full of teaching needlework classes, Bible classes and Sunday school classes. Particularly difficult were those times when the annual Conference was held and up to twenty missionaries from other stations must be accommodated and fed. The station at Thaba-Bosiu was especially interesting since it was where the kings of the Basotho were buried, and thousands of Basotho, as well as the High Commissioner, would always gather for a great funeral. The life on a mission station, she said, was very quiet, but interesting nevertheless.

In June, she heard Miss King, in front of the school governors, urge the girls to victory over the world, the flesh and the devil.

In her evidence to the Maseru court, Miss King recalled the events of September 1920. It was the custom at the end of the term to have money collected from pupils to cover their train fares home. One of the teachers had collected £10 to this end, and had locked it away. Within a few hours it was missing.

The police were called in to conduct an investigation amongst the black servants, while Miss King and her staff went through the cubicles of each pupil. Then the search took an entirely unexpected turn.

One of the staff, all atwitter, reported to Miss King that some pupils had told her that Marguerite Jacottet had mentioned a large number of letters she had received (from a *man*). On hearing this, Miss King went to Marguerite's cubicle and turned it out, finding letters in various places, some of them locked up. When she read them, she found them to be quite unfit for any young girl to receive. All were written in French, but they were not signed with a proper name. She noticed, however, that they were postmarked from Morija and she recognized the handwriting. Miss King was shattered. She knew who Marguerite's ardent lover was.

The Headmistress immediately telegraphed Marcelle, who, since her mother's death the year before, had, in loco parentis, seen to the schooling of her younger sister. Not long before, Marcelle had written to Miss King requesting that her sister be allowed to return home with Rev. Samuel Duby, and that, for reasons of family convenience, she be allowed to leave a day early. Sam Duby had duly arrived on the day before the vacation and had made arrangements to pick Marguerite up a bit later.

The telegram to Marcelle instructed her to come at once, as the school was worried about Marguerite. Miss King had meanwhile sent for Marguerite, and, after telling her firmly that she was dissatisfied with her conduct, she locked the young girl up in an empty room, until the arrival of her elder sister. She also gave orders that if Rev. Duby called again, he was to be told he could not see the disgraced girl. Duby did call and was duly given the message. A second telegram to Marcelle then asked her not to communicate with anyone else about the matter.

When Marcelle arrived, Miss King interviewed her privately in her office. She showed her the letters. Marcelle instantly recognized the handwriting. Miss King then said, 'In view of the content of the letters, I am led to believe that *improper relations* have existed between Marguerite and Rev. Duby.'

To Miss King's great surprise and dismay, Miss Jacottet reacted quite calmly and said she did not think there was anything unusual in the letters.

Faced with Marcelle's apparent complicity in the affair, Miss King's anxiety increased dramatically. She fetched a meal up to her unhappy prisoner and took the opportunity to tell her that she had seen Marcelle. She urged Marguerite to make a clean confession. The young girl broke down, admitting that the letters were not such as she should have received and confessing that she *had* had improper relations with Duby.

When Miss King reported this to Marcelle, she said she did not believe it. Precisely what she claimed to disbelieve is not clear. Marcelle then asked to see her sister, and, questioned by Miss King in her presence, Marguerite repeated what she had told the Headmistress.

Deeply suspicious of and disturbed by Marcelle, Miss King then said that henceforth her business relations would only be with the father, who had previously informed her that Marcelle would look after Marguerite while she was at school. She then summoned Édouard Jacottet by telegram.

When Jacottet eventually arrived at the school, accompanied by Marcelle, Miss King began to tell him the story. But he cut her short, saying that his eldest daughter had already apprised him of the details. So Miss King produced some of the letters for Jacottet with certain passages highlighted.

One passage mentioned a dream. Miss King had already asked what this dream was about, and Marguerite had told her it was about a child (presumably imaginary) being born to her and Duby. Apparently there were a good many other references to the dream. Miss King said that it was unpleasant and terrible to have to mention it to M. Jacottet.

She then told the missionary that she could not keep his daughter in the school any longer, and advised him to send her away where she would be under strict supervision. She added sternly that she believed Marcelle was very greatly to blame.

She also insisted that Duby be dismissed from the mission as he was a great moral danger, threatening that if he were not, she would 'expose the entire thing'. Jacottet promised that this would happen, but said it would take time, possibly three months, to arrange. Jacottet did not know, of course, that he had only a little over three months to live.

As a parting shot, Miss King then told Jacottet that his daughter was either 'very wicked or fit for an asylum'. All the girl's things – the relics of her school career – were packed up, and her father promised that the letters would be destroyed. The unhappy threesome then departed.

—◦◦—

Rumour ran through the school corridors like an excited conspirator, dodging the anxious authorities and titillating the ears and the imaginations of the impressionable young. The girls were agog. The boredom of routine succumbed to the whispered sensation of the moment. The adults, of course, tried to keep the whole episode hush-hush, but they were not successful, even if they did not realize it. A frisson of scandal had agitated the entire school, nothing quite so exciting had happened since the wall had been heightened to dissuade the boys from nearby Grey College from scaling it.

Marie Kohler, whose father was a French missionary at Cana in Basutoland, was a boarder at the time. She was only thirteen and in the Residency, so she was not close to the older girls' bedrooms in the main school. She heard the name Duby whispered, she was told that Marguerite had 'eloped'. Official sources were mute on the subject, but information was sneaked in by the day girls.

Dorothy Johnston was a day scholar. Perhaps this is why she remembers more than Marie Kohler – because she knew more. In 1996, she recalled: 'There was a big thing about Marguerite. Wasn't there a love affair? Miss King was criticized. She had allowed them to go for a weekend to the Bloemfontein Hotel. The bigger girls each had a room of their own. How terrible it was to lock Marguerite up in a room. Miss King was criticized for allowing a man to see so much of her and for taking her out of boarding school.' The Bloemfontein Hotel, she explained, was Polly's Hotel, an imposing building in Maitland Street almost opposite the main post office.

'For a little while,' continued Dorothy Johnston, 'all the girls knew about it. Wasn't the man married?' The boarders were clearly upset by the general search, which they saw as an invasion of their privacy: 'The girls thought they were looking for the money at first, and didn't suspect they were looking for letters. That was the big criticism – Miss King getting into their intimate correspondence. That was their big thing. Why did she have to go looking through our things?'

Some time afterwards, Miss King, while searching some boxes, came across two more of Marguerite's letters, one of seventeen pages, the other of fourteen. They are testimony perhaps to Duby's foolishness, but they also indicate his ardour and his serious intent, as well as the fact that the affair must have been going on for some time.

At this point, Miss King, having exposed the original plot, slips from the story. She lived to be ninety-two and died in Carolina in the Transvaal in 1962, but the effects of her intervention persisted. During her interview with Jacottet, she had extracted one more promise – that Duby's wife, Eva, be informed of the relations existing between Marguerite and her husband. Subsequently, she received a letter from Jacottet saying that steps were being taken to have Duby removed from the mission, and that Duby had spoken to his wife and had made a full confession.

CHAPTER SEVEN

CHOICES

The journey of Jacottet and his two daughters from Bloemfontein home to Morija can scarcely be imagined. Rage, remorse, sullenness, self-righteousness, obstinacy, frustration, foreboding, reproach – all mixed in one giant emotional maelstrom. By the time he got home, Jacottet was choked with grief. He was also ill. And he was faced with a terrible dilemma.

Duby had to go, that was clear, the mission was no longer big enough for the two of them. Marguerite's expulsion from school could not be concealed and must be explained. The reputation of the mission must be protected. So must that of his daughter. And what was he to make of his eldest daughter, who had helped flesh his cadette into the forbidden instinct of the chase?

One of the first things he did was have a solemn talk with Madeleine, his middle daughter. He told her that his news was sad, that the fears that had snatched at his heart when he first received Miss King's telegrams were justified – Marguerite had been disgraced by a 'gentleman of the mission', who had consequently lost his reputation in her father's eyes. Madeleine was puzzled. Who could it be?

When he told her, she could not believe it. Samuel Duby? Surely not!

Her father asked her whether she realized the gravity of the situation. Keep the affair a secret, he begged her. Then he said a truly astonishing thing. He instructed her to tell Rev. Alfred Casalis that Marguerite had been removed from school for theft! Was Jacottet prepared to sacrifice his daughter's reputation for honesty on the altar of chastity? In conclusion, he said that Marguerite was not entirely responsible for the situation and had been seduced into it.

Madeleine first went to comfort her younger sister in her bedroom. She told Marguerite that she was glad she had come home and that they would be happy together in the evenings. Then she returned to the Normal School to deliver her father's message to Casalis.

—◦⊙◦—

This was Madeleine's version of the events surrounding Marguerite's expulsion in September the previous year. It was delivered to the court in impeccable English with a definite French accent.

The court saw a striking-looking woman in her mid-twenties, not particularly tall, well built, but neither heavy nor plump. She had strong features and thick, dark-brown hair, almost black, and her deep, expressive eyes matched those of her sisters in the dock. As she spoke, in a characteristically rapid manner, she was clearly nervous.

She continued her evidence. Her father had later explained to her that he had allowed Marguerite and Duby to come back for the honour of the mission. 'Father told me,' she said, 'that he had advised Duby to make a confession to his wife.' He added that he had assured Duby he would not let the disgraceful facts be known, but that Duby must leave the mission in a few months' time. As a postscript, her father entrusted Madeleine with a sacred task: 'If after my death the facts do become known, the missionaries may not understand, so it will be your duty to let them know this action was to save the honour of the mission.'

Silence and secrecy were the price of honour. Who could foretell the consequences? This was the pastor's dilemma.

Madeleine's evidence moved on in time. It seems that Jacottet either grew somewhat erratic in his behaviour in the following months or that emotional confusion in the family translated itself into failures of understanding.

One evening, Jacottet returned to the subject of his own death, saying, 'When I am ill and feel I am going to die, I will ask my brother to come.' Did he intend to confide the whole story to Dr Jacottet so that he could set the record straight if necessary, in times to come?

Jacottet also said he would write to his eldest son Henri in London, telling him he had to fetch his youngest sister home to England. When Madeleine flinched and said, 'You will not like to tell him the reason,' he replied, 'No, not such unpleasantness.' He also said that naturally Marguerite could not stop going to visit Mrs Duby, but that Madeleine should always be with her when she did so.

Clearly, Jacottet had come to rely more and more on Madeleine as the only daughter he could trust.

Some sort of routine re-established itself, although it was punctuated by frequent quarrels. Marguerite began studying for her matriculation examinations at the end of the year. 'She was very nice,' remembered Madeleine, 'and we got on very well.'

Then, one Sunday, the sisters went for a picnic with the Duby family – an event which perhaps testifies to the great tolerance of Eva Duby, who had to suffer the presence of the young girl who had nearly stolen her husband. That night, Marguerite, somewhat incredulously, confided to Madeleine: 'I think the world is coming to an end, because Marcelle told me that father said that as soon as I finish my exam, I can go and help them [i.e. Marcelle and Duby] take stock at the Book Depot, and he has agreed to allow me to go camping on the mountain with the Duby family.'

Again, Madeleine was puzzled by her father's decisions. A few days afterwards, he confirmed to her that he had consented for Marguerite to take stock at the Book Depot, with Marcelle and Duby, but he did not mention anything about mountain camping.

—◦◦—

It had been a long day for the court, with more than its fair share of sensations. Mr Foord adjourned the hearing at this relatively quiet moment, but the onlookers anticipated more revelations from Madeleine's evidence when it resumed the following day.

That night, Lt Col. Garraway noted in his diary that poor Mr Dieterlen had had lunch with Win Garraway during the day. With this homely item of news recorded, he moved on to the more public face of the Jacottet case, observing that the preliminary examination had been going on all day, a circumstance he found 'most unpleasant'.

—◦◦—

The hearing resumed on the morning of Friday the 11th to the sound of continuous rain.

The evidence the previous day had been tantalizing, but no decisive fingers had been pointed. Madeleine's continued testimony was likely to shake things up.

She began quietly enough. She had felt aggrieved, she said, when she was not invited to the picnic that had been arranged in the mountains. But Marcelle had later placated her, assuring Madeleine that she wanted her to come, and even promising to ask their father to let her off her household chores for a few days. Having gained the moral high ground, Madeleine, with a fine perversion, replied that she did not wish to leave him, especially as there were visitors (probably the Paillards) coming to the house.

But then she came, in her testimony, to the evening before the murder, the night of the 21st. This fraught night began with a confrontation between Marcelle and Jacottet in his study. They were discussing the proposed picnic. The voices grew angrier, and so loud that Madeleine could eavesdrop without difficulty.

Jacottet vehemently objected to Marguerite going to the mountain camp. The name of Duby was frequently mentioned. Marcelle tried to persuade her father to unbend and allow Marguerite to go, but he replied that she could not go 'at any cost' and he was surprised that Marcelle should ask such a thing.

Marcelle hit back by accusing her father of being a hard-hearted man, of having no mercy, and of not forgiving Marguerite for what she had done. Jacottet retorted that he had forgiven, but there was a difference between forgiving and letting Marguerite go to the picnic.

Marcelle had the last word, and it was possibly the last time she ever spoke to her father: 'You are like that, you parsons. I hope when you die the gates of heaven will shut in your face when they ask you, did you forgive on earth?'

—∞—

Madeleine then went to Marguerite's room and found her in bed. Marguerite admitted that she had also heard some of the argument. So loud must it have been.

The elder sister consoled the younger by saying, 'Never mind, we two will stay at home.' To which Marguerite answered angrily: 'Well, if it is only polite I don't mind, but if it is going to spoil the Depot business I will revenge myself.' Madeleine tried to soothe her: 'Don't think about it. Go to sleep.'

Madeleine next went to Marcelle, who was still seething with anger. Madeleine did not say what they talked about.

—∞—

In the cool hours of the following morning, passions remained hot. It was the custom of the daughters to kiss their father every morning, but when Marguerite studiously avoided doing so, Jacottet asked, 'Will you not kiss me, Marguerite?'

Later, at about half past ten, as the day grew oppressively hotter, Madeleine was seated on the verandah, taking advantage of the outside air, when she heard a door banging in the house. She went into the passage, and, as she approached the door of the dining room, it opened 'inside against her'. She saw Marguerite and jumped back. Then both laughed. 'Did I frighten you?' asked Marguerite, to which Madeleine replied, 'Yes, you came so suddenly.' Marguerite took her by the waist and asked her to come and find the little tin patterns for cutting biscuits. They went into the pantry together.

Before she left to return to the Book Depot, Marguerite mentioned that Mr Reid and his son Harold had been there that morning, and she thought they were coming to see Jacottet.

The Reids duly arrived and had morning tea. The Paillards were also there.

After tea, they all went out on to the verandah (Madeleine called it the 'stoep') to look at the weather. Mr Reid was anxious to get back to Mafeteng, but decided to wait. The storm was threatening.

Under cross-examination from the Crown (probably represented by Inspector Bunbury), Madeleine said that after Marguerite had gone, she subsequently met Marcelle in the kitchen, Marcelle apparently having entered that room from the outside. Marcelle asked if her father had spoken about the argument the night before. Madeleine replied that he had asked if she had overheard it. Marcelle asked her to tell their father that she was taking Marguerite to lunch with Duby.

When they sat down to lunch, Madeleine served the soup. It was an old joke in the family how her father liked soup. Her father had the most; she and Harold had only a little.

She was taken ill and went to lie down for a time, but on hearing that all the others were stricken, she went to their assistance. Then, although she herself was very ill, her legs shaking and her head burning with pain, she hastened down to Duby's office to urge him to hurry to the house. When she entered his office and told him they had all been poisoned, he put his finger to his lips and said, 'Ssh.'

After they returned to the Jacottet house, she collapsed and was nursed by Duby, Marcelle and Marguerite.

In further evidence, Madeleine said that after their father's death, Marcelle had warned her that there was going to be an inquest, and that a doctor and the police were coming. Marcelle added that she had something to tell Madeleine: she said that, on his deathbed, their father had wrung an undertaking from her that, whatever happened, they would 'cover' Marguerite and Duby. Marcelle also insisted that *she* would answer any questions on behalf of Marguerite that the police might ask concerning the school affair.

On the question of arsenic, Madeleine admitted that there had been a bottle in the dining-room cupboard until a month previously, but it had been removed by Marcelle. This was because she, Madeleine, was suffering from considerable head and nerve pain, which became so bad she thought she could no longer bear it, and she sometimes felt as though she would like to do away with herself.

Marguerite had also said that she would like the arsenic for herself, her life being unbearable since she was not allowed to live with the man she loved. In addition, Marguerite had complained that her father was always finding fault with her. With her sisters vying for the lethal favours of the arsenic bottle, it is little wonder that Marcelle was asked by her father to remove it. Madeleine did not know what Marcelle had done with it.

Madeleine added that she had heard her father complain about Marcelle's behaviour towards him.

Madeleine finished her evidence by saying that she was afraid something was going to happen to her, and so had asked her uncle, Dr Jacottet, to take her away. Questioned about this, she answered that she was afraid she was going to be poisoned, but she could give no tangible reason for her fears.

—◦�〇◦—

Dr Gustave Jacottet, the dead man's brother, gave evidence after Madeleine. He was at home in Matatiele in East Griqualand at the time of his brother's death, and knew nothing about Marguerite's expulsion from school. He first heard about this from Dr Augsburger, who came to speak to him not long after the funeral.

Shocked, he went to see Duby and demanded to know what had been going on. Duby turned white and became agitated. Dr Jacottet grabbed Duby by the shoulders and repeated his demand. Duby asked him what he knew, and Dr Jacottet answered that he had heard reports of a petty theft. At this, Duby said that Marguerite had broken many of the rules at school, but refused to supply further details, stating that he had given his word of honour to Marguerite's father to remain silent. He suggested that Dr Jacottet ask Marcelle instead.

Dr Jacottet did not pursue the matter with Marcelle, however, as he had great affection for the delinquent Marguerite. Satisfied that it was not a serious matter, he did not care to know more. This is no doubt what he meant when, after returning from his conversation with Duby, he said to Augsburger, 'I have slept.' But he had clearly been deceived.

Dr Jacottet told the court that he had seen a bottle of arsenic on Duby's desk in his office. This was in full view, and Duby had actually shown it to him. He and Duby had, in fact, talked about arsenate of soda in a discussion of chemical terms. They spoke of the difference between arsenic acid and arsenate of soda. Marcelle had told him that she had brought the bottle from the house to the office herself.

It seems that it was Madeleine who later told him of the affair between Marguerite and Sam Duby. He was astounded, incredulous. He wanted to confirm her story, so he went to Bloemfontein, taking her with him, so that she could repeat her statements to his attorney (it was much later, on 24 January, that he had told Bunbury he had 'startling news for him', but must first see a lawyer in Bloemfontein before communicating it to him). He and Madeleine also went to visit Miss King, who must have left him in no doubt. On 29 January, he telegraphed Bunbury about his suspicions. It was Dr Jacottet, therefore, who had provided the authorities with their first real break and precipitated the whole crisis.

He finished his evidence with snippets of family history. He had had but little correspondence with his brother, though the latter did ask his medical advice about the nerve pain Madeleine felt in her face and head. His brother, he testified, loved Madeleine and referred to her as 'a ray of sunshine in his life', a life which had been darkened by Marcelle's studied avoidance of him, and by the clouds of gloom that surrounded his youngest daughter's frustrated affections.

His brother, Dr Jacottet said, had married a lady who had suffered from 'nervous fits', but he added that she was 'no blood relation'. The three boys were 'mentally quite sound', except for the youngest, who was 'a degenerate'.

The 'native cook', Jerita, had had a hard time of things. Arrested on the same day Dr Jacottet went to Bloemfontein to see his lawyer, she must have given evidence to the Maseru court with some foreboding. She had, she said, worked for Mr Jacottet for ten years.

On the day of the tragedy, she had cooked the lunch, which was to consist of soup, beans and macaroni. She put the food on the fire after the morning tea, and boiled some meat separately. She then went into the garden, which was at some distance from the house; she could not see the kitchen door from the garden. She was there for 'a considerable time' gathering vegetables, but was not sure for how long. When she returned, she put the vegetables away (whether in the kitchen or the pantry, she did not say).

No one came to the kitchen before she left it to go into the garden, and she 'did not see Marcelle that morning, neither did she see Marguerite'.

When the company manifested the symptoms of real illness, she went to Miss Madeleine's room and immediately saw that she was very sick.

She herself had eaten the leftovers of the soup which she removed from the dining room, an amount of about two tablespoonfuls. But she was not in the least affected by it. The dish was not full when it was sent into the dining room. She had no idea as to how the party became ill.

'Have you heard,' asked the prosecution, 'any whisperings among the natives concerning the relations existing between Marcelle and Duby?' She replied, 'I have not.'

If Jerita was nervous, the following witness must have been truly frightened. It was a strange and different world that 'the young native girl' entered, where dozens of peering faces, white and black, quizzical and intense, followed her every move. Mamaime was the 'native nurse girl' of the Paillards, and she remembered the day of the tragedy well.

After breakfast, she was washing at a tap when she saw Marcelle coming by a footpath towards the house, which she entered by the kitchen door. Jerita was in the garden at the time. Marcelle remained in the house for a short time and then left again by the kitchen door. Mamaime said that nobody else had come to the house and she had not seen Marguerite that morning. Marcelle asked her where Jerita was, and she answered that she was in the garden. Marcelle said, 'Please greet her for me.'

This version of events had been confirmed by Jerita in her testimony. She had testified that Mamaime had said to her that 'Miss Marcelle had been to the kitchen and asked where she was; she had told Mamaime to give her her greetings'.

The preliminary examination ended on a quiet note. The last witness, a man with a disturbed past himself, was Ernest Mabille. He stated that he had been at Morija since the beginning of August and had visited Mr Jacottet 'about twice' at his house, but had only 'met' Duby 'on the day before the funeral'. He said he had come into contact with Jacottet in 'the way of business', he had never heard any quarrels between Jacottet and Duby, and the former had never spoken to him about his daughters.

Marcelle, Marguerite and Sam Duby were not required to give evidence, nor did they offer to do so. Their counsel, Mr Watkeys, asked for bail, but Mr Foord said that it was not within his power to grant it, though he agreed to make a note of the application and submit it to the Resident Commissioner together with the evidence. It was the Resident Commissioner who would fix a trial or otherwise.

Garraway's diary that night recorded that the 'splendid steady rain' had persisted all day until five o'clock. The entry continued: 'The preliminary examination in the Jacottet case is, I think, finished today, and I suppose I shall have it passed on to me for necessary action in a day or two.'

In the days that followed, Garraway would have to decide whether to proceed to trial or not. It was a decision he was not looking forward to. He always got a bit fidgety in the face of high seriousness. Although he wanted to wind things up as quickly as possible, he did realize that the case was a timepiece which was extremely complex, even delicate, and needed careful handling.

He was presented with a dilemma. He could choose to treat only the narrow plot of the affair, in which case he need only examine the bare bones of circumstance and motive. Or he could, like one of the hyenas of history, scratch deeper beyond simple motive to explanation, or even meaning.

He was a regular churchgoer. He knew that the New Testament could not be understood without some reference to and knowledge of the Old, that to understand fully it is sometimes necessary to travel back to the beginning of things, and that this might be true of the Jacottet story. Being a sportsman rather than a pedantic scholar, however, his overall grasp of the story's fundamentals – not to mention the subtle connections of its details – was necessarily vague. And he had little idea what it all meant to those involved and their view of how the tragedy had unfolded. Nevertheless, that night, and in the days and nights that followed, the words of St Paul to the Corinthians ghosted his thoughts and his dreams: 'Behold, I shew you a mystery.' Perhaps even a mystery within a mystery.

Part Two

THE WORLD

——❦——

Time brings all to birth –

Aeschylus, *The Libation Bearers*

CHAPTER EIGHT

LEHAHA-LA-SONTAHA

February, 1840

I t had been a long and tiring day by the time the party of about thirty men reached the cave on the great Tsime plateau in Lesotho. It was Saturday evening, 22 February 1840. The imposing figure who led the party was dressed in a pair of velvet trousers and a green-striped waistcoat, with a long, home-spun jacket of the kind that sailors wore. Around his neck, a tricoloured woollen band was fastened, after a fashion, and around his waist a sash of red. His coarse carter's shoes were topped by a fine pair of white socks, though these were not as pristine as when they had started out that morning. He carried a bamboo lance in his hand, a powder horn slung over his shoulder, and a pair of assegais; perhaps, too, a gun. On his head were a cotton hat and a blue cloth cap with the initials S.H. stitched into it. A gift, or the discarded headgear of a soldier from St Helena? This man was Moshoeshoe, King of the Basotho.

Of the three white men in the party, the only one of note was a young man who spoke Sesotho with a French accent. His name was Thomas Arbousset, and he was one of the founders of the Morija mission station. He was more soberly attired than Moshoeshoe, as befitted his calling as a missionary. In his saddlebag was the journal he was keeping of the expedition.

The morning had started early, with Moshoeshoe in something of a hurry. But Arbousset had dug in his heels and taken the opportunity to make a point important to him. Up to this, the eighth day of the journey, he had listened carefully to the King, given him full respect, and obeyed him as the most humble of his subjects would. Now, he had silently gathered the whole group to sit on the grass, where they sang two hymns, read a chapter from the Bible, and prayed. It had become the usual morning ritual, and the point Arbousset wanted to make was that prayer is not to be postponed. Moshoeshoe had quietly joined them, listening attentively, thus giving the younger man, deter-mined in his spiritual domain, his own nod of respect in return. As he mounted his horse, Arbousset, aware that his Christian religion might seem humourless in its strictness and inflexibility, had given the King a smile. Moshoeshoe understood well what he meant. The two were friends.

The day had also been frustrating: they had hoped, after their climb from the valleys, to find the high country teeming with eland, but there were none to be seen. They had to content themselves with the majestic scenery, the plateau extending for miles until it gave way to the great range, stretching east-wards and southwards, of the Maloti, 'which hide in the skies their imposing size'; and with a certain curious phenomenon which Arbousset called 'magic circles', and the Basotho 'maphakatlali', wraths of the thunderbolt.

These perfect circles of dark-green grass seemed to attract animals because of their distinctive taste. The local explanation for this phenomenon was that, during the winter months, the violent contest between the north wind, Leboea, and the south-west wind caused tornadoes, which spun around the peaks like revenging gods, full of rain and hail and noise, lashing the grasslands with their thunderbolts. After such a wild storm, 'a superstitious pagan priest', in Arbousset's words, would come to 'dig reverently into the bosom of the earth', searching for 'thunder water' to use in purifying medicines that would protect him and his people against the fickle wrath unleashed from the sky. Although Arbousset noted the mushroom fringes, he did not recognize the magic circles for what they are.

It was unexpected to find a cave there – the group had climbed to almost 1 800 metres above sea level. The sandstone which harbours the magnificent rock shelters of Lesotho gives way, at that altitude, to basalt, where there are no caves. This cave is a great overhang of rock, in the shape of a horseshoe, light and airy. A waterfall drops into the interior, forming a pool and then a pretty stream, which meanders the whole length of the cave before it destroys the idyll by disappearing into a dark and terrifying crack in the earth, some seven metres deep. Two great boulders stand sentry not far from the pool. On the vast walls, disappearing in the fading light, inscribed by an unknown hand, were the portraits, in black, ochre, red and white, of hartebeest and eland, providing a prehistoric link between this world and the spirit world. To the Basotho, the cave was 'Liphofung', the place of the eland.

After the horses and other animals had been driven into a safe corner and the entrance to the cave sealed, against the wild, with branches of 'wilde-geld-hout trees and heather', Qacha, the butcher, chose a young ox, and drove his spear, according to ritual, through its fifth rib. The animal stamped, and tossed its head, but several other oxen were driven up against it so that it was contained, rigid with pain, in a warm surround, its blood let in a steady sacri-fice. At last, it swayed, its knees buckled, and it sank to the ground, giving out that final sigh of death.

Within three quarters of an hour, the ox had been skinned and the meat roasted on burning brushwood. Those highest in rank, 'like Homer's heroes', did not eat first, but the best delicacies – the entrails – were eventually served to them on two short switches. This was followed by the brisket, part of the kidneys and the best pieces of meat. With a morsel in his mouth and another on his spear, Moshoeshoe asked Arbousset if the taste of the Basotho food was not 'every bit as good' as that of the Mafora, the French.

The party had used all their pots in the preparation of the various dishes, so they had to look around for plates in which to pour the resulting broth. The rock floor had a number of hollows, worn away by water, and into these natural bowls the broth was poured. Arbousset was slightly taken aback by this solution, but intrigued and amused nonetheless by its inventiveness. Even Diogenes, he supposed, not renowned for his delicate living habits, might have been embarrassed by how basic the utensils were, but would still have found them effective.

After the supper, and after prayer, the men settled down to more domestic tasks like mending and washing clothes. Arbousset prompted Moshoeshoe to talk about the history of the Basotho.

—୧⊙—

Moshoeshoe may be regarded as the greatest southern African of all, at least in the nineteenth century. And, at this time, in middle age, he was beginning to reach the high plateau of his power, and his reputation was also spreading. Yet his origins were not particularly exalted, and when he was born, some fifty years before, few would have predicted his rise to rule a country.

The land itself is dramatic. It has three main features. Stretching away to the west are the 'lowlands', a great plain which is in fact high above sea level (the lowest point in present-day Lesotho is nearly 1 400 metres above sea level, making it the highest lowest point of any country in the world). Breaking up this plain are a number of hills and great plateaux, or mesas, such as the Thabana-Morena, Makhoarane, Qeme, Berea and Leribe plateaux, usually topped by a visible layer of sandstone carved by Nature into dramatic cliffs, with caves formed from the great overhangs of rock. To the east, and running from north-east to south-west, rise still more dramatically the vast mountain ranges of the Maloti (covering nearly three quarters of present-day Lesotho). At the country's eastern boundary, the mountains, here called the Drakensberg, drop away spectacularly to the plains of Natal, which extend to the sea.

Cutting through the land is a vast river system, the main course of which flows from its source in the high north-east, making its way through the eastern and southern side of the country, before heading west and north to find its outlet in the Atlantic Ocean. This is the largest river in southern Africa – the Senqu, or Orange. The other large river lies to the north and west. The

Mohokare (or Caledon) is a tributary of the Senqu and joins it beyond the modern town of Aliwal North. In the eighteenth and for most of the nineteenth century, the inhospitable Maloti were almost entirely deserted except for a sprinkling of Bushmen (or San), clever hunters and food gatherers who left their fantastical pictures on the cave walls. But, to the west, the valley of the Mohokare, before it was grievously wounded and scarred by erosion, as a result of changing agricultural methods and overpopulation from the middle of the nineteenth century onwards, was extremely fertile, with a temperate climate and an adequate rainfall.

The valley inevitably attracted the people who were moving slowly down from the north in successive waves. They were cattle-owners, agriculturalists and iron smelters. Archaeological evidence places them on the Witwatersrand by at least the fifth century. The first groups to move south of the Mohokare, perhaps around 1600, were the Maphetla (the Pioneers), the Mapolane and the Baphuthi. These were Nguni-speakers who came from the north-east, and they were not very numerous. They were followed by two large Sesotho-speaking groups, first the Bafokeng, then the Bakoena, who had once lived near the junction of the Crocodile and Marico rivers. The Bakoena took as their seboko, or totem, the crocodile – hence their name, the People of the Crocodile.

About 1550, Napo, the great-grandson of Koena, grew fed up with living, as he said, 'like a reed overshadowed by a tree', that is, subordinate to his elder brother Mochuli, so he migrated south, crossing the Lekoa river (the Vaal) and eventually settling near some Bafokeng, east of the Namahali river (the Elands). Here the Noka Tlou, a minor tributary of the Namahali, runs at the foot of a hill called Ntsoanatsatsi. Today it is called Tafelkop, and stands out on the horizon alongside the motorway between Johannesburg and Durban, midway between the towns of Frankfort and Vrede. At that time, four hundred years ago, its plateau was fringed by wild olive trees. It was to be the birthplace of several Koena clans.

Which is probably why a nativity legend clings to it. On his first journey of exploration to the north in 1836, Arbousset had visited the hill, and was told by the Basotho that their ancestors lived there, having emerged in some miraculous fashion from a cave surrounded by marsh and reeds. Ntsoanatsatsi means 'the Rising of the Sun'.

Here Napo married a daughter of the Bafokeng chief, and they had a son called Motebang. Then Motebang begat Molemo, and Molemo begat Tšoloane. In his turn, Tšoloane begat Monaheng, who begat Motloheloa, who begat Motloang. Motloang didn't exactly beget anyone, because he was killed in battle first. But his widow, as we shall see, did have a child called Motšoane, who was brought up by Motloang's young brother, Mokoteli. Motšoane was an unfortunate little chap and soon acquired the onomatopoeic name of 'Peete', the Stutterer. His main claim to historical fame is that he was the grandfather of Moshoeshoe.

Although the Bafokeng and Bakoena lived for a while in reasonable harmony at Ntsoanatsatsi, poverty and oppression, Moshoeshoe was later to say, drove his forebears thence. Napo's sons moved to what is now the Heidelberg district. Then the clan went to present-day Bethlehem; and, in the time of Monaheng, on to Futhane mountain, near what is now Fouriesburg. Monaheng died there in a cave called Moribeng. Mokoteli, with Peete, his adoptive son, brought up as the seed of his brother, moved to Mohobollo (Levi's Nek), then on to Molokong, where he died aged about ninety. Peete was of little account and scratched a living selling leqala (bergbamboo), which he carried about on his back. His sons Libe and Mokhachane were more capable, however.

Mokhachane was lucky to survive beyond early manhood. A group called the Basekake raided the Bamokoteli, captured Mokhachane and relieved him of his few cattle. They took him to their village and left him bound in a hut, waiting for his death at sunrise, while they went to feast on part of the spoils. The future of southern Africa hung in the balance. A woman, whose name and motive are lost to time, scraped a hole in the mud wall of the hut, untied him and let him out. He hid in a ravine, and his pursuers never found him.

As was customary, these two sons of Peete established their own villages. Mokhachane's village was called Menkhoaneng and was some twenty kilometres along the Hlotse river from its junction with the Mohokare. His first wife was called Kholu; she was the daughter of a Mofokeng immigrant, and came from near Botha-Bothe mountain, a few kilometres to the north. Their first child was a daughter, 'Matšoenyane. Their first son was born at a time when there was a quarrel over witchcraft in the village, so he was called Lepoqo, or Dispute. Jacottet estimated the date of his birth as being between 1786 and 1788. The couple had two more sons, Makhabane and Posholi, and Mokhachane subsequently took several more wives, who provided Lepoqo with a number of half-brothers, the most important of whom were to be Mohale (by Mokhachane's second wife) and Mopeli (by his fourth). It is ironic that to a boy of humble birth called 'Dispute', the Basotho people today owe their unity and their existence as an independent nation. Jacottet never met Lepoqo – or Moshoeshoe, as history remembers him – but he lived always in the shadow of his shade.

—◦◎—

The Moshoeshoe-Arbousset expedition had started out from Thaba-Bosiu on 15 February, seven days before their arrival at Liphofung cave. Arbousset had travelled up from his post at Morija a few days earlier. He had arranged to leave his wife, Katherine, and their children with 'friends truly worthy of this designation', Eugène and Sarah Casalis, at the mission station at the foot of Thaba-Bosiu mountain. Four years before, in March 1836, Arbousset and another colleague, François Daumas, had made their pioneering venture into the northern part of Lesotho, where they had come close to the sources of several of the great rivers of South Africa, the Lekoa, the Mohokare, the Tugela, and, above all, the Senqu. In the process, they had fixed the French language forever into the landscape by naming one of the great peaks Mont-aux-Sources. But Arbousset was disappointed that he had not actually seen 'the headwaters of the Orange River', having been within a few leagues of it. The purpose of this new trip was to remedy that disappointment, and at the same time promote his calling by taking the Word of God into this wilderness. At the beginning of 1840, he had mentioned his plan to Moshoeshoe.

The King announced that he, too, would like to make the journey to explore the mountains, and the river whose source nobody in the country, other than a few hunters, had seen. He was prompted by a 'natural curiosity' which Arbousset thought distinguished him from the majority of his subjects. He had 'a deeper yearning for complete knowledge' and 'his horizons were not confined'. It was time, too, for the King to inspect the uncertain northern margins of his domain, whence came the constant threat of his 'sworn enemies' the Batlokoa, or Mantatees as they were commonly known, under their chief Sekonyela.

After a few days' delay due either to royal privilege or royal perversity, the expedition set out from Thaba-Bosiu, at first heading northwards, then roughly in a north-easterly direction. The countryside was spectacular. The great plain, which stretched unbroken to the west, was bounded to the east by river valleys and huge plateaux, while further to the east, the great chain of the Maloti, the Blue Mountains, promised mystery and adventure.

Moshoeshoe took with him knowledge of the terrain, and an experienced though not wholly trusted guide, Mokiba, who knew the Maloti well. The King was also accompanied by his sons, Molapo and Masupha. Arbousset took with him his faith and his knowledge of a new world.

They soon crossed the Phuthiatsana river, whose current was so strong and deep that Arbousset sat cross-legged on his horse, like a tailor, as it ferried him over. They then climbed up on to the Berea plateau with its magnificent views and its fine grazing for Moshoeshoe's herds, and headed towards Thupa-Kubu, the Wood of the Hippopotamus, whose name stood as a memorial to a creature long since vanished from those parts.

But every Eden is likely to contain a fatal tree, thought Arbousset, like the fig tree in the Bible which was cursed by the Lord, a tree of knowledge or a tree of evil. So the party came to 'the sad Lithethana, or Tree of Skirts'. Arbousset could not pass it without shuddering, because of the story attached to it, a living reminder of the dreadful years the country had so recently endured.

Here bands of cannibals, Malimo, would waylay travellers on the road, swooping down on them from their 'horrible shelters, like infernal demons', to cut their throats and eat their flesh. Women had the added indignity of having their leather skirts or aprons, their lithethana, stripped from them and hung on the branches by their executioners, part spectacle, part trophy, before being 'driven or dragged to the den of these bandits'.

When it began to drizzle finely a bit later, Arbousset felt cleansed. Riding along the precipices of the plateau, he enjoyed an entirely new perspective: on top of the world, he looked down upon a cloud releasing huge drops of rain into the maize and millet fields hundreds of feet below, 'producing a noise like drainpipes', which gave him the uncanny feeling that he was in an upper room in his native town in France, listening at the window to the rain in the street.

This sense of exhilaration, heightened by nostalgia for home and security, did not last. The party soon arrived at their first destination, the cave of Malimong, or place of the cannibals. It was dark, and they were met by a jostling riot of Malimo wanting to know who they were and what they wanted, all to the backdrop din of a pounding waterfall. Ruefully, Arbousset was now reminded of a noisy market in Gascony. On second thoughts, perhaps it was Hell. Confused by this jumbled succession of feelings, sometimes pleasant, sometimes frightful, he retired to a private corner of the cave to pray to God. His dreams, in this cave of cannibals, a place both beautiful and frightening, where humanity preyed on itself, were of the darkest days of the French Revolution.

Things looked a bit more cheerful in the sunny light of morning. It was Sunday, and the mountains provided a grand setting for the throng of stoics and epicureans who gathered from the neighbouring villages to hear this babbler holding forth about strange gods. Like St Paul, he had 'a real Areopagus', truly a hill that had been presided over by the god of war. So Arbousset, paraphrasing Acts 17: 22–33, took for the subject of his sermon 'The Unknown God', and gave Him a name. Because He had made all nations of one blood, this God, Jehovah, Creator and Lord of heaven and earth, had looked upon them, even in their ignorance. And now God commanded 'mankind, all men everywhere, to repent, because he has fixed the day on which he will have the world judged, and justly judged, by a Man of his Choosing, that is to say, Jesus Christ, our Saviour, whom he has raised from the dead'.

Arbousset was fulfilling his calling. These words, these ideas had never before been heard in this place, by these people. He felt a measure of exultation. In a small way, he had chosen, and had been chosen, to bring precious knowledge to the ignorant. Hitherto in darkness, perhaps now they might see. Like the Athenians who had listened to St Paul, a few seemed to respond. Others were doubters and scoffers. One of the expedition members, Mohale, a half-brother of Moshoeshoe, a man given to drink, said that their prayers 'were merely matters of custom peculiar to white men'. Was the commandment 'Thou shalt not kill' merely custom, protested Arbousset? Or the commandment, 'Thou shalt not steal'? Or even, 'Thou shalt honour thy father and thy mother'? Mohale was taken aback, forced to question himself, examine his conscience. Publicly, he confessed his inner turmoil: 'When I hear the Gospel read, or when the missionaries explain it to me, it speaks to me, I believe in it; but when I am alone, my heart cries out, "Oh! What a strange heart it is!"'

Then the wise Moshoeshoe took his friend Arbousset to the top of Pulane mountain, and from there, surrounded by the principal cannibal chiefs as well as their own missions and temptations, they surveyed the countryside through a telescope. To the west, at the limit of their vast horizon, they could even make out, over ninety kilometres away, the peak of Thaba 'Nchu, which seemed 'like a smudge lost in the sky'. In the past, these hills had been happily and prosperously populated by tribes owing their common allegiance to the great chief, Mohlomi. Now, to the eyes of the onlookers, they were for the most part uninhabited. Distressed, Moshoeshoe said, 'At the time of that renowned king, these fertile and spacious valleys were covered with men, just as they are today covered with stones.'

'War,' he added, 'that is the great evil of this country.'

Then the son of Mokhachane put his hand over his eyes and preserved a deep silence. No doubt he was thinking of the past. Perhaps there was a moment when all intervening time pressed itself into a defining instant, and the spectre of Mohlomi rose before him.

The society Moshoeshoe had been born into was only very loosely organized, and there was no unified political system or centralized chieftainship. Villages seldom consisted of more than a hundred people, and although there was conflict, it usually consisted of cattle-raiding and was never on a massive scale. In the late eighteenth and early nineteenth centuries, one man amongst the Bakoena stood head and shoulders above the rest. He was a grandson of Monaheng and therefore a distant relation of Moshoeshoe. His name was Mohlomi. Born in about the 1720s, Mohlomi was a mystic rather than a militarist. 'It is better,' he said, 'to thrash the corn than to sharpen the spear.' At his initiation, when he was about thirteen, he was said to have had a vision, while his fellow initiates were sleeping, in which the roof of his hut opened wide and he was carried up into the skies, amongst a multitude of people, and he was told, 'Go, rule by love, and look on thy people as men and brothers.' He was also reputed to have had a dream of warning, which his father Monyane scorned at the cost of his life.

Near Hlohloloane (Clocolan) in the Free State, there are a number of Bushman paintings: when the Bakoena saw them, they said, 'Ke melimo e ngolileng moo' (The shades have written here), and so the place became known as Ngoliloe. It was the mystery of Ngoliloe which attracted Mohlomi to come and live there. Not only was he a diviner and prophet, but he was also a healer (he was reputed to have cured leprosy) and, no doubt as a careful observer of the elements, a famous rainmaker. But he had little time for the witchdoctors and selaoli, the bonethrowers, and on at least one occasion exposed their practices by hiding a shield himself and then standing back to watch while they accused all and sundry of its theft.

Thanks to the cattle he acquired through his fame as a healer and diviner, and to a number of astute marriages, he spread his leadership over a large sector of the surrounding population, whose loyalty he retained not through threat or fear, but by wisdom and tolerance. 'When thou shalt sit in judgement, let thy decisions be just. The law knows no one as a poor man,' was one of his famous dicta, handed down through the generations.

He was also a man of metaphysical curiosity, seeking for answers beyond the mundane. Arbousset captures some of the questions that occupied him: 'Where does the world end? There must be a powerful Being who created all things! There is nothing to make me believe that any one of the things which I see created itself. Does anything create itself today? Conscience is the true guide of a man. It shows him his duty always: if he does it well, it smiles at him; if he does it ill, it reproaches him. This internal guide joins us at our birth and accompanies us to the grave. Oh, the vanity of things! Everything passes away. I too shall pass away … but to rejoin my fathers.'

This curiosity and desire to learn turned Mohlomi into a great traveller. He journeyed far to the west, to the Kalahari desert, where he came across a tribe called the Majantja, the eaters of dogs, amongst whom he lived and accumulated many dogs, and married a daughter of the land for whom he paid a canine bride price. He also travelled far north to the Soutpansberg where he sojourned amongst some cannibals called the Majabatho, who drank thick milk and ate the flesh of their fellows as a delicacy. He was truly, in Arbousset's fine phrase, a 'king errant'.

Once, when he arrived at Botha-Bothe, people came from far and wide to see him. Amongst them was Moshoeshoe, newly married, brought along by his grandfather. Despite the fact that Moshoeshoe was only the son of a man 'of small account', Mohlomi picked him out: 'My son, if thou couldst forsake all, I would take thee with me whithersoever I go; but it may not be. One day thou wilt rule men: learn, then, to know them; and when thou judgest, let thy judgements be just.' Moshoeshoe, who had before this killed five of his own subjects on separate occasions, was undoubtedly moved by these words, and they led him to rethink his ways; but, at the same time, they fuelled his already strong ambition to rise above the status of his father. Mohlomi was to Moshoeshoe what Samuel was to Saul.

Even in his old age, Mohlomi, part history, part legend, was a wanderer. A few days before his death (in about 1815), he visited the Maphetla living near Morija. On the return journey, he took ill and had to be carried home to Ngoliloe. He fell into a kind of trance on the last day of his life and made his final prophecy to the assembled mourners: 'My friends, I wanted to move my children out of the way of the war which is coming, and take up my abode on the plateau of Qeme, but sickness has prevented me. After my death, a cloud of red dust will come out of the east and consume our tribes. The father will eat his children.'

Harvesting his ideas from the view in front of him, Arbousset eventually broke the silence of Moshoeshoe's reverie. 'Mong'a ka, my Master,' he said with deference, 'you are right. There is no greater enemy of nations than war. And where does war start, if not from selfish interests, which put aside the public interest? But in reality, to disregard the public interest is to disregard one's personal interests; because we can then never dare to look at ourselves with impunity. That is what we can learn from these deserted villages in all directions in this beautiful country of Mohlomi.' The greedy, earthbound hordes below had squabbled over spoils and destroyed themselves, ignorant of the fact that the sun rises for all men. 'The Gospel brings us new blessings, unknown in the past,' he concluded. 'Whoever believes them, grows in wisdom. God says to His creatures; direct your desires to the blessings from above, in the way in which a father advises his adolescent son to forget the games of his childhood in order to think about the realities of adult life. Are you able to imagine how admirable this doctrine is? Once it is well understood and accepted as a rule of conduct, the horizon of our hopes extends, our view enlarges, our heart expands, the earth is considered earth, that is, the transitory place; its pleasures cannot absorb us any more. We gather them like strangers, looking towards those that are permanent.'

Moshoeshoe gradually shook himself free from his drowsy trance, and let his eyes wander over the plain. He spoke, as if trying to make poetry from history.

'My friends,' he said, 'works that are produced by mortal hands will themselves also perish: works created by hands that do not grow old, remain. These skies have not changed; over there the famous mount Hlohloloane rests still on its original base; and between it and ourselves, the Phuthiatsana river winds today as it has always done. Is the grass in the valleys less green this year than the previous year, or are the waters of our springs less sweet and less good? Nothing changes, neither God nor his works: but man changes, and with him changes that which he creates. A generation disappears from the surface of the earth, and another generation replaces it. Mohlomi was a great king, a wise and gentle king; under his government, men grew like the grass; they were as numberless as the animals of the fields. He has faded away; a deluge of Matabele swept over his people. Oh, what an unfortunate country ours is! The tempest struck the father, and the flood of waters carried away the mother and her child. See in the distance the shadow of the clouds blown by the wind; it ascends, it draws near, it is before our eyes, it has passed; and there another shadow of a cloud rises from the horizon; it scuds along, floats, and passes away; it is the picture of our tribes. Did our ancestors know that their dwellings would remain widowed after them, or did they foresee that their great-nephews would tear the flesh of their fellow men with their teeth? Did they know that white men existed? Would Peete [Moshoeshoe's grandfather] believe his eyes if he came out of hell right now and saw that man sitting beside us, and heard him speaking in our language about a thousand things that are all true, but new? Oh! Father of Kotsoane, chief of the Malimo, you believed me when I told you: "Stop devouring my people, or I shall come to massacre all of you in your caves." Did I speak the truth that time when I assured you that you could not die of hunger under my eyes, when in front of us grew magnificent fields of corn? Will you with Moshoeshoe thank the God of peace and abundance today? I am going to tell you what I know about Him, even though I have the misfortune of knowing these wonders only in my mind.'

Moshoeshoe then spoke about religion, but the winds of unrecorded time have swept away his words.

Later, Arbousset preached again to the anthropophagi, paraphrasing Psalm 23. The audience interpreted it to mean that the hunger the country had endured in the past did not stem from God's neglect of men but man's neglect of God. The rain had not ceased, nor had the sun dimmed: it was man who had killed man, burned crops, destroyed villages. They also concluded that the man who feared God would not fear death, even in the valley of its shadow.

For the first time ever, then, this Sunday, Arbousset could proudly record, these cannibals observed the Lord's Day. So, in the evening, in order to mark the event, a final prayer of thanksgiving was said after dinner in the cave. Abraham Ramatšeatsana, 'a Mosotho of staunch faith', asked the Saviour 'to bless the word that had been proclaimed, and to grant to the Malimo, as well as to the rest of us, forgiveness of sins, faith in the Gospel, and prosperity in this life'. Arbousset, who favoured a balanced style, admired 'the extreme timidity and the ardent fervour' of this neophyte.

<hr />

Once they had put behind them the Malimo (or Bakhatla as they called themselves, after the nightjars which they deeply reverenced), the expedition's journey was touched with allegory. They passed through two Bakhatla kraals, 'built near a heap of human bones, which they had not even thought of burying yet'.

There was a saying in that country, 'Whoever drinks beer with the subjects of Mankoane, disappears there.' Since Mankoane was the wife of an early chieftain, it was believed that the Malimo had secretly been cannibals from remote times. But when Arbousset had asked Rakotsoane, the chief of the Malimo, about the origins of their flesh-eating, he had asserted that it was only a recent manifestation. 'Hunger was the first cannibal,' he said. 'It devoured us.' Without cattle, grain, game (because the plains were occupied by their enemies), they had taken to eating their dogs, then their sandals, karosses, leather shields. What the hyenas missed, famine snatched.

So they took to luring travellers. Some of the people preferred to die of hunger rather than eat human flesh; others were deceived by the bolder spirits into believing that they were devouring daman meat, or rock rabbit. Once they tasted it, they often found it excellent. Perhaps it was cursed, too, for many people died from dysentery as a result. They even turned on one another! One of the principal chiefs, Rataba, would betray his own compatriots while out searching for roots, and devour their limbs in secret in the forest; or, while parents were away from home, he would take their children, 'cut off an arm, and throw it on the fire, and would feast on it, while his wives had the rest of these victims boiling away in pots'. He had even given himself a name, Lelimo, this cannibal of cannibals.

Naturally, Arbousset, the good Protestant, was curious about their consciences: 'And what did you feel in your heart in the midst of all these atrocities?'

'Our hearts did fret inside us,' was the reply, 'but we were getting used to that type of life, and the horror we had felt at first was soon replaced by habit. Besides, conscience in times of famine is different from the conscience of today.

It is now, especially, that I feel ashamed of myself. I look at my limbs and I shiver. What! I tell myself, it was us eating ourselves! We have all purified ourselves extensively, but our conscience (letsoalo) is still there, gnawing away at us.'

Arbousset believed that they 'had not completely lost their past tastes', but he did add, with hope, that 'their condition is improving'. They were also beginning to reintegrate with the people on the plain. What helped this re-integration was the fact that, during the period of extreme famine and fighting, the cannibals in their mountain caves had preserved grain in large straw baskets, and at times had given succour to the hungry. The last word, appropriately, belonged to Moshoeshoe. They were 'the saviours of the country', he said, 'and the real cannibals were those who had brought war and devastation, the Matabele and the Mantatees'.

It was fitting, then, that the party next moved past a great reed swamp, ten to fifteen kilometres in circumference, a natural trap waiting to suck into its treacherous maw any careless hunter following an equally doomed antelope. The peaty soil harboured another hidden danger – a continuous underground fire, which every year broke out to consume the reeds above. The fearful locals called this wild and menacing slough Tebetebeng, which means 'from one quagmire to the next'.

Their next point of call was Khongoana, the 'last village of the Basotho in the northern part'. On the way, they passed through an area called Mohlafotheng, the Sesotho name for the palma christi, or castor oil plant. Arbousset was told that it was not only used by the 'quack doctors' of the country but also by many a woman, when she could lay her hands on the fairly rare plant, as revenge against a drunken husband. She would grind some seeds between stones and slip them into his calabash of beer. He would take a large draught, begin to feel queasy, and believe he had been bewitched. Only then would the wife reveal her secret. The ideal resolution would be that the one promised 'not to drink so much; the other to be less playful'. Since the castor oil seed contains the deadly poison, ricin, it was wise for the husband not to provoke his wife to more serious dosages.

On the outskirts of Khongoana, a witchdoctor had built two cairns of stones and set up two purified branches of morifi, the tree of mourning. These were the magical equivalent of lightning conductors, and, bent towards the Maloti, were designed to direct the passing storms into the mountains.

But the village was deserted, a sign of the fear that plagued the land. Strangers in these parts were to be treated with suspicion. Only hesitantly did this timid peasantry emerge from the sorghum fields where they had hidden.

As the chief, Tsomane, explained: 'Whoever expected to see travellers here? We always live alone like the damans in the rocks.' To one of these great overhanging rocks the party was shown for the night, their abode lit only thinly by some goat fat smeared around a linen wick set in a piece of broken pot. Tsomane, Moshoeshoe, Molapo and Arbousset held a discussion in the dark, bordering on a Socratic dialogue, which lasted over two hours.

Molapo and his father were surprised by the 'poor intellectual development of these poor people'. Seemingly out of nowhere, what was preying on Moshoeshoe's mind erupted: 'Lies are everywhere, and truth is nowhere: why is that so?'

'I have heard it said,' replied Arbousset, 'that man has banished truth to the bottom of a well.'

Moshoeshoe laughed. A little later, he qualified his comment: 'There is a strand of truth in men, all the rest is lies; like a tree entirely parched, with the exception of a small branch, still green.'

His son, Molapo, voiced a thought not dissimilar to Mohale's the day before: 'As for me, I am ashamed of myself in front of my moruti [teacher]; I am also ashamed of myself when I am alone; sometimes his words kill me. He tells me the truth, and my wicked heart tells me so too, and if I don't believe effectively yet, it is not because I do not want to believe … I am almost afraid when I am alone.'

Moshoeshoe understood this not only as guilt, but also as something more: 'When a man is alone, there is council within him; a feeling occurs, then another; it is a real meeting of consciences [pitso ea matsoalo]. An utterance which I have heard for a long time from the lips of my white man comes back to my memory sometimes when I go to bed, and it occupies me for part of the night: does the soul sleep? Its sleep is thought.'

Not surprisingly, Tsomane did not fully understand: 'My masters, where is this coming from that you speak in such a manner? This is no more our language. Do you also think then, like the whites, that there is a God, that this God sees us and loves us all?'

The prince's answer was a smile of pity. But he and his father gave an explanation, too. 'Why, Tsomane, don't you use your two eyes to see? Does the sun rise at the command of men or at the command of God? Or better still, does rain obey God's voice, or man's voice? If it obeyed man's voice not everyone would have it; because the best rainmaker also has his enemies to whom he would give nothing.'

The perplexed chieftain was not convinced, but as his opponents dropped off to sleep, one by one, he alone was left awake 'to argue by himself'. Which is just as well, because he not only prevented the horses from damaging his fields, but also woke the group to cover their guns and saddles when the rain came pelting down at three in the morning.

—◦⊖◦—

Arbousset was struck by what he described as 'the extreme fear that savages have of meeting one another'. This was prompted by an encounter with a lone hunter, who, on spotting the party, flung himself on his belly and tried to crawl to a hiding place. Here was a Mantatee, considered Arbousset, not afraid of lions, perhaps, but trembling at the sight of his fellow men! 'A man so solitary makes an impression on everyone!' Arbousset pondered. 'Oh yes, it is not difficult for the Lord to see this man: how could His divine providence not reach him, not reach all men?' The party itself was moving with some caution – they were in alien territory, where Moshoeshoe's authority was tenuous at best.

So they were not surprised when the inhabitants of the next village, more than three hundred 'Mahlaphahlaphas', Zulu-speaking allies of Sekonyela, fled at their approach. They were only coaxed back with difficulty by Mohale, still unsure, like other villagers further along the route, whether Moshoeshoe's party's true purpose was 'hunting or killing'.

That night, near a Mantatee village, the travellers were given shelter by the headman, Masopo, in an immense cave of reddish hue called Maoa-Mafubelu (now Pitseng). Moshoeshoe and Arbousset spent several hours in conversation with Masopo, and he spoke bitterly of Mzilikazi and the Ndebele, who had wounded him fifteen years before and stolen many of his cattle.

It is possible that Arbousset, consciously or unconsciously, had an agenda for the trip. His discussion at the place of the cannibals had been about war and evil; with Tsomane it had been about truth and conscience; now, he added a further theme. Had Masopo, he asked, forgiven the Ndebele?

Masopo's astonishment echoed in the cave. 'No, no,' he exclaimed, 'I never forgive.' But his proud recollections of his past raids eventually led him to an admission: 'We are all mad here; one devours the other. What can be the cause of it?'

'Our covetousness,' Moshoeshoe had no hesitation in replying. 'This white man tells me that all the time. He says that tigers are better than men, that at least they don't tear one another apart.' Had Arbousset read Oliver Goldsmith – 'Where crouching tigers wait their hapless prey / And savage men more murderous still than they ...'? And Moshoeshoe went on: 'The earth should be our nursing mother, but instead, we want the spear to be our mother. As for me, today I love only peace. I think war is too costly, and my senses are still very weary from past hardship.' Moshoeshoe was no longer a young man. He had the wisdom of age.

—◦○◦—

On the 19th, at nine in the morning, Arbousset addressed an audience of Mantatees, Makakanas, Malimo and Mahlaphahlaphas on the banks of a river. He told them about how Jehovah, the Master of Heaven, had created the world; the mountains, the forests, the grain; the sun, the moon, the stars; and man. And how, through Adam, 'they might love one another like brothers'. The fierce and formerly cannibalistic Mahlaphahlaphas listened to the magical names, and, in the words of the young missionary, 'their eyes fixed on me like flames of fire'.

He spoke to them about original sin, 'engendered by the disobedience of our first father', and how it was passed on by him to all his children.

He spoke of how this sin was washed away in the precious blood of the Son of Man, so that whoever knew this 'merciful Saviour' would obey Him and love Him.

Then he had them sing Samuel Rolland's beautiful hymn, 'Molim'o ratile batho' – God is always filled with love for men.

How fitting are the praises of the Lord! he thought. How wonderfully they resound in the mouths of the fierce inhabitants of the African peaks!

—◦○◦—

The humble sower withdraws when he has deposited his seed in the bosom of the earth. His heart is calm and confident as he awaits the rains of heaven.

These were the thoughts of Arbousset.

—◦○◦—

Later that day, they passed through the birthplace of Moshoeshoe. The King was filled with childhood memories. He pointed out to his companion a particular rock with a round crack in it. Mystified, Arbousset could award it no distinction. Moshoeshoe enlightened him: one day, as a herdboy of his father's cattle, he was playing here when suddenly, out of an oppressive sky, a bolt of lightning struck this very rock. The boy thought he was dead; he ran home without stopping, as though *he* had been struck.

On a beautiful plateau, he pointed out where he had ridden young calves, or run free, free as a desert gazelle.

He took his friend up the mountain of Menkhoaneng and made him drink at the cool spring of Maruru.

These kinds of memories are of such exquisite delight, said his missionary, that 'everyone preserves them enshrined in his heart as the best and most enduring of all'.

'How does the heart respond to a man who sees again the place of his birth?' he asked Moshoeshoe.

'I have joy in my heart such as and even more than if I were returning home to Thaba-Bosiu and into the midst of my family,' was the reply.

Moshoeshoe also pointed out the spot in the valley where his initiation lodge had been built and where he had spent six full moons at the circumcision school. There he had become a man, and learned how to be a father, husband and warrior.

—⊷⊶—

Menkhoaneng is a small plateau directly to the east of the modern town of Hlotse (formerly Leribe). Mokhachane's village was situated up against the plateau, which got its name from the monkhoana trees growing there. In the valley of the Hlotse below, the villagers grew millet because maize was still unknown. Horses and guns were also unknown. Sheep and goats were plentiful, but cattle were the backbone of the society, the 'god with the wet nose'. A man's wealth was largely measured in cattle, and cattle-raiding was part of a young man's expectation. Without cattle, he could not raise the bohali in order to marry. The transfer of the cattle – perhaps twenty – to the family of the bride was the central and essential action which constituted marriage.

Warfare was conducted with spear, knobkerrie and a light shield, but the fighting was seldom intense or at close quarters. The bodies of the slain did, however, provide the more potent elements of the medicines used in various rituals.

Polygamy was widespread, but few outside the chiefly class could afford many wives. Chiefs could cement or extend their power and patronage through marital alliances. There were advantages and disadvantages for the state in this system. For the husband, on the positive side, he not only provided himself with a variety of lovers and the chance for numerous children ('Our women age quickly, and then we cannot resist the temptation of taking younger ones,' Moshoeshoe once told Casalis), but he also augmented his labour supply and the amenities for hospitality; on the negative side, he might have to mediate in domestic disputes. For the women, the system, when it worked well, allowed for security and the sharing of agricultural, craft and domestic tasks in times of health, sickness and transition. Widows would usually be passed on to brothers of the deceased, and spinsterhood was little known. On the other hand, rivalries and jealousies no doubt ruined the lives of many women, particularly the junior wives, and their offspring, and widows might find themselves the bedfellows of less attractive brothers.

As regards religion, the Basotho, according to D.F. Ellenberger, who knew their belief system intimately, did have 'some vague notion of one God, supreme and omnipotent', the Molimo, though this was not a Creator god. The more immediate influences were the Balimo, the shades or spirits of the ancestors, who were regarded as mediators between the living and the Molimo. There was a prayer known to all the old Basotho: 'Melimo e mecha rapelang Molimo oa Khale!' (Young gods, pray for us to the Ancient God.)

There was a kind of continuity between life and death, the departed dwelling in an underworld (Ellenberger likened it to Hades or Paradise) where they lived more or less as they had on earth. They did, however, continue to influence the lives of the living, sometimes by intervening directly, and they demanded appropriate remembrance and respect. On occasion, they manifested their hypostasis, their continued presence, by taking the form of a snake, which species was usually treated with extreme reverence. Misfortune was often put down to the uneasy rest of the ancestors.

After a seemingly happy childhood, Lepoqo's initiation was delayed slightly because of the great famine of Sekoboto in 1803. Once he and his fellow initiates had been circumcised, they were taken to the mophato, the remote lodge specially built for the occasion, where they spent several months under the instruction of the mesuoe, who taught them the customs and traditions of the chiefdom and the duties of a husband and father. Here Lepoqo gave himself new names: Tlaputle (the Energetic One), Lekhema (the Hastener) and, particularly, Letlama (the Binder), so that his group became known as Matlama, the Binders. When they were finished, they burned down the hut and returned to society amidst great celebrations. The group of age-mates who underwent this period of trial together naturally formed a cohesive band and the association often endured a lifetime. This was certainly the case with Moshoeshoe and one of his fellow initiates, Makoanyane, who was to be his most trusted lieutenant and confidant, and who saved his life on at least one occasion.

As a visible manifestation of his manhood, and a step towards accumulating wealth, Letlama led a raid on the herd of Ramanoheng, a neighbouring chief. Because he had thus shaved Ramanoheng's metaphorical beard, he gave himself the onomatopoeic name of Moshoeshoe, the Shaver, the name he finally offered up to history and to fame. And in about 1810, his father arranged for him a marriage with the daughter of a Bafokeng chief. Quick and intelligent, Moshoeshoe was ambitious from an early age. 'When I was a young man,' he afterwards told his son Molapo, 'I had a great desire to become a chief. I longed that my chieftainship should grow and rise, and with this wish I went to Mohlomi ... I asked him to advise me on how I could become a chief.' But before he accepted Mohlomi's injunction to follow the path of peace, he believed he must acquire a strong following, by force if necessary. To Makoanyane he said, 'You are my right hand. Together we will found a new empire. Let us first render ourselves popular by mighty deeds, and afterwards we will speak of peace and clemency. In the disputes of others let us always put ourselves on the side of the strongest. If we would become rich in men and cattle, we cannot help making enemies; but they will not roar forever.'

In 1820 or 1821, Moshoeshoe moved away from his father's village to found his own at Botha-Bothe, a mountain topped by a small plateau and with adequate defences. His first child Mohato (whose praise name became Letsie after initiation) had been born around 1811, followed in 1814 by Molapo, and then a girl, Tsoamathe, and two boys, Masupha and Majara. At this stage, there was little to distinguish him from a clutch of other minor chiefs. However, that was about to change, for the cloud of red dust, which Mohlomi had predicted on his last day of life, was fast approaching.

—❧—

By 1822, Shaka had established his militaristic Zulu state in the hills and coastal plains east of the Drakensberg escarpment. The consequences would reverberate through much of southern Africa for many years to come. A number of groups had fled from his grasp westwards – the Ndebele under the rebel Mzilikazi, the Hlubi under Mpangazitha, and the Amangwane under Matiwane. In their turn, these fugitives attacked, raided and sometimes displaced the Basotho groups north and west of the Maloti. The scale and ferocity of the fighting – total warfare which swept up the aged, women and children – had been hitherto unknown.

The Amangwane pushed the Hlubi westwards. In their turn, the Hlubi bumped into the Batlokoa, who were living in the Namahali river valley under their redoubtable queen regent, 'Manthatisi. Moshoeshoe looked on anxiously as the Batlokoa moved past. He was not keen to get between the dragon and her wrath. He managed to ward off the Hlubi with a tribute of cattle, but his luck ran out in the winter of 1822 when the Amangwane arrived in the northern part of the Mohokare valley. Efforts to buy them off failed, and the Bamokoteli, outnumbered and undone by the new fighting methods, were easily routed, although Moshoeshoe managed to hide a good proportion of his cattle.

A few months later, in the autumn of the following year, the Batlokoa attacked Botha-Bothe. During the course of the battle, the Bamokoteli got amongst the cooking pots of the Batlokoa and smashed them. This therefore became known as the Battle of the Pots. It was the only limited success the home team had, and they were soon scattered and pursued, Moshoeshoe taking refuge first in Liphofung cave and then in the Maloti. When the

Amangwane crushed the Hlubi and the Batlokoa retired, Moshoeshoe was able to return to Menkhoaneng.

Paradoxically, despite his defeats, these events gave Moshoeshoe the opportunity to increase his strength. The general displacement of tribes and the influx of refugees enabled him to incorporate individuals and groups into his fold. He gathered together the strays and put flesh on their bones, building up their muscle and their nerve. On occasion, when weak, he would offer tribute; at other times, when superior in strength, he raided for cattle and increased his herds. He extended his power and patronage by distributing some of his cattle amongst his old and new followers in accordance with the mafisa system, in terms of which he allowed the *use* of the beasts but retained their *ownership*. Now, too, his innate astuteness and the wise words of Mohlomi began to turn him into the great leader he was to become. When his warriors took the herds of a rival group without his permission, he ordered them returned, thus earning a reputation for compassion – while at the same time no doubt keeping ownership of the cattle under the leasing system.

In the spring of 1823, he returned to Botha-Bothe, but before he could harvest his crops the following year, 'Manthatisi was back, along with her son Sekonyela. The Bamokoteli retreated to the top of the mountain while the Batlokoa laid siege below, destroying all the millet fields. Desperate hunger drove the Bamokoteli to eat their dogs and contaminated meat, while their besiegers, having stabbed themselves in the foot by destroying the food supply, did not fare much better. An attack by the Tlotlokoane, though unsuccessful, convinced Sekonyela to withdraw northwards, where he displaced the Marabeng from the distinctively shaped mountain named after them. There he settled down and for thirty years was a devil's thorn in the sole of Moshoeshoe.

Moshoeshoe decided he, too, must move. The lightning and the thunder were laying eggs on the plains and mountains to the north and the east. He had heard of a mountain eighty kilometres to the south-west which was reputed to be a fortress more formidable than Botha-Bothe. So he sent his brother to investigate, and Mohale was favourably impressed by the new site.

Hence, in June 1824, Moshoeshoe led his people into a new land. The Bamokoteli set out southwards, hugging the Maloti for protection. Weak to start with, many died of hunger on the way, or were devoured by wild animals, or were ambushed by cannibals driven to desperation themselves by the general destruction of crops. They made their way along the Khamolane plateau and eventually looked down on the valley of the Phuthiatsana river. Out of the navel of the valley rose the strange conical sandstone pillar of Qiloane, from which, it is said, the Basotho have taken the shape of their distinctive straw hats. Beyond it, stretched the long plateau that was their destination. Crowning the entire top of the mountain was a sheer golden band of sandstone cliff.

They arrived towards nightfall, and as people began to straggle in, the mountain loomed up above them; as if by magic, it appeared to grow. This was an illusion of the fading light, but it was awesome.

So they gave it a name – the Mountain at Night. Thaba-Bosiu.

On its top was a grassy plain, well watered with springs and large enough for substantial herds and several villages. Only six easily defendable passes gave access to the natural fortress. Moshoeshoe established himself at the northern end near the Khubelu (or Red) pass, where a dolerite dyke interrupted the sandstone, its reddish tinge contrasting with the creamy sandstone. Here he settled down in relative safety, cultivating the fields below and covering with his protective mantle his neighbours and the refugee immigrants, while extending his wealth and patronage through the mafisa system. Amongst the groups further afield over which he extended his dominance there were, to the south, the Baphuthi (under their chieftain, Moorosi). The skins of all lions and leopards killed in the hunt by any of his clients were to be sent to Moshoeshoe, as a token of submission and allegiance.

Early in 1827, a Zulu army swept over the Drakensberg, savaged the Amangwane regiments and seized swathes of Matiwane's cattle. Although Moshoeshoe continued to pay Matiwane tribute, one incident indicates his ambiguous evasions. A mortally wounded fugitive from the Amangwane royal household, suspected of having an affair with a royal wife, fled towards Thaba-Bosiu. When his pursuers came looking for him, Moshoeshoe denied that he had arrived, claiming he had been the victim of animals or cannibals. In fact, he had reached the Bamokoteli and his body was used to prepare potions for Moshoeshoe's horn of medicines.

In February 1828, four divisions of the Amangwane, like a dry and choking wind from the north, crossed over the Thuathe (or Berea) plateau and into the valley of the Phuthiatsana, heading towards Thaba-Bosiu. Two other divisions went south to attack Moshoeshoe's half-brother Mohale at Tloutle. The bulk of the attacking force forded the river and made its way to the north end of the mountain, while part of the army went further to a camp below Mokhachane's village perched on the western edge of Thaba-Bosiu.

Moshoeshoe, with his loyal Matlama age-mates at his side, and supported by the contingents of his brothers Posholi and Makhabane, and his friend Makara, drew up his numerically inferior forces at the foot of Khubelu pass. He had left his young sons, Letsie and Molapo, at the top of the pass, with the instructions, 'Remain you here and gather many stones, so that if we be overcome, you may still defend the pass.'

At first, the superior numbers of the Amangwane pressed heavily on the

Basotho, but a timely attack on the flank from Moshoeshoe and the Matlama, hidden in a fold of ground, reversed the fortunes, and the Amangwane broke and many were slain. Moshoeshoe had caught the wind in his fists. The Amangwane were pursued all the way to Maqhaka (Berea), where Moshoeshoe's brave lieutenant Makoanyane himself slew ten with his own hand.

When the remnants of his army returned, Matiwane, who had consented to the attack against his better judgement, berated them: 'I had no wish to attack my friend and subject who used to pay me tribute, but ye would have it so, and now that he has seen our weakness, he will pay no more.'

And so it was. It was a watershed for Moshoeshoe. He was now independent of his neighbours, and people began to flock to him in increasing numbers for protection. For Matiwane it was almost the end. The Amangwane, haggard with physical and emotional distress, flowed over the Witteberg, making an unsuccessful sideswipe at the Baphuthi of Moorosi on the way, into the land of the Thembu. There, on 24 July 1828, they ran into a small party of white soldiers, and, for the first time, were subjected to the ordeal of gunfire. Matiwane abandoned most of his people and fled north, where he was ambushed in a cave by Sekonyela. With his meagre force further depleted, he approached Dingane, the Zulu king, who received him affably, and then treacherously ordered his death and the massacre of all his band.

Moshoeshoe was now master of the Mohokare valley and lord of the Basotho, and he led, in 1829, a couple of raids to the south, making himself rich with Thembu cattle. While he was away on the second expedition, the Batlokoa launched a surprise raid on Thaba-Bosiu, but were driven off by the old men and boys (including Letsie) who had been left on guard. In 1831, the dreaded Ndebele of Mzilikazi came, flinging themselves against five of the passes up the mountain. They were met with avalanches of stones and hailstorms of throwing spears, and were everywhere repulsed. As they moved off, disheartened, Moshoeshoe made one of his most famous gestures. Instead of hurling insults after them, he sent them a small herd of oxen to feed them on their way home to face an irate Mzilikazi. Such bemusing behaviour was unheard of.

But while the wind from the north continued to bring red dust, the southwestern wind also threatened. When they clashed, they sent the litsokotsane, the dust devils, spiralling clockwise across the land, presaging wind and rain and hail on the Maloti.

The first to arrive from the south and west, in small groups, were the Korannas, mainly intent on poaching cattle. They came with their guns and mounted on strange new animals, like dark zebras, giving them an infuriating mobility, and allowing them to dance out of the range of spears.

Behind the Korannas loomed the threat of the whites, mostly confined for the moment to the Cape Colony, but with the occasional advance party exploring the countryside north of the Orange. In December 1832, a German naturalist called Seidenstecher visited Thaba-Bosiu and spent much of his time chasing butterflies over the plateau with a net. Then came a preacher called Martins, who had only a few words of Sesotho – God, heaven, light, burning fire – which he accompanied with vigorous pointing to the heavens themselves. He made up for his lack of Sesotho by presenting Moshoeshoe with his umbrella; then he staggered off into an unknown future, which probably consisted of being killed by cannibals – the archetype of the missionary in the pot.

Given this introduction to the strange ways of the whites, it is surprising that Moshoeshoe would have shown much interest in them. But he had no doubt heard of Robert Moffat at Kuruman and of the interesting work of the London Missionary Society amongst the Griquas at Philippolis. Late in 1832, a Griqua called Adam Krotz arrived at Thaba-Bosiu. He was a huge man, black as a Mozambican slave, and a member of the Church of Philippolis. When he was asked whether the people there had suffered at the hands of the Korannas, he said no. The Griquas had amongst them servants of God, including Rev. Kolbe, who taught them to live well and fear evil. The Korannas duly avoided them. These servants of God, he said, were what Moshoeshoe needed, not guns.

Moshoeshoe determined to acquire for himself some missionaries. So he sent a hundred cattle with Krotz on his return to Philippolis, in order to procure some of these men who talked of peace. The cattle were stolen by some Korannas, however, and two subsequent offerings were taken by Bushmen. Nevertheless, a message did get through to Mr Kolbe at Philippolis, and, whether by luck or providence, three young French missionaries arrived there a few months later.

Into the country to the south and east of Moshoeshoe's old stronghold at Botha-Bothe rode the party of Moshoeshoe and Arbousset late on the 19th. This land was inhabited by Makakanas, Nguni immigrants from the Tugela river to the east of the Maloti. They had begun to shrug off their allegiance to Dingane, partly because of expediency, partly because of disillusion with his tyranny, since he stole their cattle and hunted them down. They were becoming Sotho-ized. As one old man genially explained to the Basotho: 'Friend, I am of Setebele origin; but I am already a Mosotho in my ways, and even in language … The Makakanas are no longer foreigners in your country. I too am a Mosotho calf!' They had changed the way they pierced their earlobes, and they covered their nakedness with the tšeha that the Basotho favoured for modesty.

That night, Arbousset, exhorting the Makakanas to give up their superstitions and abandon their 'false rituals of ablutions and their belief in the lares', took as his text Matthew 5, 'Blessed are the poor in spirit'. The Makakanas, unused to these strange ideas, garbled in a hasty translation, asked, 'If the white men are wise and rich, is it because they know the God Jehovah?' To which Arbousset replied, 'Jehovah is the father of all men. Consequently, He desires all men to love Him and to honour Him, as if they were His children.'

—◦◦—

On the 20th, they came to the ruins of several ancient Basotho villages. There Arbousset was told the story of 'Maleshoane, the Mother-of-the-Dead.

She was the wife of Mahlole, who had lived there a hundred years before. When he died, she should, according to custom, have gone to live with his younger brother, Mokoteli; instead, she took as her lover a low-born Hlubi foreigner and had a son by him called Peete, derisively known as the Stammerer. His other nickname was 'Thohako', or Mockery, so he was doubly damned.

When the Bamokoteli, to whom Peete's mother returned when she tired of her lover, moved from Hlotse to Thaba-Bosiu, Peete and two of his men fell behind. They were surprised by cannibals, and, while his escort escaped, he himself was captured: 'For him there was the ghastly fate of being eaten by them.'

The story told to Arbousset at that time, at that place, was all the more poignant and meaningful because Peete was the father of Mokhachane, and the grandfather of Moshoeshoe. His death was never avenged.

In his journal, the diligent Protestant could not avoid adding a moral rider to the tale: 'Thus Africans, no less corrupted than other peoples, sometimes suffer retribution from adultery in the end.' For Arbousset, there could be a direct causal link between adultery and murder.

—◦◦—

On the same day, Moshoeshoe drew Arbousset's attention to another historical parable provoked by the sight of one of the mountains near Botha-Bothe. Thirty years before, Mohlomi had been living here peacefully with his father Monyane. A shepherd killed a springbok, and both father and son claimed it as theirs. Neither side would back down, and they declared war on one another, the defeated Monyane eventually retreating to the aforesaid mountain.

Arbousset recalled the biblical quarrel between the servants of Lot and Abraham over a waterhole, and the historical disaster when William the Conqueror turned an insulting joke into a war, and he mused that 'we have to recognize that, morally speaking, there are many levels of relationships amongst men, no matter to which nation or times they belong'. The idea that 'ambition and pride, for example, are common to all, and God knows the thousands of evils that these two vices produce in our nature all the time' gave him a partial explanation for how a trivial dispute might escalate into a deadly one, even between father and child.

—◦◦—

At four o'clock the next morning, the real world intruded on the phantasms of the past and its moral messages. A pride of lions had got amongst the horses and scattered them far and wide.

For the younger men, including Molapo, the excitement of the hunt was all that mattered. The older men were more circumspect. Coming across his favourite horse missing only its intestines, Moshoeshoe was shocked that a life could be taken so casually, wantonly, like flicking flies, for the sake of a mere morsel. 'Is that the kind of big eaters lions are?' he asked in disgust. 'They just kill for the sake of killing!' And Arbousset's epitaph for his strong and faithful Marche, dead but otherwise untouched, was that it was as though the ferocious beasts had 'only wanted him just because he was so beautiful!'

The lions, one or two of them wounded, had been pursued into a dense wood by the unthinking young men, way ahead of the rest of the party. 'Those children,' muttered Moshoeshoe, 'those children! They have gone too soon.'

Stones rolled into the wood and a fusillade of firing failed to dislodge the lions, so the two other whites in the party, and a few of the braver or more foolish Basotho, penetrated the undergrowth and succeeded in flushing them out. But their efforts were squandered when one unfortunate man fired prematurely as the beasts broke cover and merely drove them back into the same hiding place. After that, no one felt like repeating the exercise.

These were amongst the last lions seen in Lesotho, and this live sighting is the last recorded in the literature of the country. In the midst of the hunt, Arbousset took the trouble to consider in the forest two very beautiful varieties of lily, one arrayed in pristine white, the other in vermilion. Even Moshoeshoe in all his glory …

—◦◦—

And so, on the evening of the 22nd, after an exciting lion hunt and an equally fruitless eland hunt, they came to the final cave, the horseshoe-shaped cave on the doorstep of the Blue Mountains, where Qacha slew the ox.

The cave was like an old house. It had a history; it had a life story.

One morning, many years before, Makoanyane, the friend of Moshoeshoe, and Ramakonyana, age-mates just past circumcision, had come to this very cave. Investigating a clump of bushes, Ramakonyana slipped and fell down the crevice that splits the cave's floor. Makoanyane was right behind him and also lost his footing, falling on top of his friend. There they were, stuck fast in the narrow pipe, and there they remained all day. The situation was truly terrifying. Each had shattered a leg, so the pain added to their fear.

They waited and waited, sometimes with hope, more often without.

Fortunately, towards dusk, others came to the cave, perhaps to kraal their cattle, safe from the wild animals. So the cries of the trapped were heard, and they were pulled to safety and carried home. Three moons later, Makoanyane could walk again, and, some time after him, Ramakonyana.

Much later in his life, when his days were almost done, Makoanyane gave Arbousset his interpretation of the story, his words flowing as if from a spring.

> The precipice has taught me well. I ask myself whose hidden hand then kept me from dying when I fell. At that time, God was watching over me like a good father, He wanted me to live my full span of days so that I might know Him. And also the precipice of evil, that is life itself, it is full of temptations. I have wallowed in sin for a long time; I have been stagnating in the mud of covetousness. I have killed forty men in war. We put the blame on Adam. But it is we who have eaten the forbidden fruit: to the sin of our first forefather, we have added sin after sin. I say that I have most certainly broken the Ten Commandments of the Lord, and so it is … but the Lord is love, He has forgiven me. He did not die for anyone else, He died for me, the wicked Makoanyane. A child does not play twice on the edge of a precipice; that is why I am in a hurry to leave the precipice of the world, in order to follow the Son of Jehovah, my Saviour.

Arbousset thought the maxim that a child does not play twice on the edge of a precipice was 'truly worthy of becoming a proverb'.

Then, too, a man does not rub bottoms with a porcupine. Moshoeshoe had not found the cave by accident. He had been there before. At the time the Batlokoa erupted into his territory some twenty years earlier, in 1821 or 1822, he had found refuge here for six months with some of his people and cattle. When finally he was discovered, he had to flee to a mountain ridge close by, where the Batlokoa would not follow. But his troubles were not over – he was soon attacked from the east by a band of Ndebele, forcing him to return to the cave, which had meanwhile been taken over by the Batlokoa.

Moshoeshoe took charge of the battle, 'distinguished', says Arbousset, 'for his paternal love as much as for his military valour', for at the height of the fighting, he carried his little son Molapo on his shoulders, while his queen, 'Mamohato, carried Masupha at her breast, and one of his lieutenants led princess Tsoamathe by the hand.

A mighty storm unleashed itself and dampened the attack of the Batlokoa. Having lost some of his men and a large number of his cattle, Moshoeshoe slipped away in the darkness to a mountain retreat safe from both the Batlokoa and the Ndebele.

—◦◉◦—

Given this prelude, the time was right for Arbousset's most dramatic scene. His Romantic character always liked a bit of theatre, and the cave, its natural beauty enhanced by history and legend, was the ideal venue.

Early on Sunday morning, the 23rd, while Moshoeshoe donned a pair of white trousers and a blue frock coat, carried specially for Sunday services, and while his sons and the others put on clean clothes, Arbousset washed himself amongst the reeds in the secluded corner of the cave behind the screen of the two fallen rocks. When he brushed his hair in the mirror provided by the crystal waters of the pool, a pair of finches similarly preened themselves, then burst into song. A gentle breeze accompanied daybreak. The cave was filled with life and happiness, its great walls lined with moss and maidenhair ferns arranged by Nature's hand, and ghostly animal and human images by man's. As the voices of the Basotho singing the Lord's Prayer were lifted on the breeze, it would have been difficult not to have recognized in the cave, he thought, a temple prepared by Nature for the service of its Creator.

At the early morning service, Arbousset read 'the high-priestly prayer of Jesus Christ', and it would be surprising if he did not give a thought to his brave predecessors, who had used similar caves as venues to advance the cause of the Church of the Desert in the years of Protestant persecution in France.

For the divine service at ten o'clock, he mused on how the party had, over the past week, 'wandered amidst the varied and altogether wondrous works of the Creator', and so he spoke of the Creation, and of the seventh day, and of how it imposed sacred and beneficial obligations on man, with its intimations, too, of the eternal rest of the redeemed.

Afterwards, the King repeated to his retainers all that he remembered of the sermon. Then he went outside to sit on the grass, and, resting against a tree, spelled out words painfully for two hours, under the instruction of his son Masupha.

Moshoeshoe had a great respect for reading and writing. Earlier in the journey, he had said to his missionary: 'My language is nevertheless very beautiful. We are only beginning to realize this since we have seen it written down.

Thanks to the little books of the missionaries, it will not be altered: there it is written; oh! your *paper*; that paper organizes everything well.' When Arbousset laughingly pointed out that the paper was full of ink blots, he countered by saying he had noticed this, but the blots could be washed out with 'the soap of learning'. This banter eventually led to Moshoeshoe sincerely assuring Arbousset that part of his work was already done – that his children always carried with them a moruti, a teacher, in their travelling bags wherever they went.

Despite his diligent efforts in the sun that day, and on other days, Moshoeshoe never did master the art of reading.

—◦◦—

Arbousset was contented. He appeared to be getting somewhere in his work at last. In particular, Molapo, Moshoeshoe's second eldest son, seemed greatly moved. Arbousset regarded him as a worthwhile young man, who loved truth to the extent that he would not profess to a false or precipitous conversion. On one occasion, he had said to Arbousset, 'Today, I felt that Jesus loved us; but I do not want to make a fuss about it. I believe I understand, but I do not feel ...'

He was baptized later in the year, on Christmas Day, in the presence of his father.

—◦◦—

As they left the cave the next day, it was unanimously agreed that it should be called Lehaha-la-Sontaha, the Cave of Sunday, a name as euphonious as the site is beautiful.

—◦◦—

That day, the party climbed into the Maloti proper, via a great pass (now called the 'Moteng pass) and, in the afternoon, reached the banks of the Black river – the Malibamatšo – which is one of the two great arms of the Senqu. They were probably unaware that another major river lay to the east. They found a small cave which gave them some shelter; this was fortunate, because they were overtaken by a violent storm of rain, hail, thunder, lightning, and a bitterly cold wind. They spent the time talking far into the night about God and His works, and as a result they called this cave Lekhalo-la-Lipoko, the Gateway of Praises.

But fate or providence was working against Arbousset's reaching 'Mont-aux-Sources' (by which he meant not the highest mountain to the east, which is now known by this name, but Thaba-Putsoa, to the north). Many of the men were tired; others, including Arbousset, wanted to press on, for eight or ten days, following the course of the river. However, supplies were low, the countryside, which was devoid of shelter, fuel and game, looked inhospitable, and the Bushmen (Baroa) presented an ever-lurking menace.

Moshoeshoe, Arbousset and a few others contented themselves with climbing the nearest high mountain to the east, where they built a cairn of stones, had a picnic of biscuits, cheese, raisins and tea, and named the spot Nyarela (Viewpoint).

As they left this furthest, most remote point of their journey, Moshoeshoe exclaimed: 'How much of nature's beauty is unknown to us! Oh, how great God is! How terribly and wondrously does He manifest Himself through the grandeur of His works! How well have my two eyes feasted! Who knows, but that in my dreams I will not return to these proud mountains, these roaring torrents, heard by no one but He who fashions their beds, who drops them there from on high, and who follows them in their courses?'

Their return from the Gateway of Praises took them back past the magic circles. Moshoeshoe, impatient, as he often was, had hurried ahead. He set fire to some of the long grass to warn those at Thaba-Bosiu of his imminent return. The next day, beyond Pakoa, the party came in sight of a sefika, a cairn of stones, built by travellers, each one adding a stone as he passed. Following the custom of the country, Moshoeshoe, Arbousset and the others also added a small stone each, a memento of a momentous journey.

Crossing the Leribe plateau, they came to 'Mota's town. The sycophantic welcome and the eggshell dance of diplomacy that followed are explained, in all likelihood, by the fact that 'Mota was Sekonyela's brother. Moshoeshoe, according to Arbousset, had to prove his status amongst his enemies. A curious conversational manoeuvring ensued, with the lead actor assuming a stance of mock modesty, to be answered by a chorus of denials, like frogs in a pond.

'Children of Potjo,' Arbousset heard the King say, 'I am not Chief.'
  'Yes, you are!'
'But a chief must have a beautiful mouth.'
'Yours *is* beautiful, Morena.'
'What is more, he must have rich herds.'
'Oh! Son of Mokhachane, you alone are richer than all our peoples put together.'
  'No, no. I am not Chief, I am a dunderhead.'
'No, our Master, you are thinking too much about the older times at Botha-Bothe. That time is over.'

At this point, a beggar asked the King for a gift of two heifers. Moshoeshoe taunted him: 'Oh! Ah! You want to extract a present from me just to go and show it off to Sekonyela and put me in an unfavourable light, as if he did not hate me enough without that!'

The people shouted, 'He loves you!'

'Then why does he not come to see me? Listen, my friends, I am tempted to present myself before Sekonyela this very evening, so that he can see with his own eyes that I am Morena.'

At this bit of audacious populism everyone burst out laughing. 'Indeed, you are Morena, you are a great Morena.'

For the moment, the relationship of the two bulls, Moshoeshoe and Sekonyela, was all snort and scuff and no charge.

At last, Moshoeshoe and Arbousset parted, each to their daily cares and different kingdoms. It had been a memorable trip, an interlude of escape, physically demanding but with time for thought and discussion.

But something significant had *not* happened. At the beginning of his account of the journey, Arbousset acknowledges this. The King's slowness to act – one might say, his deliberation – explained 'in part why he has not yet sincerely adopted the Gospel that we proclaim to him, and which he, moreover, argues about knowledgeably, even as far as one can judge, with some belief'.

Moshoeshoe did not go all the way to full conversion. It is hard to say why. The usual explanation is that he realized such a step might irrevocably divide his nation and undermine his power, placing him definitively on one side of the split between Christians and pagans. Faced by the threat of Sekonyela, this might not have been a wise or pragmatic move. Then again, since he was living in a period of relative peace and security, he might not have felt it necessary to seek radical changes in his view of the world. He must have known as well that the missionaries would have required him to give up all but one of his many wives.

Perhaps his self-analysis was not dissimilar to Molapo's – at times understanding and believing strongly in the new version of an old God, but in moments of solitude racked once again by uncertainty.

It does seem as though he might already have gone through a critical agony of indecision in 1837, when, as the missionary Constant Gosselin wrote to Paris, he publicly 'prayed Jehovah to forgive him his sins, to convert him, and give him a new heart, and he asked the same for his wives, his children, his mother and his people'.

Arbousset would have understood this reluctance to commit totally; he would have respected and accepted it. He would not have wanted a false conversion.

There is no doubt that Moshoeshoe was deeply moved by what he saw and heard and thought about on the journey. Clearly, he responded to the idea of the magnificence of the Creation and of its Creator. He also acknowledged the importance of a new morality (or the return of an old one). But, in his reported responses, that is as far as he went.

Had he gone further, the fate of his people may have been different, for better or worse. On the one hand, freedom of choice in matters of religion was partly preserved; on the other, the chance for a unified form of the new culture, the infusion of which was inevitable, was shunned. The rapprochement between church and state was not quite as close as the missionaries had hoped it would be.

CHAPTER NINE

THE DESERT CHURCH

1832–1836

I t is hard to imagine what Adam Krotz must have thought when he rode in to Philippolis from his nearby farm one day in 1833 and first encountered the three missionaries from France. The eldest, Constant Gosselin, was over thirty years old and of an open and friendly character, but his role was mainly supportive. The two more forthcoming men were Thomas Arbousset, who was twenty-three, and Eugène Casalis, who had only recently turned twenty. They spoke some English, the rudiments of Dutch, and a mother tongue Krotz had probably never heard before. Their plans for the future, their choice of destination, were nebulous. They were plumb in the middle of an area which the map they had bought in Paris left blank, and described only as sandy and desert plains.

___

Eugène Casalis was born on 21 November 1812, at Orthez in the southern French province of Béarn, a land of great beauty, of rich valleys, clear mountain streams and high plateaux, running down from the lofty heights of the Pyrenees. Béarn was staunchly Protestant, until the massacre on St Bartholomew's Day in 1572 ushered in a period of religious repression. Although the Edict of Nantes issued in 1598 by Henry IV provided some respite, religious repression continued, and the Huguenots were excluded from the public service, their children abducted and constrained to become Catholics.

With the revocation of the Edict in 1685, repression became full-blown. The persecution of the pastors was relentless; they were ruthlessly hunted down and executed. Any of their followers who gave them sustenance, or hid them, were imprisoned or sent to the galleys. Hundreds of thousands of industrious co-religionists were forced into or chose exile. Those who remained, a small minority of the French, no more than two per cent of the population, stood together, clung to one another, banded into the tightly knit groups of the persecuted – ascetic, morally strict, suspicious, secretive, protective, sharpening their intellectual stance. Often their survival depended on it. For a hundred years, it was a life of persecution they endured. They called it the Time of the Desert. Stories of the Church of the Desert – those small communities that met in the forests and hills and caves – were what young Protestant children cut their teeth on. Literate and articulate, their elders produced numerous histories and martyrologies.

Although their lot was somewhat improved by the Edict of Tolerance in 1787, it was the French Revolution, with its emphasis on the individual rights of man, that gave them legal equality, and religious and intellectual freedom, confirmed by Napoleon's Concordat in 1802. Although young Eugène was himself a child of the Revolution, he was brought up by those who had lived through the dark times that preceded it.

At an early age, Casalis went to live with an aunt and his paternal grand-father, who, winter and summer, in spite of his eighty years, would rise very early to pray and study the great family Bible. On Sundays, Casalis would bring him his powdered wig, his three-cornered hat and his ivory cane, and help him fasten the immense buckles on his shoes. Then they would go to the church called 'The Iron Gate', and his grandfather would always pray on his knees on the hard floor, without stool or cushion. In the afternoon, his grandfather would recall the past with two or three venerable old chaps whose religious habits, like his own, recalled the Time of the Desert. This desert was not necessarily a wilderness, but a place of physical and spiritual refuge.

Casalis's own early life was not without excitement. In fleeing from the fighting when Wellington attacked the Napoleonic forces in the south of France, the small boy was dropped on his head on the pavement by his nurse. But the accident had no lasting consequences. Another accident did, however. His beloved maternal grandmother misjudged some steps and broke her thigh. She was crippled for the rest of her life. Casalis was devoted to her, holding her mirror while she completed her toilette, filling her snuff box and listening to her vast repertoire of stories, acquired over the many long years since her birth in 1736. Some of the stories, through reflection, became favourites – swaddling the child in the comfort and security of the familiar.

Once, her husband and the fugitive pastor of the area had been in discus-sion when the alarm was raised that the dragoons were at hand. Mme Labourdette took up her seat in front of the door and refused entry, asking the officer whether he could show her his search orders. He could not. While he huffed and puffed, M. Labourdette and the pastor slipped out of the window (often used for this purpose) which opened into the vineyards, and made their way to the safety of the woods. When she had bought sufficient time, the redoubtable old lady raised the latch of the front door and said to the officer,

'Sir, my door is closed against anybody who endeavours to force it without being authorized by the king, but it is open to those who, like you, have need of refreshment and repose.' While the dragoons searched the whole house, she repaired to the kitchen, and when they were done she laid before them omelettes and ham, and plenty of the best home-made wine!

Despite the oppression, she was no simple or fanatical sectarian. When some Catholic priests fled from the atheist Revolution to the mountain hide-outs nearby, she quietly sent them supplies. It is no wonder that, when she had her accident and it was feared she might die, her most ardent devotee felt guilty and in some way responsible for this misfortune. Guilt is such a powerful and curious thing, not only to the guilty.

By the age of eight, Casalis understood that 'the great business of men was the salvation of the soul', and he was acquainted with the Huguenot doctrines of justification by faith alone and salvation by grace. But his sentimental feelings were roused, too, by the reading of a history of the conquest of Mexico and Peru, and of the missionary romance called *Gamul and Leria*, a story about the sufferings of two little Africans who find happiness after their conversion.

Happy chance put him in the path of M. Henry Pyt, brother-in-law of Ami Bost (one of the pioneers of the Réveil in Geneva), who passed through Orthez on his way to preach at Bayonne. There was no suitable school for the ten-year-old Eugène, and Pyt offered to take him under his wing. Eugène's parents were naturally hesitant, but, as Casalis was to say, it is the mother whom God generally uses as the means of determining the career of His servants. Martha Casalis agreed to the childless Pyts taking her son into their household, asserting that it was in the nature of 'a sacred adoption'.

Under this man of simple, trustful, happy piety, a man who 'dwelt in the immediate presence of God', Casalis was given, for eight years, with strictness but not austerity, a thorough education in Latin and Greek, in the Old Testament and the New. Taken on charitable visits, the boy became acquainted with the poor and with prisoners. And Pyt left him in no doubt as to the existence and meaning of *sin*.

According to Casalis, Pyt educated him 'in the truest sense of the word'. His method was to allow his pupil to find out by his own best effort what he wanted to learn. He found the Man in the Child. This was also a time of revival in evangelical faith, inspired by the Scottish Haldane brothers. Casalis discovered, too, the recently written hymns, chivalrous and defiant, of César Malan (many years later, he sang to Malan his Sesotho translations of these hymns). Pyt also succeeded in captivating Casalis by studying and analysing the Epistle to the Romans. The boy realized then what it meant to be converted, and believed it was at this moment that God touched his heart.

In those days, the word 'missionary' was not a term of approbation amongst French Protestants – because of the fanatical excesses of the Jesuit 'missionaries' in France itself. But, after hearing about the formation of an Evangelical Missionary Society in Paris, the young man began to believe that his 'earthly future was decided'. Consequently, when his mentor, with whom he was travelling to Sauveterre on holiday, turned to him, on the summit of a hill, and asked him what he wished to be, the fifteen-year-old Casalis replied, 'I shall not tell you what I *wish* to be, but what I *shall* be.' And what was that, asked M. Pyt. 'A missionary,' was the categorical reply.

On their return home, M. Pyt decided to test out this determination. He told his pupil to write out for him all the reasons for his choice. Casalis filled several pages with explanation. Unbeknown to him, M. Pyt sent this off to the Missionary Committee in Paris.

M. Pyt also began to switch the emphasis for his disciple from classical studies to biblical exegesis; they compared the profane and sacred authors of antiquity (to the general benefit of the latter); and Casalis responded to the unpublished lectures of Guizot and Cousin, and to the 'warm and generous liberalism' that was then washing over the youth of France.

A crisis was reached in 1830, when M. Pyt was called to another field of labour. Casalis was faced with the choice of going to theological college at Montauban to become a local pastor or to Paris to become a missionary.

Paris in 1830 was an exciting place for a young man not yet eighteen. Not only was the Director of the Mission House, M. Henri Grandpierre, clear and methodical in his teaching, and not only was his wife a surrogate mother to whom Casalis could confide all his secrets, but also there were new friends to be made. And in July, when Paris rose up against the arrogant autocracy of Charles X, they helped build the barricades in the revolution that overthrew the Bourbons for all time and put Louis-Philippe on the throne. Then there was the cholera that swept in from Asia and carried off thousands of Parisians, one of whom collapsed in Casalis's congregation while he was preaching and vomited over his clothes as he held him in his arms.

Here he came across the first of the students at the Mission House and the first of the missionaries to go to Africa – Isaac Bisseux and Prosper Lemue, Jean-Pierre Pellissier and Samuel Rolland. And here he met his fellow student, Thomas Arbousset, who had come from near Montpellier in the south of France to the Maison des Missions in 1829.

The original idea was to send Arbousset and Casalis to Algeria, which had been invaded by the French in June 1830, after a long dispute that was sparked off when, during an argument between the ruler of Algeria and the French consul, the latter was struck by a fly-whisk. The students, who were already studying Hebrew, were thus sent to learn Arabic at the Collège de France. They also gloried in the historical lectures of Lacretelle at the Sorbonne, and the talks of Andrieux on the fables of La Fontaine, of Laromiguière on philosophy, and Champollion on Egyptian hieroglyphics, as well as the great Cuvier reconstructing antediluvian animals from a couple of bones or so. They were taught the basics of medicine, and Arbousset learned some locksmithing and carpentry. They also did missionary apprentice work in the wretched quarters of Paris and the poor villages of Picardy. Then, after a while, Algeria was off the menu, and they were told that they were to follow their pioneering colleagues to the far-distant Cape of Good Hope.

When Casalis first went to Paris, and even more so now, parting from his parents was very hard for both sides, and the courage it took for all of them should not be underestimated, given that the chances of their seeing one another again on this side of the Great Divide were remote.

Casalis went home for two months to say goodbye. On the day of his departure, the horses were brought to the door at four in the morning. After a short prayer, his mother gave him up into the care of God. When he was already in the saddle, his father called him to dismount. 'I must embrace you once more,' he said. 'No, I beseech you,' cried Eugène, 'we shall lose what little strength we have left.' But his father persisted. 'I command you,' he said. Eugène threw himself once more into his father's embrace and heard him say, 'I shall never see you again here below!'

It took two hours of riding before Eugène's sobbing stopped.

Arbousset and Casalis left Paris for London a few days later, joined by Constant Gosselin. They sailed from Gravesend on 11 November 1832, on board the 250-ton brig called the *Test*. The first night was calm, the food and wine good, the company excellent. The next eight days were rough, and Casalis was sick the entire trip. Arbousset and Casalis occupied their time in reading and mastering a course of medicine and surgery in four volumes of six hundred pages each. Aside from being chased by a pirate ship and watching the odd fish, there were no distractions, and except for one islet which Casalis identified as Trinidade, they saw no land for three and a half months. Their first view of the Cape was when they were altogether too close to Green Point and very nearly hit a huge rock.

Table Mountain was savage and stern, a frowning wall that reduced the town below to Lilliputian proportions. The strangeness of everything and the wearisome monotony of the town on their first night there made them melancholic. But the three of them prayed together and then, being young, they slept.

Next day, everything had changed. They were rested, the sun shone, there was a breeze, and the exotic fruits and flowers were of the kind that they had only seen in certain shop windows of the Palais-Royal. The people, the Malays and 'Hottentots', were equally exotic. Their stay was made even more pleasurable by the hospitality of the famous Dr Philip of the London Missionary Society and his remarkable wife Jane.

Casalis, a child of the Revolution and defender of the rights of man, was scathing, however, about the demeanour of the colonists towards the lowly Hottentots and how their religious complacency tolerated, and even justified, this treatment. His descriptions of the Dutch farmers were measured but critical overall. He was astounded that their Puritanism extended even to the condemnation of the use of braces, since they made a cross on the back! He was also saddened that all the descendants of the Huguenots who had found a new home in southern Africa after 1685 had lost their original language, as the Dutch had forbidden the use of French in all governmental transactions in 1709, and in all churches in 1724.

Dr Philip had some bad news for the young men. They were meant to go north to Motito in Bechuanaland to join their compatriots Lemue, Rolland and Pellissier (Bisseux had remained near Paarl as pastor to the descendants of the Huguenots there). But Mzilikazi and his Ndebele had devastated the area and dispersed the tribes who were their potential converts. So they proposed instead to sail to Port Elizabeth and then head north to Philippolis, to see what fate or chance or luck or providence had in store for them.

The journey by wagon north from Port Elizabeth was a long one, punctuated by occasional stops at remote Boer farms, whose owners were taciturn and spartan but simply hospitable. Casalis had the misfortune to be extremely short-sighted. He was, however, far-sighted enough to have brought along with him several spare pairs of glasses, so that when he carelessly broke a pair he could go to the wadded packet in which he kept his replacements. Alas! The first time he did so, he found they were all reduced to powdery fragments. Nor were there any to be had in Graaff-Reinet, through which they passed on the way to the Sneeuberge. Casalis's plight was not helped by the fact that he rode a one-eyed pony, so that thereafter he had difficulty telling wildebeest from lions (a potentially unhappy form of mistaken identity); and it may have been a heightened sensitivity to sound that made him feel more strongly 'the incomprehensible silence of the desert to which one never gets accustomed'.

Eventually, they reached the last outpost of 'civilization' – the hamlet of Colesberg, which boasted a doctor, a carpenter and a Swiss watchmaker. 'Where are they not to be found!' exclaimed the disbelieving traveller. There was also the German Maltitz, whose shop was probably the last before you reached Cairo.

Beyond Colesberg, they came to a great river, three hundred metres wide and two metres deep, luscious after the parched desert, and shaded by plentiful willows! It was the Orange, and Arbousset and Casalis pondered its course and wondered about its source.

After crossing the Orange, they reached the lonely mission of Philippolis, run by Rev. Kolbe. They had little idea what they would do or where they would go, but they had no doubt that God would reveal the field of labour He had destined for them. Adam Krotz may have mistaken the fierce glare of myopia for indomitable determination in the eyes of Casalis or he may have responded to the youthful energy in the three missionaries. He almost certainly felt there might be something in it for himself. Whatever the reasons or reactions, he agreed to take them north to meet the King of the Mountain at Night.

Again, their courage should not be underestimated. They knew they would be travelling through countryside of 'thieving Korannas' and other potentially hostile tribesmen, but they had no real idea where they were going or what kind of chief and his people would be at the other end. They were being led into a new land by a man called Adam.

—◦◦—

The main topic of conversation – almost the only topic – was lions. On this subject, the missionaries learned fact and folklore intermingled. They also saw the occasional Bushman and picked up the local prejudices against them – the Tswana called them 'human scorpions'. They learned a very healthy respect, almost fear, for their arrows, the necks of which were smeared with a sticky poison 'which could chill and curdle the blood of the elephant himself' if it penetrated his skin. The encounters were slightly weird. A lone Bushman, who had been squatting behind a small heap of stones or a knot of reeds, would suddenly rise up once he had determined that the newcomers were not Boers, who hunted his people down without mercy and shot them in their hundreds. Although Casalis found them 'hideous' and was reminded of 'the disgusting abortions which the amateurs of anthropology preserve in their large phials', he discovered enough humanity in himself to regret the fact that there had been lost moments in the history of the colony when they might have been 'won over', and he had a grudging respect for their single-minded determination to remain independent and utterly free, like the antelope around, even if this meant their inevitable disappearance from the face of the earth.

After a meandering journey, submitting to the hunting whims of Krotz, the party arrived at a great mountain rising out of the plain. It was called Black

Mountain – Thaba 'Nchu – and was the western boundary of the Land of the Basotho. At his first encounter with them, Casalis was impressed with the physique, dignity of bearing and grace of movement of the Basotho. The chief who welcomed them, from this mountain fastness, was Moseme. Allied by blood to Moshoeshoe, he recognized the King's overlordship. The territory of the Basotho therefore extended, by common consent, far to the west as well as the east of the Mohokare river. The extensiveness of the kingdom was one of Casalis's first impressions; its significance would become increasingly important in the years ahead, and Casalis would always be mindful of it when the land came under threat of encroachment.

From the top of Thaba 'Nchu, the missionaries marvelled at the splendid prospect, the grandeur of Nature. All around were great outcrops like fortresses, crowned by huge sandstone rocks and surmounted by vast habitable plateaux. Eighty kilometres to the east ran the splendid chain of peaks, the front range of the Maloti, which separated Lesotho from Natal. They were shown, too, the courses of the two great rivers, whose names they transcribed as the Magokaré (the Mohokare, or Caledon) and the Sinkou (the Senqu, or Orange). The first divided Lesotho longitudinally into two almost equal provinces; the second formed the frontier with the Cape. They also saw a mountain, greyish in the haze, which was the residence of the King, and which had the reputation of being impregnable. They laughed at the Paris map which had designated these spaces as barren and desert plains.

As they moved through the valleys to the east, however, the sights were less splendid, their track littered with the signs of terrible massacres. Human bones were everywhere. Broken earthenware, abandoned fields and empty villages were on all sides, the survivors having taken to the inaccessible heights. The Lifaqane had taken a heavy toll. The plains had been left to the vultures.

At last, after struggling across the Caledon, with its steep, wagon-unfriendly banks, they left their first footprints on the soil of eastern Lesotho. It was more than just a river they had crossed.

—•◦•—

Next morning, a noisy cavalcade burst in on their camp. To Casalis's eye it was a bizarre sight – the spectacle of next-to-naked men riding bareback, with the risky unease of novices, the grace of the horses contrasting with the graceless-ness of the human forms. They were also in danger of upsetting everything. The young madcaps were Letsie and Molapo, the sons of Moshoeshoe, come, with great expectations, to welcome, and to play. The horses were new to the Basotho, taken off the Korannas. How soon they were to become part of the landscape, and almost like one with their riders!

The valleys skirting the Thuathe plateau were now quite well populated, indicating a reasonably prosperous and secure existence. Soon the pentagonal hill that was Thaba-Bosiu, some 150 metres high, came in sight. It was completely isolated, separated from the plateau which served as a base for the Maloti by the Phuthiatsana river, which cut through the countryside around Thaba-Bosiu on its way to join the Mohokare. Perched on the edge of the peaks above, like a fussy line of crows, was a serious and impatient multitude. Sorghum and maize (a recent import) covered the land around. A ravine like a scar ran up the mountain, providing the visitors with a way up to its top.

There they were greeted by a fantastic figure with a huge headdress of black ostrich feathers and a long wand, who approached them growling and snapping like a dog. This praise-singer of the King, 'at once a royal panegyrist and buffoon, public crier and policeman', known to the local populace by the title of the 'town dog', parted a line before them up to the mat where a man was seated. 'There is Moshesh,' said Krotz. The impression he made on Casalis was immediate. About forty-five years of age, the upper part of his body naked, perfectly modelled, fleshy, not obese. He had allowed to fall carelessly around him a large mantle of leopard skins, lissom as the finest cloth, and a string of glass beads was bound around his forehead as the sole ornament, with a tuft of feathers fastened behind. On his right arm was a bracelet of ivory – an emblem of power – and on his wrists some copper rings. His profile was aquiline, his eyes, a little weary, were quick with intelligence. Casalis felt at once that this eagle of the mountain was 'a superior man, trained to think, to command others, and above all himself'.

For an instant they looked at each other, then Moshoeshoe rose and said, 'Lumela lekhooa' (Welcome, white man!). Casalis held out his hand, and the King took it without hesitation.

—◦◦—

Casalis was then entertained by the King's senior wife, 'Mamohato, though Moshoeshoe was careful to have his other thirty or forty wives paraded past first. At the meal, Casalis uttered his first word of Sesotho on Thaba-Bosiu: 'Monate.' His host smilingly repeated it after him. So his first word was 'Good.'

—◦◦—

The wagon having arrived at the foot of Thaba-Bosiu by this time, the missionaries invited Moshoeshoe to dinner. They served him, from their sparse larder, hashed mutton, pumpkin, and bowls of coffee of a dubious colour but sweetened with handfuls of raw sugar. Because their second wagon with most of their utensils had not yet arrived, Moshoeshoe had to eat off the saucepan lid, and the missionaries out of the pot!

After the meal, they explained to the King their business as the messengers of a God of Peace, with the most perfect assurance that He would make the incursions of enemies cease and create in the country a new order of belief and manners which would secure tranquillity, stability and abundance. On the material side, they asked for a site where they could build houses and cultivate the ground according to their own ideas and habits.

'My heart is white with joy,' said Moshoeshoe, 'your words are great and good. It is enough for me to see your clothing, your arms, and the rolling houses in which you travel, to understand how much intelligence and strength you have. You see our desolation. This country was full of inhabitants. Wars have devastated it. Multitudes have perished; others are refugees in foreign lands. I remain almost alone on this rock. I have been told that you can help us. You promise to do it. That is enough. It is all I want to know. Remain with us. You shall instruct us. We will do all you wish. The country is at your disposal. We can go through it together, and you shall choose the place which will best suit you.'

To this his chief counsellors – his maternal uncle Ratšiu, his principal warrior and friend Makoanyane, and his second cousin Khoabane – agreed. Others were less forthcoming, such as the King's father, Mokhachane, suspicious, mocking, ironically superstitious. The common people were now curious, now timid, seeing these strange new creatures either as ghosts or as the spirits magicians were assumed to contact, but astonished that they had no wives.

Because the banks of the Phuthiatsana were too steep for the river's course to be turned, thus enabling the irrigation the missionaries desired, and because there was a lack of wood for building, the area around Thaba-Bosiu was deemed not to be ideal for the first mission site. So, accompanied by Moshoeshoe, they went in search of one.

Some eight leagues (about forty kilometres) from Thaba-Bosiu, they came across 'one of the most beautiful valleys in the country', entirely uninhabited. After the mountain that overlooked it, it was called Makhoarane. Arbousset, Casalis and Gosselin decided to call it Moriah, the land where Abraham offered up Isaac for sacrifice, to express their gratitude to God for past mercies and their confidence in Him for the future. Later, it would be known as Morija.

That night, 9 July 1833, the African travellers settled into their new home, squatting like gypsies around a blaze. 'Under the arch of heaven, the sight of a fire replaces all possible elements of comfort.' Pencils in hand, they pointed at objects, using the all-purpose word, 'Ke'eng?' (What is it?)

Next day, the three raw young pioneers began the task of building a shelter and clearing the ground for fields and orchards, a task that was to take three years before they were fairly settled. These years were like a capsule, self-contained, concentrated and industrious, so that they seemed like a dozen years rolled into one.

The trio complemented one another. Gosselin was 'force and good humour personified', elementally down-to-earth, cheerful, simple and a fount of wise competence, uncomplicatedly pious. When secret melancholy crept into Casalis's soul, Gosselin coaxed him out of it. Arbousset, on the other hand, had a sweet and fervent piety, and his ardent imagination, his adventurous spirit, his quick and profound sensibility, his fevered activity, picturesque speech and occasionally eccentric ideas were the typical products of his native province, Languedoc. He also had a real flair for the dramatic. Casalis was somewhere in between: less demonstrative, more studied, intuitively sensitive to human strengths and weaknesses, cooler – like the air closer to the mountains from which he came and to which he had come. Although they held him in great affection, the Basotho did give him the nickname 'Mahloana-matšoana', Little-Black-Eyes.

Hard work endowed them with dignity. The Korannas were always an invisible threat, the lions were a hazard, and those great resurrectionists, the hyenas, a nuisance. Necessities were scarce and had to be husbanded: there was no bread, and when the salt gave out the privation was severe. Luxuries were what many would deem necessities: at one stage, Casalis might have given his kingdom for a button, and instead had to content himself with acacia thorns to secure his braces. But they kept their health and were fortified by the knowledge that they were there by virtue of a direct order from Christ. And their spirits soared when, on some savage rock, they sang a French hymn and realized that, for the first time ever, the name of their Father in Heaven had been uttered in these wildernesses.

Soon, they came to love their new home. At the foot of Makhoarane there was still a small lake where heron and other waterbirds frolicked, and otter and water snakes thrived. A little way off, leeches multiplied in the reeds, and birds from the mountain beat such determined songlines in the air, down to the bottom of the valley to feed amongst the limpid pools, that the missionaries called the beautiful stream Lerato (Love) and visited it often, in the certitude of seeing duck, teal and wading birds.

Even though none of them had the shadow of a regret, they did have a strong consciousness of exile: the nearest post office was at Graaff-Reinet, nearly five hundred kilometres away. Letters would be entrusted to travellers, black or white, and although they were invariably delivered faithfully, it would take ten to twelve months to get a reply. Consequently, it was only at the end of the first year of their sojourn that Casalis heard of the death of his beloved father several months before. Although he had died of stomach cancer, Casalis believed it had been hastened by the shock of his departure, and in the first burst of his grief there was mingled a feeling close to remorse – guilt for the death of a parent, which is the normal and natural feeling of many children. 'I seemed to myself,' he wrote, 'to have killed my father.'

Before he died, Eugène's father had made a strange comment to his wife: 'I shall see Eugène again before you.' It was his pledge that he and his son would not be separated in space, by mere geography, but that his son would henceforth live under his eye. This was a thought the Basotho would have understood readily. They scrutinized in minute detail every word, gesture and action of the missionaries, and no doubt discussed them avidly. A profound sympathy was painted on all their faces when they saw Casalis's grief, though they were puzzled when he told them that his father was now in heaven, since their own dead passed into the bowels of the earth. Nevertheless, it did make clear to them that the whites shared with them a common mortality and had, despite their capacity for what seemed like miracles, no remedy for death.

What impressed them was Casalis's iron faith that he and his father would ultimately enjoy an 'eternal reunion'. This was a revelation to them. They realized that although the Frenchmen could not conquer death, they did not fear it.

Another important river had been crossed, too. Casalis's bereavement convinced the Basotho that the missionaries were resolved to remain amongst them indefinitely. Their common destinies were now glued fast.

The missionaries did bring certain improvements in material conditions: to the domestic animals of the Basotho, they gradually added the pig, the duck, the goose, the turkey and the cat. The cat, it was said, was a godsend: in huts hitherto infested by rats and mice, the quiet assassin came to be the guardian of the hearth. The missionaries were not successful, however, in trying to domesticate local wild animals such as the quagga, wildebeest and antelope.

Apart from practical matters of survival, Casalis and Arbousset set about their primary task of religious instruction. This, of course, was not easy. At first, they had to depend on their Mosotho interpreter, Seipeami, a lazy liar whose 'follies' as their 'dragoman' led to some misapprehensions: on one occasion, by confusing 'zaligmaaker' with 'zadelmaaker', he managed to turn Jesus Christ from a saviour into a saddlemaker!

Through hard work, the Frenchmen began to master Sesotho, not only the names for things but also the verbs, those words that capture process and are so difficult to conquer. Soon they began, in the little spare time they had, to write brief abstracts of Bible history and short meditations to be delivered on Sundays, and they even ventured to compose some hymns, and to translate the Lord's Prayer. In this modest way, the written literature of Sesotho was born.

They also introduced to their new audience the act of prayer, addressed to the invisible Being. Gradually, through the call and response method, usually varied to avoid mechanical routine, they began to discover the glimmerings of reflection and sentiment. On their frequent visits to Thaba-Bosiu, they were always heartily welcomed by Moshoeshoe, who summoned them to an audience, taking the somewhat unusual step of actively encouraging the women and children to join in, despite the murmurings of the older men. At first, the women were sheepish, but eventually they grew to be the majority.

Moshoeshoe himself was fascinated by the new teaching, surprised to hear that it was based on 'facts' or 'real history'. Although he acknowledged that his ancestors used to speak of a Lord of Heaven, pointing to the Milky Way as 'the way to the gods', he and his people assumed that that world must have existed forever, and they had venerated the spirits of their ancestors, asking them for good rains, harvests and reception after death. Now they knew that God had given men and animals existence.

'You were in darkness, and we have brought you the light,' said Casalis. When he continued, 'All these visible things, and a multitude of others which we cannot see, have been created and are preserved by a Being all wise and all good, who is the God of us all, and who made us to be born of one blood,' the King's advisers were incredulous. 'What!' exclaimed one. 'That can never be! You are white; we are black: how could we come from the same father?' But Moshoeshoe scoffed at them, using the analogy of white, red and spotted cattle to refer to the idea of a common species, which prompted a discussion on the accidents of gestation. Moshoeshoe, Casalis noted, had a 'robust faith' in the 'unity of the human race'. In a speech reminiscent of Shylock, the King said, 'Black or white, we laugh or cry in the same manner and from the same causes; what gives pleasure or pain to one race, causes equally pleasure or pain to the other.'

One of the greatest obstacles to conversion, one of the largest rocks in the road, was the question of polygamy. Moshoeshoe, the greatest polygamist of all, with thirty or forty wives, was nonetheless quite happy to discuss its disadvantages, such as quarrels between the wives, the fomenting of rivalries between children, and the attempts of idle older wives to turn younger ones into domestic servants. But he warned that in condemning polygamy, the missionaries were attacking 'a strong citadel' and were unlikely to shake it, at least in his lifetime. He regretted this point of contention, which he felt would prevent the Basotho from soon becoming Christians. Casalis replied that they were in no hurry: like the poor stones that served as the foundations of the house they were building at Morija and which would never see the sun or be praised for their beauty, the early pioneers of monogamy, of whom Moshoeshoe might be one, could, with some sacrifice, be the foundations of the new family, the new city of God. But Moshoeshoe was not won over entirely.

—◦◦—

With Pellissier having moved to Bethulie and Rolland at Beersheba, there were now five missionaries in the area with overlapping interests. Consequently, at the prompting of the Paris Committee, it was decided to set up a regular Conference at which all the missionaries would meet annually. The first was held at Beersheba in 1836. One of its most important discussions revolved around the need for a missionary to be stationed permanently at the populous and important centre of Thaba-Bosiu. It was a wise decision to send Casalis for the purpose. He accepted this new task with determination, although parting from his friends Arbousset and Gosselin was not easy. Moshoeshoe also agreed readily, but was concerned that many of his people feared the new teaching and the changes to customs and institutions it was likely to bring. Nevertheless, Casalis moved in early 1836, and Gosselin soon joined him for a while to build the Thaba-Bosiu mission house in the following year. And so the mission at Thaba-Bosiu, where Édouard Jacottet was to serve for twenty years, was born.

It was not easy at first, as Casalis found himself to be no Simeon Stylites. He was lonely. Moreover, it was a belief universally acknowledged amongst the Basotho that, being a single man, he was in want of a wife. Otherwise his status would be too lowly for them to take his teaching seriously. Casalis realized that he was no St Paul either, and what he needed was 'a sister-wife'.

He had two problems. Firstly, where could he, a man without fortune and now already become 'more than half a savage', find a suitable mate? The answer to that, he decided, must be Cape Town. Secondly, as a dutiful son and employee, he believed he could not marry without the blessing of his mother and the Paris Mission. Fortunately, he had foreseen this contingency and had written to both some time before, asking, with no one special in mind, for a kind of blanket permission. After some weeks, he received a packet of letters from a man who had brought them on the end of a long reed. Dated more than six months previously and at the mercy of chance, they brought at last, but safely, his mother's consent and the Director's best wishes – the name of the bride to be filled in at his discretion! So Casalis set off for Colesberg and the Cape, in search of a wife. He married Sarah Dyke in Cape Town on 13 April 1836.

Prior to this, however, there occurred an event of profound significance. One evening at about nine o'clock, at a little distance from their house, Arbousset and Casalis overheard a young man at Morija spontaneously offer up a fervent prayer. They approached him silently in the darkness, suspecting they had heard his voice in the accents of contrition. They were right! Moved beyond words, their tears flowing freely, they fell to their knees, witnesses to a genuine conversion. The name of the convert was Sekhesa, and the day of this first fruit of their labour was 9 January 1836. It was two and a half years since they had arrived.

CHAPTER TEN

THE MOUNTAIN KING

1836–1848

'Peace,' Moshoeshoe used to say, 'is the mother of nations.' Whether it was happenstance or providence, the arrival of the French missionaries in 1833 coincided with the beginnings of a long period of relative security and prosperity for the Basotho. This is reflected in the growth of the population. In the mid-1830s, Moshoeshoe's following was estimated at about 25 000; in 1841, this had grown to perhaps 40 000; by 1848, Casalis believed the figure to have risen to 80 000.

It was a period of considerable economic growth too. With the introduction of maize, Lesotho became the granary for the population north of the Orange, livestock increased in a healthy upward curve, and new goods – clothing, farming implements and arms – began to flow into the country in exchange for grain. Traders started to take an interest in the area.

But there were also warning signs that this would not last forever. In 1833, a group of Barolong of the Seleka clan, under their chief Moroka, coming from the west, scouted out the area around Thaba 'Nchu, which was held by Moseme, whom the French missionaries had met on their way through. The Barolong were accompanied by two Wesleyan missionaries. Some Griquas under Barend Barends and Pieter Davids, Korannas under Jan Taaibosch, and Bastards under Carolus Baatje, joined them. New settlements sprang up at Thaba 'Nchu, Platberg (near Ladybrand), Lesooane (beyond Viervoet), Meru-Metšo, and Mpokoane (near Clocolan). Although Moshoeshoe regarded much of this territory as his own, he was not opposed to these developments, as the new settlers provided a windbreak between himself and the dreaded Ndebele of Mzilikazi, the cloud of red dust to the north-west. But their fealty to him was ambiguous and they were eventually to become a thorn in his side.

In addition, towards the end of 1835, the dissatisfied Boers of the Cape began to cross the Orange, looking for land, looking for independence. Some began to settle in the south-west, in the wedge of land formed by the confluence of the Mohokare and the Senqu, land which Moshoeshoe might wish to claim as his. Others moved north, skirting the outer limits of Basotho territory, marking out farms for occupancy; while yet others trekked ever northwards, agitating what flimsy stability there was amongst the Ndebele to the north-west, the Batlokoa of Sekonyela to the north, the Zulu in the north-east, and ultimately the Pedi in the extreme north.

Moshoeshoe himself was not idle. After the 1840 journey with Arbousset, and no doubt as a result of it, he began to expand north-eastwards himself, first establishing Khoabane on the northern side of the Berea plateau. Then in 1846, and with the agreement of Sekonyela, whom he was trying to woo diplomatic-ally at the time, he sent Molapo even further north.

Molapo would have to jostle with Sekonyela for living space. In the south, the Baphuthi chief, who considered himself independent but whom Moshoeshoe regarded as a vassal, provided a buffer against the southern Nguni, while Moshoeshoe encouraged his brothers Posholi at Thaba-Tšoeu and Mohale near Mohale's Hoek to secure his south-western flank against the per-sistent encroachment of the Boer farmers. The world was beginning to close in on Moshoeshoe, the intruders like an incoming tide lapping at his feet. Unlike the tide, however, there was little chance of them receding.

As the new recruits of the PEMS began arriving, so the number of stations grew. Moshoeshoe welcomed this, not only because he genuinely had no real objections to the message, but also because it happened to suit his political pur-poses and reinforce his security. In 1833, Pellissier had founded the station of Bethulie on the northern bank of the Orange, just to the east of its junction with the Caledon. This tended to block the eastward expansion of the Griquas at Philippolis. The mainly Tswana people here regarded themselves as inde-pendent of both the Griquas and Moshoeshoe, so Bethulie was something of an isolated spot of its own. Up the Caledon to the north-east, Rolland had set-tled at Beersheba. The people here were Basotho and recognized Moshoeshoe as their sovereign. They therefore formed the western edge of the Basotho influence. In 1837, François Daumas started a station at Mekoatleng, not too far from Sekonyela at Marabeng. There, at Mekoatleng, he was joined by Moletsane, the chief of some refugee Bataung, who became a friend of Daumas and a staunch ally of Moshoeshoe.

The establishment of Bethesda amongst Moorosi's Baphuthi by Christian Schrumpf in 1843, as well as Hebron (near modern Zastron) by Louis Cochet, and Hermon (near modern Wepener) by Hamilton Dyke, brother of Sarah Casalis, in 1847, completed a formidable network in the south, of both tem-poral and spiritual significance; in the north, Pierre-Joseph Maitin located at Berea alongside Khoabane in 1843, and Daniel Keck moved close to Molapo to found Cana in 1846. From south-west to north-east, then, parallel to the vertebrae of the Maloti, ran a spine of mission stations, propping up the body of Moshoeshoe's consolidating nation. It was a reasonably happy polygamous marriage – the Basotho, after all, sometimes joked that the missionaries were Moshoeshoe's wives, since he had sent cattle as bohali with Adam Krotz. Safe under his patronage, the missionaries built their houses and churches, planted their trees, vegetable gardens and orchards, and were able to spread the Word of God to an expanding area and an increasing number of people, loaned to them under the mafisa system by the King.

After the initial success with Sekhesa, there was a small but steady growth in conversions. In 1842, Morija had 28 full church members; in 1844, there were 93; and by 1848, the number had risen to 251. Casalis baptized the first convert at Thaba-Bosiu in August 1839. By 1842, there were 23 converts; in 1844, the number of full members of the Thaba-Bosiu church was 59; and by 1847, there were 128. Most successful was Rolland at Beersheba, with 463 converts by 1847. Struggling in centres of great resistance were Maitin at Berea and Schrumpf at Bethesda. Each had only 22 members by 1847. In all, there were by then over 1 200 full members of the church.

Amongst them there were some notable converts. Moshoeshoe's uncle (Mokhachane's brother) Libe, an avid opponent until his conversion in 1846, was one; Moshoeshoe's brothers Mopeli and Tšiama and his sister Ntšebo were others; then there were some of his wives, including his third wife 'Masekhonyana, as well as his brother-in-law Matete; his second son Molapo was baptized by Arbousset in 1840, and was followed by Masupha, Makhobalo and Sekhonyana; his most trusted counsellors, Makoanyane and Ramatšeatsana, were also early converts. Some of the larger fish were netted. But the big one kept getting away.

King Moshoeshoe was clearly close to conversion in 1837, but unlike Molapo later, did not quite go the whole way. Perhaps he was just too settled in his ways, and disinclined to make a radical choice in a period of comparative quiescence. He was, after all, over fifty by 1840. 'Beyond a certain age,' he said, 'one can learn new things, but one does not remake one's heart.' Casalis explained 'the tardiness of his avowal' by suggesting that he was 'excessively attached to the usages of his fathers, and still more to his possessions, which he increased, at times, by means which were not defensible'. Bitter experience of human perversity had made him a 'fatalist', and 'to struggle with success against evil' seemed to him almost an impossibility. In his eyes, his own conversion was a dream that Arbousset and Casalis entertained, and he admired but could not quite accept. While the triumph of Christianity seemed inevitable, the time did not seem right. But his profound interaction with the missionaries and the new learning gave him a wider horizon. 'Casalis,' he pronounced thoughtfully,

'I see men have been the same in all ages. Greeks and Romans, Frenchmen, Englishmen and Basutoos have all one common nature.'

—❦—

The advance of Christianity faced great opposition amongst the Basotho. Naturally, the witchdoctors and diviners resented professional competition. Chapi, one of Moshoeshoe's diviners, tried to blame a deadly measles epidemic that swept southern Africa in 1839 on the coming of the missionaries, and, painted on one side with white clay and on the other with black carbon, epitomizing to the missionaries a harlequin charlatan, he climbed Thaba-Bosiu and delivered a tirade against the intruders. Some years afterwards, the missionaries were even accused of being cannibals themselves. But there was also resistance within the royal household. Moshoeshoe's parents both undermined the teachings of the missionaries: his mother, for instance, stoked up the younger wives to keep her son on the straight and polygamous narrow by use of their physical charms; his father remained stubbornly heathen, and grumbled that the only good thing the missionaries brought was sugar – he had a sweet tooth. Ratšiu, the King's maternal uncle, also sided with the 'traditional'. More openly hostile were Moshoeshoe's half-brother Mohale and brother Posholi, a very superstitious man, who actively discouraged his followers from visiting Morija. So too was Moorosi, chief of the Baphuthi, who lived on the southern edge of the kingdom and vacillated between opportunistic vassalage and independent sovereignty – the latter facilitated by the repeated movement of his headquarters beyond the boundaries of Moshoeshoe's kingdom.

Arbousset did not make much headway with crown prince Letsie either, after a promising beginning. He had begun to turn away even before 1847, when Arbousset criticized him, in front of all the inhabitants of Morija, for the commission of a judicial murder.

Moshoeshoe soon had first-hand knowledge of the depth of this tension. When Tsenei, the sister of the first convert at Thaba-Bosiu, died, she had, at the specific insistence of her brother, been buried according to Christian rites. This was no small undertaking, as Casalis realized, given that the tomb was the 'altar' where the Basotho made their sacrifices and supplicated 'the formidable shades of the ancestors'. But Moshoeshoe responded to the inner light of her brother and personally pointed out a spot for the new 'city of the dead'.

When the measles epidemic carried off Casalis's daughter Emma, Moshoeshoe asked to see the body in the coffin before it was closed. Observing the care with which Sarah Casalis had adorned the child, he exclaimed, 'Ah! Christians only are happy, they weep, but their tears are not like ours. We see that you believe that Emma will rise again, and that death is but a stream that man crosses to go to God.' In the depths of his grief, Casalis found a grain of comfort in knowing that the Basotho had witnessed Christian parents sustained by the firm conviction that they would see their child again in a region of glory, and that this might help release the Basotho from fearful superstition and the clutching hands of the dead.

Two days afterward, death touched Moshoeshoe even closer to home. In a fit of delirium brought on by the measles, one of his principal wives, 'Mantsane, threw herself off the highest cliff of Thaba-Bosiu. Moshoeshoe begged Casalis not to leave his side, as he anticipated the day of mourning would also be a day of strife. 'Mantsane's relatives, including Ratšiu, had prepared a burial place in a cattle kraal alongside the grave of Moshoeshoe's first wife, 'Mamohato. The King spent considerable time in arguing for a Christian burial, while the deceased's brother protested against any deviation from the national customs. 'On what are these customs founded?' the King retorted. 'I should like to see the book where they are enjoined: the missionaries give us the reason for all they do. Man dies, because he received in Adam the seed of death; the dead should be buried in the same place, because it is a beautiful thought that they lie together in the long sleep of death. Man is only alone as long as he remains in his mother's womb; when he sees the light of day he clings to the breast of her who has given him birth, and from time to time he lives in the society of his fellows. You say we must sacrifice to our ancestors, but they were only men like ourselves. You, also, when you are dead, will be turned into gods; would you like us to worship you now? But how are we to worship men? And if you are but men now, will you be more powerful when death shall have reaped the half of you?' From the crowd a voice shouted, 'What the missionaries say would be excellent if we believed it, but I, for my part, do not.' Another voice retorted, 'Courage, my master: do what is right; you will not repent of it.' Casalis then spoke, saying that Moshoeshoe had given the reasons why the ancestors should not be worshipped. He challenged anyone to refute his truths then and there.

When, after a long silence, someone said, 'We will speak when the missionary is gone,' Moshoeshoe scornfully replied, 'Yes, you will conquer when there is no longer an adversary; speak now!' Eventually, Moshoeshoe ordered them to fill in the pit and take 'Mantsane to sleep beside Tsenei. Moshoeshoe had told the crowd that though he himself was not a converted man, and had long tried 'to resist the truths spoken by the missionaries', he was now convinced he could no longer 'stand against them'. To Casalis he said that he would one day rest alongside 'Mantsane and Tsenei.

It had been a moment fraught with danger. As Ratšiu had said, 'We are silent, because we will not yield.' Moshoeshoe had faced the opposition down with courage, but he was too wise not to take heed.

Nevertheless, he went ahead with other modifications to custom. In 1840, he stopped initiation schools and circumcision for his own sons and for his immediate followers. In 1841, when two of his wives, 'Masekhonyana and 'Mamosebetsi, were baptized by Casalis, they each asked Moshoeshoe for a divorce. The King tried to persuade Casalis to bend on the issue, but he would not. Moshoeshoe eventually approved the formal deeds of divorce and tried to defend the position (and his ex-wives' continued access to their former privileges) to a disgruntled crowd. His most vociferous opponent argued that the Basotho recognized only one death that could separate wives from husbands, and that was the death of the grave. This was a new kind of death which destroyed families, and they could not accept it. The life of Ramatšeatsana, the first royal counsellor to convert, was then seriously threatened. The pitso disbanded in disorder and disgruntlement.

In 1843, a deranged old woman, a relative of Moshoeshoe, had her field confiscated by her local headman, and so she cursed him. When the man died soon afterwards, of natural or supernatural causes, she was blamed and ultimately stoned to death by some of Moshoeshoe's wives. Moshoeshoe was shocked. Following the example of Mohlomi, he had always been suspicious of the machinations of witchdoctors; now he found himself trying to protect those accused of being witches. To a pitso quickly called, he warned, 'Hear me well today! Let no one ever have the audacity to come and tell me: "I have been bewitched!" May that word never again be pronounced in my presence!'

The missionaries and Moshoeshoe found common ground on a number of points which might have caused conflict in a different country. While Casalis enjoyed a good bottle of Bordeaux – he was as French as Garraway was Irish – Moshoeshoe was abstemious, believing that strong drink, snuff and tobacco were likely to produce undesirable familiarity with his subjects. A clear head was undoubtedly an advantage to a ruler.

The King had a distaste for the death penalty and rarely invoked it. He was reluctant to shed blood – the blood of his own people in particular. This extended even to the cannibals, of whom there may once have been up to 7 000 in his country. He preferred to lure them away from their hateful habits by giving them food and cattle. He was merciful to them partly because he felt responsible – once, in the dark days of the Lifaqane, the Bamokoteli had robbed the Bamaieane of all their worldly goods, and told them, 'Go ye, and eat people'; and partly because he was grateful to some of the cannibals for sharing with the

Basotho the grain they had hidden in caves, during one of the bitterest wars, thus saving them from starvation.

In addition, he found an ingenious argument to justify his policy of reconciliation, which was not at first popular amongst his people. When his counsellors pointed out that Rakotsoane (that very Rakotsoane who was present when Arbousset conducted a sermon in 1840) had been responsible for the death and consumption of Moshoeshoe's own grandfather, Peete, Moshoeshoe replied, 'All the more reason for leaving them alone. It is not seemly to disturb the grave of your ancestors!'

This reintegration of the cannibals into common society certainly eased the task of the missionaries, and the conversions of some of these outcasts made good stories, even if they were tinged with a frisson of horror. One such convert even confessed in her straitness to infanticide, sobbing: 'I am indeed a murderess, for I have eaten the fruit of my own womb.' Another made an interesting public confession: 'Oh, how vile I was! I sucked wickedness with my mother's milk, and the depravity of my parents. Later on came the terrible wars, ruin and starvation. I lived on roots, grass seed, and even ate pot-clay to try thereby to stay my hunger. The hand of the Amangwane was heavy on the land; all the tribes were at war with each other, and everyone was a fugitive. Day by day men began to eat men, and I too tasted human flesh. From that time I shunned my fellows, dreading to be eaten too. What horrible days followed that on which I cut off the arm of my mother's brother and cooked and ate it! I also ate my father's brother, every bit of him, and many others. Even as Ezekiel saw in a vision the dried bones of a whole nation draw near to each other and assume form, so, with terror, do I see the bones I have picked reunite with their fellows and rise up in judgement against me. I see the figure of one with a rein around his neck; another rises from the earth with my knife in his breast; a third appears without an arm; while another indicates an old pot wherein I cooked his flesh. Woe is me, I am afraid! I am Kholumolumo, the horrible beast of our ancient fable, who swallowed all mankind and the beasts of the field.'

CHAPTER ELEVEN

THE OXEN OF THE BATLOKOA

1848–1858

The year 1848 was fateful. Revolution swept through Europe, brushing Louis-Philippe from his throne in the process. In Paris, the PEMS stumbled, almost to extinction. In southern Africa, the British annexed the land between the Orange and the Vaal rivers. And in Lesotho, the missionaries made a serious mistake.

A small deficit in the finances caused a disproportionate panic in the Mission Society. With unseemly haste, the Mission House in Paris was closed and its seven students were packed off home. There was no real reason for this panic – it happened, in fact, before the February revolution. Its consequences, though, were dire for the Basotho mission, since the supply of new recruits dried up and the existing missionaries – already deemed too few – were put under considerable strain. They were weakened further when it was decided to send Casalis to Paris to plead their case. Had he been present in Lesotho, the incident concerning the oxen of the Batlokoa might have taken a different turn. It is worth following mainly, but not exclusively, Jacottet's version of events written sixty years later, so that the biting criticism of the mission's decisions and conduct can be seen to come from within its ranks.

In 1845, a British Resident, Major Henry Warden, was stationed at Bloemfontein to mediate between the immigrant Boers and the Basotho. For a while he was relatively successful, patching up an untidy peace between Moshoeshoe and Sekonyela, for instance. But early in 1848, the new Governor of the Cape, Sir Harry Smith, a military man, more impulsive than considered, and preoccupied with the bitter fighting in the eastern Cape, blundered in for a cursory meeting with Moshoeshoe, alienated the Boers, declared the whole land as the Orange River Sovereignty, and galloped off again, leaving Warden to attend to the details. As Warden must have known in the pit of his stomach, the devil is in the details.

The Boers soon drove Warden out of Bloemfontein, and had to be defeated at the Battle of Boomplaats on 29 August 1848 before he brought them to relative acquiescence. Then he set about trying to demarcate the boundaries between the Boers and the Basotho, as well as the other interested parties, 'without taking into account', in the words of Jacottet, 'either strict justice or the history of the country'. Part of the subsequent trouble arose because he began to favour chiefs like Moroka, who saw the fluid situation as an opportunity to establish his independence from both Moshoeshoe, who regarded him as a vassal, and Sekonyela. In 1849, Moshoeshoe had to accept, with gritted teeth, this arbitrary demarcation, in which thousands of his subjects, including Moletsane and the Bataung, were cut off on the wrong side of what came to be known as the 'Warden Line'. Would Moshoeshoe accept this line? 'Yes,' answered Letsie, 'as when a dog consents to walk after he who drags it with a rope.' It was an uneasy submission to an 'absurd and culpable policy', and Moshoeshoe was strongly criticized by his own followers for acceding to it.

The French missionaries tried vigorously to advise Warden and Smith of their folly, only to offend. They were accused of blind bias towards the Basotho. By the Basotho, on the other hand, they were accused of siding with the British when they warned against an open rupture which might lead to the ruin of Lesotho. Then the Boers and the British, both, accused them of inciting Moshoeshoe's resistance. During the course of all this, the missionaries were forced into making a choice which was little short of a disaster.

In October 1848, Moshoeshoe, like a hawk tearing apart a pigeon, ordered a massive reprisal raid on Sekonyela, who had attacked him after twenty years of relative peace. In the absence of the diplomatic and restraining hand of Casalis, who was in Paris, the missionaries, disapproving of reprisals from the point of view of both Christian ideals and politics, told their church members to disobey Moshoeshoe's order. 'They erred,' was Jacottet's circumspect opinion, 'in interfering in too marked a degree with those questions of Native policy, and in using their spiritual authority in questions with which they were not concerned. They went so far as to forbid them, under penalty of ecclesiastical censure, to partake in a war which they disapproved of, and even decided to apply disciplinary measures against all the Christians who had carried away cattle belonging to the enemy and refused to give them back.' In fact, they went so far as to withhold communion from the members who shared in the oxen won from the Batlokoa.

'Such intervention in questions that were out of their sphere,' Jacottet went on to write, 'was a serious mistake. The missionaries unquestionably exceeded their rights; they forgot that certain domains are exclusively under the control of civil authority and that the missionary, as well as any other citizen, must render unto Caesar that which is Caesar's.' While the missionaries genuinely believed that reprisals were contrary to the spirit of the Gospel, and were therefore sticking to their faith and their principles, the sad fact is that they had interfered impoliticly in a popular national war against the old enemy, the Batlokoa. 'The interference of the missionaries,' judged Jacottet, 'was thus doubly unfortunate. It is impossible to approve of it from any point of view, and the conditions under which it occurred make it all the more blameworthy. The missionaries seemed to side with an enemy particularly hated. There was already a certain amount of feeling against them, as people resented their abuse, on occasion, of their ecclesiastical power. The Christian sons of Moshoeshoe, with Molapo and Masupha at their head, bore with impatience the rather too stern authority which had been sometimes enforced somewhat indiscreetly. Instead of exercising discipline rigorously in such a crisis, it would have been far wiser to have acted more circumspectly, and to have avoided pushing the exigencies of Christian law too far. He who pulls the rope too tight, breaks it ...'

There is an irony here, or at least an ambiguity, that might be intrinsic to Protestant evangelism. On the one hand, the missionaries, in their youthful zeal to succeed and to justify themselves, had perhaps admitted too many converts before they were ready; on the other hand, they were overly rigorous with these very same people when the situation called for tact and flexibility.

The consequences were soon felt. Within a few weeks, Molapo had left the church and ceased to be a Christian. He was followed by those other sons and brothers of Moshoeshoe who had also joined, although it must be said, in the words of Jacottet, that some were already 'on the road to apostasy', having accepted the new religion a little too hastily. 'So for the first time, the mission was not in harmony with the national cause.' The effort to convert from the top down had failed. The mission had lost, perhaps forever, *the chance to become the national church of the Basotho.* What made things even worse for the missionaries was that not only was there a widespread withdrawal from the church, but also the apostates embarked on an active revival of traditional practices and began to prepare for war. In this they were encouraged by the emergence of a female diviner called 'Mantsopa, whose reputation was enhanced by the revivalist movement of the Xhosa prophet Mlanjeni, which spread to and stirred up Lesotho in 1850–51. War had, in fact, broken out in the eastern Cape. Moshoeshoe found himself caught in a difficult position. His faith in the missionaries had been subverted by the actions of other whites – their devout virtues could not be claimed for a wider white society. So, for a while at least, Moshoeshoe turned his back on them, reintroduced initiation schools, took new wives, purified himself anew with old rituals, and sought advice from 'Mantsopa and Mlanjeni.

He and others must have felt themselves vindicated when Warden, ill-advisedly listening to one side only, backed Moroka and Sekonyela, and, seeking reparation for stolen cattle, advanced on Moletsane and the Bataung with a mixed force of British, Boers, Griquas, Korannas and Barolong in June 1851. They attacked the Bataung on Viervoet mountain and, with the aid of a cannon, drove them back. However, the Basotho, under Letsie, Molapo and Mopeli, arrived to turn the course of the battle, assegaing many Barolong and throwing numbers of them off the perpendicular cliffs of Viervoet. Warden licked his wounds all the way back to Bloemfontein, but Moshoeshoe, as he had shown so many times before, was temperate in triumph. He did not follow up his victory. Soon afterwards, however, he did take on Sekonyela once more, and broke him forever.

For a while, the British now listened to the French missionaries, where before they had spurned them. They even recognized the injustices of the Warden Line and promised to adjust the boundaries more favourably to Moshoeshoe. But by the end of 1852, Sir George Cathcart, the successor to Sir Harry Smith as Governor, had overcome Xhosa resistance, and in November he moved north of the Orange with a force of 2 500 soldiers, including cavalry and artillery. On 13 December, he camped at Platberg. Cathcart was an honest and straightforward man, but not a subtle one. He met Moshoeshoe on the 15th and imperiously ordered him to hand over a fine of 10 000 cattle within three days, over and above the submission to British rule that he required. Moshoeshoe apparently could raise only 3 500 head by the appointed day, so Cathcart, giving no leeway, crossed the Caledon and headed for Thaba-Bosiu. At Berea, on the 20th, he divided his force into three, two columns heading over the plateau and the third round the southern end. On the plateau, after some initial success capturing cattle, the British were repulsed by the horsemen of Molapo. On the plain just to the west of Thaba-Bosiu, Cathcart encountered the main force of the Basotho, mounted and armed with muskets and assegais. The British were forced to retreat into a square formation and held out only with difficulty, on the verge of total defeat, but kept together by the resolution of the commander-in-chief. The Battle of Berea had been, in the opinion of Jacottet, 'one of the most important events in the history of South Africa'.

Moshoeshoe, as usual, was not foolhardy. He had seen the discipline of the British troops and knew a renewal of fighting might end disastrously. Many Basotho who shared his concern were already heading for the refuge of the mountains. This meant that Boer farmers would have easy access to large swathes of land, which might spell the end of his kingdom. So, in consultation with his counsellors, and with Casalis, recently returned from Paris, beside him, he dictated to his literate and Christian son, Sekhonyana, a letter to Cathcart. How much of it was Moshoeshoe and how much Casalis does not matter; their partnership was certainly inspired.

Thaba Bosigo, Midnight, 20th December, 1852

Your Excellency,

This day you have fought against my people, and taken much cattle. As the object for which you have come is to have a compensation for Boers, I beg you will be satisfied with what you have taken. I entreat peace from you, – you have shown your power, – you have chastised, – let it be enough I pray you; and let me be no longer considered an enemy to the Queen. I will try all I can to keep my people in order in the future.

Your humble servant,
Moshesh

The historian Theal rated this letter as the cleverest diplomatic document ever written in South Africa. It certainly allowed Cathcart, who relished the renewal of hostilities as little as Moshoeshoe, an honourable way out. Neither side was conquered; but even if he did not claim it then, the battle honour was Moshoeshoe's. By the subsequent Treaty of Berea, Moshoeshoe gained peace with Britain and maintained his independence, and the British Orange River Sovereignty was soon abandoned.

Yet again there is irony. These reverses for the British at the hands of Moshoeshoe in part convinced them to withdraw from affairs north of the Orange. This they did in March 1854, and Moshoeshoe was now left danger-ously exposed to the Boers and their new Orange Free State.

As for the mission, it had suffered a great setback in numbers and morale. 'Something had surely vanished, never to come back,' was Jacottet's considered opinion, many years after. 'The freshness and the zest with which the converts had been imbued was no longer to be seen in Lesotho, for the new converts always bore in mind the fact that evil is ever present and that a fall is always pos-sible; and they understood better that the Christian, though converted, is not yet in every respect a new creature. They were thus inclined to get used to that thought too easily and to accept their weakness and their sin too readily as something quite natural. The missionaries also would no longer know the hap-piness of the early years: they would no longer have the same beautiful and naive confidence in the future. Henceforth they would not be free from trembling while rejoicing; at each new conversion they would ask themselves anxiously whether it were sincere or not; at every new success they would wonder whether it were not the shadow of one.'

Paradise was lost, but the Church had survived.

— ∞ —

To start with, the Boers and the Basotho both needed peace. 'Peace,' said Moshoeshoe, 'is like rain.' The fledgling Boer state was weak and disorganized, and, moreover, the first president, Josias Hoffman, was a personal friend of both Moshoeshoe and the missionaries. For a year there was an uneasy quiet.

The mission tried to pick up the pieces. 'The dream of seeing the whole tribe embracing the Gospel was now over. The hopes of the conversion of the whole nation had disappeared.' That was how Jacottet was to sum up this period. 'Most of the chiefs had gone back to a kind of heathendom worse than that of the early days and believed that in that way they were increasing their own popularity.' It was 'necessary, then, to restart mission work on a new plan, aiming at reaching the people individually rather than the masses, the ordinary clan rather than the great chiefs. It would no doubt be a more humble, more difficult and slower process, but perhaps more sure and more efficient in the long run.'

Slowly, the numbers began to recover, the stations to stir themselves once more. Only Cana, short of a miracle, could not reopen because of lack of resources – a pity, because it left the whole of northern Lesotho unattended. One lay element of the new plan did have considerable success. It was an idea of Arbousset's to extend and develop the work of evangelization. With the help of several full members of the church, he started evening classes in some of the distant villages: these were the forerunners of the future annexes or outstations. There was also the possibility of establishing a Teacher Training School and an Industrial School with money promised by Sir George Grey, the new Governor of the Cape. But the mission dillied and dallied, and the money went elsewhere.

Part of the problem lay in the fact that, because of the closing of the Mission House in Paris, no reinforcements had been forthcoming since 1848 (other than Rev. Théophile Jousse, who arrived in Lesotho in 1850 and replaced Casalis at Thaba-Bosiu in 1855). The first generation of missionaries – Arbousset, Casalis, Keck, Dyke, Daumas, Rolland – were getting older and slowing down. They were tired. Arbousset, for instance, had not been back to France for twenty years. Then came another heavy blow. Sarah, the beloved wife of Casalis, ever frail but ever brave, died on 17 June 1854. She was buried under the willows at Morija, the event having to be delayed while more and more Basotho, including many chiefs on horseback, swiftly alerted by the tribal telegraph, came in to pay their respects to 'Ma-Eugène, some pressing kisses on her forehead, bathing it in tears. Moshoeshoe himself spoke the eulogy.

The following year, having never fully recovered from this loss, Casalis, Mahloana-matšoana, friend of Moshoeshoe, beloved of the Basotho, was asked by the Mission Board in Paris to succeed the late Henri Grandpierre as Director, and to reopen the Mission House, which he agreed to do. He continued to serve the mission with sensitivity and distinction until his death in 1891, but never saw Lesotho or his first wife's grave again.

'In his departure,' Jacottet wrote much later, 'Basutoland lost a tower of strength; in losing him, the mission lost one of its pillars. He had an influence on Moshesh that no other missionary ever possessed, and during his twenty-one years of service, he had done much to render the chief favourable to Christianity. He had helped him to save his people from the dangers that had at one time threatened them with destruction; he had been his best counsellor and in some respects his foreign minister. As one of the three pioneers of the Basutoland Mission, of which he was, with Arbousset and Rolland, the true founder, he had contributed in a very large measure to guide its march forward and to shape its traditions.'

Moshoeshoe is rightly honoured as the founder of the Basotho nation. Like Thaba-Bosiu, he was the Rock on which their future independence was built. After him, no one made a greater contribution to the security and independence of Lesotho than Eugène Casalis.

—∘⊖∘—

While Moshoeshoe has been recognized as amongst the most astute and diplomatic of African political leaders, he is seldom credited with the qualities of generalship. Yet it might be argued that he was ultimately more successful than any of the Zulu kings. He made effective use of what resources he had: fighting or retreating as the situation or his strength demanded; gradually building his power through incorporation, using military, economic or social means, ranging from conquest through mafisa to marriage; and shrewdly moving from Botha-Bothe to Thaba-Bosiu. But he also had those virtues of the great general – vision, flexibility, ability to adapt. Of all the southern African peoples, the Basotho adapted their fighting tactics most effectively, and partly to this they owed their ultimate independence. They soon saw the advantages of two specific innovations in regional warfare.

Sometime in 1829, Bushmen in the service of Moorosi stole two horses from a farmer near Dordrecht in the Cape. Moorosi sent one of these to

Moshoeshoe with instructions as to how to ride it. Moshoeshoe was delighted – it was the first horse he had ever owned. With some initial reluctance, he mounted it awkwardly, keeping his balance with two long sticks he held in either hand. The horse, with no better bridle than a piece of olive wood for a bit and plaited grass for reins, was gently led around. Nervous as he was, Moshoeshoe had no doubts about the significance of the newcomer, and he soon became an accomplished horseman.

He then encouraged his subjects to acquire horses, by trade and working in the Cape, and he himself acquired them whenever he could, always preferring to pay compensation in cattle. The horses were mainly of sturdy colonial stock, a mixture of oriental breed and English thoroughbred. They readily adapted to the mountains, developing into what later became known as the Basotho pony.

Firearms were the other commodity in great demand. The government of the Cape and then that of the Orange Free State tried to restrict their spread, but there was always a flourishing subterranean trade in guns and gunpowder. Although the firearms were often old and of dubious quality, by 1843 the Basotho were better endowed with guns and horses than any other African group, and it was estimated that, in addition to warriors on foot, there were 'not less than six thousand well-armed horsemen' at the Battle of Berea in 1852. This mobility and firepower became formidable in broken terrain, where coverts for retreat were plentiful. In the mid-1850s, as war threatened once again, this time with the Boers, the stockpiling of grain in woven baskets – in caves and mountain fastnesses – was a foregone conclusion.

Approaching its twenty-fifth anniversary in this uneasy time, the mission to the Basotho could still claim substantial achievement. Since the desertions of 1848 its numbers had recovered, even if the emphasis had shifted to ordinary people rather than leaders. And two keystones were now in place, tangible emblems of progress.

On 5 March 1847, the foundation stone had been laid for the church building at Morija. Most of the work was done by François Maeder, helped by Bapedi migrant workers. Because he had other buildings to put up at Morija, it took him ten years to finish the church. The building, about thirty metres long and twelve wide, was made of bricks and lime, with four interior columns – ships' masts brought by wagon from Port Elizabeth – supporting a flat roof. It had a sacristy, and another room which Arbousset designated the archives. It could accommodate about eight hundred worshippers, and the pulpit and windows were decorated by Mme Maeder. In the evening, the church was lit by three large chandeliers attached to the roof beams, a beacon of light in the surrounding darkness. Except for some benches intended for the white congregants, there were no seats, so many people brought small chairs with them. The building had cost in all about £800 by the time it was consecrated on 3 January 1858, just weeks before the birth of Édouard Jacottet in Switzerland. Maeder was exhausted, but the church, the visible sign of his efforts, stands to this day.

The other tangible achievement was the translation of the New Testament. It had always been Luther's desire, during the Reformation, that the ploughman should be able to recite scripture to himself while he ploughed and the weaver while he wove. Therefore, the Bible must be accessible to them in print, and in their own language. Within a few years of arriving in Lesotho, the missionaries had learned Sesotho to a point of near fluency, and Rolland and Arbousset had composed and translated a number of hymns. Their next task was to reduce the language to printed form. In 1837, a small elementary catechism, their very first publication, was published in Cape Town. This was followed in 1839 by translations of the Gospels according to St Mark and St John, done by Casalis and Rolland respectively, as well as a book containing fifty chapters from the Old and New Testaments by Arbousset. By 1843 Beersheba had acquired a printing press, and in 1845 M. Ludorf began printing the whole of the New Testament, which had been completed by Rolland and Casalis. The Word – or part of it, at least – was now in Sesotho.

—◦◦—

In March 1858, the Boers declared war on the Basotho. A few days later, about five hundred of them appeared before Beersheba. Rolland had asked the men of fighting age to remove themselves from the mission so that his task of serving the old, the sick, the women and children might be made easier. He also raised a white flag as an emblem of peace, while the Boers were taking up position on a small hill facing the church and threatening to open fire if all arms were not surrendered within five minutes. Rolland replied that the place had surrendered and asked a little time to deliver the weapons. But the Boers opened fire with a fieldpiece, and the bombardment lasted ten or fifteen minutes. Because they aimed at the roofs, only one inhabitant was killed, but Rolland and his people were forced to quit and the mission was burned down. Beersheba no longer existed. The Boers advanced on Morija and Thaba-Bosiu.

—◦◦—

Arbousset had married Katherine Rogers in the Scottish Presbyterian Church in Cape Town in 1837. She proved to be an excellent missionary wife, presenting her husband with six lively daughters. Their joy was complete, however, when their son was born in 1852. Moshoeshoe himself was in the church for the baptism. When Katherine appeared with her babe, the King cried, 'Ahé, welcome!' and, stooping to kiss the child, he added, 'Happy is the woman who holds a son in her arms.' With a theatrical flourish, Arbousset put his son in the King's arms and said, 'Here, he is yours, so that your name may protect him in the land.' Moshoeshoe, in his turn, said to his own son Letsie, 'Look at this beautiful little boy I hold in my arms. His father is white, I am black: have you ever seen a white commend like this his son to a black?' He then called on God to guard the child day and night. But a year later, whooping cough carried away the young life. Katherine Arbousset never quite recovered from her grief.

At the beginning of 1858, Arbousset and his family were in Cape Town. Their return journey was a little microcosm of what missionary travellers faced in those days. Although the trip to Algoa Bay was storm-free and therefore lasted only four or five days, it then took them three weeks to get their dilapidated wagon in order and to acquire trek-oxen, which were scarce and expensive. The water supply on the road to Grahamstown was so brackish nearly all of the party contracted dysentery, and as they pushed on to Fort Beaufort the sun was pitiless. At the Orange they turned eastwards towards the Witteberg, where the Wesleyan missionary Gottlob Schreiner sent a fresh team of oxen to their aid. From there, as they headed for Bethesda in the south of Lesotho, the roads were frightful, with raging torrents and deep ravines, and mountains to climb and to descend. On one occasion, Arbousset took a tumble from the wagon which was nearly fatal. They were received with open arms at the Bethesda mission by old friend Gosselin, but learned that war had been declared, as a result of which the men had headed for the high mountains with the livestock, and the women had fled. Arbousset borrowed a horse and sent a follower to scout the vicinity. He returned a few hours later: he had seen villages in flames and had heard gunfire. While he was telling his story, a thief jumped on Arbousset's horse and galloped off. 'Quel temps! Quel pays! What a time! What a country!' exclaimed the baffled Arbousset, who had just recorded the region's first instance of hijacking.

Lent an old wagon by Gosselin, Arbousset made for Morija, keeping to the high ground, since the 'enemy' steered across the plain. His wife kept to the wagon all day, lying down. Next morning, in a state of suffering, she was reluctant to resume the journey; but they did, which was just as well, as an hour later the village where they had slept was burned by the Boers, who then discovered them on the hillside and advanced menacingly upon them. But Letsie had installed himself on the ridges with two or three thousand warriors and intercepted the invaders. About thirty of them were killed, and Letsie himself lost seven or eight men. Arbousset was deeply saddened that amongst them, defending his mission and his country, was 'our excellent schoolteacher Uriel Mabitsa'.

Keep your eye on Uriel. In a murder mystery, no character or incident is there without a purpose. Uriel will make his entrance again, not in the fiery sun but as a shade. His spirit will join the banquet.

Skirting Thaba-Tšoeu, Arbousset's party reached a village an hour away from Morija. It was full of refugees, mainly from Beersheba. Arbousset gathered them and, with a large number of his flock who had come to greet him, he celebrated that Sunday with a thanksgiving service. The next day, 5 April, three months after leaving Cape Town, he entered Morija to the great joy of both his followers and himself. A message from Moshoeshoe welcomed him on his return. But Arbousset's wife was chronically sick; and one of his daughters was seriously ill from the effects of the poisonous water they had had to drink. And there was little time for recovery.

On the morning of Wednesday 28 April, Arbousset and one of the English traders who had established themselves at Morija rode out on reconnaissance. They soon had to face about, ahead of the rapidly advancing Boers, a body of about 1 400 men together with 120 wagons. Letsie had taken the bulk of his forces off the previous day to join his father for the decisive battle at Thaba-Bosiu, so the remaining, heavily outnumbered forces could only delay the Boers long enough for the population of Morija to evacuate the village.

The English traders placed their families, belongings and merchandise in the church for safety. Arbousset, knowing himself to be deeply hated by the Boers, fled up the mountain with his family, including his frail wife and invalid daughter. They had time enough only to snatch up two woollen blankets, but one got dropped in the flight. An Englishman fleeing with them turned back to retrieve it at the risk of his life. The fugitives were then joined by the English families, and six or seven unmarried Englishmen. There were fifty-five women and children in all, exposed to the bitter cold. Arbousset found them a cave to shelter in. They had truly become a Church of the Desert.

They had escaped none too soon. The Boers pounced upon Morija with a bitter ferocity. It seems they had attacked Letsie's village of Matsieng, not far from Morija, where they found, exhibited in ghastly array, parts of the bodies of their comrades who had fallen during the ambush at the Hell (Hellspoort, near Thabana-Morena) and had been mutilated for the purpose of concocting medicines of war. Though the missionaries were ignorant of this at the time, and

Moshoeshoe himself innocent of the appalling atrocity, the Boers lashed out in retaliation. Matsieng was razed and Morija took the brunt of the subsequent fury.

On their arrival at the mission, they fired their muskets and a few cannon shots. One of these landed in Arbousset's bedroom. Although they left the church standing, they broke every window, smashed the pulpit and destroyed all the books. They seized Arbousset's wagon, his furniture and all his possessions, and auctioned the lot. They then set fire to his house, destroying twenty-five years of his research in the process. How fragile knowledge and evidence are, how easily they can be lost, or destroyed by the ignorant and barbarous – and how difficult they are to recover! The attackers treated the houses and goods of the traders in the same way. M. Maeder, who had stayed, was insulted and threatened, and his precious collection of tools stolen. Only his bullet-riddled house was left standing (today it survives as the oldest building in Lesotho), along with the desecrated church which he had so lovingly put together, brick by brick, over the last ten years.

On the mountain, things were desperate. It snowed for two days without stopping, as it is wont to do on the higher peaks further inland. Arbousset managed to 'borrow' a sheep and a goat from a female parishioner one day, and a pig from a nearby village the next. A small cache of wheat was found under a rock and a little was taken.

When the sun finally shone again on the snow, black dots appeared here and there on the mountain above and around – Boers in search of their prey. They sprayed bullets in every direction and rolled rocks down from the mountain top. The men of the fugitive band decided, for the sake of their loved ones, to separate and hide on a nearby mountain. Arbousset watched from afar as his family was discovered in their cave, and his ailing daughter carried down. He also watched as one of the minor chiefs got into a quarrel with one of the Boers and was shot 'stone dead' in the valley. Arbousset and his companions crouched in their shelter as the Boers came within hearing, without discovery.

For a few days, the Boers hung around while Arbousset dodged them in the mountains. There was a lot of drinking, of plundering, of brutality. Finally, they moved off towards Thaba-Bosiu, and Arbousset rode down to inspect the devastation below. All that was left were a few household objects and books: Calvin on the Psalms, Don Calmet on Matthew and Mark, a couple of New Testaments in Sesotho, a little English Bible.

So he took his people south once more on the trail of tears to Bethesda, which they reached on 12 May, the end of two weeks of hardship and danger.

Meanwhile, at Thaba-Bosiu, on 6 May, Théophile Jousse faced with considerable trepidation the advance of the 'barbarians' who had 'profaned the sanctuary of the Lord' at Morija. His house, his gardens and the hill on which his mission stood were covered with Basotho warriors as the Boers pushed forward in their mobile fortress of wagons to within a kilometre. Despite tentative sorties and a cannonade, they made no headway beyond that. Detachments of Basotho had meanwhile slipped around the enemy forces to raid their defenceless farms to the west. So after three days, disheartened, the Boers packed up and retreated, followed by a letter from Moshoeshoe to their president regretting an unnecessary and unwanted war, but berating him for the conduct of his army: 'You call yourself a Christian in your letter to me. I have long known that you are a Christian; but the commandants of your army are not yet Christians and, if they persist in claiming they are, they will force us to believe there is no God. What! Would their Christianity consist in destroying Christianity?'

Eventually peace was brokered by Sir George Grey and a treaty signed at Aliwal North on 29 September. Although some land was restored to Moshoeshoe, he was forced to give up a great deal, too. It was a makeshift arrangement and it was unlikely to last.

As the mission at Beersheba was now firmly located within the Orange Free State, it could never recover its former vigour, and nor could Bethulie and Carmel prosper. The manse at Morija had been levelled, the village destroyed and the congregation scattered. Although Samuel Rolland stayed on in the country, he was shattered by the destruction of his beloved Beersheba. As for Arbousset, he was heartbroken, scarcely capable of reconstructing his life's work. The time had come for him to leave.

But Fate was not done with him yet. On the homeward voyage in 1860, the ship in which he and his family were travelling struck one of the Seven Stones off the Scilly Isles. Their six daughters made it safely across to the lifeboat, but Katherine Arbousset, fragile, assailed by such terrors and such trials in recent years, clung to the rigging of the ship, unable to bridge the chasm. She was drowned and her body, washed up on the Cornish shore near Newquay, lies in the churchyard at St Columb Minor.

Arbousset did find a new challenge. He spent four years setting up a PEMS station in Tahiti. He did not remarry, and died in France in 1877. 'The strongest and most courageous of a strong and courageous band' of pioneers, he was, said Jacottet, 'the true founder of the mission'. More than anyone else, he had 'pushed it and guided it into the path that it always continued to follow …

From the very first he had realized what had to be done, had understood what Basutoland needed and had grasped the character of its inhabitants. He had a clear, intuitive vision of what the Basothos could become under guidance and of the advantages that could be gained for the evangelization of the country by a judicious use of their latent abilities. In that respect, as in many other ways, he had been the real predecessor of the second generation of missionaries; he had pointed out to them the way they had to follow.'

The departure of Arbousset marked the end of the first generation. Those who remained were growing old or weak or demoralized. Only Jousse had joined the mission in the ten years before 1858, when François Coillard arrived. But, in February 1860, as Moshoeshoe escorted him south to the edge of his territories to say goodbye, Arbousset met at Hermon mission station a new recruit who had just arrived. This young man, married to Eugène Casalis's daughter, was to become the driving force of the second generation. His name was Adolphe Mabille.

CHAPTER TWELVE

THE SEAL

1858–1868

Adèle Casalis was not the only cause of Adolphe Mabille's coming to Lesotho, but she was the final one.

While her brother was the first child of the missionaries to be born at Thaba-Bosiu, Adèle was the eldest surviving daughter of Eugène and Sarah Casalis. She was born at Thaba-Bosiu in 1840. Her childhood there was a happy one, despite the leopards and hyenas that haunted and hunted the valleys and hills close to the house.

Moshoeshoe, too, was a constant visitor, coming down the mountain every Sunday, often dressed like a French admiral, attending church, sometimes even crying surreptitiously at an allegorical story about Jesus. He would join the Casalis family for dinner and go to Sunday school, scouting the alphabet for its meaning in amongst a crowd of small boys. Adèle would happily show him her Bible pictures and explain their stories, and when her grandmother sent them a Noah's Ark from France, she and her brother proudly showed him and his retinue all the pairs of animals displayed on the dining table, like a riddle from the past.

At the end of 1848, Eugène Casalis went to Cape Town on mission business, taking his family with him. Passing through Colesberg, where you could get anything from a needle to an elephant, and through Graaff-Reinet, where they stayed with the family of the saintly Andrew Murray, under whose influence the eight-year-old Adèle instantly found her future vocation as a missionary's wife, the Casalis family arrived in Algoa Bay, where they took passage on a coastal steamer, a 'mere nutshell' called, ominously, the *Styx*. Casalis left his family in Cape Town while he went on to France to try to stimulate the Mission Society to greater support. This was the period in which the Mission House in Paris had been closed, with the result that no new missionaries were being trained. On his return to Thaba-Bosiu in 1850, he left Adèle behind in a boarding school in Cape Town, where, for well over a year, she was perse-cuted and beaten mercilessly, the Bible her only consolation. Only when the mother of a fellow student pointed out her black and blue marks did her own parents become aware of the position. They immediately removed her to a more congenial school at George. She was not there for long before her father summoned her home – her beloved mother was ill, and the child she bore soon afterwards died within hours of birth. The following month, in June 1854, Sarah Casalis herself passed away.

At the funeral, Adèle listened to Moshoeshoe pour out his grief to his people: 'You say that my ancestors Peete and Monaheng are your gods, and perhaps after my death you will also say that Moshoeshoe is your god. Ah! Why do you not acknowledge the Lord of gods? Do you not know that a single seed of a tree can produce a multitude of trees? It is in this way that whites and blacks proceed from one God. That God, oh Molapo, oh Masupha, my sons, I was hoping by your means our people would come to know. But you have abandoned Him and left me all alone – I, who know not yet the truth. Will a swimmer fling himself into the Orange river to cross it when it is full, if he does not see that other swimmers are ready to follow him? Will not even a fish hesitate to cross the great sea if it is alone? Who has saved us in the wars which we have had to sustain? Was it our own arms that made us victors? No, it is the God invoked by our own missionaries who has guarded and protected us. But now the house of our missionary from which arose so many prayers on our behalf has fallen on his head. Chiefs and people, what say you to this? After having often spoken over the graves of people who were strangers to him, our missionary speaks today over that of his companion, and, as always, he speaks of resurrection and of life. He has told us that our mother, before expiring, expressed the assurance that the Gospel would finally triumph in our country. Perhaps that is a prophecy. From the heights to which she had already attained, she was able to see things which were hidden from us. Let us remember that if she has not written books like her husband, she has left her footprints for us to follow.' Moshoeshoe also said to Casalis that, though he was a polygamist, there had always been only one woman for him, and since the death of 'Mamohato he had walked 'as a solitary man in the midst of a crowd'. When Arbousset consoled him that the motherless children still had a father, he replied, 'Ah, Arbousset, you forget that little chickens need the feathers of the hen; Casalis and I, you know, have but cocks' feathers!'

So, two months short of her fourteenth birthday, Adèle became mother to her three younger siblings, cooking for them, reading to them, sewing and darning for them, until Casalis was called to Paris some two years later to take over the direction of the Mission Society. Adèle was upset, Moshoeshoe was devastated, when she left. Neither could have dared to hope that she would be back in four years' time.

According to Edwin Smith, his biographer, there were two significant moments in the life of Charles Adolphe Mabille that determined his spiritual path. Surprisingly, since he was Swiss, they both happened in England, where he went at the age of eighteen to teach French and to learn English, at Kendal in the Lake District. Perhaps, however, it was because he was in a foreign country that he experienced them so intensely. Certainly, he had been restless before leaving his native land. On the eve of his twentieth birthday, he attended a meeting of the British and Foreign Bible Society in Bowness on Lake Windermere. The lay secretary of the branch tapped him on the shoulder and asked him whether he had considered following Christ 'into the heathen mission field'. Mabille never had. But at a religious meeting in the Corn Hall at Kendal, surrounded by a number of pupils, he astonished the large gathering by rising to address them, confessing that for weeks he had been wrestling with his lost soul, but that now he was at peace since deciding to become a missionary.

Typically, the decision to become a missionary had (and presumably still has) two phases: the initial exposure to a religious teaching, involving a 'conversion'; and the subsequent more active wish to do mission work, involving a 'calling'. Mabille was different. While the exact timing and order of his experiences are not known, the suggestion that he might make mission work his calling seems to have finally triggered his 'conversion', his decision 'to live to God, with God, for God'. In any event, he wrote to Casalis, who was about to reopen the Paris Mission House in 1856, eight years after it had closed. Mabille was accepted as one of the first students.

The mission was humbly housed in the rue Franklin at Passy, and the students were guided by the firm but inspiring hand of Casalis, who was helped, after 1859, by his second wife Sophie. There, Mabille met Casalis's eldest son, also called Eugène, who was studying medicine in Paris. Dr Casalis was destined for Lesotho. So was Frédéric Ellenberger, a fellow student. Mabille became close friends, too, with François Coillard, who left in 1858 to become the first reinforcement in Lesotho, other than Théophile Jousse, since 1848. Coillard, it seems, possessed a 'racy humour', while Mabille, more single-minded, was nicknamed 'le père sérieux'. Coillard and Mabille were to have a major influence on the fate of two countries.

Above all, Mabille met in Paris the seventeen-year-old Adèle, and they fell in love. But her father refused them permission to marry. She had been ill in the spring, and, mindful of her mother's fragility and early death, Casalis felt she was too delicate to marry so young. To help her recover her health, their friend and fellow Protestant, Madame de Staël (daughter-in-law of the famous woman of letters), took Adèle off to her chateau at Coppet in Switzerland, where the young girl tasted, for a few months and for the only time in her life, the luxurious ways of a chatelaine. Though she never regretted the choice she made, she often, in later years, dreamed of that enchanted chateau.

Though separated, the lovers were given permission to write to each other, and they saw this as a true means of grace. From this time on, as she would later say, using the words of an old Mosotho woman, Mabille became her pastor, the 'father of her soul'. Both of them longed for an *active* life in the field.

Even in the Mission House, dedicated as it was to Christian love and devotion, there were some petty tensions. The French students somewhat despised the Swiss, who came from a small, rather insignificant country. On the other hand, the Swiss had the benefit of a better education system and tended to excel in class, often overshadowing the French, who came from poorer homes. Indeed, being one of the seniors, Mabille sometimes filled in for Casalis in teaching. He was strong in Latin, Greek and Hebrew, though a trifle weak, it seems, in Theology.

Four of the students who were to play a major role in Lesotho came from Switzerland. In fact, the affiliation was even closer. Mabille was born (in 1836) in Baulmes, Ellenberger (in 1835) at Yverdon, Paul Germond (in 1835) at Yvonand, and Louis Duvoisin (in 1835) at Payerne. This should not be taken as mere coincidence. All of these small towns are in the francophone canton of Vaud, whose main centre is Lausanne.

Although the Edict of Tolerance in 1787 had at last allowed Protestants to live freely in the French kingdom and to record births, marriages and deaths, it did not give them liberty to organize. During the French Revolution, the argument raged over whether there should be 'un culte dominant' – the pastor of Nîmes, Rabaut-Saint-Etienne, announced to the 1789 Constituent Assembly of which he was a deputy, 'It is not tolerance I ask for, but Liberty'; and although the state was separated from all the churches by the Constitution of 1795, the situation remained troubled until 1801, when Napoleon Bonaparte became First Consul. Strongly Lutheran areas such as Alsace had been incorporated into France and had to be taken into consideration. So, when he negotiated the Concordat with the Pope in 1802, Napoleon, not forgetting the Protestants, refused to declare Catholicism the 'dominant religion'. When Bonaparte, now become Napoleon I, toured parts of the country, he was received by Protestants with overflowing enthusiasm – for the first time, Protestantism in France had been put on an equal footing with Catholicism. In the words of the Protestant historian Charles Bost, 'Bonaparte had at least understood that violence cannot succeed against the religious idea.' A census in

1802 did indicate, however, that the persecution of centuries had taken its toll: it revealed that there were not three million, nor even two (as estimated by some pastors), but fewer than a million Protestants in the entire country.

For a while, with the restoration of the monarchy in the figure of Louis XVIII in 1814, the bad old days returned; bands of rioters in Nîmes and Uzès insulted, robbed and killed Protestants over a period of several months, before the King was compelled to clamp down after the assassination of a general. While the charter of 1815 recognized Catholicism as the state church, freedom of religion was guaranteed and the equality of Protestantism was not seriously challenged.

Assured of survival, the Protestants forged ahead, building churches and creating new societies, such as the Bible Society (1819), the Tracts Society (1821) and the Paris Evangelical Missionary Society (1822), to propagate their faith and interests. There was already a Faculty of Theology in Montauban, and the Faculty in Geneva was extended into Paris. The period is called by Protestant historians 'Le Réveil'. This Religious Awakening was fuelled from a number of sources. It was, in some ways, a Romantic reaction to the deists of the eighteenth century, who included many of the last Pastors of the Desert with their somewhat reductionist ideas and evangelical codes, and rather cold piety. No élan. Certain groups, most notably the Moravians, advocated and exercised a religious life imbued with a moving intensity.

In countries where Protestantism was free, the faithful reacted against the desiccated formalism which had grown up. Methodism in England and the United States stressed individual conversion and advocated the use of lay preachers. The strictly Calvinist Scots attacked pride with unremitting zeal, and the Moravians of Germany and Alsace sent out missionaries who preached of 'la foi de coeur et de la contemplation des souffrances du Christ'. The new religion spoke ceaselessly, in the words of Bost, 'of sin, of nurturing life itself on a continuous reading of the Bible, putting in the forefront the person of Christ', putting His humanity before His divinity. France lay open as a field for missionaries.

In Geneva, a group of Moravians, who met in the house of Ami Bost, son of the French refugee Jean-Marc Bost, had an influence on some students of the Faculty of Theology, who were also listening to certain Scottish missionaries, including Robert Haldane. They reacted sharply to the national church and its professors. Some organized themselves around the Calvinist César Malan. With a burning zeal, several preachers spread into France: Félix Neff to the Hautes-Alpes; Henry Pyt, as we have seen, to Bayonne, where he had a marked effect on Eugène Casalis. After 1830, much of the fire was fuelled with hymns and songs of De Lutteroth, Ami Bost and Malan, and the spontaneous writings of Puaux, Roussel, Bost, and, above all, Alexandre Vinet. The missionaries thus worked first in the homes of the French before they ventured out into far lands.

The revolution of 1848 brought another key debate in the Protestant church to a head. At a general assembly, in effect a true synod, the sides in Geneva ranged against each other. On the one hand, there were those who wanted the church to remain 'une église de multitude', 'a church of multitude', in which there was a general confession of faith and one could become a member without an individual examination of conscience. On the other hand, there were those who wanted the church to be comprised solely of members who formally and individually adhered to a confession of faith – a church of the professed.

The canton of Vaud, which adjoined Geneva, was also affected by these events and arguments. It had become independent of Berne and a member of the Swiss Confederation in 1802. Touched by the French upheaval of July 1830, the Vaudois populace forced on their Council a liberal constitution in 1845. The Réveil, too, stirred in the religious life of the Vaudois, who had, in the words of Edwin Smith, 'passed from one formalism to another'. Against this spiritual deadness, Smith wrote, the Réveil was a strong protest in Switzerland, just as Methodism was in England: 'Its insistence was upon spiritual experience in the individual soul, upon repentance, conversion, sanctification.'

The liberal constitution in Vaud did not grant religious freedom. So Alexandre Vinet, a professor at Lausanne, raised 'the fundamental question of the right of the State to overrule the individual conscience'. Forty pastors refused to read a Council proclamation from their pulpits; they were suspended from office; the majority of the Vaudois pastors then resigned. So, in 1846, Vinet led the formation of the Free Church of Vaud. In the small village of Baulmes, nestling in the foothills of the Jura mountains, the first services of the new church there were held in the house of the schoolmaster, Louis Mabille. His son Adolphe was ten. 'Freedom,' wrote Adolphe's biographer, 'was his natural atmosphere. He drew it in with his mother's milk.' Nothing came between Mabille and God: their relationship was fierce, direct and unmediated. Every comma in the Bible was from God.

The fact that several of the second generation of missionaries sent to Lesotho were Swiss was significant to Jacottet when he wrote about it subsequently. Up to then, almost all had been French, but Mabille, Germond, Ellenberger, Duvoisin were to bring new spirit and new methods. 'The blending of the French Christian, so enthusiastic, impulsive and full of life, with the French-speaking Swiss, sometimes more narrow, but often also more steady and more tenacious, was to give the mission a very distinctive character.' Since the four Swiss missionaries all belonged to free churches, they came to Lesotho with a more individualistic conception of the church and an inclination to demand more from its members, appealing to their initiative. Their education had accustomed them 'to envisage Christian life from a narrower point of view, but also from a deeper one'. The earlier missionaries tended to confuse church with nation: the new men were wary of this. They treasured their independence, and they would examine individual consciences and avoid blanket conversions.

The mission in Lesotho was now over a quarter of a century old. It had reached a critical moment, and new skills were needed.

Due to the intervention of the revered and beloved Maman Sophie – far from the wicked stepmother of fairy tale and folklore – Adèle's father was finally persuaded to allow a formal engagement, and in May 1859, Adèle, still eighteen, married her sweetheart. On 3 July, Adolphe, together with Paul Germond, was ordained in the Oratoire at Paris. The Paris Mission had decided to open new missions in China and Tahiti. From the time of his calling, 'the name of China' had been 'imprinted' on Adolphe's heart, and now it seemed as though destiny had arrived. But the Committee, partly influenced by Adèle's origins and knowledge of the country and language, determined that destiny should be elbowed aside and that Mabille should go to Lesotho. So, on 13 July 1859, after crossing the Channel, the young warrior of Christ and his even younger bride embarked on the *Hero*, a sailing ship headed for the Cape with a cargo of rails destined for the construction of the first railway line between Cape Town and Wellington.

The Mabilles arrived in Cape Town after a horrendous journey, marked by contrary winds and failing supplies, and lasting well over a hundred days, during which they were regarded as Jonahs and nearly thrown overboard. Their reception in Lesotho was also not without ambiguity. Although Adèle was welcomed by Moshoeshoe as the beloved daughter of his beloved Mahloana-matšoana, Mabille, soon placed by the Conference at Morija as the successor to Arbousset, was at first resented by those Basotho Christians who had regarded the latter as their 'father'.

But Mabille was enchanted with his initial view of the new country: 'We approached the Maluti, the long range with high and clearly cut peaks … It is a magnificent chain of mountains, sombre in colour, in spite of the absolute lack of trees and shrubs: it stood out in stark relief against the dark blue of the African sky. A beautiful, a grand spectacle!' He was deeply moved by seeing, for the first time, the mountain of Moshoeshoe and the mission station of

Casalis: 'Nor, during all my brief stay, could I shake off the extraordinary illusion that at any moment I might see the old residents of the house appearing from one side or another, so much is the memory of them linked with the name of Thaba-Bosiu.' Sights and places already steeped in history, touched by the shades of the past. 'Morija, with the high mountain which dominates it, with its graves, its ruins, its great church! What memories it all called up! I seemed to be coming into places known to me and loved: it was like coming back home ...'

For the young couple, life was not a bed of down. They had to live in the vestry of the church for eighteen months before they could occupy the house that M. Maeder vacated. The vestry, with its roof partially collapsed and with no ceiling, was blazing hot in summer, bitterly cold in winter, and almost no shelter from the rain that poured in. Eventually the flat roof, made of bricks and reeds and earth, collapsed, and the iron sheets Mabille used to replace it with were blown off in a hurricane. He then got hold of a dozen teak posts made from the masts of shipwrecks and arranged them in two rows of columns, anchoring the roof to the floor (a contrivance that lasted long beyond his lifetime). On the first day of 1861 their first child, Ernest, was born, and they were happy.

—◦○◦—

The old guard, the pioneers, of the mission were mostly gone. What it now needed were educationalists and organizers. These were roles Mabille was to fill massively.

Even before he arrived, when they were still rattling about on the unlucky *Hero*, he had begun to learn Sesotho from his wife, who was a fluent, almost mother-tongue speaker of the language, for it was mission policy that preaching was never to be done through an interpreter. He even managed to preach a sermon in Sesotho on his arrival at Morija, but his role as worthy successor to Arbousset was somewhat diminished when his parishioners tried to engage him in conversation afterwards and he was mute with incomprehension. He also began to compile a Sesotho dictionary. But he was surprised to find, when he did reach Morija, that the whole of the Bible had not yet been translated or printed – only the New Testament, the Psalms, and a couple of the books of the Old Testament. There and then – 'We will start tomorrow' – he set out to remedy the situation.

He also turned his hand to the organization of his parish. He extended Arbousset's policy of using Basotho evangelists in outlying villages, and began the policy of establishing outstations to which Christian Basotho were sent. In 1863, one of the very first converts, Esaia Leheti, was so appointed, to Kolo.

Mabille was convinced that the Basotho must be converted largely by Basotho evangelists, and his aim was to achieve a Basotho church. From early on, he nursed even grander ideas and had no doubts about the way they could be accomplished: 'It is impossible to dream of evangelizing the whole of Africa without the cooperation of the Africans.' To this end, a variety of training institutions were required. To train schoolteachers he knew a Normal School would be needed, to train evangelists a Bible School, and to train pastors, ultimately, a Theological School.

Mabille also realized that the spread of literacy – a prerequisite for the crowning objective of reading the Bible – would depend on the variety and production of available books. Rolland had had a printing press at Beersheba, and had published the New Testament. But the press had had bad luck with its printers and closed in 1855. Then it was badly damaged in 1858 when the Boers ransacked the mission. Ellenberger, a trained printer in his youth, fixed it and sorted out the type, which had become hopelessly jumbled (worse than a jigsaw puzzle). He took it to his station at Bethesda, where he printed some short works. Meanwhile, through his Kendal connections, Mabille himself was given a small press. In 1863, he started a mission periodical called *Leselinyana la Lesotho*, 'the Little Light of Lesotho'.

He continued working on his dictionary, a task more difficult than it seemed at first, as he had to introduce many new concepts and many new nouns into the language, either by adapting existing words to new usages or by inventing new terms. Within four years, he had mastered the language to such an extent that, by the end of 1864, he had collaborated with his able co-worker Filemone Rapetloane on translating Bunyan's *The Pilgrim's Progress* into Sesotho. After the Bible, this work was to become the most important influence on the future of Sesotho literature, and indeed African literature as a whole.

These were the beginnings of concrete achievements. Mabille (and some of his colleagues) were to have equally important, if less tangible, influences. The policies he put into effect, the changes that he wrought, stemmed partly from his convictions, partly from his character, and partly from his style.

Mabille was very different from his predecessor, though he saw himself as wearing, in the words of Edwin Smith, 'Elijah's mantle'. Arbousset, when he preached, was flamboyant, often even eccentric. He had a flair for visual symbolism. One Sunday, he wore a yoke around his neck to give meaning to the metaphor of the yoke of sin. His most famous sermon concerning the sowing of seed was accompanied by handfuls of grain being thrown in the faces of his congregation. In 1847, on the occasion when Letsie had committed the judicial execution Arbousset disapproved of, he tried (unsuccessfully) to smash with a sledgehammer the chair in the church in which the prince was accustomed to sit. He even went so far as to dig a grave for a man and threaten him with it if he did not repent of his sin. There was no boredom when Arbousset was around.

Mabille, by contrast, was zealous, energetic, severe, impetuous, dogmatic, demanding, unbending, grave. His preaching style was direct, rousing, militant, dark with damnation, passionate with compassion. 'His aim,' Smith tells us, 'was chiefly to instruct.' Mabille was essentially a moruti, a teacher. 'Allegories drawn from surrounding nature, stories taken from local life, proverbs and allusions to traditional folk-tales, picturesque and unexpected comparisons – all these things which light up a native orator's discourse were not in Mabille's manner: his anecdotes ... were drawn from European books and journals. In his ordinary preaching he was simple and direct.' He spoke to pagans, says Smith, like the prophet of old, his addresses like the blows of a fist. The Last Judgement and eternal punishment were often on his lips. Sin was, to him, as tangible as the sting of a scorpion, and as complex as chemistry.

Yet Smith points to another side of Mabille, too. The Basotho recognized how straight he was, how upright were his motives. They also came to realize that 'all his severity was the reverse side of his love for them'. He expected much of them; he refused to compromise his standards. This was a sign of his love and respect. He sacrificed a great part of his meagre salary in supporting *Leselinyana* with its windows on the wider world, and in trying to get a school off the ground. The time, energy and strength he dedicated to the cause of his parishioners seemed inexhaustible.

The fact that they had their origins in Vaud coloured in several ways the strong influence that Mabille, Ellenberger, Germond and Duvoisin had on the Lesotho mission. Firstly, their approach, with Mabille in the vanguard, and with support from Coillard, treasured political, social and religious independence. Since they were intimately involved in the fate of a whole country, small as it may have been, this was an important mindset. Secondly, they were strongly evangelical – this was their overriding concern – and their aim was conversion. They did not share to the same extent the ethnological concerns and curiosity of Arbousset, Casalis, and others. Their approach was direct. Coillard and Mabille, for instance, composed many hymns which spoke straight to the heart. Thirdly, in line with the precepts of the Free Church of Vaud, they were concerned not with the 'church of multitude', nor with collectivist religion, nor with a national church, but with the individual soul. 'Not a numerous church but a pure and zealous church was his ideal,' wrote Smith of Mabille. 'Conversion to him implied an act of will, leading to an entire change in the orientation of a man's life, with a new motive, a new driving power. And he knew that if conversion was to be a reality there must be a training of the convert's conscience.' So it was not easy to get entry into Mabille's church. He set out to interview personally all of the approximately four hundred Christians in the parish of Morija to satisfy himself of the sincerity of their faith, and he intended that the educational institutions be nothing if not thorough.

Finally, the Vaudois were single-minded: there was to be no compromise. They wanted a church 'untainted with paganism'. They had no hesitation in condemning practices and customs they regarded as sinful. These ranged from dancing to drinking beer, from calumny to witchcraft, from initiation to polygamy. Any number of animal sacrifices were no substitute for the one great sacrifice which had changed history. Any deviation from the narrow path was strictly dealt with. Mabille was given the nickname 'Ra-nkhaoli', the Cutter-off.

Moral issues were not to be seen in pastel colours. The church must be true to its discipline. This was to have consequences; oh, it was to have consequences!

—◦◦—

The conflict of 1858 left a lot of unfinished business. The poison of war was still in the system. Cattle rustling on both sides was becoming endemic, and the peace treaty of Aliwal North had not solved the land question. Quite the contrary. 'All people know,' lamented Moshoeshoe, 'that my great sin is that I possess a good and fertile country.'

The King was well over seventy. Without literacy and an effective bureaucracy, he had always had to rely on patronage to preserve national unity. Now, enfeebled, he could no longer hold the show together, no longer control his brothers, his sons, no longer call in his old favours. He had also reverted to pagan customs. He had turned to the advice of the prophetess 'Mantsopa. In the absence of Arbousset and Casalis, he distanced himself from the French missionaries.

One of the main reasons for this change was the question of polygamy. In the early 1840s, Moshoeshoe's second son, Molapo, had been the darling of the mission. He was baptized, and later had a Christian wedding. But when, like his father, he took more wives, he was denounced by the missionaries, uncompromising in their beliefs, who regarded such practices as the work of the devil. The rift was never fully healed, though Moshoeshoe did not forget what he owed them, including the horse, the gun and the book.

When, in 1862, Father Joseph Gérard of the Oblates of Mary Immaculate slipped into the country and made his way to the capital, Moshoeshoe saw an opportunity not only to acquire a new source of information but to play one church against another. Perhaps he enjoyed opening a can of worms!

There followed what King Letsie III, in his address to the National University of Lesotho at Roma in 1995, called 'an incident of ecclesiastical rage'. When Rev. Jousse, in the mission at the foot of Thaba-Bosiu, heard of the arrival of a stranger and deduced, from his appearance, that he was a Catholic priest, he stormed up the mountain. While Jousse's fury certainly gave Moshoeshoe an interesting insight into the 'passionate divisions' of white society, he managed also to effect a compromise. The Protestants had already established missions in the choice spots of the country, but the King directed Gérard to the magnificent Tloutle valley, a few kilometres south-east of Thaba-Bosiu, where he founded the mission of Roma. Curiously, the two main religions of Lesotho thus had French origins. This religious division was a legacy Moshoeshoe left his country. Whether he meant it to be a horn of plenty or a poisoned chalice is not known.

Early in 1865, the Boers ruthlessly expelled Basotho farmers from disputed land on the west bank of the Caledon before their crops were harvested, condemning them to starvation. So, not realizing how much stronger the Orange Free State had grown, and misled by self-interested advice, Moshoeshoe embarked on war. In the opinion of Jacottet, this was, during his long rule, 'the only serious case in which he failed to act with calmness amid circumstances of danger and to fathom the exigencies of the position'. It was to cost him half his country.

The war was a disaster for the Basotho. Resistance crumbled and the Boers were soon at the foot of Thaba-Bosiu once more. The mission house where Adèle had been born was bombarded. At Morija, Mabille, knowing that famine was inevitable, dug a great hole under the stoep behind the church and buried there as much grain as he could. The people of Morija fled once again to the mountain and the caves, the men to join the resistance. Morija, according to Dr Casalis, who had arrived in Lesotho the year before as a medical missionary, had become a great tomb.

An assault on Thaba-Bosiu on 8 August failed when the Boer commander, Lou Wepener, was killed, but the Boers then set about investing the mountain. After months, the suffering on top of the mountain was indescribable. Thousands of cattle and horses died, and the stench of the carcasses piled above and thrown over the sides suited only the vultures, who stuffed themselves until they literally could not move. By September, when spring brought renewal, Mabille lamented that 'the country is admirably green, but a desert, oh a desert!'

For the morale of the nation even worse was to come. Jacottet is pretty unforgiving in his assessment. Several of the principal chiefs 'deserted the national cause'. Most prominent amongst these was Molapo, 'a traitor to his father and to his country', who made a separate peace with the enemy in return for continued possession of his demesne. Then, in March 1866, the Volksraad decided that the French missionaries were to be expelled from the Orange Free State and Lesotho. This was a devastating blow. Samuel Rolland and his son (from Poortjie), Cochet (from Hebron), Dyke and Dr Casalis (from Hermon), Paul Germond (from Thabana-Morena) and Maeder (from Siloe) were escorted across the Orange to two years of exile in Aliwal North. Daumas (from Mekoatleng) and Coillard (from Leribe) were forced to go to Natal. Mabille, defiant, wanted to stay at Morija, and brave the rigours of the conflict. Immediately, he went up the mountain and sought out some of his flock in the caves. He asked them for advice. If you die, they said, and you surely will, the church will be destroyed. And Letsie said, 'I cannot protect you.' So he took leave of them, reminding them of Paul's words to the Ephesians (Acts 20: 29–31): 'For I know this, that after my departing shall grievous wolves enter in among you, not sparing the flock ... Therefore watch, and remember ...' Then they knelt, and they prayed, and they wept, and they kissed. And as he accompanied Mabille to his wagon, Esaia, in the moment of departure, welcomed him, fully and finally, into the hearts of the Basotho: 'When that young man arrived we asked each other, what can he teach us? Can he feed us with the milk of the Word of God with which our fathers [Arbousset and Casalis] fed us? Well, not only has he given us milk to drink but more, it seems to me, he has minced up some of that meat of which the Apostle spoke so that we might savour it and find it easy to digest. Yes, it seems to me that since he has been with us some of us have become *men*.'

As the Mabille family left, they were escorted by a band of savages, as Mabille called them, 'more savage than our Basotho pagans'. Mabille was particularly hated by these Boers, who derided the missionaries as 'verdamt zendelings'. For a man of Mabille's temperament, exile was torture. And he was uncertain whether he would ever be able to return to the land he now regarded as his country. Moshoeshoe must sue for peace: the 'knife was at his throat'. A treaty was proclaimed on 4 April amid the pillaged ruins of the mission at Thaba-Bosiu. Defeated, exhausted, Moshoeshoe was reduced to a strip of land between Thaba-Telle (a few kilometres to the east and slightly to the north of Morija), the Mohokare, and the southern Phuthiatsana river. It was to be known as the Peace of the Millet. The Basotho, like ants in summer, were desperate to save their crops and harvest them before winter came.

The ensuing peace, which endured until October 1867, was decidedly uneasy. The Orange Free State surveyed the Conquered Territory and divided it up into farms. Moshoeshoe never recognized this move, the Basotho in fact occupied much of the territory, and few farms were successfully settled. But the Bishop of Bloemfontein moved the Anglicans into the area to complete, together with the Catholics and other Protestants, a holy trinity.

A cyclone had swept over the PEMS. Most of the missionaries, eleven families in all, swirled into the ether, had been deposited, dazed, in Aliwal North. At Bethesda, Gosselin and Ellenberger were clinging on, but not for long. The latter crossed the Senqu in 1866, and opened a station in the south at Masitise, in a large cave which he converted into a house. In Lesotho proper, Thaba-Bosiu was in ruins, and, in any case, Jousse had been on leave in France since 1863. Only at Berea had Pierre-Joseph Maitin and his assistant Louis Duvoisin been left undisturbed. The only positive hope for expansion lay across the Drakensberg to the south-east, into No-Man's-Land, an area into which some refugee Basotho chiefs had made their way. Paul Germond made an exploratory trip there, and eventually the stations of Matatiele and Paballong were founded to serve its growing needs.

Mabille was like a caged animal. It was not long before he broke out. In August 1866, he was at Berea, under 'a sky of brass' and in a land of drought. In September, he made a sortie to Morija, but, except for admitting a few Basotho into the church, most of them the products of Esaia at Kolo, he found a picture of demoralization, where 'theft has become the normal thing' and justice was unknown. The position was untenable, so he took up his abode instead in Dr Lautré's house at Thaba-Bosiu, the only house left with a roof. There the people were eating grass seeds and roots, and digging up the bones of cattle from the holocaust of the previous year. Once the Mabille's servant, Lucia, came into Adèle's room and could not find her. She had fainted – quietly and comfortably – into the linen chest, from starvation. But in amongst the famine and fear, Adèle gave birth to her fourth child, Eugènie.

In July 1867, Moshoeshoe repudiated the treaty of the year before. 'Although I do not like war and am afraid of its consequent horrors,' he wrote to President Brand of the Orange Free State, 'I cannot consent to buy the lives of my people with the country belonging to them, where they were born, where their fathers were born likewise; besides I know of no country where they could go.'

The Mabilles could no longer stay at Thaba-Bosiu, but they refused to abandon the country, so they took their four children first to Morija, then to Berea. 'These vicissitudes make us realize,' Mabille wrote in a letter to Director Casalis, 'that we are strangers and travellers on the earth. I hope our departure

will not do harm to the advancement of the Kingdom of God and to the maintenance of discipline among our flock. I have entire confidence in the elders of
the church.'

This time Basotho resistance evaporated almost completely. At the beginning of 1868, the Conquered Territory – on the west bank of the Caledon –
succumbed; most of the fortresses fell; Moshoeshoe's brother Posholi was killed;
Qeme stronghold a few kilometres away was captured; the fall of Thaba-Bosiu
was inevitable.

At this point the (symbolic) survival of the country was in the hands of the
French missionaries – in particular those of Jousse, who had returned to his station at Thaba-Bosiu. Some of the King's sons, aware that he would never give
up, were conniving at a complete surrender behind his back. They drew up a
document to this effect. But it was not valid without the King's seal. This seal
had been given by Moshoeshoe in trust to Jousse. The missionary had been
begged by Tsekelo, one of the King's loyal sons, never to part with it, and
Jousse and Mabille were determined to protect it at all costs. Messenger after
messenger, day after day, came seeking the seal, purporting to come from the
King. Every day Jousse, as faithful as Penelope, replied, 'The seal belongs to
Moshoeshoe; he gave it to me to guard; if he wants it, let him come for it;
I will give it into no hands but his.' So they delayed, while time ticked
away. Days, hours, minutes. Only a miracle, a deus ex machina, would save the
kingdom now.

It came.

On 29 January 1868, Moshoeshoe received a letter from Sir Philip Wodehouse, Governor of the Cape. It informed the King as well as the President of
the Orange Free State that Britain intended to make the Basotho 'subjects of
the British throne'. At last! In 1842, Moshoeshoe had made his appeal to
Britain for protection. Now a favourable change in the colonial office, a fear of
Boer expansion, pressure from philanthropic and Christian circles in Britain,
representations from the French government, who were outraged at the
expulsion of their citizens and concerned to safeguard their interests, and a
sympathetic, patient, tenacious and visionary Governor all combined at last to
prompt an intervention. On 12 March, Wodehouse proclaimed Lesotho as
British territory (henceforth to be known as Basutoland), and at a great pitso
on 15 April, he solemnly proclaimed the British sovereignty to the Basotho
people. In Jacottet's judgement, 'That date is one of the most important in the
history of the tribe and of the mission. For both of them it meant salvation. Of
course, the complete independence of the Basutos was a thing of the past; but
they were saved and their future was assured … Henceforth Basutoland was
destined to enjoy the boon of peace and to possess a stable government. But it

was a weakened Basutoland, cramped and diminished. The mission, too, could revive and recover; but the amputations which it had suffered were nonetheless painful.' As for Moshoeshoe, although he had lost half his country (all the land to the north and west of the Mohokare and much of the triangle in the south-west), he believed that he had at last 'gathered his people into the "cave" of the Queen's protection'.

—⦵—

The last scene of the last act of a long drama was about to be played out. There is no doubt that towards the end of his life Moshoeshoe turned back to Christianity in a serious way. The rival churches saw this, and the Mafora and the Maroma vied, often in the most unseemly and cut-throat way, for his full conversion.

Father Gérard, who had to use inclement weather to sneak past family members more sympathetic to the opposition, nevertheless felt that Moshoeshoe had a preference for the Catholics. The Protestants were some-what disadvantaged by the priggishness of Jousse, who was convinced that the octogenarian King's decline was due to sexual activity with the young wives he had married in the recent past.

But when the Mabilles visited him twice just before his death, he began to acknowledge that he was now a believer. Once, Adèle showed him her baby, Louis, and he said, 'Delly, your child is my age-mate.' Told that Louis was now three months old, he added, 'Then he is the same age as myself. When you told me of the birth of that child, I also was coming to birth. It is only now that I am becoming a man.'

He died on 11 March 1870, two days before he was due to be publicly baptized by the Protestants, so neither side could assume conclusive victory, despite expansive claims to the contrary.

Jacottet's assessment, made through cold, clear eyes, was most dispassionate: 'Moshoeshoe gave up the ghost without having been received into the church. Those who visited him in the last months of his life and who were able to commune with him freely, were convinced of the reality and sincerity of his conversion. Others could only believe with fear and trembling. This is God's own secret.'

CHAPTER THIRTEEN

FROM PEACE TO THE GUN WAR

1868–1884

Britical rule brought security. In fact, the decade of the 1870s was something of a golden age to rival the period 1833 to 1848. The first benefit
it brought was that civil war was undoubtedly averted after the death of
Moshoeshoe. The late King had left a house divided. Letsie at Matsieng,
Masupha at Thaba-Bosiu, and Molapo to the north all had their fiefdoms and
were not anxious to pay allegiance to anyone else.

Mabille, now back at Morija, emerged from the war as a respected and
powerful figure. Where Casalis had helped give Moshoeshoe and the Basotho
tact in victory, Mabille gave them backbone in defeat. Always 'first at the
breach', Mabille became the dominant force in the mission in a decade of
'exceptional importance for the future of the church', a decade, according to
Jacottet, who was always concerned with such matters, in which 'the various
elements of its future organization took shape'.

Certainly the mission flourished. In 1864, before the war broke out, it
counted 2 211 Christian adults in its ranks. By 1872, there were 3 502; and by
1880, 5 984. In sixteen years, the following had thus almost tripled.

The Normal School or Teachers' Training College, sometimes also called
the Sekolo sa Thabeng (the School on the Mountain), was begun by the
Mabilles in 1868. They had to do all the teaching themselves. For want of a
classroom, they used the carpenter's shop. There were no school desks. There
were no books. Of the twenty scholars, only one – Job Moteane – had trousers.
But they learned Geography and Arithmetic and a little English, which was
eventually to become the medium of instruction. They sang, and recited
Sesotho fables. They absorbed biblical history. Mabille's main problem, it
seems, was to teach them the habits of discipline. If they were in trouble, they
went to the volunteer matron, Penelope Liengoane, the archetypal friendly ear
and surrogate mother, who did her job for a few pounds a year.

A site was chosen for the school building – with the permission of Matete,
the local chief – to the west of the church. By the middle of 1869, with the
help of students on their afternoons off, the school had been built, the number

of scholars had doubled, and goatskin breeches, in the interests of modesty, had been found for all. Since Mabille's main aim was to train evangelists, much of the teaching emphasized a study of the Bible as well as some church history. 'He laid stress upon what he called sacred chronology,' wrote Edwin Smith, 'for, he said, they had no notion of time and easily took Solomon to be a contemporary of John the Baptist and Abraham of Joshua.' This chronology would have extended to the idea of 'types' – figures of the Old Testament seen as forerunners or types of the New. 'I love these young men and I hope to see with my own eyes many of them engaged solely in the salvation of souls by preaching Christ,' Mabille wrote. 'This school becomes more and more important in our eyes.' Eventually Rev. Hamilton Moore Dyke, brother of Sarah Casalis, became Principal, and Dr Casalis helped with some teaching.

Like a farmer yearning to put more fields under tillage, or a businessman always seeking to expand his business, Mabille was always ready to expand the mission. The success of the Normal School stimulated another idea that had itched at him for years. In 1873, he started a preparatory school which was also a boarding school, and by 1878 it had about fifty-eight pupils. When the spread of primary schools made it redundant, it did not die but was transmogrified. A class of learner evangelists was attached to it. Soon this expanded until it absorbed the preparatory school and became the Bible School, an extremely important development of the mission's armoury. In 1871, Jousse started a girls' school at Thaba-Bosiu with twelve pupils, and by 1879 the enrolment had increased to seventy. In 1878, Germond began an Industrial School – the fourth boarding school – at Thabana-Morena, though it was later moved to Leloaleng near Masitise.

In 1875, Mabille inherited the printing press from Masitise. This enabled the now expanded Printing Works to produce intellectual fodder for his hungry flock: catechisms, Geography, Arithmetic and English books for schools; a Sesotho-English vocabulary; the first Sesotho grammar. This may not sound very exciting, but these books were the building blocks of literacy, the very first steps towards a reading public and, ultimately, an African literature. With the collaboration of Coillard, Mabille also undertook the collection and production of a hymn book, which was published in 1881. This hymnal eventually comprised 457 hymns, and by the turn of the century had been disseminated through much of South Africa, with over 150 000 copies sold. To make sure the Protestant view of history was not ignored by default, he translated into Sesotho Bonnefon's great tome of church history.

In 1862, in order to facilitate distribution, a book depot had been started. Now Mabille made the Printing Works and the Sesuto Book Depot (to use the later spelling) self-sufficient. *Leselinyana*, temporarily suspended for the war,

resumed in 1870 and became an important source of information for a growing literate population. All of these institutions, as well as the Normal School,
exist to this day. Under Mabille's strict but benign hand, Morija was a happy
and industrious place. Amongst the numerous printers he trained was Neftali
Moshabesha: 'I was one of the first to work with him when the printing press
came to Morija. What a happy time we had with him! Many people coming
from the fields would stop and listen to our singing while we composed type
and printed or bound books.'

The struggle to produce the whole Bible was a huge one. It was no easy task
translating into a new language, which was not one's mother tongue and which
had never before been used to express Christian ideas and concepts, and where
new terms had to be coined or new meanings pressed into old words. The
translation underwent many trials and tribulations, and many hands made heavy
work of it. After the New Testament first appeared in 1855, attention turned
to the Old, and parts were parcelled out to different folk: Arbousset, for
instance, having translated the Psalms, undertook Genesis and Exodus; Cochet,
Jeremiah; Maitin, Deuteronomy; and Daumas, Samuel and Ruth (though he
never completed these because of the loss of his station at Mekoatleng in the
Conquered Territory). Much of the revision of the work of others fell to old
man Rolland, and he performed this task heroically. His eyesight was failing,
his talent soon to be buried, but by dint of using three pairs of spectacles piled
on top of each other he did his proofreading, often resorting to a magnifying
glass as well. The translations of Daniel, Isaiah and Leviticus were done out of
the corner of his eye, the only place left where a little light entered! In the face
of these trials, Rolland was uncomplaining. The book of Job can have had no
more long-suffering a translator than he.

The printing of the separate books was not a straightforward affair either.
The printing press, acquired from Beersheba, had been reassembled by
Ellenberger at Bethesda in 1862, and he undertook the work. But, because of
the war, he decided to move the press to his new station at Masitise. On the
way, the wagon on which it was being carried, together with the sheets already
printed, overturned, and some of the cases of type were broken. At this precise
moment the convoy was attacked by a Boer commando, so the Basotho
defenders took some of the lead to make shot. Whether the Boers realized that
the Bible was literally on the side of the Basotho and that they were having bits
of it flung at them, the word making for flesh, is not known. Nor is it recorded
whether any of the type found its mark.

The press was only restored to working order in 1872, and moved to Morija under Mabille's control in 1875. He published the Old Testament books, in separate editions, as fast as the various translators made them available. By 1878, the last book of the Bible rolled off the press. After forty-five years of effort it was time at last for the Bible to be published in its entirety! It was decided that this would be done by Oxford University Press, under the direction of Paris and the guidance of the British and Foreign Bible Society. A single hand was needed to oversee the task. Mabille was the obvious choice. In June 1880, the Mabilles left Cape Town for France on their first leave in over twenty years. The voyage, on a steamer, took them twenty-seven days, a quarter of the time it had taken them on the voyage out. This time there was no threat to throw them overboard: in fact, they carried with them the book of Jonah in a new language.

—∽⊙—

War in the 1820s; war in 1851–2; war in 1858; war in 1865–8: the last thing the Basotho needed was war again. But war was in the air. In 1877, the Xhosa of the eastern Cape rose once more, only to be beaten and broken. In the same year, the Transvaal was annexed by the British, but the Bapedi under Sekhukhune were simmering and were only finally defeated in November 1879, by a combined force of British and Swazi. Lobengula, King of the Ndebele, was eyeing his rival Nkulumane, and also threatening Khama of the Bamangwato to the south. Of all these, the name of Isandhlwana acquired the greatest fame, for at this curiously shaped hill in the west of the Zulu kingdom, in January 1879, the army of Cetshwayo annihilated a British regiment. Even the subsequent rout of the Zulu at Ulundi in July failed to overshadow the earlier victory, and today Isandhlwana is to South Africa what Little Big Horn is to the United States.

The Gun War in Lesotho, by contrast, is now almost totally forgotten. But it did help shape the map of southern Africa, and its significance is greater than its remembrance. It was also strongly connected to other contemporaneous events. The Conservative government in Britain, spurred by Lord Carnarvon, dreamed of a Confederation in southern Africa, and the new Governor of the Cape, Sir Bartle Frere, set out to achieve this as soon as he arrived in March 1877. Disarmament of the more powerful African blocs was part of the plan, and it was such an ultimatum that provoked Cetshwayo to war.

Detecting a whiff of the disarmament rumour, Moorosi, chief of the Baphuthi in the Quthing area, south of the Senqu, disobeyed an order from the British Resident. Letsie was compelled to send a force to support the Cape army in its attempt to subdue Moorosi, because the Basotho feared that the Quthing area would be excised from their territory and given to the Cape, and that Basutoland would shrink even further. The campaign was a long one and it was only in November 1879 that Moorosi was killed, and his head taken as a regimental trophy to King William's Town.

Before then, Gordon Sprigg, Prime Minister of the Cape and an ally of Frere, had introduced into the Cape Parliament what was disarmingly called the Peace Preservation Act. This legislation, which threatened a huge fine or heavy imprisonment for the possession of almost any weapons, was applicable to everyone in theory, but was used almost exclusively against Africans. It achieved the opposite of its stated aims. In October 1879, Sprigg went personally to the annual pitso at Thaba-Bosiu. He was met by thousands of Basotho. That they wore almost entirely European clothes reflected the tremendous change that had overtaken their society in the space of a few decades. After a prayer by Mabille and an introduction by Colonel Griffith, the High Commissioner's agent in Basutoland (since 1871), Sprigg complimented the Basotho on their loyalty, announced that the hut tax would be doubled to £1, and confirmed the proposed disarmament, solely, in his view, in their own interests. He told them that they were still children and that guns were 'toys' too dangerous for Government to leave in their possession.

Most of the Basotho listeners, however, secretly believed they were adults, and became increasingly alarmed and incensed at what they were hearing. Sprigg was not listening when Letsie's son, Lerotholi, the heir to the kingship, said, 'All that I have got to say is that my gun belongs to the Queen and that I will follow the Queen about with this gun wherever she goes, and I will stick to it.' Only now did it begin to sink in that Basutoland was not being ruled directly from Britain, but came under the jurisdiction of the Cape. Mabille had not realized this. On 11 August 1871, the Cape Parliament, with London's blessing, had passed the Annexation Act, in effect annexing Basutoland to the Cape – an event which Colonel Griffith noted had 'passed almost unnoticed' in Basutoland.

And Sprigg's plans were different from those of London. He wanted to take over the area of Quthing. He pursued the policy of undermining the chiefdoms in favour of the magistracies. It also served his interests that the paramountcy, established by Moshoeshoe, had begun to vanish, with Letsie reduced to a status on a par with his brothers, Masupha and Molapo. Sprigg, in fact, envisaged the disappearance of Basutoland as a separate nation. The first step was to extract its teeth.

He and the Governor were strongly advised by Colonel Griffith and all the magistrates, by Adolphe Mabille and all the missionaries, and by all the traders not to attempt immediate disarmament of the Basotho. But Frere responded with the insidious political liturgy that all southern African politicians intoned through the centuries: 'The amount of sedition preached by their friends [i.e. friends of the Basotho] from Saul Solomon at Sea Point up to the reverend Frenchmen on the skirts of the Drakensberg is enough to inflame a much less excitable population.'

Sadly, the disarmament proposal caused divisions in the nation itself. The minority who decided, however reluctantly, to obey the government diktat, dubbed 'loyalists', included Molapo's eldest son Jonathan. At the head of the 'nationalists' or 'rebels' were Masupha, Lerotholi and Joel, a younger son of Molapo. Letsie was the pivotal figure, and he played an ambiguous role for which he was, in hindsight, roundly condemned by Jacottet. The aged Paramount Chief 'adopted throughout an attitude which he thought clever, but which was most deplorable; whilst pretending, on the one hand, to obey the Government, he, on the other hand, incited his subjects to resistance'.

As foreign nationals, the missionaries found themselves between the devil and the high blue mountains. They were damned if they supported the government and damned if they didn't. In *Leselinyana*, the only newspaper in the country, Mabille advised adherence to the law, even if it seemed injudicious or unjust. This very correct attitude of the missionaries was, according to Jacottet, dictated to them by their Christian duty and by their very functions as ministers of the Gospel. It stirred up great hostility against them, not least from the Christian Basotho, most of whom found themselves on the side of the rebels. But Jacottet added that they took this stance, too, because they were persuaded that 'the ruin of the Basotho was a certainty if they rose against the Cape Colony'.

Edwin Smith revealed for the first time, in his biography, the full extent of Mabille's out-in-the-open *and* behind-the-scenes roles in the events of the early months of 1880. There was nothing contradictory or hypocritical about them. While the government saw him as the archetypal priest meddling in politics, he was adamant about his right, even duty, to speak freely. He wrote, on 1 February, to the *Christian Express*, a mission newspaper emanating from Lovedale in the eastern Cape, to this effect: 'I will not enter into the merits of the question about disarming the natives. If, in my opinion, it is both unjust and unnecessary, who will deny me the right of expressing my opinion, as freely as the upholders of this Act express theirs? Am I to be gagged because I am a missionary? ... I am bound by sacred ties to the tribe I evangelize, and to which I endeavour to teach the highest truths, and I am bound, to the best of my ability, to protest against what I think would be the ruin of that work ... We have our rights as men and missionaries, to speak out frankly the truth as we see it. If we err, and if it can be proved that we err, we shall be the first to acknowledge our fault. But if we are right, what then?'

Mabille encouraged Letsie to exercise his undisputed right to appeal to the Queen. Frere, who vehemently blamed the missionaries for any potential future trouble, sarcastically said of the petition, which was dated 21 January, that it had clearly been drawn up 'by an accomplished European who is well acquainted with the best mode of clothing, a sentimental appeal, addressed to a European audience, with the local colours of Basotho imagery'. Like Casalis before him, Mabille's fingerprints were on the style. The petition got nowhere, nor did a subsequent delegation to the Cape Parliament.

Mabille was not opposed, in fact, to ultimate disarmament: he was steadfastly against immediate and involuntary enforcement. He came up with a unique suggestion (one which might be of use to the powers that be in present-day South Africa, confronting their own gun war). Insist on registration, and *put a heavy tax on guns*, he advised, 'and in time you will get all you want'. It might have worked. Sadly, Sprigg did not take up the suggestion, and the order for disarmament was set, first for 7 May, and then for 21 May 1880. After that date it would be illegal 'for any person within Basutoland to sell, make, mend, repair, or keep any guns, pistols, swords, bayonets, daggers, pikes, spears, assegais (or any portion thereof), or any bullets, cartridges or ammunition'. Mabille had been led to believe that no action would be taken before a delegation of seven Basotho elders and M. Cochet, appointed by a national great pitso in April, had presented their case to the Cape Parliament, and now he felt that he and the Basotho had been betrayed. He refused to print the proclamation in *Leselinyana*. For this he was vilified, and, in a speech to Parliament, Sprigg, using his favourite pejorative metaphor, accused him 'of a childishness which I would not have believed a man of his mature years to be capable of'.

Mabille replied vigorously in a letter to the *Argus* newspaper reiterating his solution to the crisis. 'It is not creditable to you, sir, I must say, that you wanted these poor people to obey your dictates blindfold; you did not care about their understanding what it is to be a British subject. You neither wanted them to petition the Governor, or the Queen, or the Parliament. You did not want them to send a deputation to Cape Town. You said that you were wise enough to govern them by yourself. Yes, a despotic sway is all you have wished to have; but in this you have been disappointed. And I glory in this that I, a Frenchman, should have been more English than an Englishman ... I must add that I am not opposed to disarmament in itself; you are aware that, in the name of Letsie, I made a proposition – which I had made long before to Mr Griffith – that a tax should be levied on each gun, which, if carried out, would have brought the greater part of the Basutos' guns into the hands of the Government in six or eight years. Such a measure would have been easily carried out and have left the Government's influence intact. But, as Colonial Premier, you have had one fixed idea in your mind, and wished to carry it through at all hazards, and on my mind you have left the impression that you strongly wished to drive the Basutos into rebellion, in order to take their country and do away with what you have been pleased once to call an "anomaly".'

In a letter to his son Ernest in April, Mabille did note an important trend. 'One would hardly believe,' he wrote, 'how this disarmament question has brought closer together the more intelligent of the Basuto and the missionaries.' With the decline of chiefly power, a new class of political leadership, educated in the Protestant schools, had begun to emerge. The influence the mission had partly lost in 1848 began to reappear in a different quarter.

—◦◦—

Basutoland was headed inexorably for war. It was one of the most unnecessary wars in southern African history. Said Letsie: 'When a child scratches itself or its mother, she cuts its nails. Whom have we scratched?'

The 'War of the Guns' ignited on 17 July, when Masupha attacked and took away the cattle of a minor chief near Cana who had obediently surrendered his weapons.

Two men were absent when the war began. Mabille and his wife were on furlough and staying at the Mission House at 26, rue des Fossés-St Jacques in Paris. Rest and relaxation did not come easily to Mabille. For many months, he spent most of the day correcting proofs of the Bible. Then he spent much of the rest of his time writing letters or articles, stirring organizations like the Aborigines Protection Society, trying to bring the war to a close. He saw it not as 'a war of heathenism against Christianity, of barbarism against civilization', nor as 'a war of races', as Sir Bartle Frere would have it, but as an unjust war. His main aim was to get Britain to intervene and assume direct rule over Basutoland. In early January 1881, he was with a deputation from the PEMS and the Evangelical Alliance which visited Lord Kimberley at the Colonial Office. Lord Kimberley gave some hope that he would intervene if the chance presented itself and if the initiative came from the Basotho.

Molapo, darling of the early church, latter-day apostate and persecutor of Christians, was the other absentee. He had died on 28 June.

—◦◦—

In the examination of any misdemeanour, the first thing an investigator looks for is his, or her, mom – means, opportunity, motive. And when a family is involved, mom, as often as not, turns out to be dad. As regards the Gun War, a case of apparent child chastisement, if not abuse, old man Sprigg certainly had clear *motives* – pacifying the Basotho, seizing Quthing, subordinating the chiefs, and ultimately obliterating the Basotho nation as a separate entity. The *opportunity* could easily be manufactured on any pretence. In his dotage, however, the poor fool had forgotten that he did not have the *means* to whip the recalcitrants into submission! He did not have the essential attributes a parent needs – speed, to catch the critters, and strength, to smack them hard. His whip was little more than string!

All Sprigg could put into the field were the Cape Mounted Rifles, an assortment of farmers and burghers, and a corps of Mfengu from the eastern Cape who had been rearmed in order to disarm the Basotho. In a series of skirmishes in the second half of 1880, these forces did not get very far in pacifying the country.

Tragically, though, this 'family' squabble turned almost fratricidal. Letsie, weak, vacillating and treacherous, supposedly led the 'matekete', the *ticketed* 'loyalists' who had adhered to the gun law. Masupha led the majority 'mabelete', the wild ones. He was backed by Lerotholi. The majority of Christians, including the octogenarian Moletsane, who had become a devout believer, went with the 'savages'. The students at the Morija Normal School champed at the bit to defend their country. Unlike most of the traders, who left the country or took refuge in Maseru and Leribe, the French missionaries stayed at their stations, and, testimony to the respect in which they were held, none were harmed. Indeed, Dr Casalis saved the lives of many wounded Basotho, thereby earning the nickname of 'Thipa ea Letsie', Letsie's Knife. The Boers of the Transvaal played their own game, supplying the 'rebels' with ammunition. Towards the end of the year, they had started their own war against the British, which culminated in the re-establishment of the Transvaal Republic.

By the end of March 1881, the war was grinding to a halt. Lerotholi was now ready to parley. Frere's successor as Governor of the Cape, Sir Hercules Robinson, was asked to mediate, but his insistence that the rebels compensate the loyalists and the traders, and that all guns be surrendered, found little favour, particularly with the ever-recalcitrant Masupha.

In the Cape, the war rapidly lost support, especially since it eventually cost nearly five million pounds and virtually bankrupted the colony. One rising political star devoted a great deal of his maiden speech in Parliament to attacking disarmament. This was Cecil Rhodes. At the same time, another star faded. Sprigg, deserted by his colleagues, resigned.

Various attempts were made to settle the dispute. The new Resident, J.M. Orpen, tried to use Letsie and Lerotholi against Masupha and Joel, but with no success. Letsie rejected fratricide. General Gordon, a mere two years from immortal fame and martyrdom at Khartoum, went to Thaba-Bosiu to try to persuade Masupha to accept a solution based on a British suzerainty, with a Resident handling external matters, and the Paramount Chief and a Council internal affairs. Gordon got nowhere.

Mabille, who returned to Morija in 1882, to the great joy of his parishioners, did play a more constructive role. The missionaries had learned a lesson in 1848, when they interfered in the war against the Batlokoa. They did not condemn out of hand those Christians who had gone to fight, and Mabille, the Cutter-off, tempered his instinctive condemnation.

In March 1883, the Cape Premier, Sir Thomas Scanlen, and the Secretary for Native Affairs, J.W. Sauer, came to Basutoland with the new Resident, Captain Matthew Blyth, to sound out the Basotho on the future dispensation: the Cape Parliament was in favour of withdrawing from the country's internal affairs but maintaining control of its external affairs – 'the Gordon policy without Gordon,' commented the *Cape Times*, 'the play of Hamlet without the King of Denmark.' Mabille believed that the general feeling of the Basotho was to return to direct rule by the Crown; indeed, many, including Mabille, believed they had never legally left it, since the Basotho had not been consulted about the previous arrangement. However, Letsie acknowledged the advice of his counsellor Setha, drawing on an 'ancient constitutional maxim' – *Morena ke morena ka batho*: a chief is a chief by his people – and decided that no definite decision could be taken without calling a consultative pitso.

Alfred Boegner, Casalis's successor as Director of the Mission in Paris, had come to Basutoland to celebrate the fiftieth anniversary of the founding of the local mission. He was present at the pitso, and left a memorable eyewitness account (summarized here by Edwin Smith).

The plateau on which the Pitso is held under a grey sky is vast in extent and set in a frame of mountains. On one side stands the camp of Captain Blyth and other officials; on the other side the native horses in their hundreds are grazing. The ground is strewn with red saddles. Here and there a European appears; the surcoat of a Roman priest, the white helmets of other visitors, the broad black hat of Mr Dyke, père [Hamilton Moore Dyke]. All the crowd talks, shouts, discusses, laughs. They are awaiting Masupha. Horsemen by the score continue to arrive – but Masupha comes not. The Pitso begins without him. The men arrange themselves in a huge hollow square, those in front sitting on the ground, those behind standing. The chiefs and missionaries take their places within the square: Letsie, Captain Blyth and the six magistrates seat themselves there apart. The Captain has a soldierly bearing and inspires confidence. Mabille opens with a prayer. Then Letsie rises. '*Lumelang!* Hail!' he cries, and the thousands of voices respond

with a long-drawn-out '*Eh!*' Letsie addresses his people by their honorific
title: 'Bakuena! Crocodiles!' and the response comes thunderously back:
'Thou art the Crocodile!'

Letsie said little, merely introducing Blyth, who in turn exhorted the Basotho
to give a unanimous answer to the government proposals. The new law, he said,
must apply to all, or none. Letsie then declared that for himself he accepted,
and deplored Masupha's absence from the pitso. The officials retired to allow
the Basotho to discuss the issues amongst themselves. This they did, and all the
chiefs committed themselves to supporting the Paramount Chief. The only
sour note was sounded by a message from Masupha expressing his hostility to
anything and everything the government proposed.

Then Mabille, pale, passionate, moved as if by divine spirit, like a 'messenger of divine pity', spoke a classical exhortation in 'mellifluous Sesotho'.

Letsie, chiefs and all you Basuto, allow me to say a word. Though I am a
missionary I am also a Mosuto, having lived over twenty years amongst you.
If I speak it is to warn you that the hour is serious, solemn, and to ask you
to show yourselves men. You have heard what was said: the new laws must
be accepted in their entirety and by the entire nation. Will you remain
divided? Cannot you act? Cannot you unite? Or are you still counting upon
something to happen in the future? Do you not see that you must give a
clear and decisive answer, here and now? Weigh well the consequences of
the resolution you take. If you do not accept these proposals the consequences will be that sooner or later your country will be abandoned. And
do not imagine that things will be then as they were before you came under
the shadow of the Queen. Once the British have gone the Boers will come
and claim the country which once they nearly conquered. They will say:
'Moyela, clear out! Lerotholi, clear out! Letsie, clear out! All this land is
ours.' And you will be servants where now you are masters. One man
troubles you – Masupha. He thinks that he has nothing to fear; he will keep
his country. So thinking, he shows himself selfish. He kills us all by his
selfishness. Son of Masupha, are you here? [Response: Yes!] Well, tell your
father: You kill us, you kill the churches, you kill the nation. And all of you,
when some day all of you are scattered abroad or serving the Boers in the
land that was yours, herding the cattle of others, ploughing the land of
others – then your children will say, and you will say to yourselves: 'A curse
upon Masupha! It is he who brought us to destruction.' Today it is not too
late. Reflect – act – be men!

But a key actor was not there: Masupha was brooding in his kraal. The pitso failed to deliver a positive decision, and Scanlen and Sauer returned empty-handed. Even worse: bankrupt, the Cape government, tail between its legs, had to send senior minister John X. Merriman to London to beg the metropolitan government to repeal the Annexation Act of 1871. The imperial government was less than keen to take over the responsibility for Basutoland, the first of the High Commission Territories, and continued to prevaricate despite the Cape passing its Basutoland Disannexation Act in September 1883. Mabille was deeply worried: 'The fact is that it is for the Basotho a question of life or death. Left to themselves there will be a civil war at once, or war with the Free State. They are afraid of their independence. And can you think what it will be for the Basotho to be under the Boers? They will lose their nationality, and by and by the larger part of their country.' Either way, this would be a disaster for the Basotho, and a corresponding disaster for the mission.

Although times were really hard for the missionaries, there were some bright spots. Membership of the church dipped by 900 during the war, but in 1882 the Bible School and the Normal School had reopened and a new development had got off the ground. Four married men, all younger than thirty, were the first initiates of the new Theological School started by Hermann Krüger, who had recently arrived. He taught them Algebra, Geometry and History, in addition to Theology and elementary Greek. A six- or seven-year study course was planned for these first candidates for the ministry.

Mabille brought back with him from France a new press, which was damaged en route but fixed in an improvised way by a Mosotho blacksmith. With five apprentices, Mabille began to publish *Leselinyana* again. It was, wrote Henri Dieterlen in the first issue, like 'the dove which came back to the ark at even-tide'. Mabille's greatest triumph was bringing copies with him of the complete edition of the Bible in Sesotho, as well as a new pocket edition of the New Testament. The full Bible was received with great jubilation at the mission. As he presented a copy to each of the evangelists, Mabille asked if they would continue to teach only what was contained in the Word of God, adding or subtracting nothing. One of them, Jeremiah, promised on behalf of himself and his colleagues, but added that he feared there would be people who differed from those who taught them and that he mistrusted the youth of the country: formerly, the converts carried their books everywhere they went, reading them at every opportunity, but the young people of today did not read, he lamented. Perhaps they would buy the pocket edition, but he was concerned this would be more for show than use. Simeon Feku was thrilled: nearly forty years before, he had gone by wagon to fetch the cases containing the copies of the Gospels of St Mark and St John which Maeder had had printed in Cape Town. When

Mabille left for Europe, the old man had wondered if he would live long enough to see the complete edition of the Bible to which he and his wife 'owed everything'. He was thankful that he had, and as tangible proof of his gratitude he put ten shillings on the table. So did his wife. A significant offering.

—◦⊙◦—

In November 1883, the imperial government asked the Basotho straightforwardly whether they wanted to be ruled directly by the Queen. At a special pitso on 29 November, thirty-five of the most important chiefs agreed; only Masupha held out for complete independence. On 17 December, Britain announced that it would resume direct rule, and Lt Col. Marshal Clarke was appointed as the first Resident Commissioner.

—◦⊙◦—

Boegner's presence in Lesotho was long overdue. No official representative of the PEMS had ever visited its eldest child, despite the latter's urgent pleas. Conference had long wanted some sign that they and the Basotho were not forgotten, nor being sidelined. In the mid-1870s, Casalis underwent a long illness, and to offer him some assistance it was decided to create the post of Deputy Director. The choice ultimately boiled down to either Jean Bianquis or Alfred Boegner. Boegner was appointed in 1878.

One of his first tasks was to visit southern Africa. Concerns, first about the health of Casalis and then about the Gun War, delayed this for four years, however. Although Masupha and the 'nationalists' were maintaining a low level of resistance, the Paris Committee felt the visit by Boegner (who had by then succeeded Casalis as Director) could no longer be avoided, and the fiftieth anniversary of the founding of the mission seemed a heaven-sent opportunity for it.

Consequently, Boegner was in a position not only to attend the dramatic pitso on 24 April 1883, but also to deliver a message from the surviving 'fathers' of the Lesotho mission, Casalis and Jousse, to the jubilee celebration at Morija on 31 May. Boegner was able to reaffirm the links between the Committee in Paris and the Church of Lesotho even as the latter moved towards greater autonomy; these links were reinforced in the twelve years ahead by a dozen new recruits, Édouard Jacottet being amongst the first.

It should not be thought that the traffic was all one way, however. At the very same time, the members of the Paris Committee held a similar anniversary celebration in sympathy with their Lesotho counterparts. In a moving appeal, Casalis exhorted this audience to transport themselves in spirit and in the imagination to Morija on that day.

But there was a more profound realization still. In a contribution to the *Journal des Missions Évangéliques*, the pastor Eugène Bersier suggested a number of ways in which Lesotho and the Lesotho mission had had a significant effect on Europe. Firstly, the Lesotho mission reminded the 'old Christian nations' that 'l'Évangile n'est avant tout ni un système, ni une institution, ni même une doctrine ... mais essentiellement une vie'. Secondly, the mission repeated to the churches of Europe, always subject to dissenting faiths and dry theological polemics, the simple fundamental of the coming of the Kingdom of God on earth, and asserted that religious unity lay in Christian action rather than words. Thirdly, the mission gave the example of a man of faith who knew where he was going and where he had come from, and Bersier severely criticized the Calvinist orthodoxy of the Boers, descended as some of them were from Huguenot Protestants who had themselves been persecuted. Fourthly, the mission counteracted racist ideas and genocides in practice.

On 19 March 1884, another great pitso was held to welcome Resident Commissioner Clarke and the resumption of the Queen's rule. It was to be a day of great celebration, the most important day in the Basotho calendar.

Letsie addressed the whole nation: 'I greet you, all Bakuena! There is sickness in this land. In this assembly there is peace. Sickness and death are brought about by men not understanding each other; peace is brought about by men knowing and understanding each other. I am as one that dreams today. Let us have the blessing of God on this meeting. Here is our father, Mr Mabille, let him pray for us.' Which Mabille did.

When it was time for Tsekelo, another son of Moshoeshoe, to speak, he said, 'We are a new people, being born a second time.'

CHAPTER FOURTEEN

WAITING FOR GODET

1858–1884

Nothing is known about Jacottet's childhood. He was born in Neuchâtel on 11 February 1858. But, like Athena from the forehead of Zeus, he springs into sight only as a young adult. The *place* where he was born was certainly significant for his future.

Most of inhabited Switzerland comprises a great plateau running between the Alps to the south and the Jura mountains to the north. The canton of Neuchâtel lies in the north-west part of the country, and Lac Neuchâtel, which defines its southern border, is the largest lake located completely within Switzerland. The small, elegant town of Neuchâtel, capital of the canton, is situated on the north-western shore, and looks out over the lake to the vast range of the Alps on the southern horizon. Behind the town lies the hinterland of the canton, with La Chaux-de-Fonds and Le Locle being the only other towns of substance. The canton of Neuchâtel is small: a mere forty kilometres long and twenty deep. It is one of the youngest of the Swiss cantons (the twenty-first to join out of twenty-three) and is predominantly French-speaking.

The modern history of the area begins around AD 1000, when the King of Burgundy gave his wife Irmengarde the 'new castle' (after which the town got its name) on a hill overlooking the lake. In the twelfth century a fine church was begun alongside the chateau, but this, the Collegiate Church, was only completed in 1276. The two buildings stand side by side to this day, reminders of the close relationship between church and state.

After a brief occupation, between 1512 and 1529, by the Swiss cantons, Neuchâtel fell under the sway of the House of Orléans-Longueville at the beginning of the seventeenth century. But the Reformation, introduced into Neuchâtel in 1530 by Guillaume Farel (the man who brought Calvin to Geneva), also introduced something of the rationalistic temper to Neuchâtel steel. This strong intellectual tendency was strengthened by the influx of skilled and energetic Huguenot refugees after the revocation of the Edict of Nantes in 1685.

In 1707, a curious twist was given to the history of the territory. Following the death of Mary of Orléans, Duchess of Nemours, Neuchâtel was given the opportunity of choosing new rulers. There was no shortage of suitors – from Auvergne and Picardy, from Savoie and Brittany, from Prussia and England. Over twenty princes flaunted their political finery. Tired of the incessant lascivious advances of France, Neuchâtel decided to place itself under the House of Hohenzollern, the rulers of Prussia. They were, after all, Protestant, they were weighty enough to keep France at arm's length, and they had the inestimable advantage of being far away! Consequently, the small principality of Neuchâtel enjoyed a prosperous eighteenth century, basking in the Enlightenment. Its publishing industry surreptitiously printed parts of Diderot's Encyclopedia, and Rousseau spent three happy years at Môtiers, a small village in the country.

It was during this period of peace and prosperity that there occurred the most significant innovation of all. Neuchâtel was not rich in natural resources, nor particularly noted for agricultural or pastoral farming (although it has long produced good wines and cheeses). In the eighteenth century, it did make fine cotton prints and lacework, and certain craftsmen excelled as locksmiths, blacksmiths and gunsmiths.

Exactly how watchmaking came to the mountains of Neuchâtel in the early eighteenth century is a mystery. Huguenot refugees brought knowledge, and enterprising Neuchâtelois travelled for their training. Daniel JeanRichard was one of the most important pioneers.

There was something in the character of the people – their determination to produce quality and accuracy, and their astringent Protestantism – which made the industry thrive. The long winters certainly helped. And perhaps a certain coldness of temperament, as well as exactitude, crept into the regional character. A division of labour developed, with different parts being manufactured on farms and in small urban workshops. Families interlocked, dynasties grew. The work was intricate and highly specialized. Le Locle and La Chaux-de-Fonds became the beating heart of the industry.

By the second half of the nineteenth century, the English were still making expensive watches for the upper classes, but this did not appeal to the Americans, who turned to the Swiss instead. With their fine workmanship and continued invention, the Neuchâtelois prospered, making such names as Tissot and Zenith world-famous.

The Swiss did not invent time. But they did perfect it.

—◦◦—

Of course, Neuchâtel was not immune to the French Revolution. In 1806,

Napoleon appointed one of his marshals Prince of Neuchâtel, and this inter-regnum lasted until 1813, though the new prince never actually set foot in his domain. But new ideas did arrive and with them a new political dispensation. There was a strong movement to join the Swiss Confederation, and in 1814 Neuchâtel was voted in as the newest canton. The Congress of Vienna confirmed this in 1815, but the position was somewhat more complicated. Neuchâtel also remained a principality of the Hohenzollerns. This was a hybrid status which was never likely to last.

In 1848, as revolutions swept through Europe, toppling Louis-Philippe in France, Neuchâtel Castle was occupied peacefully on the night of 1 March by those forces who wanted closer union with the Swiss Confederation and no foreign rule. A republic was proclaimed. A royalist counter-revolution in September 1856 failed badly (partly because of the intervention of federal troops) and, the following year, an international conference was called in Paris to settle 'the Neuchâtel Affair'. The King of Prussia finally gave up his claim on the former principality. Consequently, Édouard Jacottet was born, the year after that, into what was now a full canton of Switzerland. The population of the whole canton was then not much more than 70 000, on a par with Basutoland.

—⚬—

The canton of Neuchâtel has been compared to a gable roof. The ridge of the roof is formed by the Jura mountains (some 1 300 metres high). The south side of the roof slopes away to the lake (at 430 metres above sea level), interrupted only by an intermediate terrace, the Val-de-Ruz. At the foot of this southern side, called the 'Sunny Side' ('l'Endroit'), is Neuchâtel, described by Alexandre Dumas as 'a town carved out of a block of butter' because of its old buildings made of Hauterive yellow stone. The northern side of the roof consists of a number of valleys, running laterally and folded into the mountains. The Doubs river marks the northern boundary with France. This is the 'Cold Side' ('l'Envers'), and La Chaux-de-Fonds is popularly known as the 'cold capital' of the canton.

Whatever the value of stereotypes, there was a widespread belief in the nineteenth century that the people at The Top ('le Haut'), the people in the mountains, belied the weather in their personalities and were warmer and friendlier, had their feet on the ground, were more practical and 'in time with the world'. Paradoxically, the people on the coast, The Bottom ('le Bas'), were regarded as more formal, somewhat colder. The farmers and craftsmen of The Top gave impetus to the split from Prussia and the formation of the republic, and later, as the working class grew, to the socialist movement; the civil servants, lawyers, academics and merchants of The Bottom were supposedly more conservative. By and large, though, they were a temperate community, a mix of Enlightenment elegance and sober Reformation, with a dash of Romanticism. When the wind blows from the north-east – Le Biz – it is cold; when it comes from the south-west there is rain. This south wind – the Föhn – brings the Alps closer, you can see them more clearly. You can also blame your headaches on the Föhn.

—◦◦—

There were two men in particular whose hands were laid on Édouard Jacottet's formative years: his father, Henri-Pierre; and Frédéric Godet.

Henri-Pierre Jacottet was only twenty-seven when he became a member of the Grand Council (the legislative body) of Neuchâtel in 1855. He lost his place in the year following – was this because he had royalist sympathies? – but resumed his seat in 1859, and in 1864 became a member of the Federal Council of States.

In 1857, he had joined the editorial staff of the *Courier de Neuchâtel,* and in 1867 he became a professor of law at the Neuchâtel Academy, which was founded in 1838 and eventually grew into the University. His younger brother, Paul, was also a lawyer and later taught at the Academy, while his other brothers, Frédéric and Léopold, became ministers in the church. While he was teaching, Henri-Pierre began to compile his major work – a two-volume *Droit Civil Neuchâtelois.* He and his wife Louise-Isabelle, who was the daughter of the famous royalist and conservative Chancelier Favarger, lived a comfortable life at Hauterive, a village on a slope on the eastern outskirts of Neuchâtel, and they had seven children, three boys and four girls, although of these little Julie lived scarcely a year.

—◦◦—

Frédéric Godet was not related to the Jacottets. He was the best-known clergyman in Neuchâtel in the nineteenth century, his name recognized throughout Protestant Europe.

Born into the Calvinist faith in 1812, he was a man of intelligence, clarity, simplicity, and strong and honest will, who did not tolerate fools but never judged others from a position of assumed superiority or arrogance. He was, from an early age, destined for the church.

Godet visited Paris in 1830, soon after the July revolution. The young man, in the words of one of his biographers, found France 'too libertine, too Roman, too revolutionary, too profane: too libertine in morals, too Roman in religion, too revolutionary in politics, too profane in philosophy'. His personality kept him to a steady course: 'his faith in *the divinity of the Bible* was entire.'

In 1831, while serving in the army, he helped protect the Prussian cause against a nationalistic rebellion, so his early years positioned him as a loyal royalist. Just as the Romanovs tended to choose governesses and tutors from Lausanne and Geneva, so the Hohenzollerns recruited from Neuchâtel. It was therefore natural for a young clergyman such as Godet to look to Germany for further study; this was reinforced by his perception of France as being too decadent, so he went to Berlin in 1832. In 1834, in addition, Godet's mother was approached to look after the three-year-old Prince Frederick William, destined eventually to be King of Prussia. In 1838, Godet, having met the royal family on an occasion while visiting his mother, was appointed tutor to the young prince.

He held this position for six years, and a strong bond of trust developed between the two which lasted the rest of their lives, confirmed in a regular correspondence. Internal politics rendered his marriage in 1844 a convenient excuse for him to return to Neuchâtel, but the prince's family let him go only reluctantly, appointed him Royal Chaplain at Neuchâtel, and were ever afterwards concerned about his well-being. In many ways it was a providential return, as he was to render important service to his home town.

Like any member of the reformed churches, Godet dismissed the infallibility of the apostolic tradition as represented by the Roman Catholic Church. He never doubted the existence of sin or its gravity. He rejected the possibility of salvation through good works and believed in justification by faith alone. On the other hand, he held that the *test* of faith was conduct.

Of course, like Calvin, Godet believed that one could only know God through His Son, and one could only know His Son through the Holy Scriptures, the authentic repository of righteousness. For Godet, the conduct of Christ was what must be emulated, and this divine conduct must be translated into human conduct, the task of conscience. Intellect, emotion, will, must all be honed and harnessed to this end. But pride and zeal must be eschewed, and conscience guided by reason. Confession of faith must be circumspect, the result of reasoned certainty. 'May I proffer no affirmation,' he wrote, 'as long as I fail to be aware within myself of sufficient grounds for my contentions. May I rather dwell in doubt till God enlighten me. I shall thus best enlighten myself and be the means of bearing no false light for others. Conscience is nothing till it be tolerant, impersonal through love, as was Christ, who suffered rather than raise a material hand to prove His right. From the intellect theological knowledge should pass into life and into the heart.'

On the question of the relationship between church and state, Godet was very definite. The independence of the church was paramount. This did not, however, mean he insisted on the separation of church and state. He had no objection to their overlapping, provided everyone was in agreement and there was no conflict. In any case, he held that government should be suffused with Christianity.

As regards the kingdom of this world, the political kingdom, Godet held that sovereignty came from God. If fault there was in government, then that fault stemmed from 'man's general imperfection'. Godet's doctrine was, according to the commentator Roget, 'that when once an authority is set over a community, individuals owe to it the obedience to superior powers demanded of them by St Paul'. Said Godet: 'Obey, though the government to which you are subjected should be the outcome of violence and sedition. Refrain from trusting your own judgement as to the legitimacy of that power.' To many modern eyes this will seem unacceptably conservative.

But these were not merely theoretical positions: they grew out of immediate situations and were tested in practice (on at least two critical occasions).

From 1815, and even more so after 1848, the status of Neuchâtel was ambiguous, linked to the Swiss Confederation, but subject to the King of Prussia. Oaths of loyalty were taken to both. As tutor to his liege's grandson and as Royal Chaplain in Neuchâtel, and yet respecting the will of the republican majority, Godet felt the tension in this ambiguity more than most common citizens. An oath to him was a serious, indeed a sacred, matter. And he was pledged to both sides. Fortunately, the House of Hohenzollern was remarkably restrained in its reaction to the republican coup. Godet himself, as an act of conscience, refused to accept further remuneration, although he was allowed to keep the title of Royal Chaplain.

But there was an even more serious problem. The church in Neuchâtel was faced with a similar dilemma to the one that had confronted Vaud not long before. In Vaud, the government of the church had passed into the hands of the state, thus precipitating the secession of the 'Free Church' (one of whose founders was the father of Adolphe Mabille). Since the Reformation, the church of Neuchâtel had not been an ordinary state church: it was independent of political power, and authority resided in the hands of a 'vénérable classe' of ministers. In the 1820s, the 'Réveil' spread rapidly through the parishes: this movement was a protest against clerical dominance in the church, whether of the papist or Calvinist variety. The 'venerable company' of pastors never did comprehend the changes nor the role demanded by the laity in the practical affairs of the church. It was a matter of time before the pot boiled over. For the first time since the sixteenth century, the cohesion of the reformed church was threatened.

The King, to whom appeal was made, hesitated, and while he did so a 'free church' began to separate itself off. Then the 1848 republic allowed full liberty of worship to the dissident church. It was a knife-thrust to the heart of the company of pastors. They knew their days of rule were numbered, but they refused to allow the ancient autonomy of the church to be swallowed up by the state, so they vested their authority in the membership of the church. Godet played a key role in this. He laid down the principles for the new dispensation: the powers of the venerable company were put into the hands of the synod elected by parish members; parish ministers were to be directly elected by the people; and the Theological School fell under the synod's sway. The national church thus survived intact until 1873.

Meanwhile Godet had become the teacher of biblical exegesis in the church. He was so well respected that, when Prussia finally renounced all interest in its former principality in 1857, he was invited to lead the service which inaugurated the new parliament of the republic the following year. He remained on close terms with Prince Frederick William, although he exchanged the title of Royal Chaplain for that of Chaplain to the Republic. With a chair in the Divinity School, he began a series of commentaries on the Bible for which he became famous in theological circles.

The new crisis for the church began around 1869. This was when the 'Broad Church' (those of more liberal tendencies) began to make inroads in the canton. Up until now, the state had met the expenses of the 'national' church out of a levy placed on the community. The broad church complained that this was unfair, since all the money went to the established evangelical clergy and none to them. Godet himself felt this was unfair. He did not particularly want a separation of church and state, but he did feel it wrong, despite his own evangelicism, that all the resources of government earmarked for the church went to 'the maintenance of a clergy exclusively evangelical'. He believed that such a situation should exist only with the free assent of all the contributing members. If it were necessary to compel unwilling sections of the community, then it would be better to have separation. The Franco-Prussian war in 1870 put the clash on hold for a while, but it was merely a temporary ceasefire.

A relatively minor incident in 1872 illustrates some of the issues at stake and some of the passions involved. The entire episode was captured in correspondence published in a supplement to the *Journal Religieux* of 19 October 1872.

F. Guillermet, a pastor from Geneva, wrote to Édouard Jacottet's uncle Léopold, pastor in the national church at La Chaux-de-Fonds, asking permission to use the pulpit of his church to give a lecture. He felt constrained to add, openly, that he was of a 'liberal tendency'. Léopold Jacottet vigorously turned down the request. A few years earlier, before the 'explosion' of their religious struggles, this would have been possible, he wrote. Now it was not. Between the Christianity which called itself 'liberal' and that which called itself 'evangelical' there was an abyss. While the former claimed as essential only 'the moral side of the Gospel', the latter, to which he linked himself strongly, considered no less essential the supernatural doctrine and facts of the Holy Scriptures. His conscience as a pastor and a Christian absolutely forbade him to cede his pulpit, since this would give the impression that he was indifferent to the differences. Pastors of the evangelical persuasion should preach in evangelical churches, liberal pastors in liberal churches. This would avoid the confusion of principles.

Guillermet would not leave well alone. So he replied. He said that contrary to the principles of Jacottet, *he* would be happy to yield his pulpit in Geneva for a lecture, as his church did not rest on any specific confession of faith, and he and his colleagues believed it was good for their congregations to be exposed to a variety of Christian ideas. They were then in a position to examine all things and keep what was good. Should Jacottet not sweep away the limitations of his thought, he asked. Could a deep abyss exist between pastors who pursued the same goal? Did they not work, in the sight of God, to produce amongst their brethren the regeneration of their hearts and the sanctification of their lives? Why build a Wall of China between their endeavours when they could call on each other's services, and when there were souls and consciences to be reached and awakened?

Guillermet was so pleased with his own showing that he went even further. He published the correspondence up to that point – without asking his respondent's permission!

In return, he got a flea in one ear and a cuff around the other from an irate Léopold. He also got a lecture in contemporary comparative theology.

Léopold Jacottet first pointed out that it was not exactly true that Guillermet's church was without a confession of faith: though there was no confession of *particular* faith, the synod in 1851 had stated that their church had a rule of faith in the Holy Scriptures, in the two sacraments of baptism and holy communion, and in the Apostles' Creed.

He then spelled out a number of differences between the liberals and the evangelicals. For liberal Christians, the Bible was not a sovereign authority and a matter of faith, but instead reason and conscience could take what suited them and reject what did not; for evangelical Christians, reason and conscience must bow before the revelations made in the Holy Scriptures. For the liberals, God was chained to the laws of nature; for the evangelicals, God was free to do as He pleased. For the liberals, Jesus was the first and greatest religious originator, but also a man like the rest of us, neither more nor less the son of God than other men; for the evangelicals, Jesus was the only and beloved Son of God, the Word made flesh. For the liberals, sin was merely an imperfection inherent in human nature, for which the individual was not finally responsible; for the evangelicals, it was an outrage against divine sanctity, which earned the sinner damnation and death. For the liberals, one could be saved without faith – yes, had Jacottet not heard justification by faith denounced as a dangerous doctrine which annihilated moral obligation? For the evangelicals, there was salvation only in Jesus Christ.

Léopold Jacottet did not understand, furthermore, how Guillermet could still believe in regeneration: according to liberal Christianity, there were not even souls to save, since none are lost and God is too good to punish sinners in eternity.

As for the Wall of China, it was not the evangelicals who had built it, but the liberal pastors, when they abandoned the better part of the Gospel and the two great principles placed by the founders of the Reformation at the base of Protestantism: knowledge of the sovereign and infallible authority of the Word of God; and knowledge of the doctrine of justification through faith in Jesus, dead for our sins and resurrected for our salvation. How could Guillermet preserve a united church out of two different religions?

In this way, Léopold Jacottet set out two very different views of God and of man.

He himself did not have too many illusions about man, at the least. He cast a cold eye on the human spirit and was not blind to its dark recesses.

The crisis came to a head in 1873. The majority Liberal Party proposed changing the ecclesiastical law, reducing the powers of the synod and guaranteeing liberty of conscience to all ministers, so that they could be restricted neither by doctrinal precepts, nor by a confession of faith, nor by church discipline. The future training of pastors was taken away from the synod and put in the hands of a new Academy answerable to the state.

The most articulate opposition to this bill came from Édouard Jacottet's father. Henri-Pierre Jacottet delivered a paper to a conference on 8 April. He objected strongly to the new dispensation on legal and moral grounds, while his indignant anger bubbled below the surface. Firstly, he contended that the 1848 constitution had guaranteed that all changes which affected the foundation of the national church must be ratified by the people. The State Council (the executive branch of government) said that a referendum was not necessary, since the proposed law did not entail a separation of church and state; but Jacottet countered that, by law, any fundamental change to the church must be referred to the people's vote.

Secondly, he was aghast at the inevitable consequences of the envisaged legislation. Like Godet, he respected the rights of the liberal breakaway from the national Protestant church, going so far as to say 'their right is equal to ours'. The solution was clear: separate the church and the state, and the state could devote equal resources to both churches. But the State Council chose a different route. Its real aim was to incorporate liberal Protestantism into the evangelical church. Its avowed aim was the liberty of ecclesiastical conscience, and this was 'inviolable'. Henri-Pierre was adamant that the result would be the exact opposite: 'It is precisely in the name of liberty and equality that I reject the bill, which sacrifices these things.'

No longer would any measure of the synod be compulsory for the parishes or pastors. The synod would no longer have a say in the choice of ministers, and anyone with an equivalent licence could become a minister. Ministers would be chosen in future by a majority of 'Protestants' (now loosely defined as anyone who was not a Catholic or a Jew, including liberals, pantheists, deists, spiritualists, atheists, and the like). Once chosen for a period of six years, they could not be removed by the synod or the parish – no matter what doctrines they suddenly started preaching or even if they went insane.

In effect, the new law embodied the liberal agenda. The State Council was suggesting that the Protestant church did not have, nor need, unity of doctrine. With only thinly disguised irony, Henri-Pierre was prepared to accept equality with a religious association which did not recognize the truth, which searched for it without hope, and which was dedicated to controversy and criticism. He was even prepared for the state to devote equal resources to it. But he was not prepared to allow his own beliefs and his own church to be swamped by it. Prayer! Baptism! The Eucharist! These were fundamentals which could never be surrendered.

His third point concerned nothing less than the truth. His scorn for the relativism of the liberals was barely concealed. Beyond the democratic principles against which the bill delivered heavy blows, he placed 'another interest, which offends even more, the interest of the Truth'. For him the truth lay in evangelical doctrine. On this he could not and would not compromise.

This principle, and indeed the entire argument, was clearly communicated, in his forensic manner, to his fifteen-year-old son Édouard.

As a counter to this bill, its opponents, following Henri-Pierre, asked for a revision of the constitution in order to separate church and state. In a referendum in September, they lost by sixteen votes in an overall turnout of 13 690! The disqualification of 108 ballots further confused the outcome. The Grand Council, however, did not hesitate and immediately passed the law without conceding another referendum. The unity of the reformed church of Neuchâtel, dating back to the days of Farel, was no more.

For his part, Godet could not accept, before God, a church 'in which the pulpits would be accessible to others than evangelical clergymen'. He was no Free Churchman, but he now saw no alternative to a Free Church. On 25 September, a few days after the referendum, eighteen members of the old synod, including Godet and Édouard's uncle Léopold, seceded to form L'Église Évangélique Neuchâteloise Indépendante, the Independent Evangelical Church of Neuchâtel. The entire staff of the Faculty of Theology, headed by Godet and including another of Édouard's uncles, Frédéric, a professor, declared their allegiance to the Free Church, and on 14 October the Faculty reopened as part of the future secessionist church. On 3 November, a constituent synod met and the new church was born. Amongst the founders were members from families such as De Rougemont, Favarger, Junod, Clerc-Barrelet, Courvoisier, Jaquet, Du Pasquier, De Pourtalès and De Montmollin, as well as the Godets and Jacottets. In this way the Independent Church made of itself 'une Église libre', but not 'une Église liberale': it was a free church but it was by no stretch of the imagination a liberal church.

—◦⊖—

The strain of these events might have killed Henri-Pierre Jacottet. On 5 October, ten days after the initial secession, while climbing the hill to his house in Hauterive, he had a fatal heart attack. He was only forty-five. It was a devastating blow to his second son. Édouard adored his father and wanted to imitate the decisiveness of his character and the clarity of his mind, though at an early age, it seems, he decided to follow his uncles into the church, despite his father's misgivings.

A few years after Henri-Pierre's death, when he had taken the further decision to become a missionary, Édouard wrote to his close friend Eugène Hoffet about his father: 'It is necessary to have lived with him for a long time to know completely what he was. I have never known a man so freely guided by the single task for which he was prepared to sacrifice everything: his whole life, he devoted himself to the good of others. I am convinced that he was completely happy, although sad, too, to see me take this vocation. I was happy to be able to tell him, and to think, that I was acting under his influence. I, who am so different from him in all ways, and who have never possessed the brilliant talents that he had, would like to resemble him in this way: doing all my work, whatever the cost, I would hope that my work does not bring me into conflict with the deepest sentiments of my heart. But we do not choose our path, we must go where God leads, and I believe the path he is showing me is truly the one I shall take.'

Somewhat paradoxically, then, Édouard saw his vocation as a tribute to his father.

Hoffet, for his part, thought that Édouard inherited 'the uprightness of his mind' from his father, 'one of the most renowned men in the history of the canton of Neuchâtel'.

Jacottet received both a classical and a theological education. After passing his baccalaureate in his home-town college, he entered the Faculty of Theology of the Independent Church in 1877. There he was given an introduction to the books of the Old and New Testaments, and an exegesis of Corinthians, Philippians and I John by Godet. He was also taught the history of the church from its beginning up to Gregory I by his uncle, Frédéric Jacottet; Exodus by M. Barrelet; and systematic and dogmatic theology by M. Gretillat.

To the young men who studied under him, Godet was a 'fatherly friend', earning for himself the 'rights of a spiritual parent'. He was a man of scholarship and an admirer of natural beauty. His faith and his life, even in the highest royal courts, were simple. Even into the last years of his life (he died in 1900), his leisure was to stride up into the mountains which he loved. In the busy ebb and flow of modern 'scientific' biblical criticism, he seemed to his students like 'a solid evangelical rock'.

—◦◦—

After his father and Godet there was a third influence on Édouard, the exact nature of which is much more difficult to calculate. In May 1880, Édouard, perhaps on the prompting of Godet, left Neuchâtel to study in Germany. The University of Tübingen to which Édouard went for the summer semester was something of a curiosity, since it had both Catholic and Protestant theological faculties. The doyen of the Protestant faculty, until his death in 1860, had been F.C. Baur. Now Katusch was in all his glory at Tübingen, and Jacottet enjoyed his lectures. What he appreciated was the deep distinction Katusch made between science and faith, while at the same time showing that scientific research was also the sacred task of the Christian theologian (science here included textual, philological and historical study of the Bible and the great mass of other religious concerns). Jacottet, however, could not shake off the chill he felt while attending these lectures, since the Christian life was given so little place in them.

In October, Jacottet moved to the University of Göttingen where, for a year, he attended the classes of Ritschl, Schulz and the philosopher Hermann Lotze. Above all, he was impressed by Ritschl, and many of his letters to Hoffet bore witness to the profound influence this distinguished theologian, so significant in Protestant theology in the last quarter of the century, had on him.

Albrecht Ritschl studied at Tübingen under Baur, and for a while looked set to follow in his tracks. But Ritschl was not going to be anyone's follower, and, when he moved to Göttingen to become professor ordinarius in 1864, abandoning the Hegelianism of Tübingen, he soon drew many students to his courses. He published extensively, his most important work, which appeared between 1870 and 1874, being *Die christliche Lehre von der Rechtfertigung und Versöhnung* (or *The Christian Doctrine of Justification and Reconciliation*).

Ritschl was extremely popular amongst Protestant theologians of the nineteenth century, battered as they were on the one side by the empirical sciences (casting a great shadow of doubt on the infallibility of the Bible) and on the other by idealist metaphysics. He swept away the accumulated clutter of the centuries, the thick dust of scholastic subtleties and the false odours of Hellenistic intellectualism, and replaced them with a Christian faith of undefiled purity through the cleansed message of the Gospel. Under the influence of the neo-Kantian Lotze, Ritschl rejected metaphysics (and with it Hegelian idealism), insisting on the irreducibility of religion to other forms of experience. While he agreed with Kant that things-in-themselves were unknowable in their static form, he did not go along with the idea that we have access only to appearances or phenomena. Ritschl had his own epistemology. Things-in-themselves are knowable through their *actions* on us and our responses to them. Metaphysics could only produce an abstract First Cause, or a Supreme Being, or, in the case of Hegel, an Absolute. Knowledge of God could not be attained through pure reason. But for Ritschl, God could be found, and could only be found, through the revelation specific to the Christian religion.

Ritschl's repudiation of metaphysics and his insistence on the historical revelation of God in Christ no doubt appealed to the evangelicalism ingrained in Jacottet.

Knowledge of God comes not by reason but by faith, not by intellectual apprehension of facts but by what Ritschl famously called 'value judgements'. These value judgements 'are of the heart and not of the head', and there is in the human heart a need of God. Nevertheless, his position was not a relativist one: these value judgements are not subjective, they are related to what is really out there; and they reflect the effect real things have on humankind in terms of pleasure and pain. What is important to the religious person is the 'practical worth' of these things or objects in striving towards the ideal life.

Ritschl tended to be preoccupied more with this world than the next. As one of his commentators, Ernest Edghill, has pointed out, for Ritschl 'the best proof of Christian truth is Christian life: and were this practical proof more in evidence, the demand for theoretical demonstration would cease'. Another, Alec Vidler, adds that 'for Ritschl the Kingdom of God was ethical, rather than eschatological. He had little to say about eschatology or the last things. It was the progressive establishing of the Kingdom of God in history that absorbed all his interest. Believers are redeemed by Christ from sin, that is, from the self-assertion that spreads ruin through the social order, by being brought into the Kingdom of God so that they may participate in the work of the Kingdom. The object of Christ's redemption is not individual but the community. The Church consists of the members of the Kingdom united in prayer and worship.'

Finally, in the house of Ritschl, there was no room for mysticism, not in the study, nor in the dark pantry, nor even in a broom cupboard. His fundamental presupposition was that beneath the phenomena, the bric-a-brac of things, there was an ultimate unknowability.

—⁊⊘—

The special talent Édouard had for learning foreign languages not only allowed him to understand the German theologians who taught him, but also to do the work in his later years which his fellow students at Göttingen could not believe he had written. Speaking to Hoffet years afterwards about his linguistic studies in southern Africa, he said that his greatest pleasure 'was discovering a new language, learning it from the lips of the local people themselves and creating syntax and grammar from all the pieces'.

But he was away from home and lonely, and he did not much like the Germans. He confided his prejudices to his brother Henri, whom he envied living in gay Paris. Tübingen had 'bored him to death', he wrote. Göttingen, although bigger, was scarcely more beautiful. The houses were badly built, the roads deficient and mainly mud. When it rained the pavements became lakes. Even worse was the surrounding countryside – entirely flat, with here and there sparse hills which the locals called mountains.

About the inhabitants of this doubtful paradise, little good could be said. The people, grasping and cantankerous, were philistines, and the students all the same. If anything he preferred those in the north to those in Tübingen. In the south he felt as though he were living in the Germany of Tacitus; at least Göttingen seemed a few centuries in advance. He had been four months eating his meals at the same table and no one had exchanged a single word with him, nor did any of his companions at table know each other's names. The only redeeming factor was his friendship with Eugène Hoffet, the Alsatian, with whom he corresponded regularly.

There was also something more specific that disturbed Jacottet. He disliked clericalism in general: but here Protestant clericalism was followed blindly all along the line. And he was truly incensed at the orthodox crusade, filtering in from Berlin, against Judaism. At Göttingen, the students had made their anti-Semitic position known by adopting several resolutions at a meeting, thus making themselves look absolutely ridiculous in Jacottet's eyes. Beyond this, he continued to detest Prussia, and was concerned that the younger generation was becoming more and more Prussian.

Given his isolation, it is no wonder that he was impressed by the forceful personality of Ritschl and attracted to his ideas about community and the progressive development of the Kingdom of God. Édouard Jacottet was waiting for something to happen.

—◦◦—

This was in February. After spending the summer term in Göttingen, Édouard returned home in order to register again at the Theological Faculty in Neuchâtel, whose academic year began in October. Eugène Hoffet, who was to join him in the same class, became a regular visitor at the Jacottet house, with the approval of Mme Jacottet and to the delight of Édouard's three sisters, Isabelle, Cecile-Louise and Hélène. His manners were impeccable and he became the 'cavalier' to the four women, though most particularly to Isabelle.

Before restarting his studies, Édouard was no doubt at a loose end, so his fancy turned elsewhere. The shrewd Cecile-Louise, charming, poetic and as perceptive as Sherlock Holmes, kept a wry eye on his activities and reported them in September to her eldest brother in Paris in typically vivacious style: 'He is completely captivated by the charms of Ida, calls her an accomplished young girl and speaks of going to fetch her, in a time rather "distant".' Cecile-Louise gently and affectionately undercut this, however, by adding: 'But since many young ladies have already inspired in him an unquenchable passion which has been promptly cut as it flowered, we are very calm.'

His family clearly knew Édouard well. His adoration of Ida may have been intense, but it does not seem to have outlasted October. Towards the end of the month, the Jacottets entertained with an evening of dancing. Édouard announced that he would not dance himself: no sooner had he done so than a pair of black-diamond eyes persuaded him otherwise. The eyes belonged to seventeen-year-old Louise Barrelet, who was at the same school as his sister. At every turn, Édouard quizzed Cecile-Louise as to whether she had seen *her* at school, and chided her as 'vilaine Louise' when she said that she did not actually know Mademoiselle Barrelet!

Édouard, stepping nimbly round his pledge, danced from seven o'clock that night to one the next morning.

—◦◦—

There were three other students in their third year of studies at the Theological Faculty, one of whom was Eugène Hoffet, but the professors were the same as before. Hoffet was amazed at how hard Édouard worked. He was always trying to know and understand. He loved contradiction, and freely cultivated paradox, not as wilful obfuscation, nor to show off, but always to create a discussion from which he could benefit. In the lively interchanges that invariably resulted from his lectures on the New Testament, Godet liked to ask the opinion of the 'doctor subtilissimus', for whom he had a particular affection. In return, Édouard, while not always sharing his professor's views on dogma, nor his critical results, held Godet in the highest esteem and greatly appreciated his guidance. Happily comparing him to the lecturers he had listened to in Germany and elsewhere, Édouard always sought out Godet's advice in the most difficult moments of his career. Before the scrupulous conscience, warmth of heart and holy enthusiasm of this good and humble servant of God, all Édouard's doubts faded and awareness grew, together with a love of the truth and a desire to devote his life to heavenly things.

Godet's watchword was patience. He said man's initiative should not precede the time appointed by God, and it was, perhaps, more important to know how to wait than to know how to do. It was better to wait for God and walk with Him, like Enoch, or behind Him, than to anticipate Him, like David. This was good and steady advice for a young and somewhat impulsive student who was wrestling with the new ideas he'd encountered and with the limits imposed on human reason. Édouard's favourite saying was, 'Amicus Plato, magis amica veritas', and this is what allowed him to confront the most difficult problems without fear or hesitation. 'I have an idea of the perfect truth of Christianity too exalted for any critical analysis to overturn it; so that, for me personally, these studies do not have a bad result; I think they must be undertaken in a Christian spirit, that is, seriously, without allowing oneself to be guided by prejudice or predisposition, and asking God to show us the truth Himself. And, in the end, if all the criticisms are true, what comes of it? That the Old Testament is not the fruit of a special revelation of God? Not at all, but simply this: our human ideas are wrong on this point. I have become more and more convinced of this truth, that religion has nothing to fear from criticism.'

Having ascended to this assured overview – the great truth for him – of the relations between scientific theology and religious life, in which the echo of Ritschl can be clearly heard, it was not surprising, Hoffet noted, that Jacottet did not suffer fools gladly and found it difficult to tolerate doctrinal narrowness, either amongst theologians or in certain ecclesiastical circles. He confided to Hoffet his frustration: 'It is certainly easier to allow in dogma and traditions with the eyes closed, in the Catholic way; and if, with this, you have no life, you will be left alone. You have signed a confession of faith, you avoid with conviction any personal search which could shake one of your immutable, sacrosanct and fundamental beliefs; you have the right to live in peace; you are not dangerous, and no one troubles your tranquillity. But let one want an exact and biblical idea of Christianity, have a living and personal faith, which one looks to as a duty to enquire about what we preach and are supposed to practise, then you are a dangerous man against whom anything is allowed and to whom the duty of charity no longer applies. I am deeply saddened; but I can do nothing.' He ended this plaint somewhat dramatically, 'Ah! the light and the life!'

Nevertheless, he did appreciate largeness of heart in others and, for its sake, could forgive disagreement with his own ideas. Despite the joy he got from his scientific studies and the lengthy debates he liked to indulge in, he had deep respect for true and loyal piety, and counted amongst his close friends more than one student who could not emulate his research nor share his preoccupations.

Providence has its secrets, working below the surface of things. Sometimes it produces the opposite of what is expected.

The Mabilles were exhausted when they landed at Le Havre in July 1880. They had been in continuous service for twenty-one years, without having seen their homeland. But there was a great pleasure in store, at least for Adèle, as they made their way towards Paris to stay with her father, Eugène Casalis, now sixty-eight years old and in some pain, but still mentally alert. They were met off the train by her three half-brothers and one half-sister, none of whom she had ever seen. Over a half-century later one of these, Alfred Casalis, recalled the meeting in a letter to Edwin Smith: 'We looked upon our sister Adèle as a heroine. I still see myself at the station, fifty-six years ago, slightly awed by Adolphe Mabille's patriarchal and austere presence, but immediately at home with my big sister, Adèle, my elder by twenty-two years, who strained me to her heart, called me "my little Fred" as if she had known me all her life, her eyes beaming with tenderness. Those two noble souls very soon won their way into our hearts.'

For several months, Mabille was under strict orders from his doctors to take things easily. So at first he confined himself to the revision and editing of the Bible, and seeing it to the press. Distress at the suffering of the Basotho in the Gun War and frustration at not being there to share it, however, soon drove him to intense political activity, lobbying the British government, helping organize a petition of 24 000 signatures, and being one of a delegation to visit the Colonial Secretary, Lord Kimberley – all with the intention of persuading the imperial government to intervene to save the Basotho.

It was only in 1881 that Mabille had strength and time enough to undertake the arduous task of lecture tours to drum up support for the mission. In this Adèle and Adolphe started at home. Every day, Adèle told her younger siblings not fairy tales but true stories of Africa, while Adolphe proofread the Bible galleys and sometimes, laughingly, added an idea of his own: 'When they returned to South Africa, they left behind them, in numberless hearts, the memory of their absolute consecration to the mission and to God – a memory which later became the source of other vocations. They both literally radiated joy.' One of the people whose hearts were touched was Alfred himself, eighteen at the time, and he was to join the mission in Lesotho in 1889.

The Coillards were in France at the same time. François Coillard was trying to raise money and support for his proposed Barotse mission. His appeal was in terms of Christ's last command, 'Preach the Gospel to every creature.' Coillard and Mabille were men of great energy and passion. Both were so close to their God that they spoke as if He were in the room with them. They had a great revitalizing influence on many they came in contact with. 'What would our Reformed churches have become without M. Coillard and without missions?' asked an old French Protestant a few years later. He answered his own query, 'Nothing but a tomb.'

Both Coillard and Mabille came to Switzerland to speak. Jacottet heard neither – he was away in Germany. Their words got through to him by a circuitous route, but nevertheless struck him 'like an arrow in the heart'.

Even after he returned to Neuchâtel to resume his studies at the Faculty of Theology, Édouard was not entirely at ease with himself. In 1882, he passed his examinations and presented his thesis on 'La Théorie de la Rédemption'. Because of his somewhat radical ideas it was not accepted by his more orthodox teachers without reservation, though it did show the extent of his knowledge and deep faith. The time for his consecration was close. But certain (unnamed) experiences had made him, he said, 'excessively sceptical with regard to his preaching', feeling that he 'would never succeed', and he hesitated before the humbling task 'which I did not choose, but which I am certain God destined for me'. Now that he was so close, he said, 'I fear it and I know how unworthy I am, particularly when I see how those far more worthy than I are overwhelmed by it. Oh, if God only asked those who present themselves to recognize their unworthiness and to have the feeling of weakness! But He also claims from them the strength that comes from above, communion with Him … He says: Be always joyous, yet I am never in Him!'

Nevertheless, God seems to have been nearer than Édouard thought, and His instruments were the Lesotho missionaries. The human mind is a strange thing: it can love, and hate, at great distances, beyond the confines of the senses. Even though it usually responds to and acts on present and selfish needs, the trigger might be something remote, something fled away into the night. Édouard was an unlikely candidate for conversion. Half in love with linguistic study and scriptural criticism, he was also constantly reminded of Godet's strictures concerning a hasty decision: in no man is the grace of God inactive. By an excess of words, and by too urgent entreaty, we may hinder its action. An atmosphere of confidence, of trust, a servant of God may create between Him and the object of His care, or may find it to exist. But he may also destroy it, or prevent its appearance, and then what he may do or say is useless, nay, positively injurious to the working of the Spirit of God. Or, as Godet said, a steady flame amid embers is worth more than the quick fire of a revival. To reap a sudden reward is not good for the heart. Instead of being quickened and won slowly to God, it is lulled to sleep after a short excitement. Édouard's calling to missionary work was therefore not an easeful or painless one, as he confided in a letter to Hoffet.

It is tonight with a certain stenochoria [distress] that I write to you. I have something very important to tell you and wish to ask you for your serious advice and help. It is a grave decision that I am to take, and whichever way I choose will affect my entire career. I was greatly struck, a few weeks ago, by a paragraph which was probably making the rounds of the religious press, announcing that M. Mabille was returning to Basutoland sad at not having found a young minister willing to accompany him there to take charge of a flock. Since then this thought hounds me continuously, and I ask myself if this obsession of my mind is not a call from God, or whether it is not merely one of those Romantic ideas which one often has. I am actually totally unhappy. At first, it seemed to me a simple and easy matter; now I understand the immense sacrifice it will require, and that it is my whole life that I must give. It is impossible to ask you for categorical direction since, if I decide against, it would be better that my thoughts are not known. Besides, it would be alarming if self-consciousness caused me to retreat.

This, in my opinion, is the state of things. To begin with, there is the feeling I experienced on reading this item, a feeling which persists, even though I no longer see things dressed in that ideal mantle which covers, in the eyes of many, the work of the missions, but, on the contrary, I see clearly all that I will have to give up and the difficult task I must confront there. Then there is the indubitable fact that, with the increasingly determined cast of my mind, it is in the direction of scientific theology I will turn if I stay in Europe. And I wonder if I can really be as useful to man and work for God in studying patristic theology or reformed dogma than in giving myself entirely to mission work ... I fear that here the demon of theology will stop me from doing my work as I should, either in a large or small parish, and that, the temptation being always present, I will give in to it too easily … I ask myself if I should not make this sacrifice, if God is not asking me to. I find it natural in others, but I cannot resolve it when it is about myself. How I wish to see my life actually mapped out!

It is likely that the unorthodox ideas of Ritschl and others rendered Jacottet suspect in the eyes of his examiners; it remains to be studied if and how these ideas persisted in his thinking for the rest of his life; but it is certain that Ritschl had prepared him to turn away from a career in 'scientific theology' and dogma towards the more practical life of a missionary.

His conversion did not come in the rush of an angel's beating wings, nor in a blinding flash of light. It was a slow happening, more commensurate with Godet's admonitions. It was a wrestling of intellect and faith rather than an epiphany. A few months after reading the newspaper paragraph, he met a French soldier, returned from Senegal, on a train. The soldier, young in age, old in experience, told him of the hardships Europeans had to endure in the African climate, and of the horrors of the colonial war. Édouard was greatly moved by the conversation, which finally turned religious, and he saw in it a sign: 'It seems to me that there is something too providential in this meeting that it should amount to nothing. What beautiful work there is to be done there! This thought follows me and disturbs me. Does it mean I should go? I know that this seems quite strange, almost mad; but this meeting is not the result of chance; it is willed by God, and to what end? I know that it could be something other than God; but I cannot dispel the idea that it is indeed Him. At any rate, I feel I am closer than ever to a decision – that of becoming a missionary – and that, in deciding, I must avoid all personal desire for well-being or material concerns. This kind of sacrifice must be complete, otherwise it could emanate from within us, instead of from God.'

There is a revealing vignette of Jacottet's personality at this time drawn by his friend Henri Junod. Jacottet was regarded by his fellow students as a very forceful theologian, who held advanced ideas on the book of Daniel, for instance, and disagreed with Godet on the Greek epistles. His nickname was Faiblet, though Junod thought he did not warrant it. Everyone was sure that after a few years in a parish had knocked a bit of sense into him, he would take up a chair at the Faculty. He was one of the brightest stars, headed for a certain future at the top.

But he took Junod by surprise. One day, he invited his friend for a stroll through the beautiful village of Valangin near Neuchâtel. He began by having some fun at Junod's expense, teasing him by expounding a string of hetero-doxies. Then, suddenly, he became very serious. 'Henri,' he said, 'I am going to become a missionary; I am going to leave for Africa.' 'A missionary, you, Jacottet!' blurted out Junod. 'Yes,' came the reply, 'I feel God calling me. It is stronger than me.'

Junod, who was to become a missionary himself with the Swiss Mission in the northern Transvaal, rejoiced, and his affection for Jacottet doubled. When the news became known in the parish and in the Faculty, there was widespread astonishment, even stupefaction. The kind of surprise only God can spring.

The paradox of Jacottet is encapsulated here. Speaking at the time of his death, Junod was quite open. Jacottet, he conceded, was not equally agreeable to everyone. He was a marvellous debater, he was truly a virtuoso of paradox, and he could shock and scandalize those who took his assertions too seriously. But deep down, to those who knew him, he was a true and faithful friend; and at the core of his being, he was a humble and conscientious believer.

Junod recalled how once, when they were trying to solve some problem or another, Jacottet had fixed him with those watchful and unwavering blue eyes of his and concluded, 'After all, there is God.' Faith was belief, not proof. This great fighter, this great intellectual, thought Junod, *believed*, and believed with a bitter intensity.

—⌾—

In many ways, the families of missionaries sacrificed more than the missionaries did themselves. Édouard's mother, having given her husband to heaven and her eldest son to Paris, was reluctant to offer up her second son to darkest Africa. The contest must have been fierce, but the outcome was predetermined. Édouard was convinced from early on that he must follow the path of service marked out by his father rather than stay with his mother. 'Oh, I can tell you, it is now that I am able to realize in part all the renunciations I shall have to make and the sacrifices I face, for myself and for others. Certainly, it is more difficult to make others suffer than to suffer myself, because I know what I want, what I am doing, and I shall have, in my future career, compensations which my mother will not recognize. The more it seems that I have been called by God, and urged to go and serve him on African soil, the more my own ideas are in conflict with this call.'

In early June 1882, thoughts of Africa were still 'the order of the day', and he went to Geneva to speak with M. Théodore Vernet on that specific subject. His mother reluctantly admitted to Henri that perhaps the missionary life would suit his nature, which was inquisitive, active, and inclined to dominate.

Together with two others, Édouard Jacottet was ordained in the town of his birth on 13 June 1882. His old mentor gave the accompanying sermon. Édouard wrote to Hoffet, confirming that his agony continued. Again, in the light of what was to happen in his whole life – even to the very end – his letter is worth reproducing in full.

One of the most important steps of my life has been undertaken; I say one, but it is, in fact, two. Though not definitely having decided in favour of the mission, I felt that, finally, it was to the missionary ministry that I was consecrated. I can do no more, I feel that I do nothing and let myself do so. It is an impulse I cannot resist in good conscience. It seems to me that, like Hernani, I could say, 'I am a moving force.' But yesterday's ceremony, the speech which was so serious and yet so consoling by M. Godet, especially the oath that I took to forsake everything to follow Jesus Christ, it is this that gives me new strength within myself, as well as in others. I see the path to follow more and more clearly, a path which is difficult at the start, but will certainly become smoother for me.

It is when we feel the decisive moment approach that we can probe the depth of the sadness of such a separation. It is the naked reality which shows itself to us, the prose of life and not the glossy, poetic garment that hides all sacrifices. I believed that I could foresee all the bitterness of the decision, but the blow was even more bitter than I thought. It is extremely painful to find oneself in the presence of these words of Jesus Christ, true and painful as they are: 'He who loves his father or mother more than me, is not worthy of me' ... Dear friend, may God allow you never to know the anguish which the fulfilment of your duty may one day cause in your mother's heart. There is nothing more painful ... I have been so close to tearing the letter I have written to pieces, and to renouncing the mission forever! But I could not. The voice that spoke to me seemed to be God's. I had to follow it. I acted in good faith, with the deep conviction that it is He who has chosen for me, and not I who chose. The thought that it is He whom I follow is above all others.

The letter he refers to, which he nearly tore up, was probably the one he sent to the PEMS the day after his ordination. Reiterating his response to the anguished, and until then unsuccessful, plea of Mabille and Coillard for young missionaries, and coming clean about his mother's anxieties, Édouard asked for advice from the Committee and a meeting with them, before definitely offering his services. A note from Godet accompanied this letter: 'It is with emotion and joy that I add a few lines to those of E. Jacottet. I consecrated yesterday my dear young friend with two of his co-disciples. This is to say that I can recommend him to you honestly. He has undertaken comprehensive and meaningful studies, both literary and theological. His struggles have been deep. His faith emerged victorious, and it can now be said that it is a faith of experience. His piety is sincere and deep, his conduct beyond reproach.'

The meeting was held towards the end of June, and on 25 July Édouard wrote to the Society formally offering his services, putting no limit on the period, and adding no particular conditions. The Committee did not hesitate to accept so definite a vocation.

At this time, three other students were completing their studies at Paris headquarters: Henri Bertschy, Dorwald Jeanmairet and Ernest Mabille. They would all be future colleagues of Jacottet.

His departure for Lesotho was scheduled for early 1884. The winter of 1882–3 was spent in Glasgow, learning English and some medicine, and studying Sesotho. Within a short while, he managed to read some of the Gospels and the epistle to the Romans, no doubt in the new Sesotho translation. 'I believe that I was wrong in saying that I have nothing of the missionary in me, because I am imbued now, and every day confirms it, with a real love for the Basotho, and I am happy to think that I could devote my life to them ... As for my theology, I admit that this point concerns me greatly, but not always, and I was wrong to worry about it too much. I sometimes feel that the way I formed my vision of things, little by little, isolated me from my surroundings. However, in the confusion of my ideas, and, I can add justly, those of almost everyone else – at least those who see and think – it seems to me that one could not call enough attention to the high and eternal value of the moral life, of the life hidden in Christ and God, and to see there at the same time the beginning and the end of Christianity ... If God decides to grant me further insights, He will. This is probably a reaction in my mind and in my conscience, which have been too offended by certain exaggerations and certain dogmas ... I say to myself that the missionary must above all keep in view the good of the natives, and forsake his own personal conveniences. There are enough Societies who think they must govern and dominate; the greatest glory of the Lesotho mission has been never to do anything that looked like a good deal, always to act with the greatest disinterestedness, and I would never wish this charisma to be removed from us. Because, for those who know the story of the missions, this is a charisma so rare as to be beyond comprehension.' (Jacottet, a scholar of Greek, was using 'charisma' here in its specific theological sense of a divinely bestowed power or talent – from the Greek *kharis*, meaning grace or favour.)

'If ever you want to study this mission history,' he continued, 'prepare yourself for deceptions and a host of disillusions. There are fine acts, but, on the other hand, what stains, what acts which bruise and chill! This is, all things considered, hardly any more beautiful than the general history of the churches … The history of the missions is, however, slightly better, but it is as human, though many do not appear to have the least idea of it. And, as such, I prefer it, because it is true, and at least I have the impression that I am dealing with people and not with angels of chromolithography!'

—◦◦—

While Eugène Hoffet continued to court Isabelle Jacottet, whom he was eventually to marry, Édouard waited impatiently to leave for Lesotho. He spent some time learning how to make furniture and windows, and some time enjoying his 'beloved Alps'. He visited his uncle Léopold in La Chaux-de-Fonds, where he might have conducted an occasional service in the new church, built after the Independent Church seceded, with its grey statue of Farel in front (in modern times, some irreverent prankster has painted his footwear so that it looks as though this venerable gentleman – God forbid – has slipped outdoors in his favourite pantoufles); he might well, too, have greeted in the street a mobile little boy called Louis-Joseph Chevrolet, who would one day go off to America to see if he could make a name for himself. And sometimes he would extend the trip to take in Le Locle, a few kilometres to the west, where his uncle Charles was a watchmaker. The ride up into the Jura to these two towns was no picnic. Today the modern road tunnel has reduced the distance to five and a half kilometres; then, over the mountains on horseback, it was much longer! But it was an exhilarating trip and worth it, as Le Locle was where Louise Wilhelmine Barrelet had been born (her middle name was chosen out of respect for the Prussian king). Of all the girls who had for a moment enchanted him, she alone had retained his interest.

On 8 October 1883, in a letter to M. Boegner in Paris, Édouard announced his engagement to Louise. She had, he felt, all the gifts which would enable her to accept missionary work actively and usefully. She came from a family of undoubted piety and she knew her Saviour personally. Her parents were somewhat surprised by the engagement, and though they gave their consent, they were reluctant to let her go to South Africa so soon, especially considering her youth.

In the run-up to their wedding and departure, there appears in Édouard's letters one aspect of his complex character – a certain petulant irritation when he was under pressure and things were not going his way. This was sparked by some financial problems of the Paris Mission which meant that the departure of the Jacottets might be delayed beyond February. He replied tartly to the

Director that this was not desirable, since it was better for everyone if the difficult moments of separation were not prolonged. His mother had now accepted his course of action, but needless strain was unfair to her. Then there was the fact that arrangements had been made specifically to catch the same boat from England as the Berthouds, another Swiss missionary family, so that his wife would have the comfort of the company of fellow countrywomen. Most importantly, there was his fiancée herself, who was less certain of her own decision.

Indeed, the task Louise Barrelet had undertaken was daunting. She was going to a different world, which danced in her imagination as only a few fragments of frightening images. The companion she was about to bind herself to was a complicated and paradoxical man: he had a formidable intellect, perhaps the most brilliant mind of all the Lesotho missionaries; he was serious, academic, impatient, importunate, remote, austere, driven; he had the logicality of an organizer and a lawyer, but a quick and irrational temper; he was precise and exacting about time, but fussy in detail; he was somewhat democratic but with remnants of royalist sympathies; his progressive theology contrasted with his conservative personality; his head was progressive but his backbone was evangelical; he was leaving his mother in pursuit of his father, intent on helping build the Kingdom of God; Louise sensed in him the potential for greatness, along with a pinch of narrowness.

His own anxiety and puzzlement at her turmoil are reflected, unusually for a man so assuredly articulate, in his syntax and sense, the translation of which goes something like this: 'As for my fiancée you will not be surprised to hear that she is somehow worried about the future and that she sometimes has difficulties remaking in detail the great sacrifice that she once made in one go.'

Eventually the arrangements were sorted out – not before a string of niggling letters reached Paris from Neuchâtel – and the marriage went ahead on 7 January 1884 by civil ceremony, and in a church the following day. The Jacottets spent a few days on honeymoon at Montreux on Lake Geneva and made a brief visit to Zürich. But the ground, as Édouard said, was burning his feet. A few days before they were due to leave, a ceremony of farewell was held in the Independent Church in Neuchâtel with Rev. Coulon and Godet presiding. Édouard had never seen such a large crowd in a church of God. The building could only hold a few hundred people, but there were over two thousand outside as well. Édouard was nervous when he spoke, but delighted that missionary work was so enthusiastically supported.

On 28 January, they took the night express to Paris.

—◦◦—

Édouard was worried about their baggage as they left Switzerland (it was a constant itch of concern throughout the next two months). When he managed to detach himself from the trivia of the immediate, he checked his timepiece, and then he stared out of the window into the dark. He thought he saw a great plain peopled with the ideas of Ritschl; beyond it, like the Alps, within him almost from birth, and to which he went for inspiration, rose the grand though somewhat hard concepts, and majestic though somewhat cold vision of Calvin. What he saw was his own reflection.

CHAPTER FIFTEEN

NEW LIFE

1884

Two very different personalities still exploring each other's strengths and weaknesses, the Jacottets stayed in the French capital with the Director of the Paris Evangelical Missionary Society, Alfred Boegner, and his warm and hospitable wife.

It was customary for the mission to hold a small ceremony of farewell when any of their missionaries set out for foreign fields for the first time. So, on the evening of Monday 4 February, at the monthly service, many people gathered at the beautiful Église des Billettes to say goodbye to a missionary who was returning to work in Tahiti, and to M. Jacottet who was off to Africa. The President of the Mission Society, Georges Appia, gave a moving speech, describing, in new and original ways, the difficulties faced by the missions of the time. He pointed out that these missions were now fully grown, no longer young or adolescent as they had been in the early part of the century. Alfred Boegner himself had been present in Morija the previous year when the Basotho mission had celebrated its fiftieth anniversary. Jacottet was not going out as a pioneer – he was part of the third generation of missionaries to the country and his talents were suited to a different role.

Jacottet was expected to respond to Appia and Boegner. In the eyes of his intent audience, he seemed so serious and so spirited. He began by giving details of how he had come to his missionary vocation. Then he affirmed his strong faith: 'For me personally and those who have agreed to follow me, we are leaving because we have a conviction that we must. When God gives His children a path, sad in many ways, is it not their task to obey Him and to do so without complaint but with joy? And if it pleases Him to choose me, despite my weakness, to be one of His servants, a witness of His name in a pagan land, I would not want to see as a heavy and bitter burden what is on the contrary one of the greatest privileges that He can give me.' He remarked on the broad-based nature of the Paris Evangelical Missionary Society: 'I am not French, as you know, but our French Swiss churches are united with yours through so many links that it makes no difference. That is one of the most beautiful things about our Société, that it has brought all the sectors of French Protestantism into it. Each brings its own character, and this diversity, far from harming our work, has made it stronger and more vibrant.'

Jacottet was proud to be joining the Basotho mission in view of its great success and the 'crowd of souls brought to the faith' already. He was also sober in his assessment. 'The majority of the tribe,' he realized, 'has so far refused to give itself to God.' But he was distinctly progressive in his views, definite about the ultimate goal: 'We must also raise a new generation in Christianity, develop their conscience and intelligence, and above all try to push our young black churches toward independence, and bring them to the spiritual majority.' This was a new phase in missionary work, he continued, 'possibly not the easiest'. If the task of the later missionaries such as himself was 'less dangerous and diffi-cult' than that of their predecessors, it was also more 'delicate', and demanded tact and responsibility just as great. Finally, he was certain that the hand of the Lord was with them.

Within days, the Jacottets left for London and stayed at the Charing Cross Hotel before travelling on to the Royal Hotel in Devonshire, where they waited to embark on their Castle Mail Packets steamer at Dartmouth. The *Grantully Castle*, 3 454 tons, was only three years old, and designed to carry 380 passen-gers; built as a mailship, it could easily be converted into an armed merchant cruiser. It could take the Jacottets to Cape Town at a top speed of twelve knots.

By the time the couple reached Morija, their attitudes to the country and their own future had diverged. The months before leaving Switzerland had been a frustrating period for Jacottet himself. Delays and disappointments had scratched away at a personality that was both impatient and precise, somewhat fussy and demanding. His letters to Paris continued to niggle about times, costs and insurance. From Neuchâtel to London to Cape Town to East London, he fretted about lost and delayed baggage. But he was also motivated and driven by the fact that, once they left Neuchâtel, they were on the path he had chosen.

He thought the green and fresh countryside of England splendid, and he enjoyed the long voyage south on what he called 'a true missionary ship'. He was closest to the families of Messrs Berthoud and Jacot of the Mission Suisse Romande, brave fellow countrymen from canton Vaud, who were headed for difficult and dangerous work on the Zambezi, but he also had amiable con-versations with some English clergymen. He had at first a natural Protestant suspicion of the three Jesuit priests and seven brothers who were to reinforce the Catholic mission on the upper Zambezi, fearing his own colleagues there would probably enter into conflict with them. But, intelligent and cultured himself, he unexpectedly found Father Weld and his companions to be proper gentlemen. He found less 'choice' what he called 'l'élément colonial' on board.

When eventually the Jacottets stepped ashore at the Cape, he cursed the detestable southeaster, but within a few days he was delighted with Cape Town, though he was impatient to get on – the annual Easter Conference of the Basotho mission met in April and he was anxious to be there to start his first year in a new land with a solemn observance of the message of the empty grave. At the same time, full of gratitude to God, he had not felt so happy for a long time, finding his vocation was growing stronger and deeper by the day.

Somewhat unusually, after a few days in the Mother City, the *Grantully Castle* headed not for Port Elizabeth but for East London. Arriving there on Friday 14 March, they stayed at the Royal Hotel, and took the opportunity to make an excursion along the Buffalo river and explore the 'charming countryside'. Jacottet found the 'natives' there more pleasant than those at the Cape, and Africa continued to grow on him. They were able to leave for the north by train on the following Thursday, when their luggage finally caught up with them.

If the journey up to now was what Jacottet had dreamed of, for his wife it was more like a nightmare. While she dutifully followed her husband, Louise Jacottet had only the vaguest idea where she was going. During the Channel crossing she had been horribly ill. When the *Grantully Castle* left Dartmouth, her husband got away with a light seasickness, whereas she suffered greatly almost all the way to Lisbon. Although the subsequent voyage to Cape Town was a fair one, her stomach never settled, and her head was no better. By the time she reached East London, seasickness, fatigue and the heat had left her a little hysterical, and the 'demi repos' which was about all one could expect from a colonial hotel did not help. Jacottet regarded her condition as the inevitable consequence of a long journey.

As the train rattled northwards, she looked out bleakly on an increasingly dry land. They spent a night in Queenstown, but the line had recently been extended to Sterkstroom and they arrived there on the morning of Wednesday the 19th. They were met by the wagon which Dr Casalis, son of the pioneer missionary to Lesotho, had sent from Morija to fetch them. Sadly, Jacottet's book-learned Sesotho could not cope, and neither the driver nor the leader spoke a word of English, let alone French. They tried to communicate with Jacottet by waving their hands and pointing wildly like a pair of human wind-mills. Louise Jacottet watched bewildered as her husband, all at sea on this desert plain, tried to conjure meaning from the strange words and vehement gestures. She relied totally on Édouard, and at this moment he seemed utterly confused.

Out of nowhere, the Dutch Reformed Church predikant from Maclear made a providential appearance. This worthy clergyman in sombre black brought order to the chaos, so that the newcomers, ensconced on the wagon, were able to leave in the afternoon. Time slowed down with their new, uncomfortable, primitive form of transport. But they reached Aliwal North by Saturday night, and stayed with their PEMS colleague François Daumas. Sunday, as it should be, was a day of rest. At last, after a few days of further travel, on the morning of the following Thursday, Jacottet set foot in Lesotho.

It was a solemn moment for him as he saw, for the first time, the country where he was to spend the rest of his life.

A half-hour from the border they were met by two of their colleagues, Dr Eugène Arnaud Casalis and Hermann Dieterlen. As he shook hands with them, Jacottet felt the joy of being received into the missionary family of Lesotho. After a brief discussion and a cup of coffee, the party made its way (in Dieterlen's cart) to Morija, which they reached at nightfall and where they were greeted with the usual fanfare of flags, salutations and hurrahs. Jacottet felt able to join fully in the prayers the missionaries of Morija made to God that evening, because he and his wife were under God's special protection.

Dieterlen, then a veteran of ten years, wrote a letter to his mother every week for thirty years. He soon reported to her that the new arrival had made an excellent impression. Jacottet seemed to be an extremely intelligent man who was not content to glide over the surfaces of things; on the contrary, he had meticulously reasoned out his faith and his vocation before coming to Lesotho. He was clearly a studious intellectual, having already struggled alone with Sesotho and mastered it more quickly than others. He was up with current affairs in the country and spoke with the authority of a long-time inhabitant. 'We have in him an invaluable acquisition,' Dieterlen wrote, 'if my first impressions are correct.'

On the other hand, Mrs Jacottet, though very agreeable, was much less of a presence. Dieterlen pitied her for having to cope with a completely new way of life. Despite her obvious willingness, she was not driven by a vocation as her husband was, and there was no doubt that she would suffer spiritual and psychological torment before becoming what she must – a missionary happy with her lot. She should not weep, he believed, for the life of Europe which she had renounced.

One incident had touched Dieterlen deeply. While the party made its way towards Morija, the cart carrying him and the Jacottets very nearly overturned as they were crossing a donga. The 'poor little lady', on the edge of nervous collapse, cried out, from the depths of her soul, 'Oh, Maman!'

For Dieterlen, that said it all. She was only nineteen.

CHAPTER SIXTEEN

LITTLE CERBERUS

1884–1886

I t is worth stepping back for a moment and taking an aerial view of this little piece of earth, Lesotho. The parameters of our overview have been laid down partly by Jacottet's own hand, since he became the most prominent and knowledgeable of the mission's historians for the four decades after 1880.

The missionaries of the first generation had set about establishing the mission itself from scratch and making their faith familiar at least to the chiefs and commoners of the country. Arbousset and Casalis had been men of great curiosity, recording new discoveries almost daily.

The missionaries of the second generation – men like Mabille, Germond, Duvoisin, Jousse, Coillard, Ellenberger – had the more grinding task of making converts, of consolidating the mission, of starting new institutions such as additional mission stations, the printing works, the newspaper, schools and outstations. Most of the first generation had left by 1860 when they took over, so there was little continuity and they did not have the benefit of the experience of their predecessors. Their job was not made any easier by the series of catastrophic wars that interrupted their activities between 1858 and 1883. These were men who were products, by and large, of the Réveil, concerned mainly to evangelize, and less quixotic in their approach.

The third generation was, in one way, luckier than the second, since Mabille, Germond, Ellenberger and Duvoisin continued their work throughout the decade of the 1880s and beyond, allowing the younger men to learn from their older colleagues. Major wars were also a thing of the past. The country was now under the direct rule of Britain, though government policy had changed to one of less direct rule and influence on the daily lives of the Basotho. In the previous decade, the Cape government had deliberately undermined the authority of the Paramount Chief, Letsie, by making him, to all intents and purposes, but one leader amongst equals in a triumvirate consisting of himself and his two brothers; Molapo and Masupha ran their own territories almost as autonomous entities. The new dispensation determined to restore Letsie's primacy, as well as the power of chiefs to try cases which had been under their jurisdiction before the interference of the Cape, encouraging magistrates to consult with them whenever they could. This was to be done without military occupation forces. It was to rely almost wholly on the tact and diplomacy of the first Resident Commissioner, Lt Col. Marshal Clarke, who turned out to be ideally suited for the post.

There were, nevertheless, substantial difficulties facing the missionaries. On the political front, the 'loyalists' and 'rebels' were still at each other's throats, and Masupha flatly refused to accept the validity of British rule. He also posed a grave threat to Lerotholi, the heir apparent to the paramountcy, whose father Letsie had been weakened by age and debilitated by brandy, which was now flooding the country. The nationalist revival under Masupha, as is usual with movements trying to recapture the perceived glory of a former age, tried, too, to recreate 'the old ways', and Masupha, who had given great promise of conversion so many years ago, looked set to revert to the practices of his youth. The payment of bohali was likely to prove a crucial bone of contention in the missionaries' struggle with the traditionalists.

There was a problem even more insidious, however. Financial worries were to sap the energy and morale of the missionaries of this generation like a slow water torture; ultimately, one must surmise, they played their part in the Jacottet tragedy. In his own words, the financial burden of the missionaries during his first decade in Lesotho was 'one of the heaviest crosses' they had to bear.

While Paris paid the salaries of the missionaries – and they were never princely – those of the evangelists, trained at the Bible School and located at the outstations, had to be raised from local sources. Similarly with the teachers. Capital expenditure also had to be funded somehow, schools and churches built or repaired.

The 1870s, fuelled by relative peace and the diamond trail, had been a prosperous period for the Basotho. But the Gun War had shattered that. Church collections halved after the war, and drought brought famine and a dismal economy. In addition, when the new government took over, it had no revenue. Consequently, the subsidy to the mission's schools, which in 1880 had been over £3 000, disappeared overnight in 1883. Evangelists and teachers woke up to find themselves without salaries, or with drastically reduced ones. Many showed the depth and sincerity of their faith by carrying on at their posts regardless.

As the situation settled and taxes began to be paid, the government granted a small subsidy to the schools, increasing this as the years went by. Remarkably, the mission managed to double the number of schools between 1883 and 1892 from 60 to 132; the number of pupils more than trebled from 2 180 to 7 869; and the number of outstations also doubled from 69 to 141. The number of adult Christians also grew apace, from 4 424 in 1884 to 13 733 in 1894. Of course, this was still a small proportion of the entire population, which itself had increased from 139 000 in 1875 to 218 000 in 1891.

The 1880s saw stations established the length and breadth of the western plain, the last being Qalo in the extreme north in 1889. There were by the end of the 1880s fifteen stations – in order, from north to south: Qalo, Leribe, Cana, Berea, Thaba-Bosiu, Morija, Likhoele, Hermon, Thabana-Morena, Siloe, Bethesda (or Maphutseng), Masitise, Sebapala, and, in East Griqualand, Mafube and Paballong. Symbolically, as Qalo was established, so Mabolela was closed, thus shutting down fifty years of PEMS mission work in the Orange Free State (its stations were taken over by the Dutch Reformed Church), and concentrating all its efforts within the borders of Basutoland and East Griqualand.

This was also the period when the first real steps towards the indigenization of the church were taken. Initially these steps were faltering, but by the beginning of the following decade they became increasingly confident.

The stringent financial constraints rankled, though, in Jacottet's long memory. Years afterwards, in summing up the achievements in the face of adversity at this time, he wrote: 'We may be permitted to state that it was neither fair nor normal that this should have been so, and the mission should never have allowed its missionaries to bear such a heavy burden.'

It certainly tainted with sourness the idealism of his early years as a missionary.

—⚬—

The mission at Morija may have been long on faith, but it was certainly short of accommodation in 1884. On first arriving at Morija, the Jacottets were given the house formerly occupied by Rev. Jean Preen, who had helped Rev. Dyke at the Normal School. The house was very small and was quite a distance from the centre of the mission.

Of course, the house was lacking the fittings and facilities a nineteenth-century Swiss housewife was used to. In addition, it lacked a garden, so Mrs Jacottet had to forage elsewhere for her fruit and vegetables. However, the hospitality of their fellow missionaries was open-hearted and generous. Mrs Mabille, in particular, became like a mother to Louise Jacottet, while her daughter Aline, who was of similar age, became her close friend.

Within a few weeks, Jacottet attended his first Conference, at Masitise. The Conference of missionaries met every year, at a different venue, around Easter. Here key business of the mission was conducted: annual reports from each station were submitted, new missionaries were placed in their parishes and allocated their duties, ecclesiastical rules and discipline were discussed, conditions of service amended, the annual budget debated and agreed, and a new president and executive elected. While parishes retained considerable autonomy, the Conference did have a fair measure of control over areas of common interest, though each missionary had an equal voice in its deliberations. Jacottet had already met Mabille, Dr Casalis and Hamilton Dyke from Morija, and Dieterlen from Hermon; now he was welcomed by his host Ellenberger and his other colleagues, Duvoisin (from Berea), Daniel Keck, the younger (from Thaba-Bosiu), Kohler (from Cana), Maeder (from Siloe), Christmann (from Paballong), Cochet (who was soon to set up the new station at Mafube, near Matatiele, in East Griqualand), Preen (who was to start the Industrial School at Leloaleng), and Marzolff and Christol (who were yet to find a permanent home). Only Weitzecker (from Leribe in the north) and old Pierre-Joseph Maitin (from Berea) were absent, while Paul Germond (from Thabana-Morena) was on leave in Europe.

The Theological School, to train 'pasteurs indigènes', had had a somewhat disrupted beginning. Its existence was also somewhat controversial within the mission. Although his vision was not shared by everyone, Mabille had long believed that the eventual conversion of the Basotho lay in the hands of the Basotho themselves and the ultimate Africanization of the pastorate. To this end, he brought back with him from furlough a brilliant young man called Frédéric-Hermann Krüger. So the Theological School started in 1882 with four young teachers from Morija as its first students.

But the times were difficult, the Conference was ambivalent about the future role of the students, and Krüger's declining health had forced him back to Europe at the end of 1883. Uncertainty as to whether he would return bedevilled the planning of the School for several years.

The 1884 Conference therefore decided to let Jacottet cut his teeth on some teaching to the theological students as an interim solution. It was not to be a permanent appointment, as it was strongly felt that the Director of the School, whoever he may be in the future, should have experience of a parish. So Jacottet tried to breathe life into the embryo of the School by giving lessons on general history and a short course on the pastoral Epistles. But since the Conference had put everything on hold and refused to reopen the School formally, Jacottet felt that the students were being treated unfairly. His frustration was increased by what he described as his 'detestable Sesouto', so he also gave lessons at the Bible School and the Normal School in an effort to improve it.

His unsettled position was not alleviated when an extraordinary meeting of the Conference at the end of September once again postponed any definite decision, even though it had been informed that Krüger was too ill to return.

Jacottet's discomfort was compounded by his characteristic outspokenness, which offended some of his colleagues, particularly Rev. Weitzecker, who initially turned cold towards him. Clearly the young man's progressive ideas did not appeal to everyone, and there may have been mutterings about his teaching.

'I realize,' he admitted to Boegner, a year after his arrival, 'that once or twice, particularly in the beginning, I have been a little too sharp and maladroit, but only towards colleagues. I can say categorically that I have never said anything to my students to which the most narrowly orthodox could object ... I am not so stupid as to go and perform a work of destruction which could have grave consequences and serve no purpose.' He had, he added, always taught in a positive manner, and Mabille, who had entrusted him with giving lessons on the Old Testament to the Bible School, would not have done so had he thought his teaching dangerous for the pupils.

He felt that the only difference between himself and the majority of these gentlemen was not the substance but the form of certain doctrines.

It was not for a year – until the 1885 Conference – that Jacottet's permanent placement would be decided. The feeling that his teaching gave him merely the illusion of doing something and the demoralization brought about by his 'long novitiate' were evident in the letters he sent to Boegner. Dotted with German, Latin and Sesotho words and phrases, these letters are an invaluable source for Jacottet's thoughts and moods, since he had wrung from Boegner permission to write him non-official letters so that he would not have to sort and censor his opinions as through a sieve. Although he strongly asserted his love for the mission and his conviction that it was the right place for him to be, he was clearly irked by the fear of innovation on the part of some of his colleagues.

—⊙—

Being of an active disposition, Jacottet often climbed Makhoarane. One thing intrigued him in particular. During the last war, the missionaries had taken care of the wounded in a kind of natural fortress high above the station. There they noticed, on a huge rock, a set of tracks which resembled an extraordinary script. They identified these prints as those of a bird that must have been twice as large as an ostrich.

The missionaries speculated that when the mountains were formed, or after the Flood, there had been a muddy lake at Makhoarane. Once a great bird had come there to look for water snakes or other prey. While it searched, its feet sank into the clay, leaving their imprints. Over time, the clay hardened into stone, and the footprints with it. Even though the rock itself had shifted, the prints had lasted to this day, with neither rain, nor hail, nor sun able to erase them.

The prints became an object of curiosity, even incredulity. There was something biblical about the monstrous creature they conjured up, as though it had stepped from the Ark, speaking of birth, death and rediscovery. For sceptics who could not come to see the prints with their own eyes, the missionary artist Frédéric Christol drew sketches. Not surprisingly, comparisons were made with impressions drawn on man by the Holy Spirit, and how quickly these usually disappear like ripples on a lake after a stone has been thrown in it.

Jacottet came to the rock several times to meditate. But the Great Bird of Makhoarane remained for him a mystery.

There was one diversion from this unsettled state: his first trip into the mighty Maloti. A few months after his arrival, in October 1884, Jacottet accompanied several missionaries on a visit to the mysterious and beautiful 'Maletsunyane falls, first recorded in 1881 by the Catholic priest François le Bihan.

They rode (Mabille, Dieterlen, Dyke, Weitzecker, Jacottet, and a trader called Wells) for several days up on to the plateaux and the Hill of Thieves, then into the mountains, up ridges and down endless valleys, passing close to Thaba-Putsoa, the grey mountain, over 3 000 metres high. They were exhilarated. Such a carefree journey was like playing truant from the serious business of a missionary's life.

At night they would squeeze into a single Basotho hut – Jacottet invariably found himself closest to the door. To the close confinement and the hard floors of these makeshift hotels was added the expectation of being devoured alive by the innumerable and infinitely agile lodgers that were reputed to creep and crawl around them. The fact that no attack ever came added to the pleasure of the trip. And sheer physical weariness always ensured deep and lasting sleep.

One night their rest was disturbed when one of the Basotho accompanying them raised the alarm. 'Messieurs, Messieurs, the moon is dead!' he kept shouting. The missionaries stuck their noses out to search for the moon which had been shining with such purity and splendour when they took themselves off to sleep. And, indeed, it was gone!

It was the total eclipse of the moon which almanacs had predicted for 5 October, but which none of the travellers had given any thought to. They watched it for a while before drifting back to bed, drawn by the gravity of fatigue.

Eventually, they reached the top of the falls, which Dieterlen described as a miracle of creation. It was awesome. One by one, they crept up to the edge on their stomachs and gazed down into the abyss, while a colleague clung to their ankles to ensure their safety. From this perilous eyrie they saw the column of water propel itself downwards in a spray of white snow and lose itself in a pool which was black and ceaselessly turbulent. They estimated the height of the falls to be about a thousand feet. (The following day, when they returned with appropriate instruments, they scaled this down to 571 feet.)

After this, the main body of the visitors returned to Morija, but Jacottet accompanied Dyke right across the mountains to the east and visited Christmann at his station in East Griqualand, courageous in his isolation.

As the Jacottets settled into life in Basutoland, time began to heal the wounds of parting from home, though always a scar remained. Slowly, they started to adapt to the new land: during the drought in the summer, as the big winds swept away the clouds and the wheat drooped, they learned to desire the rain they had so often cursed in Europe. Jacottet's one fear was that life at Morija, being so much easier than elsewhere in the country, might spoil him and his wife for when they would have to move to a more remote and lonely station.

In December, to take some pressure off Mabille, Jacottet, accompanied by two evangelists, rode east over the first range of mountains to the Makhaleng river to visit an outstation which Mabille had founded there. Each night, after Jacottet had tortured his companions and the locals with his Sesotho, they slept in huts, resigned to living on coffee, bread and corned beef because of the drought, and scarcely able to close their eyes because of the insects. But Jacottet enjoyed the wildness of the mountains, which were his first love and reminded him of his homeland. His wife, however, felt that he left her a little too often to explore the neighbouring countryside.

Jacottet approached the April 1885 Conference at Mabolela with some anxiety. A place would definitely have to be found for him to start his work. There were several possibilities. The directorship of the Theological School had to be filled sooner or later; the northern part of the country had never been properly evangelized and it was a stronghold of paganism; Chief Joel was asking for a teacher and a missionary; in the south, there was concern about the future of the Bataung around Siloe (since the Catholics were making inroads there); missionary work along the valley of the Senqu and into the Maloti, it was felt, urgently needed expansion; the people of Moorosi were in danger of being lost to the mission; in East Griqualand, it was felt that the sole station at Paballong manned by Christmann was insufficient and that a second, at Mafube near Matatiele, should be established. All this meant juggling personnel.

A further problem arose. Jacottet had soon become aware of the psychological pressures on the missionary families. The most dramatic example of this was Mme Keck, wife of Daniel Keck fils. The younger Keck had taken over the station of Thaba-Bosiu from Jousse in 1882. But his wife was deeply unhappy, and she suffered, according to the minutes of the Conference, from 'an unconquerable nostalgia'. This came to a head at the beginning of 1885 in a complete breakdown, when she seems to have abandoned her family, compelling her husband to withdraw from the country. Jacottet was scornful of her behaviour. 'It is unbelievable to what extent Mme Keck shows little regret – Europe is for her the promised land, poor woman!' He felt that she had made for herself, as well as for her spouse, a future of chagrin and remorse. He did not approve of the story put out that she was a victim of the climate or the country, believing she was only a victim of herself, to be pitied, perhaps, but certainly to be blamed, too. He could not forgive her the insensitivity of leaving her family.

Nevertheless, Jacottet was concerned about his own posting. On the one hand, he dreaded the possibility of staying on at the Theological School, even though it had the advantage of being centrally based at Morija, which offered a more comfortable life. He felt his Sesotho was not fluent enough for the task, and, even more, he wanted to play an active role in pastoral work with all 'its deep joys and immediate usefulness'. The experience of this parish work was necessary, he believed, before he could teach successfully in the Theological School, and the Conference shared this view. (The post of Director of the School was only filled in 1887 when Dieterlen took over.)

On the other hand, what 'frightened' him was the possibility of being given a remote station such as the new one to be started in East Griqualand: 'I fear that my wife could not put up with the isolation.' He rather hoped that he would be sent to found the new station at Moorosi's in the south. But he was pleased that the choice was not his, and he put himself wholly into the hands of God. All he asked, echoing Ritschl, was to be useful and to be placed in some way so that he could work with all his might in the advancement of the Kingdom of God. Given their faith and the fact that his wife, despite the novel difficulties of conducting a marriage, had got over her initial homesickness, he did not think there was any need to fear a repetition of 'l'affaire Keck'.

Jacottet privately assured Boegner that he would try to stay calm and not impose his will on the decisions of the Conference. But the Keck business had alerted him to the internal politics of the mission, and he raised with Boegner the looming problem of what to do with the sons of missionaries who chose to follow in the footsteps of their fathers. Young Ernest Mabille was due to return to Lesotho after his ordination in Europe, and the consistory of Morija, no doubt under the influence of its pastor, Adolphe Mabille, had requested that the young man be stationed there. Jacottet was bitterly opposed to particular stations becoming the 'fiefdoms' of individual families and he felt that Morija was already too much a family centre. Although he welcomed the return of Ernest Mabille, he maintained that a missionary body as small as theirs risked becoming 'une petite coterie'. In the event, Lerotholi, the heir apparent to the monarchy, insisted on having a missionary, and specifically demanded the son of Adolphe Mabille; the Conference felt it could not refuse such an important chief, and in 1887 Ernest Mabille set up a new station at Makeneng (later called Likhoele).

A number of other issues occupied the 1885 Conference. Jacottet, ever alert to the wider world, was concerned about the persecution of Protestant missionaries by the colonial authorities, and he got the Conference to agree to press the Paris Committee to intervene with the French authorities on behalf of the Anglican missionaries and American Presbyterians in Gabon and the Loyalty Islands. He carried this only by a majority vote, however.

This may seem a rather obscure point. But Jacottet's sharp eye saw a lurking danger in French imperialism. It was, after all, the time when the European powers were scrambling for colonies, grabbing what they could, consolidating what they had. Jacottet strongly believed that missionary work should be disinterested and should not be used as a pretext for colonial ambitions. He also had a pragmatic reason for this stance: he feared that the Paris Mission might go along with French nationalism and pour more resources into places like Tahiti than into Basutoland, which was now a British colony and consequently scarcely furthered French national interest.

While Jacottet was annoyed at the indecisiveness of the missionaries over various issues, he was also surprised at the management of some of the finances, which he saw as their weakest side. Weitzecker, for instance, was given a torrid time by the treasurer Dieterlen for profligate expenditure at Leribe. Missionaries like Weitzecker, noted Jacottet, seemed to find it difficult to 'get rid of their European ideas of comfort and easy life'. They forgot that the money was not for them but was sacred, given by friends of the missionaries, the precious donations of widows and orphans. He decided that the Conference must find 'a little Cerberus' in this regard, and so he unofficially appointed himself the 'guardian dragon' of the treasury. His deeper motive was to find the wherewithal to finance the expansion into the Maloti. He was happy to report to Boegner that Weitzecker seemed finally to understand the point being made: but the problem of overall control of the funding was to re-emerge, and one of Jacottet's most important early contributions to the mission would be the establishment of a Central Chest.

One of the prickliest issues discussed at Mabolela was that of church discipline. It involved the question of 'les petites femmes' – the lesser wives of polygamists. The prevailing ruling was that they could not be admitted into the church as long as they remained with their husbands. Some of the missionaries argued that the rule should be abolished, but when a vote was taken only four voted for abolition while thirteen voted against. Consequently, Chief Lebenya, who had asked that his wife 'Manthakoana be allowed to enter the church, was told that this could only happen if she went to live at a certain distance from his village and if all conjugal relations ceased. But the subject of the 'petites femmes' was to keep simmering in the Conference and would come to the boil in the not-too-distant future.

At last, the Conference came to the question of staffing vacant and new stations. Providence here played a strong card. The departure of the Kecks left a vacancy at Thaba-Bosiu. Rev. Marzolff was earmarked for the post, but it was felt that a sojourn at the Mountain at Night would be prejudicial to his wife's health. Jacottet was chosen instead.

So, to his great surprise, Jacottet was to stay close to the centre of things, and to join the line of great missionaries at Thaba-Bosiu.

Jacottet was delighted. 'No solution could be more agreeable to me,' he told Boegner. 'There I have in front of me a fine field of endeavour.' He would avoid 'the nightmare of a teaching profession full of thorns and disappointments more than any other'; yet, at Thaba-Bosiu, he would be located in the centre of Lesotho and close to the missionaries, such as Dieterlen, with whom he was most in sympathy. The historical significance, of course, was not lost on him: he was walking along the path cut by Casalis and Jousse.

He came away from the Conference with three strong opinions concerning the future personnel of the mission. Firstly, he felt that the Bible School should be reorganized on entirely new foundations and receive only students better prepared to profit from a much higher standard of teaching, though he did not expect Mabille ever to agree to this.

Secondly, he was frustrated by the indecision over the Theological School and the reluctance of some of the more conservative missionaries to pursue vigorously the creation of a 'pastorat indigène'. He was even prepared, however reluctantly, to return to the Theological School after a couple of years if this was deemed desirable. Thirdly, as the first of the Lesotho missionaries (together with Dieterlen) to be university-trained, he attributed the opposition to more 'progressive' ideas to the three-year training most of his predecessors had had at Paris headquarters. He felt that students would be less likely to lose their vocations if they were given more freedom, including the freedom to pursue most of their religious studies at theological faculties of their choice – such as Neuchâtel.

Besides the normal pastoral duties of Thaba-Bosiu, which were particularly onerous in such a huge parish, Jacottet was given two further tasks by the Conference. He was to try to get the School for Young Girls reopened and he was to oversee the beginnings of evangelical work on the Senqunyane (the Little Orange). This would be part of a three-pronged advance into the Maloti: Bertschy was to establish a new station amongst Moorosi's Baphuthi at Sebapala and to further his work up the course of the Senqu; and Cochet, having set up the new station in East Griqualand, was to penetrate the upper reaches of the Senqu, where a section of the Batlokoa, under Lelingoana, had been allowed to settle by Letsie during the Gun War.

–—◦◦—–

The Jacottets left Morija in mid-May.

In spite of lacking a thousand household gadgets and goods of modern life, they had nevertheless acquired, in the course of their short marriage, a thousand items more which had to be packed in a wagon the Mabilles had lent them, as well as a buckwagon to catch the spillover. Just as they thought they had finally finished, they would find a new object – a piece of crockery or a kitchen utensil – to be packed. Since the younger Dykes were still on holiday at Masitise and the Casalis family at Mabolela, they had only the older Dykes and Mabilles to help them.

Finally all was stowed. Then, as they were leaving, both wagons threatened to capsize, and their clock, almost touching the roof of the wagon tent, was in mortal danger. Time – and their composure – teetered on the edge of collapse. But at last they got going.

They stopped halfway, overnighting at Ha Pita, and arrived without mishap at Thaba-Bosiu the following day. They found the mission house cleared and cleaned by one of the Keck ladies, and had not finished unpacking before the first visitor – one of the Cochet daughters, Mary – arrived. Jacottet immediately seized the opportunity to leave his wife in her company and ride off all the next day with Daniel Keck to be introduced to the main chiefs of his parish: most important of all was Masupha, the third son of Moshoeshoe, whose village was only twenty minutes' walk away at the foot of Qiloane; then there was Theko, a son of Letsie by his second house, who lived at Ratau, further to the east; and finally, there was Maama, another son of Letsie by his second wife, who was at Mokhokhong (Popa Ha Maama), to the south. Maama, who had fought fiercely against the Cape and the loyalists during the Gun War, was favoured by his father to succeed to the paramountcy rather than his brother

Lerotholi. He was an Anglican and had been educated at Zonnebloem College – the elite school in Cape Town for the children of southern African chiefs – but had fourteen wives. Jacottet's parish was an old and big one, and very complicated, containing as it did some of the most important people in the country.

It was fortunate that they got these initial activities over with immediately, because the following day torrential rain set in and it was still bitterly cold on their first Sunday (17 May) at Thaba-Bosiu. But they were overjoyed when Mabille arrived, followed by Duvoisin and Kohler, to conduct the formal installation of Jacottet in the parish.

The weather kept Masupha, Theko and Maama away, and the congregation was small enough to fit into the church – and happy they were, as the cold was unbearable. First Keck thanked the church and the chiefs for all they had done for him; then Mabille, with words of encouragement and exhortation, presented the new pastor; finally, after Jacottet had stumbled through a few words of 'wretched Sesotho', Esaia, evangelist of Korokoro, and Simeon Feku of Morija, bade him welcome. It was one of those ceremonies, thought Jacottet, where it is impossible to say anything new, but one is left weak with the awesome responsibility of the task to come, and the knowledge that the strongest can do nothing without the help of God.

Next morning all the guests departed, and by the afternoon even Keck was gone. Suddenly, for the first time, Édouard and Louise found themselves alone amongst their unknown parishioners. They felt a sense of complete isolation, knowing that, except for their God, they could rely on no one but themselves.

It was a solemn moment. Strictly speaking, mused Jacottet, 'it is the beginning of our missionary life.'

Jacottet now took stock of his new domain. Keck had left him a legacy of neglect. The mission buildings at Thaba-Bosiu were badly in need of repair. The church at Mokhokhong in the south of the parish was falling down, and the 'kabelo', the fund made up of contributions from the congregation, no longer yielded anything. Jacottet was also immediately faced with the unenviable duty of having to fire a teacher made unreliable by drink, and he was not sure whether the government would renew funding for the post. What worried him most was that, as a result of Jousse having mistakenly established an outstation with an inferior chief, Chief Theko was demanding an outstation at his own village. Already responsible for six outstations and four schools, Jacottet was not thrilled at the prospect of establishing a new one, but he also knew that if he did not, the Anglicans or the Catholics would, which would be 'a disastrous blow to all the work at Thaba-Bosiu'. The Anglicans were already in the process of establishing a station at Masite, round the corner from Morija, in the district of Chief Bereng, a son of Letsie (by his second wife) and full brother of Lerotholi, and Bishop Stenson had come from Bloemfontein to baptize some of the wives of Letsie himself. Jacottet lamented that the English, ignorant of the French presence, seemed to believe that there were only Catholic and Anglican missionaries and that it was their duty to further the Protestant cause through the Anglican Church, to the detriment of scarce resources and the confusion of local converts.

His first pastoral trip was a short one of two days to the edge of the first range of mountains at Machache, where he 'had the honour to sleep in the spotless bed of one of his evangelists'. His next trip, to place the evangelist Josefa from Korokoro at a new outstation deep in the mountains on the Senqunyane river, was a much more taxing one, lasting a week. 'Thanks to the winter,' he wrote, 'everything was drab and monotonous. Passing the Catholic mission at Roma on the first day and crossing the first Maloti Range, we reached Likotopong, Mr Mabille's highest outstation on the Makhaleng … From this point a forced march took us to the Little Orange and a hamlet lost among the cliffs, where we spent the night as best we could in a hut open to every wind … Next morning we proceeded downstream but by paths which would make even an alpinist shudder, especially when they must be negotiated on horseback. I have never seen anything so utterly wild and devoid of splendour. It resembles a tomb and I severely reproach myself for having brought poor Josefa, his wife and his four children to these parts.'

Sepulchral the interior may have seemed, but Jacottet was convinced of its importance and always lifted his eyes to the mountains for his inspiration. 'It is very important,' he had said from the start, 'that we lose no time in occupying all the Maloti. It is there that we can place our first Basotho ministers.' Not all his colleagues shared his enthusiasm, and he sometimes felt like 'a voice crying in the desert'. News had begun to arrive in Lesotho of Coillard's first successes on the Zambezi; with genuine admiration and a little envy for the work of pioneering a virgin territory, Jacottet saw the Maloti as his own destiny. He was quite specific about his perception of his own role as a Christian witness: 'Despite certain constraints of time,' he wrote to Boegner, 'I want to be more an evangelical missionary than a pastor. Our activity must be above all directed outwards towards the pagans.' He spent the first two months almost entirely in the saddle, so Louise hardly ever saw him. It was not a happy time for her.

Jacottet was irate when he was not given the necessary financial support for the work of expansion – to leave some areas untouched, he believed, was to compromise the whole Lesotho enterprise. While he sympathized with Paris's financial constraints, he was worried that the mission might have to fall in line with what he called the recent 'colonial enthusiasm' for 'the conquest of the world', and that Basutoland, being under British rule, would be neglected, 'abandoned little by little'. 'My heart bleeds to see the French Republic play the role of aggressor,' he said, 'and by its action in Madagascar show Bismarck how he must behave in the Cameroons.' Curiously, he saw advantages in the Basotho situation. 'Without saying it too loudly,' he continued, 'I am not unhappy having affairs in the hands of England rather than a French administration; at least we enjoy complete freedom, and have a free hand.' He did not envy the splendours of Tahiti: 'I prefer our more independent situation, freer and even stronger for it. Nothing smothers the mission and the church more than the administrative bureaucratic embrace.' He was, however, concerned about the uncertainly continued presence of Britain in South Africa, which depended on unforeseen European politics. He was also annoyed that when the Governor General did visit Basutoland, the visit was so fleeting – he had to be back in Kimberley for the opening of the new railway – that he did not have time even to meet the three main chiefs. With the British, Jacottet lamented, it was 'always half measures'.

When he did turn his attention to his parish work, he found that evangelization was going slowly, and although there was a slight awakening amongst pagans, there was nothing noteworthy in this regard. More distressing was the perception that even confirmed Christians seemed, for the most part, to be asleep. In his first year, he brought a dozen people into the church, mainly old pagans, but also some lapsed renegades. He wondered if the spiritual torpidity was his fault, but ascribed it mainly to frequent changes of missionary. The mission was still extremely small, he thought, relative to the pagan mass that surrounded it, its moral standards were in decay, and there seemed to be a nationalistic revival of many pagan practices that had previously been rooted out.

He was not pessimistic, however. 'Evil is great, but God is here,' he was convinced. 'I have not regretted for a single moment having embraced this vocation, and I know it was my choice. That often strengthens and encourages me – I need it in the difficult moments through which I often pass.' Above all, he believed that the breath of God was needed to give back life to the dry bones of the church.

The efforts of the missionaries to rid the country of brandy seemed to be more fruitful. Letsie and his sons had renounced it – though Jacottet doubted their sincerity. Maama, one of the biggest drunkards, had given it up. Masupha was Jacottet's immediate concern and despair. When Chief Mopeli, a temperance adherent from the north, travelled through the country advocating temperance, Masupha was silent. But soon after, he ordered his sons to cast out all the cantinas and made severe laws against brandy. Jacottet was hopeful that he would not bend, because the day after his pronouncement rain, so long awaited, fell in abundance, saving the harvest. A providential omen.

Throughout the year, the pot of civil war simmered. The Orange Free State, through its newspapers, poured oil on the fire. Troops, not usually available to Clarke, might be needed. Masupha refused to pay tax, and conflict with the matekete threatened. Then Peete, son of Ramaneella (who was, in turn, a nephew of Moshoeshoe), and Lepoqo, under the orders of his father Masupha, had a go at one another. The affair was messy, and eventually both troublemakers were fined a number of cattle by Clarke and Letsie acting in concert. The outcome was reckoned a defeat for Masupha. These events filled Jacottet with contempt for the leadership of the local chiefs. Letsie was ineffective; his son Theko was tactless, uncouth as a bear; curiously, only Masupha had an innate courtesy, which never left him in his dealings with his missionary. 'It is a comedy,' said Jacottet bitterly, 'too evil to be laughable.'

The year brought its share of other minor irritations to Jacottet. Paul Germond, smarting from the Conference's reluctance to allow his son Louis to take up the station next to his at Thabana-Morena, seemed to blame Jacottet, and aggressively accused him of having fixed his own posting to Thaba-Bosiu. Jacottet fiercely denied lobbying, and hoped that Germond would soon forget his grievances, which he thought should not be difficult for a missionary.

Jacottet also suffered from bouts of giddiness, which Dr Casalis attributed to the climate and to the coming of spring, and he was consequently forbidden to take too many rides. Nevertheless, his concern over the encroachments of the Catholics prompted him to make a visit to their headquarters at Roma, which fell within his parish. He was impressed by their buildings, which were far superior to those of the Protestants, but he regarded their conversion progress as slow; their discipline was flawed, and as regards liquor and marriage for cattle, they lagged far behind and were unlikely to succeed. But he was worried about Father Le Bihan's success amongst the Bataung, still important even after the death of the old chief Moletsane, and he felt that the placing of a missionary at Siloe should be speeded up.

The year also brought its share of rewards. Jacottet informed Boegner that a young visitor was expected at Thaba-Bosiu in the new year.

At the beginning of December, a false alarm caused the young couple some anxiety, so Louise went to stay with Dr Casalis and his wife at Morija. Édouard was particularly grateful, as Thaba-Bosiu did not have the resources to cope with the last-minute complications that set in.

He himself stayed on at Thaba-Bosiu through Christmas and New Year on his own. He was tired and his health was not good. But he learned something from his loneliness. 'From the experience I have just been through,' he ruefully acknowledged, 'I can declare that, in Lesotho more than elsewhere, it is not good for a man to be alone. He suffers too much in complete isolation and does not know how to handle it.' A woman's companionship was essential for mental stability.

The young visitor did eventually arrive. She was born at Morija on 22 January 1886. They called her Marcelle-Hélène. She was born at the time of the year when flocks of birds begin to threaten the just-ripening mabele crop, and the lephephe hut must be put up in the field as temporary shelter for motšosi, the scarer-away-of-birds.

CHAPTER SEVENTEEN

THE MIRROR BREAKS

1887–1892

Thaba-Bosiu was one of the largest and most densely populated of the mission's parishes, and certainly one of the most important, on a par with Morija. It was also the most difficult.

The mission station itself lay at the foot of the northern edge of Thaba-Bosiu mountain. The buildings had suffered gravely from the ravages of the Gun War and the neglect of Keck. Jacottet had to apply himself to the mending of walls and rethatching of roofs, which required an aptitude and skills he lamented he did not have.

Some of the most important chiefs of the realm – Masupha, Maama, Theko – lived within the bounds of the parish. To the south, the parish adjoined that of Morija, and the two had to deal constantly with the ever-present tensions between Letsie and Masupha, and between Lerotholi and Maama, and skirmishes between their followers. To the north, the situation was even more unstable: although there was a station at Cana, the original site of Molapo's residence, it was occupied by the less-than-certain Rev. Kohler, while the station near Leribe, where Molapo had finally settled, was also vacant.

To the east, the parish of Thaba-Bosiu stretched all the way to the first chain of the Maloti and even beyond, as people began to inhabit the mountainous hinterland. To the south-west, it extended across the Qeme plateau and further to the river border. Jacottet must ride great distances to take in his spiritual domain and to guide the catechists (or 'évangélistes' as they were called in French) under his wing.

In all this great sweep of magnificent, stately countryside, the parish as yet had only seven 'annexes' or outstations. Three lay to the west: at Boqate on the road to Maseru, the new administrative capital of the British authorities; at Masianokeng; and at Matukeng, up against Qeme. Three lay to the south at Maliele, at Korokoro, and at Popa Ha Maama. At the latter station, Jacottet managed at last to finish the building of the chapel. This was an important achievement, since the outstation rubbed shoulders with the Roman Catholic headquarters at Roma, but it failed to prevent Maama's eventual conversion to

Catholicism under the considerable influence of Father Gérard. To the east, there was only one outstation, at Metšoarong, home of Chief Khotso. Jacottet was particularly concerned by this vast area, growing in population every year, which the Catholics had obviously targeted. He was especially worried that they would get to Theko, and his first priority was to establish an outstation and school there, as Theko was threatening to go over to the Catholics if Jacottet did not do so. In the north, although the vast plateau of Sefikeng and large valley of Thupa-Kubu were home to forty or fifty villages, there were no outstations at all.

In addition, there were, under his aegis, seven day schools (each outstation chapel served as a school on weekdays) and two night schools (at Thaba-Bosiu and Masianokeng), but Jacottet had ambitions to increase them and to double the number of outstations, in order, as he said, to 'pursue the war against paganism and unbelief'. Basotho society was like a pot with three legs – circumcision, bohali and polygamy – all three of which must be knocked off before it can be tempered in the fire of the Lord.

The year 1886 ended with an event which Jacottet judged to be of considerable significance. The day after Christmas, Lepoqo died. In his thirties, he was the eldest son of Masupha, and the last surviving son of the chief's principal wife (the youngest having been killed in the assault on Maseru during the Gun War). Although the immediate cause of death was dysentery, Jacottet was certain that the real cause was alcohol. This disaster was 'one of the catastrophic fruits of the drunkenness that had already overwhelmed Lesotho'. Whether he knew it or not, he was echoing the words of Louis Duvoisin years before. Duvoisin had warned that if there were no remedy to counter the influx of liquor, the people would become a 'fruit which has rotted before it ripened', and he added that this rottenness was reflected in the land itself, as the fertile parts washed away. One of the Basotho Christians had said to him, 'Naha e ea tsofala – the land is ageing.' Now, thirty years on, Jacottet felt that the moral erosion in the people had truly found its visual symbol in the dongas that widened every year and scarred the countryside.

Although many old customs had disappeared under the influence of the missionaries, a number of the chiefs, particularly the younger ones, had resorted to the 'old habit', this despite the fact that some of them had forsworn liquor earlier that year. It was easy enough to find brandy on the other side of the Caledon, with the local police closing their eyes to the escapades of the highly-placed – wisely, in Jacottet's view, since it would be dangerous, if not impossible, to apply the letter of the law. Consequently, Lepoqo was 'often in a state of complete intoxication' – as were, Jacottet feared, most of the other sons of Masupha, and those of Letsie and Lerotholi – and he died unrepentant.

Jacottet was cynical enough to assume, however, that the warning of this premature death would not be heeded, that it would be put down instead to sorcery, to the agency of 'baloi'. The consequences of the death and the problems of Masupha's successor would only add to the Byzantine internal power struggles.

The funeral took place a few days later on a gruesomely hot day. Kohler came from Cana to conduct the ceremony. Also present were Duvoisin, Ernest Mabille and Marshal Clarke, the Resident Commissioner, with a posse of policemen. Jacottet had sent his wagon to fetch the coffin and take it to Masupha. He himself crossed the Phuthiatsana to meet the funeral cortège and greet the old man bringing the body of his son to Thaba-Bosiu. It was an imposing spectacle: more than two thousand horsemen, including Jonathan Molapo, Theko and Maama, as well as sundry lesser chiefs. The numbers had grown as the procession moved through the surrounding villages on the previous day and night.

The sight was strange to Jacottet, but at the same time wild and moving – the mourning of a whole people something so great, so powerful. He was struck by how Masupha took the blow without caving in.

By the time they reached the top of the mountain, this 'human sea' numbered four to five thousand people, and, as the body was taken past the house of Moshoeshoe to the royal cemetery, Jacottet felt the ground move underfoot. The cries of the women and the hysterical tears got to him, despite himself, and in the stifling heat he felt chilled to the marrow.

The missionaries were in a quandary, not sure how far to push their preaching in this Christian service over the grave of 'a pagan'. Such a moment, however, when the first seed of an idea might be sown, seemed too good to pass up. Kohler gave the main speech, not a funeral oration but an incisive call to conversion and repentance. Jacottet added a few words, directed mainly to Masupha, asking him to understand and accept the chastisement of the Eternal, trying to return him to Him.

Masupha exacted an unintended revenge by giving an interminable speech, repetitive, tortuous, muddled, which none of the whites understood, and which was vague enough for the Basotho themselves to translate in five or six different ways – some of them totally contradictory. He did make a half-hearted gesture to the missionaries by suggesting his son's death should not be used to kill anyone under the pretext of sorcery – an old custom abolished by Moshoeshoe but making a recent comeback.

Since Lepoqo had often eaten at the Jacottets' table in the company of his father, the missionary could not help being shocked by his sudden death. But he did not grieve. Soon after Jacottet had arrived at Thaba-Bosiu, Lepoqo had murdered four women accused of a death by witchcraft, and Jacottet had been left with a distaste he could never shake off. Nevertheless, he saw a critical opening and hoped that, in future, suitably admonished by the death of his son, Masupha, whose presence and influence bulked large in the parish and in the country, might be more accessible.

So, the following day, Jacottet went to see him and they talked seriously for nearly an hour. Jacottet was distressed by Masupha's lack of references to the Bible and the banal fatalism which he expressed in these moments. But he did get Masupha to the point where they were about to pray together. It was a crucial moment; a breakthrough might have been possible, with a slight nudge from the hand of Providence. Unfortunately, the proverbial man from Porlock, in the shape of a messenger from the government, intruded. The spell was broken: Jacottet had to leave without having 'penetrated the heart of the chief'.

Jacottet took consolation in the everyday trials and triumphs of his own small family. Little Marcelle was growing quickly. She had not yet decided to walk, though she had been crawling since she was four months old.

By the beginning of 1888, after two years at Thaba-Bosiu, Jacottet could look back with some satisfaction. In the first few months of 1887, there seemed to be little stirring in the parish, but after the Missionary Conference at Cana in Easter, suddenly a light breeze sprang up, especially in the schools. In the preceding years, the school at the main station had never numbered more than eighty or ninety children: by December, it had grown to two hundred, of whom a good third were boys, and had become the largest school in Lesotho.

Equally pleasing was the night school, which Jacottet had opened for the shepherds and other youngsters who could not attend during the day and therefore manifested 'an absolute ignorance'. Instead of the thirty or forty he expected, Jacottet was inundated with more than 130 prospective scholars. For six months, he himself taught five nights a week to give them the foundation he felt they needed, until he could hand them over, with regret, to an assistant teacher.

Progress in these peaceful times was excellent throughout the country. Between 1884 and 1892, the number of the mission's outstations throughout Lesotho doubled to 141. The number of scholars in the same period increased, according to the official census, from 139 000 in 1875 to 218 000 in 1891.

Over and above all this, Conference had heaved another task on to Jacottet's shoulders. In 1871, Rev. Jousse had started a school for girls. Mlle Miriam Cochet took charge. Her task was not so much a question of giving the girls an advanced education as 'developing their character, teaching them order, cleanliness and home duties'. The school started with twelve pupils, and by 1879 had grown to seventy. But it was yet another victim of the Gun War.

'L'école des Baroetsana' reopened in 1887 under Jacottet's general and Miriam Cochet's specific direction. The missionary was apprehensive when it started, and it was to cause him constantly niggling worries. It did not prosper. Although he himself got on well enough with Mlle Cochet, she had, to his mind, 'a very black character', acid and sharp, and the girls could not endure her. Many of the girls who started did not return. Accommodation was a problem until a new school was built in 1888. In addition, casting his eye over the limited supply of suitable females in the mission, it proved difficult for Jacottet to find, and hold on to, a deputy schoolmistress. The Mabille daughters were indispensable to their father at Morija; Henriette Cochet would be excellent, but could not leave the Cape; the Kecks, Julie and Louise, did not have the aptitude; Laure Casalis 'would not last six months'. For several years, he searched and searched for an adequate deputy. Firstly, Miss Eugènie Keck, unable to coexist with Miss Cochet, left for Europe; then Miss Lydia Lautré, who proved a huge success, let the side down by getting married to a missionary who was off to Lake Nyasa.

It was only in January 1893 that Miss Elisabeth Jacot arrived, in time for the new school year. Jacottet went to meet her in an open cart at Maseru. For Miss Jacot, this first meeting must have been unpropitious. Even before they arrived at Boqate, a huge downpour drenched them. After a struggle of over six hours on a muddy road, they arrived at the drift across the Phuthiatsana to find the river swollen and dangerous. With the help of Ben, one of the mission converts, who arrived fortuitously, they tried to cross in the cart, but, in the middle of the largest whirlpool, the horses jibbed. The torrent grew heavier, the position more critical. Ben lifted Miss Jacot on to his shoulders and carried her back to safety: then he returned to render the same service to Jacottet. Finally, the cart was retrieved.

What to do? The idea of going all the way back to Maseru or of passing the night in the hut of a local had no appeal. As for asking hospitality of the trader at Boqate, Charles Maitin – son of the missionary Pierre-Joseph – with whom Jacottet had had a run-in, 'nothing in the world' would make him do it. So he took what he felt to be 'a heroic resolution' and asked big Ben to carry Miss Jacot across the floods, flinging himself in the uncomplaining hero's wake. A quarter of an hour later, they were on the other bank, wet, without baggage, without cart, but resolved to continue. At half past eight that night, Miss Jacot, covered in mud and soaked to the skin, made her first appearance at Thaba-Bosiu. Her first day had undoubtedly been a vivid experience, but having ended well could only have filled her, remarked Jacottet drily, with good memories! Though there had been danger at the time, the two of them took the thing cheerfully and laughed much about it.

Miss Jacot proved to be an equally resolute teacher.

—⌒◯⌒—

The progress in the schools was matched in the church. 'The taste for learning', Jacottet wrote to Boegner, was also 'a sure indication of a desire to accept the Word, or at least to be placed under its influence'.

Since 1884, conversions had increased steadily, if unremarkably. But the years 1887 and 1888 brought 'a fine revival'.

The 'réveil' began in Morija, but soon spread to Thaba-Bosiu. Jacottet was gratified with the fruits of his labour. In August 1887, the inauguration of the new chapel at Mokhokhong drew a huge crowd of two thousand pagans to the services, but curiosity might have attracted many amongst them, as well as the understandable desire to share in the provisions that Maama generously offered.

But, in September, at a great ceremony of baptisms at the station itself, Jacottet felt something different as he looked down on the multitude, which included headmen and petty chiefs known for their hostility, indifference and ignorance. They seemed drawn there by an aspiration for something better, a higher life, purer than what they were accustomed to. At this ceremony, twenty adults, four of them men, were received into the church. But most remarkable of all was the rare and touching spectacle of a centenarian called 'Mamoiketsi, shrivelled up and wrinkled as the hide of an elephant, brought to the service in a cart because her legs refused all commands. This contemporary of Moshoeshoe was baptized under the name of Naomi, proof, for Jacottet, that conversion was possible up until the last moment of life. That it was a true conversion he had no doubt, as she had convinced him of it under rigorous examination. This was no cheap showmanship on his part.

Of course, there were bitter disappointments too. In no time, four of these twenty adults had lapsed. For missionaries such as Jacottet this was always humiliating and exhausting. Old Christians returned to what seemed to him to be the worst customs of paganism. Even on the station itself, he lamented, there was no lack of superstitious ceremonies.

But there were more steps forward than back. In November, a long-planned but long-delayed series of religious meetings took place over four days in the large village of Job, a couple of kilometres from the mission station. Jacottet was backed up by his elders and his schoolteachers. Of the three hundred people who attended, over thirty, to Jacottet's astonishment, opted to stay on. It was time for them to take the decisive step.

A similar series of meetings was held in the village of Masupha and on the mountain itself. Then, eight days before Christmas, profiting from a holiday that attracted a great crowd of pagans, Jacottet made a special appeal to them, as seriously and incisively as he could. The five or six hundred pagans were shaken as if by an electric shock, as the missionary and his aides began to speak. Sobs broke out on all sides: for half an hour no one could speak. Although he realized such emotion was fleeting, Jacottet knew it was a scene he would never forget.

He was also worried about being swamped by conversions, concerned that quantity would harm quality. He expressed his fears about half-sincere conversions, about a discounted Christianity reduced in value. With his emphasis on strict individual salvation, he prayed that only the truly faithful would be allowed to enter the church.

—◦○—

Tales he had of remarkable conversions under his guidance.

It was on the mountain that the most conversions occurred. Fifteen women, almost all of them widows of Moshoeshoe, now belonged to the mission. Perhaps, since the death of their husband and protector, they had become marginalized. Amongst them was 'Makena, renegade from the church for more than thirty years.

In the nearby village, Job Mokhachane, brother of Moshoeshoe and a long-time renegade from the church, bound by strong ties of polygamy and advised by counsellors who feared to see a new convert, had always hesitated to rejoin. However, when one of his concubines left him to join the church, and his latest wife also wanted to do so, he felt it was time to 'break with sin' and return to his 'legitimate' wife, whom he had abandoned a long time ago.

In the village of the station itself, there were conversions, too. Rakhopane, who had lived at Thaba-Bosiu for over thirty years, was not a traditionalist but came from a Christian family, and his children had married without bohali. He attended church services regularly, but would not convert. What held him back was brandy. As this modest réveil progressed, Rakhopane was suddenly overcome and left Jacottet in no doubt as to his sincerity.

Most interesting, perhaps, was Sebego, the immediate neighbour of the Jacottets. His mother had been a devout Christian, and the confidante of the Jousses. Sebego was an excellent fellow, assiduous in his church attendance, he read the Bible regularly, he prayed. More than once, Jacottet asked him: what prevents you from converting? He did not know, he replied. He wanted to, and he asked God for His help – but his heart did not respond. One night, he arrived at Jacottet's house, visibly disturbed. He had trouble explaining what had brought him there. He wanted, he said, to be written on the list of those who desired conversion: he wanted to be prayed for. Jacottet questioned him, he pushed. This time the mirror, in which Sebego saw only himself and what he was made of, the mirror ... broke. The pieces melted away like ice as God entered and warmed the heart of Sebego. Now, through the grace of God, said Jacottet, he became a particularly joyous Christian.

Over the last few months of 1887, in the course of this awakening, as Jacottet interviewed the applicants for admission to the church, he learned much more than he had in the previous three years. When the conversions were sincere, they were interesting. In a phenomenon recognizable to oral historians and those who take confessions, the majority of his converts seemed to him to have a new light in their eyes and a confidence in their bearing. And with it Jacottet's own confidence grew.

One prize soul eluded him, however. Although three of his most important wives and one of his sons converted, and though he himself seemed shaken for several days, Masupha, once baptized David, would not or could not break free from his traditionalism – 'it was more difficult for a Mosotho chief to convert,' thought Jacottet, 'than for a camel to pass through the eye of a needle.' Anyway, camels were pretty scarce in Lesotho. And God had shown in the past months that what was impossible to man, was possible to Him. For now, Jacottet was content.

—◦◯◦—

To see Lesotho as remote, isolated from all but its immediate neighbours, would be wrong. Jacottet certainly never made that mistake. The wider world was constantly bumping into him like a playground bully, proving that no country is an island.

Of course, the raison d'être of the PEMS was to take the Word to where it had not been heard before. If people did not hear the Word, there could be no salvation – the very essence of the evangelical doctrine of the time. But the mission also realized the importance of keeping the interest of its friends and church members by stimulating them with new challenges. So, within the financial constraints, it was always on the lookout for fresh fields to sow.

For the first fifty years of its existence, the impetus of the PEMS came from two sources: the first, via the Réveil, regarded by its adherents as a second Reformation, was purely evangelical and universalist; the second, courtesy of the Enlightenment, was philanthropic, deeply involved in the suppression of the slave trade and the abolition of slavery.

When the French conquered Algeria in 1830, it seemed a promising field of labour for the new mission, and Arbousset and Casalis were sent to learn Arabic; but soon the terms of surrender, which specified that Muslim customs and religion would be protected, diminished its attraction. In 1851, Guillaume Monod – who will reappear later in this chapter in strange garb – was sent to Algiers, but he confined his ministrations to the urban Arabs of Algiers and Oran, and to the French colonists themselves.

The mission in Senegal was started in 1863 as part of the anti-slavery movement. But it never had a 'father', like Adolphe Mabille, and tentativeness on the part of the Paris Committee combined with the country's infernal climate ensured that it never had two missionaries who overlapped for more than two years. Founded much later than Lesotho, the Senegal mission was caught up in French nationalism and military expansionism. It never fully took root. The lesson Boegner took from the Senegal mission was that its philanthropic involvement in the anti-slavery movement tended to distract it from what was meant to be its main goal of evangelization.

The mission to Lesotho had little to do with colonialism or French expansionism. Rather, it came out of the Réveil and the search for pagan territory, as well as the desire to reattach itself to the Huguenot diaspora.

But the world of 1880 was a very different one from 1830. Nationalism was on fire in Europe and colonialism was beginning to reach out with its tentacles. Stung by their humiliation in the Franco-Prussian War, the French were looking for a Greater France, and the north – Algeria – rather than the south was seen as the gateway to Africa. In 1883, Eugène Réveillaud, editor of the moderate, Protestant, republican weekly *Le Signal*, launched a bitter attack on the PEMS, accusing it of lacking patriotism and demanding that the Lesotho mission be contracted as soon as possible and its resources transferred to Algeria.

This onslaught was from within the Protestant camp. But it did not find an echo in the hearts of 'protestants libristes' – those Protestants of the 'free churches' who believed that the spiritual realm should not be mixed with the political, who believed that the churches should be separate from the state, and who consequently harboured a streak of anti-colonialism. The PEMS, dominated by the evangelical independents, rather than the liberals who doubted that religion and politics could be kept apart, held firm, and Boegner called Lesotho 'a true (spiritual) colony of French Protestantism', even if it was under British rule.

But, as French colonialism and imperialism slid around the world with the irresistible power of a boa constrictor, the PEMS was drawn ineluctably into its coils, and the Mission Society came to change its stance considerably over the last two decades of the century. A number of variables played their part in this period.

Throughout the century, religion in general and Protestantism in particular had waged war against atheism, communism, scientism, but waves of anti-Protestant feeling, often associated with French nationalists, rolled in at the end. This was an anti-ecumenical epoch, too, in which Catholics and Protestants fought bitterly for spiritual and temporal turf. And in this period French governments also became increasingly anti-clerical, and secularization grew steadily to the point where church and state separated in 1905.

When the nationalists retreated to the last refuge of scoundrels, the Protestants found themselves banished from the French-speaking family. *Qui dit protestant dit anglais, qui dit catholique dit français,* was a popular slogan of the time. As they jockeyed for position and power with the British, the French administrators came into contact with Methodist, American Presbyterian, Anglican and LMS missionaries. Frequently, they regarded them as little more than agents of the British. One of the ways of making their life difficult, short of outright expulsion, was to ensure, through legislation, that all education took place in the French language. So the English-speaking missionaries had to bring in specially trained French teachers or ask the PEMS to take over their missions, lock, stock and barrel.

Jacottet, it must be remembered, left for Lesotho a matter of months before the Berlin Conference of 1884, which divided the world up between just a few colonial powers.

—◦—

Jacottet was always alert to what was going on in the outside world. Nevertheless, at first glance, the interest he took in the Loyalty Islands in 1886 might seem somewhat excessive. Yet, when these three emerald butterflies, floating on a warm tropical sea, flapped their flimsy wings, the breeze was felt in the high, cold kingdom of Lesotho.

Jacottet himself was very aware of the connection. The French were exerting pressure on the Anglicans in the Loyalty Islands – Ouvéa, Lifou and Maré – and on the LMS in New Caledonia. The PEMS was under great pressure to step in and replace them, which would put enormous strain on resources already stretched to the limit and beyond. Jacottet could only lament the circumstances and involvement. 'In certain cases,' he wrote to Boegner, 'somewhat reluctant as I am to yield to the colonial course, where I believe I have sometimes seen more chauvinism than Christian zeal, while regretting the circumstance which forces us to act, I can only applaud our resolution in coming to the aid of the threatened missions.' Although he felt intervention was something it would be 'unfaithful to neglect' in a situation the PEMS had not sought, he warned that it would 'always, in fact, be a mission at least as political as religious'. The Loyalty Islands and their big brother, New Caledonia, would draw off resources, particularly financial resources, from Lesotho, if only indirectly.

Some of the elements that conditioned Jacottet's thinking are clear to see. Partly, and most immediately, he was concerned with the effect that the colonial thrust in the Loyalty Islands might have on the Lesotho mission; partly, his habits of thought stemmed from the French Protestant history of persecution and suspicion of the state and state religion, further reinforced by the more recent phenomenon of the 'églises libres' – the independent churches – and his own family's involvement with them; partly, he adhered very strongly to the strict evangelical code – the unchanging authority of the Gospel – and the reign of its kingdom over all narrow and temporal nationalisms, as well as their colonial extensions, placing the salvation of the individual soul high above patriotism.

Gabon and Congo threatened Lesotho even more directly than the Pacific. Although the great explorer of the area, Pierre Savorgnan de Brazza, had received help and hospitality from American Presbyterian missionaries like Dr Robert Nassau and from British traders like Thomas Sinclair and Aloysius Smith (Trader Horn), and was well disposed towards them, he nevertheless wanted to draw the PEMS into Gabon, using as a contact his friend, Henri Jacottet, Édouard's brother.

In 1887, this situation had serious implications for Lesotho. The PEMS was looking for an experienced missionary to head the Congo mission. The obvious candidates were in southern Africa. Dieterlen was one. Jacottet wrote frantically to Boegner pointing out that the Theological School had just reopened and its Director was vital to its success: if it were to close again, the already sceptical students might never return and the indigenization of the Lesotho church would receive a mortal wound. Not only was Dieterlen Jacottet's closest friend, he was also 'precious to us in all ways and a force in the mission who contributes, through his moderate way of understanding things, an indispensable balance of optimism and pessimism'.

Mabille was the other candidate. Linked to the loss of Coillard (who finally left for Barotseland in 1884), his departure would be even more disastrous. He was no longer as strong as he had been in the past – there had been a marked decline in his health in the last two years – and the new task would likely kill him. 'What would we do without him?' Jacottet added. 'It would take three men to replace him.'

While Jacottet could accede to the regrettable but necessary involvement of the PEMS in New Caledonia and the Loyalty Islands, and worry about the possible loss of his friend Dieterlen or his mentor Mabille, he reserved his irritation for Tahiti. When Casalis was awarded the Cross of Honour in 1886, Jacottet compared it to the award of the title of Chevalier of the Legion of Honour to the doyen of the Tahiti mission, Charles Viénot, in 1883. These were, he complained, merely baubles for grey hair – a judgement he believed Casalis's old friend Moshoeshoe would have agreed with.

Part of Jacottet's acerbic view of Viénot stemmed from the fact that he was a member of the colonial Council of Tahiti and did not preserve a sufficient distance between the church and colonial government. Another part of his resentment stemmed from the fact that the missionaries of Lesotho could not help making comparisons between the two missions. Tahiti cost the PEMS as much as Lesotho but catered for only nine thousand people, already 'more civilized, more advanced', Christianized, and with no outstations to add to its expenses. Poor Lesotho had a much larger, more pagan population. 'Are we wrong to fear that a strong minority of the Committee, caught in the colonial enthusiasm which not long ago pushed France to the conquest of the world, considers Lesotho only as an udder to go to, which one only takes into account because one cannot properly get rid of it?' 'If only,' he lamented sarcastically, 'we had the privilege of being under the French flag!!'

His prejudices were undoubtedly strengthened when a row erupted in November 1889 between Viénot and Etienne Girard, a missionary newly arrived in Tahiti. Girard had been a student of Godet's at the independent theological faculty in Neuchâtel; his theology, though, was very evangelical. Soon after arriving in Tahiti, he gave a sermon based on the Epistle of St Paul to the Philippians (3: 18–19) in which he warned 'the enemies of the cross of Christ' that their end would be destruction, since their God was their belly and their mind was on earthly things. A friend of Viénot's in the congregation saw this as an explicit attack on Viénot and accordingly accosted Girard afterwards.

Girard promptly wrote to the Paris Committee with numerous accusations: that the Tahitian Conference was hopelessly divided and that Viénot bypassed it; that Viénot lived in total luxury; that Viénot should more truthfully be called the King of Tahiti as regards his attitude towards the church and the way he led the governor by the nose; and that Viénot was preventing him from going to evangelize the island of Raiatea, having stated publicly that he was 'not the man for the situation' (Girard, after all, was Swiss and belonged to an independent church; Viénot was French and of a national church persuasion). Viénot counter-attacked in a letter to Paris, denouncing Girard as 'a young prophet violently inspired', whose 'religious views were Philippian'.

The initial response of the Paris Committee was to transfer Girard to Lesotho. He refused to take up the new post, however, until he had returned to Europe to present his case. This he did with such vituperation, particularly in Neuchâtel, that Boegner had to hasten there to calm the concerns of the many influential Neuchâtelois friends of the Paris Mission. Girard had added to his previous accusations that Viénot hogged most of the resources and that the preparation of an indigenous pastorate was not progressing. Boegner eventually submitted a report to the Committee prepared for him by Dieterlen, who was on sabbatical and acting as his auxiliary.

The report suggested that the Protestant churches were less prosperous than they had been twenty-five years before and that this was because of the demoralizing effect of antagonistic civil and military colonial officers, the incursions of the Roman Catholics, and the secularization of colonial schools. It added further that the Tahitian Missionary Conference was split into nationals and independents, that the emphasis had shifted from religion to education, and that it was 'a mission divided against itself'. Boegner believed that it had erred in displacing its centre of gravity from missionary to philanthropic action, and suggested that steps be taken to reinspire the evangelical faith.

Jacottet no doubt gloated if he heard – and there is no reason why his friends in Neuchâtel would not have told him – that Girard was accusing Viénot of having 'inappropriate relationships with his, Girard's, own wife and with a certain schoolmistress ...'

The suggestion that Girard be transferred to Lesotho was the kind of thing that Jacottet deeply resented. Although it was an indirect compliment to the maturity and relative harmony of the Lesotho mission, he also felt that Lesotho was sometimes used as a dumping ground for problem cases. The example of Emile Vollet might be construed as just such a case.

Vollet was a young Alsatian who was sent to the Zambezi in 1890. Somewhat weak and impressionable, he came under the spell of an Englishman from Natal, George Middleton, who had been in Coillard's party that left to missionize Barotseland in 1884. Middleton had become disaffected from Coillard and eventually went into the service of the Lozi king, Lewanika. In 1890, a British envoy, Elliot Lochner, signed a treaty with Lewanika, in the presence of Coillard, by means of which the territory passed under British control. This forestalled Middleton, who represented a Kimberley company eager for mining rights in the country. Middleton venomously accused Coillard of deceiving the king and selling the country to foreigners. Poor Vollet arrived as a bemused innocent in the middle of these accusations and counter-accusations. He precipitously and rashly took Middleton's side. He wrote letters to Middleton, which the latter used to bolster his argument to Lewanika that he had been betrayed. Jacottet regarded Middleton as no ordinary man, no common adventurer, but as an unscrupulously cunning manipulator, playing on Vollet's idealism, his evil genius.

Vollet came to Lesotho broken in spirit. At first, Jacottet was favourably impressed with him and thought the affairs of the Zambezi had been exaggerated. Vollet was not entirely forthcoming, it seems, with the Conference. When a letter came from the Zambezi spelling out the details of the dispute, Vollet was confronted with his own failings. He was mortified and thrown into a deep spiritual and psychological crisis.

Jacottet became his confidant when he hid himself away at Thaba-Bosiu to wrestle with his conscience. Jacottet was both sympathetic and ruthlessly honest with him. He criticized Vollet, amongst other things, for at first isolating himself from his colleagues on the Zambezi, for neglecting or refusing to see that discipline before the adversary is necessary in a mission, and that it is the duty of an officer to obey even orders he can only half-acknowledge. The Conference was his superior authority and he was frankly wrong to act outside of it and in opposition to it.

On the other hand, Jacottet felt that Vollet should have been given a longer transition period in the calmer atmosphere of Lesotho, before being precipitated into the febrile evangelical frontier of Barotseland (and that this should be done for other recruits in the future). Jacottet acknowledged that he knew from his own experience what it was like to make over-hasty judgements in the first days of enthusiasm. A combination of unlucky circumstances had plunged Vollet into bitter crisis.

As the days passed, a special bond grew between the two men. Unlike his colleagues, who did not delve so deeply and had less charity for Vollet, Jacottet came to believe that his initial concealment of the full story from the Lesotho Conference had not been done consciously, was not a crime, was not even selective amnesia, which might have confirmed some idea of self-interest; he felt rather that Vollet had suffered temporarily from a numbness of mind, which made him incapable of remembering the facts or understanding their full import. It was, in the words of Jacottet, as if he had been suffering from 'an eclipse of memory'.

Only after several weeks did the crisis pass. 'There was a victory over himself which is indeed one of the most difficult that is given a man to face, and which will be for him decisive and a blessing, I have no doubt,' wrote Jacottet. The time had been exhausting for both men, but the end result rewarding: 'He has the humility to pick himself up and give himself peace. It was an illness; it seems to me it is cured. May God ensure the cure is complete and that the rest of his career be entirely for the glory of the Lord. I like him greatly, I respect him much, and consider him today as a true friend. All the time he has been here I have sought to gain his confidence, borne witness to friendship; I consider myself to be a little his advocate but an advocate who does not fear to tell the truth.' Vollet survived his spiritual crisis and, after a few years of missionary work, decided to study medicine. He died in the Quthing district a few years after the man who had helped him through his worst crisis, and was buried on a mountain high above the valley he loved so much.

The cases of Girard and Vollet annoyed Jacottet. He felt that the Paris Committee accepted too easily the idea that Lesotho might take those missionary candidates who were, morally or physically, unsuccessful elsewhere. The Lesotho mission had too many of its own problems to be the home for stray dogs.

—⦁—

Two powerful personalities like those of Jacottet and Masupha were bound to chafe each other. There are two amusing stories that illustrate their posturing.

Once, when a Mosotho excused an act of omission on his part by pleading that Chief Masupha had previously given him instructions to the contrary, Jacottet retorted in a tone of contempt, 'Masupha! Who is Masupha?'

Shortly afterwards, Jacottet was visiting Masupha, and, ever willing to learn, he prompted the old chief to tell him about the days when Moshoeshoe ruled the land. Masupha paused a while, before relating the story of how two strangers, arriving at the royal kraal of Moshoeshoe, had slept the night there at the village. As they were preparing to leave next morning, the villagers asked why they had not paid their respects to King Moshoeshoe, whereupon one of them replied contemptuously, 'Moshoeshoe! Who is Moshoeshoe?'

Another pause, then Masupha completed the tale. The two travellers were taken before Moshoeshoe, who received them with 'marked courtesy'. He asked them about the country through which they had travelled and the adventures that had befallen them. Then he had two oxen slaughtered in their honour, so that they might eat their fill. After the feast was over, the strangers were sewn into the skins of the two beasts and thrown over a cliff on Thaba-Bosiu, as a message to others about the desirability of showing respect.

Jacottet took the hint that Masupha had ears even within the walls of Troy, and was glad to take his leave without being invited to dinner.

In 1889, when Alfred Casalis arrived in the country, his services were in great demand from those who revered his father. He had only been in Morija two days when he received a letter from Jacottet saying that the church and the chiefs of Thaba-Bosiu wished to see the son of their first missionary. A great 'mokete', or feast, was organized for the following Sunday to present him and his wife Caroline to the people.

There was an enormous crowd that day. At the afternoon meeting, Masupha spoke in the most glowing terms about Alfred's father, and then turned to Jacottet and said, 'My dear friend, we like you very much, but now the son of our Ntate has come, you must depart and let him take his inheritance.'

This was most embarrassing for Casalis, and, as he himself put it, 'very unfair towards Jacottet'.

—∽⊖—

While all these worries were slow to recede, Jacottet had the consolation of his family. In May 1887, at the age of fifteen months, Marcelle was filling the house with happy cries, playing with an imaginary rabbit as she waited for a toy one which Boegner had promised to send her from Paris. By the age of two, in January 1888, she had grown much and was strong; but from the point of view of intellectual advancement, Jacottet felt she was developing very slowly – she could speak only four or five words.

In the same breath, though, he could pronounce himself happy. He had been extremely fatigued for a couple of weeks, 'almost "prostrate", as messieurs the English would say', but now felt much better, especially as he had given up smoking almost entirely. His good humour was increased by the fact that his wife was expecting again, and he ventured to hope that 'this time it will be a boy'. It was.

Pierre-Henri was born on the morning of 15 April 1888. Dr Casalis chanced to be there and the birth went well. Mrs Jacottet, thanks to the good offices of Mme Mabille – who came specially from Morija to attend – and Mlle Cochet, recovered quickly. Henri was a contented baby and the Jacottets did not sacrifice too much sleep. Soon everyone said what a healthy baby he was, and even the coy father had to admit it proudly, though as he grew the little boy brought great vibrancy to the household as well as a great deal of work. Marcelle, now two and a half, was just beginning to speak. 'Am I not rich?' the father could exclaim.

By the time Rose-Germaine was born on 17 May 1889, he was a bit more circumspect. 'It aged me a little,' he mused wryly, 'to feel myself already a father of three children with all that heavy responsibility on my shoulders.'

Although Germaine established herself as something of a favourite in her father's eyes, the joy of her coming was very soon tempered by the news of the death of Jacottet's sister, Cecile-Louise.

Lovely, lively Louise. Her mother had called her 'the ornament of the family'. At twenty-five, she had had no time to make a husband happy. Her bubbly letters would no longer brighten her brother's labour-laden days. Édouard grieved for his sister and even more for his mother in her loss. The faraway death of Louise reminded him of his student years of exile in Germany: 'How sad it is to feel so far from her and how much do I understand what such a separation means!' However much he had grown to love Lesotho, and however much he remained dedicated to his calling, he would have been less than human had he not suffered from the melancholy of what he called 'heimweh'.

The death of Cecile-Louise was the first of a series that affected Jacottet greatly. Within a month of getting the news about his sister, he learned of the demise at Menton in the south of France, on 11 January 1890, of Théophile Jousse, his predecessor (between 1855 and 1882) at Thaba-Bosiu.

Jacottet's affection for Jousse went back to the time in 1883 when he visited Paris to confirm his desire to join the PEMS, and he passed a week in the company of Jousse – interim Director while Boegner was visiting Lesotho for the jubilee – and his wife. Jousse had corresponded with him regularly, giving him useful advice, and his two-volume history *La Mission Française Évangélique au Sud de l'Afrique*, published the year before, was a key reference work.

Of all the missionaries who had resided at Thaba-Bosiu, Jacottet wrote to his widow, it was the memory of Jousse that was most alive and loved. When, at a Saturday meeting, Jacottet announced his death, there was an explosion of sobs and tears so fierce that it was impossible to continue with the meeting. Solomon and Moshe and Mileka and Miriam and old Dorothea Likhima and 'Mamoretlo (who had been such a fine and faithful helper to the Jacottets) were all greatly affected. The older generation was beginning to pass away.

Next to go, on 4 September, was Silas Koma, a convert of the first generation of missionaries. He had been baptized on 7 November 1841, and had remained steadfast to his Christianity in the face of considerable temptation. In the period 1848–50, when the great defection and the return to paganism had taken place, he held firm, 'fearing not to carry the opprobriums of Christ'.

His steadiness led to his being chosen as one of the early evangelists, sent first to Malimong, then to Cana. There he was subjected to such continuous persecution that Jousse had to withdraw him to Matukeng, where he remained until his strength finally betrayed him. At Thaba-Bosiu his shrunken figure was one of the strongest pillars of support for Jacottet. Always smiling, he would arrive half an hour early for the services – until, in the last three years, he was unable to leave his hut. He was never without his Bible, morning and night, and he knew it almost off by heart. Jacottet felt humbled, whenever he visited him, to see the old man so happy in spite of his infirmities and his poverty. He and Moshe and Mareka were the last left to keep alive the tradition of the first days – what Jousse called 'the heroic time of the mission'.

Silas Koma's death coincided with a signal triumph for Jacottet: the conversion of the wife of Theko. He must have felt vindicated for concentrating effort on Theko's village. Theko's wife was the daughter of Molapo and in her youth had borne the name of Julia. She was a proud and difficult woman, and had formerly treated Jacottet quite badly when he visited her. But little by little she softened, and the founding of the outstation in her husband's village drew her closer. For some two years, she seemed to feel the desire to convert, but the indifference bred of joala (sorghum beer) and brandy made it difficult for her. Finally, however, she gave herself completely to the Lord. Few conversions gave Jacottet as much satisfaction as hers.

There were tangible rewards for the church. Theko's wife had considerable influence over her husband, and now she convinced him to establish himself on the top of Thaba-Bosiu mountain itself, of which he had always been the legal chief. But few actions escape contamination. The coming of Theko to the mountain roused the displeasure of his uncle, Masupha, who had, since the death of Moshoeshoe, considered himself chief, a de facto position uncontested since the Gun War. As his star had waned somewhat in recent times, he greatly resented this new blow. The mission lay on the route between the two – the hammer and the anvil – or, again in Jacottet's terms, between the goat and the cabbage. Jacottet feared that this might do harm to their religious work, which was their great end and raison d'être.

The Roman Catholic presence established at Masupha's village was not flourishing, as Jacottet well knew. 'In fact,' he told Boegner, 'it is a fiasco, considering the way in which it was founded and the nature of its propaganda … No one can build his house if the Eternal does not lend a hand, says our old Psalm, and the hand of the Almighty cannot be there.' Already, a dispute had led to the closure of the Catholic school, and Jacottet had the impression that Masupha wanted to come closer to the Protestants and to renew the rapport he had once had with the French missionaries. Jacottet did not plan to make his advances too easy, however.

He was convinced that the Catholics would not make major strides amongst the Basotho, 'above all amongst those who know the Word'. At first, they had been carried shoulder-high into the village of Masupha, but he felt that this had been done for short-term political reasons, coupled with the fact that a number of converts were tired of the Protestant discipline and found their worship too severe. He was encouraged that the pagans, who hoped to play one church off against the other, were beginning to realize that the Roman Catholic presence had not prevented the Protestants from extending their work right into the very house of Masupha. As was to be expected, Jacottet reserved most scorn for the Catholics, with their 'lack of seriousness', the 'shortage of safeguards which they demand of their catechumens' and the 'vulgarity of their attacks' on their rivals. Why, even the pagans could see the remnants of paganism in the customs and life of that church!

—◦◦—

The next death came as the Jacottets were preparing to receive the Conference for its meeting in April 1891, which was to be held at Thaba-Bosiu. This was no light undertaking. More than a dozen missionaries had to be housed, fed and generally cosseted over the period of a week. Jacottet dreaded this duty especially for his wife, who, although she was in good health, had a heavy load 'from one end of the year to the other', and besides always had to be watched over.

But everything had been planned well in advance, and Misses Keck and Cochet pitched in like yeomen. In addition, the deluge that preceded the Conference and the one that followed it held off for its duration, and the fine weather did not confine the participants indoors in their leisure hours. The new building for the girls' school eased the accommodation problem. As a consequence, the Jacottets took nothing but pleasure from the occasion.

Jacottet was in reflective mood at the time. He wished Boegner could see the station now. Although nothing much had changed since the Director had visited in 1883, everything had been overhauled. The one significant improvement, aside from the new school, was the stream of water which had been brought to the station (thanks to funds raised by the Comité des Dames of the PEMS in Paris) and which now decorated the courtyard; it was not a useless luxury, but on the contrary was used for all kinds of purposes by the Jacottets and the school. In one corner there was even, to the delight of the children, a fountain fed from a pretty reservoir, which had been cut from stone by a student in the Industrial School.

Jacottet's nostalgic mood was prompted by the news of the passing away of Eugène Casalis on 9 March. At the service on 13 April, attended by all the missionaries, by Chiefs Theko, Maama, Job and Ntsane, amongst others, as well as a huge crowd, their thoughts went back to the first time of the mission, and it seemed providential that the Conference was being held this year at Casalis's old station – at the foot of the mountain where for the first time the Word had been preached to the Basotho, and where the first Christians had been converted. 'It was not difficult,' mused Jacottet, 'to evoke memories of those almost legendary times in this place, which, for our mission, is almost a holy place.'

Sadly, one person – 'he who would have been before all' – was missing. The old pupil, the adopted son of Casalis, Masupha. Nevertheless, he made his existence felt. Less than two kilometres away, he organized for that day a great holiday to celebrate the baptism of his little daughter by the Catholics. It was no coincidence – he had been informed long before of the Protestant memorial meeting, but wanted to show that the Catholics had taken their place. Nevertheless, despite the food and drink he offered, the Protestant meeting was more successful. The Catholics did not leave it at that, however. The priests organized a procession, with banners flying, from Masupha's village past Thaba-Bosiu, right in front of the angry Protestants. This technicolor medieval pageant confronting the sober black and white of the Protestants was a gross provocation which scandalized even the pagans, and the chiefs had to intervene to persuade them to retreat. Jacottet was confirmed in his opinion that the Roman mission was more evil even than paganism, by becoming its surest ally and adding to it an intractable aggression.

The confrontation was for Jacottet an indication of the changes that had occurred since 1833. While eleven thousand Christians showed that the seed sown had grown into a healthy tree with thick branches, on the other side the difficulties had also grown. *Then* it had been all of Lesotho acclaiming the arrival of the three pioneers. *Now,* although the heart of the nation was still with the Protestants, the sons and grandsons of Moshoeshoe were not afraid, on occasion, to place themselves in opposition. And yet, thought Jacottet, despite failings in the mission, it had such a strong back that no wind could break it. It was founded on the rock of the Word. Its schools were so far ahead that it would take a miracle for the Catholics to catch up. Was Christ Himself not the chief of their mission? The one for whom they waited.

If there was chagrin at the provocative incidents, then the speeches that followed soon effaced them. Mabille quoted from Jeremiah. Seeiso, the son and representative of Letsie, recounted what his father remembered of the arrival of Casalis, and all the good he and his colleagues had brought the Basotho nation. He also conveyed the condolences of the Paramount Chief. Petrose Matlaha, the principal counsellor of Masupha, finding himself in an embarrassing position, nevertheless acquitted himself well. He spoke best when he spoke in his own name, this old catechist of Casalis.

Then spoke Moshe Mosetse, one of the oldest of the old, last of the first generation, baptized fifty years before. 'Do not ask me to repeat his speech,' Jacottet reported to Boegner. 'Impossible to translate – it is too Sesotho, too completely Sesotho for that. Moshe is, in fact, the Mosotho amongst the Basotho. For him this first period of the mission is an epoch always living, and his heart warms up to these old memories.'

After him spoke Abraham Ramatšeatsana, baptized six months before Moshe. Like Makoanyane (and Ratšiu), he had been one of Moshoeshoe's chief counsellors. He had also been in Liphofung cave with Arbousset and Moshoeshoe on 23 February 1840, when they named it 'Lehaha-la-Sontaha'. He was over ninety, broken and decrepit, but still with a grand air and noble stature. His head was not always clear, but on this day he made one of the most incisive speeches Jacottet had ever heard. Alluding to Letsie and Masupha, he asked that the assembled people pray for their conversion. He said that the two great chiefs must enter the church by their own efforts. Thinking perhaps of the story of Makoanyane and the crevasse, and of Makoanyane's 'precipice of evil', he exhorted them in metaphor: 'Thus when an ox is fallen into a ravine, it does not wait for someone to come to rescue it, but it makes every effort to rescue itself.' Echoes from the cave.

One of the striking things about the speeches was that the dominant note was joy, not sorrow. This, thought Jacottet, was how it had to be. The general belief was that Casalis, long ill, had entered into eternal happiness and had joined Arbousset, Gosselin, Moshoeshoe and all his children in the faith who had preceded him. The old said that they were happy Casalis was already there, and that he would look forward to welcoming them when it was their turn to enter on high.

Unlike the outburst that greeted the demise of Jousse, this response was more circumspect, a sweeter and more Christian emotion, thought Jacottet. Casalis had left Lesotho in 1854, so few present had known him personally, but all knew his name and his story. He had been the first to drag Lesotho out of the shadows of sin.

What impressed Jacottet most was the reverence and loyalty the Basotho, so often accused of ingratitude, had for the memory of the pioneer missionaries. There had been forged an alliance between the Basotho nation and the French missionaries – an alliance of a kind that existed nowhere else. This Sunday had shown to Jacottet that, despite the chicanery of Masupha and the Catholics, the alliance had not been breached and the hearts of the Basotho were still beating in time with those of the missionaries.

The significance of the death of Casalis was mainly symbolic. He had long before been replaced by Boegner as Director of the PEMS. The death of Louis Duvoisin, a missionary of the second generation, was a different matter: it led to bitter controversy.

Jacottet visited 'our dear Duvoisin' shortly before he died. He considered him a man concerning whom only good could be spoken. It was hard to believe that his days were numbered, as his face did not carry 'the imprint of death'. Dying seemed to hold no terror for him – he was happy to go where the Lord called him. Duvoisin had represented the idealistic side in the Conference, which the more practical majority often neglected. He was, in a way, the conscience of the Conference, and Jacottet would miss him.

He would not miss Duvoisin's family, however. The station of Berea had been founded by Pierre-Joseph Maitin in the 1840s. Maitin still lived at Berea: Duvoisin, his successor, had married his daughter. His son, Charles Maitin, was a trader at Boqate. Now that Duvoisin was dead, Jacottet was saddled with the temporary supervision of the parish, in addition to his own.

There was, to say the least, bad blood between him and Charles Maitin. Things only got worse when Duvoisin's widow and old man Maitin refused point-blank to vacate the station. Soon the Maitins, particularly Charles, were intriguing with the chiefs in the area, not shy to accuse Jacottet of any number of wickednesses. It took eighteen months and much correspondence to evict Mme Duvoisin and old Maitin.

This episode, and the pain it caused him, confirmed Jacottet in his conviction that it was necessary in future to prevent missionaries (such as the Germonds at Thabana-Morena, the Maitins at Berea, and the Mabilles at Morija) from regarding stations as their personal property, fiefdoms of a particular family.

Together with the experiences of Vollet and the Christmann scandal, this episode helped Jacottet fuse certain ideas into the beginnings of a coherent plan.

Gustave Christmann, a native of Ban de la Roche, in Bas-Rhin, but educated at Basle, came to Basutoland in 1875. He was very soon sent across the mountains to Paballong in East Griqualand. By 1888, unsettled by the untimely death of his young wife, Christmann was revealing himself to be a disciple of Guillaume Monod, a member of the PEMS Committee, who proclaimed himself to be the Messiah.

To say the least, this did not sit well with his colleagues. Perhaps Christmann was taking his own name a bit too literally? He wrote to Jacottet trying to defend his position, but his arguments were rejected out of hand. Jacottet foresaw 'a deplorable scandal', which would be 'a triumph for our enemies, who are numerous'. He categorically pronounced Christmann crazy ('toqué'). 'That M. Monod calls himself Christ one can believe,' he exclaimed, stunned, 'but that there are relatively reasonable people who believe him – that goes beyond limits!'

While Christmann poured out his heart in numerous missives, the Conference could not make up its mind to winkle him out, and palmed the decision off on Paris, prevarication which annoyed Jacottet greatly. Eventually Christmann did leave for France, where he died comparatively young in 1890, while Monod was forced to leave the PEMS Committee.

Jacottet attributed Christmann's madness to two factors: firstly, he had not been properly trained in theology at a fully recognized theological college, and was one of those recruits with a substandard theological education; secondly, as a widower, his long isolation in No-Man's-Land had affected his brain and his imagination.

Jacottet had for years been storing a basketful of resentment against certain conditions within the mission. What he and his colleagues lacked most, in his view, were true personal relations based on Christian fraternity. Though they helped each other, it was usually only on a superficial level. When he first arrived in Lesotho, he had hoped to find in missionaries like Mabille and Duvoisin fellowship and support from a religious point of view, a Christian rapport of the kind he had had with Junod and Godet in Neuchâtel. But it had failed to materialize, which he regretted deeply. He freely admitted that his outspoken impetuosity in the beginning had not helped, but he denied that he had deliberately provoked his adversaries. A couple of years later, he had had a long talk with Dieterlen, who indicated that he too felt isolated, thereby cementing what was already a close friendship between two like-minded people.

Jacottet felt that his colleagues were often too timid to venture on to the true terrain of conscience and the religious life. This meant that there was often a certain tension in Conference; if they prayed together more – and not just in Conference – he thought many of the things that offended them would disappear. This collegial distance was exacerbated by his own self-doubt. His work weighed heavily on him, and he decided that the evil he detected was not in his flock but in himself. He lacked the sense of leading a true Christian life, of feeling a real communion with Christ, a faith and lively hope in the life eternal. He often feared there was a gap between what he taught and what he did. For this thankless work, a man needed to be filled with the Holy Spirit. What Jacottet felt much of the time was inadequacy and guilt. Prayer, for him, was the only answer.

After a few years, too, Jacottet had learned that the mission, being a relatively small and closed community, was a beehive of concoctions and gossip. 'Lesotho,' he confided to Boegner, 'est le pays par excellence des potions et des cancans.'

The lack of collegiality, the isolation, the personal fiefdoms, the need for discipline, all this prompted Jacottet (and others) to think about the organization of the Lesotho church, and the progress from mission to church. Practical considerations also began to force the issue. Some parishes were large and wealthy, others were small and poor. Some could afford more evangelists and outstations than others. If progress was not to be uneven, it was clear that resources would have to be more evenly spread. In addition, the first Basotho ministers were coming up for ordination. Their salaries were dependent on the church as a whole rather than a local parish, and would have to be found not from Paris, but from local sources. The idea of a Central Chest, made up of proportional contributions from the congregations, had been floated for some years, but proposals from Kohler and Jacottet in 1891 were found unsuitable and premature. Eventually, in 1893, a five-member commission devised a scheme which the Conference accepted unanimously. It was a major step in the march towards church unity.

―◦◉―

Edwin Smith noted that the prestige of the missionaries was never greater than in these years: they were 'universally recognized as the saviours of the nation'. The church progressed so rapidly that soon it seemed 'the whole nation would within a measurable period be gathered into it'. Yet paganism also was undergoing a réveil and presented challenges that caused cracks in the mission and threatened to create a chasm. At the heart of it were relationships between the sexes in Basotho society, and two often overlapping issues: bohali and polygamy.

As to the former, the church had always specifically advertised marriages as being without bohali (the transferring of cattle at marriage from the husband's family to the wife's) and Moshoeshoe had recognized the validity of these marriages. Letsie, however, had begun to waver. Other chiefs wanted to undermine the disciplinary rules of the church, claiming that marriage without bohali was a severe blow to their own social system.

In 1888, when a Christian woman requested a divorce from her polygamous husband, Letsie responded by calling a pitso. On the surface, Letsie seemed magnanimous. He suggested that Christian marriages without bohali should be recognized. But the French missionaries, including Jacottet, saw this as a trap. Behind it, they detected the hand of the Catholic priests, who openly sanctioned bohali marriages. The full might of the chiefs, Letsie, Masupha, Jonathan, bore down on the missionaries, willing them to accept such marriages in turn. Mabille stood firm as a rock: the Protestant church would never countenance bohali. While the status quo was restored, from then on Christian marriages were no longer contested – a small victory for the Protestants. On the negative side for them, the pitso had conferred on the Catholics influence and prestige which they had never previously enjoyed and their own work began to flourish, often to the detriment of the Protestants.

The next crisis peaked at the meeting of the Conference at Thabana-

Morena in April 1889. It revolved around the question of the 'petites femmes', the minor wives in polygamous marriages. They were called 'lirethe', or 'heels', by the Basotho. A number of these 'heels', who wanted to save their souls through conversion, had faced dire consequences: 'This movement has excited much persecution,' wrote Mabille, who was implacably opposed to polygamy. 'Where young men and women are still under the authority of their fathers, these seek by all kinds of threats to hinder their conversion. They make them drink various medicines to cure them of "sickness of the spirit", as pagans call conversion. Those who have to suffer most are the married women and especially those who are no more than concubines. I know some who have been thrashed and thrashed again, and whose husbands have taken away their clothes on Sunday to deter them from coming to religious services ...' Several truly tragic dramas had been enacted.

The bone of contention within the missionary body was the treatment of the lirethe – whether they should be admitted as full members of the church. Up until now, they had been allowed to become catechumens, but could not be baptized or become full members unless they left their husbands. At one time this had involved a serethe actually leaving the village of her husband, but this could be so onerous – it often meant abandoning her children – that in later years she would be allowed to stay in the village with her husband's consent. But, according to customary law, she was still married and could only obtain her freedom if the bohali cattle were restored, something most of the parties were not so keen on.

Some of the younger missionaries were deeply unhappy with this state of affairs and wanted to allow full membership to the lirethe. They argued that the wife of a polygamist only had one husband herself, and, since she was allowed to become a catechumen, the principle of admission had already been conceded. In addition, on a more pragmatic level, the prevailing rule was hampering many from joining the church. They therefore proposed to the Conference the following resolution: 'The Conference, desirous of opening the door of the church to the wives of polygamists without, however, causing disorder in our own flocks, decides that, in certain cases and with all precautions taken to assure to a secondary wife the possibility of living with her husband in a manner compatible with her title of Christian, a wife called serethe can be admitted to the church.'

This certainly put the jackal amongst the sheep. The resolution was carried by ten votes to three, with five abstentions. Jacottet voted for; Mabille, Ellenberger and almost certainly Duvoisin (all veterans from Canton Vaud) voted against. Mabille was concerned for the purity of the church: 'The word of God ordains that each man have his wife and each woman her husband; and all deviation from that divine rule is impudicity.' Mabille and Ellenberger threatened to resign, so the Conference chose to refer the matter to the Committee for ratification. Letters flew to Paris like swallows heading north for the European summer.

Mabille knew what a blow his departure would be to the mission. But he wrote an anguished letter to Boegner asking to be sent to the Loyalty Islands if the PEMS did replace the LMS there: 'Who would take my great district with all its outstations? Who would take over the Printing Works and the Book Depot and the Bible School? But what is there for me to do? I cannot ask the Committee to do for others what I do not wish them to do for me: if my conscience does not allow me to receive the secondary wives while they still live with their husbands, the consciences of my brethren will not allow them to defer longer their admission.' Although he was in a minority in the Conference, he did point out that he had the support of others in the mission: 'One thing to be noted is that the majority of the lady missionaries are in favour of the old rule, which demands séparation de corps. They comprehend perhaps more than we what degradation there is for the wife in what is proposed.' On the other hand, indicative of the generation gap, his own son Ernest voted against him.

Jacottet, as usual, gave Boegner the confidential benefit of his own opinions. Although he voted with the majority, he had only recently been converted to their cause and retained strong reservations. He urged Boegner to act with extreme caution: Mabille was the kingpin of the mission, and Jacottet had told him this personally. He felt that if the Paris Committee limited acceptance of the lirethe to completely rare cases, Mabille would accept this. He also felt that it was right to change things only if there was complete unanimity, which in this case there wasn't. And he felt, with Mabille, that it was wrong to mistrust the Basotho: they should be consulted through the consistories, and a synod should sanction the change. He urged Paris to act quickly.

They did not. No reply had been received by the beginning of the following year, and a rupture was imminent. Jacottet, who saw himself in an intermediary position, believed that, given time for reflection and allowed to make his own mind up, Mabille would compromise and accept the fait accompli. Unfortunately, he said, Ellenberger was very bitter towards the Conference for 'mean and personal reasons', and would rattle the cage whenever he could to prevent an accommodation. Dieterlen agreed: he called Ellenberger 'entêté' – pig-headed. Dieterlen was one of the more ardent of those wanting easier acceptance of the lirethe, but Jacottet felt that, since Dieterlen had become Director of the Theological School, he no longer had a church of his own and did not understand certain practical difficulties.

Eventually, the Committee came to its decision: seeing that there was insufficient unity, the rule which had been in existence for fifty years should not be overturned.

In September 1890, Jacottet could report that in some areas there was a movement towards conversion. He cited the case of a polygamist who agreed to send his second wife back to her family. In five years of being in charge of the Thaba-Bosiu parish, Jacottet had not experienced such a case. It was a real encouragement, he said. But he did not record the feelings of the second wife.

On 20 October 1891, Letsie died, aged about 93. He had been a weak and vacillating king, even a cowardly one, and, unlike his father, had not been held in very high esteem by the missionaries. He had tried to manoeuvre his son Maama into the succession, but his counsellors would have none of it: 'Letsie, oa hlanya – Letsie, you are mad.' They and the chiefs, skilfully supported by the Resident Commissioner, Marshal Clarke, eventually ensured that his eldest son, Lerotholi, was received at the great assembly of the people. Lerotholi, who had made a name for himself in the Gun War as a warrior, was stronger, more decisive, and most favourable to the mission, even moving his capital from Makeneng near Likhoele to Matsieng close to Morija.

Letsie was buried on top of Thaba-Bosiu. It meant a great deal of work for the Jacottets, but by now Louise was taking such occasions in her stride. In fact, she actually enjoyed the bustle.

Their only concern was for their fourth child, Gustave-Ernest, who had been born on 13 September 1891. The poor little thing was ill with bronchitis, but eventually made a full recovery.

CHAPTER EIGHTEEN

FOQOQO

1893

I t is hard to believe that only yesterday the Maloti were still virtually unexplored. For fifty years after the French missionaries arrived, the 'Maletsunyane falls remained undiscovered. They were scarcely more than fifty kilometres from Morija as the crow flies, but they were hidden behind the first two ranges of the mountains, the massif that covered two thirds of the country and stretched eastwards to the Drakensberg escarpment, a 'barrier of spears' separating Basutoland from Natal.

Surprisingly, after Arbousset's two early journeys to the north, no serious attempt was made to penetrate this last frontier. True, the missionaries were preoccupied. And Moshoeshoe and his successor, Letsie, discouraged curiosity, preferring to keep secret their cattle pastures and hunting grounds. But a further reason was that the hinterland was practically uninhabited, except for a scattering of Bushmen, who led a nomadic life and only occasionally made a nuisance of themselves marauding for cattle, so there was no reason to go in search of souls.

As late as 1878, when he made a journey seeking a direct route from Matatiele to Morija to attend the Conference, Jean Preen could comment that 'the greater part of these mountains will never be inhabited'. The cold, he said, was too severe, and there was no firewood. He was wrong. Within two or three years, as a result of overpopulation and the Gun War, the people of the plains had hurled themselves on the mountains, and Mabille, lamenting that the majority of the migrants 'belonged to the most heathen section of the tribe and the most hostile to civilization and Christianity', was insisting that the church should follow them and 'place them within reach of the means of grace'.

The Basotho had long believed that the frost of the Maloti was inimical to sorghum and maize. But necessity proved them mistaken. At first, villages began to spread up the Senqu river valley, and across the first range of the Maloti into the Makhaleng valley, the Baphuthi of Chief Moorosi being in the forefront on the Senqu. The Gun War, however, provided the trigger for the new and sudden influx. The old enemy, the Batlokoa, at least those who had been allowed to settle around Matatiele, now sided with the Basotho national-ists. After their defeat by the colonial troops, a section of the tribe under Lelingoana was at last allowed by Letsie to settle on the upper reaches of the Senqu near its junction with a major tributary, the Seate (now the Khubelu). Letsie then sent Tlhakanelo, the son of one of his counsellors, to establish himself near Sehonghong to prevent any move towards independence by the Baphuthi immigrants, and he sent his own son Rafolatsane to ensure the same dominion over the Batlokoa. During the early 1880s, much of the region was still unexplored by the missionaries, however. So Jacottet's first two journeys into the mountains – in 1884 with Mabille and a few other colleagues, and in 1885 to place Josefa and his family at the new outstation on the Senqunyane – were through terra relatively incognita. There were parts of the mountain country he visited which were as empty and elemental as the world on the fourth day of Creation, but now people were beginning to creep in and establish themselves in the most remote places. What concerned him was that they knew nothing of the mission or of Christianity, and their paganism was probably the same as it had been fifty years before.

As the deserts of the Maloti were being populated, they became for Jacottet 'deserts' of another kind. He was convinced, after his early explorations, that it was necessary to bring the Word to the interior. He was also sure that this land not yet sown was too remote for European missionaries, who would have been resented by the local chiefs. Within a few years, a solution presented itself. With the prospect of a new field of labour, the Conference decided, in 1885, to reopen the Theological School. Overcoming its timid start in 1882 under Krüger, it reopened at Morija in 1887 under Dieterlen with three pupils – Job Moteane, Carlisle Motebang and John Mohapeloa. Fired by the youthful enthusiasm of Jacottet, fresh into the field himself, the new initiative gave renewed purpose to the mother-stations. The mountain 'deserts' would be ade-quate outlets for the energies of the pioneering black pastorate.

The headwaters of the Senqu remained largely unexplored. So in October 1887, the Resident Commissioner for Basutoland, Marshal Clarke, set out with sixteen men, including a police officer and representatives of Letsie, Jonathan and Joel (but no guides), to rectify this situation. Clarke collected three weeks' supply of bread and groceries, while his 'followers' took with them a supply of tasty lipabi – maize finely ground, roasted, and mixed with sugar and salt. Clarke also took with him the recently enrolled theological student, Job Moteane. The journal Moteane kept is the first account by a Mosotho of such a journey to the east.

Some years later, when their theological studies were over, it was decided to place Motebang and Moteane under the guidance of experienced missionaries, the former being posted to Thaba-Bosiu under Jacottet, the latter kept at Morija under Mabille (Mohapeloa, being younger, went to Lovedale School in the eastern Cape for further training).

Motebang was the first to prove his worth sufficiently to be ordained. At Thaba-Bosiu, on 2 August 1891, he became the first Mosotho to be recognized as a full minister of religion. Moteane's turn came a month later at Morija. In the words of Jacottet, the mission of Basutoland, 'slow and conservative, had waited fifty-eight years before establishing the Native pastorate'. He was clearly pleased with his part in changing the situation, although he was aware that other Societies had not been too successful when they rushed the process.

In 1892, Moteane was placed at Tlhakanelo's, and a few months later, in response to the pleas of a minor chief, Tšepe, Motebang established a new mission station at Molumong, just round a ridge from Rafolatsane's village, and two days' journey from Sehonghong. So, as the Basotho settled the Maloti, the Basotho missionaries followed. It was a proud moment for Jacottet and the mission − the Gospel had penetrated new territory.

In March of 1893, Jacottet made another epic journey across the mountains, one which had a profound effect on his temper and his outlook for the future. This time he crossed the first range through what is now Bushmen's pass, forded the Makhaleng, went over the 'Pass of the Jackals' and through the wilderness beyond to Khoanyane's village overlooking the Semena, a major tributary of the Senqu. Then on to Tlhakanelo's, having to wait a day for the Senqu, which had been swollen by recent rains, to subside. He spent three days at Moteane's station of Sehonghong, and they visited the famous cave near which Soai, the last Bushman chief, had been hunted down by Joel and Jonathan Molapo some twenty years earlier. The wall of this great overhanging rock was covered with numerous scenes of hunts and battles, in which the Bushmen were depicted as always victorious, delicate in their artistry of bow and spear, their enemies clumsy with big hands and thick legs. Crossing two important streams, the Mashai and the Linakeng, Jacottet arrived at Rafolatsane's on the 15th, where he was warmly welcomed by Carlisle Motebang.

Jacottet found the route hazardous, full of narrow paths and precipices. There were only a few bridle paths, and, rather than following them, he found it was almost easier to pick his way across the ranges from one valley to the next. Yet he was impressed enough by the journey up to this point to be almost poetic in his vision of nature 'so virgin and fresh'.

Fain would I give you some idea of this beautiful country, which is still so little known, of these mountains which are so varied in aspect. In some parts, everything is so green, so peaceful that one would imagine oneself somewhere amongst the loveliest nooks of the Gruyère; everything is fresh and charming; a carpet of verdure, flowers in profusion, brooks with water so clear that it is almost luminous, here and there thickets of arborescent growth. When one emerges from the scorched plains of Basutoland, the contrast is vivid. This is the pasture of the high Alps at its best; and above all that a blue sky, brilliant sunshine, the likes of which are unknown in Switzerland. Elsewhere, bare and stony plateaux, scarcely covered with a rare and coarse grass, marshy in parts, but waterless in general; this is a picture of solitude, almost a desert, and on every side, as far as the eye can reach, unknown and as yet unnamed summits, mountain ranges which vanish over the horizon in tangled confusion, intersected by deep and narrow converging gorges. On every hand a jumbled maze of peaks and rounded summits, a chaos of rocks and grassy slopes. The image of a world scarcely begun, as yet unfinished. Elsewhere again, wild gorges at the bottom of which roaring torrents are confined between vertical cliffs which rise to giddy heights. Beyond, the gorge widens and becomes a valley, the mountains recede and the cliffs vanish, grassy ledges rise one above the other, superimposed villages appear on them, sometimes suspended on the slopes at dizzy altitudes, elsewhere hard by the river; fields of wheat, maize, and millet lend tranquillity to the scene; great herds of cattle or flocks of sheep browse around. The landscape has changed; the presence of man has completely altered its aspect.

Journeys have a habit of turning into something else, of changing direction, of presenting the unexpected. Jacottet departed somewhat from his itinerary. With Tšepe, the minor chief of the area, he set out along the Mokhotlong river on an eland hunt, wryly defending himself against imagined criticism by saying that 'once is not habitual'. But the hunt was only a pretext: the real purpose of the excursion was to see a mysterious place called Foqoqo by the locals (the origin of the name is not known, but it may be an ideophone signifying amazement). After a few hours' ride in the wild and secluded Mokhotlong valley and a night sheltering in a remote cave, they arrived after midday at their destination. Foqoqo turned out to be the magnificent view looking eastward from the edge of the Drakensberg escarpment. Perhaps sensing a high-water mark in the tide of his life's experience, Jacottet was awestruck, gazing at this last frontier as God had created it.

Imagine a majestic rampart, perpendicular, created and flanked with bastions and jagged towers, six to seven hundred feet in height and stretching on either side as far as the eye can reach. From the Mont-aux-Sources to the borders of Natal and Matatiele this same bastion extends without a break, like a gigantic fortress. Until it passes out of sight, the eye follows this black, towering cliff, rent again and again by narrow clefts which fearless mountaineers alone would venture to scale. At our feet lies a green and smiling country, wooded here and there, still very mountainous, but infinitely less wild than the high plateau from which we view it. Beyond this are hills and then the plains. We guess the towns and the villages without seeing them. Farthest of all lies the sea, behind a light veil of white clouds. Very far away, to the left, the mountains of Zululand, the land of Chaka and Cetwayo; it is there that the terrible drama of Isandhlwana was enacted, there that the Prince Imperial died. Behind us is a bare, elevated plateau, dismal, cold, marshy, but not devoid of a certain wild grandeur.

For a transitory, enchanted moment, he held his breath in the presence of this new world, a world scarcely begun, commensurate with his capacity to wonder, geography and history joined together in a vision of the eye and the imagination, a moment of rare communion. But the gods of the mountains allow only a brief glimpse of the sublime; within a few minutes, the mists surge along the cliffs, the clouds roll in like white waves from the ocean, the vast horizon vanishes, darkness falls, and knife-like rain cuts to the marrow, leaving only a haunting memory and a treacherous retreat over boggy ground, where footprints disappear without trace. Jacottet had to turn back.

They saw no eland on the return journey west. The largest mammals were the white- or grey-bellied ice rats sunning themselves on the rocks, and the hunters returned to Molumong 'without bagging anything but a couple of inoffensive marmots'. Overhead, though, he watched that rare bird the lammergeier, half vulture, half eagle, gliding in the sky, looking to dash its carrion bones on to its ancient ossuary. Once it had marked its spot in history by mocking the Father of Tragedy; now it was being harried by lesser birds protecting their young – to the point of indignity. It almost made him sad.

On the 23rd, he resumed his travels, this time going north, fording the Senqu and its tributary the Ngope-Khubelu, visiting Lelingoana, the Batlokoa chief, and Lekunya, of the smaller Bakholokoe clan. He then reached the top of the plateau and spent a night at an altitude of 2 950 metres, before sweeping round, over the desolate plateau, to Rahane's Nek (now 'Moteng pass), making this his most complete journey through the Maloti.

After eighteen days in the heart of the mountains, with the horses exhausted, he experienced a strange sensation at the sight of the sun setting on the plains of the Orange Free State as he looked down on them. What this 'strange sensation' was he did not explain, but he added that it was 'such a different world from the one we were leaving behind us'. This was clearly an important

CHAPTER NINETEEN

DEATH AND THE FALL

1893–1898

J acottet returned from the Maloti refreshed in body and spirit: 'It made me much better, and will allow me to continue my work in a more lively way. I was very close to a physical and moral *breakdown* [he used the English word] and this diversion was necessary, as well as the bath of bracing air which I have taken, for some weeks, in the admirable nature of the Maloti. All the enchantment of the alpinist in me was recaptured.'

From a missionary point of view, he considered the trip to have been useful, too. Thanks to money from the Cape General Mission, it had been possible to supply the pastors, who were facing great hardship and privation, with many essentials. 'It is a beautiful and great work, and I have returned completely overwhelmed by it,' he said. 'We have in Job and Carlisle workers of a class, faithfulness and disinterestedness of which there is no doubt.'

Thinking of Vollet and others, he was less complimentary about new recruits from Europe. He chided Boegner for this: 'I do it only for love of this church of Lesotho, which could be so great and have such a future if it continues to be well directed; for that, it needs special personnel, who are above average.'

At the same time, Jacottet's reputation for competence and clarity was growing. He made a fine impression at the Methodist Synod in Bloemfontein in the middle of 1893, though his satisfaction was tainted by a severe bout of gastritis, which left him very tired on his return to Thaba-Bosiu.

The benefits of the journey to the Maloti and the spiritual recovery brought about by the experience of Foqoqo were consequently cancelled out, and he was not in great physical shape when the greatest fear that parents can know fell upon him and his wife.

Towards the end of August, their four-year-old pride and joy, Germaine, was indisposed for a few days. Since she had just been vaccinated, the Jacottets attributed her illness to the effects of the vaccine, and none of the symptoms allowed them to foresee what was to come. On the night of Wednesday 30 August, she was coughing, though not alarmingly. Nevertheless, early the next morning, the rather laboured manner of her coughing prompted her parents to send for the doctor from Maseru. Just before ten o'clock, an hour and a half after the messenger set out, Mrs Jacottet called her husband – the child had gone into a fit of choking. She only had time to say, 'Maman, hold me,' before dropping into her mother's arms, lifeless. All efforts to revive her over the next fifteen minutes were futile. 'Our dear little one, so strong, so lively, so happy, was no more than a little body without life,' wept Jacottet. 'It was all so sudden, so terrible, that we hardly had time to grasp what had happened.'

It was diphtheria that had taken her by the throat and suffocated her. What emptiness this caused the parents! 'The house,' said her father, 'seems dead and lifeless without her. Of all our children, Germaine was the strongest and liveliest, with beautiful red cheeks which were the admiration of everyone, large brown eyes, an air of splendid health. How hard it is to accept this instant disappearance and to know that we will never again see here this open little face.'

They buried her next day in the new cemetery below the mission station. Friends came from Morija, Berea and Cana. 'God, who has taken her from us,' said Jacottet, 'has left us with the anguish.'

But that was not all. There were the other children. The burial was on Friday. Despite their desperate precautions, by Monday morning the contagion had seized Henri. On Tuesday morning, it was Marcelle's turn. 'How could God do this?' cried their father, faced with the annihilation of his whole family. Only the baby, Gustave, remained free of the sickness. For days they fought for the lives of their children, living hour by hour with a sharp pain in their hearts. They had the help of Dr Savage from Maseru, and of Eugènie Keck, but it was terrible for them to see their older children, each like a small animal with a leopard at its throat, in the grip of the same disease that had taken Germaine. They felt that they were in the hands of God, that He must protect them.

Fortunately, forewarned by the sacrifice of their one child, they checked the disease in its first stages. Henri was stronger than Marcelle and recovered quickest. After a week, they were both out of danger.

Although he testified to his wife's great courage in this time of trial, Jacottet noted her extreme fatigue in addition to her grief. She was also pregnant. 'God save her and me,' he prayed, 'from a new loss.'

But his headaches did return. And in January, his wife was delivered of a stillborn child.

Within a few weeks, she was pregnant again.

—◦◦—

Death was not done yet. He must eat till he burst.

During a service in the church at Morija, a storm came close and lightning flashed around. A mother hardly noticed when her daughter quietly laid her head against her shoulder, but when the last hymn was ended, the child could not be roused.

—◦◦—

In 1886, Ernest Mabille had returned to Basutoland, having finished his studies at the Maison des Missions. Adolphe Mabille, in the face of Jacottet's grim opposition, wanted his son at Morija to help with his crushing weight of work. The heir apparent to the paramountcy had other ideas. While Moshoeshoe had had Casalis as his own missionary, and Letsie had had the son-in-law of Casalis, Adolphe Mabille, Lerotholi believed he was owed the grandson. The Conference felt that they could not afford to alienate the future king, so Lerotholi got 'the girl he had courted'. Ernest went to 'the place of Lerotholi'.

Nevertheless, Adolphe Mabille felt he had his family around him. In addition to Ernest and his daughter-in-law Margaret, his daughter Aline taught Algebra, Geology, History and English Literature in the Theological School; Florence helped her father in the Bible School and in the Sesuto Book Depot, taught the white children of the area and became postmistress of the newly opened post office at Morija; and Eugènie helped in the Bible School and Book Depot. In 1889, Mrs Mabille's half-brother, Alfred Casalis, his wife Caroline and daughter Renée stayed with them for six months while Mabille taught Alfred Sesotho, before Alfred went north to found the station at Qalo, the residence of Molapo's son Joel, which finally completed the string of stations of the mission.

In 1892, Louis Mabille completed the return of Adolphe's children. In 1887, when Louis had earned his baccalaureate, Adolphe had written to him saying that he should buy himself the commentaries of Godet, since 'you cannot have better books'. When Louis entered upon his missionary studies, Adolphe again gave him the advice of experience: 'Believe me, for a missionary career you need as severe a training as for the home pastorate. It is an insult to missionary work to think that any ordinary studies are sufficient. Read, if you can, outside your courses; but take care to read only books which will not lead you astray. I do not mean that you should not make yourself familiar with the new theology and know what it says; but do it as if in the presence of something suspect; and please, my Louis, pray that the new theology, which reduces the Lord Jesus to nothing, may not sweep you off your feet ... Now that there are workshops at the Mission House, try to learn some carpentry. I recommended this to Ernest, but he neglected it and now deeply regrets that he did so. Learn music well and to sing well from memory. Neglect nothing that will give you mastery with your hands. In the mission field, you know, one has to do *everything*.'

On the eve of Louis's return to Lesotho, Mabille warned him about false expectations: 'Only remember that what is called the romance of missions exists no longer in Basutoland. The work to be done is one of consolidation. Without doubt it increases: in some places like a snowball on the roll. The work grows, whether one wants it to grow or not, in spite of all obstacles. The people become more independent and their behaviour is often disagreeable. One must go on, all the same ...' This was sound advice coming from someone whom Jacottet, a more subtle man, called 'the strong man, the indefatigable pioneer, the real leader of the mission since 1860'.

Indefatigable Mabille certainly was. Edwin Smith itemized his routine:

The day started early: the first fresh hour was always spent with God. Three times a week he left his study at six o'clock to give a singing lesson at the Normal School. When he came to breakfast at 7.30 he had been up for two or three hours. After family prayers he taught at the Bible School from eight to ten or eleven. Then he went to the Printing-shop. An establishment with fourteen native journeymen and apprentices was no bagatelle: there was always work to supervise, proofs to correct, estimates to prepare, difficulties to clear up, personal squabbles to reconcile, and correspondence to attend to. Hard by was the Book Depot, the business of which had so increased that books to the value of well over a thousand pounds were sold every year. Mabille also supplied materials and furniture for all the schools in the country. Whatever assistance he had, it all meant work for him. The mid-day meal was at 12.30. Mabille generally came in late and out of breath through hurrying. He usually had a packet of proofsheets in his hand which would be laid beside his plate and corrected during the meal; often he would write between mouthfuls, while conversation went on around him. The sacred quiet time in his room with Mrs. Mabille followed lunch. People would be waiting for him when he returned to his study: some of the numerous Christians seeking advice, teachers and evangelists with their troubles, messengers from Letsie or other Chiefs to discuss some matters of tribal importance. Two or three times a week he mounted his big roan, Passy, and set off to visit one or other of his twenty-four out-stations ... At home, half an hour, or perhaps three-quarters, were given to his family after supper. About nine it was his wont to retire to his study. At midnight his lamp would still be burning: it was frequently two or three in the morning before he retired to rest. These quiet hours were given to preparing lessons, writing articles and books and letters – four hundred letters a month were a fair average. Some of them were business letters; others were personal letters of several closely-written sheets, in French, English and Sesuto.

Sunday was never a day of repose. As a rule Mabille preached in the morning to some seven or eight hundred people; and in the afternoon there was another service. With what force and enthusiasm he led the singing in his powerful voice!

—❧—

But, by early 1894, when Mabille visited Thaba-Bosiu, Jacottet remarked on his failing health and agreed to take over some of his duties. 'There is nothing that I would not do for him,' Jacottet told Boegner. 'He is one of those rare great men I have come across. Sickness does not frighten him. I have trouble imagining what we would do without him. It would be a loss completely irreparable.'

Mabille brushed aside his problems: 'As for myself, my health is not bad, but my head is more tired than usual.' To ease the old pilgrim's burden, the Conference decided to divide some of his responsibilities between Louis, who took over much of his pastoral work including the outstations, and Alfred Casalis, who moved to Morija to head the Bible School, the Printing Works (including *Leselinyana*) and the Book Depot – bearing out Dieterlen's comment that 'Mabille's work is that of two men'. This enabled Mabille to complete the second edition of his Sesotho-English dictionary, 'the fruit,' noted Edwin Smith, 'of thirty years' study of the language.'

In spite of his failing health, the Mabilles made a trip north to visit Ernest and to baptize their newborn granddaughter. When Mabille returned to Morija on 10 May, he had severe pain in the chest, and then in the abdomen. On the 13th, Whit Sunday, he could not serve communion. By the end of the next week, it was clear that the end was close. His eye was not dim but his natural forces had eroded beyond revival. Jacottet hurried to Morija, along with many, many others: Dyke and Christol and Dieterlen, Sir Godfrey Lagden (who had recently replaced his friend Clarke as Resident Commissioner) and Anglican missionaries, all the evangelists and a host of anonymous folk whose lives Mabille had touched. Lerotholi knelt at his bedside, refusing a chair, as Mabille gave him his last words of advice. Jacottet saw him on Saturday, the 19th.

The next day, Christol and Jacottet stood in for him in the church, which was full to overflowing. He died in the evening, a month short of his fifty-eighth birthday. He was buried the following day, and many hundreds filed past his body. His coffin was carried by his evangelists and Bible School students, but they did not take it to the corner of the manse garden where the missionary families were normally buried. Some years before, an old Basotho woman, one of the converts, had said to him on her deathbed: 'One thing makes me sad, my father, and that is that when you die you will be buried away from us;

otherwise, on the resurrection morning, you would rise to meet the Lord and we with you; and you would say, "Here, Lord, am I and all those whom You have given me."' Mabille had been deeply struck by this thought, lamented the separate cemeteries, and promised her that he would be buried with his people. To this day, Mabille lies, with his daughter Léonie, who died in 1890, and his wife Adèle, who survived him by twenty-two years, amongst the Basotho he loved, all waiting patiently together for the Resurrection.

Edwin Smith chose to end his account of the death of Mabille with only one obituary. 'Of all the letters written about Mabille we will quote but one,' he said. 'It was written by E. Jacottet, a man of very different temperament, perhaps the most purely intellectual of all Mabille's colleagues. Jacottet was inclined to think Mabille's theology old-fashioned; but they had much in common – reverence for Jacottet's great teacher, Godet; a zeal for the evangelization of the people in the mountains; a belief in the Basuto church, to the organization of which Jacottet devoted much thought; and a love of the Sesuto language. "A real missionary," Mabille said of him.'

It is clear that Jacottet spoke straight from the heart when he told Boegner, 'More than ever Mabille was necessary to us … He was the base of everything.' He 'sacrificed everything he had, his talents, his tranquillity, his future, for the mission' and 'there was no shadow of selfishness about him'. The death of Mabille was not just a loss to the mission, however; it was a deeply personal loss for Jacottet himself. 'He was almost a father to me,' he wrote. 'He loved me above my merits, because he saw that I understood many things as he did, that I had the same vision as he of the mission. There was hardly a question on which we disagreed.' Jacottet said he would never forget Mabille's words to him on the day before he died, nor what 'he made me promise'. A fortnight after his colleague's death, he was still stunned, his heart full. Lesotho seemed empty, beheaded, and Jacottet struggled to accept it and to understand God.

But he had gone to Cana to see Mabille's daughter, Aline, who had not been able to attend the funeral, and recount to her what had taken place at Morija. Then he went on to Leribe, where Ernest was now stationed, with the same errand. Jacottet had great affection for Ernest, who was genuinely pleased to see him too. Ernest had also been prevented from seeing his dying father by a broken leg, sustained in a fall from his horse, and was still immobilized when Jacottet visited him. Though he accepted God's will, how hard it had been for him to see his family afflicted! Jacottet was struck by the strength in the Mabille family. 'One sees,' he reflected, almost prophetically, with no shadow of dramatic irony, 'what a blessing it is for all the family to have a truly Christian father! How I wish to be able to arrive there myself.'

Adolphe Mabille was spared the scandal that erupted around his son a few months later.

An epidemic of diphtheria in the autumn of 1894 had carried off Lagden's little boy of two years, and Emma Ellenberger. This had reawakened the Jacottets' grief for their lost Germaine. Then, in the spring, they were again reminded of the immanence of death when measles successively struck the three children of the household. Heavily pregnant, Louise Jacottet was physically and emotionally exhausted. The recent death of Mrs Dyke in childbirth had made them nervous; black clouds seemed to have enveloped the mission and it was sometimes hard to discern the brightness of God. But, on 28 November, at nine o'clock in the evening, she gave birth to a daughter. It was a difficult and painful labour, but, said the relieved father, 'she is so happy to have this little girl that she desired so much'. They called her Madeleine-Henriette.

Then the pleasure in new life was tainted by the ancient sin and shame that was Ernest Mabille's.

On Sunday 4 November, when Charles Christeller ended his first service of the day at Qalo, Ernest Mabille's son Georges was waiting to see him. He handed Christeller a letter from his father begging him to come to Leribe as soon as possible, without saying why.

Christeller hastened south and found Ernest seated under an oak tree in a corner of the garden with one of the Cochet sisters. They all went inside, but from the demeanour of the pair Christeller knew that something was seriously wrong. Then Ernest made a confession to Christeller: he had got one of the maidservants, a girl called Junietta, pregnant, and she had given birth to a child which was stillborn. But he could no longer conceal his deception from his wife.

Christeller had little sympathy with what he felt was Ernest's hypocrisy. From his early years, Ernest had 'begun to go with women', a habit that persisted up until his marriage. Things had improved in the first years in Africa, but the 'demon of the flesh' had possessed him again and he had committed adultery with Junietta. Christeller could not understand how he could go on performing his duties as a minister while at the same time living in sin. Since Ernest for a while persisted in proclaiming his love for the girl, Christeller could not believe that he repented in his heart nor genuinely admitted his fault, and was angry at the harm done to Ernest's wife and children. Christeller, a bachelor, added virtuously that whoever was destined to be *his* wife would be the first woman he touched.

Christeller took some practical steps. He summoned Kohler from Cana, and they were joined by Ernest's brother Louis. A meeting of the congregation was called, at which Ernest confessed his sin publicly, and declared he would resign his ministry and quit Leribe that week.

Ellenberger, as President of the Conference, received Ernest's resignation, and an extraordinary meeting of the Conference was convened at Thabana-Morena on 18 December. It was not a happy meeting, as it had another unpleasant piece of business to attend to: Cochet at Mafube stood accused of gross financial mismanagement as well as immorality by his congregation, and he was stripped of his offices in the church and asked to leave.

It irritated Christeller that some people pondering Ernest's fate wanted to forget the whole thing in deference to the Mabille family name, but when it came to a vote on Ernest's removal from the list of mission workers, the four-teen missionaries present (one of whom was Louis Mabille) voted unanimously in favour.

What a blow it was for the whole mission! Jacottet was too dispirited, too floored to write to Boegner about it for quite a while. He had gone immediately to visit old Mrs Mabille, who had visibly aged in a few days.

Jacottet's first response on hearing of the scandal was profound commisera-tion with Ernest, but his pity was tempered when he heard more of the facts and circumstances from those who were closer to the events. Then he turned his indignation against him. Ernest was in a fallen state. Perhaps in the eyes of God his behaviour could be forgiven, but in the eyes of those below it was inexcusable. It was necessary to forget the story, even to suppress it, thought Jacottet – but how could it be forgotten? The mission had never had a scandal like this, and to think that it involved the son of Mabille, the grandson of Casalis, a man in whom everyone had such confidence.

Like all the other missionaries, Jacottet was concerned about the effect of the scandal on the mission: 'a sin of one can be an injury to all'. He was grat-ified, however, by the conduct of the Basotho Christians, and even the pagans. Everyone knew the story; no one spoke of it, except his own evan-gelists privately to him. A spirit of bereavement, almost, settled on Christian and pagan alike.

Jacottet, returning to his hobby horse, felt one or two lessons must be drawn from the unhappy events. Although he asserted that the Mabilles had always been and would always be his best friends, he felt that pride had perhaps crept into the family – in fact, he said, 'perhaps we have too much of it in Lesotho'. He was adamant that the Committee in Paris should not send missionary chil-dren back to work in Lesotho (or anywhere their parents worked). He meant sons: he was less specific about daughters.

He also suggested, with some doubt that his opinion would be generally accepted, that missionaries should not grow old in their stations, so that their children returned either as missionaries, like the Ellenbergers and Germonds, or as traders, like the Maitins. Instead of discouraging the missionaries from returning to Europe, the Committee should rather let them go back at the age of fifty or fifty-five.

Ernest Mabille left the mission to go and work in Johannesburg, but eventually, in part because of his name, in part because of his repentance, he was allowed to return as a teacher in the Normal School. It is not clear whether the real shock of the scandal was that he had had an affair with a Mosotho woman or that he had committed adultery. Some might have felt the former: all would have felt the latter.

The fall of Ernest Mabille was a sad story, with its lessons drawn and its lessons forgotten. In some ways, it was a type of things to come.

Adolphe Mabille had lived long enough to see a final ambition of his – as of Jacottet and others – begin to coalesce. Having solved the question of financing certain key activities, such as the salaries of the Basotho pastorate, with the formation of the Central Chest, the Conference began to address another pressing question – how to give a voice to the Basotho Christians themselves. The system prevailing until 1894 had been a semi-congregational one, with all common decisions being taken by the Conference, made up exclusively of the white missionaries. An earlier attempt to introduce a Synod, which met four times between 1872 and 1879, was disastrous.

The first Synod, comprising representatives from each of the local churches, had debated delicate questions concerning marriage, bohali, widows and children, made certain decisions, and sent a deputation to present them to Letsie, Masupha and Molapo. All hell nearly broke loose when the chiefs interpreted this as an attempt by the church to legislate for the entire nation. Church and state looked set to resume the old debate. Acrimoniously.

In Paris, Director Casalis, who still harboured dreams of a national Church of Basutoland, recommended caution, patience. Was not the Synod being given too much trust, too much power?

In addition to this problem, many who participated in the subsequent Synods of the 1870s did not fully understand the binding nature of decisions taken; furthermore, a legalism and a love of making laws for their own sake began to creep in. The Gun War had been a convenient excuse to stop the experiment.

In 1894, a purely consultative body was proposed, mainly by Germond, which would deliberate on questions submitted to it by the Conference, three members of which were to attend the assembly ex officio but interfere as little as possible with proceedings. Proposals would then go to the Conference, which had sole decision-making powers. 'If that proposition, which was put forward brilliantly and supported by some excellent arguments, had been accepted,' wrote Jacottet years afterwards, 'it could easily have brought the mission into very great difficulties, for there could be nothing so dangerous as the right of veto thus granted to the Conference. The Synod, consisting purely of Natives, would have deliberated in public and passed important decisions, which the Conference, consisting purely of Europeans, could have negated after discussing them behind closed doors. It would probably have introduced into our mission the racial question, which up until then had been unknown to it, and brought the Native and White people into conflict.' Mabille, Ellenberger and Jacottet had been against such a structure, regarding Germond as utopian.

An alternative was found. Missionaries and Basotho ministers would join the old form of the Synod and all would vote together. But the Conference would prepare the agenda and screen out all problematic questions. Decisions would go first to the Consistory (the body of church elders), then to the Conference, and then back to the next Synod to be finalized. Although Jacottet thought it a cumbersome mechanism, he felt that it would put a brake on hasty action.

It was clear, in Jacottet's judgement, that 'the Synod was no longer a real Synod and could not be the directing body of the church'. Though it was envisaged that its powers would be increased to a presbyterial system or to a full Synod, the interim body, useful as it was, did not fulfil its expectations fully. For an effective organizational body, the mission would have to wait a few years yet.

Death, the Devil's drilled recruit, again extended its cloak over Jacottet's days, taunting his confidence in God.

In December 1893, so soon after the death of his daughter, Jacottet had to add to his grief as a parent, the concern of a child. A letter arrived from Godet, who was writing at the request of Jacottet's sister, Isabelle Hoffet. Jacottet's mother – perhaps the most important person in his life – was gravely ill.

A malignant tumour on her leg had forced an immediate operation in Lausanne. The procedure was successful, but, when pressed by Mme Hoffet for the truth and nothing but, the surgeon had to admit that the tumour would likely reappear, in seven or eight months, and that this second manifestation would be infinitely more dangerous. Godet advised his old pupil to come to Switzerland in the course of the following year if he wanted to see his mother again.

Jacottet was not due for sabbatical – it was usually granted after fifteen years and he had served only ten. He told no one but Dieterlen about this news, and wrote to Boegner asking him to keep the situation confidential until definite decisions had been taken.

He did argue that early leave, of two or three years, might be advantageous to the mission: the canton of Neuchâtel was leaning more and more towards the Mission Suisse Romande, with its headquarters closer to home in Lausanne, and giving less support to Paris, and Jacottet felt he could play a role in helping to ward off this tendency, which threatened the morale and finances of both Paris and Lesotho. Although he assured Boegner that if there was any possibility of waiting, he would wait, there is a hint in his correspondence that he would do anything for his mother, even if it meant resigning: 'A return to the country, she being no longer there, would not be the same thing. Not only from the aspect of my heart but from all points of view. In the interests of the future of my children, of my relations with my brothers and sisters, of my links with my friends, it is vital that my mother still be there when I return on leave.'

By April, the news of his mother was somewhat better, and by early June, she was 'very well'. But the fear was always there, like a beggar tugging at his elbow, sometimes pleading, sometimes threatening, throughout the bitter days of 1894.

—◦◦◦—

After the worry and agony of her confinement and the long weeks of recuperation, Louise Jacottet was strong enough by early February for little Madeleine, herself delicate and a cause for concern, to be baptized.

Jacottet spent his free time working on his linguistic and literary studies. His book *Contes populaires des Bassoutos* was in press and he looked forward to seeing the product of years of research. 'For me, these studies are often a precious relief, above all from the terrible times like those we have just been through.' Slowly but surely, he was turning his back on the broader vistas of missionary work – just as he had turned his back on Foqoqo – knowing he could not pursue his personal ambitions to the detriment of his family responsibilities. He had grave decisions to take: about his mother; about his own health and that of his wife's; about his children's future, in particular, because he could see too clearly 'the inconveniences of this country for them'.

In May, too, after the Conference, he was given another huge and heavy task. For health reasons, Dieterlen was moved to the parish of Leribe, and Jacottet took over the direction of the Theological School. He was to finish off the studies of the second intake of students and there were still two full semesters to go. In addition, he was charged with overseeing the final stages of the revision of the Bible, the second edition of which was to be published with the help of a grant from the British and Foreign Bible Society.

To make matters worse, Mlle Cochet was in the middle of one of her black spells, and he and his wife were desperately tired. But with the first Basotho ministers placed in parishes and the Synod a reality, albeit an imperfect one, Jacottet was cautiously optimistic, if not confident: 'We will have a true church in a few years,' he said, 'the first, I believe, in southern Africa.'

An interesting view of Lesotho towards the end of 1895 was given by a first-time visitor, James Bryce, recently Chancellor of the Duchy of Lancaster and President of the British Board of Trade.

The difficulty of getting to the country was his first concern. The easiest approach was from Bloemfontein, and so he and his wife travelled through the wide and level pasturelands on top of the coach to Ladybrand. They left on a bright November morning, but the road was only a track, rough and full of ruts, and the coach, drawn by eight horses, was old and its springs had seen better days. Only by holding tight to a little rail did the Bryces survive the journey intact. The beauty of the vast landscape and the brightness of the light helped them to forget their discomfort. It took all of twelve hours to get to Ladybrand, but when the sun sank and the constellations came out in the pure, dry African air with a brilliance unknown to Europe, the hazards of the last part of the trip – some of the inclines were as steep as an abyss – seemed relatively insignificant. Next day, they rode by horse into Basutoland.

They stayed with the Resident Commissioner in Maseru (there were no inns in the country), and admired the groves of trees and luxuriant gardens of Morija, which gave the landscape softness and verdure. At Matsieng they met Chief Lerotholi, a strong, thickset man, noted Bryce, dressed in a grey shooting coat and trousers of grey cloth, with a neat new low-crowned black hat. The Bryces were impressed, considering him to be 'not wanting either in intelligence or in firmness'. The Maloti were equally impressive, reminding them of the view of the Pyrenees from Pau, and the rich variety of alpine flora delighted them.

After that they arrived at the mission station beneath the imposing bulk of Thaba-Bosiu. They were greeted by the 'Swiss pastor in charge of the mission, Mr E. Jacottet', whose collection of 'Basotho and Barotse popular tales' was already known to the visitors. 'No man knows the Basutos better than he and his colleague, Mr Dyke of Morija,' wrote Bryce.

Jacottet's voice as ventriloquist is clear enough in the Basutoland chapter of Bryce's book *Impressions of South Africa*, which he published in 1899, and Jacottet might well have influenced Bryce significantly in his attacks on the British expansionist policies that were making the coming Anglo-Boer War inevitable. But obvious mutual respect and a firm friendship also developed between the two men, and this was to have important consequences for the future of Basutoland.

Christmas Day was spent in simple celebration as usual. The festivities centred largely on the School for Young Girls.

Miss Cochet came up with a Christmas tree festival that baffled the more classical ideas of the others (Mrs Jacottet was famous for her Easter parties, where she would hide painted eggs in the pines). Miss Cochet and Miss Jacot prepared balls of wool for the girls and procured penknives for the boys. Then, from the stem of an aloe and the branches of thorn trees, they manufactured a Christmas tree. It may not have been a fir tree exactly, but the youngsters made no complaint! Little packets of sweets and small cakes were hung from the branches. When the children, shepherded by their teachers, entered the church in procession and saw the flickering candles also hanging from the tree, their faces lit up. For a moment, this uniquely African Christmas had transported them into a world of enchantment.

Jacottet addressed them with a few serious words, the presents were distributed, and Mr Dyke, who was passing through, ended with a prayer.

'I have afterwards learned,' wrote Miss Jacot to the Comité des Dames of the PEMS in Paris, 'that this simple holiday gave great pleasure to the children and to the parents. These little blacks are not spoilt.'

This was surely how Christmas was meant to be.

After protracted negotiations, the Paris Committee finally agreed to allow Jacottet early leave in 1896. Rev. Jeanmairet was assigned as stand-in at Thaba-Bosiu while he was away. He was very grateful: 'These last two years have totally upset me ... it seems to me that I could not support the "strain" much longer.' A year and a half afterwards, the disgrace of his colleague and friend continued to haunt him: 'The business of Ernest Mabille has been and continues to be so painful! If you knew what we suffer still!'

At last, though, the Jacottets left Lesotho for Cape Town around 10 April

1896. Rain hampered the initial part of the journey, and forty-one hours on the train tired them out, four small children not being easy to mollify in a confined space. But all was forgotten when they found a charming boarding house only fifty metres from the sea, 'so beautiful, so blue'. Mrs Jacottet had time to rest and gather her strength for the voyage she dreaded. They left on the *Guelph* on 23 or 24 April, headed for Southampton. From there they went to Paris, where the whole family was warmly received by Boegner and his wife. Jacottet spent a few days with the Director, holding lengthy discussions, but he was anxious to get on to Neuchâtel to see his mother.

—⚬—

They arrived 'home' towards the end of May. The joy in Jacottet's heart at the welcome given them by friends was marred only by the bronchitis that afflicted the baby. A brief period of panic ensued as she had to be kept to her room. But God soon restored her to health.

Most emotional of all, of course, was Jacottet's first meeting with his mother. She had not seen her beloved son for twelve years, and had never met her four grandchildren.

He was taken aback by how much she had aged. But this proved to be largely illusory. The weeks of anticipation, of irritation, of anxiety, through which she had just passed, combined with the sickness that assailed her, made her look worse than she really was. After a few days, when she had recovered her composure, she seemed much less changed than he had first judged. In any event, if her appearance had changed, her character had not: 'The spirit is the same, always the same heart, the same intelligence, the same conscience. I thank God for having preserved her for me. For the well-being of my life it was necessary that I see her again, she to whom I owe so much ...'

His parents-in-law, the Barrelets, he found well but much weakened. He also had the joy of seeing Godet, more lively and vigorous than he would have believed (Godet's death in 1900 was to sadden him deeply). By the rest of the community he was received with tremendous cordiality, which made him think that he could do something for the mission's cause, finding that the ground lost was not as great as he had feared.

—⚬—

After the first month of social visits, the whole family went for a holiday in the Val-de-Travers in the Jura. They had a favourite place to go to, a farm called Grands Champs, high up on the mountain above Couvet. In the lazy heat of July, Jacottet found it difficult to work.

With an idyllic two weeks behind him, Jacottet went on to Lausanne and

Geneva; amongst other things, he was looking for suitable recruits for the Lesotho mission, since the Committee had promised to finance them. After another holiday at Grands Champs, he took his family to Zürich to stay with his brother-in-law for ten days. Then he had an appointment in London on 28 September with Dr Wright, Secretary of the Bible Society, to discuss the new edition of the Bible. He stayed with a friend at Brondesbury, and then went to Liverpool to pursue some personal affairs of an unexplained nature. On his way back, early in October, he stayed at the Maison des Missions, the handsome new headquarters of the PEMS at 102, Boulevard Arago. When he had left France in 1884, the PEMS was housed in cold and cramped rented accommodation in the Latin Quarter. The new building had been specially designed for the Society in 1886. Much of his discussion with Boegner was about Madagascar.

—◈—

The PEMS was not involved in Madagascar by choice: it went into the country with all the grace of a recalcitrant child.

The London Missionary Society had had its eye on Madagascar ever since the late eighteenth century. The king of the Merina (the people of the central highlands) had organized the ruling class, the Hova, into a position where the conquest of the whole island became a possibility, and Radama I, who succeeded him in 1810, had this as his aim. The Hova never quite achieved their ambition. There was, of course, resistance from the other tribes, and there was also the hovering presence of the French, ensconced on the island of Réunion, and the British, lurking on the Île Maurice.

Radama was favourable to Western civilization, and two Welsh missionaries of the LMS arrived in 1817. But the missionary advance was checked when Radama died in 1828. His wife Ranavalona ascended the throne, and, returning to traditional beliefs and practices, with the support of the traditional ruling class, closed the country off to foreigners and persecuted the Christians.

After her death, her son Rakoto succeeded her as Radama II. Immediately missionary prospects improved. Rakoto was crowned in a somewhat dubious fashion – by the Jesuits who had established themselves in Réunion in the 1840s. The Anglicans, the Quakers and the Norwegian Lutherans moved into the country, too. The Anglicans had a firm foothold in the monarchy and large numbers of conversions were made, rather more perhaps from loyalty or fear than from conviction – a situation not always acceptable to the LMS missionaries, whose congregationalist leanings made them uncomfortable with the idea of a state church. The Jesuits had to content themselves with gains in the rural areas. But one of the consequences of the rivalry was that, to Malagasy and

French authorities alike, Protestantism was equated with the English and Catholicism with the French.

By the early 1880s, the French had a significant presence in north-west Madagascar and a few grievances against the Hova. In exchange for a free hand in Egypt, Britain gave its blessing to the French embrace of this island, and the Berlin Conference smiled benignly on the betrothal. In December 1885, a treaty established a form of French protectorate, with the European power taking over foreign affairs but leaving internal sovereignty to Ranavalona II. Although the Queen was Protestant, the Catholics entered the capital Antananarivo with pomp and procession in 1886.

Two years before, a letter from the French Marine Ministry had invited the Reformed Consistory of Paris to send Protestant pastors to Madagascar. The President of the Consistory passed this on to Boegner. This fairly innocent missive was to be the cause of – or excuse for – considerable turmoil.

The position of the PEMS was that it would not step on the toes of the LMS, its sister organization. Nor would it intrude without the express invitation of the LMS or the local Malagasy churches. Above all, the PEMS was committed to the evangelization of virgin lands, of pagans, and Madagascar already had a strong Protestant presence.

But anti-Protestantism had been on the rise in France ever since the disastrous Franco-Prussian War, where, in the usual search for scapegoats, the Protestants were accused of sympathizing with their German co-religionists. French nationalism and French colonialism fostered the propaganda. The parliamentary deputy for Réunion, François de Mahy, seized on the Marine Ministry's letter to attack Methodist Protestantism in general and the PEMS in particular. He viciously accused the PEMS of unpatriotic behaviour, because it refused to get involved in Madagascar. Pressure came from within as well: the liberal section of French Protestantism, which had never played much part in the PEMS, largely because of its strict evangelical nature, now also denounced the Society's failure to intervene.

Under great pressure to support French national and colonial interests, Boegner countered that religion, like science, extends beyond nationalism. Other prominent Protestants, such as the pastor Roger Hollard, denounced the 'colonial politics' of De Mahy and tried to define another position, based on the rights of man. Boegner even courageously defended the British missionaries, pointing to the inspirational achievements of Livingstone and the fact that French missionaries were allowed to work in territories administered or influenced by Britain, like Lesotho and Zambezia.

In 1895, when negotiations with the Hova finally broke down, the French ordered a full-scale invasion of the island. After a cruel campaign – though fever

The new year of 1897 saw him working vigorously on the Bible proofs (it was published in 1899). He was relieved to hear that Dieterlen was not to be sent to Madagascar, as 'it would perhaps have killed him', but he was disturbed that Alfred Casalis might be posted there instead: 'It seems to me that Madagascar is not the place for Casalis.'

Then, after a quick trip to Morges, near Lausanne, and a lecture to the National Church in Neuchâtel on the 17th, he was off again to Paris and Glasgow, for a meeting on 22 January. When he finally returned home in February, he found, perhaps inevitably, certainly not surprisingly, a minor crisis in his family. His wife was far from well. She was worn out and listless, and unhappy that he might go away again soon. 'My wife,' he wrote on 25 February to Boegner, warning him that he could not return to Paris in the near future, 'cannot do without me these days.'

He did get away again at the end of March, but when he returned to the family home at Boine 7, he was full of melancholy: 'Each time I return, I feel all over again the void which my mother's death has created. Here, everything speaks of her, and the house seems to me so dead, so desolate. When I am far away, I can forget. Here, forgetting is impossible.'

One source of irritation at the time was the visit of Coillard to Switzerland. There had always been a prickly relationship between the two. Jacottet envied Coillard his pioneering role in Zambezia: Coillard resented deeply the path-breaking grammars of the Zambezi languages which Jacottet had produced. Now Jacottet felt that Coillard was hogging the publicity in Switzerland for the benefit of his own mission and to the detriment of the Society.

As a break from the house that had such a grip on his heart, Jacottet took his family to visit the Hoffets in Colmar for fifteen days. Their house was in Rue de Turenne. There was another reason for going to Colmar – it had been decided that Marcelle and Henri would be left there with the Hoffets to attend school after the Jacottets returned to Lesotho. In May, Jacottet was yet again in Paris, and this time his return to Neuchâtel found his whole family in good health.

But the news from Madagascar was truly shocking. Boegner had received the 14 June telegram.

On 21 May, Benjamin Escande and Paul Minault were murdered on the massif of Ankaratra, two hours' walk from Antananarivo. 'The only thing that never crossed my mind, even as a simple possibility,' Jacottet exclaimed to Boegner, in a black-bordered letter of the kind he had used to announce his mother's death, 'was that our friends could be assassinated by the fahavalos.' He lamented for Mme Escande and for Mme Minault; he lamented for Madagascar and for the mission; he lamented for the Malagasy, who had 'massacred those who came to help them'.

Picking up some of the terminology of Coillard, he proclaimed that 'they are dead on the field of honour as soldiers'. Here, he said, 'was a tragic realization of what one had to expect over there'. Did Minault have a premonition of his sacrifice? Jacottet remembered him talking, at his farewell in the Church of St Esprit, 'of the possibility that God would ask them to affirm their faith through their blood'. But given the strength of their belief and the fact that the love of God alone could give them the courage to confront such an end, perhaps 'it was natural that these were the ones to become the first martyrs'.

At the farewell, M. De Seynes had talked of the 'possible danger' to the missionaries in the revolt. Jacottet had thought the phrase exaggerated; now he had to eat his words. Pragmatic ideas, too, disturbed him: 'This murder not only takes from us our colleagues, but will disorganize the work, and can contribute to upsetting Protestant opinion in France, and cause them to regard Malagasy Protestantism in a deplorable light.'

In early September, Boegner addressed a letter to Jacottet which forced a crucial and revealing reply. Jacottet had sequestered himself with his family in Malvilliers. Here he had an excuse to ponder on Boegner's requests contained in the letter, one long-term, the other short-term, and to delay his reply for a few days.

The long-term proposal made by Boegner was not stated directly but contained in a broad hint, and Jacottet could read between the lines. Boegner and the Committee would look favourably upon his candidature if Jacottet volunteered for Madagascar (as Director of the Theological School there). This was no surprise to him. He had considered the possibility himself for weeks, thinking constantly of Madagascar. It must have crossed his mind at times that he might, in fact, become a new martyr. But he also had some self-doubt.

He began his reply to Boegner by saying that had he 'found himself free of all shackles', the position would have tempted him greatly, and he would have seen in this splendid field of endeavour a serious call from on high. It thus took considerable will to renounce the prospect. But his reasons for turning it down were serious and solid. They were of two kinds: those specific to his own circumstances, and those of a more disinterested nature. What convinced him was that these two sets of reasons were not at variance.

The first set centred on his family. If he were alone, he said, he could decide to leave for Antananarivo. But as a married man, he would have to consult his wife, and he was absolutely sure she was not made for the task. She would follow him, but reluctantly. 'She has already sufficient trouble in agreeing to leave behind her older children – it is for her an extraordinary bitterness. If she were to be asked to separate from her other two (as I do not believe it would be wise to take them to Madagascar), it would be just too much. It is a sacrifice I have neither the courage nor the right to ask of her ...' Speaking as one father and parent to another, he said to Boegner, 'I believe that you will understand me; a pity as it is, it is certain that a married man can no longer be entirely his own master and must pay attention to the desires and aversions of his wife. It is sometimes hard: but that is no reason not to resign oneself to it.' Perhaps this was something he had learned years before, when he went to Foqoqo and came back again.

The second set of reasons was bound up with his missionary vocation. He had his work, his road to follow in Lesotho, and he believed that, after all he had begun there, it 'would be deplorable not to return'. It was for him 'a question of absolute duty'. He had played a part in preventing Alfred Casalis from leaving; he had insisted on Dieterlen staying. For him to go now would be a kind of betrayal. And since the Lesotho mission would be suffering the repercussions of Madagascar for years to come, he could not think about weakening it further.

Madagascar tempted him sorely. He was faced with a potentially life-changing choice. But he had to ask himself whether he was driven by human impulse rather than divine injunction. The 'desire of a work much vaster, much newer', where he would 'have his elbows freer than in Lesotho', was like an ambitious devil at his shoulder. It is testimony to his unswerving honesty, constancy and maturity – especially in relation to his family – that he turned away.

He had racked his brains thinking of an alternative candidate for Boegner. He had even written off to friends, including M. Godet, but had no more success than in his efforts to find missionaries for Lesotho.

He then turned his attention to the short-term request made by Boegner in the name of the Committee. Jacottet had already spent several weeks in Paris helping Boegner with his immense workload. It had been a great pleasure for him to live with the Director and get to know him even better. He had profited greatly, and was pleased that he had the trust of Boegner and the affection of him and his wife. Now Jean Bianquis had been appointed as Boegner's deputy, but could not take up the post for some time. Boegner therefore asked Jacottet to fill in as his assistant in the interim.

It cost Jacottet a great deal to refuse, but his reasons were 'so strong' that he could not hesitate. These reasons parallelled almost exactly those he had given for turning his back on Madagascar – they were simply more immediate in this case. By enjoining Boegner to strict confidence, he gave the impression that there was more to the situation than he was willing or able to express. Firstly, he could not think of putting aside the new edition of the Bible at this point. His experiences in May had convinced him that he must finish it before the new year, so that snags could be ironed out before they left Europe in March as they planned. He was needed in Lesotho to reopen the Theological School, and all the material arrangements to do with letting the house in Neuchâtel and booking passages had long since been completed. To stop work on the Bible, long and tiring as it was, would be disastrous.

Secondly, he had agreed to teach a course on missions at the Theological Faculty in Neuchâtel, and could not break his word. He also felt there was propaganda work still to be done, and only the winter left to do it in.

Most importantly, there were deep personal reasons for not leaving Neuchâtel at that moment. For reasons he did not want to detail, he said, his wife's family demanded his attention. Decisions had to be made about his mother-in-law, who was widowed and without fortune. His wife in particular needed him. 'She has, in her family, reasons for sadness and grief (as a result of circumstances rather than through the fault of people). She has need of being supported, especially as the immediate future is so black for her and as the thought of being separated from her children has been for her a frightful nightmare. I have seen that in each of my long absences there were serious drawbacks to my being away so long; there is in this entire situation that which compels me to caution and to great care. I repeat – something you who have so many children will understand – how hard it will be to leave my children for too long at the very moment when we are going to be separated from them for years.'

A couple of months later, Jacottet could assure Boegner: 'I cannot tell you how happy I am to have been able to rest here. It probably saved my whole future.' Although he did add somewhat ominously and mysteriously that 'there are things one cannot say by letter'.

At the beginning of 1898, the Jacottets now made preparations to leave in April. The strain of the last few years finally caught up with Jacottet. The dose of influenza he contracted was so bad that his wife had to write to Boegner in his place. In the only known extant letter of hers, she said, 'Clearly, my husband is tiring himself out too much, as a result of his many worries from last year, which contributed to making him quite run down.' Not least of these worries had been the recent death of Mrs Jacottet's own sister.

Jacottet was in bed for twelve days and confined to his room for another eight. 'Without ever believing myself to be ill,' he said, 'it nevertheless appears that I was indeed sick.' His doctor forbade him to travel for at least three weeks.

The illness was inconvenient. Jacottet had long wanted to visit the Faculty of Theology at Montauban, which was more orthodox and independent-inclined than those of Strasbourg and Paris. He had been offered a pulpit there on 20 January. The enforced postponement presented him with a dilemma: he had agreed to give a course of lectures at the Faculty of Theology at Neuchâtel in February, at the same time as the proposed rescheduling of the Montauban visit. He asked Boegner's advice. The latter urged him to go to Montauban – it was no doubt politically important to reinforce the alliance there and balance the liberal emphasis of the other two Faculties.

In the sermon and lectures he gave at Montauban, where he was received with more enthusiasm than he expected, he focused on what the Lesotho mission was currently going through, and, 'naturally', assessed it according to what was known of the mission of St Paul.

After Montauban, he dropped in on Paris. He had asked Boegner for a private meeting to discuss sensitive matters, where 'Lesotho is not the prime concern and where M. Coillard does not steal the limelight'.

Although he admired Coillard, there was also a certain amount of jealousy and irritation towards a man who was not shy to push his cause: 'I received a letter from Miss Bain, who informed me that M. Coillard's visit to Edinburgh unfortunately made our work more difficult for us … To be honest, I cannot help but have a certain bitterness when I notice, everywhere I go or don't go, that M. Coillard has (without wishing it, no doubt, but as a natural conse-quence of his aggressive manner) contributed to a few doors being closed on us. This is, of course, between you and me.'

During the two years of his sabbatical, Jacottet had spent several periods – a couple of them stretching over weeks – with Boegner, acting at times as a kind of unofficial Secretary General. He had always, from Lesotho, written confid-ential letters to the Director. Now the relationship had deepened.

In one such letter, Jacottet confirmed this: 'Thank you for your lovely, indeed wonderful, letter … This time you filled me in on so many things and brought me up to date on everything, which you so rarely get the opportunity to do these days. It gives me great joy to know that I can trust in your friend-ship; I am so grateful to you for that. I really need it, I need it more than you can imagine. And the bond between you and me will be one of the privileges that have made my trip to Europe worthwhile – a bond which has and will continue to do me good.'

—∽◯∽—

Disquieting stories were emanating from Lesotho. At first, they were only rumours. Had the old enmity between Lerotholi and Masupha reached its peak? Had the ancient crimes and grievances revived? Had the civil war, so long threatened, finally broken out?

On 12 January, Jacottet got his first whiff of the trouble from a newspaper, which reported a serious war in Lesotho but gave no details. On 16 January, he heard that a great and decisive battle had taken place at the Thaba-Bosiu mission station itself! This piece of news jolted him at last from his sickbed.

A confidential note from his friend Lord Bryce came on 2 February, saying that the war would not change the British government's opinion of the Basotho. But Jacottet did not know how long this would last, how long the British would stand firm. He was very concerned how the PEMS reported on the matter – he did not want even tiny 'anti-English remarks' to be published, as some of the missionaries could be 'dangerous in this regard'. 'The government is on our side,' he said to Boegner, 'we must not displease them, all the more since deep down it is probably right, and the country can only benefit from the victory of Lerotholi and the defeat of Masupha.'

The disaster was evident: the details were not specific. Villages, chapels, livestock – his villages, his chapels, his livestock – were gone. But he did not know precisely what had happened. Friends, too, had gone. By April, as they were about to leave for Paris on their way to Lesotho, he knew his losses were considerable. The war was over, but the consequences were not.

Typhoid fever had broken out at Thaba-Bosiu. Jeanmairet's children had contracted it. He begged Boegner not to mention it in front of Louise: 'I have not told my wife any of this because I do not want to worry her, all the more so since I am not entirely certain it is true. Do not bring it up in front of her when we are in Paris … There are so many things setting out to cast a shadow over our departure.'

Louise was leaving two of her children *behind*: no need to worry her about what she was taking her other children *toward*. A secret between men of confidence.

—∽◯∽—

Jacottet was always concerned about the quality and training of younger colleagues. A new recruit was a fellow Neuchâtelois, Paul Ramseyer. Jacottet knew relatively little about him, but had to admit that what he saw of his 'stubborn character' made him 'a little afraid'. Ramseyer wanted to travel with the Jacottets, but the old hand cautioned him against this: 'I advised him to wait a while, in case he was thinking of getting married.' If he went down there unmarried, he would have a very difficult life.

The policy of the PEMS on the marriage of missionaries had changed over time. In 1824, for instance, it had actually refused to accept as a candidate a young man who was the child of an adulterous union. The Society initially followed the practice of the LMS in allowing only unmarried missionaries to leave for foreign lands: they must establish their stations first, before entrusting a wife to dangerous climes and times. In 1831, Pellissier had engaged himself to a girl before he left: the Committee had refused to send him if he married. A crisis was averted when Pellissier accepted the decision. Certain conditions were also imposed on prospective marriages. When Rolland, after a stretch in Africa, wanted to marry, he was granted permission to do so because he was thirty, but only if his fiancée was 'a true Christian'. The Committee was even prepared to make confidential enquiries about prospective wives.

But reports from the missionaries in the field prompted the Society to rethink its position and a commission was appointed to examine the question. A faithful companion might, for instance, have alleviated the initial loneliness of Eugène Casalis, and he and Thomas Arbousset had not been taken all that seriously by the Basotho until they were married. Furthermore, it soon became clear that female missionaries were not simply companions but more than useful in several areas of the missionary field, including education and nursing.

In 1840, Auguste Pfrimmer was the first to leave for Lesotho with a fiancée. In the interim, the stigma of adultery and illegitimacy had been somewhat relaxed – Pfrimmer's wife-to-be was the natural child of the President of the PEMS!

By the 1890s, then, the convention had been reversed: Jacottet reflected the prevailing opinion that it was preferable for missionaries to be married from the outset. Satan's temptations could not be eliminated, but they would likely be diminished. On the other hand, he did disapprove when a missionary he knew proposed to take his young wife into the fever-ridden death trap of Zambezia.

Then a new case, on the eve of the Jacottets' departure, reminded Jacottet of the calamitous behaviour of Ernest Mabille. At the beginning of March 1898, the return of Edmond Meyer from Madagascar was announced. The *Journal* said that his sudden return was for personal reasons: it did not give Meyer the opportunity to reply. The real reason was an affair between his wife and an official at the Government Residency.

It is interesting that Jacottet had inside knowledge of the episode: 'What an atrocious affair!' he exclaimed to Boegner. But what is more interesting is his primary response, similar to the one he had had over Mabille. He remained the Confidential Man. He felt that the scandal should be hushed up as far as possible: 'Even if the Society stepped in and took stronger action with such matters (if only it could), they would only create further problems and would crush the public's trust in us. There have been too many cases these days and, in my opinion, the less you speak, the better.'

—⦾—

The Jacottets left Neuchâtel on the evening of 18 April, and arrived in Paris the next morning. Their ship for South Africa left Southampton on 21 April.

The last weeks in Neuchâtel were deeply distressing. Although Jacottet himself was happy to be returning to Lesotho, he and his wife were in 'constant pain' at the impending separation from their two eldest children. This was one of the greatest sacrifices the missionaries were called upon to make, with only one comfort: 'God will give us the strength to endure our pain. He alone can do that.'

The final days, as the actual time drew near, were almost unbearable. 'How miserable the last few days have been!' he said, on the very last day.

If the parents were hurting, think of the children. They were packed off to the Hoffets in Colmar to be sent to school. They had only each other – Marcelle, at twelve, on the edge of adolescence; Henri, a bewildered little boy of ten.

CHAPTER TWENTY

NO-MAN'S-LAND

1898–1905

The *Briton*, Jacottet had no doubt, was by far the best ship of the Union line, better even than any of the rival ships of the Castle line. It was quick, covering up to four hundred miles a day, and took only fifteen days to Cape Town. A far cry from the old *Grantully Castle*. Which was why he had chosen it, and why he had resisted postponing the journey home, despite business piling up at the end. He wanted to spare his wife as much discomfort as possible. It did not work. She was predictably prostrate, and by the time they reached Madeira, which offered a few hours of relief from the eternal torment, she could do no more than stretch out on her deckchair.

High seas, the heat of the equator and the illness of little Madeleine made the second part of the journey even more of an ordeal for Louise Jacottet. This meant that her husband was busy with his children from morning to night, a fairly novel experience for him. 'It is not exactly easy looking after two bored and disoriented children; I also have to make them eat, which is an even worse task.' On board were three groups of missionaries, headed for Namaqualand, Nyasaland and Uganda. There were also two theatrical companies, one of them little more than a 'lower class of cabaret'. Nevertheless, two of the women helped a great deal with poor Louise and the children, and the artistes were generally very kind to the Jacottets.

As the ship neared Cape Town it was overtaken by a terrible storm, with swells such as Jacottet had never seen before and would not forget for a long time. Sleep was impossible the whole night, and the entry into the harbour was delayed by a day. His faith in the *Briton*, however, remained steadfast, and he asserted that he could 'only recommend it to all those who will outlive me'.

The train trip to Bloemfontein, which took thirty-eight hours, was an easy and comfortable one. On the way, they paused at Wellington to visit the 'Huguenot school for girls', to meet the serious Andrew Murray, and to see the pioneer PEMS church in Wagenmakersvallei, of which Jacottet had heard so much. But the closer they got to Lesotho, the less auspicious the journey became. On 23 May, they left Bloemfontein in a rented cart drawn by four miserable horses of the Rosinante type. These gave up the ghost a couple of hours from Thaba 'Nchu, just as dark began to descend. The air was chilly, the night hell-dark, as they approached a Boer farmhouse. Even though these farmers were relatives of Paul Kruger, President of the Transvaal, Jacottet felt that he had 'fallen amongst the poorest of the poor', and found the house 'horribly primitive and very uncomfortable'. Nevertheless, what little their hosts had was offered with such heart-warming goodwill and hospitable favours, that to see these Boers close up for the first time modified his opinion of them: 'They have so often been spoken badly of, and at times with good reason, but they also have their patriarchal virtues, amongst which their hospitality ranks first class.' Their simple kindness found a lodging in his heart.

As they crossed the Caledon, the river was the same and not the same. They realized that it was not as easy to come back as it had been to arrive for the first time, fourteen years earlier. This time, there was the heartbreak of what they had left: 'Our two souls remain up there, it is as though a part of ourselves has remained behind,' said Jacottet sadly. 'There is a wound in my heart – eventually it will heal, but it will continue to ache. God has helped me endure this separation; may He watch over our two dear children and may He let this sacrifice be a blessing for both them and us.' There was also the heartbreak of what they had lost: 'What an emptiness in my heart when I realize that my own mother is no longer there for me, that she will no longer write to me, that I will no longer be able to tell her all that I am thinking and doing. The strongest bond that tied me to my home country has been broken.'

The bond with Europe was loosening. But in the two years of their absence, Lesotho had changed significantly too. 'To think that we had been looking forward to returning home!' he exclaimed. 'How different it all was from what we had expected.'

Firstly, the rinderpest, the 'bovine plague', had cut a path of destruction through the herds of southern Africa, just as the Lifaqane had cut through the tribes seventy years before. Around Thaba-Bosiu itself almost no beef or dairy cattle were to be seen. Those who had been rich were now poor. Those Christians who had owned the most cattle had been wiped out; those who had managed to keep one or two cows were now rich. Fortunes had been turned upside down. But there were some advantages: the pastures were luxuriant, the grass was thick and tall, the surviving cattle fat and beautiful; the country had had a chance to regenerate itself.

Jacottet had known that civil war had at last broken out between Lerotholi and Masupha, but he had not known the details. Masupha had never recognized the authority of his brother Letsie, nor of Lerotholi, who followed him as Paramount Chief. Tension between them was therefore always threatening to boil over. Finally it did towards the end of 1897. Moeketsi, a son of Masupha, fancied the wife of one of his subjects, and, when she fled to Ladybrand for protection, he pursued her into the Free State with a band of warriors, and abducted her to Sefikeng. Resident Commissioner Lagden feared the Free Staters would take things into their own hands in reprisal for the violation of their territory and spark a major incident. Provoked by a mocking wife, who said he might as well wear her skirt if he did not resist, Masupha refused to give up his son.

Lerotholi led a large force against him. With an army of equal size, Masupha retreated from Thaba-Bosiu on to the Khamolane plateau to the north-east. Lerotholi directed the attack on 6 January 1898, and his sons Letsie and Griffith were prominent in the action, which consisted of a clash of mounted men. It did not last very long, and losses were not heavy, but as the centre of his army broke, so too did Masupha's spirit. The fortifications at Thaba-Bosiu were dismantled and Masupha was prevented from re-entering his village at its eastern foot.

A huge epidemic of dysentery and typhoid fever followed closely on the bovine plague. When Jacottet had left Thaba-Bosiu two years before, the new cemetery had only four graves in it: now he counted twenty-seven! And they were only of people in his immediate area, which was home to no more than 150 or 200. He was almost afraid to ask after people: too often he got the reply, 'He is no longer here.' One of the departed was Shei Moshesh, a Christian chief to whom the missionaries could always turn for support and advice. Another was Maria 'Masenekane, former wife of Masupha, a noble Christian and the 'true light in her village', a woman who led others to understanding. The greatest blow of all was the loss of Moshe Mosetse, the old man who had been his best informant in his research on folk tales and grammar.

The small children of Jeanmairet had also hovered on the edge of death. In the struggle to keep them alive, the maintenance of the mission house had been neglected. It was one of the oldest buildings of the entire mission and was now more ramshackle than ever: the roof let in the rain, the walls were crumbling, the interior was damp. It would have been lethal to let the children live in it. So the Jacottets crowded into the little cottage that Carlisle Motebang had used as a student, and the children watched with big eyes as their father took on the new occupations of businessman, architect and bricklayer for the repairs required. 'I have never been one for working with bricks and mixing mortar,' he sighed. 'As a missionary, it is the one task I am stuck with the most.'

On the bright side, the closeness of death may have accounted for an increase in conversions under Jeanmairet's guidance: the breath of God seemed to have passed through Thaba-Bosiu. The number of young men amongst the many eager novices was encouraging, and certain villages, including that of Job

Mokhachane, had been almost completely transformed. Despite the deaths, Jacottet was overjoyed to hold his first service in a full church. Even Miss Cochet, of the dark moodiness, had proved 'a true saint' to both the Jeanmairets and the Basotho, tending the sick continuously for six months.

—◦◦—

Driven from Thaba-Bosiu, Masupha was defeated. But he would not accept it. His people were weary from months of battle and uncertainty. He returned to his old village near Qiloane, but Lagden and Lerotholi objected and wanted him out. What complicated matters was that Masupha — 'le pauvre vieux renard,' Adèle Mabille called him — was 'always drunk', so negotiation with him was no easy task.

He died in July the following year. Jacottet knew that 'the final vestige of the Lesotho of old has gone with him', and wrote an objective and not unsympathetic obituary of his old adversary — the man he regarded as having played 'one of the most significant roles in the political events of the past fifty years'.

Jacottet looked back over a life which, in the end, had brought disappointment to the missionaries who knew Masupha best. Born about 1821, he was three or four when his father moved from Botha-Bothe to Thaba-Bosiu. He went to the school of M. Casalis and even stayed at his home for a few years. He was baptized on 11 April 1841, only the seventh Mosotho to be enrolled as a member of the church. The Christian name he was given was David, and even long after his relapse he often referred to himself by the name. Educated at Zonnebloem College in Cape Town, he learned English and Dutch.

But when contempt for the conduct of the whites in the Orange Free State after 1845 transferred 'naturally' to the mission, a wave of revolt spread through the converts. A 'mass defection' also took place between 1848 and 1852, as a result of the missionaries' principled but disastrous condemnation of the war over the oxen of the Batlokoa. Masupha then, in the words of Jacottet, 'plunged himself head first into the worst forms of paganism', although he always loved and continued to read the Bible.

In the war against the Boers of 1865 to 1868, when Letsie and Molapo had all but completely abandoned the national cause, Masupha defended the mountain of Moshoeshoe with unflinching defiance. 'If Lesotho is in existence today, it is above all his doing and we owe him for that,' was Jacottet's judgement. As the true leader of the national party, it was Masupha who put Lerotholi at its head in 1880. He represented all that was 'authentically native and anti-European', and if he continued to respect the missionaries and protect the mission in some way, it was because he understood what it had meant for Lesotho. 'In the mission, he saw, instinctively yet at the same time clearly, an element of strength and cohesion, without which Lesotho would be unable to go on. On the other hand, he fought against evangelism and its principles, because he saw it, and admittedly with some reason, as a cause that ruined the old order of things, to which he held so dearly.'

To the end, Masupha remained faithful to his past, but so many civil wars and half-defeats and shabby subterfuges on both sides had whittled away his heroic status. He died 'far from the mountain that he always believed was his'.

As with his father, the rival religions squabbled over Masupha's last days. The Catholics secretly rebaptized him, but Jacottet, so concerned that a confession of faith be true even to the moment of death, was not convinced. 'He had fooled me too often for me to believe him,' he noted with cynicism, and thought that Masupha had merely listened to those who 'claimed to show him the easiest route to get to Heaven'. He scarified the Catholics for their indulgent acceptance: 'If the Catholics have been able to welcome him with open arms, if they have been able to bend their rules on his behalf, that is their affair. It is not ours. It is as though they were playing with holy procedures and making a mockery of the concepts of conversion and repentance.'

Masupha was buried, as he would have wanted, on Thaba-Bosiu, in the necropolis of the royal family. Jacottet attended, but Father Cénez conducted the ceremony. At first, Jacottet smiled when the priest claimed that Masupha had been saved on his deathbed, but his smile soon gave way to an intense feeling of sadness. 'It is this, then – a change of heart – that the "Fathers" put in place of repentance and conversion.' They were devaluing the religion of the Cross in this way, he felt.

Nevertheless, he concluded: 'Protestantism and Catholicism do not really matter deep down; what separates them, Heaven will no longer be able to recognize. The most important thing, as St Paul said, is that we have to become new creatures.'

He was talking about Masupha's end. He might just as well have been talking of his own.

—◦—

In 1898, the twenty-two-year-old Edwin Smith came to Lesotho in order to gain experience as a missionary. Born in Aliwal North of Primitive Methodist missionary parents, he had been ordained the year before.

He spent some time studying Sesotho with a Morija student, Henry Tanke, and later with a teacher, Akkim Sello. Then he met Jacottet, who was examining at the Normal School, and was invited for an extended stay at Thaba-Bosiu.

He arrived at midday on the last day of the year and spent a week in the company of the great man. The word portrait of Jacottet he drew in his diary is a fascinating and important one, and shows the eye of a fine future biographer. In his unpublished reminiscences, he summed up the impact of the visit with Jacottet on his own career.

He was the most intellectual of his brethren. Trained under the great Swiss theologian Frédéric Godet at Neuchâtel, a man of erudition, he was credited with a knowledge of twenty languages. He was the author of the Sotho grammar in current use, an ardent collector of Sotho folk-tales, and more than anyone else encouraged and fostered the growth of a native Sotho literature. By the aid of two Africans from the Barotse country he had recently (1896) compiled grammars of their languages (Luyi and Subiya) by analysing a considerable number of folk-tales dictated by them. He showed me how this was done. Not only did he help me with difficult points in Sesuto but he initiated me into the comparative study of the Bantu languages, all of which I was to realize the value of in future years.

Mr Jacottet was a great talker and for hours on end he lectured me (it is the only word I can use and I mean it kindly) *lectured* me on the problems which confront missionaries. In particular, he expounded on the principles of – and the obstacles in the way of founding – a National Church, indigenous, self-governing, self-propagating, self-supporting, linked as an integral part of the one Universal Church of Christ.

On the day of Smith's arrival, they spoke all afternoon and way into the night. Or rather, as Smith later put it, Jacottet did the talking and he did the listening.

New Year's Day was a Sunday. During the morning, people began to arrive from all directions for the mokete, and Smith was amused by the variety of costumes, which included a dress coat and a Salvation Army jersey. He had to engage in a great deal of welcoming and handshaking before the service began under the trees at half past ten. The sun was hot, and as many people as possible clustered together in what little shade there was. Altogether there were between 1 500 and 2 000 people present, amongst them, Smith was informed, a monna-moholo of over ninety-five years of age who walked the mile from his home to the mission station several times a week.

In the afternoon, a communion service was held in the church. It was a neat stone building with an iron roof and a ceiling made of reeds. Brick benches provided seating. The parish had added 500 new members during the past year, the most ever admitted in a single year, the previous highest being 350. About 500 communicants were present that day, and after Jacottet and Smith had spoken (on 'forgetting the things that are past'), the sacrament was administered.

The people came up from each side of the church in two streams. Within the rail stood four elders, two with bread and two with wine. The communicants filed past, partook of both and moved back to their seats, all in a very orderly fashion. Jacottet told Smith that he had found this to be the best system.

Chief Theko's wife sat inside the communion rail. When she first arrived there was no chair for her, so she had to squat on the floor until one was brought. Before the service ended, tired of the chair, she resumed 'her undignified position'. This contrasted strongly with Smith's experience: the rickety bench he had been provided with collapsed beneath him, with much loss of dignity. Apart from this, he enjoyed the service greatly.

In the days that followed, when he was not walking around the mountain or up it, Smith spent most of the time talking to his new friend. His summaries of these conversations provide important insights into Jacottet's preoccupations.

Jacottet proudly showed him his library of grammars and lexicons, and lamented the paucity of linguistic study on the continent. He also criticized southern African missionaries who did not learn their languages: he knew of one who had been in the country for fifteen years and still used an interpreter. (Most newcomers were treated to the joke that PEMS stood for 'Please Excuse My Sesotho'.)

Jacottet spoke with angry irony of Englishmen who believed the French missionaries were agents of the French government, and of Frenchmen who believed these same missionaries were *English* agents. He pointed out how Mabille had saved Basutoland from Boer dominance by holding on to Moshoeshoe's seal. He surprised Smith with his interpretation of what had happened when the French missionaries were expelled by the Boers and turned to France for defence. Emperor Napoleon had acted only indirectly by appealing to the British to annex Basutoland – but Jacottet felt that the French could have occupied it themselves by coming through Pondoland, which had not yet been annexed by an imperial power.

Jacottet also spoke passionately on the drink question. At that very moment, the white men who were rebuilding his house were away in Maseru having 'a jolly time'. The two whites who had visited him that morning stank of whisky. And a boy had told him last Tuesday that all the white men in Maseru were drunk! At one time there had been thirteen wagons of drink in the hills around Thaba-Bosiu, one of them 'in the charge of a missionary's daughter'.

There were laws, but the government was powerless to enforce them. Although the chiefs had once asked Clarke to make sure the liquor law was adhered to, in practice abolition lasted only two years. Drink was smuggled in to the chiefs, who began to see it as their prerogative, while at the same time denying it to the people. The penalty for smuggling was a £5 fine plus confiscation. What happened to the confiscated brandy, Jacottet asked scorn-fully. The policemen drank it.

The policemen, all polygamists, were a bad lot, and any Christian who joined them lapsed within six months.

Whatever bite there was in these innocent conversations between Smith and Jacottet soon turned septic, however. After helping the Jacottets move into the mission house and put up the blinds, Smith went away and immediately sent off a letter to England, which was published in the *Primitive Methodist* of 2 February. In it he repeated the stories about drunkenness that Jacottet had told him. An extract subsequently appeared in a newspaper in the Orange Free State.

Sir Godfrey Lagden was livid, and summoned Smith to Maseru, excoriat-ing him for publishing unsubstantiated slanders. To his credit, Smith refused to reveal his source, but later in the day signed a letter of apology to the irate officials and traders whom he had offended. Next day, Jacottet and two others added their signatures.

Smith felt he had embarrassed and compromised his friends, so he left for Aliwal North. He subsequently spent a long time as a missionary in Northern Rhodesia. He was to write grammars and several lively biographies in later years. In both these aspects of his career, he acknowledged a profound debt to Jacottet. Indeed, he stated that this 'far-seeing missionary statesman' had kindled within him the ambitions and enthusiasms which engaged him in the years that followed.

Oddly, Edwin Smith nearly died in the same way as his mentor. While improvising a potion against malaria in 1913, he added a bit too much arsenic and was seriously ill for several days.

—◦◦—

In 1899, there were two welcome arrivals. One was Jacottet's younger brother Gustave, who had qualified as a doctor. He came in the middle of the year and stayed with his brother and sister-in-law for a few weeks: his intention was to join the practice of his friend and countryman, Dr Georges Hertig, in Natal or in Pretoria (both had trained under the famous Dr Roux in Lausanne). He was an excellent table companion and brought 'good European air with him!' He also immediately proved himself useful, tending to the sick day and night. With the tremendous influx of patients to the station, it became clear to Jacottet that a missionary hospital was needed at Thaba-Bosiu.

The other newcomers were Samuel and Eva Duby, who had left Southampton on 22 July on board the *German*. Free of the seasickness that cursed so many of their colleagues, they revelled in the voyage, and by the time they reached Aliwal North, Rev. Duby was bubbling with anticipation about their new 'homeland'.

When they arrived in Lesotho, their first intention was to travel to several stations, ending up at Qalo in the north. But rumours of war hinted that it would be prudent to turn back to Morija. As they travelled around, they thought the land, after a mild winter, looked splendid, the prairies were green, the wheat ripe, and the trees round the stations laden with fruit. The year, said Duby in his lively style, would be 'a fat cow after many lean ones'.

The Dubys attended the Synod held at Thaba-Bosiu in October. Sam was deeply impressed, especially at the Sunday service, where two of the Basotho pastors exhorted a crowd of thousands, and at Holy Communion, which was administered to 750 communicants. He soon realized that he had arrived at a significant moment for the mission, a time of crisis; but at the extraordinary meeting of the Conference held at the same time, there was little doubt about Duby's future. There was only one station vacant – at Paballong, in East Griqualand.

Jacottet thought this was a pity, as he was impressed with the young man. 'Duby will be very supportive,' was his opinion. 'He is a gentleman. I deeply regret that he is going to Paballong. He would have been of more useful support in the centre. But perhaps he will be more needed there, that is to say, in restoring Paballong. It will be a difficult task.'

Because Paballong had been a flock without a shepherd for nearly two years, and because the rainy season would soon be upon them, making the mountains difficult to cross, the Dubys set out for their new world as soon as they could in December.

Samuel Duby was born in Lausanne in 1874. When he was only eleven years old, his father died suddenly. As Duby described it, it was like the points on the track of his life being switched in an instant, and he was sent flying in a new direction. In order not to be a burden on his mother, he earned a living by manual labour for the next seven years. But at fifteen he joined a youth group called L'Étoile, which gave him a community to work with and for, and at nineteen he took up his books again to study theology, with a view to becoming a missionary.

In fact, he was not sure when his missionary vocation came to him. It seemed to him that it was born with him, because the question was never posed: it was always decided. 'Be assured,' he asserted, 'I had not a single doubt, not a shadow of a doubt in regard to this vocation.'

After he had volunteered his services to the PEMS, he was sent in 1898 to

England for three months, to 'pick up as many grains of knowledge' in English and medicine as he could 'in the fields of Queen Victoria'. He found the Anglo-Saxon nature totally different from the Swiss, religious viewpoints being no exception. Since his English was rudimentary, his time at London Hospital was rather wasted, especially as the doctors there looked at him askance and were not prepared to do a French-speaker any favours. But he had so much to learn in such a short time! This excited desperation made him feel like a thief with only a few hours to pillage a chateau, who rushes through the major rooms grabbing the objects of greatest value that will fit into his pockets, hoping to sort them later at his leisure.

He married Eva Surleau from Valentigny in southern France. One of her ancestors had been a Pole with an unpronounceable name: as he was a miller, he was simply called Surleau – 'on the water'. On her mother's side, Eva had a relative who made garden and electrical tools and velocipedes and quadricycles. His name was Peugeot. Later he made motorcycles, and then motor cars. (In the Great War, still shrouded in the future, he would make aeroplanes.) Eva was tall, good-looking and pious. Sam was short, with a fair complexion, an oval face and an aquiline nose. His blue-grey eyes laughed when they alighted on a comely representative of the fairer sex.

At the beginning of July, the Dubys left Geneva, saying goodbye to Sam's beloved Lac Léman, resplendent in its undulating azure robe. Never had the surrounding mountains sparkled so. But the sacrifices they were making to the Eternal by giving these things up seemed paltry in comparison to the rewards.

On 9 July, Sam Duby was ordained in Paris. In the name of the PEMS, M. Bianquis gave the special address. Taking as his theme Christ's injunction to 'Follow me!', he described Christ as the model of missionaries, whether in the simplicity of His language, the dedication of His entire life to the last things of this world, or the spirit of renunciation through daily sacrifice in prayer and in love, which was the essence of His ministry.

In reply Duby said, 'We will announce to the Basotho the Word of the Lord, the power of salvation for those for whom He died. We shall speak of conversion as a change not superficial, but whole, inward, reaching the depths of being; we shall speak of regeneration, of the principle of the true divine life, lodged in hearts through the meeting of the soul with God – a living principle, growing, blossoming, making of unworthy and wretched man a new being who transforms himself from day to day through the power of the Spirit, on the model, the normal and perfect type, of Jesus Christ, until the day when, having achieved his development, the awakened one will attain the perfect stature of Jesus Christ, He who will bring him to life everlasting.'

Duby was a very neat and organized man. Before he left Paris, he had ordered a riding outfit with six bottoms so that he would not run out of them quickly!

—◦◦—

Jacottet thought it was fortunate that Masupha died before the Anglo-Boer War broke out. It meant that Lerotholi was in undisputed control of the chieftain-ship. At one time it had been feared that Basutoland, at the very centre of the great conflict, in the eye of the storm, would be dragged into the fighting. On one side, many Basotho saw an opportunity to avenge earlier wrongs, and urged an attack on the Boers. On the other side, the Boers tried to ignite inter-nal rivalries by inciting Joel Molapo at Botha-Bothe to rebellion. Had his uncle Masupha been alive, the nationalists might well have tried to force matters to a head, particularly in the opening stages of the war when fortunes fluctuated alarmingly. The Resident Commissioner, Sir Godfrey Lagden, had an extremely delicate diplomatic task keeping the territory neutral.

Supported by the British High Commissioner, Lord Alfred Milner, Lagden informed the Basotho chiefs that they should stay out of the 'white man's war', and only if Basutoland were to be invaded by the Boers should it be 'defended in the Queen's name'. Fortunately, Lerotholi saw that the interests of his small country lay in maintaining this course. Consequently, as Jacottet noted, for three years Basutoland remained 'an islet in the midst of agitated seas'.

There were moments, though, when the whole nation held its breath. At the beginning of the war, Lagden, believing Maseru – the seat of government – to be of strategic importance, armed its few white inhabitants and solicited the support of a strong contingent of Lerotholi's subjects. His nervousness grew when the Boers cut adrift the pont which was Maseru's connection to the opposite bank of the Caledon river.

The most dramatic incident, however, occurred in April 1900. The Boers had reached a low point in their fortunes on the battlefields of Natal and the Orange Free State, when General Christiaan de Wet presented the glimmer of a new strategy that was to change the course of the war. While General De la Rey feinted towards Bloemfontein, De Wet took a flying column of 1 500 men to the south-east to capture the waterworks at Sannah's Post and cut off the sole water supply to Bloemfontein. There, in a major skirmish, De Wet elbowed General Broadwood in the eye, foxtrotted his way south to Reddersburg, where he orchestrated the last fling of 600 men of the Royal Irish Rifles (besieged and captured), then glided across the ballroom floor to Wepener, a village on the left bank of the Caledon. It was defended by 1 900 men of Brabant's Horse – mainly Cape Afrikaners fighting for the British. They were well dug in, although Colonel Dalgety, their commander, had planned his trenches on the assumption that they would be screened from attack by the neutral ground at his back across the river. It soon became clear that the Boers had every intention of violating the neutrality of Basutoland by taking up enfilading positions on high ground on the other side of the river – a move that would have rendered Dalgety's situation untenable.

Lagden saw the danger immediately. He called on Lerotholi to resist. Lerotholi, 'always gallant and at heart loyal' in Lagden's eyes, despite his 'excessive drunkenness', hastened to occupy the ground across from Wepener with several thousand armed and determined horsemen. This deterred De Wet, who turned away northwards. This passive demonstration therefore not only saved the garrison across the river, but also preserved the integrity and neutrality of Basutoland.

—◦◦—

War heightens suspicion. Because of their nationality and the somewhat strained Anglo-French relations, the French missionaries were a little nervous about their position at the start of the war. Indeed, suspicions were raised against some of them that they had been pushing the Basotho to disobey the government – to the point where Jacottet and others felt that certain missionaries were under surveillance. An article in the *St James Budget* of 17 November 1899 accused them of having deliberately placed obstacles in the way of the British all along. For a time they truly believed they were in danger.

With his usual caution, Jacottet warned Bianquis early on to be circumspect in what was published in the *Journal*: 'There are times when the less one talks about certain matters, the better. This is one such time.' The missionaries were somewhat reassured by a letter from Lagden affirming his support and understanding in the event of unforeseen mishaps or careless mistakes being made on their part. And this reassurance was strengthened when their school grant from the government was actually increased in the course of 1900.

Jacottet was a little embarrassed by what happened to his brother. The British ambulances were effectively staffed, so, with some difficulty, Gustave got the permission of Lagden to offer himself to the Boer ambulances, with the proviso that he could not return to Basutoland before the end of hostilities. He joined the service of Dr Hollandais Coster and assisted during the combat at Ventersburg. But the Boers, as they retreated, took all his instruments and spare clothes, and left him stranded on British ground. The British treated him with 'admirable courtesy' and returned him, with an escort, to the Boer front. At Sand river, he found himself in the line of fire, with shells and shrapnel dancing wildly around him. Once again the Boers left him behind. They made off like rabbits at the first gunshot, he said. With all Europe, he could admire them from afar; closer up, their actions seemed less praiseworthy to him.

The present campaign at an end, and his instruments gone, Gustave made his way back to Basutoland with the open permission of the military, who, in fact, praised his services. But Lagden took him prisoner, held him in Maseru for twenty-four hours, gave him a few days to collect his belongings from Thaba-Bosiu, and barred him from the country. Jacottet himself could not account for this brash procedure. He could only think that Lagden might have felt his authority was being undermined. By the time the war was over, Gustave had founded a medical practice in Matatiele in East Griqualand.

Lagden certainly had no reason to doubt Édouard Jacottet's support. Along with some of his colleagues, Jacottet confessed himself to be 'extremely pro-British'. He had always hoped for a British victory, and always believed in it, even at the time when the Boers were momentary winners. This did not make him an ardent supporter of imperialism. His concern was almost entirely for the Basotho.

Three months into the war, he affirmed his faith while contemplating the worst: 'I am convinced that once again God shall save Lesotho from destruction. If the impossible *should* happen, Afrikanerism that is, it would probably be different, and it would definitely mark the end of Lesotho.' And six months later he was of the same opinion: 'From the point of view of the blacks, particularly those of Lesotho, the British cause was ours. The Boer victory would have wiped us [that is, Lesotho] off the face of the earth.' For his part, Lagden was grateful for any help he could get from the missionaries in keeping the country out of the conflict. In July 1900, when the worst of the crisis was over, he wrote to a friend: 'I felt all along that the Basotho would be a text unto nations and that, if they went mad, the black terror would envelop the whole and divert the course of the war.' Once again, the French missionaries had played a small but important part in the fate of nations.

Although by June 1900 the Boers had been 'undeniably and inevitably defeated', Jacottet feared that a guerrilla war would persist. He had high praise for Lerotholi and for the Basotho, whom he regarded as 'fine politicians'. By their firm stance at Wepener the Basotho, he thought, had managed to ward off conflict, and just as his faith in God had been justified when doubts about the war began to creep in, so he felt that 'we were not wrong to have faith in them'. He also admired the patience of the British administration, and thought that their prudence and mediation, with the help of Lerotholi and Jonathan, had managed to prevent the incipient revolt of Joel from turning into civil war and the country being dragged into the wider conflict. 'The cooperation between the government and the Paramount Chief has secured the tranquillity of the country. With all the provinces of South Africa suffering one after the other, Lesotho alone has been spared.'

Even at this early stage, Jacottet began to look ahead with some prescience. He was pretty certain that there would be a prompt reconciliation between the British colonials and the Boers. For the moment he guessed that Lesotho was safe, but, he warned, 'Everything depends on what becomes of Rhodes. If, as I think will happen, his star is extinguished, our worst nightmares will be over; if he takes hold of the reins again and regains power, we shall have everything to fear.'

In the near term, he thought that the interests of the Basotho lay with the British: 'In the new united southern Africa, Britain will carry on a single, uniform policy towards the blacks.' Dictated from London, this would 'certainly be *for* the natives, accompanied by sentiments of justice and philanthropy'. What worried him was the day 'when the colonies draw up their own policy in matters concerning the natives … For the colony, the native is generally the enemy, or rather the dependant who must be provided for, but who must also be prevented from rising to a position in which "nature did not intend him". With the South African colony, as with the Madagascan colony, the Rights of Man are not an "article of exportation".'

As for Lesotho specifically, it was clear to Jacottet that neither London nor the Cape was planning to touch it. 'If only the internal administration of the country could be improved on, if only the exercise of the power of the chiefs could be more carefully controlled, if only the abuse of authority by certain chiefs could be suppressed,' he believed, 'it is all possible. But deep down, things will never change. It is my sincere belief that Lesotho will remain as it is today for many years to come, but will be more capable of progress and self-development. Our mission can help things along; it will be, as it always has been, one of the major contributing factors to social progress. The Church of Lesotho will be the lever of the country. May God be with us, and help to render the Church worthy of its task.'

But the threat to the survival of Lesotho would come sooner than expected – within the decade. And Jacottet would find himself at the heart of the crisis.

—◦—

While the nightmarish war encircled them and the noise of cannon could be heard across the border, the missionaries remained calm. They preached, taught and lived as though everything was as before. The only new thing was the isolation. There was virtually a complete break with the outside world: the mail was seldom sent and many letters never arrived; the telegraph was cut, so messages had to be sent across the Maloti; only one newspaper in two months meant they had little idea of the progress of the war!

Provisions were scarce: sugar, kerosene, salt had all but vanished. Jacottet had, at the beginning of 1900, enough provisions to supply the Girls' School and the station for a few months, but at the Bible School in Morija, Alfred Casalis was completely without fuel.

The Jacottet children had whooping cough, but survived it. In the midst of chaos and concern, Étienne-Serge Jacottet was born on 8 April 1900. The momentary presence of Gustave was invaluable, as Dr Hertig arrived only at the last minute. What luxury, exclaimed Jacottet – a doctor for the mother and another one for the child! Both child and mother were fine.

The only mystery is that at some point in the next year or two, for reasons unknown, the child's name was changed to Charles-Claude.

No-Man's-Land always presented a dilemma for the French missionaries. It was the area to the south-east of Basutoland, across the mountains. The mountains did form a natural barrier between the two areas and should have presented a natural border to the interests of the PEMS. The trouble is that human activity is an altogether messier proposition.

After a preliminary recce to No-Man's-Land, Adam Kok and his Griqua people, harassed from their land north of the Gariep (or Orange) by a combination of immigrant farmers and severe drought, were allowed to trek eastwards in 1863–4 and settle in the relatively underpopulated area around what became Kokstad. With considerable fortitude, they found a path through the Maloti; but they were satisfied with the land where they had settled, which was much better watered than where they had come from, and soon No-Man's-Land came to be known as East Griqualand.

Frustrated in their exile in Aliwal North during the 1865–8 war, aware that their resources could not last them forever and mindful that some of their flock might need a refuge from the war if it continued in such disastrous fashion, the PEMS missionaries had looked for alternative pastures. Consequently, Paul Germond made two journeys to No-Man's-Land. The second of these, in the winter of 1867, is worth summarizing for what it reveals of the difficulties and challenges the missionaries had to face.

When one travelled in Europe, money was the chief difficulty, while transport was no problem. In Africa it was rather different, as Germond discovered – especially when he decided to take his whole family with him. 'There is the wagon to overhaul, the soundness of the axles to be carefully checked, bolts tightened up, available space estimated, a judicious choice made of the objects which it will be possible to take,' he sniffed. 'And as one is always wrong, no sooner does one imagine the task completed, than it is necessary to begin all over again. And what of the team? Let us pause to consider it. Invariably it is disorganized, an ox is sure to be limping, another sick, and it is not always easy to replace them.'

With children sick, and traversing territory where common thieves practised their terror while bands of Bushmen fought for their very existence, then travelling for a fortnight without meeting anyone, the Germond party came after five weeks to Matatiele. This was, thought Germond, 'a very pretty name for a very ugly country', with its marshy plains and cold, denuded plateau. He found in the area a mixture of Basotho, Batlokoa and Baphuthi who had moved there some years before, and who were, as so often in these circumstances, keen to get themselves a missionary: 'Every little chief wished to have me near him, for it is no small matter for an African chief to have at his beck and call a missionary to whom he can say, "My missionary, write me a letter; my missionary, do me such and such a favour." It adds to one's importance in the eyes of the tribe and one has the satisfaction of arousing the jealousy of one's neighbours.' It was clear that, in the words of Jacottet, 'a new Basutoland was springing up there'. After the war, however, no missionaries could be spared, so two Basotho evangelists were sent instead in 1869; and it was only in 1875 that M. Preen established the first station at Matatiele, followed by Christmann at Paballong in 1877. In 1884, the station at Matatiele, disorganized and almost destroyed in the War of the Guns, was moved to Mafube, halfway between the old site and Qacha's Nek, with Cochet as its first missionary.

After the Christmann debacle, Henri Bertschy had to put things right at Paballong. But when he was transferred to the Industrial School at Leloaleng in 1898, the station was left vacant for two years, until Sam Duby arrived in the new year of 1900. At the Conference at Thaba-Bosiu, he had been warned by some evangelists that the flock had been warm until they lost their shepherd. Now they shivered as under a torn blanket.

The Dubys must have been so pleased with their first arrival in Lesotho that they spent some time celebrating their new life. Certainly, Mme Duby was pregnant when they crossed over the mountains, so that it may not have been an altogether comfortable ride, although it took only three or four days on horseback compared with the five-week wagon trip of the Germonds thirty years before.

After two years of neglect, the buildings of the station had quickly decayed and needed intensive repair. Duby's immersion in Sesotho was consequently slower than he would have liked, but he managed to conduct his first service the Sunday after Easter.

What struck the Dubys most was the monotony of African life. One of the reasons for this was that, at the beginning, they had hardly any real contact with the locals: 'Not only their language, but their customs, their way of thinking, in a word their intimate life is still a domain full of mystery to us. Oh, these people are certainly not the primitive, simple-natured and easily-read people that we naively imagined before our departure.' He felt it would take him a few years to penetrate the barrier, and that the 'fundamentally private character of black people' would make conversion slow. 'Because of the way things are,' he said sadly, 'we live amongst the blacks and far from them, in constant contact but separate from them.'

The tedium of hard work, the slow progress, the lack of old friends in this first year was relieved only by the birth of Robert in June. Visits from colleagues were special, but they were few and far between in an outlying corner like Paballong. Private feasts, such as birthdays and family celebrations, took on special significance: 'The more one feels isolated, the closer one feels to oneself.'

The drought was hard that year: vegetables withered, animals died. It was matched by a spiritual drought: hearts were dry, souls languished.

All in all, Duby had to admit that 'an African Christmas does not mean a great deal to me'. Nevertheless, consolation lay in his faith: 'If nature surrounding Christmas changes, Christmas of the heart remains, thankfully, the same everywhere ...'

The drought lasted well into December. So bad was it that Duby began to dream of the torrential rain he was accustomed to at home. So bad was it that Chief Lebenya called an emergency pitso. But Duby knew that there was only one Being who could help if He wanted to, and that He was punishing them for their sins. Duby therefore decided to speak to the people himself. As the church could not accommodate one quarter of the throng – pagans called by Lebenya with their respective chiefs, evangelists with their congregations – the meeting was held outside under a particularly strong sun. The Ten Commandments were read (something done only on great occasions), a prayer was said, a hymn sung, and, as the beasts of the field groaned and the veld fires raged, Duby used the words of the old prophet Joel: 'And rend your heart, and not your garments.' Humbly, they prayed for rain.

That night, after the sun darkened, the moon darkened too, as the clouds came over and the stars withdrew their shining. Next day the rain fell, dropping from the mountains like new wine, and the hills flowed with God's blessing.

For the drought of the spirit, Duby knew that he must have the patience of the farmer in the story by St James, and wait for the early and latter rain.

Until then, he was not unhappy: 'I like Paballong. I am here and here I stay.'

—⁂—

After a while, though the church was in a deep sleep, the Dubys' solitude diminished. At first, the war seemed as remote as their station. On 28 September 1901, their second child, Germaine, was born. Not a day too soon, because Boer commandos under Smuts, Lotter and others had infiltrated the Cape, and in response the whites in the area were armed and put on alert. The defenders' camp was no more than one and a half hour's ride from Paballong. It was not wise for the missionaries to leave their stations, and if Germaine (soon to be nicknamed Gynette) had been born much later, outside help would not have been forthcoming in an emergency.

Communications with the Cape Colony were cut for a few weeks, and books and supplies were impossible to get. With his family growing, the mission house was cramped, and Duby's study was a sunless kennel, but building extensions came to a halt as all the men were enlisted to protect the borders or scout for the British. Matters were not helped by the reappearance of the rinderpest, which stopped travel by wagon between stations.

—⁂—

In September 1901, Jacottet had the opportunity to cut free from his sheltered isolation. He accompanied his son Gustave to the Cape to put him on the boat for Europe. Gustave was ultimately bound for Paris to live with the Hoffets, who had moved there, and to join his siblings Marcelle and Henri. Gustave celebrated his tenth birthday that month, too.

Jacottet found it another very difficult separation: 'Alas! We will never get used to it.'

But in his journey to and fro, he saw the eerie effects of the war: 'I returned even more horrified by the wars – whichever ones they were – that have been fought. They always leave a deplorable path behind them. Seeing all the devastation and desertion of this country is truly saddening … In all our travel through the Free State, there was neither a beast, nor a house, nor a person to be seen. Practically all the farms have been burned down. All that can be seen now are soldiers and small forts. The entire population has been taken captive, either in the concentration camps (which I did not see, but of which I have heard some very sad tales) or in commando … Censorship is stricter than ever. In spite of everything, one cannot help but admire the steadfastness of Botha, Steyn and De Wet in continuing to hold firm. But it is almost suicidal.' Although he had always wished for a British victory, and believed that a Boer victory would have been '*disastrous* for Lesotho and the future of the black *pastors'*, he nevertheless deplored 'the way in which Britain has continued the war for over a year'.

For once, Lesotho had not been sucked into strife. 'I have never fully realized just how privileged Lesotho has been,' he told Boegner. 'It is the most peaceful corner, the only fortunate part of South Africa. I am almost frightened at times when I think of how it has been spared.'

—∽⊙—

Although the cyclone of war swept past him and left him largely unscathed, the war years nevertheless saw much inner turmoil in Jacottet and precipitated a crisis that almost prompted him to resign and ask Boegner to find him a place in Europe. Like the causes of a war, like the explanations for a murder, the reasons for this crisis were neither single nor simple. No single reason was sufficient, but several were each necessary. His anguish stemmed primarily from the policy and future direction of the Lesotho mission, which was the subject of much contention in these years and on which he held strong opinions.

In 1894, the Synod, reconstituted after many years, met harmoniously. This was repeated in 1896. The Synod had a small but useful role to play in the life of the church. But a significant turning point had been reached. Until now there had been only two Basotho pastors, Carlisle Motebang and Job Moteane (though they were soon to be joined by a third, John Mohapeloa), and so it was possible to leave their exact status in the government of the mission undefined. But in 1896, the second batch of Basotho pastors – Everitt Segoete, Fineas Matlanyane, Bethuel Sekokotoana, Edward Motsamai and Nicolas Mpiti – finished their theological studies, first under Dieterlen, then under Jacottet, and were accepted into service by the Conference for a probationary period, to be followed by ordination. At one time, the two earliest pastors had been allowed into some of the sittings of the Conference, but this had proved unsatisfactory. While it did not seem appropriate for the Basotho ministers to debate issues related to Europe, it seemed equally unfortunate to exclude them from all sittings. Now there would be eight pastors, and that was a significant number. But in the Synod they would be diluted like a few drops of rain in a large pool. It was clear that what Jacottet called 'another wheel' should be added.

The solution, which was neither foreseen nor planned for, came in a few hours of inspiration during an extraordinary meeting of the Conference at Morija in October 1898. It was decided that a new mixed Conference of French missionaries and Basotho ministers was to take the place of the old Missionary Conference in all exclusively ecclesiastical questions. The old Conference would be retained only for matters involving the European personnel alone, such as salaries, transfers, leave, children's bursaries and relations with Paris, as well as related budgetary affairs and those schools which did not come under the exclusive purview of the church. The mixed Conference would concern itself with the church, its discipline, laws and finances, and would oversee the creation of new parishes and outstations, the placement of Basotho ministers, ordinations, theological students and primary schools. It would be 'the guiding hand of the church'. It was given the name of the 'Seboka' – an assembly or gathering, even a feast.

Somewhat unusually, the minutes of the extraordinary meeting do not give details of the debate, so we cannot be sure who said what, but it is certain that Jacottet argued forcefully for the new arrangement. Although the missionaries did not fully realize it at the time, this was one of the most radical changes the mission chose to undergo. Its importance was not missed by Jacottet. A few years later, in a history of the mission for its 75th jubilee, he wrote with undisguised pleasure and pride on the creation of the Seboka, letting the italics on the page reflect the emphasis in his mind: '*It was at that moment that the Mission gave birth to the Church of Basutoland.*' There was complete equality between Basotho and French missionaries: the old Conference retained no veto rights, and the only check was a two-thirds majority vote required for changes on certain specified matters.

A decade later, Jacottet was able to comment on 'the complete harmony which has prevailed between the blacks and the whites', and the fact that 'there has never been even a semblance of a colour conflict, something so rare in South Africa that it is well worth mentioning'. At first glance, it might have appeared to be an unnecessarily complicated structure – Conference, Seboka and Synod – but it worked. Jacottet thought that the Conference might be needed until the very last missionary left Basutoland, but that its importance would diminish while that of the Seboka grew. As for the Synod, which brought together representatives of the church of varying ability and experience, its influence and value were for some years uncertain, though in 1908, with the jubilee, it was used to 'exercise a truly religious influence on the whole church'. The structures of a church organization which he had dreamed about for so long were slotting into place.

This had not been achieved without a struggle, however. And there were a number of other issues that strained his patience to the limit.

Although he judged the Conference at Hermon in May 1900 to be 'the best one I've assisted with in a long time, without any conflicts or harsh words spoken', two of its decisions were major setbacks for him. Firstly, the Girls' School had grown to thirty-three students and it was expected that the number would increase to sixty. Thaba-Bosiu was unsuitable for the expansion, as its water supply was inadequate, and so the Conference decided to move the school to

Thabana-Morena. There were twelve missionaries at the Conference. Eleven of them voted in favour of the proposal; only Jacottet voted against. He felt the reasons for the move were sound and accepted what he called 'this quasi-unanimous decision', but nevertheless he 'suffered as a result of it'. On his leave in Europe he had personally raised a considerable amount of money for the school's expansion, and he felt the donors would not have given had they known he was not to be involved. His fund-raising efforts had been neither fully appreciated nor courteously acknowledged, he felt, and he hoped that the transfer would not result in the downfall of the school. In the event, it did not. But he was left with what he called 'pelo ea lla' – heartsickness, or crying of the heart.

The second disappointment touched him even more deeply. The Theological School had been closed in 1896 when Jacottet went on leave. It had not yet been reopened, which meant that for several years there had been no third intake of pastoral candidates. He saw this as a serious problem. At the time, both missions and established churches were beginning to face competition from breakaway or independent black religious movements, roughly collocated under the name of 'Ethiopianism'. Jacottet regarded the Basotho pastorate and the Seboka as bulwarks against this encroachment.

When the subject of the Theological School was broached, only five of the missionaries (Ellenberger, Vollet, Casalis, Dyke and Jacottet) voted for its immediate reopening. Had the normally progressive Dieterlen voted with them, the Conference would have been neatly split; but he decided that the salaries of the catechists and the number of outstations should be increased as a matter of priority, and the mission could not afford this as well as the considerable expense of reopening the Theological School. In the back of the Conference's collective mind when it came to making these decisions was the fact that the likely Director of the Theological School, namely Jacottet, would be in a position to provide premises – the buildings vacated by the Girls' School – if the reopening were delayed until that move had taken place.

Once again, the controversy concerning the 'petites femmes', the junior wives, and their acceptance into the church erupted. Two of the oldest and most senior of the missionaries found themselves at the extreme ends of the spectrum of opinion.

On the conservative side, Ellenberger, in a thirty-five-page document, argued that the lirethe – the minor wives – lived in impurity, and so there was no question of admitting them into the church. But there seemed to be contradictions in his position: he would admit first wives of polygamous marriages who had left their husbands, and he had even, on occasion, admitted a junior wife into the church himself. Dieterlen and Christeller, both relatively moderate on the subject, felt that when the heathen husband consented to 'this comedy', the church should admit the petites femmes without separating them from their spouses, although with certain severe restrictions. Jacottet, admitting that there was 'a lot to say for both sides, and the majority of us are irresolute in our views', put forward to the Seboka a proposal which partly closed the door to the lirethe and partly opened it. This was so obscure that Dieterlen described it, in a letter to his mother, as 'fumisterie', a practical joke. Even a vote failed to clarify what the prevailing opinion was, since not everyone fully understood its aim! Of the twenty-three votes, sixteen were in favour of admitting minor wives according to a narrow rule. What was most interesting was that all but one or two of the Basotho pastors voted against the proposal – a nice illustration of how, in a relatively non-racial context, behaviour often works against racial stereotype. These pastors, brought up early in the school of Mabille and Ellenberger, were in some respects more conservative theologically than their white counterparts. As Jacottet said of them, 'the black pastors ... are traditionalists par excellence'.

Dieterlen, although he generally regarded Ellenberger as 'entêté', or stubborn, respected him for saying 'no' so clearly. His opinion might be wrong, in Dieterlen's view, but it was sincere. Dieterlen himself wanted clarity and frankness, not subterfuge. Ultimately, the decision of the Conference was conservative: with a few minor exceptions, it upheld the principle that a second or third wife could only be baptized after divorce or, at least, a physical separation from her husband.

Yet Ellenberger was not happy, and he submitted his resignation directly to Paris. This astonished and angered Jacottet in turn, because it raised a matter more serious than that of the petites femmes itself. He firmly hoped that the Committee would not involve itself in disciplinary matters which 'the missionaries here alone can truly understand'. Acknowledging that in the same dispute years before the Conference had appealed to the Committee, he asserted that that had only been done to get out of an embarrassing situation and prevent the resignation of Mabille. This time, Paris had been approached neither by the Conference nor by the Seboka but by an individual. Jacottet was adamant that it was now a matter of *sovereignty*: the bodies of the Church, the Synod or the Seboka, must decide in these matters. What he was aiming at was the progressive development of the Church of Basutoland to *autonomy*.

The Seboka refused to accept the resignation of Ellenberger. But Kohler's position also presented it with a quandary. On taking the stance which basically upheld the status quo, the Seboka had been informed that, in certain churches, junior wives were being baptized contrary to regulations, although such practices had diminished considerably because of the introduction of black pastors and the greater unification of the churches. The missionaries and ministers were quite certain that no one would intentionally violate the regulation.

But Frédéric Kohler, at Cana, did just that. On more than one occasion. In June 1900, for instance, he baptized three wives from a polygamous marriage, even though they had in no way separated from their husband. This was officially brought to the attention of Nicolas Mpiti, whose parish was Maseru. He had no choice but to inform the Executive Committee of the Seboka.

The Executive Committee wrote a letter of complaint to Kohler, asking him to refrain from further unlawful baptisms. Kohler's reply, in a lengthy report, was to refuse point-blank, declaring he could not accept a discipline that went against his conscience. The situation was grave and dangerous, amounting almost to a constitutional crisis involving authority. Jacottet considered this to be 'an enormous faux pas' on Kohler's part and scorned his fundamentalist position: 'By demanding that the church grant agreement to polygamous men and to circumcision, etc., and by saying that to do otherwise would be to go against God, he is, in fact, going against our entire discipline. Abraham and Moses, etc. were naturally cited in the report. He declares that the Word of God asks only for faith, that we must receive and baptize all those who declare themselves to have faith in God, without asking for anything more than that. It is complete and utter infantile radicalism. But it is specious, full of sophistry, and, I fear, highly dangerous.'

Jacottet's position is interesting. On the one hand, 'truly beside himself with fret over what might happen', he was adamant that he would not keep quiet if the Seboka gave in to Kohler's demands: 'Allowing a missionary consciously and willingly to violate the rules would certainly lead to the rapid ruin of our mission. It would mean chaos, anarchy, and before long Ethiopianism would gain power as a result of our failure.'

On the other hand, he was equally concerned about the ultimate autonomy of the Church of Basutoland, of 'the absolute independence of the Seboka, then later of the Synod, in ecclesiastic and disciplinary matters'. For many reasons, he maintained, 'I sincerely wish that the Church, represented today by its Seboka, tomorrow by its Synod, would follow the autocephalous discipline.' In other words, discipline was needed over its ministers and congregations within an autonomous church.

Where discipline was defied, Jacottet was not averse to the exercise of authority.

—∞—

In two letters (privately approved by Alfred Casalis) to Boegner on 22 March and 15 June 1901, Jacottet laid out his vision and his intent with passion.

Because the letters were confidential, they represent a heightened level of authenticity.

Before the Conference at Thaba-Bosiu in April 1901, Jacottet had 'got to the point where I wondered whether I still had a place in Lesotho; whether, with all the causes that I was defending (native pastorate, Theological School, self-government to the churches), it would not be better for me just to take my leave'. Leaving Lesotho 'would truly break my heart', he said, but there were 'certain factors' which upset him terribly and which 'took certain illusions' away from him. 'You know my opinions, my desires, and what I refer to, even though the term is a little ambitious, as my programme: the consistent development of the native pastorate (in correlation with the swift reopening of the Theological School) and the autonomous Church of Lesotho. This programme is also yours ... But there was an attempt to go backwards, which almost succeeded. If the situation ever arose where the majority moved decisively for reaction, I would never concede to it. In such a case I would have to leave.'

The reason given at the Hermon Conference for not reopening the Theological School had 'never seemed good enough to me', Jacottet said, and it was just 'another attempt to move backwards'. But after the Thaba-Bosiu Conference the following year, he was a little more upbeat. The return of Jeanmairet and Louis Mabille strengthened the ranks of his supporters. Although 'up until the 11th hour the outcome was doubtful', eventually, he could happily proclaim, the majority of the Conference (though not everyone) 'gave in to my progressives and liberals'. It was decided that the School would reopen in July 1902 (it eventually opened in September). Jacottet was chosen as Director by twelve votes to two.

Piqued despite his victory, he returned to an old hobby horse. What the mission of Lesotho needed was 'worthy recruits, great in heart and mind'. This had never been the case. 'What we need,' he wrote, 'is people like Duby. We need men of true worth. We need Christian gentlemen!' But he was optimistic that the tide was in his favour: 'In fact, when the number of Basotho pastors eventually grows, they will have a greater influence on the Conference, which will prevent it from putting off our work.' He envisaged that the number of white missionaries would be reduced little by little and 'the native pastorate' built up.

He was admirably self-aware when it came to his shortcomings as a leader of the 'progressives' and as a candidate for the School's directorship. But he had the courage of his strong convictions: 'It was not my place to be or not to be the nominated spokesman. Indeed, I would have preferred it if my candidacy had not been considered, because I was under the impression, at the time, that my personality would unfortunately do harm to our cause. I am too identified with the whole issue of the autonomy of the church and all too often I unfortunately have to push too far ahead to get things done … I accepted the post of Director. I am glad that it is an activity which I enjoy and one towards which I feel I can truly give my all. But I am nervous about starting my new job. I know what is involved: the responsibility and, above all, the workload. It is too much to take on, managing a school and a church at the same time.'

—∽—

The controversy over the 'petites femmes' rumbled on late into 1901 and even into 1902. Though Ellenberger's resignation was turned down and he withdrew it (he retired to Steynsburg in 1905), Kohler continued his defiance. It looked as though the Seboka meeting in October 1901 might become a showdown. But, in the end, heeding the advice that came at him from all directions, Kohler backed down beforehand and agreed to abide by the rules. He also accepted the reprimand delivered to him. Jacottet had feared the Seboka might be faced with a terrible crisis, if the Basotho pastors gave in to the temptation of going along with Kohler, a dissident in the hot seat, and a white-black confrontation ensued. Instead, they stood firm, discussing things calmly and with common sense. Jacottet was now certain that the Seboka was 'a viable organ'. He also felt that in the long run the Kohler affair had turned out to be a good thing – it had shown everyone 'that every white and black must obey the law'. Although he was annoyed that the Conference following the Seboka demonstrated that 'several of our colleagues do not share in our achievement, revealing unwarranted sentiments of resentment, almost jealousy, towards our black pastors', he could proudly boast to Boegner that 'I do not think that any other mission is as far ahead as our own on the path of self-government and to building a truly native church'.

The matter didn't quite end there. Early in 1902, Jacottet addressed a communication to the various church consistories concerning the Seboka's decisions the previous October. By omitting a passage or two, he annoyed Kohler mightily. Kohler wrote Jacottet a letter which the extraordinary meeting of the Conference at Morija in April judged 'offensive and regrettable', ordering the former to apologize.

Later in the year, Kohler tendered his resignation. Jacottet was disgusted: 'Mr Kohler has shown a great narrow-mindedness in the whole affair, and, whilst his resignation is deplorable, given the state of mind that he was in for such a long time, I believe that he should be held to it.' At the delayed meeting of the Conference at Cana in October, Kohler was persuaded to withdraw his resignation (he retired in 1908, and died, aged eighty-one, at Cana in 1929).

—∽—

The bitter winter of 1901 was followed by the worst on record in 1902. It culminated in an unprecedented snowfall, so that the year became known forever as the year of Lehloa le Leholo (the Great Snow). Vegetation was hacked down and uprooted with indiscriminate desperation. Erosion deepened, dongas widened. This was a continuation – compounded by the rinderpest disaster – of an old process of destruction, relentless and cumulative, which struck at the very life of the fertile land.

On 31 August 1902, the Jacottets' last child, Marguerite, was born, rather earlier than they had expected. Jacottet had been worried: his wife had simultaneously been bearing a heavy workload. However, things went exceptionally well and never had she had such a swift and almost painless labour. She recovered quickly in the days immediately after the birth.

This soon changed. Mrs Jacottet was so run down that she became ill; perhaps, too, she suffered from post-natal depression – a condition scarcely recognized at the time. Certainly, there was a crisis, which lasted for months and left her husband so discouraged that he began 'seriously to consider actually leaving Africa for her'. This put great strain on him: 'It was an enormously painful test for me; my heart belongs here in Lesotho, this is where I feel most at home, this is my destiny.'

Paris allowed Miss Privat, a niece of Louise Jacottet, to join them, and she was able to pick up some of the older woman's burden. She was, thought Édouard, 'a godsend'.

In 1903, the five new students of the reopened Theological School at Thaba-Bosiu, very keen to learn, were making good progress. Jacottet felt a sense of real achievement: 'The struggle of the first few years is over. The pastors have complete trust in us, and what I am even more pleased about is the fact that those missionaries who were afraid to change their minds at first are a lot more optimistic today.'

There were other good things that happened during the year: although Marguerite was poorly for a while, she recovered, and all the Jacottet children prospered; with the support of Miss Privat, Mrs Jacottet began to feel much better; a new parish was established in Maseru, a church built, and Nicolas Mpiti placed in charge. A visit from Coillard, too, was infinitely more successful than the one five years before. Jacottet finally laid to rest some of the envy he secretly harboured for Coillard's more romantic, more glamorous task. Coillard probably also felt chastened: the Zambezi mission had lost many of its personnel to fever, and the station and its founder had come in for some fierce criticism. 'We got on more calmly,' said Jacottet, 'related to one another more easily, more cautiously, with less panache, but there was also more of a sense of true brotherliness between us. I shall always be grateful for that.'

When Bianquis was due to return from Madagascar, where he had served for a couple of years, Jacottet made an unsuccessful attempt to get him to visit Lesotho, 'our oldest and most developed mission and, in certain respects, the most advanced on the path of autonomy'. He felt the contrast would interest Bianquis: 'One a colonial mission, the other a non-colonial mission; one new, the other one old.' Almost wistfully, he expressed the desire to visit Madagascar himself, feeling the trip would benefit both missions. He had strong ideas for Madagascar, some of which may once have been 'considered dangerous and utopian' in Lesotho, but had been 'carried out so successfully that the majority of people accept them today'. The main thrust of his advice was that the mission in Madagascar must have a Central Chest: 'They cannot have a unified church, or a defined pastorate, or good finances without one.' Under the enthusiastic encouragement of René Ellenberger, he wanted to visit the Congo as well – rather more than the Zambezi.

But he was also tired: he felt himself hounded from all sides, by the vast station that was Thaba-Bosiu, the demands of the numerous outstations, the primary schools and the Theological School, the chairmanship of the Synod, and the preparation of the next Conference, which he had volunteered to organize.

The wider situation in southern Africa was also a concern to him. A conversation with Herbert Sloley, the new Resident Commissioner, in May gave him the impression 'that Lord Milner is firmly in the hands of the capitalists and risks becoming an anti-black politician'. Then, in October, he had spoken to Sloley in an official capacity, requesting a £1 000 grant for new buildings at the Normal School. It was turned down. The Resident Commissioner was keen to accede, but Jacottet believed 'it is Pretoria that has a problem, as they do not support black advancement', and he went on to lament plaintively: 'This war has done a lot of damage. The high governmental spheres have become, increasingly, more openly hostile towards the interests of the blacks. And all in favour of the capitalists.'

The war had reshuffled the political cards in the southern end of Africa once and for all, and Jacottet would find himself playing for higher stakes.

—⁂—

After the customary few days of holiday at Christmas, Jacottet prepared himself for a trip of several weeks to East Griqualand. Initially, his purpose was to visit his brother, who had started a practice there, and his sister Hélène, a noted botanist, who had come from Switzerland to keep house for Dr Jacottet. It would be, he thought, 'a good opportunity to get away and clear my head'.

But his journey soon became a mission. East Griqualand was in some trouble. The senior missionary there, Christeller, had asked to leave. Jacottet thought he was wrong to do so. 'His departure has been a tremendous blow to East Griqualand,' he confided to Boegner. 'He did his work well, was loved and appreciated by all.'

Christeller had been replaced at Mafube by Paul Ramseyer. Coillard had warned Jacottet well in advance about Ramseyer: he was an obstinate man who would not listen to anyone. Before his departure, Jacottet had received 'an extremely harsh letter' from certain critical members of Ramseyer's church, and the situation seemed very serious. Christeller, always a pessimist, thought, in fact, that it was lost. Since Jacottet judged that 'Ramseyer seems to have made the whole world go against him and is provoking almost a revolution', suddenly he had less enthusiasm for the expedition, concerned that he would be caught 'between the devil and the deep blue sea' and might have to take uncomfortable decisions. He would probably, he anticipated, 'have to act on authority'.

On his way to Matatiele, Jacottet rode straight over the mountains. He was immensely pleased to see his brother and sister, and the trip did him the world of good both mentally and physically. He found that the problems between Ramseyer and his church had been blown completely out of proportion. Certainly, a group of people had risen up against Ramseyer, whose blunt manner and choice of words were not what the Basotho were accustomed to. Jacottet had to be 'quite firm' to re-establish order, but Ramseyer was pleased at his presence as the situation was becoming intolerable. Jacottet felt that the episode might have chastened Ramseyer somewhat and might lead him to curb his incredible temper; he hoped so, because he had had the pleasure of seeing a more agreeable side to the young missionary in the process.

By contrast, Sam Duby, at Paballong, was a model of discretion and enterprise. Although he had struggled at first in a poor parish with poor Sesotho, he had by now got both these things into shape. Eva Duby was pregnant with their third child.

While bohali and beer were recurring problems, Duby was categorical about the worst offence: 'Adultery remains the sin which is the order of the day, the rodent within our churches.' Sometimes, in the moral desert, he was tempted to be discouraged, but he reminded himself that there must be and still were men who, lifted up by God alone, did not kneel before Baal.

Adultery was certainly roundly condemned by the church and its members, and the guilty were severely chastised, but it was not irredeemable. When a Basotho evangelist who had been sent to Barotseland committed the sin, he was suspended, but ultimately reinstated. This was not scarlet-letter country.

—◦⌒◦—

Duby had been midwife to a number of conversions.

Linko was an old patriarch, well over eighty, with a wizened face framed by a white beard and pierced by small, expressive eyes. Formerly chief adviser to Lebenya, he had led the singing at pagan festivals, but after a year of struggle with his conscience he had at last been filled with the spirit. Now he sang the Christian hymns with no less heart. He had had a sizeable herd of cattle, all of which he lost to rinderpest. Only the bohali of his two daughters had allowed him to recoup some of his losses. But, as he told Duby, 'I reckoned without God, who made the scales fall from my eyes.' Just like St Paul at the touch of Ananias. He could not read or write, but each week he learned and recited the biblical verses and lessons.

Yosefa, in his late twenties, with an arm crippled by tuberculosis, saddened his deeply pious mother by taking a pagan wife. For four years, he struggled with a serious physical illness, the cause of which seemed to be spiritual. Weakened by long months of suffering, he was unable to move, unable to walk. Then, on the day he declared himself beaten and vowed to serve the Lord, he was filled with joy. 'Ruined during his time of madness', as he called it, he had now set his heart right, and his faith led him gently to the evangelization of the pagan villages.

Joel, like Yosefa, had been christened in his childhood by a pious mother, who had the pain of seeing her son become distant as he grew away from what she considered to be the only things worth living for. She followed her eldest daughter to the grave without having witnessed her precious son's conversion. Day after day, both women had knelt to 'struggle with God', imploring Him in prayer to return the sheep that had strayed. But Joel's heart hardened and God seemed to be deaf.

His conversion, when it came, was dramatic.

One day, a strong and lively man arrived at Duby's study, placed himself in front of the missionary and swung his hat between his hands. His face was covered with sweat. 'It is I, Joel,' he said, 'I have just come from Semongkong, where I live. I can tell you that it is over, I am vanquished and I am giving myself to God.'

'It is well, Joel,' replied Duby, 'sit and speak in peace.'

Without appearing to have heard him, Joel continued rotating his hat even more quickly, and went on, 'Oh! If you only knew! I have seen the Lord! He spoke to me, he said to me, "Joel ..." But no, I must tell you everything.

'It was during the night, last night, it was dark, I was sleeping when suddenly a magnificent, marvellous song filled the house. Marvelling, I raised myself on my elbow to see where such beautiful voices were coming from, and there in my house, in the middle of the night, I saw a band of people clothed in robes of a brilliant whiteness. Amongst them were my mother and sister, both some years dead, who looked at me as they sang. While I couldn't take my eyes off my beloved mother, she made a sign with her hand, indicating a person whom I had not noticed before, in another corner. His radiant face lit up the whole house. He gazed on me for a long time, and called to me, "Joel!" I moved towards him. It was so wonderful to be close to him that I wanted to stay there forever, without speaking, without moving. But, once again, he called to me, "Joel! Don't you see?" And he showed me with a gesture a figure hiding in a dark corner near my bed, horrible, with the form of neither man nor beast, and equipped with a sharp staff, digging in the ground a hole, a pit. "Joel, have you really decided that he will bury your soul in the grave which he digs? Oh, believe me! It is your enemy who seeks only your death."

'Then everything vanished. I cried, I cried, as I was no longer in the presence of the one who seemed so good, so loving; I cried at the thought that I was in the hands of the monster who dug the vault for my soul. And today I tell you, moruti, that I have given myself to Jesus. I want to hear him speak to me again and stay with him, with him alone, forever.'

Since that night when he saw Jesus, Joel had had the joyous certainty of those who know and truly believe. Duby testified to it. The ministry of Joel, as an evangelist, bore 'beautiful fruit'. Joel's only dilemma, it seemed, was that he did not know how to tell which was better for him — 'to live down here below or to leave and to be with the Lord always.'

Finally, there was Tselane. Despite being unusually tall, she was, Duby noted amusedly, 'a little woman', a petite femme, second in status to a woman who had converted to Christianity. Tselane loved her husband, the neat village sheltered against the mountain, the tidy huts. But she was unhappy, because she had no children. How she envied the other women as they passed her hut with their broods. Her tears changed nothing.

Often she watched the first wife kneeling in her hut. Once, she was reciting a strange prayer: she was asking God for what she needed. Why should Tselane not try it herself? That night she prayed, naively but fervently.

Later that same night, she had a vision. In an enchanted, sunny land there was a clear lake, where a group of children were dancing, many children, all singing, all lovely. Her heart ached that such fresh voices had never been heard in her hut. Then a figure appeared near the water. His face was so bright she could not look upon it. 'Tselane,' he said, 'choose a child from amongst these – all girls – whom you love, and I shall send her to you next Christmas.'

She did not have the strength to choose, but her eyes came to rest on one of the little girls. Immediately, the vision ended.

The following day, Tselane announced to her neighbours that, when Christmas came, the Lord would give her a little girl whose face she had already seen. And so it was.

But well before then, she had given her heart to God.

—⚬—

People without rain. Men without mothers. Men without cattle. Women without children. For whatever reason, they came searching. For whatever reason, their need was great. Their conviction could not be doubted.

—⚬—

In all the great swirl of time, the great roiling river of the past, certain events seem to stand out – with hindsight – as still centres of the turbulent world. One such incident pushes its way forward in a very moving memoir compiled by Nellie Germond in 1910. She and her husband Louis had numerous children, most of them boys. Her sixth child, Jacques Louis François, was born in October 1899 at Thabana-Morena, two days before war was declared. He was soon nicknamed Loulou.

When Loulou was three, the family went by wagon to visit Thaba-Bosiu. On the way, they stopped at Morija where Paul Ramseyer, who happened to be there, took a photograph of Loulou in his pretty red and white dress, holding the small toy animals that had once belonged to Dieterlen. A moment frozen in time.

At Thaba-Bosiu, Loulou was very good, but at times he quarrelled with young Claude Jacottet, six months his junior. One day, everyone went for a picnic to a beautiful spot on the Phuthiatsana river. Loulou was delirious with delight, dancing, jumping, laughing. 'You are going to fall!' his mother called out to him. 'Be careful of the meliqoaliqoane!' But the child was so enchanted with the newness of the world that he paid no attention and skipped round and round with the Jacottets' little dog, which also leapt about in circles. Then the giddiness did get him and he took a dive and disappeared in the river. His elder sister fished him out, pale, puking and heartbroken.

Three years later, Loulou became ill. His concentration seemed to waver, then his appetite fell away, his legs would fail him and he would flop to the ground. Violent headaches racked him, and finally his beautiful eyes began to dim. The only thing that did not fail him was his sweet and generous nature and his trust in a loving presence.

Doctors confirmed the parents' fears that the illness was 'related to the meningitis type', and eventually Dr Hertig diagnosed a brain tumour. Finally, at the age of six, he died, in the presence of his parents, 'with the movement of a little dying bird'. His big eyes became beautiful, luminous, as though a veil that was covering them had been taken away. His mother was sorry when someone gently closed them.

What was the significance of that moment by the stream at Thaba-Bosiu, that comes to us like a snapshot of the mind? Loulou's mother, in retrospect, wondered if, without her ever suspecting anything, he had not hit his head on a rock when he fell that day into the river and whether that had not been the origin of his strange illness.

And there is the quarrelsome Claude, perhaps already manifesting the wayward tendencies that he was to take into the future.

Two little boys – and a gambolling dog – and two very different destinies.

There is a photograph of Claude and Marguerite taken shortly after Loulou's death. It compels attention. The young faces look so innocent, untainted, fragile, that any viewer, knowing what was to come, would want to take the picture and agitate it ever so slightly, perhaps to jog the elbow of Fate or will the past to take a different path.

—◦◦◦—

Bad news came from France at the beginning of 1905. Isabelle Hoffet was seriously ill. For the sake of her health, the Hoffets might have to leave Paris for up to a year. What was to become of the Jacottet children – Marcelle, Henri and Gustave – in their care?

Jacottet asked for permission from the Committee in Paris to take leave for four or five months at his own expense. Although it was a great sacrifice on her part to forgo the chance of seeing her children, he was strongly urged by his wife to make the trip on his own. She recognized, amongst the other reasons, that he was in desperate need of rest. In return, it would cost him dearly to leave her and the younger children alone at Thaba-Bosiu. Having obtained the Committee's blessing and put back the final term of the Theological School from August–December to November–April, he left Cape Town on the *Walmer Castle* on 31 May. The voyage placed him, happy and melancholic, between the two halves of his family. He did, however, look forward to seeing the older ones: 'The separation from our own children has caused us great sadness, but God has been kind and allowed them not to suffer.'

After a good crossing and having concluded some successful business in

London, he arrived in Paris towards the end of June. He soon found himself in deep water. Not only did he have to decide on the immediate future of his own children, but he also became embroiled in the fate of the children of his late brother, Henri. These nieces were under the guardianship of Hoffet, but were being looked after by an aunt, whose influence, it had soon become apparent, was 'detestable'. He and Hoffet had to remove them, since it was absolutely impossible for them to remain with her. It was sad that all these calamities descended simultaneously. Sometimes, Jacottet thought sadly, it seems that destiny conspires to overwhelm one man on his own. He was probably talking about Hoffet: he might well have been thinking of himself.

Something else deepened his inner turmoil. In 1904, the year of his death, Henri's book *Pensées d'automne* had been published. In it, with some measured gravity, Édouard's elder brother had given voice to the sufferings of Swiss Huguenots in exile, ill at ease in the role of mouthpiece of the 'two Frances'. Through the figures of Tristan and Iseult, he examined the remorse that follows the amorous excitement and the solitary end, despaired of by heroes, who fall into the dark abyss, 'the despair of the heart, the blasphemy of the mouth'. He struggled against the riddle, the enigma of fate; he circled tirelessly around the mystery of death, questioning a heaven black and mute. The last word – was it dissolution or was it life? While he glimpsed some light, he acknowledged himself to be 'Christian without faith, a stoic bitter and unhappy'. What kept him going was a belief in duty and solidarity, which bound him to his revered ancestors (his beloved dead). In the end, he consoled himself with Dante: 'L'âme en paix et les yeux fixes sur les étoiles.' In the mirror of his brother's agonized words, Édouard inevitably recognized some of his own fever and fret.

His solution for his own children was for Henri and Gustave to go to school in Lausanne (they were to lodge with the widow of a professor of theology), while Marcelle was to attend university in Glasgow. There is something very moving about his jealously guarding a period of two weeks in August when he could be on his own with his three children in the Val-de-Ruz. Because of the 'inexorable march of things', he said, this was 'the only moment I shall truly be with them'. After seven long years of separation, these two weeks of bonding were made even more precious by their brevity.

This poignancy was reinforced by something else that Jacottet experienced. After twenty years in Lesotho, he was beginning to identify with it almost completely, to think of it as home. Now, his mother and other relatives and friends were gone; Vaud and even Neuchâtel were switching support away from the PEMS to the newer Swiss Mission; he began 'to find himself a stranger in [his] own country'; it was a land he no longer belonged to. This was a disturbing feeling.

His movements were slowed down by pains near his heart. These were not entirely new, but they felt more severe. It was something that seemed to run in his family.

He spent some of his time raising money for a mooted move of the Theological School to Morija, and, at the end of August, he accompanied Marcelle to Scotland. She registered at the University of Glasgow to do a master's in English Literature. He was pleased to leave her 'in excellent conditions' at the university residence of Queen Margaret Hall in Bute Gardens, Hillhead. As he headed away, he felt there was at least one less thing to worry about.

One worry overcome, two more pounce. In Lesotho, Lerotholi died, meaning that Louise would have to cope with the influx of mourners to the inevitably huge funeral at Thaba-Bosiu. And Alfred Casalis, a stalwart of the mission and one of his colleagues Jacottet respected most, resigned, partly under the weight of work that the combined portfolio of the Bible School, Book Depot, Printing Works and *Leselinyana* imposed, but mainly for family reasons: he and his wife Caroline had five children and did not wish to be separated from them during their formative years. Their youngest, Freddy, who was now nine, needed higher schooling, determined as he was to become a missionary himself. It was 'a great blow' to Jacottet just before his return to Lesotho, though he sympathized with Casalis, having complex family problems of his own.

All too soon the time came for him to leave Europe. He was not entirely happy. He had not pursued as much of the mission's business as he would have liked. His love for his children was strong: but there was never any doubt that there was one thing stronger. 'It will be hard to leave my children again,' he wrote to Boegner from Neuchâtel, 'but it is duty. And God will help.'

CHAPTER TWENTY-ONE

THE BOOK OF GOLD

1905–1908

On his return home to Thaba-Bosiu at the end of 1905, Jacottet 'marvelled' at what his wife had done in his absence. Louise Jacottet had been 'an enormous help in maintaining the work' of the station.

Almost immediately, he was off to an extraordinary meeting of the Conference at Morija (where he admired for the first time the fine new spire that had at last been built on to Maeder's church). At this Conference it was necessary to choose someone to take over the Bible School, the Book Depot, the Printing Works and *Leselinyana* at Morija. Alfred and Caroline Casalis, who had been finding it difficult to place their children with family in Europe, had decided to return to France. The resignation of this amiable and competent man saddened both him and his colleagues, but his mind was made up. 'Placed between his duty to the mission and his duty to his children,' the Conference minutes recorded, 'he did not hesitate, he must concern himself with his children's education.'

There were four candidates for the vacant post, but Bertschy and Marzolff soon withdrew. Duby told the Conference that he did not present himself as a candidate and did not want his possible departure to affect the work in East Griqualand, but he put himself at the meeting's disposal. Christeller, in turn, stated his preference for remaining at Maphutseng (Bethesda); the work at the Bible School and the Printing Works held some attraction for him, but he was put off by the demands of the Book Depot. In the end, Jacottet scotched Christeller's candidacy by pointing out that his sabbatical was coming up, which would render him ineligible. Duby was chosen unanimously. Jacottet strongly supported the move, as he thought Paballong was not important enough for Duby's talents.

—◦—

Ninety years afterwards, Duby's daughter Gynette recalled – as one of her very first memories – riding away from Paballong on horseback, held in someone's comforting embrace. That was her father. They rode high up into the mountains, the long, difficult journey to Morija. There was snow, too. It was March.

The job Sam Duby was taking over was one of the most onerous of the mission.

Firstly, there was the Bible School. Mabille had had faith enough to start this school in 1882, as the Gun War ravaged the country. It began with twenty-nine students. Its practical aim was to produce evangelists to man the outstations that had been developed since 1872. Its spiritual aim was to acquaint the students as deeply as possible with the Bible and to imbue them with its spirit. Less attention was given to teaching them mathematics or the names of the Himalayan mountains, the provinces of China or the islands of the Pacific Ocean, so long as the sacred flames of the love of God were kindled, and burned truly, in their hearts.

The School was not confined to the Basotho. From hundreds of kilometres away, over inhospitable, sometimes threatening terrain, came Xhosa from the Colony, Barolong from Thaba 'Nchu and the northern Cape, Bapedi and Magwamba from the northern Transvaal, Bamangwato from the land of Khama and the fringes of Lake Ngami, Ndebele from Matabeleland, and, furthest of all, Barotse from the Zambezi.

Sesotho became the language of instruction, and, over three years, the trainee catechists were given a general introduction to the Bible and the history of Israel, a brief survey of the Old Testament, and a study of the whole of the New Testament, the life of Jesus, the principal periods of ecclesiastical history and the fundamental doctrines of the Christian religion. The course was, wrote Alfred Casalis, 'to show them the origin of sin and its spread in the breast of humanity, to make them aware of the promise of salvation, to reveal, through the vicissitudes of the story of Israel, the messianic plan, the threats, the promises and the final appeals of the prophets, then the realization of salvation in the person and work of Jesus Christ, the continuation of that work in the foundation of the church and its later development'.

Courses were divided in two: religious studies were the domain of the Director; primary learning, after 1894, was in the hands of Henriette Cochet, helped by Nathan Sekhesa, Mikhael Mofokeng, and others. In the quarter century since its founding, some five hundred students had graduated from the Bible School.

There were stories of remarkable achievement and heroism associated with the School. Ntesang Ra-Gaugane and his friend, Seakhane Ra-Olerile, gathered enough money from the sale of animal skins to venture on the long journey from Bechuanaland to Morija with their families. While their wives became ardent students of Caroline Casalis and their children entered the primary school, they threw themselves into the three years of study. Then Ntesang went to preach in a remote part of Matabeleland where some Ndebele, seeing him as a threat to their traditional religion, killed him in front of his wife and children. A martyr of the Bible School.

Then there was the time a young Mosotho teacher entered the office of the Director leading an old man. It was his father, who wanted to become a student. The teacher then took the old man to his class, sat him down on a bench, and, in an act symbolic of the turmoil of the generations, the child began to teach the parent. The father had paid the fees for his son's studies; now, in his turn, the son paid for the father. The older man stuck to his task, becoming one of the School's best students and an evangelist of great worth.

The Bible School was never funded by Paris, nor the government, nor the Lesotho Conference. A committee of women based in Geneva sent an annual sum they had raised, and a large donation from a benefactor in Geneva allowed a great study hall to be built in 1898. But the cost of food, fuel, furniture, repairs and salaries always seemed to outstrip income, and Casalis and his successor, Duby, were constantly weighed down with financial worry – the burden of the modern missionary.

There was also a shortage of suitable material in Sesotho to stimulate the students' interest. A series of commentaries was therefore commissioned and printed: the first, on *Luke*, was published by Duvoisin in 1894, and was followed by texts on Paul's *Epistles* (by Marzolff in 1907), *John* and *Jude* (in a single volume by Duby in 1911), *Acts* (also by Duby in 1911), *Romans* (by Dieterlen in 1912) and *Corinthians* (by Jacottet in 1912). Later, Duby added others on *Revelation*, *James* and *Timothy*.

But a further concern was the fate of the catechists once they had left the refuge of the Bible School to take up their duties in some remote backwater. How was their interest, their enthusiasm to be sustained in a sea of antagonism? It was a problem. Some became backsliders, even apostates. It was Duby who came up with the fine idea of vacation Bible courses, refresher courses, which turned out to be a great success.

In the time of Duby, the Basotho still called the Bible School 'Sekolo sa Mabili' – the School of Mabille.

Then, too, Duby was in charge of the Printing Works and the Book Depot. The press had occupied a brick building, which Maeder had erected below the church, from 1874 onwards. By the end of the nineteenth century, however, it was clear that the printing business was at crisis point: the press was so old and inadequate that many of the mission's books had to be printed in France and England; the printing office was too small; a trained printer was a must.

On sick leave in France between 1901 and 1903, Casalis had been charged by the Conference with raising funds for a more spacious building and a new press. Substantial donations made possible the purchase of the steel structure of a complete building, as well as new printing machines powered for the first time not by hand but by a Japy paraffin motor – the first internal combustion engine ever to be installed in Lesotho. Casalis also recruited an experienced printer, Charles Labarthe.

The airier, cooler, lighter building improved the conditions of the printing workers, and the speedier plant meant that a large number of new books and new editions of old ones were published from 1904 onwards. Below the new spire of the old church, the equally new press hummed.

In consequence, the Book Depot took on an even greater importance. Annually, it sent out over six thousand post parcels and over one hundred cases of books; more were sold over the counter. In 1911, some sixty thousand Sesotho books (not counting Bibles and New Testaments) were sold from the Depot. What was even more impressive was that the Printing Works and the Book Depot were self-supporting, and had, since 1870, Jacottet could proudly proclaim, 'not cost a single penny to the Paris Society or the Basuto Mission'.

Finally, there was the newspaper. Mabille had started *Leselinyana* in 1863 as a monthly in Sesotho. Except for breaks in 1865–9 and 1880–82 because of the wars, it has been published continuously into the twenty-first century, and has a rightful claim to being the oldest African vernacular newspaper in southern Africa. In the 1880s and 1890s it began to appear twice monthly, and in 1909 Duby converted it into a weekly with a circulation of around two thousand.

March of 1906 was a busy month for Jacottet as well as for Duby. It began with a visit from Lord Selborne, the British High Commissioner in South Africa. In meetings with the missionaries, Selborne established a close rapport with them; at a pitso in Maseru, he heard the chiefs praise the missionaries in glowing terms: 'They are assuredly Basotho even if their skins are white.'

At the end of the month, Jacottet participated in a meeting that would mark one of his most important and lasting achievements.

Ever since his exposure to scientific and historical language studies, especially in relation to the Bible, he had taken a keen interest in linguistics. In 1893, when he had made his greatest journey to the east, to the furthest border of Lesotho and the edge of the Drakensberg, he had consciously put aside his early desire to be a pioneer, an explorer-missionary like Livingstone or Coillard, harrowing new lands in order to cultivate fresh souls. Such men, driven by ambition and pride, wanted the glory of virgin conquest. Thwarted in this, Jacottet turned to the study of language as a more abstract and intellectual substitute. Just as he could focus on the organization and expansion of the church, so he could examine and organize the rules of a language and extend its frontiers into limitless generation.

To the chagrin of Coillard, who regarded Barotseland as his domain, Jacottet produced the first study of the languages of the Upper Zambezi. And without ever having visited it! His information came from extensive interviewing of two visitors to Morija from the Zambezi.

Now, in 1906, he spent much of his time gathering his vast knowledge and writing a grammar of Sesotho. This would be published as *A Practical Method to Learn Sesotho* and for many years remained the preferred text for English-speakers learning the language.

There had long been discussion and controversy over Sesotho orthography, and many attempts had been made to standardize it. Eventually, in frustration, the Resident Commissioner of Basutoland, Herbert Sloley, called on the four bodies most interested in the question to meet in Maseru: the Roman Catholics were represented by Father Cénez; the Anglicans by Canon Spencer Weigall; the independent newspaper *Naledi ea Lesotho* by Cranmer Sebeta; and the PEMS by Jacottet and Nicolas Mpiti.

They met behind closed doors on 26 March.

The Conference on Sesuto Orthography soon recognized unanimously that 'however desirable it may otherwise be, it is not practically possible to arrive at a uniform spelling of Sesuto as spoken in Basutoland on one side, and Setswana in Bechuanaland, and Sepedi in the Northern Transvaal on the other side'. The differences between these dialects, they judged, were too great, and it was hopeless to expect an understanding between numerous bodies holding quite conflicting views. The Conference was of the opinion that 'to arrive at a uniform system of spelling Sesuto proper is the most that can be hoped for now, and that such an agreement will go a long way towards minimizing the inconvenience arising from want of harmony in the matter'.

There were many points of contention on which definite decisions had to be made. One example will suffice. There were three possible ways to write the name of the people of Moshoeshoe's clan: they could either be the 'Bakuena', the 'Bakwena' or the 'Bakoena' (the pronunciation was the same). 'Bakwena' was clearly influenced by English orthography (indeed, Moshoeshoe could have written his own name 'Moshweshwe'). Where then did the spelling 'Bakoena' come from? From the French missionaries, in fact. They were used to rendering the 'w' sound as an 'o', in spellings like 'Loire', 'noir' and 'ouest'. Thanks to these divergent rules, children of the time learned to spell their national language differently depending on whether they went to Anglican, Catholic or PEMS schools!

Two of the representatives at the Conference were French-speakers; the two

Basotho had been educated by the PEMS; only Spencer Weigall, a close friend of Jacottet's, was English. What is more, Jacottet, with his immense knowledge of Sesotho and other African languages, and with the pressure of his personality, almost certainly dominated the exchanges. When the meeting was over, the 'French' spelling had been accepted.

It is also from the French that we get the hyphen in Lesotho place names – hence 'Thaba-Bosiu' as contrasted with the South African 'Thaba 'Nchu' – and indeed in names of French origin like 'Mont-aux-Sources'.

One oddity is that two spellings were retained for the national language – an English one ('Sesuto') and a Sotho one ('Sesotho'). Here the Conference members were influenced by English usage, which then favoured 'Mosuto' and 'Basuto', as reflected in the official name of the country. When Independence came, such spellings fell from grace, although 'Sesuto' still curiously survives a century later in the name of the Morija Sesuto Book Depot.

Despite opposition, the recommendations of the 1906 Conference on Sesuto Orthography are still largely in effect to this day in Lesotho (as opposed to a different practice in South Africa). Wherever a signpost stands, a book is printed or a letter written, the fingerprints of Jacottet and his colleagues can be seen. His hand is on the language.

Jacottet was also busy with the third intake of pastoral students in the Theological School. While he was in Europe the year before, their studies had been deferred, and now he had to catch up the lost time. There were five of them: Samuel Moeletsi, Joel Mohapeloa, Moshe Moletsane, Joel Ntšasa and Azaele Buti.

Jacottet's students had great respect for him. One of them at least – Joel Mohapeloa – loved him dearly, and told his children frequently that Jacottet was an extremely intelligent man and 'a great moruti'. He and the others saw, in Jacottet's fierce espousal of the cause of Basotho ministers, that he was much more forward-looking than his colleagues (even some of those who came after him), who were less active in advancing the Basotho people and the status of the church. While they recognized his difficulties in getting church members to understand what their membership demanded, they admired the fearless way he spoke his mind, even though it made him unpopular in some quarters.

Joel's son Makibinyane (Prof. J.M. Mohapeloa) – who was born at Molumong, where Joel had been posted – remembers his father saying that Jacottet might well have been of the same calibre as Mabille. There could be no higher praise than that.

Jacottet was not without a humorous side. Joel Mohapeloa often told one story with great fondness.

One day, the students were at table with their tutor. Jacottet turned to Samuel Moeletsi, a man much older than Joel and more set in his tastes, and invited him to say grace.

'O! Re se re lebohile,' Samuel said. 'We've already said grace.'

'Ke ne ke nahana hore ha u bona nama ...' Jacottet replied. 'I was thinking that when you saw meat ...' The unstated implication was that when Samuel saw the fare, he would want to say grace again. Jacottet knew how fond the old man was of meat, and was gently pulling his leg about it. Sometimes there was just the ghost of a smile on his lips.

When the training of this cohort was completed by June 1906, Jacottet turned to another preoccupation, the moving of the Theological School to Morija (the water supply at Thaba-Bosiu had always been inadequate). In that same month, Paris gave the project a definite go-ahead. By this time, the school had proved so successful that the Mission Suisse Romande had asked for its own students to be trained there. Consequently, the next intake of seven students – three of them from the northern Transvaal – was to be the biggest so far.

Negotiations with the local chief of Morija for an appropriate site and the usual struggle for finance caused some anxiety and delay, and the constant shuffling between Thaba-Bosiu and Morija for months tired Jacottet out. So busy was he that the 'perpetual hurricane' in which he lived swept him into 1907 almost before he knew it.

The new year started with a relatively unobtrusive event. In January, Sam Duby published in *Leselinyana* the first instalment of a book by the man who worked for him in the Book Depot as a clerk and proofreader. The instalments ran until September, when the completed work was published by Morija as a book. The publication was momentous. *Moeti oa Bochabela* was the first novel ever to be written by a black African anywhere in Africa. A new branch of African literature was born.

The man who had 'made the paper speak' was Thomas Mofolo.

Moeti oa Bochabela (The Traveller of the East) was described by Alfred Casalis as 'a kind of poem in prose' by a man with 'a remarkably observant nature, interested in the natural world, the seasons, the habits of animals'. It has, too, the immediacy of the conversion stories that Duby and others witnessed, and visions are woven into its very fabric. Duby himself called it 'a Mosuto's dream'.

Like his contemporary, Solomon Plaatje, Mofolo sought to extend the timelessness of the traditional African fable into the new form of the novel, in this case an allegorical one. There is no doubt where the novel began: it began when Adolphe Mabille, with the considerable help of his student and assistant, Filemone Rapetloane, translated *The Pilgrim's Progress* into Sesotho. Bunyan's book was the inspiration for Mofolo and gave him the outline for his story.

But that is not all: there is something deeper, something that burns beneath the surface. The novel is driven by the uncompromising strength of Calvinist Protestantism, by the certain knowledge of the real existence of evil and sin in the world, and the single path of the just to Redemption. Consequently, it is a novel of extraordinary power.

It is the story of Fekisi, a man who wanted to walk in dry places.

It was a time when people ate each other, a time when lying, stealing, adultery were commonplace and not acknowledged as sin. A time of darkness. The whole nation seemed to be travelling the same path of destruction. Like Christian, only one man stood up against the lack of truth around him, as he tended the cattle he loved so much. His neighbour Phakoane drank and beat his wife, but Fekisi always spoke the truth. His heart was pure. His cattle loved him, they knew his voice, they knew he loved them, he herded with love.

In August, the coldest month of the year, the month of dust and wind, the month of suffering, which tested the best herdboys to the limit, Fekisi began to ask questions, especially when Phakoane's son was killed by lightning.

What are the clouds? Where do they come from? What is this lightning which splits rocks and mountains? The wizards do not make rain, nor does it come from the ancestors – who makes the rain? Why does it fall impartially for the bad and the good? There is some secret, he thought, which I must seek till I find it.

Fekisi had been told that the ancestors were those who had died and were with God. God was just and pure, and rejected all evil things. God wanted people who were just. Why then did people who had knowledge of evil commit sin?

Then, in November, when the rains had come and life had quickened, Fekisi looked at the sun hurrying on his road, like a traveller going where he longs to go. Who guided it on its journey? What is this heat which makes things grow? Because the sun is life itself, it is like the bread we eat and the water we drink. His heart was saddened by the paradoxical beauty of this land of his.

He asked himself, where did the God his elders spoke of live? Did he live at Ntsoanatsatsi? The place where many Basotho said they came from? Ntsoanatsatsi – the Rising of the Sun.

So he went to the tellers of tales. To the men he could trust. One old man, too feeble to walk, told him the story of Kholumolumo, the marvellous monster who ate all the people, who ate all the animals. When it had eaten everything it sat down, its belly weighted to the ground, only its tongue moving. Its belly was so big it covered all of Basutoland, and even beyond. Only one woman escaped, and she hid in a cave. She was pregnant and she gave birth to a male child. When the boy grew older, he killed the monster and plunged his knife into its vast belly. A voice cried out. He plunged it in again: a dog howled. He plunged it in again: an ox bellowed. From the great rent he had made, out tumbled people, dogs, cattle, every living thing. And they thanked the boy and made him their chief. Then, out of their weakness and out of their jealousy, they killed him.

Fekisi was also told the story of Sankatana, the boy whose ox was taken by his enemies and killed. But the boy tapped its skin and the ox rose up alive, whereas those who had eaten its flesh died. When Sankatana went home, his mother offered him bread to eat, but the ox warned him that it was poisoned: instead, his father ate it and died.

The Basotho believed in a God, but the tellers of tales told Fekisi that He dwelt far away because of people's disobedience. It seemed that He lived on the other side of Ntsoanatsatsi. All they knew was that Ntsoanatsatsi was towards the east, in a great reed bed in the middle of much water, and that a huge fountain rose where the sun emerged. Man also came from the reed bed.

One night, as the women began to scrape out the pots for the final meal of the day, Fekisi went up a little hill above the village and gazed at the evening star, Sefala-bohoho. Later, as the dawn approached and the cock began to crow, there appeared one brilliant white star, which outshone all others.

Fekisi was sick with love and a thirst for God. He thought of how badly people treated each other, and how, in the fable of the boy and Kholumolumo, the people had killed their saviour. No wonder God stood aloof from people on account of their growing wickedness.

So Fekisi began to think he must leave people of such great evil, people who had fallen into ditches.

Then came the feast the chief arranged for his son after his time of circumcision, the feast of the heir, Vanity Feast. How could it be that animals, which had no intelligence, kept the commandment of God, that water, with neither life nor spirit, ran in one direction only, but man alone turned from the law of his Creator?

The feast brought drunkenness and fights over girls. There were murders political: Sebati was found strangled, and a faint rumour connected the crime to the chief himself; there was murder domestic: Phakoane came home and killed his wife with a battleaxe. Fekisi's grief turned to anger. A great fire was consuming him inside. There was no country more beautiful than Basutoland, but he began to think he must leave these people who ate each other, this place where truth was unknown, where to steal was to help oneself, where sin was life, even amongst the chiefs, and where drunkenness was food.

Suddenly the sun nearly disappeared. It became red, it became like blood, as if great drops of blood trickled down, like water. Finally, there was darkness. Then came a tremendous noise like a great rock rolling down a mountain. Fekisi remembered what the old tellers of tales had told him: if a person calls to God, he will be heard. So Fekisi, learning to pray, called to God. And a small voice replied, louder than the thunder.

That night he dreamed a dream. Far away, he saw Ntsoanatsatsi in the light of dusk, and the great reed bed, surrounded by the marsh of many waters. As he gazed, the form of a man passed before him, wrapped in a transparent mist. As he gazed, the beauty of the man's face blinded his eyes, and tears fell from them. Fekisi knew he must go where every living thing wanted to go.

Then in spring, in the month of December, the world quickened with anticipation. When he went to view his cattle on a special day at full moon, they all stood up at the same time and looked, with great longing, to the east. He sensed they could hear something unknown. Then he praised his cattle, he praised white-faced Tšemeli, the finest of the herd, he praised her for her singing, the god with the wet nose.

Then he took his olive-wood stick, trusting it for his protection, and he went away secretly, leaving behind his blanket for his cows as a comfort and promise, so they would stand still at its smell and allow themselves to be milked, and he fled across the marsh to the east, looking only ahead, looking for righteousness, looking for God.

His mother mourned him; his father mourned him; the young girls mourned him, for he was tall and straight; the mothers of the young girls mourned him.

But he said to himself: 'Of all these things there is not one which matters. There is nothing that I can do. If I had not left them, I could not have lived as I wished. The voice said, I should look for God, and if I had not left them it would be that I refused the order of the great one to be with my elders. If they are righteous people then, indeed, they are not lost; if they are not righteous as they should be, it is their fault – theirs only – it is not mine. They will die alone, each on his day, one by one, each alone.'

He passed through his own country and then through the country of the Batlokoa. Only once, when the sun touched the tops of the mountains, did he look back to his native land. He felt it was the last time he would ever see the mountains of home.

He passed through deserts, he passed over mountains. Then he came to the edge of the mountains where the country fell away, stretched out into the distance, far, far away, where the sun rose. He could not see Ntsoanatsatsi, but he knew it was near where the sun was rising. It was no longer where he came from, but where he was going to.

So he prayed, a real prayer, in faith and expectation. He prayed as though he was speaking to an earthly chief. He imagined God to be a person of flesh and blood like all chiefs: 'Lord, I have left my home to look for Thee.'

He passed over plains with dangerous animals and plains without animals. Driven on by thirst, he followed a lone hartebeest with its ears drooping and eyes hanging out, till it led him to a spring in a marsh, and he drank. 'What is this for which that antelope leaves the herd, and travels for days, crying, crying for it?' he asked. 'What great strength does this water have? I myself have drunk, and now my eyes are clear. I am a man.'

But the desert went on and the lion came. 'Whatever happens can just happen,' he said to himself. 'When a person is in trouble truly God fights for him and cools the anger of wild beasts, even of the lion itself.' But the desert went on, beautiful, cruel.

Until finally he came to a long, grey-black line. It was water. Water as far as the eye could see.

He slept, he dreamed of a voice encouraging him to go on, he walked in the burning sun, he starved, he had a fit, he fainted.

When he revived, he found three men standing beside him. They were white with grey eyes and hair like the manes of horses. They spoke a language he did not understand.

They asked him where he had come from, and he said, 'From Lesotho, towards the setting of the sun.'

They asked him where he was going to, and he said, 'To Ntsoanatsatsi, where God lives.'

Because he was ill they took him on their ship, and on a voyage to the east they taught him how to read and write and they gave him a book of laws. He read the story of the Son of God, of his suffering and patience and mercy, of his life and death and his rising from the dead – that Man with gentle eyes.

In his turn, Fekisi told them of Sankatana and Kholumolumo. And they told him there was no Ntsoanatsatsi here on earth.

The faith of the man astonished them. After all, these sons of Christians were used to the Word of God, often they prayed not from the heart but from habit. But Fekisi was a poor man, emerging out of darkness, a true sinner, so his prayer was from the heart, not from fear of authority.

Fekisi knew only Basotho, Batlokoa, Zulu and Baroa: the voyage took him through lands where people were brown and yellow and white. All of them, the known and the previously unknown, the creatures of God.

When the ship arrived at its own country, the city of righteousness, the faithful city, Fekisi was taken to a large and beautiful building where there was no chief, but where God was chief. He went often to this house of prayer and he found peace there. A feast was announced and Fekisi prayed for an end to his journey, but for days he found no answer, no voice, no dream. Nothing.

Then, on the day of the feast – the most important of all days for the nation of the east – he watched as people passed before the altar of ransom in the house of God, and the whole congregation fell on their knees and covered their faces. The voice of the pastor said, 'You have not come to a mountain which may be touched with hands ... you have come to Mount Zion, the home of the living God.'

Fekisi rose from his seat and took two steps forward. His eyes were bright; his whole face changed; it shone with glory; it was the face of a child newly born.

At that moment a form which he had glimpsed twice before came down from above, transparent and white like a mist. But now, in an instant, he saw not the form but the Son of Man, in His own person, in the house of God.

'Ahé! My Jesus! How I have longed for Thee!' exclaimed Fekisi. 'Let me go home with Thee, to the home of God.'

And from the mist the gracious voice replied, 'Today, thou shalt be with Me in My Kingdom.'

As the congregation, in fear, uncovered their heads, the pastor approached the altar trembling. They found Fekisi looking up to heaven. The mist had disappeared; his face was full of joy.

His spirit had gone home; only his body remained in the house of prayer.

There were echoes here that moved Jacottet, a depth of feeling and power of imagination far beyond anything that he might have expected.

Though there is strong evidence that Thomas Mofolo, born in 1876, was of Christian parentage, both Alfred Casalis and Hermann Dieterlen were categorical that his parents were pagans. Casalis, in his unpublished auto-biography, said that Mofolo had some trouble persuading his parents to let him attend school and that his father refused to pay a penny for his education.

The first school attended by Mofolo, who had been baptized by Dieterlen in 1877, was at Qomoqomong in the Quthing district in the south. The first major influence on him was Everitt Segoete, the teacher-evangelist there. Segoete trained initially at the Bible School. A couple of years later, he would join the second batch of students at the Theological School, and be taught first by Dieterlen and then by Jacottet. Segoete's influence on Mofolo was considerable: he opened his eyes to a wider world, he instilled in him religious doctrine and he almost certainly introduced him to the idea of literary form in writing. In 1891, for instance, Segoete published an allegorical piece he quite likely showed to young Thomas. He also wrote many pieces for *Leselinyana* and eventually published a semi-autobiographical novel in 1910 (he was the model for the teacher Mr Katse in Mofolo's own semi-autobiographical novel, *Pitseng*).

After Qomoqomong, Mofolo went to school at Masitise, studying under Ellenberger. Then, in 1894, he enrolled at the Bible School at Morija, where he boarded with Alfred and Caroline Casalis. In 1896, he went on to the Normal School – the Teachers' Training College – at Morija. After that, he joined Casalis in the Book Depot, where he worked (with at least one interruption for the Anglo-Boer War) as a secretary, proofreader and general 'factotum'. When Sam Duby arrived, he was happy to inherit Mofolo.

'Then, one fine day,' wrote Dieterlen a couple of years later, 'he set himself to compose an imaginative work, completely original, and which first appeared serialized in *Leselinyana*.' Of course, the conception was not quite so miraculous. For one thing, the day might not have been so fine. The serial publication of the novel began in January 1907: the action of its first part takes place between the cold winds of August and the sunny rains of December. This is obviously symbolic. But in August 1906 even Paris knew that there had been a drought of several months, which had been particularly severe on winter crops – a fact that might have deepened Mofolo's sense of symbolism.

Nor did Mofolo's work come out of nowhere. He had been able to draw on *Leselinyana*, a deep pool of writing created by the slow spread of literacy over the years. Others besides Segoete wrote for it. Azariele Sekese, for instance, recorded proverbs, tales and customs in the newspaper, and published a collection of them in 1893. He advised his readers 'not to cling to the old house and remain there alone' lest they be caught by Limo, but neither should they allow 'the memory of the old house' to be erased entirely. These sentiments were shared by Jacottet, who believed strongly that 'care must be taken not to allow the Basuto to lose touch with their past and to become denationalized ... their national history must be saved as far as possible.'

In 1895, Jacottet had published his *Contes Populaires des Bassoutos*, which contained folk tales and proverbs collected by himself, Dieterlen and others, and translated into French. Then, in 1896-7, in the *Bulletin de la Société Neuchâteloise de Géographie*, he published 'Moeurs, coutumes et superstitions des Ba-Souto', which was an annotated translation of Sekese's earlier work.

At the same time as *Moeti oa Bochabela* was appearing, Jacottet, no doubt in response to and as part of a widening nationalist cause, sketched out an extremely ambitious project for the publication of eight to ten volumes of collected history, folk tales, proverbs, songs, customs and grammar, to be prepared by himself and others. He had already begun working on the first volume. Although this was the only one of the projected series ever to see the light of day, it was extremely important, indeed almost seminal. (It had a significant influence on the thought and writing of Blaise Cendrars, for instance.)

Jacottet followed in the footsteps of Bleek and Lloyd, Bishop Steere and Dr

Theal, Sekese and Junod, all of whom he was very much aware of. He noted that 2 500 years before, Herodotus had drawn gems 'from the treasures of Egyptian folklore', and he was not averse to criticizing, however humbly, his predecessors such as Bleek, for his belief that animal stories were unknown to the Bantu; Callaway, for his assertion that the Zulu were 'a degenerate people' declined from a higher state (whereas Jacottet believed they had 'advanced from a lower grade of civilization to the state in which Europeans found them'); and even Casalis, who, despite a wonderfully full and accurate description of Basotho life, tried, 'probably unconsciously', to 'render the Ba-Suto and their customs more acceptable to European taste'.

In reproducing tales collected by Dieterlen, Sekese and himself, Jacottet's methodology was precise and uncompromising: to give 'an absolutely accurate image of the true language of the people' by reproducing 'the ipsissima verba of the Natives themselves, the very Se-Suto as it is spoken in everyday life, without any admixture of European ideas or speech'. Even the parallel English translation of the Sesotho text, he made as literal as possible.

Because Lesotho had been fairly isolated, he felt that the tales told by the old men and women were not only 'still wonderfully free from all foreign admixture', but that some were also 'very, very old'. Indeed, he thought that some existed in a form that must be not dissimilar to those 'at least two thousand years ago' – a symbolic and magical number for a Christian.

Jacottet used several informants. One of the best was old Moshe Mosetse, born before 1810, whose death he had mourned while he was on furlough in Neuchâtel in 1897. Moshe's death was for Jacottet not just the end of a generation, even the end of an era: it was also the end of a continuous, relatively pure tradition of two thousand years. Never again could storytelling recapture its original innocence; henceforth, sources would inevitably be corrupt. While his linguistic studies might shape and generate the future, his literary and historical studies tried to recapture and preserve the past. This lone volume, *The Treasury of Ba-Suto Lore*, which he published in 1908, is a fragment from before the Fall.

Jacottet was pleased. Whereas there had been a paucity of reading material not so long before, he rejoiced that 'during the last few years certain young Basuto have begun to create a literature of their own' and that 'the appearance of a genuine native literature will reveal the native mind to the European public as nothing else will be able to do'.

Joel Mohapeloa (as seen through the eyes of his son, Prof. J.M. Mohapeloa) had no doubt about Jacottet's influence on Mofolo, his students and others. He got them to participate in what he was doing. He encouraged them to write things that were useful to read. He showed them what was written elsewhere.

He encouraged them to think beyond the school desk. He would read and edit their work. He helped them to publish. Segoete, Mofolo, Z.D. Mangoaela – they were almost a school of writers in the first decade of the new century. Indeed, the pupil may even have followed the teacher's methodological lead, since Mofolo seems to have talked extensively to an old man called Fekisi Makana, who lived up in the mountains and who gave him many stories.

In his turn, Mofolo acknowledged his debt to Alfred Casalis, Duby and Jacottet. On the abstract level of pure allegory, the three white men at the end of *Moeti oa Bochabela* represent missionaries in general; on a less symbolic level, they are clearly Arbousset, Eugène Casalis and Gosselin; on the most immediate level, touched as Mofolo was by them personally, they are Alfred Casalis, Sam Duby and Édouard Jacottet.

—◦—

Throughout 1907, the Catholics were on the rise, the Protestant personnel on the wane. Christol and Kohler were due to retire the following year; Marzolff was chronically ill; Dieterlen and Dyke were ageing. The latter was shaken, too, by riots amongst the students at the Normal School towards the end of the year. Germond and Jacottet were chosen to go on a deputation to the Zambezi, but Jacottet, who would dearly have loved to go, was too busy, so Duby went instead.

The best thing for the Jacottets was the return in March or April 1907 of Marcelle, after nearly ten years' absence from Lesotho. 'That changes our whole life, as you can imagine,' Jacottet wrote to Boegner. It is not certain whether Marcelle completed her university course at Glasgow, and there is some evidence that she taught in Scotland for a while, but she found herself happy to be back and her return certainly made her parents happy.

In August, the Theological School reopened and the Jacottets finally made their move to Morija. The new house that Jacottet built was a bit narrow, but better than he had anticipated. It was up against the mountain between the Normal School and the Bible School. From its dominant position, it looked down on the mission and the valley beyond. Water came from a spring quite high up on the mountain. Behind the house a stable was erected, and the orchard and vegetable garden were also at the back, near the kitchen. The house was L-shaped and faced north. The sitting room dominated the short arm of the L and had a large fireplace. In front, too, were the dining room and two bedrooms, including that of Édouard and Louise. A long verandah ran in front of these rooms. A small room and the kitchen were behind the sitting room. Also at the back were a large pantry (separated from the kitchen by a passageway), a bathroom and another bedroom. On the corner at the back, furthest from the kitchen, was another large room completely isolated from the rest of the house, with access only from an outside door. This was to be the classroom of the Theological School. It was not the coldest of houses (except when the winter wind blew) as the surrounding rock retained the heat of the sun. The square huts of the students would be built off to one side, a couple of hundred metres down the hill.

For the moment, with almost no vegetation around it, the house stared out rather bleakly.

—⊙—

The parting from Thaba-Bosiu, after twenty-two years of service there, was bittersweet. It gave Jacottet pause to think on his achievements and failures.

When he had taken over from the much-revered Jousse, the country in general and the parish in particular were suffering from the disastrous effects of the Gun War. Masupha's village, only two kilometres away, was still in open rebellion, the civil war not yet over. For eight or nine years thereafter, skirmishes occurred frequently and were a constant threat – kept in line only by Resident Commissioner Clarke's tact. Only after 1898 was Masupha's district calm, and only through God's providence did the country avoid the calamity of the Anglo-Boer War, so that the latter part of Jacottet's ministry passed in peace and calm.

In 1886, there were six outstations; in 1907, seventeen. The parish stretched all the way to the Maloti. There were now nine hundred pupils in school. Two thousand adults had been baptized. God chose some; God alone did all.

Jacottet asked himself whether inner progress matched this external picture. He lamented the passing of the older generation. They had had a moral seriousness and an admirable Christian strength. Their conversions were not easy, their sacrifices, in the face of pagan hostility, were real (Mofolo's conversion, it should be noted, took place when many of the older converts were still alive).

Now, it seemed to him, there was less individual Christianity, but there was perhaps more true comprehension, fewer renegades. There was less likely to be an awakening like the remarkable réveil of 1887 or the slightly lesser one of 1898.

He was pleased about the progress of church autonomy. He had always encouraged the catechists and elders of the consistory to take on maximum responsibility. He quietly prided himself on the fact that the church at the Masianokeng outstation had been built entirely with local collections.

But all the Jacottets' children except Marcelle had been born at Thaba-Bosiu, they were leaving many good friends, and they would miss the busy swallows that had found a nest for themselves over the entrance to the mission house. Above all, they were leaving the two little graves at the bottom of the hill.

Despite their losses, despite mistakes and things left unfinished, they had seen their dream grow slowly in their hands. Jacottet was realistic, however. The fine illusions of youth were gone: 'At my age,' he said, 'one no longer has the hope of restarting so long a career. The road shortens before my eyes.' He looked forward to the new challenge; but part of their hearts – those of his wife and himself – remained in Thaba-Bosiu.

—◦◦—

If the last two years had been tough, the next two were to be much tougher. In May 1908, Mrs Jacottet went to Europe for a year's well-deserved leave. She took thirteen-year-old Madeleine with her. Jacottet accompanied them to Cape Town to see them off.

Mrs Jacottet settled in Lausanne, no doubt to be near Gustave and Madeleine. (Henri, who had been studying at the University of Lausanne, had just moved to London, where he had enrolled at Birkbeck College.) Jacottet missed his wife greatly, although Marcelle ran the house in her absence and looked after Claude and Marguerite well, and helped him teach in the Theological School.

In April 1908, Jacottet had been elected President at the Conference in Morija. Consequently, he inherited the final preparations for the great jubilee to be held in October to celebrate the founding of the mission in Lesotho seventy-five years before. Guests were invited from sister churches and missions as far afield as Barotseland and even Madagascar. The French consul (who eventually declined on account of his wife's illness), British government officials, chiefs, brother missionaries and their families, Basotho ministers, catechists, elders, teachers – all had to be invited to Morija. Above all, a delegation from France, headed by Bianquis, now Secretary General of the PEMS, was to grace the occasion with their presence, and had to be housed and fed. The logistics were daunting.

In organizing the celebrations – particularly who got to do what – and the itinerary of the delegation, Jacottet frequently incurred the wrath of some of his colleagues, who felt they were not being given their due. How to satisfy everyone? 'Such conjunctures and sad combinations are my unhappy occupations,' he grumbled. He loathed the details of organization, too. For instance, over one and a half days in July, he wrote thirty-five letters – never his favourite activity!

As a permanent memorial to the jubilee, a commemorative book was planned. It was to be a handsome, beautifully illustrated limited edition and was to be called the *Livre d'Or*. A number of people were commissioned to write pieces for it. In France, Frank Puaux set about a chapter on the origins of the mission, while Dieterlen and Kohler combined to do sections on the Basotho in the past and in the present. Bianquis was to produce an account of the jubilee celebrations themselves and the visit of the delegation from France. But the heart of the book – making up nearly half of its 689 pages – was a history of the mission to date, and this was assigned to Jacottet.

It was one of his most important and more permanent contributions to the mission and supplemented Jousse's earlier history written for the fiftieth anniversary. Through all the busy period of preparing for the jubilee, he also worked at this magnum opus. At the same time, he was putting the finishing touches, not without pain and hard work, to his *Treasury of Ba-Suto Lore*.

At one stage, he got Dieterlen to read his contribution and make comments. The latter, who was in a rather dark frame of mind, wanted him to make it a bit more pessimistic. Dieterlen was struggling with his own sections and, by the end of August, wanted more time. Jacottet was against this, wary of his own prevarications, and concerned that if it were not done now, it might never be done. By October, he had finished most of his task, and when the delegates departed in December they took with them two hundred pages of his manuscript. Bianquis also took with him, hot off the press, the first copies of the *Treasury*.

Jacottet was modest about all the effort that had gone into the history section. He hadn't written it: God had. He had merely held the pen.

—⁀○—

Amidst all this activity and achievement, there was a matter that concerned Jacottet, something he realized he would have to watch in case it grew larger and turned malignant.

As early as 1906, the young men whom the High Commissioner, Lord Alfred Milner, had brought from Britain and introduced into key positions in his administration – his 'Kindergarten' – were discussing the desirability of unifying the four southern African colonies, an idea soon picked up by the Prime Minister of the Cape, John X. Merriman, and Jan Smuts, the indispensable right-hand man of General Louis Botha, Prime Minister of the Transvaal. By early 1908, it was clear that some form of unification was likely; whether it would be in the form of a federation or a union was more opaque. In May, an intercolonial conference met in Pretoria and Cape Town, and reached agreement on the composition of a national convention to be held in October in Durban. The conference decided that Basutoland (as well as Bechuanaland and Swaziland) should not be incorporated immediately into the new grouping, but would be absorbed later on 'as a matter of course'.

That Jacottet was alive to the huge repercussions and potential dangers of this course of events is evidenced by a reply he sent in May to a letter from his friend Lord Bryce, now British ambassador in Washington, asking him what ought to be done for the welfare of the Basotho in the circumstances. He seized the opportunity to catch the attention of someone in the corridors of power.

First of all, he pointed out how, when Basutoland was proclaimed a British possession in 1868, and, more particularly, when it became a colony in 1884 and it was proposed to rule the country with the help of the chiefs, most white South Africans regarded it as 'doomed to failure'. Instead, it had become 'a splendid experiment', ensuring a tranquil oasis during the Anglo-Boer War and since, with a happily peaceful succession following the death of Letsie, and the successful creation of the Basotho National Council in Maseru. He was not uncritical: more money was needed for education; 'more influence could be given to the people' and it would be good 'if the commoners had a little more say'. But on the whole, he thought that the present system of government had 'answered so remarkably well that we cannot wish for another'.

Then he went on to the prospects for the Basotho if federation did take place. He told Bryce quite categorically that if Britain did not carefully define and safeguard the interests of the Basotho, it might mean 'their extinction' as a country: eventually, they would meet with 'very scant justice at the hands of the governing race' and would be treated as 'an inferior race created to serve'.

He envisaged four possible scenarios. Firstly, Basutoland might be annexed to the Orange River Colony or the Cape (Botha had proposed that Swaziland be incorporated into the Transvaal). With the experience of the Gun War fresh in his mind as he wrote his part of the *Livre d'Or*, he was convinced this would mean war once again.

Secondly, Basutoland might be handed over to the future federal government of South Africa as a protectorate, a solution he felt was favoured by 'a large number of thinking men' in South Africa. This would be equally disastrous, as a subject race 'is always governed for the benefit of the governing race'. Incorporation in this way should be opposed 'as long as full electoral rights [have] not been given to the Natives'.

Thirdly, the High Commission Territories might be treated as independent partners in the federation, on the same footing as the other colonies but under the direct rule of the imperial government. This option, which more or less reflected the situation as it was, would secure the rights of the Basotho to their own country, and was probably the course favoured by Jacottet.

Fourthly, Basutoland might stay outside the federation. This was the position preferred by the chiefs, who were already alarmed, Jacottet had heard, by the current rumours. He could accept this option himself, but thought there was a risk Basutoland might be 'squeezed out of existence'.

Whatever course was chosen, he insisted that the Basotho must be consulted.

He ended by reminding Bryce that the mission had, throughout its history, pursued only 'the good of the country and its people', and that its 'highest aim' had been 'to try to convert this tribe to the Gospel of Christ'. As for himself, having lived in Lesotho for nearly twenty-five years, he intended 'to devote to this work the rest of [his] life'.

Of course, the Tempter heard him, and decided to test him. Not immediately, naturally.

A few months later, just as the jubilee was about to descend on him, he was tentatively offered a professorship in the Theological Faculty in Neuchâtel. It was his chance to return to his birthplace and to his initiation school, a chance to regroup his family. In addition, the position was more lucrative. He had only a few days to telegraph his acceptance.

No telegram was sent. He had no hesitation. 'Duty is clear,' he told Boegner. 'My heart is in Lesotho, too.' He had the support of his wife, who wrote from Switzerland to say she thought he must refuse.

In 1898, Jacottet had left his two eldest children in Europe to pursue his chosen path. He had done the same again with Gustave in 1905. Now, for the third time, with Madeleine there, he was in a position to put his family and his personal wishes first. But he was resolute. Remembering his condemnation of Alfred Casalis and others, he said, 'I have rebuked several who have left. I do not have the right to leave, even to find my children. And I appreciate how loyally my wife has understood and accepted this.'

Later, he reaffirmed his position: 'I, too, have children. I suffer from being far away from them. Now I have refused my last chance to return to Europe. If one does not want to make sacrifices, rather abandon the mission.' This suffering was sanctified by God.

Jacottet, as President of the Conference and prime organizer of the jubilee, went to Bloemfontein to meet the delegates from Europe. Their travel was a far cry from seventy-five years before. The boat voyage (on the *Armadale Castle*) now took only eighteen days. The train, complete with sleeper coaches – a long undulating millipede, as the Basotho described it – took a day and a half from Cape Town to Bloemfontein. An overnight stop in Bloemfontein was followed by a leisurely journey to Maseru over the new railway bridge across the Caledon.

There were six delegates – Bianquis, Frédéric Dumas (one of the longest-serving members of the Paris Committee), Alfred Bertrand (an honorary member of the Committee) and his wife, Alexandre Bonzon of the church at Pau, and Mme Escande, widow of the Madagascar martyr whose place Jacottet had once nearly taken.

After a night spent under the roof of the Resident Commissioner, the delegates arrived in Morija on Saturday 17 October. It was spring in Lesotho. En route they admired the great Qeme plateau to the west and the line of mountains to the east, stretching naked in the sun, and were surprised by the near-complete absence of trees, except when they approached the mission station. As the cavalcade rolled or galloped towards the new spire it was greeted by local chiefs on their hardy ponies and by long files of students, boys and girls from the various schools. French, Swiss and English flags flew bravely, as well as the Bakoena flag, which showed a black crocodile on a white background.

On Sunday, Bianquis preached in the old church with nine hundred people packed in a space designed for seven hundred. On Tuesday, after a day of rest, a large party rode a couple of kilometres around the mountain to visit Letsie II in his home, high up like an eagle's nest at Phahameng. His Majesty welcomed them without ceremony, and sat with some of his counsellors and the missionaries on the verandah of his house. He and Jacottet made short speeches of greeting.

That night at eight o'clock, in Newberry Hall, one the buildings of the Normal School, the official welcome meeting was held. One hundred and forty whites attended, the largest number ever seen in Morija. Toasts were made, and at the end of the evening rousing versions of 'La Marseillaise' (in French) and 'God Save the King' (in English) were sung by the Normal School students. The storm of emotion that greeted the former led to an enthusiastic encore.

Next day was the first of the two-day celebrations. It was the most solemn day, the public day. Beneath a benevolent sky the crowd began to gather, some sheltering under the two gigantic pines planted by Arbousset and under the willows, eucalyptus and smaller acacias, until there were more than five thousand people, a whirl of costumes and colours. Close to the rostrum were the Basotho pastors, the catechists, the students of the Bible School and Normal School. On the right were many young girls and young women, some with babies in their arms, dignified and upright. Beyond were many interested pagans.

At nine o'clock, Jacottet formally opened the proceedings. He read from Genesis 13: 14–17, the ancient promise of God to Abraham: 'Arise, walk through the land in the length of it and in the breadth of it; for I will give it unto thee.' He went on to recall some of the memorable happenings of the last seventy-five years, gave thanks for the numerous examples of God's blessings, welcomed the various representatives, and underlined the way the French church had endeavoured to give an indigenous character to the Church of Lesotho. Then followed nearly four hours of speeches, suitably translated into French, English or Sesotho.

Herbert Sloley complimented the missionaries on their achievements and hailed the unique spectacle in Africa of a tribe living in peace and prosperity.

Letsie, in Bianquis's eyes, did not rise to the dignity of the occasion. As his eyes were somewhat bleary and his speech somewhat blurred, it was not clear what he said exactly. He did, however, seem to thank God for bringing the missionaries to the country.

Bianquis thanked Letsie and all the chiefs for remaining faithful to the heritage of Moshoeshoe and for recognizing the alliance contracted so long ago between the Bafora (the French) and the Basotho. He advised the chiefs that it was their duty to lead by example: it was God's wish that they, together with 'the elite of the Basotho people', accept the Christian religion. 'We love you and we shall always love you. We have loved you and we have in the past raised you as a nurse does her child. Now you are no longer a child, you have grown up. The Church of Lesotho has already left its time of first infancy: it approaches its majority. When a young man grows up, his father gives him a field to plant; when a young chief grows up, the great chief gives him a small tribe to rule; this have we done with you. But the young man continues to respect his father and to follow his advice, while working for his own family.' He finished by exhorting them to grow, like a young warrior, and brandish the spear of God's Word.

Then the two most venerable figures of the mission spoke. The little old man, Feko, had been Arbousset's first shepherd at Morija. He was now over ninety. His eyes sparkled in his wrinkled old face; he leant on a long stick. He had been fifteen years old and already circumcised when the missionaries arrived, 'trundling with them a white house'. With a fine mimicry, he compared the first efforts of the missionaries to convert blacks to a kingfisher trying to trap a frog. He described the first convert: 'He stood up, covered in red ochre; his wife also stood up.' Then, pointing to a small clay pot, he recalled that, when the foundations of the first church which he had helped build at Morija were laid, the names of Christians who had contributed to its construction were placed in a couple of pots and sealed by Arbousset in the foundations.

He was succeeded on the rostrum by Adèle Mabille, the eldest child of Casalis, the first white child born in Lesotho, called also by Moshoeshoe his 'daughter'. Now she was regarded as the 'mother' of the Basotho. On behalf of the women of Lesotho, she hailed the jubilee. She made a solemn appeal to the men of the tribe and directly to Letsie: become Christians and drive away the enemy that threatens to ruin the nation – brandy. Finally, she invoked the memories of her mother and of her husband, Adolphe Mabille, who both lay beneath the nearby trees. Bianquis was reminded of Deborah, a 'prophetess of Israel', industrious as a bee and of a wise discrimination.

Mme Mabille was followed by Letsie's brother, Griffith Lerotholi, first a convert, then a renegade with many wives. In complete contrast was the uprightness of bearing, dignity of word and attitude of Litia, son of Lewanika and heir to the Barotse throne. Setha, the local chief of Morija, Rev. Jalla of Zambezia, and old man Ellenberger brought the speeches to a close.

At two o'clock, a great banquet was held in the hall of the Normal School. Toasts to the government of Basutoland, to the Basotho chiefs, to the Paris Committee, to the mission hosts were given by Jacottet, Duby, Dieterlen, Dyke. The President of the Chamber of Commerce ended with a prayer to God. Nearly ten thousand people were fed that day, stretching the resources of the Morija mission to the limit. But the people had not come just to eat; their spiritual enthusiasm did not flag throughout the day. That night, a huge crowd assembled before the church, where they heard Everitt Segoete compare the Church of Lesotho to the people of Israel and beg them to keep themselves pure, with God's help, from the stain of paganism.

The second day was devoted to more strictly and intimately religious services, and a plaque commemorating the three pioneers was unveiled by Jacottet and a granddaughter of Arbousset. That night, in the church, the last ceremony was held, including many addresses. Dieterlen finished it all off by bringing to the notice of his listeners the centenary in twenty-five years' time, but reminding them of the most important jubilee of all – the meeting with the Lord Jesus.

—◦◦—

Next day, Friday 23 October, as the pilgrims began to disperse from Morija, and the world began to return to normal, the formal business of the church began.

A special meeting of the Synod was held, with Jacottet presiding. The atmosphere was convivial, and the Paris delegates listened attentively to a discussion generally optimistic in tone. But it was not all plain sailing: there were lapses to pagan customs like circumcision; many people found the Fora church too rigid and were attracted to churches that were laxer in their acceptance of members and in their discipline; the kabelo (the collection) suffered in a largely non-monetary economy; there was a gross imbalance of women to men in the church (there were 13 442 women to 3 718 men); there was the poison of alcohol.

The Seboka met on both Saturday and Monday, with the Paris delegates and the two missionaries from the Zambezi as special guests. They were deeply impressed by this mixed conference of European missionaries and Basotho pastors, the highest authority in the Church of Lesotho. There was one major point of discussion – the soured relations of the Lesotho church with its 'daughter', the Zambezi mission. Eventually, it was agreed that the collaboration would be resumed, but conditions for the future treatment of Basotho evangelists were carefully spelled out.

The Seboka also discussed the evil effects of alcohol and the smuggling of brandy into the country. The only really discordant note of the whole jubilee had been the inebriated state of Letsie. The missionaries and pastors quite justifiably saw that liquor might destroy Lesotho. They passed a resolution calling on the government to do more to halt its illegal importation and on the chiefs to set a better example to their subjects.

Neither heeded the call – the first because they could not, the second because they did not want to – to the ultimate detriment of the country.

—◦◦—

The delegates spent the next two months travelling through most of the country (except the mountains) visiting as many stations and outstations as they could. As regards Jacottet's work specifically, they were deeply moved by the historic site of Thaba-Bosiu and 'the most intelligent improvements' he had made. They praised the Theological School for 'the richness and solidity of the studies asked in Lesotho of its future indigenous pastors'.

Of the mission as a whole, they noted that the population of the country had grown from a tribe of forty-five thousand to a nation of over four hundred thousand. The mission numbered seventeen thousand members and seven thousand catechumens. It had built two hundred and thirty churches and annexes. In the beginning, Paris had underestimated the enormity of the task – the missionaries had had to educate as well as evangelize. As a consequence, the large majority of schools were still Protestant in 1908.

But the great mass of people, particularly the chiefs, were resistant to Christianity. The growth of the mission was seriously constrained by financial shortages. And the Catholics were catching up. Fast.

—◦◦—

The delegates left on 20 December. Bianquis was headed for the Rand. Jacottet suggested he stay with Ernest Creux of the Swiss Mission in Pretoria, since he warned that 'English Protestants do not generally celebrate Christmas. On this subject they have still got old puritan ideas.'

The Jacottet Christmases were certainly not puritan. But the year culminating in the jubilee had been exhausting. Having to entertain a houseful of guests for long periods had tired Jacottet out, and Marcelle was weary too.

Relieved at last of the delegation and other guests, Jacottet and Marcelle welcomed a quiet Christmas with the little ones.

CHAPTER TWENTY-TWO

THE PRICKLY HEDGEHOG

1909

P aris had been wooed and won. The Director was happy with the way the jubilee had gone. He felt that for some years the PEMS had stagnated, but, with the help of God, the celebration in Lesotho would stimulate renewal in the Society and in the local mission.

The jubilee was not without cost to the Jacottet family, however. Marcelle was still in a 'state of fatigue' into the new year as a result of her efforts, a fact which came as no surprise to Bianquis, who considered that she had been excessively overworked. Happily, he joked to Jacottet, there was no question of starting the jubilee again.

Jacottet himself had little time to recuperate before he was plunged into the major crisis which had been simmering for quite some time over the question of the relationship of Basutoland to the proposed Union. In what followed, he would play a key, if unacknowledged, part in the history of his adopted country – perhaps the most important contribution he ever made to its future.

The potential threat had not gone unnoticed by the educated elite in Basutoland. Until 1904, they had taken their guidance from *Leselinyana*; thereafter they had a new star to follow, when *Naledi ea Lesotho* began publication in Mafeteng. Responding to a letter that appeared in some colonial newspapers recommending the incorporation of Basutoland into the Union, *Naledi* published two articles in June 1908. Given what it suspected of the future 'native policy' of South Africa, *Naledi* understandably did not favour incorporation. The chiefs were also uneasy, and, after a meeting of their Lekhotla la Mahosana (Council of Chiefs), Letsie wrote in May to Resident Commissioner Sloley for clarification.

Lord Selborne, who had succeeded Milner as High Commissioner to South Africa, responded by suggesting that he considered it desirable for Lesotho, together with Bechuanaland and Swaziland, to be transferred to the proposed Union, or else their 'island' status would lead to friction between South Africa and the imperial government.

Selborne's reply was not what the chiefs wanted to hear. They suddenly feared that their house was built on shifting sand. So they drew up a petition to be delivered personally by a delegation to His Majesty, King Edward VII.

In fact, Selborne had jumped the gun. The Colonial Office's position was reflected in a marginal note on Selborne's report: 'Lord Selborne is in too great a hurry in this matter. Basutoland is a very prickly hedgehog and it is not at all certain that the S.A. Union when it is made will be anxious to handle it. The Basutos are already asking questions, they are warlike and armed.'

Up until the middle of 1908, most people believed unification would take the form of a federation, but after that the tide turned and the current ran strongly towards union. Aside from Natal with its insular quirkiness, only a few voices were raised in defence of federation or in favour of a colour-blind franchise. One notable exception was that of former Cape Prime Minister, W.P. Schreiner; another was that of his sister, Olive Schreiner, the novelist. In a long essay in the *Transvaal Leader*, she mentioned that in smaller states there tends to be 'more personal freedom, more individuality and a higher social vitality' than in larger states. Deeply distrustful of South African politicians, she feared for what she called 'the root question in South Africa' – the policy towards Africans. With both these positions Jacottet sympathized greatly, and, while preferring the maintenance of direct imperial rule, his was a voice for federation as the best alternative, long after there was much hope for its implementation.

The four colonies, together with Rhodesia, met in Durban between 12 October and 5 November 1908, and in Cape Town between 23 November and 3 February the following year. What added to the pre-existing anxiety and made response more difficult was the fact that the Convention's proceedings were held in secret.

—❦—

With its ear close to the Council of Chiefs and to Basotho opinion, the Protestant mission, as one of the few major voices listened to seriously by the High Commissioner, was soon closely involved. Jacottet was in the forefront of its thinking and its representations, and he became the chief spokesman.

In a meeting with Selborne in October, Jacottet stated his clear preference for the continuation of direct imperial rule, which had 'answered so well in the past', having ensured a quarter of a century of peace and prosperity, and he pointed out the risks attendant on incorporation. In response, Selborne gave him to understand that it would not be possible for Basutoland and 'the other Native Territories' to remain forever outside a united South Africa.

So Jacottet wrote to Selborne after this meeting, the first of his memoranda on the subject to the High Commissioner. This was just a few days before the Convention began. (Although Selborne was not to be party to the Convention debates, he was in Durban, received minutes of the proceedings, and had discussions with delegates on the questions of the franchise and the Territories.)

Jacottet accepted, at least for the moment, that for Basutoland to remain outside the Union for any length of time was 'a practical impossibility'. Given this, he was anxious that the conditions for any future incorporation should be hammered out and guaranteed *now*, when the imperial government could still enforce such guarantees.

In suitably understated language, he warned Selborne that there was already 'a feeling of anxiety' amongst the Basotho chiefs and the nation. Favouring federation rather than union, the most important thing he wanted was for the land of the Basotho to be secured under every possible circumstance, and under no condition was any part of it to be confiscated or disposed of, as it had been, under compulsion, when Moshoeshoe was King. Other guarantees were required: 'Europeans' should be excluded from owning land, and there should be strict limits on 'European' immigration; no discriminatory laws should be allowed; the revenues of the country should be used for the benefit of the country; and the existence of the National Council should be ensured. Furthermore, the consent of the Basotho nation – through the chiefs and the National Council – should be obtained before any important changes were made to these conditions.

Jacottet apologized for the length of his submissions, but he was acting, he said, 'for the good of the tribe', of which he felt himself to be a member. This responsibility, he concluded, lay heavily upon his heart. Selborne graciously acknowledged his contributions, and after the initial round of discussions at the Convention wrote again to assure the missionary that most of these conditions had been secured, in particular that transfer would not be immediate, as Lionel Curtis and Jan Smuts, to name but two, had originally wanted.

Perhaps it is worth pausing for a moment to examine Jacottet's motivations.

He had been in Lesotho since 1884. Being so close to it, he knew well the causes and effects of the Gun War and fervently wished to avoid a repetition.

He had also come to identify with the Basotho, and to think of himself as an honorary member of the tribe, bound by sacred ties. In a sense, though obviously to a much lesser extent, he saw himself following in the tracks of Casalis as a kind of foreign minister. Like Mabille before him, although his main concern was with the salvation of individual souls, he was fiercely protective of this small nation scarcely begun.

For buried deep in his psyche was the thought of his own homeland, his canton and his country, and their struggles for independence. Selborne had described Basutoland as 'a very prickly hedgehog'. Adolf Hitler later identified the same quality in Switzerland when he called it 'the little hedgehog'. A tiny creature with a fierce, resistant spirit. And Jacottet had imbibed a double dose. He even went so far as to suggest that the remoteness of rule from faraway Britain was advantageous, just as Hohenzollern governance had been to Neuchâtel: a distant sovereign power was less likely to meddle too often in local affairs.

Many times, but most notably in 1893, he had travelled through Lesotho. To its very edge. He had embraced the boundaries and he honoured its integrity.

There was a touch of royalism, too, in his responses – echoes, from his past, of a kind of democratic constitutional principality. So he passionately wanted to protect this mountain kingdom, ruled as it was not by one but by *two* Kings.

—◦◦—

In January 1909, the chiefly deputation to England was on the brink of departure. The original purpose had been to present a petition protesting against the notorious Proclamation No. 47 of 1907. This Proclamation provided 'for the banishment or confinement of any person whose presence in Basutoland may be considered undesirable by the High Commissioner'. Ostensibly this was designed to deal with undesirable whites, but in a private letter to Jacottet, Lewis Wroughton, the Acting Resident Commissioner, rather injudiciously for a government official, spelled out the unspoken rationale of the Proclamation: 'This is intended to be used (and has already been used) against undesirable *whites* but it *can* undoubtedly be used against any *Mosuto* who may behave in such a way – politically or otherwise – as to render his presence in Basutoland a danger to the peace, order and good Government of the Territory.' Indeed, an attempt was made to banish Chief Mocheko Moorosi of the Baphuthi to Matabeleland in terms of this Proclamation.

But now impending union and incorporation became the deputation's primary concern. The great fear of all interested parties – the chiefs, the commoners, the educated, the missionaries – was that the engine of Union would steam ahead without 'native policy' having been settled, allowing the future government a free hand to introduce draconian legislation, and that the Basotho would be treated on the same terms as the blacks of South Africa.

Jacottet had spent the early part of the month pleasantly traversing the southern Maloti on a visit to Matatiele. On his return, he was immediately contacted by Letsie, who wanted him to join the deputation to England (the

King himself had a phobia for foreign travel and never even went as far as Cape Town). Jacottet went to Matsieng on Thursday 14 January, where he found Letsie 'hopelessly drunk'. The following day, he was approached again by three royal messengers with urgent requests to go. But he consistently answered that he could not go without the approval of government, nor at such short notice. He also needed to be told the specific instructions of the delegation, so that he would know what he was letting himself in for.

A small dust-devil of telegrams and letters between himself and the Acting Resident Commissioner elicited a decidedly lukewarm response from the latter. Jacottet himself felt the delegation had little chance of success, as he believed eventual incorporation was inevitable, but he agreed with its aims and would have consented to go had he been given a little more time. He did have reservations that the chiefs, in their desire to continue being ruled by Britain rather than by white South Africa, had their own interests at heart rather than those of the nation.

—◦◦—

On 29 January, just as the delegation was departing, a second key memorandum was sent to Lord Selborne via Wroughton. This was a combined PEMS response signed by Jacottet as President of the Conference and countersigned by Sam Duby as Secretary. Fearing that the mission might come under rule other than that of the imperial government within a few years, and hinting at the historical tension between the missionaries and the Boers who would constitute the majority of their potential future rulers, the memorandum not only reiterated Jacottet's stance on the inalienability of Basotho land, on free trade, the use of revenues, and on liquor, but also insisted that incorporation not take place without a charter embodying these most necessary rights and reservations; in fact, it went further in suggesting that the National Council should be secured in the charter and even that the means should be found to give it 'a more representative character, and to gradually increase its powers so as to lead eventually to representative institutions'. This, they claimed, was one of the most important points, as it was 'necessary to have the people at large more interested in the government of their own country'.

This highly progressive stance did not find favour with Selborne, who undermined it in a letter to Lord Crewe, the Secretary of State for the Colonies, in which he wrote: 'H.M. Govt. are the trustees and at all times will be far better judges of what is really to be to the advantage of the Basuto people than the Chiefs and Council can ever be. These uncivilized natives have not the knowledge or the education to form a sound judgement under the complicated conditions of modern civilization and politics.'

Jacottet's third memorandum to Selborne on 18 February was a direct response to the Draft South Africa Act, and especially to the attached Schedule, which more directly related to Basutoland. While praising Selborne for securing provisions to do with land, liquor, free trade and the continued existence of the Council, Jacottet was clearly agitated about the future nature of the governance of Basutoland, distrusting the new relationship between the Crown and the prospective form of Union government, and believing that South Africa would have too great a say in the Territories' affairs. He also pointed out that Basutoland should be treated differently from Bechuanaland and Swaziland, since it was 'a country which has a real National unity and has advanced much'. Finally, he nudged Selborne with the reminder that proposals similar to those in the Draft Act to redirect Basutoland's revenues had led to the Gun War in 1880, and might well once again lead to 'dangerous agitation' in the country. You don't play twice on the edge of the same precipice.

Meanwhile, the Basotho deputation had arrived in London on 6 February. Lodged in an excellent hotel, furnished with a special cook and outfitted with fine new clothes, they were fêted with sightseeing tours and dinners, twice met with the Secretary of State for the Colonies and once with the King; a proposed trip to PEMS headquarters in Paris was cancelled at the last moment, however, to the genuine regret of Bianquis. But the High Commissioner had already negated their original purpose by sending a telegram to the Colonial Office defending the banishment Proclamation and denying that he intended it as a sword of Damocles over the heads of the Basotho: his real fear, he claimed, was a bitter succession struggle on the death of Letsie, who had no male offspring.

At the beginning of March, Selborne attended a great pitso in Maseru, where he explained to a doubting and anxious public gathering of chiefs the conditions of the proposed transfer. The chiefs were alarmed to find that the guarantees were not as binding as they would have liked. Afterwards, Selborne granted Jacottet a private interview where the missionary spelled out his own objections, as well as an official audience where the wishes of the mission were set out.

It is possible that Jacottet was becoming wary of Selborne's intentions at this point, because he began lobbying members of the British government and parliament directly. Long letters went off to Lord Crewe, to Sir Francis Hopwood of the Colonial Office, to Sir Charles Dilke, a respected and experienced Liberal MP, and to his old friend James Bryce in Washington.

Even as he was growing concerned about Marcelle's health, the tempo of his efforts, far from flagging, actually increased, and on 12 May a flurry of correspondence flew off to Dilke, Hopwood and Crewe, and to a new recipient,

James Keir Hardie, a Labour MP. He also alerted local Free State political figures like Dewdney Drew, as well as the former Prime Minister of the Cape, W.P. Schreiner, to a disturbing development. He had uncovered a new, and potentially mortal, danger hidden in the Draft Act – more specifically in Article 150.

Despite Selborne having stated expressly at the pitso in Maseru that Basutoland would remain as it was and not be annexed to any colony (or province) after incorporation, the gist of Article 150 seemed to be that the future Union government *could* annex the whole or part of Basutoland to the Orange Free State or the Cape, 'so breaking up the unity of the country and blotting it out altogether', and this could be done by a simple majority of the Union parliament. Jacottet was horrified: implicitly, this provision annulled any of the guarantees. The argument revolved around the interpretation of the word 'Territory' in the Article. Did it refer to Bechuanaland, Swaziland or Basutoland, or did it mean 'Territories within the Union' already, for example, Zululand or Transkei? Despite assurances from Selborne that 'Territories' referred to the latter in this instance, Jacottet was not convinced. He was always distrustful of the designs of South African politicians on 'native policy', a distrust shared by Schreiner, who wrote to him complaining that the 'narrow and illiberal provisions which deface' the Draft Act 'deprive it of any fair claim to be considered, as it might have been, one of the World's great Liberty documents'.

Eventually, as a result of lobbying and of debate in the House of Commons on the part of those Jacottet had corresponded with, success was achieved. In October, the Chairman of the Basutoland Chamber of Commerce, in his written congratulations to Jacottet, observed that what was now Clause 149 of the Draft Act had been altered so that the word 'Territory' was deleted. The manager of the influential trading company Fraser's, whose headquarters were in Wepener, while regretting that the imperial government had 'given away practically everything on native policy', nonetheless thought that 'the thanks of the whole community' were due to Jacottet for what he had done in getting the amendment to the Draft Act: 'That this alteration has been secured is a great thing.'

Without Jacottet's vigilance, this ambiguity might have been fatal to Basutoland.

The threat of incorporation nevertheless hovered for many years. Indirectly, it made the chiefs more dependent on imperial rule and more subservient to the colonial officials, whose moods they watched as nervously as they did storm clouds over the Maloti. The colonial administration also found it easier to resist demands for constitutional progress. In mid-1918, rumours that Lesotho was to be taken over were as wild as winter veld fires, and General Botha's proposal to incorporate Swaziland fanned the flames.

But Basutoland never did join the Union. Its legacy of independence was in no small part due to Édouard Jacottet, though his contribution is now forgotten and unsung. He had helped to prevent the small country from being swallowed by its larger neighbour.

CHAPTER TWENTY-THREE

A BREACH OF FAITH

1910–1914

Relieved as he was that the immediate danger to Basutoland's independence was over, and quietly pleased that his own efforts in its defence had not been insignificant, Jacottet nevertheless feared that 'the special position of Lesotho' would not last forever.

To this specific concern, at the beginning of 1910, was added another general worry. The missionary body was weakening and none of the vital replacements that were needed had come. His wife was chronically ill and he himself was exhausted to the extent that he no longer took pleasure in his work. As Easter and the Conference at Thaba-Bosiu approached, he looked forward to relinquishing the presidency after two arduous years: 'I have had enough,' he said, 'more than enough.'

As one of his final acts in office, he felt impelled to write a formal letter to Boegner, as Director of the PEMS, expressing his 'purely personal' views. The true aim of his life had been 'to help in erecting an edifice in Lesotho worthy of the Kingdom of God, to walk on such a beautiful path as we have, tracing the footsteps of our precursors, Arbousset, Rolland, Casalis and Mabille'. His dream was to continue to build 'a true local church in South Africa, probably the first of its kind' in this subcontinent.

He pointed out that, despite a substantial church membership, there were still nearly half a million souls to convert in Basutoland, and that the church was 'on the verge of becoming a national influence over the country, the pagan multitude and the government'. But he warned that the 'vast and heavy superstructure that we have built up is in danger of collapsing on our heads'.

The problem was the ageing and ailing missionary corps. Of the seventeen men presently in Lesotho, Dieterlen and Dyke were over sixty, Marzolff, Auguste Jaques, Jeanmairet, Bertschy and Jacottet himself were over fifty; Germond was about to turn fifty; Barthélemy Pascal, Christeller, Louis Mabille, Ramseyer and Théophile Verdier were over forty; all the rest, Duby, Bertrand Moreillon, Henri Baltzer and Georges Dieterlen, were over thirty. Moreover, Marzolff was virtually disabled, Dieterlen was often ill (he subsequently suffered a couple of heart attacks), Dyke was old and tired, Germond had tuberculosis which slowed him down, and Jacottet was getting warning signals from his body that his health might fail.

Over and above this, what worried Jacottet was the quality of the younger echelons: Christeller was a hard worker, clued-up and clear-sighted, but he seemed to lack the ideal drive and spirit, being too critical and negative; Louis Mabille, for all his work and devotion, knew himself that, unlike his father, he was not made to lead; Baltzer was a puzzle, doing things well or not at all, but he could never be relied upon; Georges Dieterlen was an unknown quantity. For the rest, it was the old lament of Jacottet: they simply were not up to scratch, intellectually or spiritually. The only exception was Duby, 'the most reliable'. Otherwise, leadership lay with Dieterlen, Dyke and Jacottet – and *their* days were numbered.

In his letter to Boegner, Jacottet mentioned the continuing dangers of Ethiopianism and the expanding threat of Catholicism. He begged the Director for 'a larger, younger workforce, a workforce of true worth', and, if priorities had to be established, 'not so much the quantity as the quality'. He concluded with a passionate plea: 'I will say it again: this grand and beautiful work, the work of three generations, has to be able to continue: it must be given the means of continuing. The worst thing would be to wear it out to a small fire.'

—◦◦—

One of Mabille's daughters had been assisting Duby in the Book Depot, but she left in December 1909. He was fortunate to find a ready replacement in Marcelle Jacottet, who started in February of the new year. Her father was pleased: he thought she would do well and that Duby would help her to learn quickly. As Duby was due to go on leave in 1911, it was important for him to have someone reliable and experienced in place to shoulder the responsibility in his absence.

The Depot was extremely busy and was in the process of printing a new series of reading books in Sesotho. It was also about to publish Thomas Mofolo's second book, *Pitseng*, which had been serialized in *Leselinyana* in 1909. It is likely that Mofolo had submitted a further manuscript for publication late in 1909 or early in 1910. It is almost certain that this was the basis for his third – and most famous – novel, *Chaka*.

Duby (in particular) and Jacottet were justifiably proud of their protégé. In a review of *Pitseng* in the *Christian Express*, Jacottet wrote that 'it is highly gratifying to watch the beginnings of a good and genuinely native literature'. He had no doubt where praise should be bestowed: 'All missionaries and others interested in native progress must feel grateful to the editor of the *Leselinyana*, the Rev. S. Duby, to whose encouragement and zeal this is mostly due. In encouraging and fostering, as he is doing, the birth of a genuine native literature, he is rendering to the whole native race an inestimable service which we should never forget.' He was probably modest about his own contribution.

Pitseng was a semi-autobiographical novel, and represents many of the central ideals and concerns of the mission at the time. Somewhat more realistic than *The Traveller of the East*, it nevertheless has some of the same elements of journey and vision.

—⊙—

The book begins in snow and almost ends in snow. A young teacher-evangelist and his family are making their way towards Pitseng, a village where Christians are few and their lives hard. The snow forces them to take shelter in a cave. But, with great courage, the young man leaves this refuge to rescue a number of people in dire straits.

The area he has come to in order to teach and preach is backward and in desperate need of his ministration. Whereas there is progress in the rest of Lesotho, in Pitseng it is still a time of utter darkness and the observance of old customs. Elsewhere in Lesotho it is a time of enlightenment, a time of schools; in Pitseng it is as it was in the olden days, a time of circumcision rites and drinking parties.

But the new evangelist's reputation for self-sacrifice and his inspiring sermons soon fill his church with converts. He becomes known as Mr Katse, after the hat he wears made of the skin of a wildcat (it was the missionaries who introduced the domestic cat into Lesotho).

He preaches inspiringly about love and marriage – this is the central theme of the novel – and in one particularly eloquent sermon he extols Christ's love for the church as the ideal model for personal love. Lovers should mate for life in the sanctity of marriage.

His words find a home in the hearts of two young people, Alfred Phakoe and Aria Sebaka, who now take over from Katse as the central characters of the book.

Alfred goes off to training college in the Cape, where he has a dream-vision of an exceptionally tall person in snow-white garments gliding over the ground without quite touching it. He also learns that Mr Katse has given up his post. This seems inexplicable, until he remembers that the teacher has always struggled with his eyesight and must have gone blind.

In a letter to Alfred, Katse presents him with a riddle. It finally becomes clear that the answer to the riddle is the union of Alfred and Aria. Much of the novel is concerned with the state of morality in the country. Mofolo criticizes the laxity of morals and the undermining of traditional ways and parental authority, which have been the unintentional consequences of the coming of Christianity. At the same time, he attacks certain malign practices in the old ways, such as bohali. He defends the best of the old ways, but as a devout convert is convinced of the efficacy of the Word of Christ. His implicit desire is for a marriage of the two. The paradox at the heart of the book lies in the question of choice and custom, but the non-negotiable message is the unshakeable sanctity of love and marriage.

Both Alfred and Aria have to resist many sexual temptations on their way to their eventual union (which comes after Alfred hears her beautiful voice *before* he sees her). Meanwhile, Alfred has to hurry away to Molteno where Mr Katse lies dying. He arrives just too late, but the appearance of the morning star as Katse dies signals that his soul lives on.

On his return to Pitseng, heavy snow forces Alfred to take refuge in the same cave used by Katse in an earlier time. Symbolically, he has taken Katse's place. The wedding of Alfred and Aria is celebrated in beautiful weather after fresh rains. Their love is holy and blessed by nature.

Pitseng is one of the unsung masterpieces of Protestant literature. Basotho readers have been known to weep at the beauty of the language. The voice of the omniscient narrator – appropriately, given the subject matter – soars on angels' wings over the mountains of Lesotho.

The publication of *Pitseng* in book form was due to be announced in *Leselinyana* on 9 April. Mofolo was at the peak of his craft and set for an illustrious literary career. But on the very eve of his greatest triumph, he fell.

On 23 March, Mofolo fled away from Morija, leaving behind his wife and a note of remorse for Duby.

The Reverend Duby,

Sir, everything you will hear from Rev. Mabille, communicated by letter, truly comes from me. I have tried many times to be brave and tell you but I was overcome by shame. I am leaving at this very instant to go and hide myself so that this matter will come to light in my absence, and shall return when it has simmered down a little. At this moment I am going to my father in the Orange River Colony (at Villiers). Also, Reverend, I remind you that Matšaba has already paid the ten pounds and you will get it from me. When I come to my father I will sell a few cattle to obtain that money.

I plead and say oh, even though I have wronged you so much, do please have mercy and exercise patience and do not let your heart be angered. I have been your ward over many years, and even now I continue to be your ward, please have pity on me.

With disappointment and shame.
T. Mofolo

Mofolo had shown himself to be as human as Ernest Mabille. He had had an adulterous affair which could no longer be concealed.

At the exit to the cave, a deep crevice had opened up between sanctity and human weakness, between aspiration and achievement.

—∽⊝—

Duby was devastated. 'Last Monday,' he informed Boegner, 'one of your secretaries at the Depot, Thomas Mofolo, the author of the charming piece *The Pilgrim of the East*, which I will publish in English soon, was accused of adultery, and disappeared. This is a terrible matter. Mofolo was not only one of the most intelligent natives of Lesotho, but was also well known, thanks to his position, and known even beyond the borders of the country, thanks to his books. Furthermore, he was my right hand. Teacher at the Bible School, official reporter for *Leselinyana* and in charge at the Depot of all native correspondence, regular colleague in our newspaper through his writings, which are greatly appreciated by our readers, Mofolo was a vital man, the right man in the right place. Now he is gone, having abandoned all his work. I find myself in a most difficult situation.'

It was not just in the work situation that Duby was hurt: 'You will under-stand how much something like the fall of Mofolo affects my wife and me, as we considered him our child, whom we raised with energy and moral spirit. The whole mission feels affected: we shall certainly learn some salutary lessons from this terrible failure, but we shall have lost some of our strength. We are trying to find Mofolo and make him come back and repair, however possible, the damage he has done. I hope that despite the shame he feels, he will return and arrange his affairs like a man of honour and a Christian. Poor Mofolo!'

Mofolo's behaviour and reaction to his disgrace are of considerable interest in view of the events ten years later. He was almost overwhelmed with shame, full of self-abnegation to the point of disappearance, spiritually as well as phys-ically, and full of fear, too, at having to face his real father and his putative father. In fact, he so dreaded seeing his father 'crushed' by his shame that he changed his mind about going home. On 27 April 1910, when he responded to a letter that Duby had addressed to him, exhorting him to return, he was in Livingstone in Northern Rhodesia.

He began by expressing gratitude for Duby's support and understanding. He had been very astonished to learn that his job was even being preserved for him at Morija, because he had expected only 'harsh, stern words' from those he had disappointed. His letter continued:

> Now, sir, I am at a loss what to say. What made me leave Moria was a dread of my disgrace and of being exposed. I found it difficult to look at you face to face after being so debased and wiping off the trust that you had in me. I know very well that you trusted me very much. I thought about this matter for two days while I was in Moria, wishing very much to tell you about my affairs, but I was unable; I was afraid to see your face becoming saddened and your heart broken. I was afraid.
>
> Also, I thought about my father, poor man, and also of all my relatives who trusted me, and I wondered how much pain they would feel, how disappointed they would be when they heard my news; and I knew it would be too much for me to see tears in the eyes of my elders. Then I began to realize that the pain resulting from my action did not affect me alone, but passed on and went to break the hearts of many who loved me, who sympathized with me; and it brought sadness and weeping to the hearts of my parents and all my relatives.
>
> Also, another important thing was the fear of being exposed. I thought also of those who would rejoice when they heard the news, because such are also to be found, and they are many. When I thought of these, I feared to be ridiculed, and I dreaded their songs. When I put all these things together and viewed them in their totality, I considered myself to be as good as dead, an unfortunate, miserable sinner ...

Mofolo went on to say that he could not entertain the thought of returning to Morija: 'As regards the path leading back to Lesotho, it is dim, it is black, it is a confusion of dark, billowing clouds.' He was planning to leave for Johannesburg instead, where the climate was cooler. He asked Duby to convey his apologies to Mme Duby and Mlle Cochet, whom he had also hurt, and concluded, 'The life I have lived in these past few days has been one of sorrow, which I do not even wish to tell to anyone; that is the bitter fruit which has resulted from my guilt, my guilt which is so great, which is great indeed.'

Some people tried to dilute his fault by pointing out that his wife had been nursing a child and custom forbade intercourse while she was doing so, but it is clear from this letter that Mofolo's acceptance of the Christian faith had instilled in him a deep moral intensity, and the ideas of wrongdoing and guilt were embedded within him to the point of almost total self-annihilation.

He eventually arrived in Johannesburg, where Ernest Mabille, who was a labour recruiting agent on the mines and who would readily have sympathized with his situation, ultimately helped him to become a recruiter in northern Lesotho.

Mofolo's was not an isolated case. Adultery seemed to penetrate into the very homes of the missionaries. At Paballong – the station with the worst reputation in the whole mission – the Dubys had had no such trouble with their maids; but here at Morija – which Duby called 'the Jerusalem of Lesotho' – they had had three cases in a row. This caused them considerable anguish. Eva was unwell, and Sam was getting headaches and heart palpitations. The fall of Mofolo could not have helped.

One of Duby's temporary headaches, though, was solved when he appointed Z.D. Mangoaela in Mofolo's place. Mangoaela was humble and pious, and 'a good man on the literary side'. (If we allow ourselves a glimpse into the future, however, we see that Mangoaela himself was accused of 'immorality' in 1918. Jacottet defended him by saying that there was no precedent for dismissal from the Book Depot for such an offence, but Christeller brought up the Mofolo affair. When it came to voting in the four-member committee, Jacottet and Matthey voted to retain Mangoaela, Christeller voted against, and Duby abstained.)

Another, more serious concern was who would replace Duby at the Book Depot and Bible School while he was on leave in Europe in 1911–12. The Conference at Thaba-Bosiu in April solved this. The cycle of the Theological School was coming to an end. With Marcelle safely ensconced in her administrative role at the Depot, this institution – along with the Bible School and the newspaper – would become the Jacottet family business for eighteen months. With military and militant precision, the Jacottets moved into the house set aside for the Director of the Bible School the day after the Dubys moved out, allowing them no scope for indecision.

—◦◦—

The Duby family embarked at Durban on 9 March, taking the slightly longer route up the east coast of Africa so that they could relax, recover their battered health and arrive at Valentigny 'after the cold March which we dread'. With the warmth of Dar es Salaam and Port Said behind them, the Mediterranean was so fresh that they had to take refuge in the dining room. 'We were not expecting such a change, especially not so suddenly,' lamented Duby. 'The humid fog is already making us miss the beautiful blue sky and the warmth that we felt in Lesotho!' The children, who came to believe that European weather was always so dreary, were naturally disappointed: Duby prayed that they would soon see a better day!

After landing at Naples, they went to Rome – Duby wanted to be there at Easter – then on to eastern France, via Basle. Although Duby's sister-in-law, headmistress at a local school, had prepared 'a small place' for them in Valentigny only two minutes from the woods, and they were happy to be once more 'amongst their own', the homecoming was tinged with sadness for Eva, whose parents had died a few years before, while their daughter was so long and so far away. She was also expecting her fourth, and last, child. Sam soon hurried off to see his elderly mother in Geneva, and found her in bed with a bad pulmonary congestion.

In the next few months, Duby did a fair amount of travelling, particularly to Switzerland, Paris and London. The Lesotho Conference had given him permission to look for a colleague to relieve him of some of the burden of the distribution and accounts at the Book Depot. A candidate from Brussels was proposed, but Duby was 'not enthusiastic' about him. Instead, Duby told Bianquis that he had found someone else who might be suitable – 'a charming character' with over ten years' experience in a bank, a married man with a child, who had unexpectedly offered to become his second. Somewhat mysteriously, he added, 'I cannot tell you his name now but I do know him.'

The summer months they found almost unbearably hot, which was strange for them living as they did in a hot country. Duby spent his time working on various literary tasks, including a French translation of *Moeti oa Bochabela*.

In 1911, Jacottet himself went strangely silent in his correspondence (though he was active, visiting Adams College, the American Board mission school at Amanzimtoti), but Duby was kept in touch with regular news of the Book Depot by Marcelle. 'Things are going as well as expected at the Depot,' he agonized to Bianquis, 'knowing my successor and knowing how little this type of work interests him. I fear that Miss Marcelle, who has tremendous willingness and into whose hands the burden of the Depot falls, may be obliged to ease up if her father is not of more help.' He could not explain Jacottet's muteness, except to say that he was obviously not meant for what the English call 'business' and that 'he is greatly changed'. Unfortunately, Duby did not elaborate on what he meant by this.

What did emerge soon was that the mysterious candidate for his second in command at the Book Depot was none other than his own brother, Théophile.

The year ended with Duby running the house and caring for the children, as Eva was still weak from giving birth to their son Georges, who had been conceived in Lesotho.

—◦—

Like the periodic years of drought and famine, 1912 was another of those when Death stalked the PEMS, seeming to devour more than was necessary for his mere survival.

At the beginning of January, Jacottet spent eight days in the Maloti with the manager of the Printing Works, Charles Labarthe. For both of them it was a wonderful break and they got to know one another well. They also got on well. For Jacottet, Labarthe was a good example of the Protestant work ethic, full of strength and vigour: his only fault seemed to be that he would never allow himself to rest, and he had to be forced – almost literally – to make the trip into the mountains. Then, a few months later, he suddenly died. This was a blow to Jacottet. Labarthe had set the Printing Works in immaculate order and equipped it admirably, had trained his workers well, and left a legacy of published new books or new editions of old books which would do him honour. It would be difficult to replace a man who was a printer, bookbinder, illustrator and artist all in one.

On Sunday 25 February, having just finished a powerful sermon in the great church in La Rochelle, the ever-ailing Alfred Boegner, the greatest supporter of the Lesotho missions, slumped in his chair and died. Jacottet was almost 'overcome with grief'. 'I cannot begin to wonder how the mission will be without him,' he wrote to Boegner's successor, Bianquis. 'A great strength has disappeared along with him; he was a moving spirit like few others in the Protestant world … And his support of Lesotho dies with him … If there was never a question of suppressing us, it was mainly his doing. He loved us and looked after us without sacrificing the other missions.'

Over and above this, the Jacottet family was clearly taking the strain. Louise, who was not doing very well and should have been resting, had to take over the domestic management of the Bible School when the incumbent's contract came to an end. Jacottet himself complained that he had to take over all that Duby did (a healthy and growing *Leselinyana*, a larger publication schedule than in any previous year, a flourishing Bible School) with even fewer staff than Duby had, not to mention all the extra demands his central position in the mission dictated. 'I alone, together with my daughter, manage all of this,' he complained. The increased workload he illustrated with a single example: in the first two months of 1910, 510 parcels of books were despatched; in 1911, 880 parcels; and in 1912, 1 375 parcels. 'The progress made is frightening, and it is we who are responsible for it. From eight o'clock in the morning to eleven o'clock at night

I am at work, and it is not easy with a tired head to get all my correspondence done.' Ominously, he added, 'My daughter is doing Duby a great service; without her I would already have collapsed. She, too, has too much to do. I am really worried about her tiredness but she wants to take no break at all.' Jacottet at last had first-hand knowledge that Duby needed an assistant!

—◦◦—

There is a common belief that Mofolo left the mission in 1910 because his book *Chaka* had been suppressed. This myth has been exploded by the research of Rev. Albert Brutsch and Mofolo's biographer, Daniel Kunene. There is now no doubt why he left and it had nothing to do with missionary censorship. On the contrary, Duby tried to get him back, while Jacottet wrote a most favourable review of his second novel and looked forward to his further success.

There is a puzzle, though, as to why *Chaka* had to wait until 1925 for publication. Conspiracy theories are occasionally appropriate, and may be backed up by hard evidence; but, especially where publishing is concerned, problems are much more often rooted in practicalities. In this case, a possible explanation for the delay may lie in the circumstances that followed Mofolo's disgrace. He went away first to Northern Rhodesia, then to Johannesburg. It was many months before he returned to northern Lesotho, but never, it seems, to Morija. It would be quite natural that the publication would not go ahead in his absence. In 1911–12, his mentor Duby was away and Jacottet was overwhelmed with the increased production in the Printing Works and the Book Depot. Perhaps, too, the manuscript was not in final shape, and interest in and opportunity for the book might well have simply lapsed.

After *Chaka*, Mofolo never published another book. It had a strange subsequent history. Victor Ellenberger produced a superb French translation of it in 1940, grasping the essence rather than translating it mot à mot, but the Germans, thinking the portrait of the tyrant Shaka resembled Hitler a bit too closely, destroyed most of the copies, so that it was almost impossible to get hold of until it was reprinted after the war.

Increasingly over the years, *Chaka* has come to be regarded as a pioneering work and one of the most important in African literature. Like the Roman plays of Shakespeare, it examines a pre-Christian world and follows the progressive moral degeneration of its central figure, a terror to all those around and ultimately to himself. Its importance for the Jacottet story is the silent question that lurks everywhere within it. Can any ordinary person – even the most powerful in the known world – without true faith become a genuine saviour? Although Shaka was the main protagonist of the book, its true Hero stands beyond its pages.

Mofolo had written a Christian novel about a pagan world.

Because of the protestations of Jacottet and others, the mission had been marginally strengthened: André Oechsner de Coninck brought an element of youth and gaiety to counter the pessimism of many of the more experienced missionaries; the more intellectual Rev. Guiton seemed 'a man of real worth' and 'someone we can count on completely'. Meanwhile, the sickly Louis Mabille was moved to a quieter station, while Christeller took his place in the parish of Morija.

But with the death of Robert Henry Dyke in July, the third generation of the mission, except for Dieterlen and Jacottet, was finally gone. For thirty years, Dyke had been 'one of those people we could always count on'; year after year, the Normal School had grown under his direction. Replacing him caused a minor predicament.

F.M. Reid had recently led the school extremely well while Dyke was on leave, but Jacottet did not think he had the calibre to reorganize the school as it needed; moreover, Reid was neither a French-speaker nor a missionary. Duby and Christeller were already placed in key positions. Baltzer was a possibility, but his two-year stint at Thaba-Bosiu had not been successful and he had made a poor name for himself amongst the locals. Guiton was regarded as too young and inexperienced by the majority, though he was supported by Jacottet as being 'no ordinary man'.

The obvious candidate was Jacottet himself. His seniority, his status and his capabilities were self-evident, the teaching staff would accept him, and the whole community, black and white, would approve. But he refused the position emphatically, and gave a number of reasons.

He was not sure that he had the 'special virtues' needed for the task, although he did feel he was still capable of adapting to it. He felt he was too old – one should not take on a new position at the age of fifty-five. The Theological School was also due to commence a new cycle in 1914 and he would be difficult to replace there. For long the School had been his favourite child, had been 'the very centre' of his life and work, and he was determined that it should not collapse. If he went elsewhere, he believed it would not last long. He was adamant that the Basotho pastorate should be strengthened and unflinching in his belief that the future of the Church of Basutoland lay in their hands.

Then there was the question of his leave.

He was irritated that he had already had to postpone his leave for two years to accommodate Sam Duby. So he was determined to take it in 1913 for the sake of his health. Furthermore, his wife would not countenance any delay. It is clear that Jacottet was worried about her. 'She is not doing too well, and between you and me,' he confided to Bianquis, 'I must say that her health is worrying me more and more. I do not think that I should ask her to accept a position where she would have to do too much (as she would never manage to come out of her shell, nor would she cope with her part of the work) and it would risk making her even more ill. At this stage, after all the sacrifices that she has made, the sorrows that she has had, I do not think I have the right to ask her to make this new sacrifice.'

These were the main reasons for declining the principalship. He also admitted to a personal passion: 'My special talents are driving me more and more towards dedicating my last years to the literature of Lesotho, to help Duby in this, who depends on me. I know that I can be of great service to him, more than anyone else. And I have observed for a long time now that the literature as it is today is probably the most useful and important part of our work.' By 'literature' he meant not merely imaginative or fictional work but the word in its widest sense, written matter in general.

At a special Conference held at Morija, Guiton, Jacottet's choice, was appointed to the post at the Normal School. Dieterlen's health meanwhile forced his resignation, and he went to minister to the lepers in their settlement at Botšabelo outside Maseru.

———⚬———

In France, baby Georges kept the Dubys confined to Valentigny. Sam spent much of the time perfecting and correcting the proofs of various Sesotho publications – a Bible dictionary, an edition of the New Testament, a pocket Bible – and writing commentaries on *Acts* and *Revelation*.

He did manage to fulfil a long-held dream and visited the Holy Land in April. He was now happier with the way Jacottet was running the Book Depot, but his peace of mind was disturbed by one scrap of news. Jacottet informed him that Letsie was terminally ill. That the King's brother Griffith was designated to succeed him was not a happy prospect. Sadly, thought Duby, the Protestant mission would not gain much from that change. 'Griffith seems to me,' he wrote to Bianquis, 'somewhat a creature of the Catholics, whom he favours by preference, and he is above all a drunkard whose health is affected by drink and immorality, which will not allow him to reign for long.' And he concluded: 'What a sad spectacle these Basotho chiefs are!'

As the time to return to Lesotho approached, the 'horrible question' of what to do with their two older children – that constant dilemma for missionary parents – worried the Dubys greatly. 'It is so abnormal to have to break up a family like this!' he complained. The possibility of his wife and he separating for a while was even considered. If satisfactory places could not be found for them, Eva might have to stay in Europe.

Eventually, however, some arrangements were cobbled together. Furthermore, it was decided that Sam's mother would accompany them to Lesotho and live with Théo and his family in a new house that was to be built for them.

The voyage home in December was a good one. Everyone, including old Mrs Duby, benefited from the open air. Georges began to walk on board ship and then complicated things by wanting to go everywhere.

The Dubys eventually arrived back in Morija on 21 December. One person who was extremely pleased to see them was Marcelle: she was in desperate need of a holiday and seemed to Sam to be 'at the end of her tether'. A new house was built below the Bible School for Théo Duby, and in its grounds was constructed what became known as the 'square rondavel'. Marcelle seems to have lived in it for the next few years. Its four corners, cut by four winds, suited her nature. She had a watchdog which she called Waldo, probably after a favourite character in Olive Schreiner's *The Story of an African Farm*.

—◦◦—

Letsie II died on 28 January 1913, in circumstances of 'mystery and unsavoury gossip'. In truth, he seems to have died in a Scotch cart after emerging blind drunk from a canteen in the Orange Free State. The House of Moshoeshoe had become the House of Atrophy. The succession was by no means cut and dried. One favoured candidate was an infant born of one of Letsie's more senior wives. His name was Tau – 'Lion'. But this whelp died a sudden and mysterious death soon after the King's burial. Griffith Lerotholi was offered the regency and the opportunity to raise seed – in accordance with the custom of levirate – for his deceased brother by his senior wives. Griffith rejected this as against his Catholic faith and asserted, in his famous statement, that he intended 'to sit on the throne with both buttocks'. He was eventually accepted as Morena e moholo in April.

Jacottet was in Bloemfontein when Letsie died, but managed to get back for the funeral. He was not unduly worried by Griffith's succession, since he felt that the new King needed the Protestants and would temper his antipathy: 'His Catholicism does not appear profound, I doubt that it will last for long. Twelve or thirteen years ago, he was Anglican, or baptized Anglican, which is the same thing. In any case, it has been said, and certainly been reflected in his attitude towards us as well, that his personal Catholicism will not have any influence on the way he is towards us; the official situation remains the same, we are "the mission of the tribe". Griffith is striving to make us see ourselves in this light. I admit that I would prefer it if he were not a Catholic, but, in truth, it has little importance. The general opinion is that it will not last.'

With or without substance, dark rumours went abroad that Griffith had had a hand in the premature death of Tau. Had he been poisoned? These rumours were to become significant a few years later when Jacottet died, and Griffith was once again, if only momentarily, suspect.

—◦⊖◦—

The trip to Europe on leave was weighing Jacottet down. If it were not that Claude must be taken to school, he might not have had the heart to go. Since he would no longer find much of his family left, and since his children were scattered in London (Henri), Zürich (Madeleine) and somewhere in Germany (Gustave), so that he would have little time to spend with each, he dreaded the prospect. 'Will I ever have a true pied-à-terre?' he asked rhetorically. 'I dare not even think about it. When one becomes a missionary, even if one stays in one mission, any sense of home is lost. One literally becomes a wanderer and traveller on the earth!'

He sailed from Cape Town on 5 March on the *Walmer Castle*, leaving Mrs Jacottet in Morija for the year he would be away. He took with him Claude, who was recovering from a bout of measles. His intentions were to go to Paris, then on to see the Hoffets, who were now ministering in Jarnac, near Cognac, north-east of Bordeaux, and after that to Switzerland. But first he spent a few days with his eldest son in London.

Fluent in French, German and English, Henri had chosen a career in language teaching. After spending three years at school in Alsace (1898–1901), he attended the Lycée Charlemagne in Paris until 1905 and then went to the Gymnase Classique of Lausanne. In 1908, he graduated with a 'Bachelier-ès-Lettres' in Classics at the University of Lausanne. After that he taught at the High School for Boys in Croydon, where the headmaster found him painstaking and persevering, agreeable and obliging. At the same time, he attended classes at Birkbeck College. When his father arrived, he was teaching at Hazelwood Girls' School in Acton, where the headmistress, in her turn, found him to be 'an excellent disciplinarian and a thorough and painstaking teacher'. He was on the point of resigning, however, in order to complete his BA degree at London University, where he had a reputation for having 'a real and refined literary taste'. After an initial hiccup when the examiners could not read his atrocious handwriting, he was to be awarded the degree later in the year with a first-class pass.

In the following months, Jacottet criss-crossed Europe from Scotland to Switzerland on numerous errands, lecturing in Paris and visiting the Aborigines Protection Society in London, as well as meeting old friends Sir Godfrey Lagden and Lord Bryce there.

His one respite was a few weeks in July and August at Grands Champs, near Couvet, where he was joined by Claude (who was doing well at school), Madeleine and Gustave. For once, he was with 'half a family'.

News from South Africa was grim: Prime Minister Botha's 'brutality' did not augur well for blacks or missionaries. So Jacottet's departure from Neuchâtel in February 1914 filled him with foreboding: 'Every time I have to leave my children it becomes more and more difficult. It is my greatest sacrifice … It has never been so difficult for me to leave before. Perhaps it is because I have the feeling that I shall never return!'

—◦◦—

Jacottet got back to Morija in early March 1914, four days before the Conference convened. He was immediately nobbled as the new President. As he himself said, 'No sooner had I returned than the burdens of Lesotho and its responsibilities fell once more on my shoulders. I feel so far away from Neuchâtel and from the time of rest that I had there, which did me the world of good.' One of his first acts in office was to reprimand the missionary Ramseyer for a series of anti-Catholic letters published in a magazine, which would not have pleased Griffith had he seen them.

Jacottet found his family well: 'My wife is doing better than I expected, although her health is still not that good. I was astonished by all that she had done during my absence. Never has our establishment been so well organized.' His daughters, Marcelle and Marguerite, were very happy to see him and were both well, though Marcelle's workload continued to be very heavy. 'So I'm back to my family and home,' he wrote, his contentment tinged with sadness, 'but I will always think back on those I left behind in Europe, my three sons and one of my daughters. My heart is always split between two continents.'

But there was also some progress. The journey from Maseru to Morija could now be done by motor car. Not only did it cut the time to a mere two hours, but it also allowed him to take all his personal luggage with him.

—◦◦—

In the months after his return, Jacottet was beset by all kinds of problems. The Basotho National Council put pressure on the mission to soften its stance on bohali (Jacottet saw Griffith's hand behind the manoeuvre). There was trouble at the Normal School, which was not helped by the prospect of Reid leaving to become a school inspector.

The good news that Alfred Casalis was to return in 1915, after nearly ten years' absence, was offset by the imminent departure of Baltzer for health reasons. This departure was precipitated when a scandal – almost certainly an adulterous one – burst around Baltzer's head. The details of his transgression are not clear, but Jacottet, as President, had to catch the fallout. His instinct was to support Bianquis in keeping the whole deplorable affair under wraps, on condition that the guilty party resigned immediately: 'The more I think about it, the more I realize that this horrible story must remain a secret.'

—⊸⊘—

The worry over the Baltzer scandal may have put undue pressure on Jacottet. The strain worsened a few days later, at the beginning of July, when Duby went down with appendicitis and had to hasten to London for a delicate operation.

Years of stress and overwork finally demanded their retribution.

On 9 July, Jacottet was struck down by a violent headache. This was followed by a feeling of nervous helplessness, from which he recovered only slowly. At the time, he himself feared that it was 'une congestion au cerveau' – a congestion of the brain. His brother, Dr Gustave Jacottet, said it was nothing, there was a problem with his circulation which sometimes affected his brain, and rest would cure it.

But Jacottet was not entirely convinced. Four days later, he wrote a short letter to Bianquis, which took him over half an hour to finish. It is likely that he had had a minor stroke.

As a consequence, Édouard and Louise went for three weeks' rest to the seaside at East London. While they were there, at the beginning of August, the world was overtaken by a crisis that seemed to match the storm in his own brain.

CHAPTER TWENTY-FOUR

THE COMING HOUR

1914–1918

T he outbreak of the Great War had immediate effects in Lesotho, surprising perhaps for a small country so far away from the main theatre. The younger missionaries – Guiton, Oechsner de Coninck and Georges Dieterlen – left within days for Europe to join up or serve their country in whatever way they could. Verdier (head of the Industrial School) was already in France, and the disgraced Baltzer also signed up for the army. Emile Vollet, whom Jacottet had helped through a spiritual crisis in earlier times, showed he was not lacking in courage, when he lied about his age, claiming to be younger than he was, in order to qualify for service (meanwhile, his son was claiming to be *older* for the same reason!). Alfred and Caroline Casalis, who were due to return to Lesotho, decided to stay on in France to help the war effort.

With Sam Duby still in London waiting for his appendix operation (it took place on 25 August), the mission was faced with a personnel crisis. Jacottet, as President of the Conference, hurried back from his convalescence in the eastern Cape, deeply distressed by 'this terrible war which could destroy everything'.

He had no doubt where his loyalties lay. Notwithstanding his family's sympathy for the Prussian monarchy, as a young boy he had suffered with France over the disaster of Sedan and had seen Alsace, Switzerland's neighbour and a stronghold of French Protestantism, torn from the arms of France. As a French-speaker, he had not enjoyed his university days in Germany, and German support for the Boers over the years had, he felt, harmed the cause of the Basotho, which he had long ago made his own. 'The only sentiment common to us all,' he said, within days of war being declared, 'is the desire that Germany will find the ruin that she deserves.'

As the executive of the Conference, Jacottet and Christeller immediately made the decisions necessary for manning the various mission posts. Inevitably, Jacottet had to take over the position he had so firmly resisted – the principalship of the Normal School, vacated by Reid in September the previous year. There was no one qualified to take over the Industrial School – which was saddled with a deficit of £700 as a result of the financial negligence of

Verdier – and so, with typical resourcefulness, it was 'manned' for a time by the wife of Georges Dieterlen.

Even more serious than the personnel problem was the financial one. With Paris soon threatened and the PEMS in understandable turmoil, the position was grave. The mission stopped the Society's bank account and refrained from drawing anything from Paris. Stringent cuts were made, and the number of scholars at the Normal School was reduced from seventy to twenty, thus eliminating the need for a matron. Fortunately, people rallied to the cause. Friends made substantial donations, and when Jacottet's brother went off to the front, Dr Long of Maseru volunteered his medical services to help the mission.

The very first days of the war, with the 'admirable defence of Belgium and the entry of the French into Alsace', brought encouraging news. Dieterlen, as befitted his nature, was pessimistic; Jacottet was optimistic. But the subsequent disasters in Belgium and Alsace, and the near-thing saving of Paris by General Gallieni (a name Jacottet knew so well from his connection with Madagascar) in the next few weeks caused Jacottet 'a continuous nightmare', only exacerbated by the paucity of information and the strictness of the British censors. Nevertheless, the news received via the cable linked Lesotho with immediacy to Europe, and helped make this a *world* war.

One brief life seemed like an omen of the destruction to come: the baby boy of Mrs Guiton, born two months before term, died within a few hours. Mrs Guiton, chronically unable to cope with missionary life, and even more so without her husband, withdrew into herself, prompting Jacottet's opinion that many of his colleagues might not return after the war and that the Basotho would see their departure as weakness in the mission. (Guiton, in fact, never did return – he died in the war in 1917.)

The new brutality of this war, the scale of its devastation, was first brought home to Jacottet with the ruin of the cathedral at Reims, which he regarded as 'a terrible disgrace for humanity', and he felt that Germany, demonstrating its savagery in this act, had 'lost all rights to human respect'. Conversely, he was proud of the 'truly admirable calm' which the French public had displayed in calamity, 'far from the attitude of 1870'. Even if the war 'must go on for months', he believed that Germany, 'the common enemy of mankind', awaited a crushing defeat.

What an extraordinary relief he felt, then, when he learned that the fall of Paris had been averted and the German armies had retreated beyond the Marne! In a burst of pride, he hastened out of his house and put up the French flag, to 'display it in broad daylight'. He fervently hoped that he would not have to take it down again, even though the prospect of a German rout soon faded.

Closer to home, Jacottet contemplated with relative equanimity the possibility that South Africa would have 'a little war of its own' with the invasion of German South West; in fact, he thought it would be 'a blessing to no longer have Germany as a neighbour in the future', though he did have some concern for the German missionaries in the Transvaal and some sympathy for the German farmers interned in concentration camps in the Cape.

The general madness seemed to spread even to the leper asylum set up at Botšabelo. Serious discontent broke out there, and every night the lepers, men and women, sang the song of war, until the police were forced to intervene when rioting erupted. Dieterlen, who had just moved there as minister, found himself in a difficult position and tried to interpose himself between the warring parties. Eventually nearly two hundred lepers upped and left, with no one able or willing to stop them. In a state of sheer nervousness, Dieterlen could not sleep and eventually fled to Morija. At least his return strengthened the mission ranks, however debilitated his health.

By the end of the year, Jacottet reflected the general frustration of all: 'The long battle of the Meuse discourages us so often. We want to hear news of a real, sound victory. Always hoping in vain, one ends up almost believing it will never happen. In spite of everything, I still believe that the war will end in victory. But when will it end? And what will remain standing when it does? I am not referring to Germany; after all that I've heard, I cannot help but hate it with all the strength of my being. Only now are people beginning to discover the extent of its barbarity and its brutality – you have only to open your eyes to realize that it has always been that way.' Hearing about casualties only made things worse. Boys of the Monod and Escande families (the latter having already given a martyr to Madagascar) died at the front, and Noël Christol, son of Frédéric Christol of the Basutoland mission, was reported killed.

As for his own battle with his health, Jacottet felt he had conquered and was on the mend, though it seems inevitable that a change in his personality must have occurred. One good thing did result from his suspected stroke. His handwriting, a spidery scrawl at the best of times, had become a penance. Now he complained of writer's cramp. To the delight of his correspondents, he took to using a typewriter.

—⚬—

For a while Jacottet ran both the Theological School and the Normal School simultaneously. It was too much for him, however, along with all his other responsibilities, and in May the former was closed for six months.

Even though the Jacottets moved temporarily into the principal's house of the Normal School so that he could more easily concentrate his efforts, he was not ideally suited to his new role, which he regarded as the least attractive on the mission, and circumstances conspired to make his tenure less than happy. In 1915, for instance, two disgruntled and mercenary teachers left the school, and then published calumnious accusations in a Free State journal, which fell mainly on Jacottet himself.

The running of the school was divided between a headmaster and a principal, the latter position normally reserved for an ordained missionary. Fortunately, by the middle of the year, the headmastership was occupied by the reliable Mr Johns, an import from England. Johns's wife was an older woman and an invalid, and Jacottet felt that she would be better than the younger wives, who were often discontented and sowed discord. The departure of the Oechsner de Coninck women and Mme Guiton, Jacottet regarded disdainfully as 'a stampede'. But overall he saw the financial position of the mission as nothing short of 'tragic'.

The principalship proved more difficult to fill. There were two candidates. Edwin Smith had suddenly become available. With his experience in central Africa, he was a favoured possibility. Charles Matthey, who had been in Madagascar, was the other. Jacottet was dubious about Matthey: he was from Neuchâtel and Jacottet knew the typical mentality of a teacher from his canton – pedantic, fussy, loath to adapt. The principal, in Jacottet's experience, required the gifts of leadership and a lofty mind, so that he was able to see all the problems of the School from on high and seize any opportunity to effect the changes so drastically needed. In Smith – 'a missionary of the first rank' – he saw these qualities. Sadly, the demands of his daughter's education in England ultimately prevented Smith from coming.

The problems were compounded at the beginning of 1915 by the untimely death (from acute appendicitis) of Nicolas Mpiti, the tireless minister of the key Maseru parish. While not having the religious worth or originality of a Sekhesa, Mpiti, who had been in the second group of theological students and completed his studies in 1896, had had practical talents which made him indispensable in the mission's relations with many of the chiefs, and, at the same time, acceptable for morning tea at the Resident Commissioner's. He had been, in other words, a master of the delicate and difficult intricacies and intrigues of Maseru. Now Jacottet had to spend a lot of his time in the capital filling in the gap and performing many of the parish functions, until Edward Motsamai was moved into the post.

Jacottet's burden often seemed heavier than that of Bunyan's Christian, without any hope of the promised progress. Repeatedly, he warned Bianquis that he would not be able to carry the Normal School beyond the end of the year. Often he complained that his head was 'very tired'. When he looked around, there was little consolation: the corps of missionaries was aged and its ranks thinning; Bertschy was ill; the Book Depot had become 'a prison' for Duby as he became more and more absorbed in it, so that he could not give the youthful leadership the mission so desperately needed; and, although Louise's health was holding up for the moment, not only did she have to perform some of the matronly functions at the Normal School, she had also assumed responsibility for three young teachers who now boarded in the Jacottet household – almost certainly the reason why Marcelle moved into the square rondavel in the grounds of Théo Duby's house down the hill. The best that could be said was that his two daughters – Marcelle and Marguerite – kept their health, and a further vacation in East London restored some of his own vigour.

In May, Jacottet's woes worsened. Dieterlen by chance came to visit and found that the students of the Normal School, stirred up against Jacottet, were on the point of open mutiny. That night several stones were thrown on to the roof of the house. It was Dieterlen's opinion that the students were in the wrong, and their actions could easily have led to their expulsion and the closure of the school. Their prime grievance probably concerned material shortages, but the temper and temperament of the temporary principal, not really suited for the task, could not have helped. (In Jacottet's defence, it should be recorded that he was the only missionary who allowed soccer to be played on Sundays!) Within a couple of days, the simmering rebellion was over, although the odd stone continued to come down from the heavens.

Although by the second half of the year things were going well at the Normal School and some good teachers had been employed, it did seem to Jacottet like 'the calm before the storm'. He knew that if the Theological School did not reopen there would be a major crisis, with no new recruits joining the ministry, and therefore fewer Basotho pastors to replace the dwindling numbers of whites.

In the light of what was to happen later, there is one telling interlude from this period. Even though Jacottet was desperate for young, fresh recruits to reinforce the mission, he made an exception in the case of David Lescoute, an artisan-missionary. If Lescoute had come to Lesotho, he would have been posted to Berea, where the church needed rebuilding. However, there was a simple fact which made it seem preferable that he be discouraged from coming: he and his wife had just had a child – but not just any child. Having conferred with the Conference executive, Jacottet wrote to Bianquis: 'Madame Lescoute being, as you know, *une femme de couleur*, her children will never be admitted into the European schools (that is the Liberalism of this country!). And the child would find itself constantly in a terrible position, too European to be taken into the ranks of the natives, but always unable to be accepted as a white.' In the opinion of all, in his interest and that of his family, Lescoute 'would do better to remain in France, where his child would have the same rights as everyone else'. Jacottet was critical but realistic about the society he lived in.

When he cast his eyes further afield, he saw no ray of light either. With the war on the Western Front now a stalemate of trenches and barbed wire, it had become apparent to the Allies that they must launch an offensive, which would also take some pressure off the Russians on the Eastern Front. But, by May, the British attacks at Neuve Chapelle and at Aubers Ridge, and the French assault on Vimy Ridge, known as the Second Battle of Artois, ended in huge loss and no gain. The landings at Gallipoli were a complete disaster; the sinking of the *Lusitania* emphasized the hidden depths of the German threat.

If only there was the possibility of a decisive victory! But even the entry of the Italians into the war on the Allies' side was scant consolation and made little difference to the fortunes of the war. 'May God guide all and give to the Allies the necessary patience,' Jacottet prayed. 'What strikes me is the endurance and composure of France in the midst of this torment. If ever a people deserved to triumph it is surely hers. She will emerge reborn but, alas, at what price!' He also feared for his native land. What effect would the war have on Switzerland? Would it join in the fighting? And on whose side? He wondered, too, if *any* part of the world would escape.

The war, he was coming to realize, 'is as sad as it is long'. He was angry that the report of the death of Noël Christol was false – he had in fact been taken prisoner. How could people be so crass as to announce the death without substantial evidence or confirmation? This was not the only case of its kind. Rumour exacted a heavy price.

So when the news came that Alfred Eugène Casalis fils was missing, Jacottet's letter to his old friends Alfred and Caroline about their son was a model of tact and caution.

—◦○◦—

Freddy Casalis had been born at Morija in February 1896. Fifteen months younger than Madeleine Jacottet and a few years older than Claude and Marguerite, he had had a happy childhood playing with them and the other children of the mission, until he left with his parents at the age of ten.

But that contentedness had stayed with him, and, combined with the deep piety of his parents, made him sure from an early age that he would become a missionary, like his father and his grandfather. So his classical studies led him to the Protestant Faculty of Theology at Montauban. He was in his second year there when the war broke out.

Almost immediately, contrary to his nature and to his pacifist and idealist

beliefs, he volunteered: 'I am a soldier,' he asserted, 'of my own free will.'
Contrary almost to his vocation, he nevertheless felt that he had been 'called'.

It is an indication of the chaotic state of the French army that he was issued
with a filthy uniform, and a greatcoat gaping at the seams and with a huge hole
in the back, the work either of a bursting shell or a burning cigar.

He entered the army in the first week of 1915. Within two months, he had
reacted to his typhoid inoculation with a terrific abscess, and had gone down
with measles, with bronchitis, and with a dubious case of mumps. Nevertheless,
he was reassuring: 'My dear little mother,' he wrote to Caroline Casalis, 'don't,
I beseech you, be worried about me.'

Not yet nineteen, he could reassure his parents – in a series of letters to
them – that he and his peers had 'a common will to deliver humanity from war'
and that their watchword was 'Christ and France'. He often used the word
'devoir' in the weightier French sense of a higher calling, and sometimes
dreamed of 'the France that is to be'. And he was ready to open his eyes to
Death, learning 'to live with It always at our elbow, so that Its coming shall not
take us by surprise'. Indeed, It might be 'the honoured guest' who would lead
him into 'Life'.

Military life simplified everything. It changed him: he made intellectual
sacrifices, abandoning his instinctive dry, scholastic aloofness, his hair-splitting
quibbles about words, and was forced into points of intellectual contact with
simple peasants – his companions in his company – who had 'never heard tell
of Idealism, or Spirit, or Matter'. He came to love his comrades, finding riches
in the depths of their souls, and learned to accept – without a pang – things he
thought he never would: 'All of us now know we are *on active service*. And our
service is sacred.'

Freddy and his fellows were taught how to make single entrenchments and
how to attack in skirmishing order. At a word, they would fling themselves to
the ground with their packs in front of them for cover. The even numbers
would start firing while the odd numbers, still prostrate, would hollow out a
trench, deeper at the head than at the feet, piling the loose earth up in front of
them as a screen. Once this was big enough to hide a man lying down, the roles
would be reversed between those firing and those digging. Speed was essential,
not easy when they were lying flat on their faces. They learned, too, to move
with packs weighing some twenty-four kilograms.

His greatest desire was to receive communion at Easter. This he did. 'I think
I am ready to go,' he wrote, 'I mean, morally speaking.' Within days, his unit
was moved close to the front near Verdun.

He did not fear Death: 'I believe the dead live close to the living, invisible
but present.' Moreover, his forebears, the Huguenot martyrs, had not been

afraid to die. For those left behind, he added, the struggle was no less real and they must pray – for prayer was a conflict and a combat.

Before he left for the front, he was buoyed up by a meeting with an old friend from Basutoland, Roby Dieterlen, also on military duty away from his mission in Barotseland, and recovering from a wound.

Freddy, now nineteen, did not see action himself at Verdun, but it rained, it snowed, it froze, and he heard the distant cannon and saw the results on all sides in villages burned and destroyed. Up above Heippes-sur-Meuse, not far south of Verdun, he climbed a hill which the Germans had occupied, and where the fighting had been fierce. On the summit there was a multitude of graves – three thousand men, it was said, sacrificed like animals on the mountain. On the principal mound stood a tall cross of carved wood with numerous inscriptions; on another large cross of white wood there was a wreath with the words, 'In Memory of Roger Couve'. He did not need to say it, but Couve was another well-known Protestant missionary name.

Yet, in the midst of slaughter, the countryside was beautiful. He would some-times find himself whistling Grieg's 'Le Matin', and sometimes, when not on cantonnement d'alerte, he and his friends could stretch out in the sun, or doze in the shade of some plum trees just in bud, or the philosophers amongst them could fish in the nearby brook. Once, on a route march, they entered a wood where they rested. Amongst the debris of hard fighting, Freddy picked some periwinkles and anemones which he sent to his parents: 'The periwinkles made me think of Morija,' he told them. 'You remember the shady walk leading from the terrace of the Mabilles' house to the little gate under the eucalyptus trees!'

Then, towards the end of April, his battalion was moved across country in cattle trucks. The train skirted the edge of Paris and Freddy caught sight of the Eiffel Tower, so close to his parents' home. After twenty-four hours they arrived in the vicinity of Arras, to the north of the Somme, to the south of Souchez.

On the first day of spring, Freddy had his 'baptism of fire'. During the night the artillery had begun their 'grande valse', and, in the morning, 105 mm shells began to land nearby like great pots crashing to the floor. After a while the 'Jack Johnsons' came in volleys, 'falling like the swing of a scythe', so that all the men would cower down in a 'carapace generale', creating one kind of shell as pro-tection against another.

Next day, 2 May, Freddy found himself for the first time in the 'famous trenches'. He was struck most by the diversity of sounds: the dry, sharp, vibrant detonations of the German guns; the deeper, fuller booming of the French; the cannon, the Maxims, the mortars; the shells passing and exploding; the smack of bullet on metal; the rockets; the aeroplanes; and, in the corn fields between the opposing lines, the larks singing as if nothing else were going on.

He was stationed in the ruined village of Roclincourt (directly east of Arras), sharing his straw with the rats that swarmed there. Within a couple of days, he no longer paid any heed to the artillery duel overhead. He was changed. The abstract being that had been him was falling away bit by bit. As they risked their lives every moment, the men around him showed themselves as they were, everything artificial dropping away, only the essential remaining. Bragging neither of their goodness nor their badness. 'I am learning to *live*,' Freddy exclaimed.

The British were preparing their attack on Aubers Ridge. It was scheduled for 9 May. The day before, Freddy knew that the big attack was imminent and that the French would provide support at various places along the line before their own main offensive on Souchez and Vimy Ridge a week later. The artillery bombardment was incessant. The bombs whizzed through the air, just above the trenches, with great heart-rending sobs, exploding further off with dry crashes so that everything flew to pieces – earth, wood, iron – spitting out splinters in all directions. 'We must mount the breach at the bayonet's point,' he told his parents.

At ten o'clock precisely, on the 9th, the battalion at Roclincourt went over the top. Freddy Casalis ran side by side with his lieutenant: two or three times the bayonet charge went in, but without success. The bullets that greeted them, drawing no distinction between good and bad, mowed the men down.

Three days later, Freddy's outstanding and popular commanding officer, Major Charles Schmuckel, reported him – 'this modest boy with his kindness, his calm and quiet courage, his intellectual and moral value' – missing. Schmuckel, who himself had only three days left to live, gave Freddy's parents 'a gleam of hope' that their son had been taken prisoner.

It was not to be. Alfred Eugène Casalis was found in a common grave hollowed out on the battlefield close to where he fell. Four months after joining the army, he was dead. He had made the final sacrifice.

An unfinished letter was found in his greatcoat. He had been waiting for this moment of trial from the day he enlisted: 'Since that day, my life has been one tense and anxious watching for the Coming Hour.' The last words that he wrote were: 'The attack cannot but succeed. There will be killed and wounded, but we shall go forward and go far …'

—❦—

His death meant that Alfred and Caroline Casalis would not be returning to Lesotho while the war continued. They could not leave their two sons – Freddy buried in Artois and André still fighting in the army.

His death, together with that of his friend Roby Dieterlen (at Artois in September 1915) and his brother André (at Mesnil in 1918) and many others, deprived the girls of Morija – Madeleine, Marguerite, even Marcelle – of the young men they might reasonably have expected to marry.

His death touched the hearts of Édouard and Louise Jacottet with an icy hand and made them even more anxious for their eldest son.

—❦—

At the beginning of the war, Henri Jacottet was teaching at Battersea Polytechnic, which he had joined in January. When the old professional army, the backbone of the British Expeditionary Force, died at First Ypres, the country had to turn to its citizens for its 'New Armies'. In autumn 1915, Henri volunteered for active duty, something he was proud of – he had not waited for the conscription which was introduced in January 1916. Nevertheless, he stayed on teaching at the Polytechnic until the summer of 1916, when he underwent his training at Douvres in France.

In September, he went to join his unit – the 1st Battalion of the Royal Fusiliers, 17th Brigade, 24th Division – on the Somme. This was the year in which the greatest battles of attrition on the Western Front had begun. In 1915, the French commander, Joffre, equated his strategy to 'grignotage', or 'nibbling away' at the enemy – otherwise translated as 'trying to bite through a steel door with badly-fitting false teeth'. But the new year brought, inconceivably, an escalation of death, which Georges Duhamel, a doctor at the front, described as like having a mad dog in the house. Falkenhayn, the Chief of the German General Staff, knew that the fortress of Verdun was such a symbol of French pride that they would never surrender it; he therefore set about attacking it, aiming to suck the French army into its defence, so that, in his famous words, 'the forces of France would bleed to death'. His offensive began in February 1916, and, along with the French counter-offensive, lasted the rest of the year, leeching the blood of Frenchmen and Germans alike.

Joffre pressured his counterpart in the British army, Douglas Haig, to hasten an offensive in his sector in order to lighten the task of the French. On 1 July, a combined British and French attack began on the Somme. Within an hour, thirty thousand British men were dead or wounded, and by the day's end this figure had doubled (one third of them dead). They were fighting over a patch of ground hardly large enough to bury them in. The campaign lasted through to November.

Henri arrived in mid-September, but was not involved in this campaign. Fortunately for him, his battalion had just pulled out from Montauban, in the front line, through Dernancourt to Buire-sur-l'Ancre, where it entrained for Bessus for much-needed rest and retraining. The weather was fine, the country-side around was cultivated not devastated, and the local people were friendly.

The peacefulness was in contrast to the mayhem which had erupted a little to the east, where for the first time ever tanks were being used in battle, a development described by a German prisoner as 'not war but bloody butchery'.

Within a few days of Henri's arrival, the battalion was moved north to Artois and positioned in the front line facing Vimy Ridge, east of Souchez, a town marked indelibly in French consciousness, where many of its sons, including Freddy Casalis, had been slaughtered in May and June 1915.

There, Henri had his first taste of the trenches. For the next few months he learned about the enemy's artillery and 'pineapples', and to take cover when a sentry's whistle announced the coming of the 'minnies'. He shared his clothes with his personal lice and his trenches with rats the size of rabbits. He learned about gas and saw the human condition sardonically encrusted on the chemical. He learned about mud and he saw death every day, even though, at this time, he was in a relatively quiet sector. Even on Christmas Day, under sunny skies, three of his battalion were wounded.

Henri was trained as a Lewis gunner – he was very proud of this – and spent much of the winter getting used to the light machine gun, with its circular drum of forty-seven bullets firing at 550 rounds per minute. But it meant that, in addition to the thirty kilograms of equipment each pilgrim carried into the front line, his burden was often increased with extra ammunition or other accoutrements.

Faced with a certain fate and the muddy desert the men called 'porridge', callousness crept in. Bones of the dead would sometimes protrude from the walls of the trenches and would be used as pegs for haversacks – you had to hang them somewhere, said Henri, as if it were a picnic. Many men, like Roby Dieterlen, were blown to pieces and were never found, so where were the flesh and bones to have life breathed into them? Even when the bones were gathered into great ossuaries, as they were at Verdun, who was there to breathe life into them?

Fresh troops were often brought up to the front line one way; the wounded, blinded by poison gas or shrapnel or horror, brought back another. Sometimes, from these blind trenches, Henri would have to emerge like a mole in the night to patrol that deadly zone between the lines, checking for gaps in the barbed wire or any suspicious signs of enemy activity.

In the dark, in No-Man's-Land, you would move only with fear. Once, Henri lost his way. He did not know which side was which. The great silence threatened to swallow him. Darkness. Silence. Out of the darkness, out of the silence, there came a whistle. He peered ahead. He was a few steps from a German blockhouse. The sentry was whistling like a madman or a fool.

—∞—

One evening in Morija, at almost exactly this time, Hermania Sekhesa (the mother of Bethuel) was preparing little Georges Duby for bed. She often told him a story. She had a great store of them. There were plenty about animals like the clever little hare; there was the one about a woman who had such a thirst she drank all the water in the world; and there was the tale of the child with a moon on his breast.

But tonight Georges wanted his favourite, which he never tired of hearing. It seemed to be a story within a greater story. So she told it to him once again. In Sesotho, as usual, and in her inimitable style.

There appeared a huge animal called Kholumolumo. It ate the people, the whole nation. It went on eating the people, swallowing them whole; it swallowed the cattle too, and the dogs and the fowls. It is said that there was a woman in child sitting on the refuse heap; she smeared herself with ashes. Then she left the refuse heap and went into a calves' kraal. Now when the animal had eaten the people and finished them, it was still looking about, and came to look in that kraal. There it found that woman, but it thought she was a stone, as she smelt like ashes.

Then after a time it went away, having finished all the people; it went on and arrived at a mountain pass. It could not go through that pass as it had eaten too much.

Now that woman stayed alone, and she gave birth to a child. She went out and went to the kraal to get dry dung. The child was a boy. When she came back she found that a full-grown man was sitting there, having his clothes on, and his spears. The woman said: Hallo man! Where is my child? He answered: It is I, mother. His mother said: Why! my child, I did not know you. He said: And now, where are the people gone? His mother said: They have been eaten by Kholumolumo. – And the cattle? – Also. – And the dogs? – Also. – And the fowls? – Also. – Where is it? She said: Come out and see, my child.

Now the child went out and stood on that kraal; the mother also climbed on it. She pointed out to him, saying: Do you see yonder in the pass? The child said: I see, mother. She said: That object which is filling the pass, as big as a mountain, that is Kholumolumo. He went back into the stable, took his spears and said: I am going now to see that animal. His mother cried and took him by the hand, saying: My child, do not go to that animal, it will swallow you as it has swallowed all the nation. – No, mother, you will see.

He went, came to a flat stone, and sharpened his spears. He left there and went on. Now when the animal saw him, it opened its mouth to swallow him. He went alongside it. Now as it was unable to rise, he went round and arrived behind it, while it was still opening its mouth. He took a spear and stabbed it; he took another and stabbed it. It lay down and died.

Then he took his knife. A man cried: Do not cut me. He left and began at another place; a cow made: Muu! He left and began at another place; a dog barked: Koee! He left and began at another place. Kokolokoloo! cried a hen. This time he persisted and opened the belly of that animal. All the people came out of it, also the cattle.

They went back to their villages saying: This boy is now our chief. Now this boy was living with those men. After a while they hated him; they made a plan to kill him. All the nation were hating him. They planned, saying: Let us take hold of him, kindle a big fire in the public court, and throw him into it. When he came they said to him: Chief, come and sit down here. He said: No, I sit down here. He sat down. They looked at each other, those men. When they tried to seize him, he escaped them, and they took another man, and threw him into the fire. As for him, he was standing there, and said: What are you doing to that man?

Now they said: What shall we do? They dug a hole. When they had dug that hole they put straw over it, and over the straw they placed an old mat. When he came, they said: Chief, come and sit down here; chief, come and sit down here. He came; the seat of the chief was there; he sat down there. He sat down, that young boy. They were expecting to see him fall down, but he did not fall down.

They said: What can be done? They said: We must throw him down a precipice. So on a certain day they planned to throw him down a precipice. They had made a plan, and said: Come and see what is at the bottom; let the chief also come and see. He went in front of them. They said: This time we will throw him down. They arrived at the precipice; as they tried to push him he escaped them, and they threw down another man. He said: Why do you throw that man down? They said: Pe! Now they were sad. He went down to that man, took hold of him and made him stand up.

They said: What must be done? He was going round all the villages, but all the villages had made a plan to kill him. After he had made a tour of the villages, he arrived at the last village. They said: It is right. They made a plan; they decided to have a big hunt. At the place where they were going to sleep, they said that he should sleep at the back part of the cave. Then they gathered, they gathered, they gathered much wood, there was much of it.

When he was asleep, they heaped the wood on both sides; leaving no space open. Then they kindled it. He said to them: What a big fire you have made! Now they were glad and said: Today we have worsted him. He rose and said: What a big fire you have made! They laughed and said: Today he is lost. He rose, went out and stood in their midst. They seized him. He did it purposely. They killed him. It is said that his heart went out and escaped, and became a bird.

When she had finished, Hermania was quiet for a while. Time was of no concern to her. She always laughed at the missionaries' obsession with the clock and the calendar. Like many of the Basotho it was space that made her anxious to the point of fear. The night especially preyed on her fears and terrorized her. It was not indifferent: it was malign.

Now Hermania did something she had not done before. She took Georges by the hand and guided him to the window. He was puzzled. It was a dark night and he could see very little outside. 'Ssh!' she said. 'Listen.' Georges could hear nothing.

Then he did hear something. It was a voice a long way off, on top of a hill, calling. Then he heard another voice further off, picking up the message and sending it on. Echo mail. Like a chorus. All the way to Matsieng, and the Mountain at Night, and beyond.

Georges did not know what was being said on this occasion, but now that he was aware, he knew he would be alive to the sound in the future.

—◦◦—

When 1916 began, Eva Duby was ill; in fact, she had been ill for some time. Jacottet was still running the Normal School, with resentfully gritted teeth.

At the Conference in April, he was relieved of this duty and Matthey was appointed principal for two years. Jacottet was freely to admit that his judgements were wrong: he had earlier mistakenly thought the intellectual Guiton was right for the job; he initially thought Matthey was wrong for it, only to change his mind at a later stage.

He did not escape being elected President for a third successive term, however. He was now as old as Mabille had been when that stalwart died under the crushing load of his work. Jacottet felt his age, often complaining of his tiredness. A six-week holiday at Lourenço Marques with Marguerite in July and August brought only temporary relief from a heavy winter, a winter that had done for old Mrs Duby, Sam's mother. At Lourenço Marques, Jacottet became friendly with a missionary called Paillard.

He got on well with the new Resident Commissioner, Robert Coryndon, and counted it a great honour to be invited, as the only outsider, to lunch at the Residency when the High Commissioner, Lord Buxton, visited Basutoland. He noted with satisfaction that the Catholics seemed to have been snubbed, perhaps because of their intrigues involving Griffith, perhaps because a number of the priests were German.

Like everyone else, the Jacottets always looked for the post with anxiety. Although the cable and newspapers gave fairly immediate news of the progress of the war, they now had the personal worry of Henri in the firing line. Letters were agonizingly slow and out of date by the time they arrived, and Henri was by no means as diligent a correspondent as Freddy Casalis had been. As the struggle at Verdun intensified, they awaited the arrival of each post with apprehension.

Then, towards the end of the year, the mission was confronted with a situation which Jacottet and his colleagues had never considered before. The imperial government requested South Africa to send up to ten thousand blacks to work as labourers in the French ports, thus releasing more soldiers for the front. Basutoland was expected to supply one or two thousand. Jacottet was not averse to this, but he was disappointed that no chaplain from the PEMS was chosen as one of those to accompany the Basotho (though Ernest Mabille did go with them).

The letters of Freddy Casalis had been collected into a slight volume and published as *A Young Soldier of France and of Jesus Christ*. His father sent six copies to Sam Duby, who gave one to Z.D. Mangoaela, the assistant who had succeeded Thomas Mofolo, and distributed others amongst his helpers and printers. The book, he reported, 'did them much good' and moved them deeply. Nevertheless, recruitment amongst the Basotho was very slow. Jacottet attributed this to internal politics and to the people's fear of the sea.

Eva Duby was still unwell, and this weighed heavily on her husband. He feared that her sciatica might immobilize her leg completely. For the Dubys, it had been a long, difficult year.

The beginning of 1917 was marked by the usual Allied setbacks. The Germans launched their unrestricted U-boat offensive with spectacular results; the disastrous campaign in Champagne by the new French commander, Nivelle, led to his quick dismissal; fifty-four mutinous French divisions refused to go to the front after Nivelle's folly and agreed only to defensive fighting (the new commander Pétain had a difficult job restoring confidence in the army). The only real hope was the entry, in April, of the Americans into the war, though the benefits would not be tangible for a long time; the only real early success was the capture of Vimy Ridge by the Canadians (Henri's battalion helped to hold the left flank of the thrust). Henri had been in hospital at Étaples earlier in the year, but had rejoined his unit by then.

The French paralysis gave Haig his chance to switch his attention from the Somme to Flanders, which was his long-preferred zone for attack. Consequently, from the trenches before Loos, at the end of April, the 1st Battalion of the Royal Fusiliers was marched away to Bethune, and then transferred to Brandhoek, directly to the west of Ypres. There it spent most of May.

Before the eventual assault could be made on Passchendaele, Messines Ridge – to the south-east of Ypres – had to be taken. Twenty tunnels were dug under the German positions, and early on 7 June huge mines were exploded in each tunnel.

For days beforehand, the 1st Battalion trained for its role in the attack. It was not part of the initial push, but, attached as it was to the 24th Division, was in reserve behind the 41st Division, whose objective was to take Ravine Wood beyond St Eloi. To great joy, the town of Messines was taken in the first wave.

The battalion reached its own assembly point on the Voormezele road by 12.30 a.m. At zero hour, 3.10 a.m., the men heard the mines blow in front of them at St Eloi, at Wycheate beyond, and Hill 60 to their left.

Apprehensive, but chafing at the bit, the battalion received orders to move forward forty-five minutes behind schedule, at 12.15 p.m. Because they were late, they had to hurry to reach Damme Strasse, where they re-formed and corrected distances. Five derelict tanks were stranded there, 'like huge tortoises floundering in the mud'. The day was sweltering, with not a breath of breeze.

The assaulting companies moved forward from Damme Strasse in artillery formation, followed by the supporting companies. Then the leading companies advanced in extended order at intervals of four paces. They kept close behind the friendly barrage of artillery fire in front of them, and discovered most of the enemy wire had been cut by the Allied bombardment.

They continued to move forward in perfect order 'as if on drill attack', finding what little opposition they encountered greatly demoralized. D Company rushed a strongpoint and captured two machine guns and twenty-five prisoners, though their captain was cut down only one hundred metres short of their objective, which was Odyssey trench. Beyond this, stronger opposition was encountered, and Henri saw two officers, displaying the utmost gallantry, killed. He also saw the tireless padre doing fine work amongst the wounded, and the medic perform an amputation, unfazed by this being his first experience under fire. Heavy shelling and machine-gun fire swept the ground covered by the battalion, making communication difficult.

By 4.30 p.m. all the companies reported their objectives secured. Messines was described as 'the most brilliant and perfect battle of the whole war', yet its cost in lives was just as high. From a fighting strength of 27 officers and 805 other ranks, Henri's battalion alone had 189 casualties, of whom 30 were killed and 14 missing.

Bodies were not the only casualties of the war: ideas died too. Somewhere along the blind trench of his own war, Henri mutinied against his past religion and lost his faith, though not the continuity of his personality. The communism he subsequently espoused retained all the strict habits of his hidden puritanism, his atheism not far removed from the stern face of his father's God.

—◦◦—

Henri was not the only one in the family to doubt the rock of inherited faith. If her eldest brother had encountered a mudslide, Madeleine stepped on to shifting sand at the very least.

She had come to Europe – probably England – in 1908, when she was fourteen. She was on the point of returning to Lesotho in 1914 when the war broke out and she found herself stranded in London. She was lucky, however, to get a job as second French mistress at The Lodge, a high-class finishing school for young ladies run by Miss Mary Ellen Mason at Banstead along the Brighton Road.

The anglicization of Madeleine extended to her determination to be confirmed in the Anglican Church towards the end of 1917, and she wrote to her parents saying that she found there the satisfaction she did not find in any other church. This took the Jacottets by surprise, and her father's response was most interesting.

Although he was unsure that she had thought the thing through sufficiently, and although he and his wife were hurt by it, he insisted that he did not want to influence her decision. In these affairs of faith, he added, everyone must decide for themselves before God, and she must look to her own soul for guidance. 'I would prefer you to be a good Christian in another church than a less good Christian in ours,' he assured her. All he asked was that nothing be said or done that could be interpreted as placing blame on the church of her father, and that, in moving to Anglicanism, she 'search for the evangelical rather than the ritualistic side of this church'. In giving her his authorization, 'in so far as you need my authorization', he tempered his obvious disappointment by reminding himself and her that relatives on his mother's side were Anglican clergy, even bishops.

He was a bit more tart when he discovered that she had gone ahead anyway and had been confirmed before receiving the reply of her parents. Nevertheless, he continued to reiterate that the heart and conscience must decide in these affairs, and that the rapport between them would not change unless she had taken on board High Church ideas, which he deplored and which might prevent her from rejoining her family's faith. (In later years, Madeleine went the whole hog and converted to Catholicism!)

Marguerite's religion was less of a concern. She always professed to be heartbroken when she had to return to school in Bloemfontein – almost without exception, the girls of the mission preferred the freedom of station life to the strict discipline of the schools – but Jacottet thought that she had more interests and less monotony at school. In addition, her faith seemed fierce – the school magazine published an extract of a play called *Conscience*, which she either wrote or translated, on the massacre of St Bartholomew. The gist of it was the innate strength of the conscience and its inescapability.

—◦◦—

Although he had at last managed to unshackle himself from the Presidency, and the Theological School had a large new intake, Jacottet was still pessimistic about the future: the ageing corps of missionaries continued to worry him; Louise, chronically ill for many years, had a weakened heart and fretted constantly over her eldest son; a son of Resident Commissioner Sloley, a son of Boegner, a son of Mrs Jacot were dead or missing.

The tensions in Switzerland also distressed Jacottet. He felt the chasm between the German- and French-speaking sides widening and feared that the short-sighted policies being pursued would not only draw the country into war but also, even worse, into the orbit of the Central Powers. This seemed to him to be 'almost high treason'.

His pride in the Basotho was also shaken. Equivocating and dissembling for so long, the chiefs had, in his view, deceived the government with false promises. Now the mask was lifted: the chiefs refused to raise the thousands of men requested for the Native Labour Contingent, and barely a hundred Basotho joined.

He could find no single clear cause for the debacle. He felt that the government had been too slow in speaking strongly in favour; and he believed that if the chiefs had pushed for it, recruitment would have been as certain 'as a letter in the post'. Furthermore, the Boers, under the 'miserable' Hertzog, were spreading rumours not only that Germany would be victorious, but that the labour contingent was a British plot to lure away the able-bodied Basotho men, so that the country could be seized behind their backs. Finally, there was 'a huge suspicion' that the Catholics, with their supposed German sympathies, had unholy influence and could do whatever they wanted with 'the unhappy Griffith', whom Jacottet regarded in any case as 'a being without will power and without intelligence'.

Jacottet had an even deeper concern. He knew that the government in Maseru was indignant. In his opinion, the chiefs, by refusing to cooperate, had signed their abdication: 'I cannot prevent myself from believing that it is the suicide of the tribe.' Once more, a monster that haunted his sleep was beginning to stir – the threat of Lesotho being swallowed by the Union. 'Now when the Union wants to take Lesotho, no one will stand up to oppose it,' he warned.

He could scarcely believe that the Basotho, always so politically acute, had refused to listen. He had misjudged the younger generation entirely. Although a score of the few recruits who did go were from Morija (and some of them were scholars of the Normal School), he considered that 'it is a humiliation for me that Lesotho has in this way refused to do its duty'.

Jacottet was tired and he was getting old. He was a proud man, but the war had left even him disillusioned with some of the things he loved. 'Switzerland and Lesotho, my two countries!' he cried in despair.

Above all, he was concerned for Henri. Only peace would bring peace of mind, and at the beginning of 1918 Jacottet could not see it coming: he feared that the unhappy Allied soldiers must suffer a fifth winter in the trenches. Madeleine's letters were a lifeline: she was closer to Henri, still dilatory with his correspondence, and could give them snippets of extra information about him.

Life in Lesotho, on the other hand, was mundane. Only the daily domestic worries intruded. Marcelle and Marguerite were well. The summer was not too hot. The orchard yielded more peaches, apricots, nectarines, plums and apples than the family could handle. All they could do was pick them and give them to whoever asked. The smaller fruits only Marguerite picked with diligence. Though she groaned at the task, she would not allow anyone else to do it. She looked on them almost as her personal property.

—∞—

On 19 October 1917, Private Henri Jacottet, having now joined the 13th Battalion of the Royal Fusiliers, was back in Ypres. He was lucky enough to arrive too late to participate in the massacre at Passchendaele. After a winter of mud and ice and cold, he found himself, in March 1918, on the infamous Menin Road beyond Clapham Junction, and towards Gheluvelt, when the whole line was attacked. His dugout became his hovel and his home, a fragile refuge from the surrounding world blasted by man-made storms. The Germans entered the trenches of the battalion alongside, but in the end the line held – though No. 3 Company of his own battalion lost all its officers and a good proportion of its men.

Then, on 21 March, came General Ludendorff's great offensive – codenamed 'Michael' after the patron saint of Germany – which hit the British at the old Somme battlefield on a ninety-kilometre front with sixty-five divisions. The British Fifth Army in the south reeled back, leaving the right flank of the Third Army to the north dangerously exposed. Hermies, Bapaume, Flers, Thiepval, Albert – all in Allied hands since the Germans had retreated to the Hindenburg Line in 1917 – fell within a few days. Even Paris, only one hundred kilometres away, was bombarded with long-range artillery. The situation was critical and reserves were rushed in from wherever they could be found.

On 26 March, the 13th Battalion of the Royal Fusiliers were bathing and cleaning up at Manawatu Camp near Ypres when they got orders to ready themselves. Next day they entrained for the south, and on the 30th settled into their billets at Rossignol Farm between Gommecourt and Bucquoy in the northern part of the Somme sector. On April Fool's Day, the Germans rushed the bombing posts held by the battalion, which repulsed them with some difficulty, and then friendly howitzers cleared the enemy from the trenches.

Three days later, the battalion found itself in the front line touching the south edge of Bucquoy when German aeroplanes dropped bombs on the village and the two forward companies were subjected to a heavy bombardment. It was clear an attack was imminent. It came the following morning, 5 April.

Shells from 77 mm and 105 mm guns slammed into the whole front line, obliterating the trenches of No. 1 Company. At 8.45 a.m. bombing attacks and three waves of German troops were beaten off with Lewis guns and rifle fire. At ten o'clock the line was reported intact, but it was soon discovered that the 8th Lancashire Fusiliers, flanking them on the west side of Bucquoy, were retiring, which made the situation precarious – the Germans had entered the eastern side of the village. With its left flank bent back, the battalion was forced to destroy its own dugouts with bombs and withdraw along a sunken road.

While the enemy had gained the high ground, they did not press the attack. By 2.15 p.m. the Lancashire Fusiliers had regrouped to the point where they even undertook a small counter-attack, in which they lost both their commander and second in command and got nowhere. By five o'clock the line had stabilized and the Germans did not attack during the night.

It was a small action in the larger scheme of things, which, over a fortnight, cost each side a quarter of a million casualties. But it was not without significance. Ludendorff's desperate offensive was running out of momentum: it had gained sixty kilometres of territory, but had not broken through.

Once again, Henri had stared into the face of his enemy and survived. He had associated himself forever (even if anonymously) with the proper names of history and the war – Souchez and Vimy, St Eloi and Gheluvelt, the Menin Road and Clapham Junction, Rossignol Wood and Bucquoy. How long could his luck hold or providence protect him? Would his hour come? And when?

At the Residency, there was a changing of the guard at the end of 1917. Robert Coryndon, posted to Uganda, was to be replaced by Edward Garraway.

Edward Charles Frederick Garraway was born in County Waterford in Ireland and studied medicine at Trinity College and the Adelaide Hospital in Dublin. He came to South Africa in 1888, aged twenty-three, and, after short stays in Knysna, Kuruman and Edenburg, he joined the Bechuanaland Border Police and saw some fighting in Matabeleland in 1893. At a loose end, he was inveigled into the Jameson Raid by 'friends' and captured by the Boers, who treated him exceptionally well because of his medical training. He was somewhat bitter about the ruin of some of his friends' careers because of the Raid, and blamed Jameson and other leaders, admitting 'we were nothing but pirates, and richly deserved hanging'.

The excitement did not end there. He was part of the column that relieved Mafeking in the South African War. But after his marriage in 1905, he became Military Secretary to Lord Selborne and headed for a more diplomatic career, eventually being appointed Resident Commissioner for Bechuanaland in 1916. Garraway was suited to the outdoor life – he loved riding, fishing and hunting. He was amiable, informal and popular, lightly humorous and ironic about himself, without being deeply introspective.

He arrived on the Maseru train at 6.30 p.m. on 15 December with his wife Winifred and their two young daughters, and was met with befitting ceremony by his departing predecessor and a police escort. A few days later, he was visited by Griffith and a number of his counsellors. 'They seem an intelligent lot,' Garraway noted in his diary. But within a week a new deputation of messengers from the Paramount Chief had approached him on what he called 'a thorny subject': 'I'm afraid there is a great deal of unrest on the subject of the Basuto entering the Union and I will have a certain amount of trouble.' He was 'careful to give a very diplomatic answer'.

Just as diplomatic was his handling of a group of Basotho representing the PEMS in Maseru, to whom he conveyed his 'sympathies and feelings'. Of more immediate concern to himself, he noted that he must go gently because of the altitude and regretfully admitted that polo was out that day!

Over the months that followed, a pattern emerged in his way of governing: he avoided confrontation, and wrath was turned away with a soft answer. When a local jockey was killed by accident at the races and some 'unpleasantness' ensued, Garraway had to intervene, 'much as I dislike being dragged into it'. On another occasion when a deputation of Indians came to him and 'let off much steam over their grievances', he realized that often he 'had to skate over somewhat thin ice'. Nor did he relish the Byzantine national politics and the nitty-gritty of administration. The three-week-long meeting of the Basotho National Council in September, for instance, hung over him like a cloud, 'for I believe I have to attend and sit it all through'. On the other hand, he grew fond of the Basotho, especially the old men like Mohalanyane, the chief near Thaba-Bosiu.

Garraway was less sanguine about the restorative qualities of his new homeland. From the start he suffered from rheumatic pains, which he attributed either to the damp weather – or to the 'lebese', the thick milk which he was served. In early May, he made his first trip into the mountains. It was so cold that not even six blankets, a Jaeger fleabag, a heavy overcoat and a hot-water bottle were enough to keep him warm. The thought that they might at any minute be enveloped in a snowstorm, which could cut the unwary off for days at a time, was enough to chill the blood.

During winter, when measles, mumps and chickenpox were rife in Maseru, he came to the wry conclusion that 'I certainly do not consider this place much of a health resort'. This prejudice was confirmed by the presence of other hidden dangers, such as the ptomaine poisoning that Win Garraway suffered, which her husband attributed to the breakfast polony. Garraway's own heart was not strong and sometimes affected his mind. On one occasion, after Dr Long, whom he liked and trusted, had given him strychnine as a stimulant, he gave his staff a hard time, and the next day, not surprisingly, he was 'equally poisonous'.

Garraway was always supportive of the activities of the PEMS, albeit with a touch of humorous condescension. On 28 August, he had a long day at Morija. He took Winifred with him and she chattered happily all day in French to the Christellers, the Jacottets and the Dubys. After speeches to five different schools, Garraway himself ended the day distinctly grumpy. As a relaxed Anglican, his sympathies were definitely Protestant. When the newspaper editor and writer Solomon Plaatje (himself brought up in the Lutheran Church by missionaries of the Berlin Missionary Society) visited him from Kimberley on 2 October, he was pleased that Plaatje strongly agreed with him that 'the Paramount Chief is much too seriously influenced by the Roman Catholic priests'.

Naturally, he followed closely the course of the war and the macabre world-wide dance of death. He was quietly satisfied when he could record towards the end of August that 'the Huns are still retiring steadily', that the Allies had rejected an Austrian peace note in September, and that the Germans and their allies were now 'getting it in the neck'. But his joy at the unconditional surrender of the Bulgarians at the beginning of October was tempered by the sadness of a swift and lethal disaster much closer to home.

CHAPTER TWENTY-FIVE

SACRIFICE

1918–1920

Although he was nearly always exhausted, Jacottet could congratulate himself on the simple fact that he had celebrated his sixtieth birthday, 'an age which almost no one has ever passed in my family'. Nevertheless, he assured Bianquis that he felt himself 'still young of heart and intelligence, as well as physically', and asserted that his capacity for work was undiminished.

According to Mrs Jacottet, Marcelle devoted all her strength – physical, intellectual and spiritual – to the Book Depot. Dieterlen reported to head-quarters that she was 'up to her neck' helping Duby with multiple tasks. But it was Mrs Jacottet who gave her husband most cause for concern at home. She had a period of several weeks which were so bad that he even feared the worst. Her condition seems to have been a combination of heart problems and ner-vous collapse, but much of her exhaustion came from sheer anxiety about the physical safety of her eldest son, thousands of miles away.

―◦◦―

By July 1918, Ludendorff's offensives on the Western Front had finally petered out. It was time for the Allies to counter-attack and their commander Foch wasted no time in doing so. Even Jacottet, far away in a colonial outpost, sus-pected its coming and guessed that it was the turn of the British to shoulder most of the responsibility. This merely strengthened the Jacottets' anxiety.

On 8 August, the attack began south of the Somme with overwhelming numbers of tanks and men, mainly Australians and Canadians. The German line buckled. More importantly, its troops were at last demoralized beyond the point of regeneration. Ludendorff called it 'the black day of the German army'.

By the beginning of September, the Allied armies had won back all the territory they had lost earlier in the year, and more. The 13th Battalion of the Royal Fusiliers, which had fought in a major engagement near Achiet-le-Grand on 23 August and taken over five hundred prisoners, had by 4 September advanced far to the east of Bapaume. They were closing in on the Canal du Nord, which at this point described an angular S-bend. They were just to the south of the small town of Hermies, with their right flank on the canal and its northerly bend in front of them. One platoon even crossed the canal on the right. As they advanced, they came under heavy trench-mortar fire, then equally heavy machine-gun fire.

Four officers were wounded in this action, and twenty other ranks killed. In the British Cemetery on Hermies Hill there are over a thousand graves, neatly arranged like beds in a dormitory. Privates Byrne, Lees, Farmer and Bridger and Lance Corporal Handy, Henri's comrades-in-arms, were buried there the following day, which the battalion spent patrolling, pushing forward to establish outposts and consolidating their position.

They were then relieved and moved back for a few days. On the 10th, the Lewis gunners spent their time refitting their equipment and training. The next day they advanced again. As they moved along the roads they came under heavy fire from enemy guns. Henri found himself in an open area which is today a peaceful mealie field – it would have reminded him of the soporific beauty of Lesotho.

That is when the shell came out of the blue sky.

—◦○◦—

The Spanish influenza pandemic probably originated in Asia late in 1917 or early in 1918. At first it was relatively mild, but in August 1918 it turned nasty, and, helped by the worldwide communications of war, spread rapidly. Up to half a billion people contracted the flu, and in 1918–19 at least twenty million died from it, more than the war had killed.

How it entered South Africa is not known for sure, but infected migrant labourers from Mozambique were thought to be a major source. Ironically, members of the Native Labour Contingent, returning from France on the troopship *Jaroslav*, were strongly suspected as another source, since a number of them died of pneumonia or influenza within a few days of disembarking. The Reef mines, Cape Town, Bloemfontein – despite its reputation as a model town for health – were desperately affected. An estimated death toll of a quarter of a million, some five per cent of the total population, is probably conservative. All in the space of a few weeks.

The scourge fortunately reached Bloemfontein during the late September holidays, so there were very few girls at Eunice, which immediately became a temporary hospital, while several of the staff turned nurse. One teacher died as a result, as did several old girls of the school. Happily, Marguerite escaped the contagion.

By early October 1918 the insidious Spanish flu was everywhere. In his first acknowledgement of it on the 7th, Garraway noted that it was already spreading rapidly in Lesotho and he had attended a concert in aid of war funds that night 'much against my inclination'. Two days later, he was doctoring his maid in the absence of the only available doctor, who was himself laid up. Reports from the whole territory were very serious.

Soon two of Garraway's 'kitchen boys', a second housemaid, his groom and his 'motorboy' were all down with the 'fell disease'. A telegram from the Paramount Chief on the 16th reported that he had lost his secretary and his son-in-law, and that he himself had been struck down. By the 18th the first whites had begun to die in Lesotho: the wife of a carpenter, followed by Mr Johns the baker, Hughes, a clerk at Fraser's store, and a widow with children. A week after his telegram Griffith was still ill. Garraway badly wanted to see him, but was cautious: 'I don't like to go out there, where the disease is raging, and have to sit in a room full of germs and smells.' He had, however, helped start two soup kitchens, which he hoped would be 'of some help'.

Griffith did survive, but he was still incapacitated on 6 November, as the epidemic at last began to abate. This happy state of affairs coincided with auspicious signs concerning the war.

On Monday the 11th the flu was gone and the war was over. 'I celebrated the receipt of the news in the proper manner,' Garraway recorded – no doubt with his favourite Jameson's! 'It is very difficult to realize,' he mused, 'that all the awful fighting is really at an end and that our gallant soldiers and sailors can sleep in peace tonight.' The following day was proclaimed a public holiday in South Africa and Garraway decided to follow suit. This benign bit of bureaucratic flexibility brought down on the unhappy head of the Morija postmistress the Gallic wrath of M. Jacottet.

He dashed off a 'strong complaint' to the Government Secretary in Maseru that very day: his messenger had gone to the post office only to find it closed for the public holiday. It was particularly galling, he said, not to get one's newspapers and other important correspondence at a time 'when the political affairs are so important'. He was irritated, too, that the traders had been informed of the holiday but not the missionaries.

Mrs Barclay, the postmistress, defended herself: she had only heard about the closure late the previous day, and she had in fact opened the office for a few hours on the morning of the holiday to attend to essential business.

Under Garraway's direction, the government replied to Jacottet in suitably diplomatic terms. The matter seems to have died there, although there must have been frosty interactions in the post office for some time to come.

Jacottet's behaviour might seem excessive, but it is indicative of the tetchiness that his minor stroke had added to his peremptory and autocratic nature.

In addition, it is further evidence of the almost obsessive worry he felt for his children, particularly Henri.

—⁓—

Henri did not end up alongside his comrades in the Hermies cemetery, but it was touch-and-go. A piece of shrapnel from the exploding shell had gone through his thigh, fortunately cauterizing it in the process. He was taken to a Canadian front-line hospital and then transferred to England. It was over two weeks before his parents were informed, and even then they did not know how serious the wound was. Only later did they discover that the projectile had missed the bone.

They had hardly recovered from the shock of Henri's wounding when Marcelle became ill. A letter of Sam Duby's on 20 March 1919 informed Bianquis that she had been in bed for sixty days and that she would need several more weeks of convalescence. Jacottet gave a few more details: 'My daughter Marcelle has had a strong attack of typhoid fever. She has passed more than ten weeks in bed. The fever has never been very strong but its persistence eventually became disturbing. She has recovered now, she passed several weeks of convalescence in Bloemfontein and will definitely return next week. She will have been almost four months away from her work.' This was in May. Jacottet added, rather ominously, 'It was an immensely tiring period for my wife, but fortunately, she has not been too greatly affected.'

The illness deepened the crack which the war had opened in the continuity of Marcelle's life. She returned to the Book Depot, but was clearly not right. A few months later, around October, there is some evidence (though it is not conclusive) that she went to France, probably to recuperate. All was not right with Mrs Jacottet either. In September, Jacottet expressed concern that she was 'suffering somewhat'. For five or six weeks after that she felt poorly, but her state did not seem alarming and her husband had few qualms about going to Johannesburg on business on 27 October.

That day, Sam Duby went to fetch her to stay with him down the hill, so that she would not feel isolated while her husband was away. Eva Duby herself was overseas at the time, so Sam was probably helped by his sister-in-law, Margot. But when Jacottet came back a week later, he found his wife so weak that she could not return the few hundred metres home – even by car. She preferred to stay in the small airy room which the Dubys had provided. Jacottet also decided to stay in the Director's house. On 10 November, Louise Jacottet was visited by Dr Long from Maseru and she wanted to know from him the exact seriousness of her heart condition. As delicately as possible, he told her that the end was near and it was only a question of days. She took it, according to Duby, as 'good news'. He added: 'From then on she felt relief. She was admirable in her calm serenity and joyous submission to the will of the Father. All those who had the privilege of seeing her during those last days will not easily forget what they saw and heard in her room. She already lived partly in the hereafter and, for her, earthly things more and more lost their importance and interest.'

She died peacefully, and without pain, on 15 November. Bertschy, Jeanmairet, Germond, Colin and all the Basotho pastors in the area assisted at her burial. On the morning of her funeral, where before there had been terrible drought in Lesotho, the heavens wept. Despite this, the crowd in the small cemetery was huge. They came from Maseru, from Thabana-Morena, from the surrounding villages – but especially from Thaba-Bosiu where the Jacottets had served for more than twenty years, where their children had been born and where their memory was ineffaceable.

Rev. Colin, who was now at Thaba-Bosiu, described the way the congregation received the news of her death. The church bell was rung to call the people there. The evangelist Salomone Tau made the news known. The scene was sad but beautiful. Their mother had left them: their pain was deep, their tears were full. Even a pagan said to Colin, 'I am thankful to God for having given me such a mother. By her life she showed me that it was a matter of loving, working for and serving others.'

From the first, she had taken charge of the mission station and dealt with the material questions, which were so important. The Jacottet house had always been open to visitors, white and black, local and foreign. Later, when responsibilities grew, her heart grew bigger: she became the mother of all the Basotho pastors, their wives, the students of the Theological School. She was the life of the missionary meetings and of the Red Cross during the war.

She spent so much of her time in the garden, she was called by the Basotho 'Makhoiti – Mother of the Moles. When she was sad and missed her homeland, she played Chopin on the piano in the moonlight. Apparently she had a terrible temper, which would rise quickly but subside soon, like the passing of a summer storm.

Her compatriot, Rev. Jeanmairet, saw her as a model missionary's companion: 'Our sister was, in the words of the apostle Paul, a woman who was submissive to her husband, who did not make her voice heard at meetings, but who was happy to be the devout colleague of her husband. She has left us with great regret – the example of a kind woman, devoted to all her work.'

Jacottet stayed on at the Dubys' for several days. He received wonderful support from his friends, but his health had been shaken. He was stunned. The heavy blow had affected him more deeply than he let on, thought Duby:

'When he has returned to his house, he will find it sad and empty! That is when he will realize the loss. Poor Mr Jacottet! God console him!'

It was not an easy time for anyone at the mission. The Dubys had been presented with a thorny problem: what to do with their children, who were coming to the end of their schooling. Gynette went into nursing; Robert had decided to study medicine in Britain, but after a year he fell out with his English benefactor. The situation of the Duby children was critical and it was possible that Sam, like Alfred Casalis, might have to leave Lesotho. In mid-1919, it was decided that Eva would go to Europe to see what could be done. She took little Georges with her.

While she was there her health suffered greatly. The price of eggs, milk and meat made a good diet difficult to follow, and worry about her children gnawed at her stomach. Furthermore, whereas she had planned to return to Lesotho in November, failure to solve the problem of her children's education meant that she was caught in Valentigny in the 'terrible cold' of the winter, which she dreaded. It was only by late January 1920 that Robert was settled into medical studies in Switzerland, and Eva, fretting 'while my husband is alone in Lesotho', could plan to return in February. On the voyage back, when he was not engrossed in his sketching or his newly acquired jigsaw puzzles, Georges, with a wicked twinkle in his eye, teased the young girls on board mercilessly.

The eight months of her absence had been a particularly difficult time for Duby. There had been trouble at the Printing Works.

During the war and after, the cost of paper and printing materials had skyrocketed; the engine that ran the old printing machine was long past its guarantee date and might break down at any time; the Printing Works were supplying the Book Depot with only a fraction of the books required. Then there was the question of the printer in charge. Getting skilled workers had proved expensive, especially when they wanted funding for European leave, or upped and died, leaving widows to be pensioned. Sam Duby therefore preferred to recruit locally. He was soon to be grievously disappointed.

The problem he found with the locals was drink. The present incumbent, Mr McLean, a man who knew his work, waited impatiently for his Christmas holidays in order to go off and get drunk in a city on the coast. Invariably, he would return with delirious attacks. His predecessor, Hamerton, had been worse! Neither, lamented Duby, felt any attachment to the mission. They were purely mercenary and brought the Basotho printers under their influence in more ways than one. Duby therefore agreed to return to the former system, and a young Swiss, who was to serve the mission faithfully for many years, was sent to England to learn English and to study the secrets of modern printing and binding at Nelson's, the famous publishers. He was also to get acquainted with the monotype machine which Duby was intent on buying. This move was too late. A crisis broke out long before Jacques Zurcher arrived in Lesotho.

McLean returned from his Christmas holidays determined to continue them well into the new year of 1920. He invited all the Basotho printers to go and drink with him at his house, stoked them up to insist on higher salaries and then swanned off to Ladybrand without authorization. The printers needed little prompting. On 12 January, they handed Duby a letter demanding a minimum increase of £2. 10s. a month and insisting on an answer the next day.

Duby saw this as 'an ultimatum in every sense'. He told the printers that the Board of the Printing Works – comprising the Morija missionaries, Jacottet, Christeller and himself – would meet in a few days' time to consider the letter. The printers said they would have nothing to do with the Board and if Duby did not respond immediately they would stop work. He refused, so fourteen of the sixteen declared a strike and left work on the day *Leselinyana* was to be printed.

When the Board met, it agreed it would not submit to such behaviour and 'blatant ill will', and decided to dismiss the workers and pay them off with their January salary. 'Evidently,' noted Duby, 'this was not the solution they had hoped for.' The furious strikers threatened to sabotage the machines and burn the Printing Works. The government and the Paramount Chief were informed, and Griffith gave them a severe scolding.

The mission decided that it would free the Works of the 'bad elements' and determined that the major agitators would never be readmitted. But it was a nasty incident, and the dismissed workers, believing them to be behind the Board's decision, threatened to kill both Jacottet and Duby.

With his wife having been ill so long and now absent, it is almost certainly at this time that Sam Duby, while leaning heavily on Marcelle for advice and sympathy, took up with the sixteen-year-old schoolgirl, Marguerite. It was a relationship which he was to regret deeply and which ultimately destroyed him.

Jacottet, too, was suffering from a lost mate. 'The loneliness,' he told Bianquis, 'is vast.' For the moment, Marcelle was minding his household (the family had moved back to their old house in 1917), but Madeleine, keen any-way to return from England, had been summoned by her father and had applied to Paris for funds to subsidize her fare.

Jacottet did not consider retiring, especially when the upstart Ramseyer made a thinly disguised attack on the oldies of the mission. Rather, he took inspiration from Foch and Clemenceau, and, closer to home, the rejuvenated Bertschy and the evergreen Jeanmairet. In addition, he underlined his alienation from Europe. 'I feel myself more African than ever,' he asserted. But sorrow had weakened him. His stride had slowed; he could no longer ride. In February, a severe attack of angina reminded him that his family's old enemy lurked within the dark passages of his heart.

Despite this, he was once again elected President of the Conference. While the sixth intake of Theological School students was nearing its graduation (though only five of the eight were ever ordained), the Normal School continued to worry him. Like the Printing Works, the great difficulty was the personnel: the English teachers had no missionary vocation, while the only thing that interested their Basotho colleagues was the lolly (he used the argot 'galette'). What it needed was either missionaries with years of teaching experience or teachers with the missionary spirit. Instead, the school survived only through expediency. When the headmaster Johns resigned, the sole hope for the school was the return, on 3 January, of Alfred Casalis. Jacottet predicted that, despite the fact that his wife would be able to help him, Casalis would face a difficult year. He did not foresee how difficult it would be – both for Casalis and himself.

Jacottet's family was scattered. Marcelle was at Morija, Madeleine on her way home, Marguerite about to be received into the church in Bloemfontein. Henri had become a teacher of French, German and a little Spanish (which he did not speak) at Brentwood School in Essex, while Gustave, who was to take up a job in the Swiss Bank in London, had got married the previous September.

The child who worried him most was his youngest son. Claude had spent the war in Switzerland, but it was not a happy sojourn. Jacottet confided his own distress to Bianquis in language where the figurative and the literal – metaphor and grim reality – are about as indistinguishable as they can be: 'The cadet causes me considerable chagrin. Sadly, he is perhaps not all there. It is likely that we will send him to Canada. It has been one of the greatest vexations: it poisoned the last years of my wife's life and perhaps hastened her end. It is a heavy cross to carry and I ask myself how I bear up. At least my wife no longer suffers from it now. But it is too sickening for me to go on about it.'

Characteristically, he added, 'Naturally, this is between us.'

—❧—

Garraway returned from a holiday in Ireland in a relaxed mood. He was pleased with the escort of Basutoland Mounted Police under Sub-Inspector Bunbury which greeted him at the station and with the beaming domestics waiting at the Residency. He was less enamoured with Griffith, who he thought was 'full of his own importance' after a visit to England. Jacottet chimed in with a similar conclusion: Griffith, he felt, 'believed himself to be at least the equal of George V'. Garraway and Griffith were like two cocks in the same hen run: Griffith griped that he had not been apprised of the impending visit by the High Commissioner; Garraway 'let him blow off steam' and then scratched back by telling him 'that it was his duty to come in and greet me, which he never did, and that I had told him that I expected him to do so, when I would have told him all about His Excellency's visit'. But the scores were levelled at the track a few days later, when the Paramount Chief's horses won two of the races and the Resident Commissioner's Petronella came in sixth!

Jacottet thought that Griffith had returned from Britain less attached to the Catholics, but he soon had to backtrack. At the Conference where Jacottet was re-elected President, Griffith had called on him and offered an olive branch. But when the priests noticed such moves they redoubled their efforts. They took advantage of Griffith's relapse into his old drinking habits and a sudden bout of fear on his part concerning mortality. In May, what Jacottet privately called 'the Great War' between the Catholics and the PEMS broke out. Using Griffith as their instrument, the Catholics plotted what Jacottet, with a Protestant sense of persecution, interpreted as 'a kind of Revocation of the Edict of Nantes'. On 'detestable pretexts', the Catholics pressed the Paramount Chief to shut down nine or ten PEMS schools in Griffith's old district of Phamong. He also closed an Anglican school for good measure.

When his messages of protest got nowhere, Jacottet, a formidable figure in his old spider cart with its high body and slender wheels, hastened round the mountain to Matsieng to confront Griffith. 'We had a stormy interview,' he recorded. 'He spoke most disagreeable words to me. But faced with my refusal to budge he understood that he must give in himself. Our schools have reopened. The affair was very serious.' According to Jacottet's intelligence sources, the interview convinced Griffith that Jacottet was in earnest. Later in the year, Griffith seems to have moderated his attitude towards Jacottet, partly because he might be a strong ally in resisting incorporation into the Union, partly, or so Jacottet felt, because he had stood up to him – Jacottet phrased it colloquially: 'Poing le vilain et il t'oindra.'

For Griffith, the sore must have festered. In pondering who might have killed Jacottet some months later, Garraway considered this dispute as a possible motive.

In early June, Jacottet went to Maseru as examiner for the public service Sesotho examinations, and lunched at the Residency. Garraway was careful to send him down to the examinations 'in a charitable frame of mind'. Evidently he was successful, as all the candidates passed. But next day Garraway got an earful from Jacottet in a formal interview about the closing of the schools.

—◦⊙◦—

Jacottet was reluctant to take on the Presidency again. He felt himself to be an 'expiatory victim'. But the decision was almost unanimous and expressed with so much goodwill that he felt constrained to accept.

The Conference was no longer split into factions, no longer divided over questions such as bohali, the Theological School was about to add to the Basotho pastorate, and the pride of the mission, the Seboka, was in excellent shape. 'I am increasingly struck by the spirit of the Seboka, especially when I know that, throughout South Africa, the black race is full of bitterness and hatred against all that is white. Alas, they have sufficient cause.' He believed the Seboka could be a model for other institutions in the south. But the mission faced one ongoing danger. With the harvest so great, too few young white missionaries were offering their labour. Chiefs at this time, thought Jacottet, preferred white to Basotho pastors. It was also necessary to have strong men, but ones 'who think'. They must come soon or the wisdom and knowledge of the past would be lost: 'If we do not have time to mould them and give them tradition before the old have disappeared, I do not know what will become of the mission.'

—◦⊙◦—

In mid-1920, there was a certain amount of coming and going which was of some significance. Dr Hertig popped in to see Garraway on his way to Portuguese East Africa for the shooting expedition that would keep him away until the end of the year – which is why Augsburger was on hand instead of Hertig when the Morija poisoning occurred.

In July, Jacottet took himself off to Lourenço Marques for five or six weeks. Since the death of his wife, he had been 'spiritually, intellectually and physically exhausted' and needed the rest. His house would be closed up: Madeleine had taken up the offer of a friend to accompany her to the Victoria Falls; Marcelle went to Cape Town to learn about the monotype printing machine that was to be introduced into the Printing Works; she took Marguerite with her.

Jacottet thought his youngest daughter, his 'cadette', would get a job as a typist at Morija after she finished school at the end of the year. He felt Morija offered her better opportunities and a better life than Europe.

Tension, even sexual tension, was never far from the surface in a closed community like Morija. At this time it was simmering in the Duby family. Many years afterwards, Georges Duby used to tell an illustrative story in which he was an unhappy and unwitting agent.

One morning in September it was suddenly, gloriously spring. His mother suggested to Georges that they go for a walk to look for mushrooms. Since she knew everything – seven decades later, Georges said of her teaching skills that she could teach French 'even to a stone' – she would certainly be able to find edible ones and avoid those 'destroying angels' which one ate with long teeth. Georges's best friend, Scott, dashed ahead of them. The Great Dane was so boisterous only Sam Duby could handle him. Like a gangly puppy himself, Georges lolloped beside his mother.

Up the mountain they went, the mission laid out below them like a 'toy village' – the post office, the Normal School, the Bible School, the Printing Works, the church with its thin and elegant spire.

As they came over the edge of the first terrace, up towards the dinosaur footprints, Eva and Georges suddenly saw an explosion of mushrooms, like seashells in the sunlight. '*Attention!*' said Georges's mother, 'pick only the ones with pink underneath.'

Every receptacle was filled – baskets, pockets, shirts, even hats.

Mushrooms for dinner, mushrooms for breakfast, mushrooms for lunch. Until no one could bear to eat another mushroom. Even Scott was sick of them.

Now Sam's brother Théo had brought with him a wife, Tante Margot. She was, in Georges's view, 'very pretty'. Eva could not compete and was, deep down, just a little jealous. Eva and Margot did not get on too well. So Eva decided, on this occasion, to offer 'an olive branch'. She sent Georges round to the other Duby household with a big dish of mushrooms.

When Margot opened the screen door, Georges blurted out: 'Mama has sent you this present. We've had enough. The maids have had enough. Even the dog has had enough.'

To which Margot replied, with some venom, 'Take them back to your mother. We shall survive, even without the dog's dinner!'

The door banged shut.

Eva no doubt learned that diplomacy, particularly between sisters-in-law, was an affair of subtlety and not to be entrusted to an eight-year-old. The messenger was not killed, but he was certainly in the doghouse for a while.

Within a few days, though, he had to make way for his father, whose disgrace was infinitely more serious.

—◦—

Garraway visited Thaba-Bosiu when an uncle of the Paramount Chief died. He climbed up the mountain to view the body lying in the old house of Moshoeshoe and listen to Alfred Casalis read the service in Sesotho. He found it 'an uncared-for spot' and the graves of Moshoeshoe and other chiefs 'only rough heaps of stones'. He also went to Roma, which he found very pleasant, 'although there were several unmistakable Huns amongst the priests' with whom he had to shake hands.

—❧—

With exquisitely ironic timing, the past came back to taunt the immediate future. Ernest Mabille, penniless and desperate for work, wanted to return to the mission. Several of the missionaries in Lesotho did not mind him coming back as a teacher; they did not even mind him going to Zambezia as a missionary; but they did object to him returning to Lesotho as a minister. Their main concern was the Basotho pastorate. It was necessary to indicate to them in no uncertain terms that if they fell, or risked taking their vocation too lightly, they would never be readmitted. This lesson would be lost if a white were allowed back in, 'particularly one whose fall had been so grave and dismal'.

At a meeting in April, the Schools Committee, consisting of Jacottet, Casalis and Duby, assisted by Bertschy and Colin, recommended his engagement, but on the express condition that he was not considered as a missionary. They knew that there would be objections from others if this was not made crystal clear. As Jacottet said, 'Ernest had been deprived of his rights as pastor in Lesotho and they had never been restored.'

Unfortunately, Casalis had given the Mabille family, particularly the blind old grande dame of the mission, Adèle Mabille, the wrong impression that Ernest would return as a missionary. Casalis compounded the problem by publishing the decision in *Leselinyana* in maladroit fashion, calling Ernest a 'moruti', a pastor. The situation escalated when Jeanmairet objected, and Jacottet had a struggle to damp things down at the Conference. Of course, the pride and position of the Mabille family made the circumstances even touchier.

The whole affair made a bad impression when elements of it leaked into the public domain. The most interesting thing about it, however, is something that can only be speculated upon. As he sat debating the fate of Mabille at the School Committee meeting in April, did Sam Duby think of his own adultery? If his dalliance with Marguerite had already begun, could he not help thinking of it and how did he come to terms with it? How could he in all conscience keep silent? To what extent did he feel guilt?

If his affair with Marguerite had not begun, was his judgement tempered by prescience or humility? Did he have any inkling that he, too, was about to fall?

—❧—

Secrecy. Confidentiality. Suppression. These are normal proclivities for those who hold office in any organization. But in the last year of his life, Jacottet, already prone to keeping things tight, used more than his fair share of them.

When the return of Ernest Mabille was first mooted and began to cause dissension, Jacottet urged Bianquis not to publish too much and to keep his correspondence under wraps, partly to avoid hurting the Mabilles, partly to avoid agitating the Basotho pastorate.

As the 'war' with the Catholics continued (the PEMS had asked the government to introduce a regulation excluding the building of rival schools within four miles of already established ones) and as the Catholics seemed to redouble their attacks, aimed with particular venom at Jacottet himself, he strongly advised Bianquis not to publish reports on this subject in the *Journal*. He had been conditioned by the worldwide conflict of the past few years: 'As in war, it is necessary to censor everything.' After all, the Catholics, 'like the Boche', read the *Journal*.

The same applied to his family. The mental health of Claude was a problem and an embarrassment. He must be sent to Canada and the whole matter swept under the carpet.

Then, when the scandal of Marguerite and Sam Duby broke, Jacottet made it clear to Duby that he must leave the mission. But, in order to protect Marguerite's reputation from further tarnish, the affair was hushed up as far as possible, and he gave Duby a few months to settle his affairs and leave quietly. It was a fatal mistake.

Garraway, too, had his problems, although they were of a lesser order than Jacottet's. The civil service was restless for a while, but Garraway was not very sympathetic. He regarded it as merely bureaucratic resistance to change and it took him some effort to keep an even temper. However, when he discovered that the Government Secretary had simply sat on correspondence from the various departmental heads and had left over two hundred letters unanswered, he had to acknowledge the justice of their grievances.

Garraway also had to persuade Griffith to send his sons to Anglican rather than Catholic schools. He had to traverse the tedious terrain of day-to-day politics, complaining on one occasion, after an endless series of interviews, that 'truly the natives have the knack of knowing how to distract the unfortunate white man'. But another white man could achieve the same effect: one hot and trying day in October he had to entertain Mr Jacottet, 'who first had an official interview with me, and then came to luncheon, where poor Win shared my trial with me'.

Sometimes, it was flies that were the problem: in October, after thousands had been slain, the Residency was 'still black with them'. At other times, it was the domestics: in December, while dining with the Bosworth Smiths, Garraway noticed that his wife had laid a new and beautiful single-feather ostrich fan with diamond-encrusted handle on a side table, and was later horrified to see a parlourmaid use it to dust crumbs off a tablecloth. Only a desperate lunge effected a hasty rescue.

—◦◦—

In September, Jacottet received an overture which might have altered the whole course of his life and averted the fate which waited for him around the corner. The University of the Witwatersrand in Johannesburg officially offered him the chair in Comparative Grammar of Bantu Languages. The salary was nearly triple what he was earning and the work would have been particularly interesting for him, as it appealed to the heart of his own speciality. But he did not hesitate in turning it down: 'I am needed here,' he said, 'and I am not one of those who desert in open battle.'

On 29 November, Jacottet wrote his very last extant letter to Paris. In many ways it was a sad one. The present felt secure: the scholars of the PEMS out-numbered those of the Catholics by four to one and schools by 290 to 60, and he believed that, since the sons of Griffith were to be diverted to Protestant schools, the 'danger of having a catholic dynasty' had been averted. But he feared for the future. (In fact, as Catholic strength grew, particularly in the 1920s, the extremes of enmity also increased, and to this day some of the coun-try's fault lines, political and social, run along the Protestant/Catholic divide.)

Perhaps his melancholy was brought on by having to report the death of Frédéric Ellenberger, the very last of the second-generation missionaries (except for Mrs Mabille). 'It will be our turn soon,' he mused, 'we of the third generation.'

—◦◦—

December 15 was the third anniversary of the arrival of the Garraways in Lesotho − 'three good years,' Garraway reckoned. The only noteworthy event of the day was a visit from Rev. Jacottet, 'who was as usual'. Thunder growled all around. It was the last time they met.

—◦◦—

The Garraways were gearing up for Christmas − on the 22nd the festive season began for the children.

On the following day the news came of Morija's falling towers and Agamemnon dead.

Part Three

THE DEVIL

———∞———

And now I go, an outcast driven off the land,
in life, in death, I leave behind a name for –

Aeschylus, *The Libation Bearers*

CHAPTER TWENTY-SIX

WHITE DEVIL

O n the night of 11 February 1921, Lt Col. Garraway noted that the evidence from the preliminary examination in the Jacottet case was due to be delivered to him shortly. The previous night he had remarked that the case was 'most unpleasant'. Now what he had dreaded was about to happen: he had to make a decision. The thread of three people's lives was in his hands.

But then, in re Jacottet, his diary goes silent. His decision took nearly three weeks. For Marcelle, Marguerite and Sam, languishing in the Old Gaol in Maseru, the hours must have been like long days and the days like months. Added together, these pieces of time approached eternity. Marcelle, in particular, seems to have suffered from her confinement, and emerged markedly changed.

Finally, on 3 March, the three of them were brought before the Assistant Commissioner's Court, where they were informed that 'there was insufficient evidence to commit them for trial'. They were consequently released, but given to understand that if further evidence came to light they were liable to be rearrested on the same charge.

It was not a verdict of guilty; nor was it a proclamation of innocence. To this day, no one has ever been tried for, or convicted of, the poisoning.

—◦◦—

Poisoning is as old, almost, as time. Poison and food got together as early as the Garden of Eden, when serpent joined forces with apple. Occasionally, the poison is taken intravenously, as in the case of Cleopatra and the asp, but more often it is swallowed.

There are two great traditions of poisoning. The first is the political. It has its roots deep in classical times.

—◦◦—

Poison courses through the veins of Greek myth. Aconitine was called 'the Queen of Poisons' by the Greeks; its alternative name was 'stepmother's poison'. It was, according to legend, derived from the saliva of Cerberus, the monstrous guard dog of the entrance to the lower world (since Cerberus had fifty heads, there must have been a plentiful supply). One of the twelve tasks of the great hero Heracles was to descend to the House of Hades, steal this 'infernal watchdog', and show him to Eurystheus of Argos (who had contracted him to perform these labours), thereby completing the conquest of Death. On the way back, captor and captive paused a while in the cave of Acone. Medea, the ogre's daughter, and Hecate, underworld goddess of witches, were also associated with aconitine.

Antimony, a toxic metallic element, was a popular poison in Roman times. Cups used at feasts and orgies were cast in antimony: the acid in wine would dissolve the poison, and this caused the vomiting required by the sated participants so that they could resume eating. This was a somewhat benign usage; often poison was used for a more sinister purpose.

If Suetonius is to be believed, the catalogue of poisonings amongst the Caesars was a long one. Philemon, the slave-secretary of Julius Caesar, tried to poison his master. Drusus, the son of Tiberius, was poisoned by his wife Livilla. Tiberius himself died from a slow, wasting disease some believed to be poison administered by his successor, Caligula. And the great Germanicus, triumphant commander of the Roman army in Germany, had dark stains on his body and foam on his lips when he died, aged thirty-three, which pointed to an untimely end; this was given great credence because his heart was found intact amongst his ashes after he was cremated (everyone knows that a heart steeped in poison is proof against fire). Augustus himself may have died at the hands of Livia.

If the murder of Tiberius by means of cyanide brushed on to some figs was only remotely and technically parricide – since Tiberius was merely Caligula's *adoptive* grandfather – Caligula got the parricide thing right in regard to his grandmother, Antonia, whom he killed either with unkindness or poison.

Caligula's affection for his subjects extended to his instructions that those he ordered to be executed should be administered many small wounds rather than one conclusive one. 'Make him feel that he is dying!' he would say. Those closest to him often had cause to feel a frisson of mortality: he never kissed his wife or his mistress without murmuring the chilling reminder, 'And this beautiful throat will be cut whenever I please.'

After he himself had been murdered, a huge chest belonging to Caligula was found, packed with a variety of poisons. When his successor Claudius threw it into the sea, vast numbers of dead fish washed up on the neighbouring beaches.

Claudius, who had only survived to become emperor by playing the imbecile to avoid arousing the suspicions of his rivals, had reason to regret his marriage into the family by way of Caligula's sister, Agrippina the Younger. She was one of his wives who 'were unchaste but remained unchastened'.

Agrippina repaid him by poisoning him at a family banquet with a dish of mushrooms – his favourite food, but called by the Greeks 'the Poison of the Gods'.

If Caligula was bad, Nero was really nasty. He had a woman in permanent employ to do his poisoning for him. He also contemplated poisoning the entire Senate at a banquet, which might have been the politically correct thing to do but was not the done thing.

Nero lusted after his mother, Agrippina the Elder, and some reports had it that he did commit incest with her whenever they rode together in the same litter. Afterwards, because of her critical demeanour, he tried to poison her three times, but each time she had previously taken an antidote. Then he tried unsuccessfully to have her drowned. Finally, she *was* murdered and it was made to look like suicide.

A riddle appeared on the walls of Rome:

Alcmaeon, Orestes and Nero are brothers,
Why?
Because all of them murdered their mothers.

The ancients sometimes used poison as a means of official execution. Socrates was forced to commit suicide by drinking hemlock, because he had introduced strange gods into Athens. During Tiberius's reign, various of his condemned victims drank poison in front of the Senate. And poisoners were made by the Romans to die by their own poison.

Although the occasional 'doctor', having readier access to poisons, was involved in such killings, the ancients nevertheless had no means of detecting or identifying poisons. The only vaguely reliable method of prevention was the institution of tasters, who would sample beforehand everything their master or mistress ate. The statistics on mortality rates of these tasters have not survived, but it must be said that few of them left their memoirs.

While the impulse to poison appears to be a constant, fashion and availability have caused the type of poison to change. In fifteenth- and sixteenth-century Italy, the favoured poison of the egregious Borgias was orpiment, a name derived from the Latin 'auripigmentum', or gold pigment. A yellow metal consisting of arsenic trisulphide in monoclinic crystalline form associated with realgar, it was sometimes called 'yellow arsenic'. The poisonous properties of white arsenic, on the other hand, were discovered by the alchemist Paracelsus in the early sixteenth century, when he used it with gay abandon as a medicine. From the Middle Ages onwards, arsenic became the poison of choice. It was called 'the White Devil'.

In the second half of the seventeenth century, a series of poisoning scandals rocked the court of Louis XIV. One poison dispenser told a police officer, 'All these women are crazy. All they can think about is doing away with their husbands.' For instance, Marie Madeleine d'Aubray, Marquise de Brinvilliers, 'one of the most winsome little monsters in criminal history' (according to one of her chroniclers), poisoned her father when he interfered in an extramarital affair she was openly flaunting. She tested her recipes on patients of Parisian charity hospitals, before eliminating her father and her brothers on her way to the family fortune. Suspicions of similar activities spread to various viscountesses and duchesses, and even the King's mistress, Mme de Montespan, was incriminated. Arsenic became known as 'la poudre de succession'.

For the Elizabethans, poison was not only a convenient means of getting rid of small enemies, but was also the favourite metaphor for the corruption of the state. The poison poured into the ears of Hamlet's father was the 'juice of cursed hebenon'. This was either henbane, which the great herbalist of the seventeenth century Nicholas Culpeper warned 'must never be taken inwardly', or it was a distillation from the yew tree, which Culpeper's *Complete Herbal* described as 'the most active vegetable poison known in the whole world', more potent even than laurel-water. If the poison was henbane, then the antidotes might be goat's milk, honey-water or mustard seed; there is no indication that Hamlet's father had any of these to hand. If it was yew, then he would have had no time to milk a goat, raid a hive or concoct a mustard syrup. The poison poured literally into the head of Denmark's government infects the whole body of the country, only to return ultimately to the perpetrator as Hamlet stabs his uncle with a poisoned rapier and then pours the cup of poison down his throat: 'Then, venom, to thy work.' In a fine bit of personification, the poison is evil, or Satan, as well as an instrument of divine retribution.

The dramatic possibilities of murder by poison were again taken up in the 1750s, when an anonymous author published his play *The Fair Parricide*. The plot concerns the murder of a father by a daughter because he is opposed to her liaison with an army captain of questionable reputation. Though the author does not doubt the *fact* of the poisoning, he does lean towards the judgement that there was no *intention* to murder. The historical trend of opinion has been against him.

Francis Blandy was an attorney at Henley-on-Thames in Oxfordshire, the adoring parent of a single daughter, Mary, born in 1720. She was lively and intelligent, with a good figure and bright black eyes, but with a plain face further blemished by smallpox. To enhance his daughter's prospects, Mr Blandy made the fatal mistake of spreading the word that she came with a dowry of £10 000. This huge sum raised her status in the marriage market considerably by ensuring that prospective grooms would gaze lovingly beyond her looks; it also, inevitably, attracted the wrong suitor. Captain the Hon. William Henry Cranstoun was an ugly little fellow with morals to match, though he did have the inestimable advantage of being the fifth son of a Scottish peer. He and Mary met at the house of Lord Mark Kerr, Cranstoun's uncle, in 1746. In the following year, according to Mary Blandy's own account, he proclaimed his passion for her. Sadly, this glorious proposal came trailing rather murky clouds.

The problem was that he was married, sort of. Three years previously, Cranstoun had 'privately married' Anne Murray in Edinburgh. Unfortunately, she was Catholic and Jacobite, and such a marriage might have hindered his chances of promotion in the army at the time. Hence the need for secrecy. She claimed the marriage was valid; he that it was a 'pretended marriage' and invalid. The birth of a daughter would seem to support her view.

Cranstoun, perennially in debt and not averse to borrowing from his enchanted fiancée, tried to persuade his father-in-law-to-be that he had never been married. 'As I have a soul to be saved, I am not, nor ever was!' The Commissionary Court in Scotland, however, was less interested in his soul's salvation and more interested in the dry commonplaces of the law, declaring Cranstoun and Anne man and wife, and their daughter legitimate. Although Mr Blandy was apprised of this fact not by Cranstoun but by Anne, the cunning little captain continued to pay court to Mary with the help of Mrs Blandy, into whose favour he had insinuated himself. The latter, however, fell ill in September 1749 and died, of intestinal inflammation, within two days. Her dying words to her husband were, 'Mary has set her heart upon Cranstoun; when I am gone, let no one set you against the match.'

Despite discovering the existence of a second daughter of Cranstoun's by a Miss Capel and stumbling upon a love letter from a further lady in his trunk, Mary's faith in – perhaps obsession with – her lover endured. But her father, stretched to the limits of his tolerance, began to make unkind remarks to them. Perhaps his irritation was aggravated by his gout, gravel and heartburn, and sudden loss of breath.

Well over a year after Mrs Blandy's death, the fortunes of the couple had not advanced appreciably. In Scotland, Cranstoun had begun to consult the famous Mrs Morgan, a woman skilled in the art of love philtres (what William Roughead calls the Scottish equivalent of the *poculum amatorium* or love philtre of the Romans). He duly sent Mary a gift of 'Scotch pebbles', which were at the time the 'extreme of fashion', together with some 'powder to clean the pebbles with'. This was coded language for the love-powder which Mary was to feed surreptitiously to her father, ostensibly to make him kinder to her and Cranstoun. These arrived in June 1751, and Mary consented to slip the powder into her father's tea.

At about this time, Mr Blandy suffered great pains and was often sick; on one occasion, a maidservant drank the tea he'd left untasted and was violently ill for days; on another day, an elderly charwoman also drank his tea and was promptly sick almost to the point of death. But the philtre did not seem to be working in the cause of altered psychological states.

On 4 August 1751, the maidservant made gruel for her master on Mary's orders. The next day Mary was seen stirring the gruel, as no doubt a dutiful daughter should, and that night Mr Blandy was seriously ill. When suspicion turned to poison, Mary was seen to burn a packet she afterwards said contained letters from Cranstoun. But the servants rescued a small parcel containing some white powder. Mr Blandy himself was told of the suspicions and said, 'Poor lovesick girl! What won't a girl do for a man she loves?' Mary duly implored his forgiveness, to which he replied, 'I forgive thee, my dear, and I hope God will forgive thee; but thou shouldst have considered better than to have attempted anything against thy father.' Probably poisoned on the nights of the 5th and 6th, Mr Blandy died on 14 August. Mary made a foolish attempt at flight, but was apprehended and taken to Oxford Castle to await trial.

The Sheldonian Theatre being unavailable, the trial was held in the fine Hall of the Oxford Divinity School. The poison had already taken its toll of another innocent. The old charwoman was too sick to attend, but the maidservant did give evidence despite the fact that she was 'worn down to a skelliton'. Although the prosecution's opening statements condemned this crime 'of so black a dye', and proclaimed it worse than a common murder because it was perpetrated by a child 'who has murdered her own father', the motive given for the crime was simple enough: the life of Mr Blandy was 'an obstacle' to the union of the lovers.

The trial is considered most noteworthy amongst forensic commentators because it was 'the first one of which there is any detailed record in which convincing scientific proof of poison was given'.

This scientific evidence took several forms. Firstly, there were the symptoms which the consulting doctors witnessed in the dying Mr Blandy, such as vomiting and purging. Then there were the signs of an unnatural death revealed by the post-mortem: his back and other parts were livid, the fat on the muscles of his belly was loose and inclining to fluidity, the 'cawl' was yellower than natural, the heart had purple spots, there was no water in the pericardium, the lungs were blotted in some places with pale ink, but in most places with black ink, the liver and spleen were greatly discoloured, the bile was of a dirty yellow colour, inclining to red, the kidneys were stained with livid spots, the stomach and bowels were inflated and contained nothing but a slimy, bloody froth, and the internal coat of the stomach and duodenum was prodigiously inflamed and excoriated; on the other hand, there was not the least trace of natural decay in any part whatever. Finally, there were the tests that the doctor did on the powder saved from the fire. These tests showed that in appearance (milky white), texture and taste (gritty and almost insipid), smell (garlicky) and in its chemical reactions with other substances (spirit of sal ammoniac, lixivium of tartar, spirit of vitriol, spirit of violet) the powder was identical to white arsenic. The doctor did not find arsenic in the body, because there were no means of testing for it at the time.

Despite the dubious value of the experiments, neither the prosecution nor the defence questioned the fact that Mr Blandy had been poisoned. Mary Blandy herself did not doubt it. Her guilt or innocence turned on a single point: did she know of the true contents of the love-powder? She claimed that she did not, that she had been duped by her conniving lover. The evidence against her was substantial: she had previously seen the poisonous effects of the philtre, she had made contradictory statements and implied confessions, she had burned the letters and the powder, and she had tried to flee. In addition, she had sent a damning letter to Cranstoun warning him to 'take care' what he wrote in case any 'accident should happen' to his letters. She need not have worried. Her gallant companion soon skipped the country, never to return. He died in Flanders the following year, after a short but agonizing illness. He did gain a small measure of immortality, however, in the character of Didapper in Henry Fielding's *Joseph Andrews*. The single crucial question did not exercise the minds of the all-male jury for long. They did not retire but consulted together for five minutes before returning a guilty verdict.

In the month before her execution, Mary Blandy conducted a correspondence with another condemned prisoner, Elizabeth Jeffries. Although their circumstances were similar, there was one key difference, which was noted by contemporaries such as Horace Walpole: Jeffries had murdered her uncle, but he had 'debauched' her; Blandy had killed 'so tender a parent, that his whole concern while he was expiring, and knew her for his murderess, was to save her life'.

There was a sad irony in all this. After he died, it was discovered that Mr Blandy's estate was worth nothing like £10 000. He had therefore conspired in his own death.

At the foot of the fatal tree in the yard of Oxford Castle on 6 March 1752,

Mary Blandy declared to the spectators that she was 'guilty of administering the powder to her father, but without knowing that it had the least poisonous quality in it, or intending to do him any injury'. As she ascended the ladder to the gallows, she said to her executioners, 'Gentlemen, do not hang me high, for the sake of decency.'

—◌—

One of the major problems the Blandy case had highlighted was the absence of infallible tests for poisons. The only test available in the case of Marie d'Aubray, Marquise de Brinvilliers, for instance, was to feed the suspected poison to an animal.

In 1775, however, Karl Wilhelm Scheele began to rectify the situation. In an admirably concise description, the historian of homicide Colin Wilson explains that Scheele discovered 'he could make an acid from arsenic by dissolving the oxide ("white arsenic") in nitric acid or water containing chlorine, and when zinc was dropped into arsenic acid, a dangerous gas that smelt of garlic was given off – arseniuretted hydrogen, or arsine'. Thus, the presence of oxide in the contents of the stomach could be revealed as a distinctive gas in a few easy steps.

Ten years later, Samuel Hahnemann went further. He learned that 'when sulphuretted hydrogen is bubbled into arsenic acid, the result is a yellow deposit – yellow sulphate of arsenic (which the ancients knew as orpiment, and used as a caustic and depilatory)'. When heated, this produces white arsenic: 'So a mixture containing suspected arsenic could again be identified by three simple steps: dissolving in nitric acid, mixing with sulphuretted hydrogen, and heating – alone or with charcoal – to produce white arsenic.'

Johann Metzger then discovered that 'if substances containing arsenic were heated, and a cold plate was held overhead, a white layer of arsenious oxide would form on the plate', and if the arsenic was heated with charcoal until it was red hot 'metallic arsenic would be deposited on a cold plate, or in the cooler part of the test tube – the so-called arsenic mirror'.

This was fine for testing a substance, or the stomach contents, but did not help when the arsenic had been absorbed into the body. Metzger therefore cut up a suspect stomach, boiled it in water, and carefully filtered it. The liquid was then treated with nitric acid, which would convert arsenic acid, which could in turn be given the appropriate tests.

—◌—

Many famous murders produce their novelist or dramatist. Adolphe d'Ennery's play *La Dame de Saint-Tropez*, for instance, based on one of the most famous of all arsenic cases, argued vigorously for the innocence of his heroine.

The story of Marie Lafarge has all the trappings of a Romantic novel: aristocratic society, lovers who worship at a distance but do not speak to each other, illicit love letters, a stolen diamond necklace, ghosts of long-departed monks, a dramatic trial, a heroine imprisoned, and martyrdom. If Charlotte Corday, murderess of Marat, was, in the words of Lamartine, 'the Angel of Assassination', Madame Lafarge was to become 'l'Ange de l'Arsenic'.

Marie Lafarge was born Marie-Fortunée Capelle, of noble rank but in an illegitimate line. Consequently, despite her name, she had little fortune to speak of and occupied only the fringes of high society, envying her friend Marie de Nicolai her legitimacy, her money and her prospects. Steeped in the Romanticism of the time, particularly the writings of George Sand, Edgar Quinet, Lamartine and Victor Hugo, Marie Capelle acted as a kind of go-between for the furtive, though never consummated, love affair, conducted entirely at a distance, of her friend and a young, poetic stranger who followed them in the streets. Marie herself longed for such an ardent admirer.

She was dark-haired and vivacious, ni laide ni jolie. But, although there were one or two men who did show vague interest, by 1839, when she was twenty-three, her high-ranked family began to worry that their by now orphaned relative might live to be an old maid and so prove to be an unwelcome burden.

The De Foy matrimonial agency was approached and she was soon manoeuvred into meeting Charles Lafarge, a youngish widower (although she did not know that) from the Limousin area. Within a few days, the banns of marriage had been published without her knowledge and her relatives had press-ganged her into accepting his proposal. His occupation as ironmaster sounded ruggedly romantic, even if she did not understand what it meant, but her dream of a Byronic figure as a husband contrasted sharply with his face and stature, which she found 'most industrial'. She consoled herself with a vision of his estate, Le Glandier, with its imposing house and its Gothic ruins.

The marriage got off to a disastrous start on the journey south from Paris. Charles Lafarge's uncouth manners and rough advances Marie found abhorrent, and she rebuffed him with withering disdain. Arriving at Le Glandier in the rain, tired and miserable, she found it dilapidated and rat-infested, as tasteless and drab as her new mother-in-law. She wrote a letter to Charles saying that the marriage was a mistake, that she had another (imaginary) lover, and that she would either take arsenic, which she had on her, or, like a true Romantic heroine, vanish and end her days mysteriously in some far and foreign place. She refused all his attempts to assert his spousal rights, and soon had the household and the district in an uproar with her high-handed ways and Parisian fashions. She humbled her husband to the point of canine obsequiousness, insisting they live like brother and sister, rather than husband and wife, and, having established her dominance, set about refurbishing the house at great expense.

Charles Lafarge contributed to his own misery. Although he had invented a process for smelting iron, which had great potential in the coming age of railways and iron bridges, his ironworks was on the verge of bankruptcy, and he soon went through his wife's scant fortune, ably aided by her own profligate demands. Marie herself was frustrated with her lot – divorce laws being what they were, there was no way out of her marriage. In December 1839, Charles was in Paris trying to patent his invention and raise money to capitalize on it. While there, he became violently ill after eating part of a cake sent from Le Glandier (there was later great controversy over whether Marie had sent this cake or not). Coincidentally, on 12 December Marie had written to a chemist in a nearby town complaining that they were being devoured by rats and that the paste made of nux vomica which they were using did no good. Could he trust her with a little arsenic?

When Charles returned home his wife fussed over him, nursing him with favourite dishes and taking personal responsibility for his drinks. She also got 4 grams of arsenic from her chemist, along with some gum arabic, followed later by 64 grams – enough, no doubt, to kill every rat in a very wide radius. Later she gave a packet to the gardener.

By this time, Charles was vomiting continually and was greatly afflicted with diarrhoea and headaches. When one of the family saw Marie stirring white powder into his glass – Marie said it was a little 'fleur d'oranger' – it was shown to the doctor, who tasted some. It was acrid and left a blister on his tongue. He burned a little of it and it gave out a smell of garlic, which is characteristic of arsenic. The family became deeply suspicious and accusations of poisoning were thrown about, aimed particularly at Marie. Charles himself, frequently losing consciousness, his heartbeat irregular and his extremities cold, was informed of the suspicions. He died on 14 January 1840.

A small sample of the gum arabic that Marie kept in a little malachite box and from which she had once given a dose to her husband was found to have traces of arsenic. Arsenic was found in the dregs of egg and milk she had prepared for Charles; it was even found in the bread and wine. The only place it was *not* found was in the packet given to the gardener – this contained nothing more than bicarbonate of soda, which might well have helped rather than harmed the rat population! Marie could not explain what had happened to the 64 grams of arsenic (it takes about two grains – 0.13 grams – to kill someone). The doctors at the autopsy detected arsenic in the stomach of Charles Lafarge, but there were doubts about this finding. In the course of a search, a diamond necklace that had been reported stolen from Marie's friend, Marie de Nicolai

– now Vicomtesse de Léautaud – was discovered. Marie always claimed that the vicomtesse had given it to her to sell, so that she could buy back her love letters to the ardent admirer of her earlier, more indiscreet days.

Marie was arrested but vehemently proclaimed her innocence, characterizing herself as 'la pauvre calomniée'. Her name and her cause were trumpeted throughout Europe.

Her trial was held in Tulle in September 1840. Her case is intriguing for its human drama. But it is more important for another reason. Had she come to court a decade earlier, the outcome of her trial might have been very different. Till then there was no reliable means of identifying arsenic in human remains.

However, in the early 1830s, an English chemist by the name of James Marsh, building on the work of Scheele, had devised an apparatus and procedure for confining the gas produced when arsenic reacted with zinc. This proved capable of detecting the smallest amount of arsenic – a thousandth of a milligram. Marsh published his findings in the *Edinburgh Philosophical Journal* of October 1836.

After a barrage of accusations and plenty of evidence of an incriminating kind, the trial was going badly for Marie. Then one of the chemists who had examined the exhumed body of Charles Lafarge delivered his report. They had used the newly discovered Marsh test. They had found no traces of arsenic whatsoever.

The courtroom burst into an uproar. There was even spontaneous applause. Marie's shoulders lifted as if an angel had carried off her burden.

Her lawyer exclaimed: 'So, the liquids in the stomach, the substances vomited, the stomach itself, the intestines – in fact, the entire body has been submitted to analysis; and not an atom of arsenic is there! This might have been settled eight months ago, and there would have been no accusation.'

Marie's release seemed a formality.

But the judges were not happy. One of the chemists had maintained that, despite the negative results of the Marsh test, all of Charles Lafarge's symptoms had pointed to poisoning. A further expert was to be called in.

Mathieu Joseph Bonaventura Orfila was born in Minorca in 1787. After studying at Valencia and Barcelona, he got his degree in medicine in Paris, aged twenty-four. He pioneered the science of toxicology when he published his *Traité des poisons ou Toxiologie générale* in 1814.

Orfila hurried down to Tulle and with the help of two trusted colleagues he conducted his experiments over four days. The drama of his appearance in the witness box – black-coated and hawk-nosed, with a bald head and pursed mouth, like some sour bird of prey – was enhanced when a great storm erupted overhead. The courtroom grew dark, the thunder crashed, bolts of lightning and sheets of rain were thrown down from above. 'Arsenic,' he said caustically, 'exists in the body of Lafarge.' He indicated that the Marsh test undertaken by the other chemists had not been carried out properly. The amount he had found – half a milligram – was minute, but it was undoubtedly there; and he showed that it was neither the arsenic normally found in the human body (which exists only in the bones), nor was it derived from the reactives used in testing or the earth in which the coffin had been buried. The smallness of the quantity he attributed to the continual vomiting of Lafarge and the enormous amount of water he had drunk. This is an extremely important point: finding a small amount of poison may indicate that a much larger amount has been ingested and subsequently purged.

Marie's defence collapsed and she was condemned to life imprisonment. Curiously, this gave her the Romantic fame she craved. The martyrdom of the incarcerated aristocrat was better than the mundane life of the bourgeois. Her memoirs met with some acclaim, and many prominent figures protested her innocence. She played up to this, cultivating a pious aura. 'There is no worse despotism than that of virtue,' said the Angel of Arsenic. But the dark, secretive world of the arsenic poisoner was no longer quite so secure, thanks to the clear light shone on it by scientists like Marsh and Orfila.

It may be argued that the Lafarge case was a transitional one. Until then, arsenic had been relatively difficult to come by and the tradition of poisonings – at least the recorded ones – had been largely political and in the upper ranks of society.

But from the nineteenth century on, arsenic would be used for many other purposes. In commerce, it was used in the making of glass, in the mixing of artist's paints, in taxidermy and the preservation of skins and certain museum artefacts, in pharmaceuticals, in acid-resistant copper and antimonial lead alloys. In medicine, it was used in small doses (a fiftieth of a gram) for a variety of ailments, and in much larger doses (though in organic combination) in Salvarsan for syphilis. It was not unknown as an abortifacient. Above all, it was used in sheep dip, flypaper and weedkiller.

As it became easier to obtain, so arsenic became less the *powder of succession* and more the *ingredient of malice domestic*. Domestic murder is the second great tradition of poisoning.

Poison has certain advantages as a murder weapon. Since it can be administered at a distance (placed in food or drink which may only be consumed days or months afterwards), there is some latitude to establish an alibi. Seldom are there eyewitnesses to the actual introduction of the poison. On the other hand, the use of poison usually entails a fairly intimate relationship with the victim and casts suspicion on a small handful of potential culprits.

Because of its almost inevitably secretive function, poison is often called the coward's weapon. John Glaister, one of the authorities on poisoning, points out in his book *The Power of Poison* that it differs from many other crimes which are committed in the heat of the moment: 'The innate character of the crime of homicidal poisoning demands subterfuge, cunning and, what is equally important, usually a period of careful planning, and also not infrequently the repetition of the act of administering poison. On this account, it immediately singles itself out and is relegated to a category of crime which stands alone. Its characteristic being one of premeditation, it is a method of murder which therefore cannot be the subject of extenuation as some other forms of killing can, but, when proved, must severely be rewarded by stringent punishment.' In addition, this cold premeditation means that a plea of insanity has seldom worked as a legal defence.

Poison is also popularly regarded as a woman's weapon. In *The Daughters of Cain*, for example, Renée Huggett and Paul Berry suggest that the characteristics one might expect to find in criminal women are vanity, dishonesty, craftiness, sensuality, a violent temper, contradictory religious tendencies, a capacity to lead a double life, and a tendency to place themselves in involved situations. Allied to this, they suggest, might be certain basic traits common amongst all criminals, such as an instinct for self-betrayal, an impulse to return to the scene of the crime, an attraction to aliases going beyond the bounds of mere precaution, and an indifference to consequences, even to death. They might have added to the general characteristics a certain blindness to external reality, leading to unbelievably stupid mistakes.

Perhaps it *is* true that, at least historically, men have preferred more direct, and women more indirect, methods of killing; but, even if some of the controversial generalizations made above are valid, it is by no means true that poison is exclusively a woman's instrument.

In March 1912, Frederick Henry Seddon and his wife Margaret were tried at the Old Bailey for the murder of Eliza Mary Barrow. Miss Barrow was a middle-aged woman of independent means who rented rooms from the Seddons. At the beginning of September 1911, she became ill from what two doctors described as 'epidemic diarrhoea'. Her condition remained serious though reasonably stable until the night of the 13th when it deteriorated markedly, culminating in her death early the following morning. One of the doctors was happy to issue a death certificate blaming natural causes.

Frederick Seddon's failure to notify relatives, his haste in burying the deceased, the disappearance of her ready cash, the transference of most of her assets to Seddon in return for an annuity which would cease at her death, a will made two days before she died, and his furtive obstruction of any enquiries, awakened the suspicions of these relatives. Two months later, the police began to investigate and Miss Barrow's body was exhumed. Its remarkable state of preservation was an external indication of what was to be found.

The senior scientific analyst to the Home Office, Dr William Henry Willcox, gave evidence, which was tested but not shaken by the famous defence counsel, Sir Edward Marshall Hall. Using the Marsh test, Willcox calculated that there was 0.11 of a grain of arsenic in the stomach and 0.63 of a grain in the intestines. In all, he calculated that he found 2.01 grains in the whole body – just enough for what is usually regarded as a fatal dose – and estimated that, because the body normally rejects the poison by vomiting, purging and urinating, there might have been up to 5 grains taken within three days of death.

He described the symptoms of acute arsenic poisoning as faintness and collapse, severe pain in the abdomen, severe vomiting and purging, sometimes cramp in the ankles and a great thirst, depending on the amount of vomiting and diarrhoea. One would expect acute pain in the abdomen within thirty minutes. The maximum period that might elapse between the fatal dose and death would be three days; the minimum period a few hours, five or six. Arsenic would be found in the heart, liver, kidneys and muscles, as well as the stomach and intestines – perhaps in fingernails and hair, too. Willcox had not the slightest doubt that Miss Barrow's death was due to arsenical poisoning.

There are several interesting factors in the Chinese puzzle (the words used by Seddon himself) that was the Seddon case. Firstly, not only was there no evidence that Seddon had administered arsenic directly to Miss Barrow, but there was also no evidence that the Seddons actually had arsenic in their possession. Nevertheless, the judge in his summing-up maintained that, although the jury 'must be very slow to convict upon circumstantial evidence', there are crimes 'committed in darkness and secrecy which can only be traced and brought to light by a comparison of circumstances which press upon the mind more and more as they are increased in number'.

Secondly, the prosecution did believe they knew where the arsenic came from. Although the defence disputed this vigorously, a chemist claimed to have sold the Seddons' daughter arsenical flypapers. These were not the sticky hanging strips (which probably did not contain arsenic), but Mather's flypapers (which did). Mather's flypapers were designed to be moistened and left lying around in saucers. The defence not only challenged the identification of the Seddon daughter by the chemist, but drew out the fact that he had failed to keep a poison register and to record the alleged transaction.

Thirdly, because the circumstantial evidence was gossamer thin, the prosecution played more strongly on the motive – the financial interest that Mr Seddon may have had in Miss Barrow's death. But they went even further, suggesting that the *conduct* of the accused, before and after the fact, might be a significant part of the circumstantial evidence.

Fourthly, the defence, in time-honoured fashion, raised the possibilities of suicide or accident: deliberately or not, Miss Barrow might have drunk the contents of the flypaper saucers (the prosecution scathingly pointed out that she might have had to lick them!). More reasonably, if no less predictably, the defence insinuated that death might have been caused accidentally by the maid, whom they continually characterized as an incompetent and wild eccentric, a woman who was unable to keep jobs for long and whose mental condition bore comparison with her brother, who had spent twenty years in an asylum. The prosecution countered that it was most unlikely that she had had the opportunity to deliver a fatal dose of arsenic (by inadvertently infusing flypaper water into the Valentine's meat juice or the tea).

Finally, there was the question of whether husband and wife had acted in concert, and, if so, the precise apportionment of blame. In this regard the judge said, 'If any acts were done by either of them, or by both of them with the knowledge and acquiescence of the other that these acts were being done in furtherance of the common purpose, both are guilty.' In the event, Mrs Seddon was acquitted; Mr Seddon was found guilty and hanged.

Eureka weedkiller, a pink powder consisting of sodium arsenic, introduced into wine, was allegedly the poison taken by Mabel Greenwood in a small village near Carmarthen in Wales in 1919. Suspicion fell on her husband, Harold Greenwood, a solicitor, when he proposed marriage to another woman within a month of his wife's death and remarried within four. Mabel's body was exhumed ten months after her demise, and eighteen milligrams of arsenic – or slightly more than a quarter of a grain – were found in the body (the muscles were excluded from analysis). Although this was short of the two grains usually believed to be a lethal dose, Dr Willcox, called once again as an expert, was quite categorical at the inquest that Mabel had died from acute arsenical poisoning. Willcox estimated three quarters of a grain in the body and said the shortfall was attributable to distribution, vomiting and purging. He suggested at the inquest and at the trial that, in respect of the speed of poisoning, if the stomach is full and the arsenic is in solid form, death is more likely to be delayed; if the stomach is empty and the arsenic is in solution, distribution and death are likely to be quicker. In this case, from the width of distribution he concluded that the arsenic was probably taken in a dissolved state. From the fact that very little arsenic was left in the stomach (less than one thirtieth of a milligram, which is less than one hundredth of a grain, i.e. more than twenty times less than was found in Jacottet's stomach), Willcox inferred that the poison would have been taken more than three hours before death – probably nine or ten hours.

He asserted that the final cause of death was heart failure from 'the prolonged diarrhoea, due to the effects of the poison'. In answer to the question whether 'an affection of the heart' of the kind suffered by Mabel Greenwood would make any difference to someone who had taken arsenic, the scientist replied, 'Very much. It would diminish the resistance of the person to a great extent. A small dose would produce much greater effects than on a normal person.'

As in the Seddon case, the defence was led by Marshall Hall, but this time it was more successful. The circumstantial evidence proved not quite strong enough, and Marshall Hall laid a trail of doubts concerning tainted gooseberries and prior health problems. But in finding Greenwood not guilty, the jury still clearly had reservations about his innocence and took the unusual step of handing the judge a paper which stated: 'We are satisfied on the evidence in this case that a dangerous dose of arsenic was administered to Mabel Greenwood ... but we are not satisfied that this was the immediate cause of death. The evidence before us is insufficient, and does not conclusively satisfy us as to how, and by whom, the arsenic was administered.'

It is often assumed that arsenic is a cumulative poison, which is administered in small doses over a long time. One such instance of chronic poisoning took place in Scotland and was popularly known as the Oxgang Farm Case. Robert McMillan had been ill, off and on, for some time, but his condition became serious on 29 December 1939, to the extent that he had to take to his bed. He died on 6 January in the new year. Medical testimony established that he had ingested a massive dose of arsenic. The stomach and intestinal contents contained solid arsenic crystals, which must have been taken orally. In cold water, white arsenic is minimally dissolved (about 0.1 per cent dissolves); in boiling water, over several hours, up to 12 per cent will dissolve, but on cooling it will crystallize out again, leaving only 2 per cent in solution. In McMillan's stomach and intestines 11.06 grains were found and in his liver 2.33 grains. As the liver cannot take more than 3 grains and the amount steadily declines thereafter, the forensic analysts had no doubt that a massive dose had been given within twenty-four hours of death. The 11.06 grains in the stomach and intestines were more than enough to kill, but were not the cause of death: as one expert said 'it is the amount absorbed that kills, not the amount found'. It was clear that McMillan was poisoned twice, on 29 December and also within twenty-four hours of his death.

But other evidence was produced which indicated that, because of its distribution in his hair and fingernails, arsenic had been 'passing out of the man's body into these structures for at least four months prior to death'. The conclusion was obvious – there had been chronic poisoning over months and acute poisoning in the few days just before death. This almost certainly ruled out accident or suicide, two of the defences so popular in such cases. That left murder.

Suspicion fell on the wife of the deceased, Margaret McMillan. So she was arrested and tried. In England, one can only be found guilty or not guilty; in Scotland, however, there is a third alternative. The case against Margaret McMillan was found to be 'not proven'.

Chronic poisoning is insidious, slowly sapping the vitality of the victim; acute poisoning is sudden and shocking, giving the sufferer little time for farewells or reflection on the last things. Both are, of course, reprehensible. There are particular difficulties if you want to murder by chronic arsenic poisoning. You have to get the quantities pretty close to right (and they vary from person to person) so that the symptoms resemble natural selection rather than a series of cataclysmic lurches.

On the question of chronic poisoning there is a footnote to be added. As early as the first century BC, Mithridates, King of Pontus, took poison in order to build up immunity, hence bequeathing us the word 'mithridatism'. In Styria and the Tyrol, where arsenic used to be plentifully available as a result of iron-ore smelting, the locals actually ate it, supposedly as an aphrodisiac or a cure for impotence. One man was observed to consume five grains in one day – over twice a normal lethal dose!

Throughout history, one of the factors that poisoners have relied on is the difficulty of diagnosis. The symptoms of arsenic poisoning, for instance, are so similar to various other maladies, from gastro-enteritis, dysentery and cholera to food poisoning, that numerous murders must have gone undetected.

Since arsenic is white, has little odour (the garlic smell can easily be eradicated) and is only mildly sweet, it is easily disguised. Mary Blandy did it with gruel, Charlotte Bryant with Oxo (the beef extract).

Charlotte McHugh was a nineteen-year-old Irish girl who met Frederick Bryant when he was stationed with the Dorset Regiment in Londonderry before Irish independence and partition. Fourteen years and four children later (with a fifth child on the way, courtesy of a lover), she was living in a remote farm labourer's cottage near Sherborne in Dorsetshire, her looks vanished, her illiteracy consigning her to a life of tedium. Only her casual pickups at the local alehouses brought moments of excitement. Her husband generally seemed to ignore her. In these circumstances, she met her gypsy lover, Leonard Parsons, who even moved in with the Bryants for a while at the suggestion of her husband.

In May 1935, and again in August, Frederick Bryant was assailed by acute attacks of what the doctor diagnosed as gastro-enteritis. On 21 December, he again became very sick. At three o'clock next morning, a friend heard Charlotte prompting her husband to take some Oxo made from a cube given to one of her children the previous day. Twelve hours later Frederick Bryant died – of arsenic poisoning.

Evidence was never produced at her trial that she had bought arsenic (although Parsons had since tried to buy some for a sick mare, and a tin of weedkiller had been bought a few days beforehand and signed in a poison register with an 'X' that police were sure was Charlotte's mark). Charlotte was hanged in July 1936. Her motive remains mysterious. The prosecution argued that Parsons had told her in November he was leaving her for good, and the murder was an attempt to clear the way for getting him back. More likely it arose from a lifetime of frustration and a half-formed desire for freedom.

—❦—

MOM. These are the three main ingredients generally looked for in the diagnosis of a crime. Means. Opportunity. Motive. It is clear that the last of these is often the most difficult to pin down. It is often when evidence, including circumstantial evidence, is weakest that the detective, in the first instance, and the prosecution, in the second, must push hard enough for a motive.

Yet in many murder cases it has not been necessary to find or to prove a motive. And often the motive given, as in Charlotte Bryant's case, is neither very strong nor very convincing. In his summing-up to the jury in Major Armstrong's trial, the judge said to them: 'It is usual to look for a motive in any crime, but you will never find, in such a crime as this, a motive which you or I, I hope, would think an adequate motive. That does not prove that it is not a perfectly sufficient motive for another person with a criminal mind.'

Some motives are fairly readily identifiable and assignable. In *Murder and its Motives*, Miss F. Tennyson Jesse slots them into six categories: gain, revenge, elimination, jealousy, lust for killing, killing for conviction. John Glaister adds a seventh: sex. In recent times it has become possible and popular to add at least one other: child or sexual abuse. Of course, in practice, these motives often overlap.

The most interesting aspect of any murder, then, is likely to be not who or how, but why. It is also the most difficult to untangle, and often daunting, or even frightening. Because beyond the seven motives of Tennyson Jesse and Glaister, there is another possibility, terrible to contemplate: what if there is no why?

The most infamous poisoner in South Africa was Daisy de Melker, whose main motive was money. After exterminating her first two husbands with strychnine, for insurance and savings, she did not baulk at filicide, and preferred arsenic for her twenty-year-old son who wanted to inherit the estate. She was hanged, five days after Christmas in 1932, before ever she could be tried for several suspicious deaths in Rhodesia.

The struggle between poisoners and the law has always been one of hide and seek. If one can talk about an overall strategy in the war against poison, then it has had three prongs.

Firstly, there was the frontal attack by scientific method in the detection and identification of poisons through the Marsh test and its successors, the Reinsch and Gutzeit tests, for arsenic, and through alternative tests for other poisons. The second, flanking attack has involved the control of poison. In 1851, the British parliament passed the Arsenic Act, which laid out the conditions of the sale of arsenic. All arsenic, other than that for agricultural use, had to be coloured with soot or indigo. Registers, with details of the purchaser, were required to be kept. The final, pincer movement was the introduction and tightening of rules regarding the registration of death.

Before the Criminal Evidence Act was introduced in Britain in 1898, the accused remained silent in court. The Act at last allowed them to give evidence in their own defence, but they were not obliged to do so. A decision not to testify was not meant to prejudice their case. This change in the law brought somewhat ambiguous choices and benefits. The personal testimony of convicted arsenic poisoner Major Armstrong may well have weighed against him, and who knows what might have happened had accused poisoner Madeleine Smith taken the witness stand. Indeed, the editor of the *Notable British Trials* volume on the Seddons was almost categorical that Frederick Seddon's appearance on the stand, together with his cool demeanour, was decisive in his conviction: 'If Seddon had not given evidence himself the Crown would have failed to prove a case sufficient to secure a verdict of murder against him, and without his evidence few jurymen would have dared to bring in a verdict of guilty.'

In a murder case there is always confusion about the facts, the motives and the personalities, and interest and even sympathy often surround the accused or the culprit. In literature, *Macbeth* is the exemplary model. One may be carried away by an intellectual interest in the mind of the murderer. But before sentimentalizing the position of any murderer, we should not overlook the fact that in all instances another voice has been silenced – that of the victim.

The full horror of a murder by poisoning is often glossed over. As in the example of Hamlet's father, not only is the victim 'cut off even in the blossoms' of his sins, but the manner of the death is also hideous. The effect of the henbane or yew, in the words of the dead king's ghost,

> Holds such an enmity with blood of man
> That, swift as quicksilver, it courses through
> The natural gates and alleys of the body;
> And, with a sudden vigour, it doth posset
> And curd, like eager droppings into milk,
> The thin and wholesome blood. So did it mine;
> And a most instant tetter barked about,
> Most lazar-like, with vile and loathsome crust
> All my smooth body.

If the choice is cyanide, a vegetable poison distilled from laurel leaves, or the stones of certain fruit such as peaches, apricots, plums and cherries, then the blood is blocked from absorbing oxygen and the victim will die from asphyxiation. If it is hyoscine, extracted from the plant henbane, and related to deadly nightshade, it will cause giddiness and respiratory failure, as Dr Crippen discovered. If it is chloroform (as in the case of Thomas Bartlett) or hydrochloric acid, it will burn the mouth and throat and cause hours of frightful agony. If it is morphine, derived from white poppies via opium, it will induce a deep narcosis, combined with sweating and convulsions. If it is phosphorus (used to poison rats, until its banning after the case of Louis Merrifield), then a tiny amount will cause damage to the liver, haemorrhaging, thirst, delirium and a coma. If it is cantharides or 'Spanish fly', derived from the *Lytta vesicatoria* beetle and also used as an aphrodisiac – employed, it is said, by Mme de Montespan – it will cause fatal shock. If it is strychnine, it will attack the central nervous system or the brain, causing the characteristic arching of the back and intense pain, while the victim remains conscious. Its legacy is the 'risus sardonicus', the sinister smile of death, on the lips of the corpse.

Before he died from arsenic, Mr Blandy felt a grittiness in his mouth and an excruciating burning in his tongue and throat, stomach and bowels, his belly swelled prodigiously and he felt exquisite pains and prickings in every part of his body, external and internal, which he compared to an infinite number of needles darting simultaneously into him. As his body tried to expel the poison, fits of violent vomiting quickly weakened him. He had cold sweats, hiccups, an intermittent pulse, difficult respiration, bloody stools, 'gleety excoriations and ulcers' surrounding his fundament, and angry pimples round his lips. (In its chronic form, arsenic will head for the extremities, including the hair and fingernails, will cause blisters and lesions, and numbness in feet and hands.) Blandy eventually attributed his teeth dropping out to the poison, and likened himself to a rabid dog unable to drink.

In his book on Blanche Taylor Moore, the modern-day psychopathic murderess from North Carolina, Jim Schutze describes with chilling realism what he calls the 'chemical drama' of arsenic poisoning. Starting with flulike symptoms of sore throat and diarrhoea, the victim may become sweaty, nervy, skittish. Inside, Schutze suggests, the victim is being eaten alive, cell by cell, because 'the secret of arsenic is that it loves life, races to life, embraces it, combines with it quickly and consumes it hungrily, converting it chemically, molecule by molecule, from life into death'. In its attempt to fight off and expel the monster within, the body will try to vomit it out and purge it, but the poison soon 'boils off' the inner lining of the stomach and bowel, the walled organs and blood vessels turning to mush as all the fluids begin 'to leach in the open areas of the body cavity', causing 'chaotic electrical storms' in muscles and the nervous system, and 'sprinting even deeper into the physical and chemical structure' that is life. For most of the process, the victim might remain conscious, 'slipping in and out of the madness caused by slow oxygen starvation'. Towards the end, however, the suffocation of the brain may allow hallucinations or merciful unconsciousness.

When the poison is ingested as an arsenate – the molecule in its pentavalent form – the kidneys try to break it down in order to excrete it. But, in so doing, they are also signing a death warrant, because they hold back minute amounts of the much more poisonous trivalent form. As this cannot be so readily excreted, the body tries 'to seize it instead and bind it up … where it would do the least immediate harm, particularly in the bones, hair and nails, where it would reside harmlessly though permanently, or until the hair or nails were cut'.

Since it was arsenic that killed Jacottet, then, once unleashed, the monster within gnawed away with grim purpose (undeterred by sex or rank or religion), the anonymous agent of man or woman, king or commoner, spouse or stranger, teacher or pupil, parent or child, printer or printer's devil, master or servant. The arsenic simply did its job. There was no way of telling, by interrogating the

CHAPTER TWENTY-SEVEN

REVELATIONS

B roken pieces of information reach us in the middens of time. But other expressive sherds (Egypt, Pompeii) are carefully stored – in jars, on walls, in memories. Morija has been lucky in its curator of collective memory. He has been tending its archival garden for over fifty years, collecting, organizing, preserving, growing: it is largely owing to him that the small but fine documentary collection at Morija complements the large repository in the old Maison des Missions on Boulevard Arago in Paris. The two collections dovetail almost perfectly. It is also because of him that there surfaced, three quarters of a century after the event, one of the most important pieces of evidence in the explanation of the Jacottet murder.

Albert Brutsch was born in Geneva in 1916. In his home town he studied at the Theological Faculty, which was an autonomous branch of the University. After his confirmation, he had attended church youth groups and had been particularly attracted to a missionary youth group. At the first field meeting they studied Lesotho, using a book based on the *Livre d'Or*, which was very popular at the time. So Jacottet was not unconnected with the future destiny of Albert Brutsch. The young man had listened to missionaries, on furlough, giving talks, and through his participation in the youth groups he received notice of missionary youth group conferences in France. The first camp he attended was in 1937. The second, in 1938, was at La Force, the asylum for Protestant invalids started by John Bost in France in the nineteenth century, where Alfred Casalis had been Director for some time after leaving Lesotho in 1926. Casalis, though retired, was present at the conference, and M. Zurcher, in charge of the Morija Printing Works, was specially invited. Zurcher gave a lecture and showed slides of Lesotho. 'What determined my candidacy for the PEMS and the mission was La Force,' Rev. Brutsch said recently. He wrote off to his parents and said, 'Now I am clear about my calling.' He also mentioned his intention to go to mission headquarters in Paris, on his way to northern France to do parish work (like Arbousset a hundred years before) in the mining areas, thus gaining experience.

Through his service in the missionary youth organization – he eventually became chairman of the whole federation in the Suisse Romande area – he met

Aline du Pasquier, a social worker, who was from a Neuchâtelois family. When he finished his theological studies, he made a formal application to join the PEMS. By this time much of France had been overrun by the Germans, so Brutsch never did the additional training at mission headquarters which was usual at the time. Nor, of course, did he have the opportunity of going to Britain to improve his English.

After his marriage and his ordination in 1941, he was duly posted to Basutoland. But getting there was easier said than done. To get to southern Africa, he had to take ship in Portugal. The British gave him a visa to Basutoland, but the Portuguese refused him one. So he and Aline went to live in Neuchâtel: the Portuguese consul in nearby Berne was Swiss and Protestant, and so regarded their application more favourably. A Portuguese visa finally having been obtained, Brutsch now found the British one had meanwhile expired. Then to get to Portugal they had to cross France, and to do this they had to get permission from the Germans. Finally, having reached Portugal safely, they were delayed while their ship waited for the Portuguese Minister of Colonies, who was on his way to São Tomé where he had plantations. They stopped there, and then in the Congo Estuary, where some Belgians who had escaped through France and Spain disembarked. The only people allowed to leave the ship at Cape Town were the Free French representative of De Gaulle, who was evading the compulsory labour service under Vichy, and his wife and son. From Lourenço Marques, Albert and Aline travelled by train to Johannesburg, in July 1942, then on to Marseilles siding, where they were met by R.A. Paroz. Conference had decided that Brutsch would spend his induction period under Paroz, a distinguished linguist, at Thaba-Bosiu.

Here, in the former home of Casalis, of Jousse, and of Jacottet, the eldest daughter of the Brutsches was born. Here Albert spent eight months learning Sesotho and studying the history of the mission. He was a committed missionary; but he also had qualities necessary for a good historian and archivist – patience, meticulousness, integrity, reverence, and, most important of all, curiosity. He is the most trustworthy of witnesses.

Albert knew of Jacottet, of course. He had read his books; he had learned from his grammar; he even had a postcard, sent three decades before, to Aline's aunt by Mrs Jacottet, showing the house at Koapeng, Morija. But he was soon reminded that Jacottet had a living influence on the Basutoland church, and that some of his outspoken and controversial ideas had not died with him.

Albert accompanied Paroz to a meeting of the local Presbytery. Before the more administrative business, a one-day retreat was held to give the ministers some additional training. Paroz gave a lesson on the value of liturgy in the service, because he felt it was being somewhat neglected at the time. Part of the liturgy had been introduced by Henri Marzolff, missionary at Bethesda until 1909, to win the respect of his prospective bride, who was from Alsace where liturgy was perhaps more in demand. When Paroz was explaining to the ministers the value of liturgy, one of them, Ezere Masaase, of the Class of 1917 (Jacottet's last class) at the Theological School, shook his head disapprovingly and said, 'Our teacher, Jacottet, told us that the liturgy was the "dot" [the dowry] of Mrs Marzolff.'

After his training, Albert was sent as missionary to the parish of Cana, in the district of Teyateyaneng. The station at Cana had been reopened in 1873 and occupied by Frédéric Kohler, who remained there till 1908. Albert stayed there until his first furlough in 1949. Subsequently, he was posted to Leribe, and then in 1953 to Morija, where he renewed his association with Jacottet by becoming Director of the Theological School.

Soon after Albert's arrival at Cana, he met an old catechist who lived close by; Benjamin Lesia was well into his eighties, retired, blind, and helped along by his wife, who was much younger than he. Her name was Jerita.

They had been married on 6 May 1924, while Benjamin was catechist at Malimong, an outstation of the Cana parish. Jerita Mabitso was living at Matsieng at the time. The Morija parish register, in which their marriage was recorded, gave his age as sixty-four, hers as thirty-seven. In fact, she was older. Her birth was entered in the Morija register (under No. 934) as: Gerita Sara (daughter of) Rafa and Delina, 28 February 1884, at Matsieng. She was baptized at Morija on 1 June 1884 by Adolphe Mabille, and confirmed at Matsieng in 1902. She was therefore nearly two years older than Marcelle.

Jerita had nursed her husband in his blindness for many years. His obituary notice in *Leselinyana* in 1949 mentions that she regularly read the newspaper to him. Albert Brutsch was intrigued by them (to be fair he was intrigued by almost everything!). So he turned to one of his best local sources of information, the grandson of Kohler. Charles Jacot-Guillarmod knew the area well; his father had a trading store above the Cana mission, on a hill next to the chief's village. He was studying entomology, but when his father died he reluctantly returned to run the store.

So it was from Charles Jacot-Guillarmod that Albert first heard about the murder of Édouard Jacottet, and about Jerita's connection with it.

Albert enquired further, but people were reluctant to talk about the death. The missionaries had put a blanket over the story and the subject was strictly taboo. He did learn one more thing, however, which stuck with him for fifty years. The affair between Marguerite and Duby was not the only one. Marcelle, too, had had an affair … and her lover was one of the students at the Theological

School, where her father was the Director, or one of the students at the Bible School, where Sam Duby was the Director.

It is not known who the student was. Whether he attended the Theological School or the Bible School, it is probable that he was married. The affair was almost certainly conducted in the relative seclusion of the square rondavel (in the grounds of Théo Duby's house), where Marcelle lived before moving back to her father's house when her mother died.

———

In 1938, seventeen years after the Jacottet murder, Macmillan and Co. in London and Little, Brown and Co. in Boston published an obscure novel called *Love at the Mission*. It was by an equally obscure writer called R. Hernekin Baptist.

It is set in a fictional British colony called Bantusiland at a somewhat isolated mission located in mountainous terrain and run by French-speaking missionaries of the 'Swiss Mission'.

The pastor of the mission, Monsieur Oguey, is a language scholar and translator of the Bible who has three daughters, one of whom is at an English-speaking boarding school. They have a cook called Fani. Living nearby, and trapped in a stultifying marriage, is a younger pastor of the same mission, M. Verdin. Three miles away is a rival mission station run by Father Rudolph, who has brought from East Africa an enigmatic servant called Achmed.

Oguey's eldest daughter (Hortense) has an affair with Rudolph's servant; Verdin falls in love with the middle sister (Madeleine); the youngest sister (Estelle) returns from school. Hortense craftily arranges for Madeleine to spend a camping picnic alone with Verdin on the mountain, but their father finds out and forbids his daughter to go. Hortense is furious.

Four visitors descend on the mission for lunch: Father Rudolph, M. Verdin, the Native Commissioner of the country, and the Inspector of Education, a Mr Meadows. A mushroom dish, provided by Mme Verdin, is served. Pastor Oguey eats and dies immediately, while Meadows – the only guest to accept the food – becomes sick but pulls through. Strychnine proves to be the cause of death.

Pastor and Mme Verdin are arrested; Madeleine is arrested; Achmed is arrested.

———

There is no doubt as to the real origin of the tale.

Of course, there are differences between the novel and the real events of the Jacottet murder. The substitution of strychnine is an obvious one: Oguey dies almost immediately, with no clue himself as to the cause or reason for his death. More subtle is the way Mr Baptist clouds the whole story with his own interpretation and his own ideology. He clearly knew some of the details of the events: one of the ways of illuminating his interpretation is to check known facts against his changes, whether deliberate or not.

For effect, the mission was made smaller and more isolated from the outside world than Morija in fact was. The rival mission nearby (paralleling Masite) was changed from Anglican to Roman Catholic. Although Father Rudolph was inspired by the figure of Spencer Weigall, he is German and in no way resembles Jacottet's friend. Although he was on amicable terms with Father Cénez, his colleague at the Conference on Sesuto Orthography, Jacottet was less than likely to have a close friendship with a priest of 'the old enemy'. Nor is there any evidence that there was ever a servant such as Achmed, a Mephistophelean figure like the Parsee in Herman Melville's *Moby Dick*.

The marriage of the Verdins (the Dubys) was distorted: Mme Verdin is presented as Swedish and much older than her husband, whom she mothers. Verdin is much younger, and more innocent and timorous than Sam Duby. For some obscure reason the adulterous affair involves Madeleine, the middle sister, rather than the youngest. Hortense (Marcelle) is also made younger than she actually was.

The mother of the fictional missionary family is presented as having died many years before. This allows the author to portray the daughters as untutored, undisciplined, wild, and lacking a female role model. This is reinforced by the representation of Pastor Oguey as distrait, ineffectual, naive, though a 'gentle scholar' and 'saintly'. Furthermore, he has never been up the nearby mountain and 'vaguely fear[s] it'. Jacottet would have recognized none of this in himself!

In order to highlight certain social, religious and racial ideas, the cook (who is made to be fifteen to twenty years older than Hortense, instead of the eighteen-month gap between Jerita and Marcelle) is much more of a 'heathen' than the third-generation Christian granddaughter of Uriel Mabitsa, who was killed defending mission and country against the Boers in 1858. She it is who becomes the mother substitute for the family.

The guests at the lunch are all adult males and there are no sons in the missionary family. Oguey, like Lear, has only three daughters. Because strychnine is used, he dies in minutes (rather than hours, which is usually the case with arsenic) and his eldest daughter 'confesses' to the Catholic priest and is imprisoned.

—◦—

Little details, however, indicate some close knowledge on Baptist's part: the polo-mad 'Native Commissioner' drinks whiskey rather than whisky; there is a rondavel and an 'inner door' between bedrooms in the mission house; the girls not only wear ugly, slightly 'foreign' dresses, but their father also expects morning kisses; the railway siding is called Paris rather than Marseilles; the name 'Oguey' is a small town in Switzerland and 'Verdun' a farm near Marseilles in the Free State; there is an awareness of the martyred past of the Huguenots; there is poison in the pantry.

But the novel also adds supporting evidence to a number of other key elements in the real-life murder. Most importantly, it confirms Albert Brutsch's story of Marcelle's black lover; it is also therefore evidence that there were two affairs, one by Marcelle, one by Marguerite, whereas in popular memory, or what remained of it, these were sometimes conflated into a single relationship between either Marcelle or Marguerite and Duby, thereby providing a rather simplistic motive for the murder; and it hints that Marcelle might have harboured a dreamy passion for Duby before turning to an alternative. It is unequivocal in its assertion that Marcelle was instrumental in pushing Marguerite into the affair with Duby.

Baptist had definite ideas about the motives for the murder. This was 'no common crime of jealousy', he wrote. But it did arise out of a fierce rage and a strong desire for revenge on the part of Marcelle, a wish to hurt her father.

The overwhelming explanation for Baptist was a darkly sexual one. He was concerned with the transition from maidenhood to womanhood, that period when a young woman needs the advice and guiding hand of a mother or older woman to calm the sexual fears that arise when the hawk is in the farmyard, or to control the 'secret lusty life' of the young. If this mentoring is absent, he suggests, an untrained nature might erupt in violence.

Baptist accurately set the novel in the few years just after the Great War. From the vantage point of 1938, looking back over the intervening decades in which the world had been vamped and revamped, he felt it necessary to remind his audience that 'the fashion had not yet arisen when it became almost a convention for young girls to be the bolder of the two sexes'. If in 1918 cosmopolitan women were restrained, then, given the repression of the Protestant mission, their country sisters were doubly so.

He saw the bitterness and anger of Marcelle springing from the deep well of unsatisfied sexuality, making her determined to become the female saviour of her sister and ensure the smooth passage of her first love. When this is thwarted by her father, the thought of murder is 'like the embryo of a monstrous birth'.

Baptist invented a symbol for the secret ways of the subconscious, especially its violent impulses. It was a white rock, halfway up the mountainside, which appeared and disappeared, like a puzzling omen.

R. Hernekin Baptist was, in truth, not a he but a she. The pseudonym came from an obscure source. In 1829, Stephen Glover published a two-volume *History, Gazetteer, and Directory of the County of Derby*. The second volume printed, amongst other things, family trees of prominent families in Derbyshire. In the pedigree of the Allsop family of Allsop-in-the-Dale there was recorded living in 1715 one Baptist Trott, son of Hester Alsopp (variant spellings were normal at the time). On the same page but on a different branch of the tree there is a record of John Alsopp, living in 1598 but dead in 1610, having been married to 'Margaret dau. of Remer Hernekin, of Groningen, West Friezland'. These discrete names were welded into her nom de plume by Ethel Howe, who was born in Derbyshire in 1875 and who claimed descent from the Allsops. In the late 1920s, she became internationally famous (under the name of Ethelreda Lewis) as the co-author – with the old adventurer Aloysius Smith – of the three best-selling Trader Horn books.

But she grew weary of the superficial media attention and resented the fact that her novels were indifferently received. She did not want her subsequent books to be read on reputation alone; she even came to resent the fame the Trader Horn trilogy had brought her. So Ethelreda Lewis changed the name she wrote under.

There was another reason for this, too. Some of her writing might be construed as political and she was married to a civil servant who was not supposed to engage in politics, an unwritten rule that extended to a spouse.

Her husband was a forensic chemist. In 1921, he was the government forensic chemical analyst in Bloemfontein.

A singular aside can be added to this story. There is little doubt that Ethelreda Lewis had read Charles Dickens's *Bleak House*, in which the first fictional detective, Inspector Bucket, appears to solve a murder. He successfully identifies the French maid as the culprit. Dickens modelled the plot on a true crime committed in London in 1849 by a lady's maid called Maria Manning. She was hanged for the murder of her lover (the motive was avarice). Her maiden name was De Roux and she was not actually French, but Swiss-born. Dickens immortalized her under the name of Hortense.

So it is possible that when she wrote her book – one in a long line of fictional murders based on fact – Ethelreda Lewis dressed Marcelle in a disguise culled from a similar story.

—◦⊙—

Although they competed in Switzerland for money and recruits, the relationship of the Mission Suisse Romande with the PEMS was invariably cordial. The Swiss Mission had its roots in a missionary society started in Yverdon in 1821, which was followed by an institution founded in Lausanne in 1829 to train missionaries to serve other Societies. In 1869, two young theological students, Ernest Creux and Paul Berthoud, offered their services as pioneer missionaries to the Free Church.

When the Franco-Prussian War disrupted the activities of the PEMS in 1870, Adolphe Mabille appealed to the Mission of the Free Church for reinforcements. Consequently, Creux and Berthoud arrived in Lesotho in 1872 to work, at least for the moment, under the auspices of the Basutoland Conference. In 1875, they did what Mabille's heart burned to do: they went north to open new stations in the Soutpansberg amongst the Bapedi of the northern Transvaal. Valdezia became the first of these Vaudois stations. Elim followed, and in 1883 the Free Churches of Geneva and Neuchâtel joined those of Vaud to form a fully fledged independent society, the Swiss Mission.

Considerable resources were also put into Mozambique. The Paillards were missionaries of the Swiss Mission; Augsburger was a salaried medical employee.

Alexandre Jaques was a second-generation missionary born at Valdezia. In 1926, he married Lucy Rosset, who was also born there. In 1933, they had a daughter, Pierrette, who was born at Elim. Alexandre died relatively young, but Pierrette was looked after by her mother, an open and delightful person who shared most things with her daughter, including a wide store of stories. Amongst these was one about the death of Édouard Jacottet.

Pierrette was in her late teens or early twenties when she heard it. Her mother told it to her not to warn her or scandalize her, or anything like that, but rather for its tragic qualities. When, out of the dark cavern of time, Pierrette remembered it fifty years afterwards, she cast light on the Jacottet mystery of a quite startling intensity, providing a clue of great importance.

Without any prompting whatsoever, she said in an interview that all she remembered her mother telling her were the dramatic outlines of the story: 'One of the missionary's daughters had a relationship with a black student, had become pregnant, and her father had been poisoned with poison in the soup.' While she uncertainly recalled that the lover was one of the 'évangélistes', not one of the fully qualified pastors, she added, 'That my mother said it was hushed up is very clear in my mind.'

Her mother also said that there had been an abortion.

—◦⊝◦—

That this tiny piece of information survived the bleak amnesia of the past is a small miracle. Its potential significance is enormous. But without corroborating evidence, what is its value?

'Truth,' said Mark Twain, 'is stranger than fiction, but it is because fiction is obliged to stick to possibilities, truth isn't.'

In a strange twist to this strange case, we need to resort to fiction to confirm the truth!

—◦⊝◦—

Ethel Howe was born the daughter of a cultured but impoverished bookseller in Matlock Bath in Derbyshire. She had little formal education, but learned the important things at home from her fond and intelligent parents. As an occupation she took up physical culture, and while teaching eurhythmics in Cambridge she met a German-born South African who was a chemistry student at Trinity Hall. They became engaged in 1897, but because Joseph Lewis owed a relative money borrowed to finance his studies, and because he was a scrupulously honourable man, he refused to marry her until he was out of debt. It was therefore five years before he could send for her to join him. They were married in Cape Town in December 1902.

There are hints that Ethel Howe had had one dark and disastrous affair, probably before she met Joe; during the long five years of waiting, she may also have had some sort of breakdown. This may account for the fact that some of her books, including *Love at the Mission*, were, with some prurience, fascinated by the seamier side of the unchecked libido, particularly in young and adolescent women. After stints in Cape Town and Grahamstown, Joe was transferred to Bloemfontein in 1916 and the Lewises lived at 6 Second Street, beneath Signal Hill. With a small family, they were happy there, attracting a circle of interesting friends, and enjoying plenty of bridge, lectures, music and play-reading.

Joe was a gentle, kind, self-effacing, well-respected person, quite without material ambition. They never had much money, but he gave Ethel the emotional stability she needed, until his death in 1931. They complemented each other: she was bold and imaginative, he was a careful realist with a sound analytical approach.

Ethel started publishing newspaper articles and poetry soon after her marriage. Then she and her husband began writing scientific articles together – he would write the technical part without having to think about style, and this would form the body of the essay, while she would compose the introductory and concluding paragraphs. They called this 'topping and tailing', and their efforts were published in the *Cape Argus* and the *Friend*.

Three or four years into their marriage, however, her feeling of security was rudely threatened when Joe had an attack of epilepsy. Prone to hysteria, she concealed her husband's state of health from her children, and they never saw these attacks, which happened late at night. The epilepsy remained dormant for many years, but recurred after they came to Bloemfontein, triggered, she thought, by the altitude.

Incredibly, she never told her husband the true cause of his fits. After witnessing the first one, she said to him, 'You never told me you had a weak heart,' and he subsequently carried this idea with him until it became a habit of mind. In those days, epilepsy was both terrifying and shameful. Mrs Lewis herself was not immune to this prejudice. Epilepsy, she felt, was 'a destructive word, it had the power to hurt and suggest'. So when the attacks returned in Bloemfontein, she persuaded the doctor, 'an unimaginative man', to tell her husband they were heart attacks! Although Joe slowly threw off the condition as he perhaps acclimatized to the altitude, it had frightened her into believing that she might one day have to fend for herself. So it was in Bloemfontein she began writing her first (unpublished) novel. And her next novel, *The Harp*, was published in 1924 under the name of Ethelreda Lewis.

Thus began a novelistic career out of which came *Love at the Mission*. The immediate impetus for the book may have been the rivalry with her friend, the novelist Sarah Gertrude Millin. In 1934, Millin had published her novel *Three Men Die*, based on the life of the notorious poisoner, Daisy de Melker. She had picked out the theme of 'sex and destruction', but the De Melker story, driven as it was by avarice, had nothing of the complexity and allure of the Jacottet story. Ethelreda felt she could do better, be more profound, than Sarah Gertrude.

The Lewises were in Bloemfontein in 1920 and 1921, so Ethelreda, who wrote articles for it, had ready access to the *Friend*, which covered the preliminary hearing in the Jacottet case in some detail, and she must have read the reports. Even more likely is that she got intimate details from the horse's mouth.

Poisons were Joe Lewis's passion and hobby, and he was an expert on them. So much so, that he would abandon his usual quiet reserve at dinner parties and enthral the guests with the supposed aphrodisiac effects of mistletoe. Or he would recount the extraordinary case that had come to his attention where a miner gave his girl a tablet of blasting gelatine, ending with the craftily naive speculation as to whether the end result was an explosive bang.

He was also interested in what kind of poisons the Bushmen and the 'native doctors' used. A few months after the Jacottet hearing, in his presidential address on African poisons to the South African Association of Analytical Chemists in Johannesburg, Joe amused his audience with a story that showed professional jealousy was not confined to 'civilized society'. A witchdoctor came before the court, accused of killing his patient with a potion made from the shrub *Acokanthera*. The only definitive test was observing its physical action on the heart, so the analyst had conducted his experiments on mice, and referred repeatedly in his evidence to Mouse No. 1 and Mouse No. 2. When the accused was asked if he had any questions, he replied with haughty demeanour and ready wit, 'What! Ask him questions? He's only a mouse-doctor.'

In her third novel, *The Flying Emerald*, Mrs Lewis had already drawn on Joe's experiences in South West Africa. Now, in 1938, she did it again. In later years, the Lewises' son Martin told his wife Ruth that Joe had first come across the Jacottet story 'in his laboratory'. So it is possible to see the novel *not just as fiction but as a potential source of evidence*.

There is a passage in *Love at the Mission* the significance of which would be obscure without detailed knowledge of the whole case, and especially of Pierrette Jaques's statement concerning the pregnancy and abortion. It is worth quoting *in extenso*.

The appearance of a white lover on the threshold of Mam'selle Madeleine's life was the signal for Fani to burst into joyous song over work. To her the fact that a stout young woman, said to be Monsieur Hugo's wife, had once or twice accompanied him to the Mission was nothing. Like Mam'selle Hortense who, it was said, would certainly have come to grave trouble had not Fani been at hand to help her young mistress with her knowledge of the most ancient of all arts, the lore of the body practised by savage women from immemorial times: practised in proud and decent silence, and without loud outcries of boastful triumph and surprise at women's new-found and shameless wisdom.

Fact and fiction slip in and out of the passage – like the white rock which appears and disappears on the mountainside – but here is evidence corroborating Pierrette Jaques's statement. Moreover, the two sources are *independent* of one another: it is next to certain that Pierrette's mother knew nothing of the novel. Possibly it might be argued that a rumour, true or false, was spread and picked up by both women. On the other hand, it seems likely that Ethelreda got her knowledge in the confidentiality of the marital bed and that the sources of the knowledge were quite separate. And there is something authentically specific about the point she is making.

This information, however, immediately raises another question. Who did the abortion? Was it one of the mission doctors? Was it Hertig, who, like Augsburger, was not averse to the brutal removal of a tonsil and its equally callous disposal on a rubbish dump? Or was it done through the Basotho community? Was it arranged by Jerita, or Marcelle's unidentified black lover? This passage is the one indication that it was done in some fashion by the Basotho, possibly women, practising the ancient arts.

—❧—

Georges Casalis, the grandson of Eugène Casalis and the son of Dr Eugène Casalis, was also a doctor. He took a special interest in matters to do with Basotho women and reproduction. In 1896, he published an article in the *South African Medical Journal* on menstruation, parturition and related subjects amongst 'the native women of Basutoland'.

He began by pointing out how Basotho women, 'like all women', are unwilling to divulge what they 'rightly consider' to be the 'secrets of the sex'. In fact, much of the information that he imparted in his article had come not from the women themselves but from 'an old native doctor, whose reputation as a wizard extended far and wide' and whom he had had to ply with presents before he was forthcoming. Georges Casalis had some interesting things to say about abortion.

Abortions amongst the Basotho women were frequent, he wrote. Of the hundred women he examined, more than half had aborted at one time or another. The 'native women', he concluded, did not consider the casting off of a three-month ovum as anything but losing blood, this idea coming from the prevalent opinion that the child is formed in the blood. As his friendly medical colleague put it to him: the blood collects in the woman for three months, hardens, becomes flesh, and the child is formed in the centre. Up to the third month, it is not a child, only blood, and can be destroyed without prejudice to anyone: bringing back the blood of a woman who had run the risk of impregnation was therefore considered quite a natural thing to do. Traditional courts would not condemn it. What Casalis regarded as an 'abominable custom' was therefore allowed to thrive on a grand scale, and 'a native doctor is nowhere unless he possesses some powerful medicine to bring back the blood'.

What were the means to induce abortion? In recent times, desperate

Basotho women have been known to resort to drinking bottles of ink or washing-up liquid, or even to the use of arsenic. But at the turn of the century, all manner of herbs were tried, the more favoured of which were aloes and a species of ranunculus.

The bitter aloe, *Aloe ferox*, is found in the south of Lesotho. In spring, its spikes of red flowers cover north-facing hillsides, making them one of the most splendid seasonal sights of the countryside. The juice from the leaves has a purgative as well as an abortifacient effect.

One species of ranunculus very commonly found in the lowlands of Lesotho is *Ranunculus multifidus* – 'hlapi' in Sesotho, 'buttercup' in English. Growing in damp places, along stream banks and in seepage areas, it has yellow flowers with waxy, shining petals. Young girls rub the sap on the skin, generally below the knees, and then cover the smeared skin with a bandage. Next day a blister appears and when this dries out the skin is black and is regarded as a 'beauty spot'. Since the plant must contain an active irritant to scorch the skin in this way, it may well bring on an abortion when administered internally.

Two other yellow-flowered plants found in the lowlands and belonging to different families also bring about abortion: *Senecio vulgaris* or groundsel (resembling ragwort) is said to act something like ergot, bringing on contractions in the uterus; and *Gnidia burchellii*, a common woody shrublet clustered with flowers and found at the base of sandstone cliffs, causes fatal gastro-enteritis in browsing animals and is also an abortifacient.

These are the plants most likely to have been administered to Marcelle if inducement was by means of herbs. On the other hand, Georges Casalis recorded one case where a small flexible reed had been used with success.

It is extremely doubtful that the drugs given were invariably or even frequently successful. They were often poisonous, and when mixed with other concoctions certainly so. The women who took them often became ill, were in pain, and even died.

Whether Marcelle procured her abortion through herbs or through direct intervention with a reed or some other instrument, it was undoubtedly an extremely unpleasant and probably toxic experience.

CHAPTER TWENTY-EIGHT

A VERY DIFFICULT POSITION

On 3 March 1921, a month after their first arrest, Resident Commissioner Garraway released his three detainees, Marcelle, Marguerite and Sam Duby. What lay behind this decision? What was he thinking?

Some indication lies in a letter he sent to Prince Arthur of Connaught on 9 April, and which the High Commissioner sent on to Winston Churchill, Secretary of State for the Colonies, on the 19th (Churchill received it on 10 May). Garraway's letter furnishes some sensational details which never emerged in the public record, though they must have been known to at least a few people in Lesotho at the time.

Garraway gave his reason for not pursuing the case further, spelled out what he regarded as a plausible motive for the crime, discussed the possible source of the murder weapon, and revealed some sensitive information about the Jacottet family.

He told the High Commissioner that the charge had been withdrawn because 'no evidence was available which could in any way connect these persons with the actual administration of the poison, although there was sufficient evidence to establish a motive for the crime'.

He added that he had obtained the assistance and advice of an 'expert detective officer' from the South African Police. This expert, whose identity was not revealed, had failed to discover any further incriminating evidence and was 'of opinion that there would be no case for a successful prosecution'. The calling-in of this detective might account for the delay between the end of the preliminary examination and the dropping of the charges.

Garraway was definite about a possible reason for the murder: 'The motive for the crime might have been that the late Jacottet had discovered that his youngest daughter, Margaret [sic], had been seduced by Mr Duby, and that he had given the latter instructions to leave the mission in three months time.' He added some important fragments: '... the girl had refused to give Duby up, although he is a married man with a family, and she and her sister, Marcelle, have continued to work in Duby's office, and had frequent and violent scenes with their father, the last one occurring the evening before the tragedy took place.'

As regards the poison used, the government analyst stated that it was arsenate of soda. A bottle of this was found in Duby's office, 'where it had been for some time, and where anyone knowing of its existence could have obtained it'. Garraway admitted that 'there was no evidence available that any person did remove it from where it was kept, but the three accused all knew of its existence, and that it had been removed from Mr Jacottet's house, by Marcelle, and taken to Duby's office as there had been conversation on the subject of the danger of a third Miss Jacottet taking poison, on an occasion when she was suffering from neuralgia'.

Garraway then gave a few insights into the Jacottet family history. Firstly, he said that 'all the Jacottets appeared to be of a neurotic and unbalanced disposition'; secondly, 'their mother was weak-minded'; thirdly, 'one brother is described by his uncle who gave evidence at the Preliminary Examination as being a "degenerate"'. Fourthly, and most startling of all, the brother 'had been in trouble in France for attempting to poison somebody'!

—◦⊙◦—

There are many interesting things in Garraway's letter.

It reveals that the authorities had no doubt that a 'crime' had been committed and that the poisoning was not accidental. They had definitely identified the poison and also linked the poison taken from the Jacottet house with that in Duby's office. They also confirmed that it was Marcelle who had been responsible for the transfer.

While he possibly misunderstood or short-circuited the way the mission worked – Jacottet as President would almost certainly have consulted at least his executive before 'giving instructions' to Duby – Garraway puts the blame more on the older man than the young girl. In his view, Duby seduced Marguerite, rather than vice versa; and he does not favour the possibility of an equal mutual attraction.

As for his suggestion that there might be inherited instability in the family, he does link it to the maternal side. While he starts his sentence saying 'all the Jacottets' appeared neurotic and unbalanced, he finishes it by speaking of 'their mother'. The phrase 'all the Jacottets' therefore refers to *the children*, not the father. He makes no comment, one way or the other, about the father.

The attribution of 'nervous fits' to Louise Jacottet by Dr Jacottet in the preliminary examination now becomes a little clearer. The 'weak-mindedness' makes these fits sound less like epilepsy and more like depressions or nervous breakdowns, major or minor.

Equally intriguing is what Garraway omits. For example, he mentions neither Marcelle's affair with the student, nor the abortion. Is this because he did not know (whereas others did)? Or did he suppress the information, perhaps for reasons of sensitivity?

Then again, nowhere in the letter does he look outside of the trio arrested or the Jacottet family for the murderer. Rather than clearing anyone, the letter actually circles round the suspects, stopping just short of accusation.

Did Garraway know who did it, or did he have a very strong suspicion?

In his last diary entry mentioning the case before he received the evidence from the preliminary examination for consideration, Garraway lamented the fact that he could not turn to a formal judiciary: 'These are the occasions on which one would like to have a Judge Advocate here, as I had in Bechuanaland.' While it is clear, therefore, that Garraway was uneasy about his legal skills, it is nevertheless legitimate to call into question his stated reasons for not bringing any or all of the accused before his court.

His stance was certainly not unreasonable. It was no doubt extremely difficult to 'in any way connect these persons with the actual administration of the poison'. Poisoning cases are notoriously difficult in this respect: few poisoners are actually seen either administering the poison directly to the victim or introducing it into the intermediary agent used, such as food or drink. But he must have known that many poisoning cases had been successfully prosecuted on circumstantial evidence alone.

Could he not have put some pressure on the accused? Would he not have obtained a reasonable confession in the end? One, after all, was a schoolgirl; another, a man who had lost almost everything; and the third, if she were innocent, would surely have wanted to establish the truth. Did Garraway push as hard as he might have to identify the perpetrator? Or was he being disingenuous to His Royal Highness? Did he know and deliberately keep quiet? There is some slight evidence for this conjecture.

At some stage during the proceedings, Garraway wrote a letter (which has not yet come to light) to the former High Commissioner, Lord Buxton, who knew Jacottet personally, outlining some of the case's details. On 8 March 1921, Buxton wrote back as follows: 'I was very sorry indeed to hear of the Jacottet tragedy. It is a most extraordinary story, and puts you in a very difficult position.'

Perhaps this is an innocent remark. But Buxton's phrasing is curious. He does not say Garraway has a 'very difficult decision' (with regard to the evidence, for instance); rather, he says he is 'in a very difficult position', which seems to imply a political or ethical dilemma.

Here it might be well to recall something Pierrette Jaques has said. Without having to be prompted, she affirmed unequivocally that her mother had told her 'the whole case had been hushed up, strings had been pulled'.

Furthermore, Garraway must have known that one of the three accused almost certainly could *not* have administered the poison.

—◦◦—

If Garraway did know who poisoned Jacottet or suspected who did, as seems very likely, why did he not let the law take its course?

Perhaps, in part, it was because of the law and its consequences.

There has always been some dispute about whether Lesotho was a British Colony or a Protectorate. An old joke had it that Swaziland was a Protectorate governed as though it were a Colony, and Basutoland a Colony governed as though it were a Protectorate. Whatever the position, it is certain that British criminal law does not enter the Jacottet case.

In Lesotho in 1921, there were two parallel legal systems: one was customary law, the other Roman-Dutch law. Deciding which law applied to which person often entailed complicated argument – sometimes the wearing of a blanket or a suit settled it!

In this case, since whites were the accused, and it was a matter for criminal law anyway, there is no doubt which system would have prevailed. Lesotho shares Roman-Dutch law with South Africa, Swaziland, Botswana and, of all places, Sri Lanka. Thanks to the Code Napoléon, it does not share this set of laws with the Netherlands!

The use of Roman-Dutch law went back to the period of Cape Rule, and its continuation after Basutoland became a separate colony was confirmed by a Proclamation in 1884. Had the Jacottet case proceeded, it would almost certainly have been a full murder trial before the Resident Commissioner. Appeal would probably have gone to the High Commissioner, then to the Privy Council. But it would have gone to the Privy Council on a point of law only, though there had been no other murder trial of a white person in Lesotho before this time and there was therefore no precedent.

Had Garraway, knowing or suspecting who the perpetrator was, decided to proceed, he would have foreseen that the chances of a guilty verdict were high and that appeals would be likely to fail.

Murderers were hanged in Lesotho. The condemned cell in the Old Gaol was a rondavel: it is still there, somewhat dolled up, and now part of the Food and Nutrition Coordinating Office. It is where those about to be hanged spent their last night.

In this period, poisoning was regarded as a particular abomination. Frederick Seddon was executed for arsenic poisoning in England in 1912;

Major Armstrong, whose wife died of arsenic poisoning in Wales at the very time when Garraway was starting to consider the evidence in the Jacottet case, was hanged for her murder in 1922.

Garraway was a political man: he wanted to minimize any damage to the mission, which was so important to the education and social structure of the country. He was also a humane man: he shied away from confrontation and tempered the sentences he dealt out with understanding and mercy.

To hang a white woman, the daughter of a missionary, in Maseru, in 1921, was unthinkable.

CHAPTER TWENTY-NINE

THE GIFT OF DISCORD

G arraway had taken his decisions, but, of course, many of their effects were unforeseen.

The mission had already suffered – in the death of Jacottet, the scandal of the murder, the arrest of Jerita, and the shame of Duby and the two sisters – a series of terrible shocks. And more were to come.

At the time of the hearing, Garraway had lunch on successive days with Alfred Casalis and Georges Dieterlen (Hermann's son) and noted that 'these poor mission people are in a very sad state owing to this horrible case'. Each missionary reacted in his own way. Louis Germond was critical of Garraway's decision to hold the preliminary examination in public instead of behind closed doors, which would have saved the mission from being dragged need-lessly into the great scandal that had ensued, with all its titillating details. Louis Mabille endured many days of shame when he dared not look his parishioners in the face and scarcely felt he had any right to preach. Unlike the wounds of war, this wound might never heal. He was even more concerned for his mother, old, blind Mrs Mabille, for whom the murder of Jacottet was a par-ticular and bitter blow.

Charles Christeller was surprised that, as was the English way, the accused were not questioned at the hearing, and he was also irritated by the sensation-alist headlines indulged in by all the newspapers, including the Sesotho ones. The shame of the Jacottet and Duby families tarnished the mission in general, he thought.

Louis Germond probably spoke for all when he put 'the terrible drama' into its cosmic context. While the specific perpetrator of the deed remained elusive, the mastermind was certain: this 'torment of hell' had been unleashed by Satan, who was as elemental and implacable as the poison which had corrupted the body of Jacottet. The only antidote, for the moment, was prayer.

One of the main consequences of Garraway's decision not to prosecute was that it created a state of uncertainty. Several of the missionaries expressed the wish that the mystery of who had been responsible for the murder could be cleared up. Dark rumours circulated. Everywhere, for instance, it was said that Marcelle was Duby's mistress.

So it was almost inevitable that deep cracks appeared in the missionary temple which had so recently been unified. It was Christeller who sparked the controversy that divided the community into two camps and threatened the very existence of the mission.

—∞—

Makhoarane seemed to have grown darker since Jacottet's funeral as all the missionaries met for a Conference brought forward to 2 March because of the shadow that hung over the mission. It had been over two weeks since the conclusion of the preliminary examination, and the three under suspicion were still in jail. The length of their incarceration led most people to believe they were guilty or, at the very least, to think that the authorities believed so.

The Conference began by paying tribute to Jacottet for his thirty-six years of service, recalled the energetic spirit which had driven him to succeed in education and politics, to excel in writing mission history and to become pre-eminent in the study of African languages, and lauded his achievement of producing several cohorts of Basotho pastors. Surprisingly, but honestly, tribute was also paid to Duby for his long and faithful service before his fall, and for his 'conscientiousness to excess'.

The Conference had many practical decisions to take as well, but its afternoon deliberations were affected by the arrival of a government telegram (sent to Dr Jacottet) announcing that Marcelle, Marguerite, and Sam Duby would be released the next day.

It was nevertheless decided, inevitably, that Duby be dismissed from the mission on the grounds of his immorality and that Marcelle be relieved of her duties because she had knowingly concealed the relationship between Marguerite and Duby (Paris had, in any case, insisted on their dismissal).

Two key posts had therefore become vacant – the Sesuto Book Depot, Printing Works and Bible School, and the Theological School. Alfred Casalis, who had had long experience with the former, years before, was the logical choice to take over from Duby. Christeller, a small, dapper man whose nickname was 'Cri-cri' (Cricket) because of the way he spoke Sesotho with a broad French accent, was the favoured successor of Jacottet, but he was not keen on the job. He did not want to give up his church, which he loved, and he did not feel he had the right temperament: 'The Theological School reminds me a little of a school of prophets in the desert. It is not a life of action, and Jacottet suffered from it and showed it.' While he had tremendous respect for 'the great strength' that was Jacottet, he also had reservations. He had not forgotten Jacottet's malicious gossip about his own courting of a much younger girl many years before and could not have missed the irony of Jacottet's discomfort at having his own daughter seduced by an older man in much more disgraceful fashion. He managed to avoid the job for the moment, and the ageing Bertschy took over the Theological School as a temporary measure (Christeller did eventually act as Director between 1927 and 1933, during which time he and his family lived in the former Jacottet house).

The next day, the Conference, with Christeller dissenting, sent a telegram to Garraway asking him to do everything he could to help Dr Jacottet 'protect his niece, Marguerite'. It also decided to pay Duby three months' salary as the equivalent of a return passage to Europe, and noted that Marcelle had an unpaid account with the Book Depot in excess of her salary.

The Conference also debated the appropriate behaviour towards the three released prisoners, now technically innocent. Resolutions were made: Duby was warned that neither of the Jacottet sisters would be allowed to live in his household nor work in the Book Depot; the demoiselles Jacottet would be allowed to live in their father's house for as long as it took them to pack their trunks, in the case where they were free to leave Lesotho; or for as long as the executive of the Conference saw fit, in the case where they were not free to leave. Duby was given until the end of March to settle his affairs, and the Bible School was to be reopened in August. Marcelle immediately asked for an extension for herself and Marguerite, and was given until 15 April. The Conference also accepted the responsibility – at Christeller's suggestion – of paying for Jacottet's coffin.

Pleasing to Paul Colin, who reported on the Conference to Paris, was the attitude of the Basotho pastors. They assured the French that they did not regard themselves as a group apart and were as touched by the events as their white colleagues. Many ordinary Christians, too, assured their pastors of their understanding. Man might fall, they acknowledged, but truth stood firm.

On stage, therefore, the missionaries might have been reasonably pleased with the outcome of the Conference, were it not for what went on behind the scenes.

Ever since he had sat in the crammed courtroom with Alfred Casalis, Christeller had been brooding on the case. Consequently, he became Duby's prime – if not only – defender. 'I can say to you,' he told Bianquis immediately after the hearing, 'that I do not believe *at all* in the culpability of Duby in the poisoning.' All he could see against Duby was the unfortunate coincidence that Jacottet had died almost exactly three months after giving him a three-month ultimatum; and he refuted this motive by claiming that Jacottet had actually extended the period of grace he had given to Duby until September 1921.

He went even further: he was not at all convinced of Marcelle's guilt either, despite the testimony of Madeleine. He felt that the cook was hiding something and that her rearrest might make her talk.

In championing the cause of Duby and Marcelle, he gave them character references: 'I have known Duby for twenty-two years, I have continually seen him with Marcelle. She was independent and did not seem like other young girls, but I have never been shocked nor did I ever suspect anything. I respected them too much for that.' He added that he found it painful to see a life of hard work and honesty such as Duby's finish in dishonour: 'Duby is not a murderer, he was certainly not a *sensuel*.' To show his solidarity and compassion, the Christellers took Eva and Georges Duby into their own home.

So far, so good. But then Christeller dropped his bombshell. He appeared to accuse neither Marcelle, nor Marguerite, nor Duby, but *Madeleine* of the murder.

What he actually said, and how he said it, are in dispute. Moreillon, Colin and Ramseyer were adamant that he had made the accusation. Christeller himself said he had merely pointed out, without accusing her directly, that there was as much evidence to indict Madeleine as there was the other three. It is possible that the three missionaries misunderstood what he was saying, but it must also be noted that Christeller was back-pedalling when he made this defence.

Paul Ramseyer met him in private at the time of the Conference. His description of the dramatic encounter is worth recalling.

The proofs which Christeller possesses, I know them. Christeller begged me one day to go and hear them. He said he thought highly of me and wanted to make me understand why his opinion was contrary to that of everyone else. So I passed an evening in his office, listening to all that he had to say.

When he had finished speaking, I asked him, 'Is that all that you have to tell me?' – 'Yes.'

'Oh, well, my poor Christeller, I do not understand you. I knew all that you have told me. And if, in fact, your knowledge stops there, I am much better informed than you are. I know many things of which you have not said a word.'

I then asked him from whom came the information that he had. He replied: 'From Duby, from the wife of Duby, from Marcelle Jacottet and from Dr Augsburger.'

For myself, I got mine from all the missionaries, from the magistrate of Maseru, from Mrs Barclay (postmistress of Morija), from Dr Augsburger, from Hertig, from Ernest Mabille, from our doyenne Madame Mabille, from two or three black pastors, from Dr Jacottet, from Théophile Duby (brother of Samuel) and from his wife; and from newspapers (accounts of interrogations etc.); I have, what is more, had long conversations with M. Paillard of the Swiss Mission, who narrowly missed being killed himself, and whose wife's health has been entirely wrecked by the poison which she swallowed at the Jacottet house.

I warned Christeller that if he really had evidence of the innocence of Duby and Marcelle, and of the guilt of Madeleine, it was his duty to produce it and act on it. He replied, 'I will do it; I am ready to go to court.'

I greatly fear that Dr Jacottet will request him to go to court, to give his 'evidence', and that poor Christeller will pay dearly for his blindness and foolhardiness. One cannot with impunity accuse someone falsely of parricide.

On April Fool's Day, a month after the release of the accused, Ramseyer had many interesting things to say in one of his letters. Almost in parable form, he told the story of what had happened at the marriage of two mission teachers in East Griqualand. For some reason a Christian shopkeeper brought along his hunting gun and decided to add an embellishment to the festivities by firing it. The first shot hit a young man in the thigh. It was an accident, but Ramseyer knew that 'evil works everywhere in secret' and that 'Satan played his part in this wedding'. The youth was taken to Matatiele, where it was decided that the smashed leg must be amputated to prevent the spread of gangrene, which had soon set in. Both the patient and his parents would not listen, refusing to believe a broken leg could lead to death. As a result the young man died and the unhappy shopkeeper was dragged off to prison, no doubt to be judged and punished.

Ramseyer could not help adding a moral to the tale: 'He will undoubtedly be punished more severely than those who wilfully killed Jacottet! Yet the police of Lesotho have no doubt that the murderers of Morija are Duby and Marcelle Jacottet. They have even been given back their freedom!' In passing, therefore, Ramseyer gives weight to the contention that Garraway and the police believed they knew who had committed the murder.

Ramseyer also asked, half-rhetorically, why, if Marcelle and Duby were really innocent, they did not go after those who had accused them and put them in jail. As a reply to himself, he quoted the words of a Mosotho chief whom he had met in far-off Matatiele: 'Duby and Marcelle Jacottet are the only true culprits. They will never hunt down those who have blamed them, because they know too well that that could force the light to burst upon themselves.'

On 24 March, Alfred Casalis had written to Ramseyer giving him some details of what had transpired since the Conference: 'The Dubys are preparing to leave. The sale of their things will take place next Wednesday [30 March], and I think that Samuel will not delay his departure after that. We have passed through difficult and dark days. Even he for whom we have the greatest sympathy and pity does not redeem his sin by his attitude and the attestation of his repentance. I have seen him several times and cannot categorically say that he has manifested repentance and remorse. Hertig says that he has found in him a repentant! ... Humiliated, yes; upset, yes; upset at having ruined his life and lost all that he will leave behind here. But I have seen nothing more, and as for Mme Duby, she continues to tell untruths and has adopted an attitude completely incomprehensible. Marcelle still scatters her lies and tells everyone, whites and blacks, that it was Madeleine who killed her father.'

Casalis had never spoken directly to Christeller about what he regarded as his 'strange attitude' and, on that basis, could live in peace with the pastor of Morija parish – a diplomatic stance which was to prove very useful. However, Casalis did talk to his niece, Florence Mabille, about Christeller's 'proofs', and had never seen her so angry.

Something Christeller may have said also made Dr Jacottet livid. Christeller, claimed Ramseyer, dared to suggest that Édouard Jacottet would have allowed Duby to remain at his post, despite his infamy, and would have allowed Duby to give Marguerite a post at the Depot. In a stormy meeting, Dr Jacottet asked Christeller for an explanation, and, when he got one, thundered, 'Sir, you insult the memory of my brother!'

Ramseyer added further details to this (coincidentally refuting Christeller's suggestion that Augsburger supported the Madeleine-as-murderer theory). It seems that, throughout March, Marcelle continued to make claims about her father's dying words. 'Marcelle dares to say, in her lying divagations,' was Ramseyer's uncompromising version, 'that before his death, her father called her to him to tell her that he counted on Duby to take care of her and Marguerite!' Ramseyer refuted this strongly by recounting something that Augsburger had told him: on the afternoon of 22 December, before Jacottet sank into a coma, Duby had passed along the passage in front of the door to the bedroom where the stricken man lay. At that moment, as Augsburger was taking his pulse, Jacottet must have noticed Duby just for a second, because he clenched his fist, and across his face flashed an expression of dreadful anger, which ended in a distressing sigh.

Ramseyer could not restrain his own ire at Marcelle's insulting suggestion: 'She dares to claim that it is Duby, the seducer of his minor daughter, to whom Jacottet would have wanted to entrust his children!!' With an intriguing touch, he added, 'One must believe that Marcelle Jacottet has a special madness by which, it seems, certain women are at times afflicted. But Duby is not mad; nor is Christeller.'

Casalis also informed Ramseyer that Jerita had told all and sundry (and the whole village repeated it) that she had been paid to keep silent. But when pressed to be more precise, people became evasive – as the Basotho were wont to do, said Ramseyer, in such circumstances and when faced with direct questions.

Some Basotho were cynical when Ramseyer discussed the case with them. 'Ah! If it had been one of us,' they cried, 'the law would not have been closed!'

A last word from Ramseyer about Marcelle's habits is even more intriguing, even stunning. 'Have you been told,' he asked Bianquis, 'that Marcelle Jacottet gave Mme Duby expensive presents, and ran into debt? Mme Duby knew about the conduct of her husband with the Jacottet girls and never refused a present from them. I would never finish if I told you all that has been said to me, even if I told you only what has been proved true so far; no one had permission to enter the bed chamber of Duby but Marcelle alone. It was Marcelle who tidied up this room, and that after the death of Jacottet etc. etc.'

In some respects, at least, Marcelle had become a second wife to Duby. A petite femme.

Revelation and rumour had come to Ramseyer and his colleagues in a series of seismic shocks. In one memorable line, he said it was like living on top of a volcano. But in the time it took to get to the end of his sentence, he realized that the eruption had already taken place, and corrected himself: it was like being carried away on an ocean of molten lava.

―⚬―

It is worth comparing Ramseyer's views with those of Bertschy, expressed on the same April Fool's Day.

On the one side, Ramseyer saw Duby as the villain: 'Duby is the cause, the author (not the actor) of the crime.'

On the other side, Bertschy saw him as the victim. When Duby returned to Morija, Bertschy, who was about to take over the Theological School for the next intake of students, found him older and broken. The impression Duby gave him was that he had not been implicated directly in the poisoning of Jacottet. What a pity it was, thought Bertschy, to lose such an intelligent and tenacious worker. 'The Jacottet daughters have been his ruin,' he concluded.

As regards the dangerous liaison between the older married man and the innocent young girl, Bertschy suspected an initial unhealthy relationship between Duby and the elder sister, then went on to make yet more startling revelations.

Although we could not know what passed between Duby and the eldest daughter and we are reduced to conjecture, she has certainly furthered his relations with the youngest. She was devoted to him to the point that she would pass through fire to be of service to him, but their behaviour was always of a perfect correctness. Moreover, thanks to the presence of Mme Duby and of the Jacottet parents, at least until the death of the mother, no suspicion could arise in our minds. With us Mlle Jacottet was amiability itself. She is of a remarkable intelligence.

One argument the doctors (Hertig, Jacottet and Augsburger) used in declaring her abnormal was her fixed idea that certain people wanted to seduce her; she accused the most honourable people from a period when she was still just a young girl. Knowing the people in question, this appeared quite incredible; as for lying, she did it without scruple, something she was plainly guilty of.

He does not identify those Marcelle accused of seduction or attempted seduction. It is clear though that both Marcelle and Marguerite had a passionate relationship with Duby – of whatever kind.

—•◦•—

Both Christeller and Louis Mabille saw the hand of Providence in the return of Alfred Casalis to Lesotho. He was the new rock of the mission. Certainly, his steadiness was needed in the months after Jacottet's death. He was the obvious person to take over the Presidency, the running of the Book Depot and the Bible School, and the interaction with the authorities on behalf of the mission.

Consequently, when E.G. Dutton, Master of Court, published an edict announcing a meeting to be held in Maseru at ten o'clock on 8 April before the Assistant Commissioner, and requiring all relations of Marguerite Jacottet to attend in order to appoint a tutor or tutors dative to the said Marguerite, many eyes began to turn towards Alfred Casalis to take on this responsibility too. He assented with extreme reluctance, after three tiring trips to Maseru, and only when he was begged to do so (by Dr Jacottet and Madeleine, amongst others) in order to keep Marguerite out of the baleful – to some, satanic – influence of Marcelle, and until Henri could arrive to take charge of her and return with her to England. Alfred and Caroline welcomed 'this poor child' into their home towards the end of April, dreading the responsibility but accepting it in memory of their old friend, her father. Casalis was careful to inform the chief of Morija village of this event, so that there would be no gossip.

Ernest Mabille had taken over the Normal School temporarily and, ironically, proved to be 'just the man', and Caroline Casalis joined the teaching staff for a while. Sam Duby had gone, and around 2 May Marcelle also left Morija 'to establish herself in the Colony'. Before she left, she gave her dog Waldo to Jerita, and their grey cat to Hermania's small son Bethuel (he called it Masiba, because it was soft like feathers, but it kept wandering back to its old home). Marcelle also cleaned out all the money immediately owing to her late father, including Marguerite's share, as well as a sum of money in a savings bank account in Marguerite's name. She left her sister with six shillings in her pocket when she arrived at the Casalis home (Marguerite would later get a small sum when her father's estate was wound up). So, lamented Casalis, 'Marguerite is twice a victim.'

After ten days, Casalis sensed a relaxation in the young girl: in the warm embrace of Caroline and two other boarders, Misses Bowie and Henriette Cochet, she appeared happier. He had high hopes that she would pick up the pieces of her life again.

But there were other worries. Although some tried to deny it or pretend it away, Jacottet's murder had had a strong effect on the Basotho, particularly in his old parish of Thaba-Bosiu. The present incumbent, Paul Colin, was in trouble – his wife was struggling, physically and psychologically, from the loss of their eldest son, and desperately needed leave in Europe (Colin insisted that he himself would stay on alone). Casalis saw this in part as the perennial problem of young wives adapting with difficulty to the strange and daunting conditions of a new life, but equally believed the separation of husband and wife to be bad and dangerous.

Colin was determined to stay because the murder had made dramatic inroads into his congregation and many parishioners had reverted to paganism. Others showed a distinct antipathy and discourtesy to the Colins.

Then a further sequence of actions, by no means of his own making, began to snap at Casalis's heels. Dr Jacottet caught a whiff of Christeller's allegations against Madeleine, and, already incensed by Christeller's contentions concerning his brother's supposed last wishes, his hackles rose. At his instigation, Madeleine, who had gone to Matatiele to keep house for her uncle, threatened to sue Christeller. This merely added to the misery in Morija. Casalis had had almost more than he could take.

Henri arrived in Cape Town on 30 May. Casalis and his wife were worried that Marcelle, having gone there to wait for him, would poison his mind and persuade him to give her Marguerite. 'To leave her to Marcelle is to lose her,' Casalis said. 'I have in my hands crushing documents to prove it to Henri Jacottet. You can have no idea what Marcelle is: she has no moral sense whatsoever.'

The endless stirring of the pot had a deeply disturbing effect on Marguerite.

A month after coming to the Casalis home, she said to Caroline in a flood of hot tears: 'It would have been much better for me to have confessed to the killing of my father, even though I am innocent of it. I would have been hanged and my suffering would have been over.'

Casalis was shocked. 'Is it not heartbreaking,' he asked Bianquis, 'to hear a child of eighteen speak in this way?' Then, in a rare outburst, he went on to condemn his late colleague for failing as a father: 'Ah, my dear friend, it is fine to have been an influential missionary, a "porte-nom" in missionary and linguistic circles etc. But having allowed to grow up around him children in such moral and spiritual neglect is atrocious.' So vehement was Casalis that it prompted him, in bitter mockery of all that he stood for, to think the almost unthinkable: 'It would be a thousand times better if the Society took only celibate workers (when all is said and done, the Catholics and the Anglicans have admirable men who live in the most austere celibacy in their missions, in the midst of the most depraved populations) rather than sacrifice children who have not asked to be born, born to live either far from their parents, or with parents who do not have the time to spend with them and who allow them to experience the depraved influences of their milieu.' He looked for his solace in II Corinthians 4: 8–9.

Once Dr Jacottet had got his teeth firmly into Christeller's flesh, he was not about to let go. He wrote to Ramseyer, Moreillon and Colin asking them for depositions about Christeller's statements to them. Casalis and a couple of others tried to persuade him to drop the matter in early May, but on the 14th Madeleine appointed George Elliot Underwood and George Marais of Matatiele to act as her attorneys in proceedings against Christeller.

On 10 June, her attorneys issued a summons in the court of the Resident Commissioner of Basutoland requiring Christeller to make an appearance in the Court within ten days of its receipt. She demanded payment of the sum of £2 000 for slander, plus the costs of the suit. She quoted three missionaries who had heard the slander: Christeller had said to Paul Colin on or about 3 March, 'I am convinced that it is Miss Madeleine Jacottet who poisoned her father and I have proofs in hand'; on or about 4 March he repeated, as has been seen, almost the same words to Ramseyer; and on or about 7 March he told Bertrand Moreillon, 'Well, I have proofs that it is Madeleine.' All of these statements, according to Madeleine, were wrongful, unlawful and malicious. (It is interesting to note, in passing, that the allegations were made to the three witnesses separately and on different days, so if all three mistook his words, as Christeller claimed, they were mistaken on three separate occasions.)

The summons was served on Christeller on 11 June at his residence in Morija by Sergeant M. Sekese of the Basutoland Mounted Police.

Christeller hurried off to Bloemfontein, where he engaged McIntyre and Watkeys – the attorneys who had represented Marcelle, Marguerite and Duby – to act on his behalf. They assured him he had a strong defence, and he was adamant that he would not retract, nor would he publish apologies in several newspapers as requested. Bertschy, Ellenberger and perhaps Germond were prepared to act as witnesses for him. Christeller's plea, which was submitted to the court on 21 June, was that he had not said what was claimed, but that what he had said was: 'There is no evidence against them – there is as much against Madeleine.' He added that if the court found that he had uttered the words as alleged, nevertheless they were uttered on a privileged occasion on a matter of common interest, he had a duty to do so, and they were uttered without malice. Whatever the outcome, Casalis felt the honour and reputation of the mission – cleft in two – might be destroyed forever. He did, however, get Christeller to agree to the formation of a 'jury d'honneur', before which he and Dr Jacottet would appear.

Casalis then decided to go to East Griqualand in a last-ditch effort to persuade Dr Jacottet and Madeleine to call off their hunt and to save the mission. It would take him three days to get there by train and postcart, and he was exhausted before he started. The reason he was doing it, he said, was not for the scrapping dogs: 'If it were a question only of the men, I would let them sort it out themselves. But the mission before all and above all.' He was not very hopeful of success, because the good doctor was hot-tempered and as likely to show him the door as listen to him. What complicated things was Henri was due to arrive on 21 June (the day Casalis proposed leaving) or the next day, and so he had to leave his wife, already worried by the strain imposed on her husband, to sort out Marguerite's affairs with Henri. The load he took with him was the thought of so many blows delivered to the work of his father, of Arbousset, Mabille, Coillard, Ellenberger, Rolland and others. It was the weight of the whole of the mission's history.

Casalis arrived in Matatiele presenting himself not as President of the Conference, but as a friend of Madeleine and the temporary guardian of Marguerite. He was welcomed with equal friendship.

He suggested to the doctor and his niece that the defamation suit would cause yet another great scandal by pitting missionaries against each other. He also suggested that it would have the opposite of the desired effect: in defending himself, Christeller would have to attack Madeleine, and her name would inevitably be sullied, whereas until now all those who had heard the arguments had had a most favourable impression of her dignity, impartiality and openness. He pointed out that the one who doubted her was precisely the only one who did not know her at all and who had been absent when the events occurred.

Unhesitatingly, Madeleine replied that for the mission, for the missionaries who had promised to bear witness, and for the memory of her father, she would withdraw the action. With perfect cordiality and good humour, Dr Jacottet supported her. The three of them then drew up a draft letter of apology which Christeller was to address to them, on receipt of which they would drop the suit. The letter would receive no publicity and would be seen only by the Lesotho missionaries and Bianquis.

Casalis took the arduous journey back. After a day of reflection, Christeller agreed to send his apology. In it he asserted that he had never said Madeleine was the poisoner, only that there was as much evidence implicating her as there was Marcelle. He also denied hawking false rumours about her, and regretted any harm he had involuntarily caused her.

When Casalis returned home, he found that Henri Jacottet, in the fifteen days he had been there, had organized all the travel documents Marguerite needed to go to England, where he and his younger brother Gustave would look after her. Alfred and Caroline felt that, since Marguerite had a great affection for her eldest brother, all would go well with her: 'I am happy that this poor child leaves in an excellent state of mind and we hope that she will lift her life. She has certainly broken with the past, and her qualities of pluck and intelligence will flourish once she is decidedly far from those who lured her into sin, and whose responsibility for that is huge.'

On Monday 11 July, Marguerite and Henri left Lesotho forever. First love is often the most intense, and it took Marguerite a long time to get over it. But she never lost the love of the countryside which she had learned there, and, soon after arriving in England, she enrolled at Swanley Horticultural College in Kent, eventually graduating top of the class. (Henri, who was terrified of public speaking, had to give the oration and nearly funked out, but was forced to go by Madeleine, who had also gone to live in England.) Nor did Marguerite lose her great regard for the Basotho – she and Madeleine often had fun carrying things like pots of water on their heads! And when she died (in Cambridge in 1986) she was, to the great consternation of the nurses, speaking Sesotho. Only when she heard some French did she calm down. Dr Jacottet paid for everything: he paid for Henri's return voyage and for Marguerite's single ticket; he gave her a small 'trousseau' before her departure and arranged a modest allowance for her to live on and to pursue her studies; he paid for Madeleine's lawyers and he paid for the defence team of Marcelle and Marguerite (but not for Duby). And when his brother's effects were put up for auction, he bought his library of language books and presented them to the mission (where they reside to this day in the archives – a generous and lasting donation from a man who was by no means rich).

As soon as she received Christeller's letter of apology, Madeleine telegraphed her acceptance.

Had not the time come then, sighed Casalis, for the turmoil to be laid to rest alongside Jacottet, so that they could 'bury even the memory'?

—◦⊝—

Sadly, not. For Christeller, 1921 must have been his own personal Year of the Lemming. Certainly, he felt there was unfinished business: his rancour turned on those who had borne witness against him, Ramseyer, Colin and Moreillon, and others. He accused them of being behind the defamation action and demanded they acknowledge that he had never said what they claimed, that they had 'intensified and condensed' his words, thereby distorting them. He expected a retraction.

Ramseyer wrote a pleasant letter to Christeller expressing his joy that the action had been dropped by Madeleine, to which Christeller replied with what he called an 'ultimatum', which he also sent to the others. Ramseyer and his colleagues felt they could not back down and so the mission was once again riven, the two camps no longer understanding each other, nor even listening. Ramseyer thought he knew why Christeller, acting at first from the best of motives, had behaved as he did. He speculated that Christeller's reasoning had gone something like this: he wanted to clear Duby; Duby was completely innocent of the murder of Jacottet; that could easily be proven if it could be shown that Jacottet had not been poisoned by either of the daughters who had had relations with Duby; Madeleine Jacottet had had no relationship with Duby; now, could it not be shown that she could as likely be guilty? Why not? Christeller had then got caught in a determining spiral from which he could not escape.

An extraordinary Conference was scheduled for the beginning of October, and Casalis took the desperate step of sending a telegram to Bianquis telling him that his presence was vital to avoid a complete implosion. Ramseyer wrote to Bianquis in the same vein. 'The mission is very sick,' he said, again detecting Satan's hidden hand, and Dr Bianquis was the physician needed.

In the event, Bianquis himself fell sick and never came. The Conference met earlier than scheduled and spent the whole of 21 September behind closed doors, coming eventually to 'une entente complète', and Casalis was able to send the recuperating Bianquis a cable announcing, 'Affairs arranged fraternally.'

And so, at last, the matter died, though, in private, Ramseyer's blood still boiled with indignation whenever he thought of 'l'affaire Christeller'. Only Louis Mabille, the most sensitive of the missionaries, ultimately chose to leave Lesotho. He had always found Jacottet a clever but rather cold man, often off-hand in his greetings and farewells, but he felt the pain of the Jacottet family more than his colleagues and thought the whole affair had not been treated seriously enough. It was the principal reason for his departure.

The mission survived but was never quite the same after the death of Jacottet – the burial of the prince did not bring adequate renewal. He had once said to Ramseyer, in the context of the ageing corps and the lack of new blood, 'Après moi, le déluge.' Ramseyer had rebuked him severely for this comment. Now, when he remembered Jacottet's apparent arrogance, he wondered whether it had not been prophetic.

CHAPTER THIRTY

LEFETOA

After the accused were released, charge and counter-charge, cannonade and hand-to-hand combat generated curtains of fire, and smoke stifled clear vision as effectively as mustard gas strangled the throat. Let us try to see things more clearly by outlining the major events of this whole unhappy saga.

The Marguerite-Duby affair and Marcelle's complicity were uncovered at Eunice High School towards the end of September 1920. At Miss King's insistence, Marguerite was removed from the school, and Jacottet compelled Duby to confess to his wife and gave him three months to leave Morija. Jacottet told Madeleine about the scandal, but asked her to keep it a secret and to suggest to Alfred Casalis that Marguerite had been expelled for petty theft. He also asked Madeleine to explain to any missionaries who queried his actions after his death that he had taken them for 'the honour of the mission'.

Sometime in November, six weeks to a month before the murder, Madeleine, who suffered acutely from 'head and nerve affection', had threatened to 'do away with herself', so appalling was the pain. Marguerite had also threatened suicide because she 'could not live with the man she loved'. Jacottet thereupon instructed Marcelle to remove a bottle of arsenic from the dining-room cupboard. This she did, and the bottle ended up in the drawer of Duby's desk in his office at the Book Depot down the hill.

In the months between the Eunice incident and the murder, there were several stormy rows between the two implicated daughters and their father. Despite the scandal, Jacottet allowed Marguerite to work in the Book Depot – probably towards Christmas for stocktaking – even though this involved close contact with Duby.

On the night of 21 December, there was a huge argument between Marcelle and Jacottet over whether Marguerite could be allowed to accompany her and Duby on a picnic or camping expedition up the mountain. It ended with Marcelle saying that she hoped the gates of heaven would shut in her father's face when he died. Marguerite admitted to Madeleine that she had overheard the argument and that she did not mind so much about the picnic, but if it interfered with working at the Book Depot she would revenge herself. A little later, Marcelle, who was still very angry, told Madeleine that she hoped 'something would happen' to her father, although she expressed some remorse afterwards.

Next morning, Marguerite baulked at kissing her father (the seal of their bond) at breakfast, and then she and Marcelle went to work at the Book Depot. There Marguerite stayed all morning, Duby is reported to have said, until he suggested that the two sisters lunch with him. F.M. Reid and his young son Harold arrived at the Book Depot on business, then went to have tea with Jacottet at about 10.30. The Paillards also arrived at some point during the morning (it is not clear whether they were staying at the Jacottets or somewhere else, but the latter is almost certain, as it is most unlikely that the Jacottets would have argued so vehemently the night before with guests in the house). At some stage Madeleine, who had been sitting on the stoep, went inside, where she was startled by Marguerite coming out of the dining room, and they both went into the pantry looking for the little patterns for cutting biscuits. Marguerite warned Madeleine that the Reids were coming for tea.

Jerita put the food on the fire after tea, then went into the garden to collect vegetables. She said that she saw neither Marcelle nor Marguerite that morning, nor had anyone come into the kitchen before she went into the garden. The young maid of the Paillards, Mamaime, said that Marcelle had entered the kitchen and asked for Jerita, but she had not seen Marguerite that morning. Madeleine said she had seen Marcelle, who said she had come to tell her father that she and Marguerite were lunching with the Dubys.

After tea, the Reids, Jacottet and Madeleine (as well as the Paillards) went out on to the stoep to watch the approaching storm. It was such a deluge that the roads were awash, and Reid, who was anxious to get back to Mafeteng, was forced to accept the hospitable offer of staying to lunch.

At lunch – Duby said it was at twelve o'clock, Reid said it was at one – Madeleine ladled out the soup. Her father had two helpings as was his wont (it was a family joke), she and Harold Reid had the least. All of them got sick, and Madeleine sent a message to Dr Augsburger, who arrived about two o'clock. She either sent a message or went herself to fetch her sisters and the Dubys.

By five, all were out of danger except Jacottet. The doctor departed at six, leaving Marcelle with her father; by the time he returned, his patient was in a coma from which he never recovered. He died at 3.10 in the morning, in the presence of Marcelle, Duby and the doctor.

Next morning, Augsburger telephoned the authorities at ten o'clock and had a conversation with Duby about suspects such as Griffith, the printers and the family. When Augsburger suggested to Duby that the murder might have been committed at the instigation of the Paramount Chief and the Catholics, or might have been the result of 'delayed revenge' by the dismissed printers,

Duby agreed with these possibilities, favouring the first. When Augsburger said that he 'was persuaded that the poisoning had been done by one of the members of the family' and enquired about Claude's madness, Duby asked him 'never to speak about it to anybody in Morija', to which the doctor agreed, provided his silence did not interfere with justice.

The post-mortem was held, probably in the afternoon, and a quantity of the stomach contents was dispatched to the government analyst in Bloemfontein. Inspector Bunbury went into the kitchen and Jerita pointed out to him the ingredients of the soup: Quaker Oats, Lemco (a beef extract made by Oxo), salt and (possibly) cooked beans. He took samples and sealed them. In the separate pantry he found open packets of Cooper's Dip.

Jacottet was buried on the day before Christmas. On the 27th, a sleepless and tormented Duby wrote to Bianquis, apparently still mystified at the cause of death. On 3 January, the *Friend* reported that it appeared 'that through an accident some sheep dip became mixed with a soup powder'.

At some stage Dr Jacottet arrived from Matatiele, where he had his practice and where he had been at the time of the murder (it would probably have taken him two or more days to come, and so he almost certainly arrived after Christmas). After talking to Augsburger, who told him he suspected a family member, a troubled Gustave Jacottet went to see Duby, but came away happy (neither Augsburger nor Dr Jacottet are specific about the timing of these meetings and it is not clear whether they occurred separately soon after the murder or whether they took place towards the end of January when Dr Jacottet precipitated the arrests). Madeleine asked her uncle to take her away, because 'she was afraid of something'.

On 7 January, the analyst's report confirmed arsenic and pretty well ruled out Cooper's Dip. On 12 January, Bunbury interviewed Duby on the whereabouts of Marcelle and Marguerite, and on 24 January arrested Jerita. But a flurry of activity from Dr Jacottet, who had now been told about the Eunice scandal by Madeleine, led to Bunbury issuing a warrant of arrest. On 2 February, he went to Morija to execute the warrant, but found his suspects away picnicking at Masite. A search of Duby's house revealed nothing, while in the Jacottet house only a letter (addressed to Marguerite and dated 19 February 1919) from one R. Wasse or Wyss and 'relating to an affair of the heart' was found. In Duby's office desk drawer, Bunbury found a bottle labelled arsenic, which he sealed and sent to the government analyst, who later confirmed it as the poison. The three were arrested and remanded for trial. A preliminary examination was held in the court of the Assistant Commissioner in Maseru, starting on 10 February. On 3 or 4 March, the accused were released and no one was ever brought to full trial.

So who did murder Édouard Jacottet?

—◦○◦—

The mystery has most of the ingredients of the locked-room kind of puzzle that would have teased Sherlock Holmes or Miss Marple. There are only a limited number of people who can reasonably be suspected. Here is the list:

Griffith, the King
The printers dismissed from the Printing Works
M. Paillard
Mme Paillard
Mamaime
F.M. Reid
Harold Reid
Sam Duby
Édouard Jacottet
Jerita
Marcelle
Madeleine
Marguerite

Means. Opportunity. These two elements must be present in order to be able to identify who did the *actual* poisoning. So some on the list can be eliminated forthwith.

The idea of the King or of grown male printers sneaking around the kitchen or pantry of the Jacottet house surreptitiously slipping arsenic into the food is ludicrous. The same holds true for Duby – he was pretty much persona non grata with Jacottet, and even if he did visit, he almost certainly would not have gone beyond the more formal rooms. Having said this, none of these can be excluded from being part of a *conspiracy* to murder. But if they were involved, they would have needed an agent to do the actual deed.

To all intents and purposes, several others can be quickly exonerated. The Reids were at the lunch only by way of an unpredictable act of Nature. Similarly, the Paillards were there merely as ill-starred guests. The same can be said for Mamaime; although it is faintly conceivable that she could be used as an agent, the use of a young girl with no certainty of ever being in the Jacottet house or of being given a suitable opportunity (let alone the means) stretches credibility beyond reasonable bounds.

Before homing in on the only five left who could have committed the murder – Jacottet himself, Jerita, Marcelle, Madeleine, Marguerite – some of the circumstances surrounding the means and opportunity must be clarified.

Firstly, the means – the poison itself. There were only two known sources of arsenic in the Jacottet house: the Cooper's Dip in the pantry and the bottle of arsenic that had been removed in a very open, visible way at least a month before (any other arsenic present would have had to be smuggled in). Under questioning, Bunbury stated that the poison used was almost certainly not the sheep dip, 'as Cooper's Dip is so yellow that it would have been detected in the soup'. Dr Lewis, the analyst, was thorough and an expert in poisons: had he considered the possibility of dip, he must have tested for it. So the possibility of an accident, as the *Friend* suggested on 3 January, is not feasible.

It is certain that Marcelle and Marguerite had reasonable access to arsenic (the bottle in the Book Depot); for Édouard Jacottet, Madeleine and Jerita it is less certain. They would have needed to siphon some off from the bottle before it was removed a month earlier (suggesting indeterminate or long-range planning); or to bring some in from another source (none of the three is likely to have had easy access to the drawer in Duby's desk).

In Jacottet's case, if he had specifically instructed the arsenic to be removed, why would he reintroduce more himself? In any case, a scenario where he murdered himself and risked the lives of four friends (including an innocent boy) and his favoured daughter is far-fetched. He came to his last meal not as executioner, but as host.

In Jerita's case, either she took some of the arsenic a month before for some long-range, nefarious plan, or she too might have brought some in. But white arsenic was much more difficult for Africans to get hold of – it was a scheduled poison and must be signed for; and why would she need to do so when Cooper's Dip was readily available in the pantry, and its use could much more easily be passed off as an *accident*?

As for Madeleine, the arsenic had been removed specifically to prevent her from being able to use it. She herself claimed that she did not know what had happened to it. Ostensibly, the arsenic that had been kept in the dining-room cupboard was for killing flies and for doctoring horses. But there is a now little-known use to which arsenic was put on both sides of the turn of the century: women used it secretively as a cosmetic, to get rid of such things as pimples (Madeleine Smith, famously accused but acquitted of poisoning in Glasgow in 1857, is thought to have made such use of it). Madeleine Jacottet might possibly have had her own secret store for this purpose. It is also known to have been used as a tranquillizer and an abortifacient.

All five might therefore have been able to put their hands on the right kind of arsenic, but only two – Marcelle and Marguerite – can be said to have known of its whereabouts and have had reasonably easy access to it.

A key element in the matter of opportunity is timing. On the day following the murder, Bunbury took samples of the ingredients of the soup and sealed them. It is a highly reasonable (though not absolutely certain) assumption that these were sent off for analysis together with the stomach contents. Nothing more was said about them. It is thus a further highly reasonable assumption that no arsenic was found *in the ingredients.*

If, in the less than likely event that the poison *was* in one of the ingredients, then one can postulate three scenarios: it was put there some time before on the general chance that it would be used at some time in the future (this would be the choice of outsiders only, who were aiming at the Jacottet family in general); it was put there by Marcelle or Marguerite as a result of the argument the night before (this is a weak supposition, since they could not have known with any certainty that the ingredients would be used that day and would therefore have run the risk of poisoning *themselves* in the future); it was put there by someone taking advantage of the argument the night before to murder Jacottet and point the finger of suspicion at Marcelle or Marguerite. Realistically, this last could only have been Madeleine (Jerita had no need to put poison *in the ingredients* if she was intent on murder).

In poison cases and in exercises in speculation there are almost inevitably conflicting theories. Certainly, there is sometimes room for them. If anyone wishes to come to a conclusion different from the one postulated here, the clue of the ingredients might well be one of the best places to start.

That said, the most likely — almost overwhelmingly likely — scenario is that the poison was introduced *while the soup was being made or after it was made.*

—✦—

The Reids arrived about 10.30 and had morning tea with Jacottet. The soup was made by Jerita *after* the tea. Jacottet was not seen in the kitchen that morning (he was unlikely ever to be seen there!) and was probably in the company of the Reids and the Paillards till lunch in any case. He had almost certainly therefore no means and virtually no opportunity. He was never a serious suspect anyway. One down, four left.

Marguerite does seem to have been in the house during the morning, despite Duby's assertion to the contrary. Madeleine claimed to have encountered her. She *could* have brought arsenic up from the Depot, she *could* have slipped it into one of the ingredients in the pantry. But she *could not* have put the poison in the soup: she was there after the Reids had arrived at the Book Depot but before they came to tea with Jacottet, and the soup was made after the tea. (In a cynical scenario arguing that Madeleine lied about seeing Marguerite in the house in order to cast suspicion on her, the same would still hold and make Marguerite doubly innocent.) Jerita specifically stated that she had not seen Marguerite in the kitchen that morning and Mamaime makes no mention of it. There is no necessarily sinister message in her being in the dining room (there was no arsenic there) and she might have been coming in from the verandah. What was she doing in the house? She might have been looking, as she said, for the biscuit patterns to lend to Eva Duby (she certainly made no biscuits in the house that morning), and she might well have come to warn her father that the Reids were coming to tea. She left before the soup was made, so she could not have put the poison into it directly. Two down, three left.

Did Jerita (an apparently loving person) want to kill Jacottet and the five others herself? It does not seem likely. Was she an agent for someone? Would she, a good servant of the Jacottets for ten years and a devout, third-generation Protestant, further the cause of the Catholics? Almost certainly not. Of her Catholic King? A very faint perhaps. But would Griffith seriously have wanted to kill Jacottet over the spat about the closure of schools earlier in the year?

Was Jerita the agent of the printers? Their threats of revenge tended to be more direct, and they had perhaps more reason to resent Duby than Jacottet. As in the Jack the Ripper case, it is possible to multiply the suspects almost ad infinitum – Eva Duby might well have wanted Jacottet out of the way – but all would have had no chance of administering the poison and would have had to use Jerita as agent.

Much more likely is the possibility that she was acting on behalf of Marcelle, Marguerite and/or Duby (from his interviews with the Basotho staff, Henri believed she might have been cajoled into it by Marcelle). She may have acted as an agent before, if and when she helped Marcelle to procure an abortion. But she says she did not see Marcelle or Marguerite that morning (much less Duby). This is pretty well supported by the evidence of Mamaime. So how could she have conspired with them? One can only postulate the slim possibility that it was before the two women went to work. More significantly, where would she have got the arsenic from? Marcelle or Marguerite had to go and fetch it from the Depot, and she did not see them during the morning.

There is one great mystery that surrounds Jerita. Why was she unaffected by the two tablespoonfuls of soup she claims to have consumed after the meal? Was she simply impervious to a small amount of arsenic? Was she lying? One rational explanation would be that the arsenic was introduced not into the pot but into each *helping* of the soup. This could have been done in two ways. Madeleine might have done it while she was dishing out the soup. But why would she make at least five, possibly six, individual actions when she could have done it with one? Did she really, while they were in her very presence, individually poison five other people, four of whom she could have had nothing against and one of them a child?

Or might the arsenic have been in the condiments, more specifically the salt cellar? How pure was the salt, or with what was it seasoned? Could the victims, in a bizarre way, have poisoned themselves? Bunbury did take a sample of the salt from the pantry for investigation, but he did not mention taking salt from the dining room. There is no mention of a salt cellar being on the table anyway. According to Jerita there was already salt in the soup, and what are the chances of all six people, including a child, taking additional salt?

In the end, though, there is probably no mystery at all. A simple experiment makes the point. Even the most niggardly of soup helpings is at least eight tablespoons, a moderate one twelve to fifteen, and a decent one perhaps twenty. Jerita, at most, got a fraction of the poison the others ingested.

Jerita did have the opportunity and may, at a pinch, have had access to the means. She cannot be ruled out entirely. The same must be said of Madeleine. By her own admission, she was momentarily in the kitchen and she did serve the soup. Though arsenic had been removed from her immediate grasp, she might have had her own private store, or, with a little ingenuity, been able to procure some.

Marcelle certainly had very easy access to the means: she worked with Duby in the Book Depot and had taken the poison there herself. She also had a clear opportunity to plant the poison: she was in the kitchen after the soup had been made and while Jerita was in the garden. She did not have the *sole* opportunity, since Madeleine may have had just an outside chance and Jerita a clear one. But she comes close to being the only one who had the means *and* the opportunity.

Perhaps that is as far as one can go. And so, given the extreme difficulties of proof with only circumstantial evidence, and the fact that there was room for some doubt, it was sensible as well as humane for Garraway not to pursue the case. It was also not unreasonable for Christeller to maintain that there was as much – or as little – evidence to indicate that Madeleine was the murderer rather than Marcelle.

But, if one stands back in a dispassionate way, can Madeleine seriously be considered as a candidate? Even if it is conceded that she had the means and opportunity, it would have required incredible cynicism on her part to do such a thing, including poisoning four innocent people. She would also have had to fake her own sickness. This deserves a closer look.

At first glance, there is circumstantial evidence that she might have done exactly that. She was able to get a message to Augsburger and might even have gone herself to get the people at the Book Depot to help. Despite apparent illness, she recovered as quickly as the other four survivors. But there are strong arguments to counter this.

Reid gave an impartial account of the meal. The soup did not taste strange.

M. Paillard was the first to complain, followed by Harold, Jacottet, Mme Paillard and Reid himself. At some stage he asked Madeleine how she felt and she replied, 'So far I am feeling quite well,' but she 'spoke in a tone of voice that she might not have been'. One might have expected Jacottet to complain first, since he had the most soup and was the most affected, or Mme Paillard, who might have been served first as the only female guest, but the famous standard medical text of the time, John Glaister's *Medical Jurisprudence and Toxicology*, states that the onset of symptoms is regulated by several factors, such as the form in which the poison is taken (in solid form, in suspension or in solution), how much is ingested, and whether a meal has been consumed recently (this arsenic was mixed into a fairly substantial gruel). Usually the symptoms appear within an hour, but, even when large doses have been given, their appearance may be delayed (by as much as ten hours). Consequently, there is no absolute prediction of how victims will react. None became ill *immediately*, because Jacottet had time to have two helpings. It was quite possible for Madeleine, who took less soup anyway, to have begun to feel discomfort slightly later. 'In subacute poisoning', Glaister points out, 'the symptoms are less intense and many may be absent', which could explain Jerita's non-reaction after only two tablespoonfuls.

Madeleine says that she took ill and went to lie down. Jerita testified that, when the company became ill, she went to Madeleine's room and saw that she was sick. On hearing that all the others were in trouble, Madeleine went to their assistance. She then sent to or went to Duby's office to urge him to hurry to the house. She described herself as very ill, her legs shaking and her head burning with pain, which accords with Glaister's list of symptoms of nausea, faintness and a burning pain in the stomach and epigastrium. She told Duby that they had been poisoned, to which he replied, 'Hush.' She accompanied him back to the house. At some stage she collapsed (either in the office or the house) and was nursed by Eva, Marcelle and Marguerite. On his arrival, Augsburger saw 'the terrible state in which all the party were', and added that 'Miss Madeleine tried to assist him with her father, but was too sick to do much'. If she was faking her illness, Madeleine gave a fairly convincing performance in front of the good doctor and at least four others.

Madeleine is an unlikely candidate for murder. She had minimal opportunity and access to poison. She was suicidal, rather than homicidal. And there is an additional powerful reason for discarding her from the suspect list. Her lone accuser, other than Marcelle, hardly knew her, if at all: Madeleine was in England for many years, and Christeller himself was away from the time she returned in 1920 until after the murder. No reason was ever adduced as to why she would want to kill her father. Jacottet, in writing to his brother, always spoke of her with great affection, and, with his other daughters assuming the roles of Goneril and Regan, he referred to her as 'a ray of sunshine in his life'. She had willingly returned to Lesotho early in 1920, she seemed content teaching at the Normal School, and, as far as we know, no lover was about to be banished.

There are minor mysteries to be cleared up as well as the major one. Why on earth did not Duby or Marcelle get rid of the bottle of arsenic in the Book Depot after the poisoning? One obvious reason is that several people knew of its existence and to dispose of it would actually have roused suspicion.

Why did Jacottet die and the others not? The explanation at the time was that he took two helpings of his favourite soup and therefore got more of the poison. This is probably a sufficient reason. But he was also older, exhausted, and in ill health – Mabille had died of overwork at a younger age! – and his family had a history of heart trouble. The others were younger and fitter, although M. Paillard, after the poisoning, was consigned to atrophy and early death.

Why did the others not die? This points to the likelihood that the dose of arsenic was not a large one. It might also point to the possibility that it was not meant to kill – in which case the murderer must have had considerable knowledge of poisons and their effects. Alternatively, the murderer might have miscalculated the amount of arsenic needed to kill.

But there is another reasonable explanation. If, as seems almost certain, the murderer was Marcelle, she would either have taken some arsenic from the bottle in the Book Depot, or, more probably, have taken the bottle with her – the most convenient method. The bottle had already been used, so it must have been less than full, perhaps even tending towards empty. Whatever mood she was in, a small kernel of rationality would have told her that she should not use all the poison, she must return *at least some* so that the bottle with its contents could be produced. If all were used, the source might seem obvious. In other words, there may not have been enough poison to do the job clinically.

If Marcelle did do it, why did she poison all six? Who was her target? If it was her father, how did she know he would be the only one to die? On the one hand, it is unlikely that she knew the Reids would be at lunch (the storm and the invitation to lunch came late). The same may be said for the Paillards. On the other hand, she might well have known about the Paillards. Her target must have been her father. Madeleine might have been included, but she seems to be of peripheral concern.

There are two possible explanations. Poison is secretive. Marcelle (or whoever was responsible) might have wanted to get away with it, either by having the murder mistaken for accidental food poisoning or by diversifying the possible intended victim or victims and the motives. Most classic poisoning cases, as forensic commentators like Glaister suggest, involve this kind of calculation. But this explanation does not dovetail with the circumstances of the Jacottet murder. There is no evidence that there was chronic poisoning. And the act does not seem to have been carefully planned.

Most likely is that this murder was an act committed in rage. She did not care who else she got, as long as she got her father. She used the poison as if she were pulling the trigger of a gun.

—◦○◦—

How easily could Marcelle actually have done the deed?

In 1911, G.K. Chesterton published the short story, 'The Invisible Man', in his collection, *The Innocence of Father Brown*. In it, a man is murdered in a house which four men, who are watching, swear no one could possibly have entered. Only the small, dusty-looking priest, Father Brown, is able to show how it could have been done. While the witnesses cannot believe that an invisible man could have entered the house, Father Brown shows how someone invisible to them could have done so, *someone so familiar that he is not seen*: the postman.

It is quite possible that Mamaime actually did see the fatal act, but did not register it.

Amongst the scores of activities that made up domestic life, that sewed together its habitual rhythms, that swept its thoughtless surfaces and dwelt in its accepted places, as natural and familiar as the brushing back of a wisp of hair, was the womanly action of lifting a lid to tend the soup, that most universal of dishes. What could be more natural than the mistress of the house checking on the well-being of the family? This unassuming gesture, unnoticed, unremarked, would slip gently into the stream of irretrievable time.

—◦○◦—

Over seventy years after the murder, there were still a few people alive who had been in Morija on that day or who were closely associated with the dramatis personae.

Of course, they were children then, or at the most young adults. And seventy years washes away a lot of topsoil. Gynette Germond, warm, generous with her time and recollections, expressed the difficulties so well. Her memory, she said, was like a whole lot of tiny little boxes, unfortunately with lids. Now some of the lids had got rusted. They wouldn't open! Such a tug was necessary before they would budge, but sometimes one did, eventually. The testimony of the children must therefore be approached not necessarily with scepticism, but certainly with circumspection.

Georges Duby remembered Jacottet as a tall figure with a grey beard who was very strict and who never smiled at him. Kathleen Beaumont, the daughter of a trader at Morija, on the contrary, described him as 'a nice, kindly man' and his wife as 'a very pleasant lady'. Sara Molise, whose father donated part of his land, which abutted on that of the Bible School, for the Duby house, remembered Jacottet preaching one day in the church and exhorting the congregation not to imitate whites, but to live and die as Basotho. She described him as 'bohale' – angry, fierce, sharp, though with a touch perhaps of boldness and fearlessness. One of Jacottet's gardeners, now an old man, said that the missionary used to 'whip' them for stealing peaches from the orchard, and he too used the word 'bohale'. But, without exception, they also called him dignified.

Marcelle seems to have been the tallest of the sisters. She wore glasses and had blue eyes like her father, whom she most resembled. Kathleen Beaumont found her somewhat remote and peculiar, a bit of a square peg – she was frightened of Marcelle and sometimes ran away from her. Marguerite she found to be more open. On the other hand, in the Sekhesa household, according to Bethuel Sekhesa, whose mother was Georges Duby's nanny, 'Marcelle was a favourite. People liked her, there's no doubt about it. They were sorry over the whole affair. They never spoke of it in a spiteful manner.' As a child, Marguerite would often go to Sara Molise's house to play traditional girls' games, even though Sara was four or five years younger. According to Gynette, Claude was always unpopular and nobody liked him. Marcelle had a nickname amongst the Basotho – 'Lefetoa', the one who has been passed by, or, rather unkindly in common usage, a spinster.

The closest and most interesting reaction to any of the characters came from Georges Duby. Marcelle, he said, was not particularly good-looking, inclined to be plump, with a mass of blonde hair. He remembered her striding energetically to the Book Depot each morning. She was, he felt, obsessed with the job, if not with his father as well. She gave Georges wonderful presents, such as a beautiful bugle and 'a wooden Meccano set'. She called herself his godmother. But Georges thought it all a bit unfair, that she was being overkind to him in order to ingratiate herself, so he resisted it with some awkwardness. And he felt his mother's resentment. He added that his mother was somewhat cold sexually and he thought it understandable that his father, whom he adored, might in a moment of weakness or need turn to someone else for affection.

Without exception, these witnesses said that the Morija community was keen to suppress the whole story. Sara Molise said that the Basotho carefully refrained from telling their children anything of the scandal, and to this day Bethuel Sekhesa says, 'We Africans, especially our family, don't discuss things in front of our children. The Dubys were father and mother to me. I must keep their secrets.' And in his autobiographical memoir, published in 1967, Abraham Moletsane, mentioning the murder, wrote, 'Presently we heard that M. Jacottet had died in very sad circumstances ... It is best not to dwell upon things which undoubtedly harmed Morija.'

Kathleen Beaumont thought that the authorities hushed things up because it was 'bad for the image of Europeans'. Henri Jacottet's son, Julian, was told by his father that he had agreed to pull strings to get the whole thing dropped, provided that Marcelle disappear and never contact the family again. Verdier, of the Industrial School at Leloaleng, said to his fifteen-year-old daughter Elsie, 'Don't talk about that man,' as though Jacottet had gotten himself murdered.

Without exception, too, these witnesses, with only minor variations and without any prompting, were unequivocal about who was responsible for the murder. Sara Molise said she knew, as a child, that the two girls killed their father. Kathleen Beaumont gave a more detailed version: Marcelle had influenced Marguerite, and having decided to poison the soup they arranged to be out for lunch. When they heard there were to be visitors they watered down the soup, but were too late to alter the menu.

However, two children who were somewhat closer to the principal characters disagreed in emphasis. Jeanne Dieterlen said that her parents 'lowered their voices' when speaking of the murder, 'but even the children knew Marcelle did it'. And Bethuel Sekhesa, whose mother was in the Duby household and whose aunt (Mapansi or Doris) was at the same time in the Jacottets', agreed: 'Old people said it was Marcelle, not Marguerite.' He added, 'Marcelle may have thought: if I get rid of him, I'll move a rock from in front of me.'

According to his son, Henri was sure it was his sister Marcelle.

After his release from jail, Sam Duby spent time tidying up his business in Morija. But he did so in desultory fashion, neither his head nor his heart being in it. When he did send a letter to the President and members of the Conference on 6 April, he apologized for the delay in writing, but said he had not had the strength to do so and had returned to Morija 'totally broken physically and morally', in agony to think of the consequences of his misconduct for so many innocent people. He readily acknowledged that he had failed in his duty at a critical period in the history of the mission: towards God, his family, his colleagues.

But he also referred to the horrible weight of what he vehemently maintained was an unjust accusation of murder, and thanked those who considered it 'a dreadful judicial mistake'. He swore before God that he had had no part in the poisoning, and had not even known about it.

Although he was unworthy of their trust, he asked his colleagues to pity him.

When he left Morija soon afterwards, he went to Durban. He was on his way to Lourenço Marques, where he was to enter into partnership in a banana plantation with a local called Da Silva. Eva hoped that the sea air would restore his shattered nerves. She stayed on for a while in Morija winding up their affairs, but she did visit him on the Natal coast. She was in for a shock: 'The state in which I found my husband made me ill and I wondered if he would ever recover,' she wrote not long after.

Despite her desire to care for him, she felt that he needed to work above all. Nevertheless, it was hard for her to see him leave alone for a foreign country, on a Portuguese boat, not knowing what awaited him. She herself was anxious that her older children be kept from knowing the true reason for their father leaving Lesotho. The reason she gave – that it was for health reasons – must have seemed strange to anyone who heard that he had gone to malarial Mozambique.

On her return to Morija, Eva, loyally, perhaps blindly, stood by Duby. She found Marcelle, having partaken of the bread and water of affliction in prison, greatly changed: 'I am sure that her relations with my husband have always been proper and I do not believe that she had anything to do with the poisoning of her father, but the time in prison, and the long weeks of idleness for someone so active, seem to have done her much harm. I have discovered that she completely abused my trust and that she acted in a way I did not think her capable of. In addition, the few people who still held some sympathy for her have broken off all contact with her.'

Duby was soon defrauded of most of his money by his Portuguese partner, so he moved to Cape Town, where he became business manager to the garage of Lane and Thompson in Mowbray, while living first in Rondebosch, then at 21 Union Street, Gardens. 'Alas,' he wrote to Casalis, 'nothing will ever replace my work at Morija.' His wife stuck by him.

On 18 December 1923, as the third anniversary of Jacottet's death loomed, Duby's heart gave in.

CHAPTER THIRTY-ONE

MURDER IN HER EYES

P erhaps there was not one murder but three.

In the two centuries that preceded 1920, amongst the numerous murders documented in European and American society, in which even infanticide was not unknown, the killing of a parent by a child was almost unheard of. The bond of parent and child is, almost universally, a sacred one. That is why two cases which were exceptions proved so fascinating and caught the popular imagination to such an extent that they became part of folklore.

In 1893, Lizzie Borden of Fall River, Massachusetts, was found not guilty of murdering her parents. Few people today, including the major commentators, believe in her innocence. One hot morning in August the previous year, Lizzie killed with an axe the stepmother she hated; over an hour later, after he returned home, she killed the father she loved.

Her name is known to most Americans to this day through the nursery rhyme that resulted, with the simple but mesmeric rise and fall of its iambic tetrameters.

> Lizzie Borden took an axe
> And gave her mother forty whacks.
> When she saw what she had done
> She gave her father forty-one.

Allowance must be made for the exaggerations of poetic licence and the demands of rhyme: in fact, the blows to Mrs Borden were about half as many, and to Mr Borden somewhat less than that. But the reason Lizzie became so notorious is that the act was so unusual.

In 1752, Mary Blandy, unhappy daughter of foolish parents and the 'innocent dupe' of the scoundrel, Captain Cranstoun, was found guilty of poisoning her father and was hanged in Oxford Castle. In America, Lizzie Borden, the 'neighbourhood parricide', was the household queen of horrid crime; in England, Mary Blandy (before her notoriety was eclipsed by Jack the Ripper) was the same. Scores of books and articles, plays and even a ballet, bizarrely enough, have been written about Lizzie; numerous pamphlets about Mary appeared at the time, as well as the play, published in 1753, whose title gave her the name she has come to be known by – *The Fair Parricide.*

> Guilty, or guiltless, who can surely tell;
> A spotless Angel, or a Fiend of Hell? –
> To Heav'n alone we'll leave her dubious Case,
> And strive to mend the World, through her Disgrace.

At Mary Blandy's trial, Serjeant Howard, one of the prosecutors, expressed his horror of the deed. 'Of all kinds of murders that by poison is the most dreadful, as it takes a man unguarded, and gives him no opportunity to defend himself, much more so when administered by the hand of a child, whom one could least suspect, and to whom one might naturally look for assistance and comfort. Could a father entertain any suspicion of a child to whom, under God, he had been the second cause of life?' Turning to the Oxford University students who were spectators at the trial, he could not help adding, 'See here the dreadful consequences of disobedience to a parent.' While this moral does not seem wholly adequate, the mystification of prosecutor Howard was real.

Down the years, acting against nature itself, these women – Lizzie Borden and Mary Blandy – have posed a mystery. In the dark night of the soul, what force, what urge, could override the primal flinch from parricide?

—◦○◦—

Motive. William Roughead, who wrote an introduction to the published text of Mary Blandy's trial, thought that in her case the motive presented 'little difficulty': Mary murdered for love, Cranstoun for money. But he nevertheless felt that Mary remained inscrutable, keeping her secrets hugged close to her, and leaving us 'but a catalogue of ambiguous acts'.

Victoria Lincoln, one of the liveliest commentators on the Borden murders, has pointed out that Lizzie, like her mother, suffered from temporal epilepsy, 'severe migraines and seizures of apparently unmotivated rage', which occurred with 'predictable, almost clocklike regularity'. Lincoln suggests that the murders, especially the first one, of her stepmother, might have taken place during such a fit, aggravated perhaps by the fact that Lizzie was menstruating at the time. She argues that stress – over a simmering property dispute in the family – might have brought it on.

In Marcelle's case, Garraway, while pointing out certain hereditary problems in the family, was content that the motive for the crime lay in Jacottet's discovery of Marguerite's seduction, the ultimatum to Duby, and the arguments between Marcelle and her father.

But, through the ages, children without number have had such bitter disputes with their parents; not until recently have many of them gone beyond a raised voice or a slammed door. Something must have pushed Marcelle further, something made her cross the lethal line.

Motive may be reductionist or insufficient, and a search through the deserted battlefield of human motives may not uncover a full explanation (though to explain is not to excuse). And beyond even explanation there is meaning, that most ungraspable of phantoms.

—❧—

By 1920, the house of Jacottet at the foot of Makhoarane had begun to take on a lived-in look, like an adult's face. Its stones had weathered in conformity with the mountain. The garden, tended by Mrs Jacottet, had been softened somewhat with circular, rock-ringed flower beds, but now, at the end of the year, it was ragged from a year's neglect, and the moles tunnelled beneath, blind and destructive, leaving here and there their strange eruptions.

In spite of the garden and the half-grown pines, the house still stared impassively down the hill, guarded, as though a sound would curse it.

Since the death of Mrs Jacottet, the house had been managed less well. And she, who had clung to it for life, was gone as a mediator. However tempting it is to caricature Jacottet as a patriarchal autocrat, it is clear that he was not altogether in control of the household. He might have looked to his daughters for solace: but, to his chagrin, Marcelle, with conscious intent, spent much of her time away, probably at the Dubys; Marguerite was sulkily intractable in her youthful rebellion; and Madeleine, his temporary Cordelia, had been troubled with physical pain. If he tried to restore the house to strict discipline, his daughters did not give an inch in the toe-to-toe arguments that led up to Christmas. If anything, he gave ground in allowing Marguerite to help out at the Book Depot. By day the house sprawled in sullen and oppressive heat; by night it turned its face to the dark. Only occasionally, past the windows, a passer-by might glimpse a figure or catch a meaningful gesture.

In the hard ground, deep, below even the old moles, lay the trauma. Did it grow with the roots of the dog roses, or was it put there inadvertently by the builders? Did the house of Jacottet wither because of the successive droughts and lack of healing rain?

—❧—

It does seem likely that there was a legacy of instability in the family. Garraway had noted that 'all the Jacottets appear to be of a neurotic and unbalanced disposition'.

Mrs Jacottet suffered from her 'nervous fits' and was 'weak-minded'. This could have been epilepsy or depression, or both. She suffered, too, from a chronic though undefined illness. Most likely it was some form of depression. In the early years, at least, she clung to her husband with a desperate embrace, holding him back from his ambitions. In consequence, reinforcing the effects on her of having been torn from her maternal roots at a tender age, he protected her and treated her like a child at times.

Whether her children suffered from epilepsy is not known, so a comparison with the case of Lizzie Borden is tantalizing but tenuous. However, Ramseyer seems to have picked up the idea that Marcelle – perhaps like Lizzie – was afflicted periodically by 'a special madness' common to certain women.

Claude was the most obvious problem. Characterized by his uncle Gustave as 'a degenerate', he had been shunted off to Canada around 1920, and we know frustratingly little about him. In 1931, he was sentenced to ten years' imprisonment for armed robbery in Montreal and sent to the St Vincent de Paul penitentiary. In 1936, suffering from 'aliénation mentale', he was transferred to the Hôpital de Bordeaux. After 'une crise d'agitation maniaque aigue', he died there on 8 July 1939, of acute oedema of the lung and a cerebral haemorrhage. By that time his family had no idea where he was or whether he was alive or dead.

From Édouard Jacottet and his father, some of their descendants also seem to have inherited a fragile heart.

Or was it something else? To this day, many Basotho, including some Christians, believe that the Jacottets were the victims of dark and malevolent forces and that the family was bewitched, though no one knows by whom.

One of the most disturbing sherds of evidence came from Bertschy. He mentioned that Marcelle had a 'fixed idea', an obsession, that certain apparently honourable people had designs on her as a young girl, and she had accused them of attempting to seduce her. He added – echoing both Ramseyer and Alfred Casalis – that she frequently lied, evidently without scruple.

The most obvious conjecture for explaining this behaviour is that she had suffered some trauma in childhood or adolescence, perhaps an untimely or inappropriate relationship.

Indeed, there *were* distressing moments in her early years. Although slow to walk and, for a girl, slow to talk, Marcelle seems to have been a contented enough child. But when her livelier four-year-old sister Germaine died and she witnessed her parents' grief, she would, as a seven-year-old, almost certainly have felt some guilt, and might well have seen her own diphtheria, which followed immediately afterwards, as a punishment, even a punishment from God.

At the age of twelve, Marcelle was left in Europe by her parents and saw neither of them again for seven years. Her upbringing was in the hands of the childless Hoffets: her only companion, Orestes to Electra, was her younger brother Henri, so their relationship was a close one. Nevertheless, this severance from her family during the testing years of adolescence must have been traumatic in itself (Alfred Casalis, after all, put some of the blame for the murder on the sending away of the children). The Hoffets, in Henri's opinion, were very cold, and Eugène Hoffet was dry and boring. If any inappropriate relationship did take place in Marcelle's life, it is likely to have been as she approached womanhood. This might explain her ambiguous relationship with other men. Did she lose her way in the maze of sexual etiquette? Did she acquire a 'reputation'? Did her seeming inability to follow a path of moral rectitude stem from some insidious exploitation of her vulnerability? Was she seduced or molested or even raped by a stranger or acquaintance? Or did a father figure betray her trust?

There was a hint of trouble in the wider family. In 1905, Jacottet, it will be remembered, had to intervene when his nieces – the daughters of his late brother – came under the 'detestable' influence of an aunt, who tried to turn them against Eugène Hoffet, their guardian. He helped Hoffet bring these nieces back from living with her, and expected to be vilified himself for his role in the affair.

It must be stressed that this is surmise extrapolated from symptoms alone – her accusations of seduction, her collusion with her sister, her apparent amorality and disregard of the truth, even, perhaps, her promiscuity. There is no *direct* evidence to support these accusations of Marcelle's, nor can any specific individual be suspected.

In fact, the evidence specifically points away from her own father. Bertschy, in the relevant passage, used the plural 'people' three times for those Marcelle accused. This implies either a couple in tandem, or two or more separate individuals on separate occasions. The impersonal usage actually deflects suspicion from Jacottet himself. But such relatively public charges were decidedly uncommon in that day and age.

Beyond this, in the absence of further evidence, one cannot go. Perhaps Marcelle's accusations of lascivious approaches were hysterical; perhaps they did indeed happen. Certainly, her role almost as pander in the seduction of her youngest sister, vulnerable as she was after her mother's death, was bizarre.

—◦◦—

The abortion was, without a shadow of a doubt, traumatic, a process of suffering that lasted many weeks, if not longer.

The choice to abort is difficult in itself. Alone and insecure, who is there to turn to? How can considerations of superstition and old wives' tales, thoughts of inevitability and irreversibility, the deep desire for a child or the concern that this may be the last chance, be confronted or dismissed? Guilt at being pregnant is more than likely: stirred by messages from the past, from parents, from religion. Anger, too, is common: at being caught out, at being a woman, at the man who has caused this mess, at men in general, at having to make a decision. Because of the child, the father.

The further along the pregnancy, the more difficult the decision becomes, as fantasy might give the embryo, the foetus, the baby, a sex, a name, even a personality. Then, in the darkest hours of sleepless night, comes the fear – of the unknown, of danger, of infection, of death. As for the abortion itself, the environment is inevitably alien and hostile. And, although the choice is hers, the consequences, unpredictable, sometimes unimaginable, are not.

Afterwards, the body takes time to adapt to changes, the mind often takes longer. Some women even feel that they are still pregnant. Initial numbness of emotion might be followed by a succession of possible reactions. Depression is frequent; anxiety and sadness normal. While relief is possible – the lifting of an unacceptable burden – grief and loss, in body and soul, are inevitable for most. Loss of childhood and innocence, loss even of the self. A woman might even go in search of her baby; sometimes the ghost of the lost child haunts the house and her dreams. As with the pregnancy, so also after the abortion guilt is more than likely, anticipating punishment. In time, too, there may be anger, especially if the inner conflict is unresolved – a desire for revenge, blood for blood.

The deliberate termination of pregnancy does not preclude grief and the need to mourn this little death. Such grief has been known to resurface months, years, even decades later, especially in repressed societies where the mother has not seen the foetus, or where its final resting place is obscure. This grief might reignite with memory on random occasions (the pregnancy of an acquaintance, the onset of a period) or on specific anniversaries (of conception, of the abortion).

If mourning is not open or complete, if there is no catharsis or acceptance, if there is suppression or denial, behaviour might become extreme. Believing she has transgressed the sacred bond of motherhood, and having denied herself the elemental cry of birth, a woman might become a different person, or even negate her existence altogether. The deeper the denial, the greater the potential anger.

And it is not unknown for a woman to believe that she has 'killed a baby' or admit to 'having murdered my own child'.

Some or many of these feelings were undoubtedly Marcelle's lot. But their enumeration remains merely theoretical and superficial. It scarcely touches the naked fact and intensity of the fire unhealed within her. No child was born. The abortion brought no deliverance.

—◦☉◦—

In 1914, the mad dog of war was unleashed in Europe. The masters had made their choice: they could not choose the consequences. Once free, it could not be stopped. Its appetite was insatiable.

What it demanded was sacrifice. So, like Abraham, fathers sent their sons to the altar. The angel of war lit them to their beds of pain. Mud and clay were their ashes and their urns. For the British the place of sacrifice was the Somme, for the French it was Verdun.

Daughters, too, were doomed, like Iphigenia before the fall of Troy. The war hurt women, being kept from men, and they had to do the jobs of men.

The result was revolution. Not on the streets of St Petersburg, nor in the factories of Germany, but in the home and on the domestic front. The younger generation began to turn against their elders.

After the armistice, armaments gave way to accessories, guns to gadgets. Manufacturers, financiers and the barons of the press waved aside the feudal lords of the past and peddled the new. The open and weather-beaten automobile was roofed and closed, and soon the radio would find its way into every home. Alcohol and cigarettes, cosmetics and silk stockings would, for women, be the signs and symbols of emancipation.

By 1920, consumerism's gains were fairly modest. Marcelle would still have worn black stockings, cotton underwear and low-heeled shoes. Her skirt, tight at the ankles, was unlikely to hang more than six inches from the ground. She was, after all, a missionary's daughter. But she would have known that, in the centres of fashion, those six inches had become twelve, and silk and rayon were already on the way. On 21 December, Ladybrand held its first women's suffrage meeting, which drew a bumper audience.

Marcelle, being her father's child and trying to keep in touch with a wider world, might have heard that Scott Fitzgerald had published a novel called *This Side of Paradise* and that the 'Freudian gospel', its flame lit from the fuel of ancient myth, was the new evangelical creed. Biologists and anthropologists were there to remind her that man (and woman, too) is an animal with extra cunning, and that moral codes are merely relative.

If the fathers of the war knew what they were doing, could they be forgiven? If they did not know, who was left to forgive?

The greatest casualty of the war was God.

In the end, the real action of the Jacottet story contracted into the space of twenty-four hours.

On the night before the murder, the idea of forgiveness was on Marcelle's mind. She turned what seemed a trivial matter – a picnic up the mountain – into a test of her father's forgiveness. In her eyes, her father was a hard-hearted man, he had no mercy, he had not forgiven Duby. In *his* eyes, he had forgiven. But that did not mean he should let Marguerite go on the picnic.

So it is that arguments revolve around an apparent trifle, while the passions in fact run as deep as the heart's core and smoulder below the surface of the swamp that is a family's – no less than a country's – shared heritage.

Yet again, as so often in the last three months, the little war was renewed, the fighting, with numbing repetitiveness, over the same inches of terrain, a tragic stalemate of misunderstanding and missed opportunities.

Many famous murder cases are remembered for a single noteworthy remark: in the story of Mary Blandy, it was Cranstoun's handwritten note referring to 'the powder to clean the pebbles with'; in the case of Marcelle's contemporary, Major Armstrong, a timorous solicitor in the sleepy little town of Hay-on-Wye in Wales, it was his 'Excuse my fingers' as he handed his rival, with nice delicacy, an arsenic-laced scone at tea. In the Jacottet affair, the memorable and pointed statement, wrathful, enigmatic, is the one Marcelle flung at her father at the end of their final argument: 'You are like that, you parsons.'

It is the most direct statement by Marcelle ever recorded. Clearly, it came from the heart, from the depth of her disgruntlement. She might have meant that the missionaries were rigid and unforgiving; that they were unchristian in their hypocrisy; that they had refused to believe her or her past cries for help; that they were against enjoyment, against fun, against life itself. She might have meant all of these things. Those men of stones.

But probably the most significant feature of the denunciation is that it was directed not at her father alone but at the missionaries as a group, at the mission in general. It is the frustrated cry of a woman trapped – she was the new protestant against an old regime, one that was autocratic, patriarchal and unbending. She felt herself smothered by *all* that had gone before, the oppressive weight of the past. She wanted to blame something outside of herself, and she was prepared to pull down not just the house, but the temple, too.

And so she hoped that the gates of heaven would be shut in her father's face. Her frustration, impotent as a straw in the wind, had turned to anger. Her final thrust at her father, trying to get through to him, was a direct challenge to his most firmly held belief.

The argument came to an end, but without any conclusions. The father and his three daughters wrapped themselves in their own resentments and their own vindications. Sleep, if it came at all, was troubled.

That night Marcelle lay alone on her bed, bitter beyond words. Her conversion from grief and guilt to frustration and anger had taken place, almost imperceptibly, over a long time, as she contended with the inner conflict between the competing roles of murderer and victim. Now, in a few short hours, she nursed her revenge, listening only to the hiss of the lamp. When she finally turned it down, the silence was almost but not quite complete. The house breathed murder.

—⊙—

Next morning, the midnight fury of Marcelle had not abated. She knew what she would do.

Was there a murderous conspiracy in the Book Depot that morning between Marcelle, Marguerite and Sam Duby? Garraway contemplated the possibility of common purpose but claimed he could not prove it, nor could he point to which of the three had actually administered the poison. Subsequently, Duby denied vehemently having had anything at all to do with the poisoning, nor any knowledge of it. Prevailing opinion afterwards attributed innocence to Marguerite and blamed the malign influence of Duby and her eldest sister for her lapse of moral conduct.

Most likely, the three, disgruntled and harbouring their discrete grievances, fed on each other's anger that morning. Marcelle, in her unbalanced state, might have interpreted this as tacit support. Using the Reids' impending visit to the Jacottet house as her excuse, she seized the bottle of poison with passionate resolve. She stepped out of the Book Depot and headed on her own mission up the hill to the kitchen of her father's house.

Eight hundred and twenty paces from door to door, perhaps a few less for a tall woman with murder on her mind. Her footprints laid themselves with fierce precision in the dust of the well-trodden road. Each step was a choice of sorts which might have been reversed. But she was driven by a great emptiness that consumed her from within.

She passed the rondavels of the theological students on the left and crossed the stream, which had been reduced to a trickle by the drought. She looked up. The vault of the sky was a desert of clear and pitiless blue. Only a wild dark cloud was coming up over Makhoarane, covering part of it with its wings and causing a few shadows to play along the bare and stony walls of the mountain. What had started out as a womb of life appeared now for all the world like a cave of death from which she must escape.

She reached the little gate and pushed her way up the small hill to the house, past the dog roses and the circular flower beds which were her mother's memorials. By now she was determined. The accumulated impedimenta of her past and present life crowded into a single moment. In her mind's eye, a woman possessed by an eidetic vision, she could see her father reach to taste and ...

By the time she entered the kitchen, she had made her final choice. After that there were just consequences.

The god of hospitality must have blinked when this seasoning was added to the soup. The accidental guests, no less than the object of revenge, were subjected to the terrible drama within, vomiting in the harsh light of the summer sun. The poisoning was indiscriminate.

Perhaps Marcelle did not know that there would be outsiders for lunch; perhaps she wanted to disguise her deed as food poisoning; perhaps she did not care, even for her sister. Perhaps there was a special vengeance in turning the soup into a sacrificial broth for what was to be her father's last meal.

While a poisoning may have crossed her mind in the preceding months, it does not seem to have been carefully planned with the sinister stealth of most poisoners. This was a murder done in anger. She approached the house with murder in her eyes. Then, venom, to thy work.

—◦◎◦—

The night that Jacottet died, young Georges Duby lay awake with the moon across his chest. That afternoon and evening the whole world had been in uproar. Now there was an uneasy hush. No mouse stirred, though something did catch his attention. He strained to hear. After a short but intense period of concentration, he began to recognize the voices carrying from hill to hill, far into the dark.

For Jacottet, there was so little time to say goodbye. So little time to summon up and review the past – his youthful aspirations, his loves and fears, his struggles and his studies, his call to serve, his duty, complex and sometimes conflicting, to family, to the Basotho and to God, the achievements of his predecessors and his own. So little time to invoke those he admired – Arbousset and Casalis, Godet and Boegner, Moshoeshoe and Mabille – and those he loved. So little time to make a final account of his life. All that history seemed to settle in this one moment of catastrophe. His death was quick and agonized. But in that short time before he died, his physical agony was compounded by his mental anguish. Because he did not die in ignorance.

At five o'clock, he made the remark which so startled Dr Augsburger. He said, 'We have been poisoned.' Was this his last epiphany, a lightning flash of insight? He must have *known*.

The revelation was appalling. If he did suspect Marcelle, as surely he must have, then he was presented with the shattering realization that his daughter might be beyond redemption. Damned. In his last moments of consciousness, as his moral world was being shut down to the elemental and beyond by remorseless chemistry, this single thought – of his own destiny and that of his eldest daughter – became his sole concern. Now, at last, he understood the sacrifice that Morija required.

What went on between him and Marcelle in those last hours was known only to them. Augsburger said he left Jacottet alone with Marcelle between six and seven o'clock, but that Jacottet was unconscious then and never regained consciousness. So it was left to Marcelle to testify as to how he died. She said he had told her that 'whatever happened they must cover Marguerite and Duby'. Marcelle, however, was a self-interested messenger and therefore an unreliable witness.

If Marcelle is to be believed, Jacottet's last testament was one of forgiveness. This flies in the face of all his habits and beliefs. More characteristic was his behaviour the night before. Marcelle's salvation lay not in his forgiveness in this world, but in repentance and in the grace of God in the next.

Marcelle chose: her father was chosen. Was her *choice* justified? In this world, judgement would range widely along a spectrum between determinism and voluntarism, between an indulgent and a vengeful justice.

Whether Jacottet's faith was justified is a secret, as he himself would have wanted, between him and his God. His death came, with bitter irony, out of the blue and from the source he might least expect, from as close as could be, from his daughter, almost from within …

No simple motive, but an explanation for the murder lies in possible early trauma, in abortion, in grief and guilt and anger and frustration. All or most of these, together, are sufficient grounds to explain it.

One missing piece niggles away at the completion of the puzzle, however. We do not know when the abortion was carried out, and therefore its precise influence on the tragedy is obscure. Or is the timing known? Has the answer to the mystery slipped past us like a shadow in the dusk?

On 17 May 1919, Jacottet informed Bianquis that Marcelle had had an attack of typhoid fever, which put her in bed for ten weeks and required several more weeks of recuperation in Bloemfontein. Altogether, she had been away from work for nearly four months. 'The fever,' he wrote, 'was never very strong, but its persistence ended up causing considerable disquiet.' Certainly this recuperation period seems long for typhoid. And the disease, which is usually spread through unclean water, often causes an epidemic; isolated cases like this one are rare.

Could this be not typhoid fever, but the after-effects of the abortion? Is one allowed to speculate about the little mysteries, if not the great? Are we not obliged to end on the conditional? If ...

If the 'typhoid fever' was, in fact, the time of termination, then the abortion probably occurred sometime in mid to late January 1919. As there were no scientific tests for pregnancy on the mission in those days, it is likely that Marcelle remained uncertain about her condition for a good while. Added to that, she might have been reluctant to admit it to herself, let alone to others. Conception was therefore most likely in October or November 1918.

In times of war, women often become more fertile, so it is possible the thirty-two-year-old Marcelle was responding to some deep maternal call. This might have been pricked into life by the wounding and uncertain survival of Henri, to whom she was so close (he was wounded in September). Or it might have been a response to the end of a war that had carried away so many – so many who might have been lovers, husbands.

One can only imagine the turmoil the pregnancy provoked in Marcelle's mind, the rush of joy and pride, the fear of carrying such a child in a race-obsessed part of the world, the guilt – the Protestant guilt – of a missionary's daughter. In the end, fear outweighed love, too late for time's redemption.

Once the decision on the abortion had been taken, there were those days of doubt and trepidation. Abortion was risky, whether by herbs or direct inter-vention. She could not go to the mission doctors so, in all likelihood, she turned to Jerita. In all likelihood, too, the procedure went at least partially wrong and she was bedridden for ten weeks, either from the physical or from the psychological effects, or both.

The further along the pregnancy, the greater the grief and guilt. Did she see the foetus? Did she know how and where it was buried? Did she know if it was a boy or a girl? Did she give it a name?

One thing is certain: she could not openly mourn her loss.

Secrecy. Jerita knew. Her mother had to know. Perhaps Eva Duby knew. It would be impossible to keep the secret from the women of the house, and they were the only ones she would confide in. Ultimately, the rumour might spread even to a female novelist in Bloemfontein and a missionary's wife in the Soutpansberg. But a remote patriarch within the home might just be duped with the story of typhoid fever. The cost of this success would be high: guilt would be driven even deeper. Guilt was the poison feeding hungrily on the conscience, searching remorselessly into the heart of motivation. The house became a cauldron of repression and intrigue.

The death of Marcelle's child was murder in her eyes.

—❧—

Conditioned by the death of Germaine in 1893, Marcelle expected punishment. It came.

Jacottet himself had said that Marcelle's illness was 'a period of great fatigue' for his wife. Probably it drained her of her last resources. The strain of secrecy cannot have helped. When Louise Jacottet died in November, Marcelle must have seen it as a judgement. A feeling of guilt at the death of a parent is quite normal; having contributed to the death through causing her mother overwork and worry would have compounded the feeling. First she had killed the life within her; now she had helped to kill her mother too.

—❧—

Althaia, who slew her child. Scylla of Megara, who killed a parent. Clytemnestra, who wanted revenge for a child who was sacrificed. Three in one. An unholy trinity.

The forces that prompted this act of murder – that gave birth to chaos out of order – were immense. The passage of time, given intensity by a determined imagination, sealed its inevitability.

There is a pattern to the timing of events. It is one that was deeply embedded in Marcelle's mind. It is a pattern of anniversaries.

In November and December of 1918 and January of 1919, Marcelle was pregnant. As the mission contemplated the advent of the festivities and celebrated the most significant birth of all, the birth of the Saviour, Marcelle was tortured by the agony of her impending decision: to thwart the birth of her child, potentially her own best salvation, and kill the mother within her. Secrecy allowed no mourning for Althaia, and burning passion was buried deep.

In November 1919, a year later, her mother, who had helped her through the months of desolation, died, so that, as others celebrated, she mourned. The two deaths were welded together in her mind, crime and punishment. Scylla, seduced into a situation that choked her for choice.

In November and December 1920, in the weeks before Christmas, as others began to relax and rejoice, Marcelle was as wound up as a fine watch, unconsciously waiting for her anniversaries, womb-memory stirring. It was no coincidence that Jacottet died three days before Christmas.

—◦⊖◦—

The last choice was left to Henri. He had spent about three weeks in Cape Town, perhaps on legal business, before proceeding to Lesotho. He did not relish the visit. He was weary of the world. He still had the weight of a Lewis gun on his shoulders and the shadow of death hooding his eyes. He had seen the faceless and nameless die without number. Now he must face up to the death of one man. What did one death mean amongst so many? Other than that this one man was his *father*?

From Morija he wrote a postcard to the woman who was to become his wife: 'Tired to death of this wandering about.' Too tired to make heavy choices. The responsibility for Marguerite was burden enough.

What went on between him and Marcelle when he arrived at the Cape left no record. The two eldest Jacottet children were close, coupled by the loneliness of their adolescence in Alsace and Switzerland. Now he was convinced that his sister had broken one of the most sacred of all taboos, and his reaction was to recoil from the word and act that could scarcely be whispered – parricide.

So he cut her off from the family, or what was left of it. He told Marcelle to disappear and never contact the family ever again.

She tried to see him anyway, before he and Marguerite left Cape Town on their 'voyage home'. She came to the docks, but he would not talk to her. He went up the gangplank, through the traditional tangle of streamers, ties of joy and sorrow, without looking back.

When the mailboat pulled slowly away from the wharf, he did not see her as she stood silent in the crowd, fading, soon no longer to be seen, never to be seen again.

—◦⊖◦—

The house at Morija is still there, but it is much changed and split into two apartments, with a reshaped interior and a new roof. The garden is a desert.

The mission station at Thaba-Bosiu was hit by a cyclone in 1957. Several children in the village were crushed to death in their beds by the enormous stones hurled into the air. The missionary stationed at Thaba-Bosiu at the time had been under heavy fire in the war and he knew what to do – he survived by standing in a doorway. So did his kitten. A piece of grass, a straw in the wind, was flung with such ferocity it embedded itself in a tree, like an arrow from the bow of Paris.

The mission station has been rebuilt and life goes on, as if nothing happened.

Sources

Questions still lie unanswered. While a mountain of sources has been climbed, the Jacottet story by its nature opens into an ever-widening terrain of research beyond the limits of one researcher's lifetime. Of the sources that have been investigated, only the main ones, or the ones of some particular interest, can be mentioned here. At least three of the most important pieces of the story have been buried by time.

The first are the official government files on the Jacottet murder, where one might have expected to find statements, forensic reports and other evidence. In the 1970s, the Lesotho National Archives, the single most important repository of the country's history, were temporarily housed in the basement of the Roma Campus of the National University of Lesotho. Although their preservation was characterized mainly by neglect, a loose order did survive for most of the material. Despite several frenzied searches, the Jacottet files could not be found (other than the civil action that Madeleine brought against Christeller).

Then, in 1997, the University decided to surrender its protectorate over the documents and informed the government that it must take back its property. The move was carried out by convicts from the Central Jail known neither for their archival skills nor for their loving concern for ancient criminal court records and other administrative dockets which hold some of the authentic voices of Basotho history. Bucket lines were formed and the files – vast quantities of them – were piled haphazardly on to trucks. They were then split up, part being taken to the High Court and dumped in a damp cell beneath the adjoining Magistrate's Court. The rest were piled inside a house in Maseru West which had previously provided temporary offices for the Traffic Commission. Their fragile condition and equally brittle organization have undoubtedly been considerably undermined. If the Jacottet file was ever amongst them, it is likely to have been buried deeper and might remain so unless some freak accident, whether from seismic activity or erosion, lifts it to the surface for some future forensic palaeontologist to discover.

Alternatively, being of a sensitive nature, these files might have been kept under more private and immediate surveillance by the Resident Commissioner. Certainly, the contents of Jacottet's stomach were kept in a jar in the Resident Commissioner's office or elsewhere in government custody for many years in case the whole affair was resurrected. If the files do one day resurface – which would be a most welcome occurrence – they may confirm or contradict some of the conclusions of this book.

The archives of the Swiss Mission in Lausanne also provide difficult if different problems. Designed along the lines of the most devious maze to deceive secret agents from repressive regimes where the Swiss Mission was trying to help, amongst others, political activists and refugees, they prove equally puzzling to the most innocent of scholarly researchers. There is a file devoted to the correspondence of Frank Paillard, some of which is quite interesting. But on the flap of the file a note recording the receipt of five letters from Paillard has been crossed out, as though the letters were transferred somewhere or destroyed. They are certainly not in the file, nor can they be found elsewhere. Since one was dated 3 January 1921, and others in February, March and May, they were surely about the poisoning and possibly contained important clues. Their disappearance may be evidence of some kind of cover-up, although similar correspondence of the PEMS in Paris is available and does not seem to have been tampered with.

The third missing source is the most important of all – Marcelle herself. When Henri told his sister to disappear and never darken the family's door again, she did exactly that. The only glimpses of her thereafter are fleeting. Georges Duby said that when his father finally arrived in Cape Town, he applied for a job at the publishers Maskew Miller (or Juta's), but Marcelle had got there before him; another rumour was that she had dropped out in 'a native area', perhaps looking, for a third time, for some comfort in the Basotho community.

In 1957, Henri wrote to Albert Brutsch at Morija asking him if anyone had any information about Marcelle. A relative had died leaving money to several members of the family, who now needed the signatures of both Marcelle and Claude (who had also disappeared – and died – in Canada). The sum due to Marcelle was modest – a little more than 8 000 francs. Clearly, Marcelle had not kept in touch with Madeleine or Marguerite either. The only information that Henri could give was that when she had arrived in Cape Town in 1921, Marcelle had taken the name of 'Hélène Favarger' and that she might also have called herself 'Marcelle (or) Hélène Barrelet'. When no positive information was gleaned, Marcelle was finally declared legally missing by the cantonal Tribunal of Neuchâtel in November 1958.

The question remains to this day: what did happen to her? Did she change her name again? Did she marry? Did she have children? Where and when did she die? Will someone, somewhere, someday, in the vast sands of time, spot a footprint of hers? Or did she, the last victim of the tragedy, silence herself forever?

General Sources

A number of sources have been used extensively throughout the story. The two main repositories, which complement each other, are the Bibliothèque du Service Protestant de Mission (Département Évangélique Français d'Action Apostolique or DÉFAP) at 102, Boulevard Arago, Paris 14ème, and the Morija Museum and Archives in Lesotho.

The key collections at DÉFAP include hundreds of pages of letters from Jacottet and Duby (first to Boegner, later to Bianquis), and from numerous other missionaries and associates, including Arbousset, Bertschy, the Casalis family (Eugène, Dr Eugène and Alfred), Christeller, Christmann, Coillard, Dieterlen, the Ellenbergers (D.F. and Victor), Louis Germond, the Mabilles (Adolphe, Ernest and Louis) and Paul Ramseyer; as well as the minutes of the PEMS Committee, the records of the Comité des Dames, the multi-volume diary of Hermann Dieterlen, lettres circulaires aux réunions de couture, and the comprehensive collection of books and pamphlets related to the mission, as well as journals and clippings.

Crucial in Morija are the minutes of the Conference, the Seboka (Synod) and the School Boards, the letter books and the account book of the Sesuto Book Depot. Morija also has an extensive collection of books, pamphlets and ephemera, and a valuable collection of unpublished biographical notes on most of the missionaries compiled by Jeanne Jaques. Albert Brutsch facilitated access to the private letters of Hermann Dieterlen and his own private notes on church records (births, marriages and deaths, etc.), the pastoral students and life histories. The collection that Jacottet made of African grammars and dictionaries, which was repurchased by his brother, is scattered through the library.

Private collections hold certain invaluable sources: Julian Jacottet generously gave access to documents related to his father Henri's career, to scores of family postcards and to photographs, paintings and other material; Ann Patey equally generously allowed access to memorabilia belonging to her mother (Marguerite) and her aunt (Madeleine), including certain important letters, certificates and photographs; Paul Ellenberger let me copy sections of the unpublished memoirs, entitled *Souvenirs*, of his father Victor; André Casalis also allowed sections of his father Alfred's unpublished reminiscences, entitled *Petits Étapes sur le Chemin de la Vie*, to be copied; and Hélène Nixon gave me the diary of her father, Charles Christeller, which is now in the Morija Museum. Rev. John Young shared extracts from his own doctoral thesis and from Edwin Smith's journal, and Prof. Daniel Waley scanned the papers of Lord Buxton for correspondence related to the murder. Rhodes House, Oxford, holds the papers of Sir Edward Charles Frederick Garraway, KCMG (MSS Afr. S1610).

The continuous runs of *Leselinyana la Lesotho* and the *Journal des Missions Évangéliques* are invaluable sources, and *Le Petit Messager*, the *Basutoland News* and *Molepe* were also consulted.

For obituaries on Jacottet see the *Journal des Missions Évangéliques*, the *Dictionary of South African Biography*, vol. 1 (Cape Town, 1968), pp. 406–7, and the *Journal Religieux* (February 1921). Particularly valuable is a clipping entitled 'Édouard Jacottet: Souvenir d'un ami' by Henri Junod (provenance unknown).

Many, often multiple, interviews provided otherwise unobtainable information. Many of these people have been mentioned in the Thanks.

Numerous secondary sources have been consulted. The most central were the *Livre d'Or de la Mission du Lesotho* (Paris, 1912); V. Ellenberger, *A Century of Mission Work in Basutoland, 1833–1933* (Morija,1938); Edwin Smith's fine biography, *The Mabilles of Basutoland* (London, 1939; reprinted Morija, 1996), and Jean-François Zorn's comprehensive history of the PEMS, *La Grand Siècle d'Une Mission Protestante: La Mission de Paris de 1822 à 1914* (Paris, 1993). For the early history of the PEMS see also Jean Bianquis's three-volume *Les Origines de la Société des Missions Évangéliques de Paris* (Paris, 1930, 1931, 1935).

For general works on Protestantism specifically alluded to, see Charles Bost, *Histoire des Protestants de France* (Carrières-sous-Poissy, 1992), and Frank Puaux (ed.), *Les Oeuvres du Protestantisme Français au XIXe Siècle* (Paris, 1893).

Ample influence has been exerted by certain central texts on Lesotho itself, including R.C. Germond's *Chronicles of Basutoland* (Morija, 1967); D.F. Ellenberger's *History of the Basuto* (London, 1912; reprinted Morija, 1992); G. Theal's three-volume collection *Basutoland Records* (Cape Town, 1883); Sir Godfrey Lagden's two-volume *The Basutos* (London, 1909); Stephen Gill's excellent *A Short History of Lesotho* (Morija, 1993); and David Ambrose's meticulously researched *Maseru: An Illustrated History* (Morija, 1993).

On nineteenth- and early twentieth-century Lesotho politics, Elizabeth Eldredge, *A South African Kingdom: The Pursuit of Security in Nineteenth-Century Lesotho* (Cambridge, 1993), and L.B.B.J. Machobane, *Government and Change in Lesotho, 1800–1966* (London, 1990), were consulted; on law, W. Maqutu, *Contemporary Family Law of Lesotho* (Roma, 1992), Patrick Duncan, *Sotho Laws and Customs* (Cape Town, 1960) and V. Sheddick, *Land Tenure in Basutoland* (London, 1954).

Essential reference works are G. Haliburton, *Historical Dictionary of Lesotho* (Metuchen, N.J., 1977); Shelagh Willet and David Ambrose, *World Bibliographical Series, vol. 3: Lesotho* (Oxford, 1980); and David Ambrose's section on Lesotho in *The Guide to Botswana, Lesotho and Swaziland* (Johannesburg, 1983).

Particular Sources

Part One

The primary sources for the murder, the trial and surrounding events, in the absence of the police file, are the newspaper reports. The principal ones consulted were the *Friend* (3 January, 8, 11, 12, 15 February, 4 March 1921), the *Star* (8, 11, 12 February 1921), *Die Volksblad* (15, 18 February 1921), *Diamond Fields Advertiser* (8, 12 February, 4 March 1921), *Leselinyana* and *News of the World*.

Glimpses of Marguerite's school career can be seen in the *Eunice High School Magazine*, 1915–20, and the history of the school in Helen O'Connor's *No Other School So Dear* (Bloemfontein, n.d.). The various editions of Braby's *Orange Free State Directory* provided general information on Bloemfontein and Lesotho.

Garraway's impressions, reactions and confidences derive from his diary and assorted correspondence, including letters from Alfred Casalis, Edward Motsamai, Lords Milner and Buxton, and Prince Arthur of Connaught, and biographical details from an introduction to the papers by J.C. Williams. Also yielding information were interviews with Dorothy Smith, née Johnston, and Suzanne Pulane Lorriaux (interviewed by David Ambrose) and Lady Alethea Eliot, daughter of Lord Buxton (interviewed by Peter Sanders), a memoir of Fred Reid, son of F.M. Reid, letter books of the Morija Sesuto Book Depot 1913–21, and a letter from Alfred Casalis to Sam Duby, addressed from Johannesburg and dated 24 December 1920.

Part Two

Chapter 8: Lehaha-la-Sontaha

This chapter would not exist without the moving journal which Thomas Arbousset kept in February 1840. His text is enhanced by the awesome scholarship of David Ambrose and Albert Brutsch in their edition and translation, *Missionary Excursion* (Morija, 1991). See, also, Alain Ricard's introduction to his edition of the journal, *Excursion Missionnaire dans les Montagnes Bleues* (Johannesburg and Paris, 2000). For

Arbousset's first exploratory journey in 1836, see *Narrative of an Exploratory Tour* (Cape Town, 1846) and for a discussion on whether he reached Mont-aux-Sources see Albert Brutsch, 'Arbousset and the Discovery of Mont-aux-Sources', in *Lesotho: Basutoland Notes and Records*, vol. 7 (1968), pp. 49–56. David Ambrose has produced a description and history of the cave Arbousset named Lehaha-la-Sontaha (now known as Liphofung cave) in a monograph called 'Report on the Hololo Valley Historical Site "Liphofung"' presented to the Lesotho Highlands Development Authority. The site is well worth a visit and has recently been provided with a visitor centre. At the small tourist information centre at Thaba-Bosiu a pamphlet entitled 'Preservation and Presentation of Thaba-Bosiu, the National Monument' provides some useful information on the mountain. Two excellent biographies on the founder of the Basotho nation – Leonard Thompson's *Survival in Two Worlds: Moshoeshoe of Lesotho 1786–1870* (Oxford, 1975) and Peter Sanders's *Moshoeshoe: Chief of the Sotho* (London, 1975) – have been drawn from enthusiastically.

Chapter 9: The Desert Church, Chapter 10: The Mountain King and Chapter 11: The Oxen of the Batlokoa

In addition to D.F. Ellenberger's *History* and Germond's *Chronicles*, the main sources for the early history of the mission in Lesotho have been Eugène Casalis's *My Life in Basutoland* (London, 1889) and *Les Bassutos* (Paris, 1859), translated into English as *The Basutos* (London, 1861; reprinted Morija, n.d.). For biographies of Arbousset see Georges Gallienne, *Thomas Arbousset 1810–1877* (Paris, 1933) and Henri Clavier, *Thomas Arbousset* (Paris, 1965).

Chapter 12: The Seal and Chapter 13: From Peace to the Gun War

Edwin Smith's book on the Mabilles is central to any study of the second half of the nineteenth century in Lesotho mission history, as is Jacottet's contribution to the *Livre d'Or*. For the history of the Sesotho Bible, see Albert Brutsch, 'The New Testament in Sotho, 1855–1955', in *Basutoland Witness*, vol. 9, no. 4 (October–December 1955); for an account of the Printing Works see Jacques Zurcher's pamphlet, '111 Years: Morija Printing Works' (Morija, 1972); for early educational work see J.M. Mohapeloa, 'The Beginnings of Education in Lesotho', in *Lesotho: Basutoland Notes and Records*, vol. 7 (1968), pp. 5–18.

Relevant biographies include Hermann Dieterlen's *Adolphe Mabille* (Paris, 1930, first published in 1898) and Édouard Favre's *Les Vingt-Cinq Ans de Coillard au Lessouto* (Paris, 1933).

For the Catholic side of things, see Aimé Roche, *Le Cavalier des Malouti: Joseph Gérard O.M.I. 1831–1914* (Lyon, 1955); Gerard O'Hara, *Father Joseph Gérard* (Mariannhill, 1988); M. Ferragne and G. Brossard, *Father Joseph Gérard, O.M.I. Speaks to Us from South Africa and Lesotho 1854–1914* (Maseru, n.d.); F. Mairot, *Suivez le Guide: Petite Histoire des Missions de Lesotho* (Mazenod, n.d.); M. Deltour, *Les Basotho à la Fin du Siècle Dernier* (Roma, 1988); D. Levasseur, *A History of the Missionary Oblates of Mary Immaculate* (Rome, 1989).

The 'incident of ecclesiastical rage' at Thaba-Bosiu was mentioned by King Letsie III in a speech to the National University of Lesotho at Roma and published in *Lehlaahlela* (May 1995), pp. 13–14.

For the introduction and progress of Anglicanism, see Canon R. Dove, *Anglican Pioneers in Lesotho* (Mazenod, 1975). See, also, Sister Josephine's unpublished typescript 'St Barnabas Mission, Masite: One Hundred Years', which also contains some information on Spencer Weigall.

Chapter 14: Waiting for Godet

There are any number of works on the history and society of Neuchâtel. One of the most comprehensive is the three-volume *Histoire du Pays de Neuchâtel* (Hauterive, 1989). Other works consulted include L. Thévenaz, *Le Pays de Neuchâtel: Histoire* (Neuchâtel, 1948), and A. Bardet et al., *Le Pays de Neuchâtel* (Hauterive, 1995), as well as two books of photographs by Jürg Schetty, *Neuchâtel: Belle Époque* (Auvernier, 1975) and *Neuchâtel ... il y a 100 ans* (Auvernier, 1994). For the specific history of the Reformation in the canton, see F. Godet, *Histoire de la Réformation et du Refuge dans le Pays de Neuchâtel* (Neuchâtel, 1859), and for a political overview see Rémy Scheurer et al., *Histoire de Conseil d'État Neuchâteloise* (date unknown).

Information about the Jacottet family, particularly Édouard's parents, has been taken from a family tree and unsigned memorandum in the private collection of Julian Jacottet, and from the *Dictionnaire Historique et Biographique de la Suisse*, vols 3 and 4 (1926). Obituaries of Henri Jacottet père appeared in *L'Union Libérale* (7, 14 October 1873); of Isabelle Jacottet in *Feuille d'Avis de Neuchâtel* (10 November 1896); and of Bernard Barrelet in the same publication (4 December 1896). These newspapers also revealed other significant data. For the distinguished academic career in the Faculty of Law of Henri Jacottet père, see the *Histoire de l'Université de Neuchâtel* (Hauterive, 1994), second volume.

Details of Édouard's early family and love life derive from the papers of his brother, Henri Jacottet, lodged in the Cantonal Archives in the Citadel in Neuchâtel, which contain letters from his mother, his sisters Louise and Isabelle, and from Édouard himself.

Of interest, too, are the books by his father – the impressive two-volume standard legal text *Le Droit Civil Neuchâtelois*; and by his brother Henri – a travelogue called *Souvenirs d'Algérie 1881* (Neuchâtel, 1882).

On the life and thought of Godet reference was made to his biography, *Frédéric Godet 1812–1900*, by Phillippe Godet (Neuchâtel, 1913), and to a monograph, 'Frédéric Godet, Swiss Divine and Tutor to Frederick the Noble', by F.F. Roget (London, 1914).

On the church schism the core texts are Charles Monvert, *Histoire de la Fondation de l'Église Évangélique Neuchâteloise Indépendante de l'État* (Neuchâtel, 1898); *Souvenir de l'Inauguration de la Tour et des Cloches du Temple Indépendant de La Chaux-de-Fonds – Le 8 Octobre 1882* (Geneva, 1882); Gottfried Hammann's section 'Églises et Communautés Religieuses' in the third volume of *Histoire du Pays de Neuchâtel*, pp. 219–56; Valérie Siegenthaler, 'Transformation de la Place de l'Église dans la Société Neuchâteloise de 1848 à 1873: Une Perspective Donnée par la Presse' (unpublished thesis, University of

Neuchâtel); and the pamphlets 'Conférence sur la Situation Actuelle de l'Église dans la Canton Neuchâtel' (La Chaux-de-Fonds, 1873), 'L'Église Évangélique Neuchâteloise Indépendante de l'État: Ses Origines et ses Principes' (Neuchâtel, 1892), 'Le Projet de Loi Ecclésiastique' by Henri Jacottet (Neuchâtel, 1873) and 'Les Deux Maisons' by Léopold Jacottet (Neuchâtel, 1874). For the exchange of letters between Léopold Jacottet and F. Guillermet, see the supplement to the *Journal Religieux* of 19 October 1872.

Jacottet's records in Germany were supplied by the Eberhard-Karls-Universität at Tübingen and the Georg-August-Universität at Göttingen. On Ritschl, I simply could not have done without Ernest Edghill's *Faith and Fact: A Study of Ritschlianism* (London, 1910); Alec Vidler's *The Church in an Age of Revolution* (London, 1961); Karl Barth's *From Rousseau to Ritschl* (London, 1959); the *Concise Oxford Dictionary of the Christian Church* (Oxford, 1977); and the *New International Dictionary of the Christian Church*, edited by J.D. Douglas and Earle E. Cairns (Grand Rapids, 1974, new edition 1996).

On Jacottet's career at the Theological Faculty in Neuchâtel some information can be found in certain index cards and manuscript notes in the Bibliothèque des Pasteurs in Neuchâtel, in the *Bulletins du Synod Indépendant* (1872–90) and in F. Godet's pamphlet, 'La Fidélité dans Le Ministère: Sermon prononcé pour le Consecration de MM. Béguin, Écuyer et Jacottet' (Neuchâtel, 1882). *Le Petit Messager*, vol. IX (1884), also contains a short description of Jacottet's response to the call for missionaries by Mabille and Coillard.

Chapter 16: Little Cerberus

The giant bird of Makhoarane was first publicly reported in an article called 'Nonyana ea Makhuarane' by Hermann Dieterlen published in *Leselinyana* on 1 July 1885. It was afterwards quoted extensively by 'E.C.' (Eugène Casalis) in an article entitled 'L'Oiseau de Makhoarane (Morija)' in the *Journal des Missions Évangéliques* (1885), pp. 366–8. For a discussion of its significance in palaeontological history as the earliest discovery of fossil footprints in sub-Saharan Africa, see David Ambrose, 'A Tentative History of Lesotho Palaeontology', in *Journal of Research*, National University of Lesotho, Occasional Publication no. 1 (August 1991).

Chapter 17: The Mirror Breaks

The 'Who is Masupha?' story appeared in E.A. Dutton, *The Basuto of Basutoland* (London, 1923), p. 82; and Alfred Casalis told Edwin Smith the story of how Masupha wanted to replace Jacottet with Casalis in a letter from Cannes dated 10 June 1938 (Morija Archives). Information from Maitin's diary comes courtesy of Peter Sanders.

Chapter 18: Foqoqo

For various journeys into the Maloti see the chapter entitled 'The Last Redoubt' in Germond's *Chronicles*. Jacottet's 1884 journey can be found on pp. 414–16, his 1893 journey on pp. 423–30. For Job Moteane's 1887 journey see five issues of *Mehloli*, starting with vol. 1, no. 4 (December 1989). For other early comparable trips (by

Catholic missionaries), see *Trans-Lesotho: Accounts of the Trips of the First Missionaries in the Drakensberg*, edited by M. Ferragne (Roma, 1975); and 'A Journey from Qacha's Nek' by Inspector J.M. Grant, unpublished typescript copied from original diary by R. Webb.

Gilbert Tsekoa of Molumong trading store pointed out aspects of the geography of Rafolatsane's village, Carlisle Motebang's mission at Molumong, and the environs.

Chapter 19: Death and the Fall

James Bryce's meeting with Jacottet is described in the chapter 'Basutoland' in his *Impressions of South Africa* (London, 1899) and a brief meeting with Jacottet is also recounted by Alfred Bertrand in *En Afrique avec le Missionnaire Coillard* (Geneva, n.d.).

The description of Christmas at Thaba-Bosiu was made in a letter Mlle Jacot sent to the Comité des Dames of the PEMS.

Information and correspondence related to the new edition of the Bible can be found in a small red notebook, in annual reports and in the minutes of the Translation Sub-Committee of the British and Foreign Bible Society in the Society's archives in Swindon. William Canton's *A History of the British and Foreign Bible Society*, vol. 4 (London, 1910) and A.P. Smit's *God Made It Grow: History of the Bible Society Movement in South Africa* (Cape Town, 1970) are also relevant.

Chapter 20: No-Man's-Land

The defeat of Masupha is described in Major G. Tylden, *A History of Thaba Bosiu* (Maseru, 1945), and David Ambrose, 'Masupha's Village', in *Lesotho: Basutoland Notes and Records*, vol. 9 (1970–71), pp. 20–24.

For the military movements in the O.F.S. and their proximity to Basutoland during the Anglo-Boer War, see Thomas Pakenham, *The Boer War* (London, 1979). For Lagden's particular view of the war and Basotho participation, see pp. 599–612 of his *The Basutos*. The quotation about the Basotho being 'a text unto nations' is taken from a letter to Dr Stewart dated 20 July 1900 (Lagden papers, Rhodes House, Oxford, MSS Afr. S211, Box 3/1, pp. 214–16).

The dancing incident between little Loulou Germond and Claude Jacottet was recounted by Nelly Germond in an unpublished memoir called *Loulou*, written in 1910 (a copy of which was given to me by the family). The assessment of Henri Jacottet's intellectual stance derives directly, in translation and summary, from Albert Berchtold, *La Suisse Romande au Cap du XXe Siècle* (Lausanne, 1963), p. 302.

Marcelle's registration at the University of Glasgow is recorded under Entry no. 356 in the Matriculation Album (Women). She paid a guinea on 24 October 1905, presumably to register in the Arts Faculty (the Album is housed in the University Archives). On a formal list of students (in a class of seventy-nine) Marcelle was recorded as studying *both* literature and language, so she probably was there not just to improve her English.

Chapter 21: The Book of Gold

For Jacottet's involvement in church organization and his interaction with burgeoning Ethiopianism, not dealt with here but an important part of his work, see his pamphlet 'The Native Churches and Their Organizations' (Morija, 1905); and 'The Native and European Churches: Is Union Desirable?', published in two parts in the *Christian Express* (July and August 1907). His prominent role in the General Missionary Conferences (the first of which was held in Johannesburg in 1904) was well documented in the successive reports of the proceedings (printed in Morija, 1904, 1906). He was, for instance, a member of the Missionary Conference's commission on 'Uniformity and Discipline', which dealt with questions ranging from the African spirit world, through sin and baptism and the indigenous church, to polygamy and prickly-pear beer. For a conceptualization of Ethiopianism in southern Africa, see James Campbell, *Songs of Zion* (Oxford, 1995), as well as Pastor C. Nontshinga-Citashe, *Brief Outline of the History of the Ethiopian Church of South Africa* (Morija, 1957).

Thomas Mofolo first published *Moeti oa Bochabela* in book form at Morija in 1907, and the English translation was produced in London in 1934 as *The Traveller of the East*. It is this translation which is drawn on extensively here. No study of Mofolo is adequate without access to Daniel Kunene's *Thomas Mofolo and the Emergence of Written Sesotho Prose* (Johannesburg, 1989). Useful, too, is Kunene's *The Works of Thomas Mofolo: Summaries and Critiques*, African Studies Center, University of California, Los Angeles, Occasional Paper no. 2 (1967). See also T. Mofolo, *Chaka*, translated by D. Kunene (London, 1981), and *Chaka: An Historical Romance*, translated by F.H. Dutton (London, 1931). Albert Brutsch has compiled extensive notes on Mofolo's life and family. Jacottet's review of *Moeti oa Bochabela* appeared, under the initials 'E.J.', in the *Christian Express* (2 December 1907). Jacottet's review of *Pitseng* was also published in the *Christian Express* (1 July 1910). Duby's phrase 'a Mosuto's dream' comes from the Book Depot Letter Book, 10 October 1917. In *Basutoland Witness*, vol. 4, no. 2 (April–June 1951), Z.D. Mangoaela confirmed the idea that Casalis, Duby and Jacottet 'may have encouraged [Mofolo] to write'. For a general discussion of imagery in Basotho heroic poetry, see D. Kunene, *Heroic Poetry of the Basotho* (Oxford, 1971).

The recommendations of the orthography meeting on 26 March 1906 were printed in a pamphlet, 'Orthographical Rules for Sesuto' (Morija, most recently reprinted in 1985).

Jacottet published his *Grammar e nyenyayane ea Sesotho* at Morija in 1908; and his *A Grammar of the Sesuto Language* (with Z.D. Mangoaela) was published posthumously in *Bantu Studies*, vol. 3 (1927). It contains a very interesting introduction on dialects, orthography and the development of Sesotho literature. *A Practical Method to Learn Sesotho* saw the light of day at Morija in 1912. Amongst his other linguistic writings was a paper on 'Bantu Phonetics' in the *Christian Express* (September 1907). An unfavourable review of J. van Oordt's book *The Origin of the Bantu* in the *Christian Express* (April 1908) elicited a defence by the book's author in June, which in turn provoked a tart letter from Jacottet in July.

That he did not always turn the other cheek when his scholarship was attacked was also illustrated when *The Treasury of Ba-Suto Lore* was published in Morija and London in 1908. An approving review of it was printed in the *Christian Express* in February 1909. But in April a letter from someone calling himself 'Mosuto' pecked at some parts of Jacottet's opus. In the following issue, Jacottet delivered a concise, cutting retort.

A brief review of Jacottet's *Contes Populaires des Bassoutos* appeared in the *Bulletin de Folklore*, vol. 2 (July–December 1895).

After some delay, the handsome *Livre d'Or de la Mission du Lesotho* was published from the Maison des Missions in Paris in 1912. According to the page facing the title page, 100 copies were numbered, but more must actually have been printed since the minutes of the Paris Committee, recorded on 5 February 1912, note that it already had 152 subscriptions. I have a copy numbered 45; I have a second copy without a number, which seems to confirm that quite a few extra copies were produced.

Chapter 22: The Prickly Hedgehog

The main source for Jacottet's role in the Union affair is his correspondence with Boegner, contained in a file in the Morija Archives. Secondary material comes from Arthur Newton, *Select Documents relating to the Unification of South Africa* (London, 1924), and L.M. Thompson, *The Unification of South Africa 1902–1910* (London, 1960).

It is worth noting Jacottet's mood at the time of Union. In response to various urgings by the World Missionary Conference in Edinburgh, Jacottet, amongst several others, commented in the *Christian Express* (October 1910). He reiterated a long-held belief: 'It is more and more my absolute conviction that it is only on the platform of the constitution of true Native Churches that we can arrive at a real understanding, that it is only in that way that we can build the first foundations of the great Native Church of the distant future ... which I have always looked upon as the *raison d'être* of the mission.' When the Dutch Reformed Church felt it could only unite with other churches 'at the expense of the coloured members', Jacottet believed it would be better to have no church union at all than to compromise, and in March 1911 he wrote a sharp letter accordingly: 'I am exceedingly sorry to have to pen these few lines. I have good friends in the Dutch Reformed Church, and have for it a deep-seated respect; it is painful for me to have to reflect today on its action. But I am sure that the case is too serious for any feelings of friendship to hinder me from speaking out what I so strongly feel to be the truth ... To accept and *legalize* a colour line in the constitution of a Christian church is one of the saddest things seen for years in this country.' Jacottet's political stance was in harmony with his deeply felt religious position. 'I am afraid the action of the Dutch Reformed Church has put immense difficulties in the way ... as it will be well-nigh impossible for most of us to join hands with a church which has so completely and officially identified herself, as a church, with racial prejudice.'

Chapter 23: A Breach of Faith

The quotation about the 'utter darkness' of Pitseng was translated and quoted by Daniel Kunene in *Thomas Mofolo and the Emergence of Written Sesotho Prose*, op. cit., p. 89; and Mofolo's letters – also translated by Kunene – come from pp. 29 and 31–2. The assessment of *Chaka* owes an indirect debt to J.C. Maxwell's article on *King Lear* in *Modern Language Review*, XLV (April 1950), pp. 142ff.

For a hint about the mysteriousness of the death of the toddler Tau and the succession of Griffith Lerotholi see L.B.B.J. Machobane, *Government and Change in Lesotho*, op. cit., pp. 106–7. Oral sources confirm that the suspicion survives to this day.

Chapter 24: The Coming Hour

A more comprehensive look at the disturbance in the leper asylum at Botšabelo, 'Mutiny among the Lepers: Public Health Policy on the Control of Leprosy in Lesotho and Popular Response, 1912–1920', by L.B.B.J. Machobane, appears in *South-South Journal of Culture and Development*, vol. 1, no. 1 (June 1999), pp. 114–33.

While a wide range of secondary sources on the First World War have been consulted, the following had a close influence: Alistair Horne, *The Price of Glory: Verdun 1916* (London, 1962; reprinted Harmondsworth, 1993); Paul Fussell, *The Great War and Modern History* (Oxford, 1975); Geoff Dyer, *The Missing of the Somme* (London, 1994); Lyn MacDonald, *They Called it Passchendaele* (London, 1978; reprinted Harmondsworth, 1993); Paddy Griffith, *Battle Tactics of the Western Front* (New Haven, 1994); Anthony Livesey, *The Viking Atlas of World War One* (London, 1994); Les Coate, *Ypres 1914–18* (Brighton, 1982); Les Coate, *The Somme 1914–18* (Brighton, 1983); and Albert Grundlingh, *Fighting Their Own War* (Johannesburg, 1987).

For specific information on Henri Jacottet, as well as a few notes in his private papers, the following primary resources, all from the Public Records Office, Kew, are relevant: Medals List (WD329/765); War Diary, 1st Battalion, Royal Fusiliers, 1–11 June 1917 (WO95/2207); War Diary, 13th Battalion, Royal Fusiliers, 7 March to 26 April 1918 and 1 August to 19 September 1918 (WO95/2538). Henri's regimental number was G25865. He was attached to the 1st Battalion from 13 September 1916 to 30 June 1917; to the 11th Battalion from 17 to 18 October 1917; and to the 13th Battalion from 19 October 1917 to 16 September 1918. He seems to have been retired from the army in February 1924. Information from the war diaries was supplemented by details from H.C. O'Neill, *The Royal Fusiliers in the Great War* (London, 1922) and the official history of the war published by the Imperial War Museum, *History of the Great War based on official documents by direction of the Historical Section of the Committee of Imperial Defence: Military Operations, France and Belgium 1918*, vol. IV, 8 August to 26 September, The Franco British Offensive (London, 1947). Together these sources allowed me to identify, probably to within a hundred metres, the point where Henri and his shell intersected – still a mealie field.

Also examined were the on-site burial registers of Tyne Cot, Thiepval, Hermies and other war cemeteries.

On The Lodge, where Madeleine taught, see *Banstead: How a Village Grew and Changed* by the Banstead History Research Group (Banstead, 1993), pp. 41, 63.

Chapter 25: Sacrifice

For the Spanish influenza, over and above Jacottet's own letters and Garraway's diary,

H. Phillips, *'Black October': The Impact of the Spanish Influenza Epidemic of 1918 on South Africa* (Pretoria, 1990), proved immensely helpful.

Georges Duby's anecdote about the mushrooms was told first in a personal interview, but also appeared as a story entitled 'The Olive Branch that Fizzled', in *Tomorrow* (June/July 1995), p. 42.

Part Three

Chapter 26: White Devil

According to the classification employed in bookshops, 'True Crime' can usually be found alongside 'Crime Fiction'. Though not quite so numerous as their fictional neighbours, the 'true crime' volumes nonetheless occupy a good share of shelf space. Quality is not always – indeed, perhaps not often – their most notable feature. They are satisfied to remain, as Edgar Allan Poe put it when he investigated the murders in the Rue Morgue, at the level of the ingenious, rather than pursuing the analytical. He makes this distinction clear in his analogy of playing whist. The difference is in the extent of the information obtained. The ingenious player confines himself to the rules, the cards and the game itself. The analyst does not reject deduction from things external to the game – he examines the countenance of his partner and compares it to those of his opponents, noting every variation; he notes the manner in which cards are thrown on the table; he orders the sequence of all the events, shuffles them, and ties them to the reactions displayed.

Countless works of true crime have been consulted here – my own collection runs to over five hundred titles. But a debt of gratitude must be paid to a few, specifically: the *Notable British Trials* series, especially those on Mary Blandy, the Seddons, Madeleine Smith, Harold Greenwood and Major Armstrong; Martin Beales, *Dead not Buried: Herbert Rowse Armstrong* (London, 1995); Henry Blythe, *Madeleine Smith: A Famous Victorian Murder Trial* (London, 1975); R. Huggett and P. Berry, *Daughters of Cain* (London, 1956); R. Dreisbach, *Handbook of Poisoning* (Los Altos, 1980); R.G. Jones (ed.), *Poison!* (London, 1988); B. Lane, *The Encyclopaedia of Forensic Science* (London, 1992); B. Marriner, *Murder with Venom* (London, 1993); Anne Moir and David Jessel, *A Mind to Crime* (London, 1997); Francis Mossiker, *The Affair of the Poisons* (London, 1970); Jürgen Thorwald, *Proof of Poison* (London, 1966); A. Vincent, *A Gallery of Poisoners* (London, 1993); Colin Wilson, *Written in Blood: A History of Forensic Detection* (London, 1990). Also the *Penguin Medical Encyclopaedia* (London, 1972) and the *Penguin Encyclopaedia of Crime* (London, 1993) were consulted.

Of even greater importance were John Glaister, *The Power of Poison* (London, 1954), as well as *Glaister's Medical Jurisprudence and Toxicology*, edited by E. Rentoul and H. Smith, 13th edition (Edinburgh, 1973); and Suetonius, *The Twelve Caesars*, translated by Robert Graves, revised by Michael Grant (London, 1957, 1979). For an explanation of arsenic testing, Colin Wilson's *Written in Blood* (particularly pp. 57–8) was the clearest. For a description of George Marsh's discovery of an effective test for arsenic, see Philip Paul, *Murder under the Microscope: The Story of Scotland Yard's Forensic Science Laboratory*

(London, 1990), p. 73. The idea and quotation about the chemical drama of poison come from Jim Schutze, *Preacher's Girl* (New York, 1993).

Patricia Pearson's *When She Was Bad: How Women Get Away With Murder* (London, 1999) brushes away any sentimental idea that women are less lethal than men.

Chapter 27: Revelations

The archival papers of the Swiss Mission of the Northern Transvaal are housed in the Historical Manuscripts Room, William Cullen Library, University of the Witwatersrand.

Love at the Mission by R. Hernekin Baptist was published in Boston in 1938.

For some biographical material on Ethelreda Lewis, see T. Couzens, *Tramp Royal: The True Story of Trader Horn* (Johannesburg, 1992), particularly Chapters 1 and 16; and Ethelreda Lewis, *Wild Deer* (Cape Town, 1982), particularly the Introduction.

Joseph Lewis wrote numerous articles for the *Friend* and the *Star* under the pseudonym of 'D. Sc.'. In reality, it is almost certain that Ethelreda Lewis actually wrote the articles based on material supplied by her husband. One such article, on 'Poisons of South Africa', appeared in the *Friend* on 7 July 1921, indicating that Dr Lewis was very much concerned with the subject at the time of Jacottet's death and that his wife was undoubtedly discussing it with him. He was particularly interested in 'native poisons' and cases involving them. A number of these were recorded in his private papers (in his wife's handwriting), some of them making the link between poisons and witchcraft. In an unpublished typescript, he examined the history and use of mandrake from the early Babylonians and Egyptians, through the Greeks and Syrians, to the Middle Ages and Shakespearean times.

Dr Georges Casalis's article, 'The Phenomena of Menstruation and Parturition among the Native Women of Basutoland', was published in the *South African Medical Journal*, vol. 4, no. 2, pp. 30–32. Information on plants used by the Basotho to induce abortion came from private correspondence with Dr Sumitra Talukdar of the National University of Lesotho, and derives from M. Schmitz, *Wild Flowers of Lesotho* (Roma, 1982), J. Watt and M. Breyer-Brandwijk, *Medicinal and Poisonous Plants of Southern and Eastern Africa* (Edinburgh, 1962), and J. Varela, *Traditional Medicine in Lesotho* (Antwerp, 1985).

The name 'Jerita' might derive from the Afrikaans 'Gertruida'; alternatively, it may have come from the biblical 'Jedida', mother of Josiah (II Kings 22: 1).

Chapter 28: A Very Difficult Position

The letters from Garraway to Churchill and to the High Commissioner in Cape Town are held in the Public Records Office, Kew (CO417/665). See, also, acknowledgements of communications on 11 January, 22 February and 10 May 1921, in the South African High Commissioner Register 1921–2 (CO545), reporting Jacottet's death and conveying the High Commissioner's sympathy, the impending arrest of two of the Jacottet daughters and Duby, and the release of the arrestees, respectively.

Knowledge concerning the legal system and the right of appeal derives from correspondence with David Ambrose.

Chapter 29: The Gift of Discord, Chapter 30: Lefetoa and Chapter 31: Murder in Her Eyes

The record of Madeleine's summons on Christeller is contained in the Civil Record 1920–21 (Lesotho National Archives). It includes Madeleine's complaints and Christeller's defence plea.

For Ramseyer's life story, see Eugène Hotz, *Paul Ramseyer: Missionnaire 1870–1929* (Paris, 1930).

The hint that Marguerite had an earlier affair with someone called Wasse or Wyss was mentioned only at the trial and there is no other evidence for it. The name of Wyss, at least, was not unknown to the Swiss Mission. There was an R. Wyss at Rikatla in Mozambique at one stage. This was probably Mlle Rosa Wyss, who was a nurse in Lourenço Marques between 1914 and 1920 (see *Bulletin de la Mission Romande*, vol. 32, no. 421 (May 1921), p. 159 – there is a photograph of her on p. 157).

The soup was made of beans, flour and Lemco. For Lemco, as an extract of beef, see *The Oxoid Manual of Culture Media, Ingredients and other Laboratory Services* (London, 1971).

Abraham Moletsane's memoirs are to be found in *An Account of the Autobiographical Memoir by Morena Abraham Aaron Moletsane*, edited by R.S. Webb (Paarl, 1967).

Sam Duby and Marcelle, as representatives of the Book Depot, corresponded with and ordered goods from Lennon's Pharmacy in Bloemfontein. While the arsenic might have come from many sources, Lennon's was the most likely. Efforts were made to find the store's poison registers, which would probably have been signed by whoever received the poison (though this would not necessarily have pointed any accusatory fingers). Lennon's was taken over by S.A. Druggists, and a phone call to Lew Morris of this company determined that poison registers had to be kept only for five years, and it was '100 per cent certain that the poison registers don't exist'.

Garraway signed the new passport for Sam Duby on 1 April 1921, enabling him to leave Lesotho – forever.

Direct and indirect references throughout the book to Herman Melville's *The Confidence-Man* come from the Signet Classic edition (New York, 1964); to Cyril Tourneur's *The Revenger's Tragedy* from the Mermaid Dramabook, Hill and Wang edition (New York, 1956); to John Webster's *The White Devil* from The Revels Plays, Methuen edition (London, 1960); to Aristophanes's *The Frogs* from the Penguin Classics edition, translated by David Barrett (London, 1964); and to Aeschylus's *The Oresteia* from the Penguin Classics edition, translated and edited by Robert Fagles (London, 1977). But it must be emphasized that all the people in this book are real, and any resemblances to fictional characters, living or dead, are purely coincidental.

Thanks

And you who haunt the vaults
where the gold glows in the darkness,
hear us now, good spirits of the house,
conspire with us – come,
and wash old works of blood
in the fresh-drawn blood of Justice.
Let the grey retainer, murder, breed no more.

Aeschylus, *The Libation Bearers*

Had the Jacottet murder occurred in America (Lizzie Borden) or France (Marie Lafarge) or England (Mary Blandy), there would have been several books produced about it, as well as many journalistic pieces, television documentaries, and perhaps a movie. But Lesotho in the early days was remote and inaccessible, and nowadays it is neither central to the world nor fashionable.

No biographies were ever produced on Jacottet either, though some were written about lesser mortals like Paul Ramseyer. Jacottet did deserve one, as most of the missionaries would have agreed. But the mission was embarrassed and, not unreasonably, wanted the whole affair forgotten. There *was* a blanket thrown over the murder and a taboo arose about speaking of it, but for reasons not all self-serving.

When Sam Duby left the mission, Gynette Duby was nursing in France. She did not know that her father had been arrested for murder and believed he had left Morija for health reasons. She joined her parents in Cape Town in order to help them. Eventually, she moved to Lesotho and married Sam Germond, a doctor.

Gynette Germond was such a nice person that nobody wanted to tell her about her father. And so the story slowly died.

But there was always the chance that a dog might come along to scratch up the corpse planted in the garden. After many decades, the Jacottet story was all but forgotten; it lingered only in obscure places like the novel *Love at the Mission*. Even then it was well disguised: what story was the novel based on?

The person who solved this particular mystery for me when I went in search of it was David Ambrose of the National University of Lesotho. He did not know the novel, but immediately recognized its outlines as based on the life and death of Jacottet. David is the encyclopaedia of Lesotho. He knows everything about the country, he collects everything, he shares everything generously. He and his wife, Sumitra Talukdar, an expert botanist, run a household the locals call 'The Hamerkops', after those birds that collect everything for their nests, from reeds to ribbons. The Ambroses are the scholarly equivalent.

Just as helpful has been Albert Brutsch. Over fifty years he has protected the documents of the mission in the archive and its history in his head. One of the great pleasures of researching this book has been to sit, for many hours on many occasions, listening to his memories and going through the mountain of material he collected for me, in the peace and quiet of his house at Morija.

His successor as curator of the Morija Museum and Archives, Stephen Gill, is one's ideal of an archivist: not only has he made all the material available to me, but he also actively hunted for new material and, in enthusiastic discussion, generated many helpful ideas.

David, Albert, Stephen – the three wise men of Lesotho.

From the descendants of those intimately involved in the story, I half expected hostile rejection over so sensitive an issue. Instead, with one exception, they helped me in every way they could. Key elements of the whole story would have disappeared forever were it not for Julian Jacottet and Ann Patey (and her husband Tony), Georges Duby and Gynette Germond. I hope I have not done anything to hurt them; they deserve nothing but gratitude from me. I am only sorry that Georges and Gynette did not live long enough to read this. Gynette only discovered by accident at the age of ninety (thankfully not from me) that her father had been arrested for murder. I interviewed her several times over a period of four years and came to appreciate why the story was kept from her by so many – she was one of the nicest people I have ever met. Georges, always with that wicked twinkle in his eye, was generosity itself. Ann is a journalist, so she understands the problems and sensitivities of investigation. Nevertheless, her cooperation has been beyond what I could reasonably have expected. So has Julian's.

I am also grateful to other members of the families: Ilse and Ted Germond, Fleur Rorke, Yvonne Stegmann, Paul Germond, Patrick Rorke, André Casalis, Paul and Annette Ellenberger, Eddie Verdier, and Elsie Mabille (née Verdier). Ted Germond lent me Sam Duby's annotated Bible, which played a large part in Ted's own life choice as a missionary doctor, something Sam might have considered a small step towards his own redemption.

Some people contributed to the research with ideas and encouragement, and with something more as well: hospitality. François and Hedy Augsburger in Donatyre, Switzerland, were unbelievable in this regard, as were Jenny Wall in Warnham, West Sussex, and Barbara and John Cowap in Oxfordshire. In the same breath and for the same reason I must also thank my son-in-law Per Bohlin, my generous friend, the late Nick Visser, and his wife Pippa, Kelwyn Sole and Rochelle Kapp, Brian and Maureen Bamford, all of Cape Town, and Gerda and John Wollheim near Fouriesburg, as well as my wonderful mother-in-law Pauline Blanchard-Sims in Harare, and Barbara and Peter Rundle.

Biography can be extremely, sometimes cripplingly, expensive. Without the help of the following institutions this mystery would not have come close to being solved: Pro Helvetia (for research in Switzerland), the Maison des Sciences de l'Homme (for research in Paris), the Institut Français d'Afrique du Sud, the Ernest Oppenheimer Memorial Trust, the Stella and Paul Lowenstein Charitable and Educational Trust, the Centre for Science Development, and, recently and extremely generously, Investec. I am also grateful for the prize given to me by the Traveltour Media Awards (R.C.I. and South African Airways) which, fortuitously, allowed me to put finishing touches to the study. Above all, I thank the Institute for Advanced Social Research (formerly the African Studies Institute) of the University of the Witwatersrand, which was my intellectual home for many years and the demise of which I so deeply regret. The Institute and the University have supported me way beyond my just deserts.

Many other institutions have also graciously given me access to their archives and facilities: Archives de l'État Neuchâtel; Archives Nationales du Québec; Archives, University of Glasgow; Bible Society of South Africa; Bibliothèque des Pasteurs, Neuchâtel; Bibliothèque du Service Protestant de Mission, Département Évangélique Français d'Action Apostolique (DÉFAP), Paris; Bodleian Library, Oxford; British and Foreign Bible Society, Swindon; Cantonal Archives, Neuchâtel; Commission d'Acces à l'Information du Québec; Cory Library, Rhodes University; Eunice High School, Bloemfontein; Greater Johannesburg Public Library; Historical Manuscripts Archives, University of the Witwatersrand; Imperial War Museum; Le Directeur de l'État Civil, Gouvernement du Québec; Morija Museum and Archives; Musée de Mascarons and the Rousseau Museum, Motiers; Musée Neuchâteloise; Museum Africa, Johannesburg; Mutare Museum, Zimbabwe; National Maritime Museum, Greenwich; National University of Lesotho Library; Orange Free State Law Society, Bloemfontein; Public Library, Bloemfontein; Public Records Office, Kew; Rhodes House Library, Oxford; Royal Commission on Historical Manuscripts, London; South African Library, Cape Town; St Michael's School, Bloemfontein; Tower of London; Universitätarchiv, Eberhard-Karls-Universität, Tübingen; Universitätarchiv, Georg-August-Universität, Göttingen; University of Fort Hare Library; Wellcome Institute for the History of Medicine Library, London.

One of the associated benefits of writing biography is the ordinary and extraordinary people one meets along the way. The following people not only provided invaluable information but also rendered the whole enterprise a pleasurable and privileged one for me (if I have inadvertently omitted anyone, I hope they will forgive me): Margie Adam, John Alexander (St Michael's School), Cliff Allwood, Clare Amm, Carol Archibald, Ursula Armstrong, Miriam Asmal (Pro Helvetia), Roland and Veronika Augsburger, Maurice Aymard (Maison des Sciences de l'Homme), Kevin Balkwell, Maude Barry, Miriam Basner, Irmela Bauer-Klöden (Eberhard-Karls-Universität, Tübingen), Charles Marc Bost, Bill Botha (Lennon's), Chloe Bovey-Delhorbe, Helen Bradford, Marco and Olenka Brutsch, Sturla Bruun-Mayer, Micky Bulkely, Jim and Andrea Campbell, Derek Casalis, Lyn Cawood (Childline), Hugh Cecil, Patrick Chabal, James Christie (a long-time friend and adviser), Mrs G. Clay (Newtimber Place), Margot Couprie, Pierre Couprie, Christian Delord (DÉFAP), Barry de Wet (Free State Law Society), John Monaheng Diaho, Joffre Dias (Département Missionnaire, Lausanne), Ann Dubovsky, Rosemary Duby, Bob Edgar, Elizabeth Eldredge, A.F. 'Wiggie' Ellenberger, Etienne Ellenberger, Pat and John Ellison, Doris Fenn, Yvonne Flather, John Gallagher, Françoise Gibson, Sylvia Grech, Jeff Green, Sue Grenfell, Robin and Bella Guy, Brigitte and David Hall, Dorothy and Lawrence Hall, Ian Hamilton, Gertrude Harris, Sue Hickey, Colin Hickling, Isabel Hofmeyr, Jonathan Hyslop, Brian Ingpen, Natalie Jacottet, Paul Jenkins, Di and Mick Jones (Malealea), Patricia Jones (River Hotel, Oxford), Sister Josephine (St Barnabas, Masite), Saida Keller-Messahli (Pro Helvetia), Cynthia and Denis Kemp, Dr Tom Kleffman (Georg-August-Universität, Göttingen), Pat Klepp, Mike Kokot, Thomas Laely (Pro Helvetia), Pauline Pulane Leqheku,

Christopher Lowe, Hilda Mabille, Moira MacKay (Archives, University of Glasgow), Judge I. Maisels, Prof. R.G.S. Makalima (Fort Hare), Marilyn Masters (Bodleian Library), David Maughan-Brown, Barry Mendelow, Corinne Mendelow (née Paillard), Santu Mofokeng, Joel Mohapeloa, Prof. J.M. Mohapeloa, Carolyn Mondel (Library, University of the Witwatersrand), Jean-Paul, Françoise and Sylvie Montmollin, Lew Morris (S.A. Druggists), Cynthia Morrison (Toy Library Association), Colin Murray, C.R. Namponye (Howard Pim Library, University of Fort Hare), Pierre des Ormeaux (photographer, Ladybrand), Kate and Ken Owen, Florence Paillard, Sheila Park, John Parkington and Sandy Proselendis, Nick Perren (of John Murray Publishers, for constant and patient encouragement), René Péter-Comtesse (Bibliothèque des Pasteurs), Michelle Pickover (Historical Manuscripts, University of the Witwatersrand), Jan Piggert, Edwin Pons, Hélène Prince (DÉFAP Library), Karen and David Reid (grandson of F.M. Reid), Alain and Bérénice Ricard, Neil Robertson, Jacqueline Robinson (née Paillard), Ingrid Roderick (British and Foreign Bible Society), Eugène Roy, Mother Mary Ruth (St Michael's School), Peter Sanders (such a generous scholar), Karel Schoeman, Judge Peter Schultz, Karen Shapiro, Charlene Smith (whose ear got bent permanently out of shape on certain aspects of the murder problem), Jim Smith, Hans Steenkamp, Robin Stein, Beth and Neville Thorn, Laurent Tissot (University of Neuchâtel), Gilbert Tsekoe, Pat Tucker (unfailingly encouraging), Sister J. Tully, Mims Turley (Bible Society of South Africa), Claude Vanderlinden (Temple Farel, La Chaux-de-Fonds), France Vassaux, Phillipe Vassaux, Gawie Vorster (Destine Private Investigators), Prof. Daniel Waley (biographer of Lord Buxton), Pamela Watkins-Pitchford, Ray Westlake (Westlake Books, Newport), Michael Willis (Archivist, Brentwood School), Sheila Wilson (Port Alfred Museum), Patricia Wollheim, Rev. John Young.

In addition to the key family members mentioned earlier, certain people appear in the main body of this book or are close relatives of those who do. A special thanks for their contribution is due to Marie Deenik (ex-Eunice), Jeanne Jaques (née Dieterlen), Pierrette Jaques, Meshack Kotele, Georges and Louise Mabille (Sauve, France), Kathleen Maughan-Brown (née Beaumont), Sara Molise (whose ancestor was eaten by a cannibal), Hélène Nixon (née Christeller, who taught me French at university many years ago and gave me such support in these research endeavours), Jacqueline Ramelet (née Paillard, of Montcherand, Switzerland, the last person alive who was actually in the Jacottet house on the day of the murder – she was fifteen months old at the time), Bethuel Sekhesa (who inherited Marcelle's cat and who called his horse Marcelle to remember her by), Dorothy Smith (ex-Eunice), and the saintly Eleanor Wilkin (of Malta, daughter of Ethelreda and Joe Lewis). In this regard I am also grateful to my wife, Diana Wall. In the course of the research for this book we discovered that she is related to the Bost, Mabille and Casalis families, and to Caroline Casalis and Freddy Casalis in particular. This gave me an intimate connection to the story and made me feel even closer to the people involved.

Open-hearted help came from Eunice High School: Paul Cassar (headmaster), Norine van Arkel (teacher) and Vicky Cross, Christine Stewart, Dorothy Wedderburn and Ella White (ex-students).

Thanks, too, to those hardy souls who helped me with translations: Françoise

Browne, Brigitte Hall, Ulrike Kistner, Craig Stevens and, particularly, Louise Flynn (who worked far beyond the call of duty, taking an interest in the whole project); as well as those who helped me produce the physical text, but went further with timely suggestions and encouragements: Linda Davidson, Arlene Harris, Pat King, Celeste Mann and Marie Joubert.

Along the way I have been inspired by four fine scholars who have become and, I hope, remain my friends: Guy Butler, Ian Phimister, Ivan Vladislavić and Brian Willan. Editing is an exact science, a skilful craft and a dying art. Ivan is a supreme scientist, craftsman and artist. Any faults in this book I shall therefore pass on to him for blame. As for publishers, the Scottish scientist and novelist Norman Douglas said of them that they are like wives: one always wants somebody else's. In my case, Douglas is wrong. Stephen Johnson of Random House enthusiastically took on this book for better or worse, and supported its production with enormous generosity. The jury is out on my neighbour's wife, but I do not covet his publisher.

The production team Stephen Johnson chose was terrific: as project manager Douglas van der Horst combined sympathetic humour with meticulous professionalism; as designer, imaginative and creative, Abdul Amien abided persistent editorial intrusion with stoical equanimity; as final proofreader Tessa Kennedy, while ruthlessly eliminating widows and orphans from the text, endured the endless absurdities of the author with gentle tact. Ivan Vladislavić continued to treat the work way beyond what might reasonably have been expected of him as if it were one of his own. Stephen, Douglas, Abdul, Tessa, Ivan (as well as Anne Westoby and Leonie Twentyman Jones) – thank you.

Jill and Tony Traill have a special place in the Jacottet story: they nearly died with me in the greatest snowstorm in Lesotho history since the Great Snow of 1902, when they accompanied me on the trail of Jacottet's 1893 journey into the mountains. We three need to thank all those people, known and unknown, who helped in our rescue. In the course of that experience, I felt I became more than just a passing visitor to Lesotho. In a small way, I became part of it.

Over many years, four people have been my friends and my inspiration: Marshall Walker, Tony Traill, Belinda Bozzoli and Charles van Onselen. There is a touch of greatness about each of them (although they would scoff at the idea) and it has been a privilege to know them. Charles van Onselen, in particular, made the research for this book possible with practical support and with advice always available. He, like no one else I know, understands the tyranny of those pitiless mistresses, research and writing, and the extreme difficulties of trying to reconcile time-driven epic with timebound tragedy.

This book is dedicated to my children, who have given me the privilege of being their father. They cannot be blamed for not making me a better one. They have all contributed to the book with encouragement and discussion, Edmund with careful reading and comments, and Kate in particular with research in Canada. I would like them to share this dedication with the memory of my brother Roy, a man of dignity, intelligence and integrity, who also died before his time.

My wife Diana is the verdant island on the other side of the world to which I go – my Tahiti.

—◦○◦—

Two other people deserve respect – Édouard and Marcelle Jacottet.

It would have been easy enough to produce a sensationalist, 'true crime' murder story. But that would have glossed over the complexity of the history and the depths of motivation. It would have been unfair to the protagonists.

This study began with routine research, continued in intellectual curiosity, but ended in a desperate attempt to render justice, however painful, to them. There is little doubt that there is more evidence to be found which would either augment, confirm or refute some of the conclusions presented here. The Jacottets did not get to choose their biographer. Had they been able to do so, they would surely have plumped for someone in the mould of Sherlock Holmes or Auguste Dupin, with his unmasking of the 'Neufchatelish' sailor and his maniacal orang-utan, rather than, as it turned out, someone from the school of Inspector Clouseau. The comic inevitably overwhelms the tragic.

I have learned a great deal from their tragedy. Being someone of no fixed religion myself, not the least of these lessons is a new respect for the courage and achievements, despite their human faults, of the missionaries themselves. In recent years, they have been an easy target for criticism, but the fact is that most of them gave up a familiar life to go to unknown places in order to give to strangers the most precious thing they had.

Jacottet's death had a devastating effect on the mission, to the point where one oral version has it that it was almost sold to the Dutch Reformed Church in the 1920s (Griffith spoke out strongly against this move). Chronically short of funds, the church declined to the point where it has today been described by one of its prominent members as 'a valley of dry bones'. With the loss of Jacottet, part of the spirit went out of the mission and not a little of the church died with him. But part of it did survive, and that part owes much to him too.

About and within Marcelle there is abiding mystery. Having denied herself the elemental cry of birth, was there anything left for her but death? Was she God's instrument or the Devil's revenge? Was she at the end of a long line of domestic poisoners or at the beginning of a new trend? Although Marcelle, in her modern passion, may well have hated her father when she slew him, I suspect she might have loved him, too. Édouard Jacottet was not a bad man, his achievements were considerable, and he kept faith to the end. The picture of him that I take away with me comes from the obituary written by his friend and colleague, Henri Junod.

Rest then in the harsh sun of Lesotho, dear friend, who loved the blacks so well and who gave them so much. I hope that someone will plant on your grave one of those purple lilies from the mountain of Thaba-Bosiu or an amaryllis, beautiful and red, from the Malotis which you were so fond of. The Basotho will not forget you. The fruits of your ministry will for a long time mature in the breast of the tribe. And we shall meet again, in the clear light, at the foot of God's throne.

Index

DATE DUE